The **MYSTERY** of
HISTORY

Volume I
Creation to the Resurrection

By Linda Lacour Hobar

BRIGHT IDEAS PRESS
Dover, Delaware

Text, Copyright © 2002, Linda Lacour Hobar

Library of Congress Catalog Card Number: 2002106320
ISBN: 1-892427-04-4
First Edition

Printed in the United States of America

Bright Ideas Press
Dover, Delaware

www.BrightIdeasPress.com
info@BrightIdeasPress.com

ACKNOWLEDGMENTS

We wish to thank George R. Sparks, Director of the Museum of Biblical Archaeology in Columbus, Ohio, for access to the museum's unique and amazing collection of Biblical artifacts for use in this text. Special thanks also go to Emily Harkey for photographing the museum collection.

Scripture taken from the New King James Version. Copyright © 1982 by Thomas Nelson, Inc. Used by permission. All rights reserved.

(Credits continue on page 469, which constitutes an extension of this copyright page.)

I lovingly dedicate this study of history
to my children,
Heather, Kyle, and Ashley.

It is for your knowledge of the Gospel of Jesus Christ
and for the knowledge of generations to come
that I am inspired to write.

I love you all "the most"!

Now to him who is able to establish you by my gospel and the
proclamation of Jesus Christ, according to the revelation of the **mystery**
hidden for long ages past, but **now revealed** and made known through
the prophetic writings by the command of the eternal God,
so that all nations might believe and obey him—
to the only wise God be glory forever
through Jesus Christ!

(Romans 16:25–27)

Acknowledgments

I want to take this opportunity to thank both the big people and the little people who were brave enough to first try this curriculum and participate in The Mystery of History Club. There were many days that the picture of your sweet faces kept me going. Your feedback as busy mothers, teachers, and students played a huge part in helping me shape this curriculum to be what it is today. Thank you!

- The Yeager Family: Matt and Wendy, Ellie, Tabi, Hannah, Lydia, and Josh
- The Schoch Family: Chip and Sharon, Stephen, and Matthew
- The McDowell Family: Dave and Jenn, Quinn, Breann, Kayla, Delaney, and Keegan
- The Messer Family: John and Theresa, Dan, Zachary, Meredith, and Carolyn
- The Clark Family: Steve and Christina, Dayna, Bryn, Tristan, and Skye

Back row: Stephen Schoch, Dan Messer, Quinn McDowell, Matthew Schoch, Kyle Hobar *Front row:* Ellie Yeager, Breann McDowell, Ashley Hobar, Tabi Yeager

I especially want to thank Wendy Yeager for inspiring me to write this book. You are a great friend as well as a faithful sister in Christ. Your enthusiasm and your "history-loving" girls made a great difference in helping me finish. I can't wait to see what God has in store for you.

I want to thank Cynthia Brandon for your hours of preliminary work on the computer and your encouragement along the way.

I thank Dr. James Vardaman for your great knowledge and love of history, which planted a seed in me years ago at Baylor University. I appreciate, too, your input to the original manuscript.

I also want to thank Ivy Ulrich-Bonk and Christy Shaffer for bringing these pages to life through your artistry and design. I'm so pleased.

I especially want to thank Kathryn Dix for your countless hours of editing. With your incredible ability for detail work, you really put this book together. And you did all of this hard work with a good sense of humor and such graciousness toward my inadequacies. Thank you.

I thank Maggie Hogan for being so friendly at homeschool conventions, which led to our great working relationship. You are a true encourager, a "dream" publisher, and a gift from God. Thanks!

I, of course, thank my own husband and children, Ron, Heather, Kyle, and Ashley, for allowing me to be a less-than-perfect mom and wife this year. I'd much rather stare into your eyes any day than at a computer screen. Kids, thank you for riding the white board through the house, drawing sea horses on the TV, keeping sled dogs in the closet, bombarding me with erasers, and still scoring high on your tests. Our laughter together changes my life. Honey, thank you for the priceless video. It is one of the nicest things anyone has ever done for me. Lord willing, "the best *is* yet to come."

Last, I thank the Author of all history who really wrote this story. Thank you, Lord, for allowing me the awesome privilege of retelling the events You ordained. I learned more than my students ever will. Thank You for choosing to reveal Yourself through history so that life might not be such a mystery.

CONTENTS

SEMESTER I
CREATION AND EARLY CIVILIZATIONS ◆ 1

* All items listed in bold type are key people (or events) and dates to memorize. There are 12 key items in this volume.

QUARTER 2 — The Mystery Expands: 1175 B.C. to 627 B.C.   97

Around the World 97

* All items listed in bold type are key people (or events) and dates to memorize. There are 12 key items in this volume.

SEMESTER II
THE CLASSICAL WORLD   ◆   193

* All items listed in bold type are key people (or events) and dates to memorize. There are 12 key items in this volume.

* All items listed in bold type are key people (or events) and dates to memorize. There are 12 key items in this volume.

* All items listed in bold type are key people (or events) and dates to memorize. There are 12 key items in this volume.

* All items listed in bold type are key people (or events) and dates to memorize. There are 12 key items in this volume.

* All items listed in bold type are key people (or events) and dates to memorize. There are 12 key items in this volume.

PREFACE

It is with great joy that I welcome you to *The Mystery of History*. But there are a few disclaimers I would like to make.

First, if I waited for this book to be perfect in every aspect, it would never make it to print. The story of the world is beyond the scope of any of us because only the Creator knows the truth of His Creation. But even with the unintended flaws and oversights, I think you'll still find much beauty here. Not because I wrote it, but because the Lord is the author of the original script! He is perfect.

Second, for the sake of easier reading, I frequently use the terms "man" or "mankind" (and sometimes "his" or "him") to refer to male and female alike. This is in no way intended to make one gender sound superior to the other. Nor is it intended to disrespect the unique makeup and design of the sexes.

Third, all Scripture used in this text was selected from the New King James Version. With the numerous choices there are today, as well as the various viewpoints toward versions of the Bible, I tried to choose one that would appeal to a wide range of readers without compromising my own standards for the accuracy of the Word.

Fourth, although I have tried to write this text as a true history of the world, it would be negligent of me not to mention that I undoubtedly have left my own bias in the book as a natural result of my heritage. Though it is not intentional, this book leans much more heavily toward the history of the Western Hemisphere because it more directly relates to the development of my own culture.

Furthermore, without apology, this book is quite obviously written from a Christian worldview because of my personal faith in Jesus Christ. Much care was taken in accurately explaining opposing faiths in this text with dignity and respect yet through the grid of what I believe the Bible says is true.

With that in mind, I hope that you not take my words as your final source on the Scriptures but rather look to the Word itself by conducting as much of your own Bible study as possible. I suggest that owning or having easy access to a thorough Bible encyclopedia and/or an illustrated Bible dictionary, as well as a Bible concordance, may prove to be very helpful in executing the many research possibilities in this curriculum. Even younger students can benefit from sketches and photos found in these special resources. (There are so many available that it would be unfair of me to recommend one over another.)

In closing, this book is long. But at every thought of cutting a lesson or two to shorten it, I found myself pale and weak in the knees. It's all here for a purpose, a purpose that is beyond me. The story isn't mine—it's the Lord's. To Him be the glory and may He help you with your school hours each and every day to accomplish that which will most minister to you and your family and bring you to a greater knowledge of our Lord and Savior.

For the sake of the Mystery,
Linda Lacour Hobar

LETTERS TO THE STUDENTS

Younger Students (K–2nd Grade)

Hi! My name is Mrs. Hobar. I wrote this history course with someone just like you in mind. You see, I have a little girl who is about your age. I really wanted her to understand history, and I also wanted her to begin to understand God. I think that God is the reason for **all** of history. So I wrote about them both.☺

I wish I could meet you myself and tell you some of the neat things I have learned about history. I don't ever think it's boring! Instead, I think it's fascinating! Why? Because history is just a great story. It's full of adventure, drama, life, death, and even romance. You know, the mushy stuff. History is all about people and how they have lived since the very beginning of the world!

Do you know how many people have already lived? No one but God knows for sure. But the number is way bigger than a million. In fact, it is bigger than a billion! Together we will learn the stories of some of these people. Some were good like King David, and some were very bad like Sennacherib. Some people lived to be very old like Noah, and some people only lived short lives like King Tut.

And out of all those people who have ever lived, each of them was once a child like you, special and unique. I believe that God hand-designed every person who has ever lived! And you know what? That includes you! I'm so glad God thought of you when He was busy creating the universe.

In closing, remember this: The name of this course is *The Mystery of History*. I named it that because I believe, that through God, there are answers for all the questions of life. I think the mystery behind everything is God Himself trying to help us know Him. So, when you see the title of your book, think about the Lord revealing Himself to man. He did it best through the life of Jesus Christ who lived and died for our sins so we could be with Him forever in heaven.

If you have never before trusted Christ to be your Savior, read with your teacher the points of the Gospel ("Would You Like to Belong to God's Family?") in the Appendix of this book. God desires that each of us know Him personally. In doing so, you too will understand the Mystery of History!

If you ever have questions or want to write to me about something neat YOU learned in history, write me at:

Linda Hobar
3008 Larchwood Ct.
Maineville, OH 45039

I would love to hear from you! I hope you enjoy your study.☺

Middle Students (3rd–5th Grade)

Hi! My name is Linda Hobar. I just want to write you a personal note and tell you why I wrote this history course. First, I want you to know that I wrote it for you! Although we haven't met, I think about you every day as I sit as the computer, putting my notes down into sentences.

In fact, at times like that, I actually pray. I pray that God would have me write exactly what a student like you needs to know about history. I never want to bore you. I never want to insult your intelligence. And I never want to make you not like history! I want to write about things that are really worth knowing.

That is not an easy assignment. But I believe a lot of history is worth our knowing because it points to the Creator of everything. That is why I wrote this curriculum. The title of my book implies that there IS a mystery to history. Do you know what I think it is? I believe the mystery to all things is God trying to reveal Himself to man. Since the Garden of Eden, He has been showing us just what kind of a loving and personal God He is.

History really is a great story. We'll learn of good guys, bad guys, and everything in between. We'll read about treachery, murder, explorations, royal marriages, and so much more! I believe each and every life God created has had a plan and purpose. It really is astounding to think about just how many people God has created. We will only be able to cover a fraction of them.

More importantly, we will be learning about God's hand and direction in the course of this world we live in. By now you are old enough to have seen both the blessings of life and the tragedies. There is a lot of suffering in this world. Even in that, I think we can see God at work.

One of the greatest works of God was His coming to earth in the man of Jesus Christ. I hope you already know Christ personally and have allowed Him to be the Lord of your life. Apart from Him, there is no forgiveness of sin. And we are all guilty of it! If you're not sure about your salvation, please read the points of the Gospel ("Would You Like to Belong to God's Family?") in the Appendix of this book.

In knowing Christ, you will be sure of your eternal place in heaven. What better knowledge can you have than that? And you will better understand the Mystery of History! If you ever have questions or want to share with me YOUR thoughts on history, please write me at:

Linda Hobar
3008 Larchwood Ct.
Maineville, OH 45039

I hope to hear from you. Enjoy this course! ☺

Older Students (6th–8th Grade and Up)

Hi! What I have to say might surprise you. You may be expecting some "rah! rah!" letter from me on how you ought to love history and all that. But, you know what? I won't bother. I was your age once and as a young teen, I didn't give a flip about history!

I'll tell you why. At your age, as far as I was concerned, the world revolved around me. I didn't mean for it to. It just did because I was only beginning to figure out where I fit into this big drama that we call "life." I was way too concerned about how I was doing in playing the starring role of "me."

Maybe you are more mature than I was and you do care about things beyond your own life. I hope you do. I think one definition of "maturity" is simply recognizing one's place in the lineup of life. Maturity is accepting our roles and responsibilities whether we like them or not.

So, what's the point of my letter? I want to challenge you. You can be mediocre in this life and live just within your own perimeters, or you can GROW. You can learn! If you learn, you will probably change. You'll change the way you see things and the way you wish things could be.

I want to see world-changers develop out of you. That's my challenge! Maybe you won't love this history course. You might not even like it. But will you give it a good chance? Will you allow yourself to really think about other cultures, other people, and other philosophies? Will you turn off the TV and the stereo long enough to listen to what is going on in the world and care about it?

History is in the making all around us. It is the ongoing story of man since the beginning of time. He's been around for about six or eight thousand years. Some good, some terrible. Some events in history are flat-out terrifying, and others are heartwarming. But it is all real.

Besides being the story of man, I believe that history is the story of God. I titled this course *The Mystery of History* because I think there ARE answers to the questions of life. Who made us? Why are we here? What is our purpose in existing? The mystery of life lies in the Gospel itself, which is God revealing Himself to man. One of the greatest ways He did that was through Jesus Christ His Son.

I hope that you have already reached a point in your life where you have trusted Christ as your personal Savior. In that decision, you will have secured your eternal destiny! But, if you are not sure where you stand with knowing God, please take time to read the points of the Gospel ("Would You Like to Belong to God's Family?") in the Appendix of this book. Though maturity is looking beyond yourself, wisdom is occasionally looking within yourself. I do recommend examining your relationship to God regularly.

So, I guess I AM writing a rah! rah! letter about history after all. I hope you get the big picture of it in this or any course of study. Are you being challenged to care about the world around you? What does the world need from you? What do you have to offer it instead of what does it have to offer you? I challenge you to study with integrity. Study to really know something of value, to be wise, and to be a world-changer.

Keep in mind that I wrote this history curriculum for several age groups. I expect you, as an older student, to do more than read my lessons. That would be too easy for you. This course is just a guide for you if you are in high school. Take the research activities seriously and stretch yourself. Some are real easy and others will take some time to complete. And always read original sources when you can. Don't take my lessons as the final word.

May the Lord bless you in your study. If you ever have a question or thought you want to share with me, write me at:

Linda Hobar
3008 Larchwood Ct.
Maineville, OH 45039

I would get a kick out of hearing from you!

LETTER TO THE TEACHER

My dear friends,

First, I want to commend you for your desire and commitment to educate your children. Homeschooling is a sacrificial phenomenon that is only really understood by other homeschoolers. Relax. I am one of those other homeschool moms. My desire is not to overwhelm you with another curriculum but to help make your teaching easier. What you will find in these pages is a friendly format. I have done the work for you in researching, creating activities, and laying things out in a concise manner. I want to explain three things to you: Why I wrote this curriculum, how it is laid out, and suggestions for its use.

I. Why I Wrote This Curriculum

I have been homeschooling for 11 years. During that time I have learned many heart lessons about patience, anger, love, and sacrifice. I have also learned many head lessons like the names of cloud formations, how to dissect a cow's eye, who found the Rosetta Stone, and when Cleopatra lived. One thing I figured out was that my children and I could learn just about anything at one sitting. However, to *remember* that information and use it again was an entirely different matter. I began to feel discouraged at the end result of my children's education. What content were they really absorbing after all the countless hours we had put in for the sake of a "better education"?

Of course they could remember their math facts and how to read. Those were skills they acquired at young ages and then kept using over and over again. But, what about other pieces of information? Why was I bothering to teach some things that were only good for their short-term memory banks?

Granted, some learning is only useful for the short term. Like the parts of a flower for example. They may not need to know that to get by in this world, but they can learn the information in one afternoon to appreciate God's perfect design of plants. But weren't there SOME things really worth their time to have a greater knowledge of and to remember for the long run?

To me, all these questions run along the path of man's bigger question of "why" he exists. For a kid it comes out as, "Why do I have to learn this stuff?" It's a great question! (Please don't scold them for asking.) The only answer I can come up with as to why we are even here on earth is **to know God and to make Him known.** I believe that IS why we are here and that IS why we learn. If that is the case, then the STORY of God and man is worth our extra attention.

I concluded that I wanted my own children to have a deep knowledge and appreciation of world history. In my opinion, it is the story of God and man at its best. As others have already put it, history is "HIS-Story." I believe that throughout the ages God has revealed Himself and His purposes through an exact plan in time. It is really beyond our comprehension. But, by studying history, we can appreciate this awesome God and be better prepared to make Him known. That, my friends, is why I write. I named this course *The Mystery of History* because according to the scriptures, **the Gospel of Jesus Christ IS the mystery behind all history.**

I also wrote because I discovered a personal passion for the topic of history. In college I sat under two outstanding world history professors who had the gift of telling great stories (Dr. James Vardaman and Mr. Robert L. Reid of Baylor University). They first captivated my attention toward history. I then found as I taught my own kids that at times I would weep over the things we were learning because they were so moving to me. Who can be untouched by the stories of the slaves in America? Or the Trail of Tears that the Native Americans took with their families as they were moved from their homeland? I still cry at the part of the story when Joseph revealed himself to his brothers and when Joan of Arc gave her life as a martyr.

History is oftentimes sad, but it is real. I am enthused by the great stories of God's justice, of man's patriotism, and ultimately of martyrdom itself. We live such cushy, comfy lives of which I have no complaints. But in order to fully appreciate our luxuries, our freedom, and our God, we must know what life has been like in the world otherwise.

II. The Curriculum Layout

With that in mind, consider how I have laid out this curriculum. There is a specific reason for every aspect of it. I will begin by explaining a typical layout for a 3rd or 4th grader through 8th grader. However, in the next section I have provided adaptations for both younger and older students. This curriculum could be a framework for all grade levels.

Step #1—"Around the World" Summaries

You will observe that at the beginning of each quarter, there is a summary of events around the world to introduce the time period. This is also a place to make mention of some great and wonderful things that just didn't make the final cut. For example, the Seven Wonders of the Ancient World were scattered throughout different times and countries. The man who categorized the Seven Wonders is introduced in an "Around the World" section. He was not important enough to include in a lesson of his own.

There will not be any test questions from this material nor are there activities for these summaries. These pages are just bonus materials to help students grasp the incredible world in which we live.

Step #2—Pretests ("What Do You Know?")

Students begin each week by taking a Pretest—titled "What Do You Know?"—to expose them to new terms and names that they may never have heard before (such as *The Epic of Gilgamesh*). These pretests are no longer than eight questions and are broad-based in content. They are not meant to discourage students but to prick their curiosity. All the answers will be revealed as they continue their study. The pretests are also designed to somewhat stump the students who "think" they know it all. (You may or may not have one of those kids in your home. Most do.) I don't recommend recording grades on these pretests. Many of them we only do orally with no record kept at all as to right or wrong answers.

Step #3—Lessons

There are about 100 lessons in one volume of material. Approximately three lessons should be covered each week to accommodate a traditional 36-week school year. These lessons are written on about a 6th-grade level. They may be read out loud by the teacher, the student, or both. On some hectic days (which we all have), the lesson may only be read independently by the student. I would prefer that to be the exception. Reading and learning the lessons together will be more beneficial.

One thing I observed in my years of homeschooling was that in some subjects, I couldn't teach what I didn't know. History was certainly one of those subjects. I often found myself scrounging through reference materials trying to get a date on an event or a better synopsis of something. My kids could easily tell when I wasn't prepared. If I turned them over to textbooks, they were bored and quickly forgot the material. If I followed many of the numerous "activity guides" to history, we were bogged down on cool projects but not getting a big picture of the significance of key people in specific time periods.

I also felt that the approach of reading "fictional historical novels" left my children with greater knowledge of a person who never existed than of true figures. We also found gaps of time and gaps in cultures that were never written about.

I still recommend reading lots and lots of historical novels for enrichment and for the feel of daily life in a particular time period, but I don't recommend depending on them for facts. For example, we have loved the American Girl series and learned a lot about early American life through these stories. But, we wouldn't necessarily understand the American Revolution, the Civil War, or the Great Depression through these stories alone.

Last, I chose lesson topics that I hoped would help a child from a Christian home to incorporate his or her beliefs into a historical framework. From my observation, we are most often locked into a Sunday school-only mentality toward people such as Joshua, Ruth, and Jonah, for example. We usually treat these fascinating Bible stories separately from other history.

But isn't it interesting to know that Joshua lived in the same century as the legendary King Tut? Ruth lived about the same time as Helen of Troy. And Jonah lived just about when the first Olympics were taking place in Greece. I firmly believe that this kind of knowledge helps the people of the Bible to seem more real. And in a world that most often criticizes the authenticity of the Bible, that's important.

Though it has been a tremendous undertaking, I have researched and written for you what I believe are the key things that a student ought to know for each lesson. I had many choices of topics but felt these were some of the most significant for developing a Christian worldview.

Step #4—Activities

After every lesson, there is a corresponding Activity section. You will quickly see that the activities are broken down by age groups. This is done simply to accommodate families with children at various grade levels, which includes most homeschool families. I will elaborate in the next section on my definition of the age groups and my deeper reason behind the breakdown.

For now, note that the activities are written as a means to REINFORCE the material just learned in the lesson. I believe that younger children, in particular, will learn and retain information better if they can touch, taste, smell, burn, dye, or do whatever with it. The activities were created to involve many of the senses and to be fun for the little guys. This is their first exposure to school and learning. I want them to love it!

The activities should also appeal to various learning styles. The teacher and student may want to choose the activities that most interest them. Skip the ones that will cause them to grumble. (Unless it's just time to force-feed some research!) Some busy days just won't allow time for any activity with the lesson. Don't sweat it!

Last, if you are not familiar with Bloom's Taxonomy, you might want to read more about it in the next section, "A Classical Approach to Education." Bloom's Taxonomy is simply an approach to education that involves thinking on many levels, from simple to more complex.

I have kept Bloom's theories in mind in creating the activities as many of them require the children to process the information learned in the lesson by application, analysis, and synthesis. I particularly do so for the older children. An example would be when I ask the older children to consider the modern-day pro-life movement in comparison to the Egyptian midwives who saved the Hebrew babies from death by the pharaoh's orders. Other examples include the creation–evolution debate and Christian apologetics. These are obviously not "fill-in-the-blank" issues but ones that demand deeper thinking.

Step #5—Memory Cards

At the start of the Activity section for every third lesson, I remind students to make their Memory Cards. These are simply fact cards made by the students on 3-by-5-inch cards. They are designed to help students handle information learned earlier in the week. They will also use these cards for future games and drills and as a study aid. I have more information on these cards and how to make them in the section titled "Memory Cards."

Step #6—Reviews ("Take Another Look!")

Upon completion of three lessons (and hopefully after a few activities have been done), the students are ready for a review time. The review sections—titled "Take Another Look!"—offer guidelines for timeline work and map work that correspond to the material just studied. Though some families may prefer to do some timeline and map work each history day, I personally prefer to "pull out" the necessary supplies, timeline, and maps only on a review day. Furthermore, by spreading out the activities in the Review section, you are allowing more time for the students to absorb the material. You particularly will want to utilize the map work for the sake of geography skills. Geography is generally a weak subject in American schools.

For the mapping exercises, I'm including 10 outline maps that have been especially designed for *The Mystery of History*. (These maps are located in a special section at the back of this book.) Because each map is used several times, you'll want to photocopy them in the quantities recommended below for each student:

Map #	1	2	3	4	5	6	7	8	9	10
Quantity	3	8	1	6	4	7	4	1	1	2

You'll also need to have on hand atlases from which to obtain the information to record on your maps. I recommend both a Bible atlas and a historical atlas. Also, a globe is helpful for seeing the big picture.

Encourage your students to be creative with fine-tip markers, colored pencils, neat handwriting, symbols, drawings, and so forth. You may want to copy a few maps for yourself and color right along with your students in the beginning to help set a standard for neatness and creativity. Have fun with it! A well-done map is a piece of art!

And don't be surprised if you enjoy the timeline more than your children do. You see, for your kids, it's all new information that happens to be taught in order. But, for most adults it's a revelation experience to see history put on a timeline because most of us received a smattering of history here and a dose of Sunday school there. When we mesh the two together, we are amazed. Most adults have also learned far more American history than world history. It's exciting to put into perspective things that we have only had glimpses of in our own education.

I have a separate section on a suggested layout for a timeline if this is a new endeavor for you.

Step #7—Exercises ("What Did You Miss?")

At the end of every three lessons, you will find a page of exercises (or a quiz; I explain those next). My point in including these is for the review of the material already studied. Please appreciate the great value of this approach. I feel the exercises will help pull together the individual cultures that have been taught in chronological order. For example, there will be multiple lessons on famous Egyptians, but they won't all be taught at the same time. They will be taught in the order in which the people lived. But I think it will benefit a student to stop and put these people all together on a page under the kingdoms in which they ruled.

On the flip side, the exercises will also help to place famous people with their contemporaries from other parts of the world. You will find that I am not a stickler for the memorization of dates, but I am very much concerned that children have a broad grasp of time periods. For example, the period of the prophets from the Old Testament is the same time period during which the Mound Builders were active right here in America.

Last, the exercises are designed for the children to use the book for assistance. So if I do ask for a date, they can look it up. This should help them develop basic study skills.

Step #8—Quizzes ("What Did You Learn?")

The next item in the curriculum layout (which alternates weekly with the Exercise) is a quiz titled "What Did You Learn?" Pay close attention to what I have to say about these quizzes. To me, this is THE MOST unique feature of this curriculum. Each and every quiz is designed to review material from the very beginning of the course. They are *cumulative* reviews. I have never come across this format in any other history curriculum. I have seen the idea of cumulative review only in other subjects, such as math.

I would expect a child from 3rd or 4th grade to 8th grade to begin to receive real grades for his quiz performance to motivate good study habits and to develop test-taking skills, which are sometimes lacking in the homeschool environment. I don't believe in testing for the sake of busy work. Nor do I believe that tests can always reflect true learning. However, these cumulative quizzes will help a child to practice the retention of those facts that I believe are worth remembering. (For grading suggestions and format, see the section titled "The X File: Tips on Grading" later in this frontmatter.)

I tried to avoid overly specific questions that would discourage the average student but to include questions challenging enough to captivate the brighter student. Overall the quizzes are not so difficult that most students couldn't perform well. They are meant to BRING BACK to mind topics and names that a student might otherwise forget. Generally, the selected questions are asked in the chronological order in which the content was studied so that even at a glance, the children see an outline of when events took place. You will observe that the quizzes become longer throughout the text and appear more complex. However, the questions are not necessarily harder. The format is just more intimidating. By all means, give assistance to those students who would be overwhelmed.

Step #9—Quarterly Worksheets ("Put It All Together")

By the end of each quarter, students will have learned many lessons. To help them sum it all up without confusing who is who, the students are asked to complete a worksheet at the end of each nine-week quarter. They ARE expected to use the lessons to answer the questions! The worksheets are similar to the exercises but vary in length and depth.

Step #10—Semester Tests

At the conclusion of each semester, the students are given a long test. The test covers material just from the previous two quarters studied. The semester tests vary from the quizzes only in length. Each semester (which is two quarters, or half of one school year) covers one major time period.

There are ultimately 10 time periods in which to study. My intent is to write five volumes of this history curriculum in which two time periods are covered in each volume. (Pray that the Lord will allow the completion of this project!) For your information, this is the probable breakdown for this and future volumes. Exact dates are subject to change.

1. Volume I: Creation to the Resurrection   Creation–A.D. 29
2. Volume II: The Early Church and the Middle Ages   A.D. 30–1460
3. Volume III: The Renaissance and Growth of Empires   1461–1707
4. Volume IV: Revolutions and Rising Nations   1708–1914
5. Volume V: The World at War and the Present Day   1915–Present Day

Step #11—Student Notebooks

Besides *The Mystery of History* book, which students and teachers use together, each student should have an individual three-ring Student Notebook. This notebook should contain eight dividers, one for each of the seven continents and one for miscellaneous items. This notebook will grow over time. As students complete an activity or map that is on paper, they file it under the appropriate continent.

Subsequent dividers can be made out of regular notebook paper and labeled with individual country names, such as "China" or "Ancient Greece." I will often tell the student to file a project under the continent name and the country name, for instance, "Asia: China" or "Europe: Ancient Greece." I want the student to really "own" the notebook as a scrapbook of his studies. In it he will file maps, reports, photos of activities, and some exercise pages. It would also be a great place to file pictures of family vacations and brochures from special places.

III. Suggested Schedules and Adaptations

Younger Students

For those whose oldest students are still in the kindergarten to 2nd grade stage, I would consider choosing two to three lessons a week to read and doing one to three corresponding activities. (The curriculum would last more than one year at this pace.) Some children with shorter attention spans may prefer one small bit of work a day. That could mean reading the lesson one day and doing the corresponding activity the next day. I would not necessarily suggest that younger students take pretests or complete the exercises or the quizzes unless they are particularly inclined to sit-down work. The questions of the pretests, exercises, or quizzes could be skipped altogether or presented orally instead and kept "fun" like a game show. Memory Cards could be made by the teacher and pulled out for games or drills.

Timeline figures could be made for favorite figures in history but not for all. Maps could be done on an "as-interested" basis. Many of the geography skills involve only "finger mapping" where a student finds a spot on a globe or map with his finger but is not required to transfer this information to paper. These exercises would be very appropriate for children to learn about the basic makeup of their world without stressing them out over more paperwork.

To summarize, here might be a typical week for a family with the oldest child being the age of kindergarten up to 2nd grade.

Mon	Tues	Wed	Thur	Fri
Oral Pretest; Lesson 1	Activity 1	Lesson 2	Activity 2	Timeline

A variation to this format could be:

Mon	Tues	Wed	Thur	Fri
Lesson 1; Activity 1	No history	Lesson 2; Activity 2	No history	Mapping

Or:

Read Lesson 1	Read Lesson 2	Read Lesson 3	Do one activity from Lesson 1, 2, or 3	Oral quiz

Middle and Older Students

For the family who has the oldest child in 3rd–8th grades, a schedule might be as follows:

Mon	Tues	Wed	Thurs	Fri
Pretest; Read Lesson 1; Activity 1	Read Lesson 2; Activity 2	Read Lesson 3; Memory Cards	Review; Exercise or Quiz	OFF

The activities may be skipped sometimes as in the example above on Wednesday. The other activities are chosen based on what is best for the 3rd–8th grader as well as any younger siblings. If the activities are simple, a family may have two children doing a fun, hands-on project and two working on more challenging research—whatever accommodates the family as a whole.

Another sample week (that fits what we most often do) would look like the one below. My children are older and have longer attention spans. Therefore, it is a better use of our time to do a lot of history on one day rather than a little every day. Besides, my kids love science and don't want to share those days with history!

Mon	Tues	Wed	Thurs	Fri
Pretest; Read Lesson 1–2 Activity 1 *or* 2	Science day, no history	Read Lesson 3; Activity 3; Make Memory Cards	Science day, no history	Review; Exercise or Quiz

For those who may have **high schoolers**, this material could serve as a **framework** for further research and study on their part. Some of the "Older Student" activities are perfectly suitable for the high schooler whereas the quizzes and mapping would not be challenging enough for them.

Most high school students will want one year of world history and one year of American history on their high school transcript. Economics and government are generally taught together to comprise the senior year of high school. That would total three years of history in high school.

I opt instead for teaching history in four years. I would teach what I call "World History and Geography" in two years (9th and 10th grades) and what I call "American and Modern History" in 11th. The senior year can still be reserved for economics and government. My reasoning for two years of world history rather than one is simply that I believe it is too vast a subject to teach adequately in one year!

Therefore, if a high schooler chose to use *The Mystery of History* as a framework for study, it might look something like this:

Volumes I–III	9th and 10th grade
Volumes IV–V	11th grade

A CLASSICAL APPROACH TO EDUCATION

I want to expand on the design of this curriculum in regard to the classical approach to education. For those of you not familiar with that philosophy, let me explain.

A classical education is one that is language-centered, which means that students will do great volumes of *reading, listening,* and *writing* to learn. Furthermore, a classical education observes three stages of training the mind. The three-stage process is called the "trivium" of learning. I will briefly describe each.

Stage one is referred to as the **Grammar** stage. It would primarily describe children in the grades of kindergarten through 3rd or 4th grade. The authors of the book *The Well-Trained Mind* consider these ages as those that are most **absorbent.** They believe it is not so much a time of "self-discovery" as it the accumulation of new ideas, new words, new stories, and new facts. This can be a fun stage for a teacher. At the same time, the immaturity of this age range can create a battle for "how" this information is obtained!

Stage two is referred to as the **Logic** stage because children of this age group are beginning to process information they've obtained and to **question** it. This group would include 4th and 5th graders through about 8th grade. The reason that students begin to ask more "why" questions at this stage is because their ability to think abstractly has been further developed. They should begin to process things more logically. Unfortunately, some children question authority at this stage as well!

The third stage of the trivium of learning is referred to as the **Rhetoric.** These are students from about 9th grade up. By this stage, students should be **applying** information that has been learned. The challenge I have found at this last stage is in the interest level of the student. "Ability" does not always equate with "desire"!

In summary, the grammar student absorbs information, the logic student questions information, and the rhetoric student should be able to analyze or defend information. Of course, these stages are only generalities. Learning styles, personalities, and maturity can certainly affect the way any student learns.

In this curriculum, I have considered the trivium of learning and hoped to incorporate it throughout. Here is how.

The **grammar stage:** I believe the *reading* of the lessons *is* the primary source of absorbing new information for these students. The activity is then designed to be fun and to reinforce what they have learned. This student may be interested in the activity for either "Younger Student" or "Middle Student." The Memory Cards will be especially helpful in capturing the new information the student has learned.

The **logic stage:** Again, the reading of the lesson is the primary source of absorbing new information. However, these students will find that the "Middle Student" and "Older Student" activities force them to a more in-depth handling and processing of the information. Some activities are merely fun, whereas others are designed to be thought provoking. The biweekly exercises and quizzes complement the handling of the material when the student is required to make lists, compare dates, and so forth. Memory Cards will be essential in summarizing and organizing what the student has learned.

The **rhetoric stage:** This begins for most students in high school, but I know there are some mature 6th through 8th graders who are ready to touch on this level of interpreting and applying information. Therefore, some of the "Older Student" activities were written with them in mind. Many are research-oriented or at least require further reading and writing. I wrote many of the older activities with the hope of developing a strong Christian worldview in a student. I especially want the older students to become masters at expressing thoughts.

One last aspect of classical education is the process of repeating the presentation of some material at each level of the trivium. In other words, a good classical education would provide information to a student in the younger years, repeat it on a higher level in the middle years, and repeat it again at an even higher level of learning in the older years.

Not all curricula will fit that mold. My hope is that *The Mystery of History* will. If a family's oldest child is in preschool, I would hope that they could cover Volumes 1–5 of this course until 3rd grade. If they waited until kindergarten to begin, that would require some skipping around because there are only four years in that time span. In both instances, I would hope the pressure would be low on the written work but high in listening and reading the lessons and high in doing some of the activities for enrichment and enjoyment.

Ideally, that same student could repeat *The Mystery of History*, Volumes 1–5, between the years of 4th grade and 8th grade as a true **day-to-day curriculum.** That would include pretests, lots of activities, all the quizzes, and use of the Memory Cards.

Last, a high school student could once again repeat the material in *The Mystery of History* as a skeleton or framework for further study. It would require three years to complete Volumes 1–5 (as described in the "Letter to the Teacher" section).

I also want to elaborate on "Bloom's Taxonomy." Benjamin Bloom was an educational psychologist in the 1950s. He helped educators identify six different classifications of learning. They range from lower-level learning to higher level in this order: Knowledge, Comprehension, Application, Analysis, Synthesis, and Evaluation.

Interestingly, in his study, Bloom concluded that 95 percent of all test questions in the average classroom only required students to think at the lowest level of learning, that of recalling information. He observed that higher thinking skills were not being required of students.

I just want you to know that I've kept Bloom's theories in consideration when writing my material. But I don't feel I solved the problem through my tests. You will notice that they, too, are primarily focused on the recall of information. That was intentional. I want the students to review over and over again the many characters they have studied.

However, in an attempt to require some higher-level thinking, I created activities after each lesson that would challenge the students' minds to apply, analyze, synthesize, and evaluate information. An example would be that of the activity on Cleopatra in which students are asked to creatively write diary pages of either Cleopatra herself or Julius Caesar when he met her. The students have to really think about what these characters thought and felt in order to accurately portray them in writing. For more examples, see the "Letter to the Teacher" (Step #4—Activities).

If you would like more information and better definitions of Bloom's Taxonomy, I recommend looking for it on the Internet. There are numerous sites available that explain Bloom's theories in better detail.

I hope many of you make it for the long haul in home education. As I write this material, my own three children are each in one of the three stages of the trivium. Presently, Ashley is 8 years of age, Kyle is 12, and Heather is 15. Each stage has its own rewards and challenges. I love them all (the kids and the stages!) and find the training of the mind to be a fascinating adventure. Enjoy it!

MEMORY CARDS

I. Making the Cards

Ideally, students will make "Memory Cards" as a tool for reinforcing the material they have learned. (Younger students whose hands tire of written work may be the exception.) By making your own cards, your cost for this study is kept down and the students learn!

For one volume of study, obtain about 100, 3-by-5-inch ruled cards. White cards will be sufficient. There are 10 time periods to study in the five volumes of *The Mystery of History*, so you will need 10 colored markers to distinguish these eras from one another. These are the colors I will be using on my cards. Follow if possible because I may refer to the colors in future memory games.

• Volume I-A	Creation and Early Civilizations	Dark green
• Volume I-B	The Classical World	Red
• Volume II-A	The Early Church	Light purple
• Volume II-B	The Middle Ages	Gray
• Volume III-A	The Reformation and Renaissance	Light green
• Volume III-B	The Growth of Empires	Dark blue
• Volume IV-A	Revolution and Independence	Dark pink
• Volume IV-B	Rising Nations	Black
• Volume V-A	The World at War	Orange
• Volume V-B	The Modern World	Dark purple

Using a dark green marker, set up the cards for Volume I-A to look like this sample.

(Front, blank side)	(Back, lined side)
	Vol 1-A 7
The Sumerians	(summary sentence of Sumerians in pencil)
	c. 3500–2500 B.C.

The front of the card is simply the name of the lesson as given in the Contents. The back of the card should contain three or four items.

1. The upper left corner should give the volume number and either an "A" or a "B." An "A" refers to the first semester of study, or first time period of that volume. A "B" refers to the second semester of study, or second time period of the same volume. Each volume will cover two time periods, or semesters, of study.

2. The upper right corner should give the number of the lesson as given in the Contents and on the lesson page itself. There are about 50 lessons per each semester.
3. The middle of the card leaves space for one- to three-sentence summaries of the lesson. (Use pencil or pen for this because the marker will be too broad.) This activity of writing the sentences will vary for different ages. Younger children may help the teacher by narrating a sentence summary. Middle and older students can do more of this independently. I encourage the use of their book.
4. The very bottom of the card should give the date of the lesson or its approximate time span.

II. Using the Cards

The exercise of making the cards is in itself valuable because the student records the information and is reminded of the lessons studied. The cards also serve to help a student develop good organizational skills. In preparing for quizzes and tests, the cards can be used as study guides.

I recommend that a student (or siblings who share the job) make the cards at one time about every three lessons. **I remind students of these cards on the activity page of every third lesson.**

Families and groups should incorporate review of the cards in some systematic fashion. The cards could be pulled out, shuffled, and refiled. They could be brought out before quizzes to see what topics need to be studied. They might be used in games of trivia. Use your own imagination.

I do not necessarily expect every date and lesson to be memorized. Maybe some of you will choose to be that industrious. I prefer instead that a student be able to place a lesson in the proper **time period**. That is the reason for the emphasis on the specific marker color on the card. The colors will help the mind to visualize where a piece of information **fits into history**.

However, there are 12 significant dates I do recommend that students memorize. I will make reference to them throughout the text.

III. Storing the Cards

I recommend two methods of storing your cards. First, the Oxford Company that makes the 3-by-5-inch cards also makes a small two-ring binder for the cards. It is called the "Oxford Index Card Binder." Office supply stores as well as some superstore grocers carry them. (It appears to be item No. 73501.) This binder could easily hold cards for one volume. It would serve to keep the cards very handy while that period of time was being studied. Besides that, the binders are cool gadgets to make school a little more exciting.

Second, after completing one volume, those 100 or so cards could be filed in a standard 3-by-5 card file that holds approximately 600 cards. The binder would then be free for the next volume's cards. The card file could be used again and again over the years to review previously learned material.

The Mystery of History

WALL OF FAME
TIMELINE SUGGESTIONS

As mentioned earlier, part of the Review for each week consists of adding timeline figures to the "Wall of Fame." Though I have seen many beautiful timelines created for homeschoolers that could wrap around a wall in one's home, we have never had the space for such a luxury. Even if I had the space, I'm not so sure that I want to "see" the timeline on an everyday basis. I will share the one method that has worked best for our family.

We opted to make a foldable timeline out of a sewing board that can easily be stored in a closet or tucked behind a cupboard and brought out when it is review time. In fact, we have two of them. One board is for B.C. figures and the other for A.D. figures. Here are the details for the assembly of it. (I did not create the idea of using a sewing board and would love to give credit to the person who did. I just don't know who came up with the idea!)

1. To make a timeline just for this volume of study, only one foldable sewing board would be necessary. The board is about 2 yards in length and 1 yard in width. The outside is decorated with measurements but the inside is blank. The blank inside is where you will build your timeline. Fabric boards or sewing boards can be purchased at most fabric stores for about $10.

Ashley is getting ready to work on our foldable timeline made from a sewing board.

2. You now have two options for placing dates on your board.

   a. The dates could be marked with different-colored markers directly onto the blank inside of the sewing board.

   b. Or, you may opt to adhere laminated strips of paper onto the inside of the board with dates written on them. The advantage to laminated strips would simply be that when necessary to move figures around, which we occasionally do, the tape on the figures will not tear the laminated strips (but it will sometimes tear the bare cardboard). Your budget may dictate which method to choose as some cost is involved with laminating.

3. If you are going to make strips, follow these next instructions.

   a. Purchase two pieces of standard-size poster board. I recommend the same color to keep things simple.

   b. On the first poster board mark off 15 strips that are 1½ inches wide and 18 inches long. DO NOT CUT THEM YET, DO NOT CUT THEM YET, DO NOT CUT THEM YET. (You will want to laminate them first!)

   c. Repeat this step on the second poster board and again, DO NOT CUT THE STRIPS YET, DO NOT CUT THE STRIPS YET, DO NOT CUT THE STRIPS YET!

   d. You are now going to write a beginning and ending date on each of your 30 strips using a dark marker.

e. Follow the pattern as given. STILL, DO NOT CUT THE STRIPS YET.

99 B.C.	0

(Blank)	(Blank)

299 B.C.	200 B.C.

199 B.C.	100 B.C.

499 B.C.	400 B.C.

399 B.C.	300 B.C.

699 B.C.	600 B.C.

599 B.C.	500 B.C.

(Make identical strips of the years 899 B.C. to 700 B.C. because this is when the Kingdom of Israel divided. Students will be placing figures such as the prophets on the top line to signify the Northern Kingdom and on the bottom line to signify the Southern Kingdom. This will become clearer as we approach the subject.)

899 B.C.	800 B.C.

799 B.C.	700 B.C.

899 B.C.	800 B.C.

799 B.C.	700 B.C.

1099 B.C.	1000 B.C.

999 B.C.	900 B.C.

1299 B.C.	1200 B.C.

1199 B.C.	1100 B.C.

1499 B.C.	1400 B.C.

1399 B.C.	1300 B.C.

1699 B.C.	1600 B.C.

1599 B.C.	1500 B.C.

1899 B.C.	1800 B.C.

1799 B.C.	1700 B.C.

2099 B.C.	2000 B.C.

1999 B.C.	1900 B.C.

2299 B.C.	2200 B.C.

2199 B.C.	2100 B.C.

2499 B.C.	2400 B.C.
Blank	Blank

2399 B.C.	2300 B.C.
Blank	Blank

f. Now that the strips are properly labeled, you will take them to a copy store and kindly have them laminate the entire poster board for you.

g. NOW YOU MAY CUT OUT THE STRIPS!

h. Lay them out on your sewing board as shown on the preceding pages, working from the bottom up. I used a very sturdy double-sided adhesive to adhere the strips.

i. On the bottom of the first panel of your sewing board, you may want to come up with some creative lettering for the Seven Days of Creation. We will not be giving these days of Creation a date. You may use the scraps of poster board that were already laminated or use any colored paper.

j. At the other end or the top of your timeline, you may want to creatively spell out "Before Christ" with special emphasis on the letters "B" and "C." This will quickly identify your timeline. (Instructions for an A.D. timeline will be in Volume 2.) A few figures will overlap the two major divisions of time.

4. If you are not going to cut strips but rather "draw" them on the cardboard, follow the directions for the spacing of your lines as shown on the preceding pages.

5. When we do use the timeline, I find it easiest to use the blank side of 3-by-5 cards. You can cut three figures out of one card if you angle the figures slightly. I recommend (though it is not necessary) that you color-code your figures. For example, the Oxford Company sells a pack of 300 assorted color 3-by-5 cards. These colors could be used at your own discretion or you could follow my suggested code below. In a corner of your timeline, set up a key to correspond to the major cultures we will study.

Israelites	Purple
Egyptians	Salmon
Greeks	Green
Romans	Blue
Chinese	Yellow
All others	White
(Persians, Macedonians, etc.)	

6. Throughout the text I give guidelines for adding detail to your figures. Your children's interest level may dictate how extensive you get on decorating your figures. I have most certainly made several figures myself over the years to move the process along.

7. I do recommend that you trace and cut a pattern similar to the one below for convenience. I often have the pattern traced ahead of time for the children but not always cut out. For example, if we add a trumpet to the figure of Gideon, it is easiest to draw it attached to his hand, and *then* cut it out.

8. On review day we most often are in need of creating just three figures. We follow the directions for each and simply tape them on at the appropriate place in time. Some families prefer to make the timeline figures on the day that they study the corresponding lesson. I prefer the exercise later in the week as a means of bringing back information taught earlier in the week.

9. On the top center point of my timeline, I used a hole-puncher to create a hole just large enough so that I can "hang" my timeline on a nail on the wall while we are using it. I highly recommend this! It could also remain flat on the floor. It is large though!

10. PLEASE TAKE NOTE AHEAD OF TIME: I give instructions for a very special timeline project on the last Review page of the book. It involves running a piece of yarn throughout the entire timeline at the end of the course to display the lineage of Christ. You might want to stop and read it now so you will be thinking about the figures you'll include ahead of time.

Kyle is shown with the foldable timeline hanging during school hours in our classroom, better known as the dining room.

THE X FILE:
TIPS ON GRADING

To aid you in the philosophy of grading and record keeping, I have created a diagram that I hope you'll find helpful. As you can see, at the younger grade levels I believe that grading and daily lesson plans should be loosely kept. The main reason is that teacher involvement is naturally high. The teacher should know how well lessons are being grasped because of one-on-one interaction. Younger students need most things read and explained to them. Enjoy this time; it's rewarding to be directly interacting with their young minds. Their questions and perspectives are amazing.

On the other end of the spectrum, the older student should be well into studying independently. Therefore, grades and lesson plans are absolutely essential in giving them guidance and in knowing whether or not they are learning the material. Teacher involvement will be low because there are usually younger children to be taught and because ultimately, most teachers are "mothers." We are not biology teachers, algebra teachers, or Latin teachers. We can give guidance and help. But I have observed that successful older homeschool students are those who find that THEY must take the responsibility to learn. They become self-teachers, which is a great achievement in and of itself.

I believe the middle years are the more trying ones as teacher involvement naturally goes down and the need for grades and efficient record keeping goes up. Middle students need to be weaned from too much teacher involvement (assuming the student can read and follow directions), while at the same time they still need to be well taught! Too much help from a teacher can lead to students becoming lazy with their work and leaning on the teacher to get it done. Not enough help can lead to student frustration and poor understanding. It's a delicate balance requiring frequent adjustments because subjects vary in their need for teacher interaction.

To summarize, for younger students I don't feel it is necessary to keep "grades" per se, and my lesson plans are loosely kept to allow for creative bursts. For the middle student, however, I record grades in essential courses and maintain basic lesson plans. For the older students, I feel it is absolutely necessary to record grades and map out the work to be completed through detailed lesson plans. Thus a shift takes place from teacher to student as the diagram represents.

With that philosophy lesson behind us, let me give you a systematic plan for keeping the grades that you decide to keep. I don't mean to insult you, but I will be very specific. For some of you, this is new territory.

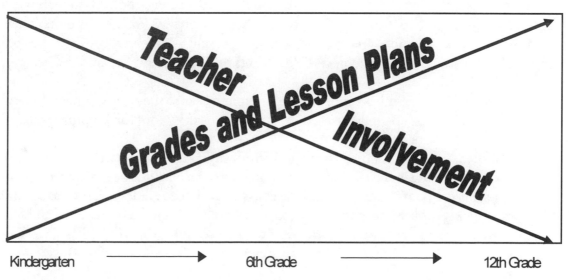

Kindergarten   →   6th Grade   →   12th Grade

Beginning with the pretests, I would grade one just after it was taken, but I would not necessarily RECORD the grade. I would simply let the student take the pretest and grade it with a 100 if they are all correct. Or, give them a fraction on the top of the page made up of the number of questions answered correctly over the total number of questions on the pretest. For example, 6/8 means the student missed two questions. The purpose of the pretest is not to measure what they know. It is to spark interest.

For the quizzes, however, I would begin to record these grades and accumulate them. **The quizzes ARE designed to measure what they have learned.** First you have to grade them with a fraction to represent the number of questions answered correctly over the total number of questions on the quiz. For example, 14/18 means that the student missed 4 questions. If you punched those numbers into a calculator, you would do 14 "divided by" 18 "equals" 78. On a scale of 1–100, a 78 means something to a student. You may decide on your own grading scale as to what you believe is a fair letter grade. I keep it simple with 90–100 being an A, 80–90 a B, and so on.

As I go through the year, **I choose to record the fractions,** not the final letter grade. This is why. The fractions will automatically "weigh" the quizzes, tests, and worksheets fairly. You see, the worksheets and tests are longer, giving the fractions greater denominators. A test grade may look like 28/36. They missed far more than the earlier quiz I described. They missed 8 questions instead of 4. But, if you put 28/36 on a calculator, it also equals 78. The student answered more questions correctly because there were more questions! Hope you follow that.

Through the year I keep track of their fractions so that at any given time I can stop and calculate their present grade. I simply add ALL the denominators of the fractions and write this number down. Then I add ALL the numerators of the fractions and write this down. Next, I divide the numerator sum by the denominator sum and voila! I have a numerical grade that I can now give a letter grade based on my grading scale.

If you think that your student does not perform well on quizzes or tests, **consider stacking up his or her grade average with credit for lessons and/or activities.** If he reads his lesson, he could get a 10/10 to average in. If he completes an activity, give it a 10/10. If he gets sloppy on activities, give him less credit, like a 7/10. That will bring down his average, as maybe it should. Use the grades as you need them to motivate, reward, or punish.

I like to use grades to reward hard work done, like reading, being creative, or having studied hard for a test. You can determine what to grade and when to grade and throw them all in the same pot for an average every nine weeks. At the end of this section, I have provided a grid on which to record grades. Some days may remain blank. If you have two graded pieces fall on the same day, just record them together. Add the numerators and the denominators separately. They will average out the same.

In regard to special activities or **projects,** I recommend establishing a point system. For example, if your student is going to do a particularly hard project, make it worth 50, 75, or 100 points. Then break it down such as neatness = 10 points, creativity = 10 points, content = 15 points, research = 10 points, and so forth. Then your student might achieve 43/50 points on a special project, and that fraction can be averaged into his grade.

I do present my children with a **report card** every nine weeks so they know where they stand. This gives ample time for pulling up grades if need be. It is also a healthy tool for keeping family members informed as to how the students are performing.

I find this form of record keeping the least painful way to track the work my middle and older students are doing. For a student below 4th grade, I don't bother at all with the grade average. For middle or older students, I use this same method in all the courses that I keep grades for, such as spelling, math, and so on. I can quickly look at the grade record to see what the student has completed and what I have graded. I may only actually grade their work every week or so and at that time fill in a week of grades. But, with one glance at the grade record, I can pick up where I left off and stay on track.

GRADE RECORD

STUDENT _____   GRADE _____

SUBJECT _____   YEAR _____

First Quarter

	Wk 1	Wk 2	Wk 3	Wk 4	Wk 5	Wk 6	Wk 7	Wk 8	Wk 9
Mon.									
Tues.									
Wed.									
Thurs.									
Fri.									

Second Quarter

	Wk 1 (10)	Wk 2 (11)	Wk 3 (12)	Wk 4 (13)	Wk 5 (14)	Wk 6 (15)	Wk 7 (16)	Wk 8 (17)	Wk 9 (18)
Mon.									
Tues.									
Wed.									
Thurs.									
Fri.									

Third Quarter

	Wk 1 (19)	Wk 2 (20)	Wk 3 (21)	Wk 4 (22)	Wk 5 (23)	Wk 6 (24)	Wk 7 (25)	Wk 8 (26)	Wk 9 (27)
Mon.									
Tues.									
Wed.									
Thurs.									
Fri.									

Fourth Quarter

	Wk 1 (28)	Wk 2 (29)	Wk 3 (30)	Wk 4 (31)	Wk 5 (32)	Wk 6 (33)	Wk 7 (34)	Wk 8 (35)	Wk 9 (36)
Mon.									
Tues.									
Wed.									
Thurs.									
Fri.									

SEMESTER I

CREATION AND
EARLY CIVILIZATIONS

CONTENTS

THE MYSTERY BEGINS:
CREATION to 1199 B.C.

AROUND THE WORLD

Are you curious about unusual or peculiar things? Do you wonder about the mysteries of life or unexplained phenomena? Are you inspired by stories of great love, courage, and heroism? If the answer to any of these questions is yes, you are going to enjoy the next nine weeks.

As we begin to study the history of the world, we will examine ancient wonders like Stonehenge and the pyramids. We will consider mysteries of the Ice Age, dinosaurs, and the Tower of Babel. We will become acquainted with some unusual characters like Hammurabi, Nefertiti, and the famous King Tut. At the same time, we will read about some familiar Bible heroes such as Noah, Moses, and Joseph.

So, if you were zooming over the earth about 8,000 or 6,000 years ago, what would you find? I think you would find many groups of people, spanning many parts of the globe. Though man may have first started out in the Garden of Eden, he quickly reproduced and populated the earth. Animals and dinosaurs were all over the world, too.

The earth was different back then, though. The Bible says that a large canopy of water vapor covered the world like a greenhouse. So rain wasn't needed like it is today. This healthy globe helped man to live to be hundreds and hundreds of years old. Do you know the age of the oldest man who ever lived? The Bible says that a man named Methuselah lived to be 969 years old! That is a lot of birthdays.

However, the Bible states that God caused a Great Flood to destroy all that He had created. For man had become exceedingly wicked. That is, all except for one man, the grandson of Methuselah whose name was Noah. The ark that Noah built under God's guidance was large enough to house himself, his wife, his sons and their wives, and representatives of all the animals of the world. All these creatures were spared from the Great Flood.

Things changed after the flood. In particular, the earth got very, very cold. We refer to that time period as the Ice Age. But, men still flourished greatly and spread out once again all over the world. With so much frozen ocean, land bridges were easily exposed, enabling men to travel to all corners of the earth and repopulate.

3

These early men and women accomplished some amazing things. Some of the archaeological remains that are still standing today provide evidence of early man's great ingenuity. For example, there is a rock formation named Stonehenge in England that still baffles archaeologists as to exactly how it was built. And of course there are the magnificent pyramids in Egypt that speak volumes to us about the past. Many structures like this stand as witnesses to the great mind of early man.

Did man ever evolve from other species or live primitively in caves? I don't believe the Theory of Evolution supports itself very well. However, I imagine there were some men and women in the world who liked the shelter of caves. These people would naturally appear to be more "primitive" than those who were building great monuments. Just like today, people were very different around the world. Some nations were wealthy while others struggled to exist. Cultures have always been influenced by the natural resources available to them.

One of the more advanced early cultures we will study is that of the Egyptians. Their greatest resource was the Nile River. As the Nile provided water for their crops, thousands of people were able to grow grain and establish permanent homes. Scattered cities grew into a great nation. From their pyramids to their elaborate temples, we will see men who thought big.

Besides the Egyptians, there were people such as the Kushites who established their own civilizations in northern Africa. The Egyptians and the Kushites sometimes fought over who was in control. We don't have much record of the early people who lived south of the Sahara because they didn't leave behind written records and huge monuments like the Egyptians did. And like simple tribes that still exist today, some early groups of people just kept to themselves.

In present-day Pakistan, there once was a very advanced civilization that thrived in the Indus Valley. It is from the name of the Indus River that India derived its name. Just as the Nile was a great resource to the Egyptians, it was the Indus River that gave so much life to its residents. These early inhabitants of the Indus Valley even had homes with running water and toilets. Yet, after some time, they "disappeared" into history. They vanished either because of flooding in the valley or because of outside invaders. Nobody knows for sure.

Farther east in Asia, there were certainly many people living in what we now know as China. They relied on rivers, too, to help in their survival. The Huang He, or Yellow River, provided rich, fertile soil for their crops. We will study the unique features of this people and some of their best-kept secrets.

South of Asia, in the vast waters of the Pacific Ocean, there were numerous small islands inhabited as early as 1800 B.C. These early people probably migrated from nearby lands such as Australia and China. Skilled craftsmen made boats sturdy enough to carry themselves as well as plants and animals to their new homes. Settled islands included Indonesia, the Marianas, the Solomon Islands, and Micronesia. How brave these early settlers must have been to travel the distances they did following the stars and sea currents.

And throughout this time period, the Lord was unfolding a great plan to Abraham, who fathered the Jewish nation. Abraham lived in Mesopotamia in a country named Sumer. Sumer sat between two great rivers, the Tigris and the Euphrates. The area has been nicknamed the Fertile Crescent because of how rich the land was.

How do we know about the lives of all these ancient people? We know of them mostly through what they wrote down about themselves. You see, in Egypt hieroglyphics were developed as a means of communication. In Mesopotamia, where Abraham was from, there was cuneiform writing on clay tablets. The early Chinese created a symbolic alphabet containing thousands of characters. The Indus Valley had its own form of writing, too. It is amazing that there are written records of things that happened so long ago. But we are so grateful that there are. It again shows us the ingenuity of the first civilizations. They were far more than "cave people."

But there is yet one other great source for knowing how people lived long ago. It is through the written words of the Bible, which I believe to have been inspired by God and recorded by men. There are so many incredible stories from the Bible, that I could never fit them all into this one curriculum. As we go through the chapters of history, you will want to read along in your Bible at the same time. Moving stories of faith like those of Job, Joseph, and Ruth are considered great literature and still give comfort to people today. But more than that, I believe that the Bible is also the greatest history book you'll ever read.

As you cover these fascinating topics and cultures in the next few weeks, stop and think about how amazing mankind and the world in which we live really are. And yet, even more awesome than all of that is the One who created it all, God Himself.

☑ WHAT DO YOU KNOW?

Pretest 1

Pretests are meant to be fun and to spark your curiosity. Before we study our lessons this week, what do you already know? Just like they do on the television game show *Jeopardy,* I am going to supply you with an answer. You come up with the right question from the list at the bottom of this page. This is not meant to be a recorded grade. Answers are in the Appendix at the back of the book so you can see how well you did!

1. The book of the Bible that explains how man was created.

2. The day of Creation in which the sun, moon, and stars were created.

3. The day of Creation in which God says He rested.

4. The first two people God created.

5. The children of Adam and Eve.

6. The name of a man who made instruments and taught music.

7. Sin and death entered the world.

8. The person mentioned in the Bible who crafted bronze and iron.

    What is Day 7 of Creation?
    Who is Jubal?
    What is Genesis?
    Who is Tubal-Cain?
    What is Day 4 of Creation?
    Who are Adam and Eve?
    What is the result of Adam's disobedience?
    Who are Cain and Abel?

CREATION

LESSON 1

Creation is an amazing topic that far surpasses our own understanding. For ages, man has asked the question of *how* he was created. Scientists today debate this question with every idea imaginable. Some say we evolved out of microscopic matter or pond scum. Others theorize that we came from another planet. Many believe that life began with a "big bang," or explosion in the universe, that set things in motion.

A better question for mankind might be "*Who* made us?" For Christians, this is easier to answer. Christians believe that a loving and personal God created each and every one of us. And Christians not only believe they know *who* made us, but also *how* we were created, *when* we were created, and *why* we were created. Isn't that incredible? According to the Scriptures, there *is* an answer to the mystery of life!

"*In the beginning God created the heavens and the earth.*" Genesis 1:1

Beginning with HOW, the first verse of the first book of the Bible tells us "In the beginning God created the heavens and the earth." Further on, the book of Genesis says, "and the Lord God formed man of the dust of the ground, and breathed into his nostrils the breath of life; and man became a living being." Wow! There it is. God Himself tells us this is how life began.

As for WHEN, Genesis 2:4 says, "This is the history of the heavens and the earth when they were created, in the day that the Lord God made the earth and the heavens..." Genesis, Chapter 1, states that He created these things in this order:

Day 1—Light, naming it "day" and the darkness, "night"

Day 2—The firmament, calling it "heaven"

Day 3—The seas and the Earth; grass, seed-bearing herbs, and fruit trees

Day 4—The sun, the moon, and the stars

Day 5—Sea creatures and birds

Day 6—Cattle, creeping things, beasts, man (male and female)

Day 7—God rested

And WHY did God make all of this? There are *many* answers to this question that are found all throughout the scriptures. But, for now, I will mention two. Genesis 1:28 says, "Be fruitful and multiply; fill the earth and subdue it; have dominion over the fish of the sea, over the birds of the air, and over every living thing that moves on the earth." This passage implies that we are to multiply and rule the earth. That is one reason why we are here.

More importantly, I believe we are here to have a relationship with our Creator in which we understand and know Him. Jeremiah 9:23–24 says, "Let not the wise man glory in his wisdom, let not the mighty man glory in his might, nor let the rich man glory in his riches; but let him who glories glory in this, that he understands and knows Me, that I am the Lord." That, surely, is another reason why we are here.

This simple but strong container was used for oil or spices about 3200 B.C. Surprisingly, it has survived for thousands of years!

About 5,000 years after Creation, the apostle Paul wrote in the New Testament, "bring to light . . . the mystery which for ages has been hidden in God, who created all things." (Eph. 3:9) So, my friends, in our study of the history of the world, let us attempt to "bring to light" the mystery of Creation to others. People *do* want to know *how* we got here, *when* we were created, and *why* we're here.

ACTIVITY 1

1A—Younger and Middle Students

To help you remember the seven days of Creation, make a Creation booklet to keep.

Materials: Bible, 4 sheets of white paper (8½ by 11 inches), rubber cement, scissors, markers, crayons, pens or pencils

Carefully follow the directions below to assemble your booklet. Read the directions through one time before you begin. This project may take more than one day to complete.

1. Fold each sheet of paper in half and then in half again, so that you have a "booklet" measuring 4¼ by 5½ inches.

2. Stack the folded booklets together, all opening in the same direction. The folded edges should be at the top and the left side.

3. Pick up the first booklet and put rubber cement on the back of it. Glue it to the front of the next booklet. Repeat this step until all four individual booklets are glued together to create one booklet.

4. Now open your book to the first page. Lift the top half of the page up and you should have a full-sized page in front of you. With your scissors, start on the crease at the very top of the page (where the crease looks like a little "mountain") and cut HALFWAY down the middle of the page on the crease (until it starts to look like a "valley"). Repeat this step for each piece, so that you have a "top" and a "bottom" half for each page.

5. Now you have a cool book that you can open up to write or color in. On the cover, write the word "Creation" in big letters.

6. Open the book and, on the left-hand page, write out Genesis 1:1 if you are a good writer. If you are younger, just write the reference or let your teacher write the verse.

7. On the right-hand page, in big print, write "Day 1." Now, lift the page you just wrote on, and you can either draw a picture of what God created on the first day of Creation, or copy the verse right out of the Bible. You can use the top and bottom of the lifted page. You'll find Day 1 in Genesis 1:2–5.

8. Continue this for all the days of Creation until your book is full. Hunt through Genesis 1 to find all the things God made on the different days.

9. On the outside back cover, be sure to put your name and either the date you made your book or your grade. It will be fun to look at when you are older.

10. File this booklet in the pocket of your Student Notebook.

1B—Middle and Older Students

Research the theory of evolution or the big bang theory. Who proposed these theories? What are the arguments for and against these theories? Use "Answers in Genesis" materials as an excellent resource. Attend one of their conferences if possible. (The Web site for materials and conference information is www.answersingenesis.org.)

If you write up a short paper on your findings, file it in the "Miscellaneous" section of your Student Notebook.

1C—Older Students

Research the phenomenon of natural selection. Familiarize yourself with the term and write at least one paragraph to define it.

In the famous book *The Origin of Species,* Charles Darwin identifies natural selection. However, he interpreted it as a means to prove evolution. From what you have learned about natural selection, where do you think Darwin was in error? Do you believe he was in error with the theory of evolution? Know what you believe and be able to defend it.

c. 6000–4000 B.C.

ADAM AND EVE

LESSON 2

Do you have a picture in your mind of Adam and Eve? From Sunday school, most of us have visions of them hiding behind fig leaves, naked and ashamed. I think we need to remember this part of the story of Adam and Eve's disobedience to God! But, there's more I hope you will remember, too.

It says in Genesis 1:27, "So God created man in His own image; in the image of God He created him; male and female He created them." My friends, those words are very powerful! Powerful because we are told that we were created in the image of God Himself! That makes each and every one of us special and of great value.

The Bible also says that Adam and Eve lived in a beautiful place called the Garden of Eden. We sometimes call it Paradise. It may surprise you but Adam probably kept pretty busy in the Garden. God instructed him to tend and keep the Garden as well as to name every living creature!

As you know though, Paradise had some rules. The Lord God said, "Of every tree of the garden you may freely eat; but of the tree of the knowledge of good and evil you shall not eat, for in the day that you eat of it you shall surely die." (Gen. 2:16–17) Well, there was a crafty serpent in the Garden who made Eve question that rule. And the rest is history. "When the woman saw that the tree was good for food, that it was pleasant to the eyes, and a tree desirable to make one wise, she took of its fruit and ate.

She also gave to her husband with her, and he ate. Then the eyes of both of them were opened, and they knew that they were naked; and they sewed fig leaves together and made themselves coverings." (Gen. 3:6–7)

Because of Adam and Eve's disobedience to God, sin and death entered the world. God then cursed man by requiring him to work harder than he ever had before. He said, "Cursed is the ground for your sake; in toil you shall eat of it all the days of your life. Both thorns and thistles it shall bring forth for you, and you shall eat the herb of the field. In the sweat of your face you shall eat bread until you return to the ground, for out of it you were taken; for dust you are, and to dust you shall return." (Genesis 3:17–19)

Women were cursed by experiencing pain in childbirth and by not desiring to be mastered by their husbands. "I will greatly multiply your sorrow and your conception; in pain you shall bring forth children; your desire shall be for your husband, and he shall rule over you." (Gen. 3:16)

That's the world *we* inherited. That's the world *we* live in! We can't really imagine the perfect world that Adam and Eve had lived in before. By their sin, they forfeited life for death, pleasure for pain, abundance for toil, and perfect fellowship for conflict. The results are evident in the world around us.

But, what else is there to know about Adam and Eve? Let's start with the Garden of Eden. Have you ever wondered where it was? Most historians believe the Garden of Eden was somewhere between the Tigris and Euphrates Rivers in present-day Iraq. The land there is also called the Fertile Crescent, or Mesopotamia.

Do you wonder when Adam and Eve lived? No one knows for sure. But we can estimate that they lived as far back as 6000 B.C. You see, God in His great wisdom has kept a running list in the Bible of all the fathers and their sons from Adam until Christ! (See Luke 3:23–38.) Using this information, we can come close to knowing when Adam might have lived. It's just a matter of counting backward.

Bible scholars think Adam lived to be over 900 years old! This is important to know because he could have learned a lot from God in all those years. We even think that the first account of Genesis was written by God through Adam and passed down for generations. Without TV or radio, people had time to memorize and learn many things.

Today, we cannot imagine a person living to be 600 or 900 years old! But if that is true about Adam, we can assume that the stories Adam had of God were passed almost directly to Noah! You see, although Noah was born a long time after Adam, their lives would almost have overlapped! This means that the stories of Creation and God could easily have been passed down to Noah and preserved after the Great Flood.

It is also important to know that across the world, archaeologists have discovered signs of early man, all dating to around the years 5000 to 4000 B.C. This shows us how quickly man reproduced and began to travel. It is possible that by the time Noah lived, there were already millions of people who had populated the world.

Historians think that by 5000 B.C. man was already cultivating corn in Mexico; there were people living in Nubia, Africa; the Catal Huyuk people were living in Anatolia (present-day Turkey); the Yang Shao period had started in China; and the Pacific islands were already being colonized. There is still a lot we don't know about this time period.

We do know, though, a few things about the children of Adam. The best story to know is that of Cain and Abel. Read more about them in the Bible. You can find their story in Genesis, Chapter 4.

Unlike anyone else who has ever lived, Adam and Eve knew God before sin entered the world, and then they experienced the result of sin. Though none of us have ever met them, through the account of the Bible, we really do know a lot about them.

ACTIVITY 2

2A—Younger Students

To help you appreciate the difficulty of creating a human or an animal, take some simple Play-Doh modeling compound and try to shape it into a man, woman, or animal. Be sure to use some of the modeling compound from Adam to help make Eve because God used the rib of Adam to create Eve. If you really like your creation, take a picture of it and put in your Student Notebook under "Asia: Iraq (Mesopotamia)." That's where the first people lived.

2B—Middle Students

To appreciate the difficulty of creating anything, take Play-Doh modeling compound or clay and make up your own animal unlike anything on earth. Then try to come up with a name for it like Adam did. It says in Genesis 2:19–20 that God gave Adam the job of naming all the animals! Take a picture of your animal and file it in your Student Notebook under "Asia: Iraq (Mesopotamia)."

2C—Older Students

1. Do a simple word study on "Adam" and "Eve." Find out what their names mean. Write down this information and file it under "Asia: Iraq (Mesopotamia)" in your Student Notebook.
2. Do you know the life expectancy of man today? Read Genesis 6:3 to discover the time span that God decided man ought to have. Use an almanac to discover the average age of man today. Compare it over the years.

---

c. 5000 B.C.

JUBAL AND TUBAL-CAIN

LESSON 3

Today we will learn about Jubal and Tubal-Cain, a couple of guys worth remembering in history although you may have never heard of them before. In fact, their names may sound kind of funny to you.

Jubal and Tubal-Cain are important in that they help to show us how intelligent early man was. This is important because Christians believe man was created by a brilliant and personable God! We don't believe that man somehow evolved from a lower form of mammal. If we did, then early man would probably not have been much smarter than the animals.

In Genesis 4:21 we learn that Jubal was "the father of all those who play the harp and flute." This means that he was a musician and that others were playing music, too.

Think about what you already know about music. Is it easy to learn music, to make instruments, or to teach others how to do those things?

If you've ever had music lessons, then you know it can be very difficult. But, that is exactly what the book of Genesis tells us that Jubal was doing.

Genesis 4:22 says that Tubal-Cain was "an instructor of every craftsman in bronze and iron." So, Tubal-Cain was a bronze- and ironmaker who excelled well enough to teach others his trade.

Consider for a moment the making of bronze or iron. Iron is formed by the "cooking" of iron ore deposits with limestone and "coke." (Not the popular soft drink of course.) The coke material comes from the heating of coal without air. All in all, ironmaking is a very complicated and dangerous process. Yet the Bible tells us that Tubal-Cain not only knew the craft of bronze- and ironmaking, but that he also taught the skill to others.

Isn't it neat that God gave us a little insight into the ingenuity of early man? The Bible clearly mentions it in just these few verses (which demonstrates how important it is to know the Bible!). Though some men and women may have lived simple lives or lived in caves for shelter, it is highly unlikely that all early people were "cavemen," as some would like us to believe.

This terra-cotta sheep was used as a child's pull toy and would have originally had wheels on it. It was made for a boy or girl about 2,000 years before Christ lived.

The Bible also mentions the formation of early cities with names such as Babel, Nineveh, Erech, Accad, and Calah. The existence of cities indicates that man was fairly civilized. Genesis 10:12 even states that Calah was a "principal city." It must have really been built up compared to the others.

Jubal and Tubal-Cain were only a few generations from Adam and were already masters and teachers of difficult trades. These inventions and the rise of cities would have required some great thinking and planning. And that in itself is something for us to think about!

ACTIVITY 3

ALL STUDENTS

It's time to make your 3-by-5-inch Memory Cards for Lessons 1-3. Follow the directions for making these cards given in the section "Memory Cards" in the front of this book. I think it will be easiest for you to make three cards at a time, so I will remind you every three lessons to make your cards. You may prefer to make one card every time you read a lesson. You decide what works best for you! The cards are designed to help you remember the lessons and to be used in games; they are not intended to be a burden. Your teacher may opt to write the cards for younger students. Try to use GREEN markers on the front side of the cards for the first semester ("Creation and Early Civilizations"). We will use RED later to distinguish "The Classical World," the title of the second semester.

Field Trip Possibility

If you have an ironmaking plant or factory in your area, set up a visit and learn about the process.

3A—Younger Students

Do you play an instrument? Play *Name That Tune* with your siblings or teacher. With any musical instrument, try to make the sounds of a familiar song and have others guess the song. If you can, use a recorder or flute (one of Jubal's instruments).

3B—Middle Students

On a piano, stringed instrument, or recorder, play an octave scale. That is the name we give to eight sounds that repeat themselves over and over again, going higher and lower. You can remember that an "octave" is eight notes because it is like the word "octopus," a sea creature that has eight legs. Both of those words come from the Latin word "octum," which means eight! If you can read music, write out the notes to an octave and file it under "Asia: Iraq (Mesopotamia)." Title the page "Jubal Teaches Music."

3C—Older Students

Archaeologists often use the terms "Bronze Age" or "Iron Age" to describe particular time periods in history. The making of bronze and iron is obviously relevant to understanding the progress of early man.

Research the process of making bronze or iron. Emphasize the difficulty of the process so as to give early man credit for being intelligent! File your findings under "Asia: Iraq (Mesopotamia)."

TAKE ANOTHER LOOK!

Now it's time to review the people, places, and things we have studied so far. That will be easy this week because we just got started together. But, over the months to come, this will become more challenging.

First, though, you should know these few details. Time is counted backward up until the time of Christ. We call it "B.C."—which means "Before Christ." "A.D." stands for "Anno Domini"—which in Latin means "in the year of the Lord." A.D. refers to everything since the birth of Christ, not his death.

Sometimes you will see the abbreviation "c." or "ca." before a date. It stands for "circa" and means "about." So, if a date is not known exactly, the date given may have a "c." before it. You will see this frequently in our early lessons, which are hard to place in time.

You will also notice that I often give only one date for a person's life. The truth is, of course, that people live for many, many years. But, to keep the timeline simple, in most cases I am having you learn one significant date rather than life-span dates. For example, when we learn about Julius Caesar, I will place the date 49 B.C. by his name. He was born many years before then, but he became an important conqueror of Rome in 49 B.C. So I picked that date to remember him by.

Out of all the important dates we will study together, there are 12 that I would like you to memorize. I'll tell you about them as we go along.

Wall of Fame

Put figures for the following people and events on your timeline in the order given. (For details on constructing a timeline, refer to the section "Wall of Fame Timeline Suggestions" in the front of this book.)

1. *The Days of Creation (c. 6000–4000 B.C.)*—On your timeline, make a circle for each day of Creation with a sketch of what God created on that day. Line these up on the bottom (beginning) of your timeline. (Though I have placed an approximate date on these events, set them on the first blank strip of your timeline.)

2. *Adam and Eve (c. 6000–4000 B.C.)*—Create the figures of Adam and Eve (using the pattern provided in "Wall of Fame Timeline Suggestions" in the front of this book). Make them of pure white to depict their innocence before disobeying God. Write the names Adam and Eve on them and give each one a gold cross because they are in the lineage of Christ. Put a question mark on them for the date. Glue small leaves on their figures to represent their shame after the fall. Then place them on the first blank line of your timeline.

3. *Jubal and Tubal-Cain (c. 5000 B.C.)*—Give Jubal a harp and Tubal an iron rod. These figures may also be placed on the first blank line of your timeline.

If you enjoy timeline work, you could add the men listed in the Bible between Adam and Noah. There are eight men listed in Genesis, Chapter 5. They all lived to be verrrrrrrry old! One of them was Methuselah, who the Bible says is the oldest man that ever lived. See if you can find out how old that was. Put his age on the timeline figure if you can.

SomeWHERE in Time

In a separate section at the back of this book, you'll find 10 outline maps especially designed for *The Mystery of History*. Please photocopy them before using because you'll need to use most maps several times. You'll also need to have on hand atlases from which to obtain the information to record on your maps. I recommend both a Bible atlas and a historical atlas. Also, a globe is helpful for seeing the big picture. Use color-coding, drawings, symbols, and words to complete your mapping projects. While filling in your maps with fine-tip markers or color pencils, be creative and have fun! A well-done map is a piece of art!

For the entire year of mapping assignments for one student, you will need to photocopy:

Map #	1	2	3	4	5	6	7	8	9	10
Quantity	3	8	1	6	4	7	4	1	1	2

1. Can you name the seven continents? Get a map or globe now and name them with your teacher. It will be important to know them throughout this course as you keep a Student Notebook for organizing all your papers and projects. You will file them according to the continent and country that you studied. If you have not done this already, set up a Student Notebook with eight dividers.

    Make a tab for every one of the seven continents and one tab for Miscellaneous items. I would put the tabs in alphabetical order in this manner:

    ### Africa, Antartica, Asia, Australia, Europe, North America, South America

    If you really enjoy coloring projects, use Outline Map 10, "The World," to color, cut, and paste an outline of each continent and glue it to its divider as well.

2. Find the present-day country of Iraq on a globe. Trace with your finger the Euphrates and the Tigris Rivers. Scholars believe that the land in between those rivers is where the Garden of Eden was. While you have the globe out, be sure to find where you live, too.

3. On a map of the ancient Middle East, find some of the very earliest cities ever built, such as Babel, Nineveh, and Calah. Transfer these cities onto Outline Map 6, "Turkey," and label them in your best handwriting. File this map under "Asia: Iraq (Mesopotamia)" in your Student Notebook.

WHAT DID YOU MISS?

Week 1: Exercise

These exercises and review quizzes are a regular part of this course of study. But listen! They can be fun! These questions will help you to go back to ALL the people and events you have learned and REMEMBER them.

When you come to a "What Did You Miss?" exercise, you are expected and encouraged to use your book to find the right answers. The number of questions will increase as we study more people and events. There are 16 exercises to keep you sharp throughout this volume of study. This first one is easy.

1. Cut out the pattern below to make seven identical circles on heavy paper.
2. Draw and color a way to depict each of the seven days of Creation on the circles. For example, Day 7 might be a picture of a bed to symbolize "rest."
3. On the back of each circle, write the answer like "Day 1: Day and night," and so on.
4. Store your circles in a small bag and keep them in the pocket of your Student Notebook. Use them like flashcards to drill yourself on the order of events in Creation.

 **WHAT DO YOU KNOW?**

Pretest 2

Match the following items by placing the correct letter next to the number.

_____ 1. Noah

a. A time period when the earth was colder

_____ 2. Shem, Ham, and Japheth

b. The name of a dinosaur found in the Bible

_____ 3. Rainbow

c. The sons of Noah

_____ 4. Glacier

d. Symbol of God's promise

_____ 5. Canopy

e. A righteous man

_____ 6. Ice Age

f. The scientist who named dinosaurs

_____ 7. Sir Richard Owen

g. Something that is suspended in the air

_____ 8. Behemoth

h. A giant sheet of ice

The Mystery of History

NOAH AND THE FLOOD

LESSON 4

The story of Noah and the flood is probably a very familiar one. Most of us as young children learn about all the animals coming on board the great ark "two by two." We see pictures of doves, rainbows, and Noah with his wife, smiling when the sun comes back out.

These are indeed great points of the story to remember. But, there is so much more to think about than just the happy ending. Consider with me the reason behind the flood. It says in Genesis 6:5–6 that "the Lord saw that the wickedness of man was great in the earth . . . and that He was grieved in His heart." In Genesis 6:3 we see that God had already shortened man's life span to 120 years instead of 800 or 900 because man caused Him strife. (We don't actually see shorter life spans until some time after the flood.)

The Bible says that God was so sorry His creation had become evil that He decided to destroy it all. Except, and this is the best part, "Noah found grace in the eyes of the Lord . . . Noah was a just man, perfect in his generations. Noah walked with God." (Gen. 6: 8–9)

I would love to know exactly how Noah stood out from all his peers. Just how bad were all the other people? What made Noah so different? The Bible clearly says it was his faith. Genesis 6:9 says, "Noah was a just man, perfect in his generations. Noah walked with God." And the result of his godliness was that all living creatures and the human race were saved from destruction!

You see, the Bible says that the flood was so bad that "all flesh died that moved on the earth . . . all in whose nostrils was the breath of the spirit of life, all that was on the dry land, died . . . only Noah and those who were with him in the ark remained alive." (Gen. 7: 21–23)

This stone churn was designed to rock back and forth and make butter out of cream. It is from about 4000 B.C. Maybe Noah had something just like it on the ark.

The ending of the story of Noah and the ark is tremendous. The Lord made a very neat promise to us after the flood. It says in Genesis 9:11, "Thus I establish my covenant with you and with your descendants after you [that's us] . . . Never again shall all flesh be cut off by the waters of the flood; never again shall there be a flood to destroy the earth." And the Lord placed a rainbow in the sky to remind us of this covenant. It's no wonder that rainbows are so beautiful. They come from God.

You should also know for historical reasons that there are many other cultures that have stories about a flood in their history. As many as 270 flood stories are known in the world. There are stories in India, China, the islands of the Pacific Ocean, and even in Native American folklore about people who survived a "great flood." The names of the survivors vary, but the story line is much the same. It kind of makes you go "Hmm"!

It is also important to grasp the facts of the flood because it helps to support the validity of the Bible. Fossil records all over the world demonstrate that at one time water could have covered the whole earth. For example, sea fossils have been found on the tops of mountains!

The flood could also help explain what appears to be the "aging" of the earth. In other words, the world may look older than it is to some scientists because of the damage of the Great Flood. A fancy word for the Great Flood of Noah's time is "Deluge," with a capital "D." Understanding the Deluge is important in defending the Creation theory. Evolutionists and creationists disagree on the age of the earth. What do you think?

In closing, when you hear the story of Noah, does it remind you of another one? We often see God repeating things in history so that we understand them better. Think about Noah again. God saved the whole world through this one man. God does this again later through the man of Jesus Christ. That's what we call a "parallel" in history. I think the moral of the story is that God really does hate sin. But, He will provide a way to save us from it.

ACTIVITY 4

4A—Younger Students

Noah had a great challenge in "pairing" the animals that God brought to the ark. Play the card game of "Concentration." Taking a deck of playing cards, lay all the cards out in rows, face side down. By turning over only two cards at a time, try to match pairs together.

4B—Middle and Older Students

The Bible gives some amazing detail on the flood. Use a Bible to find the answers to these questions. On a separate piece of paper, write your answers in complete sentences. Answers to these questions can be found in the Pretest Answer Key in the Appendix.

1. How many days total did it rain when God flooded the earth?
2. How old was Noah when the flood covered the earth?
3. What bird did Noah send out of the ark first (a raven or a dove)?
4. Who closed the door of the ark?
5. How many cubits high did the water rise?
6. How long did the flood last?
7. How many times did Noah send out a dove?
8. What was the first thing Noah did when he got off the ark?
9. How many people were on the ark?
10. What was God's promise in Genesis 8:21?

File your answers in the "Asia: Turkey" section of your Student Notebook because that is where Noah landed.

The Mystery of History

Can you imagine how much food and water Noah needed on board the ark to feed all the animals? I can't imagine it, but the author of the book *Noah's Ark: A Feasibility Study* has. In the study John Woodmorappe determined the amount of food, water, and other supplies that would have been needed for Noah, his family, and all the animals. The figures are staggering. Investigate it for yourself. (*Noah's Ark: A Feasibility Study* by John Woodmorappe. Available through Answers in Genesis Publications. Their Web site address is www.answersingenesis.org.)

c. 3500–2500 B.C.

THE ICE AGE

LESSON 5

To some scientists the Ice Age is a mysterious phenomenon. It appears we have evidence that large parts of the world were once covered by lots of glaciers and ice. A glacier consists of thousands of tons of ice layered in sheets and can cover miles and miles of land or water. But why did the earth ever grow that cold, and why did it warm up again? To understand it all, we must go back to how the world might have been before the Great Flood, or Deluge.

It says in Genesis that before the flood there was not **ever** any rain! We may find that hard to believe when we consider the world, as WE know it. But this fact could easily be true if the atmosphere was different back then. Many scholars believe it was very different.

Some scientists speculate that there was a type of large cloud, or blanket of vapor, that covered the whole earth. The book of Genesis even describes it. It says, "For the Lord God had not caused it to rain on the earth, and there was no man to till the ground; but a mist went up from the earth and watered the whole face of the ground." (Gen. 2:5–6) Do

you know how a greenhouse works? It keeps moisture in and is usually warm all throughout. The blanket of vapor over the earth did much the same thing. It insulated the world so there was no need for rain. (This may help explain one reason that man was able to live so long. He may have been protected from some of the sun's ultraviolet rays.)

Now that you understand this, think of how catastrophic it was when the heavens poured down rain for 40 days and 40 nights. It caused many great changes in the earth. All those tons of new water could have carved out miles and miles of new canyons and

This pot is decorated with a ram's head. It is from about 3100 B.C. and was probably used by someone during the Ice Age.

gorges. And, water was not only coming from above. The Bible says in Genesis 7:11 that "on that day all the fountains of the great deep were broken up, and the windows of heaven were opened." That passage may be describing great volcanic upheavals where the earth's crust was fractured. This entire catastrophe apparently went on for the whole time of the flood until God stopped it, as it says in Genesis 8:1–2.

As for bringing on the Ice Age, the Bible says that God had removed the vapor cloud covering the earth. That means that the planet would have then had **seasons** for the first time! As you may know, it is naturally colder at the poles of the earth because they are tilted away from the sun. During the Ice Age, these polar regions extended much farther than they do now. It is so cold that glaciers still exist at the north and south poles.

So, immediately following the Deluge, several factors could have brought on the Ice Age. There would have been extra moisture with all the water, the colder temperatures at the north and south poles, the colder climate everywhere from volcanic ash in the air, and the new uplifted mountains with snow. As the water began to freeze, it could have kept the earth colder, making even more water freeze. It is thought that so much of the water was frozen toward the north and south poles that it caused the oceans to be shallower.

An important thing to remember about the Ice Age is that the presence of it does not have to conflict with a Christian viewpoint of Creation. During the Ice Age, man did not cease to exist. The entire earth was not covered by ice, just large parts of it were. The Ice Age was a real time period when men, women, children, and animals lived. Many of these people may have migrated during this time period searching for a more desirable climate. Land bridges that once were covered by ocean water would have been exposed, so man could travel easier from one continent to another.

Scientists themselves do not agree on the causes or the length of the Ice Age. Most geologists do agree that it ended slowly. Again this could make sense if there had been a great flood. It would have taken time for the earth to warm back up after it. It would also have taken time for the plants, which add to the warmth of the earth, to all grow again.

Regardless of how the Ice Age began, how long it lasted, and how it went away, the Ice Age was a true phenomenon that early man was a witness to.

ACTIVITY 5

5A—Younger Students

Have an ice cube contest!

Materials: Ice cubes

To help you remember the Ice Age, have a contest in your family to see who can hold an ice cube the longest. No cheating with mittens or gloves! Put an ice cube in the palm of your hand (or on your belly if you are brave) and watch the second hand on a clock at the same time. Record your results just for fun. If one cube seems too easy, add more. (You might do this over a sink or towel to catch the drips.)

5B—Middle Students

Create your own greenhouse.

Materials: Jar with tight-fitting lid, rocks, weeds, dirt, water

A greenhouse is a good demonstration of the climate of the world before the Great Flood. Take a simple jar with a tight-fitting lid. Fill it with some rocks, weeds, grass, and dirt. Add about one-quarter cup of water and screw the lid on tight. Set the greenhouse near a window or outside in the sun.

As you observe it over the next few days, you will see condensation form on the sides of the jar. Water vapor in the jar will attempt to evaporate but be unable to because of the lid.

The vapor cloud over the earth was somewhat like that. It was a "canopy" that prevented water from escaping into the atmosphere. The land would have been more moist and lush than what we know today, making conditions ideal for vegetation and animals.

5C—Older Students

Fossils are a fascinating topic of study. Some scholars believe that the presence of fossils all over the world supports the theory of the great flood. Fossils may be the result of layers and layers of dead organisms buried under tons of water and rock from a flood! Research the fossils that are common in your area if there are any. Notice the dates often given for fossil records. What evidence is there to support the dating of these fossils? Look into it! For more information, contact Answers in Genesis.

Created on 5th and 6th days

DINOSAURS

LESSON 6

Dinosaurs have been extremely popular in the last few decades. It's no wonder. They're cool; they're huge; and they're magnificent creatures! But when did they live and why did they die? Did they live alongside early man? These are good questions to wonder about.

First of all, modern man didn't even know about dinosaurs until the 1800s. It all began when an English woman named Mary Mantell went for a walk and found a tooth like nothing anyone had ever seen before. She and her husband, a doctor, found other teeth and bones in the same area. With great anticipation, they sent these to scientists to study.

An Englishman, Sir Richard Owen, believed that these bones were of an animal unlike any of that day. So, in 1840 he gave these unknown animals the name "dinosaurs" meaning "terrible lizards."

Since then of course, thousands of dinosaur bones have been found and studied. We have a pretty good picture of how many might have lived. But there are some mysterious things about them worth our consideration.

First, when would the dinosaurs have been created? The Bible says that

Dinosaurs--a mysterious part of God's wonderful Creation.

God created sea creatures and birds on the fifth day of Creation. On the sixth day He created the beasts of the earth. We must assume then that dinosaurs were made on the fifth and sixth days of Creation. That means that man and dinosaurs must have lived at the same time! This is important because most scientists disagree on this. They seem to think that dinosaurs lived so long ago that they could not have coexisted with man.

Guess what, though! In the Bible God gave us a great description of two dinosaurs that could support the fact that man lived with them. Read about the Behemoth in Job 40:15. It closely describes what could have been an Apatosaurus or maybe a Brachiosaurus. And Job 41:1–8 tells us of Leviathan, a great and fearsome beast that sounds a lot like a huge dinosaur. Job probably lived about 2,000 years after the flood. It is not unlikely that some of the great giants still roamed the earth then.

Another presumed mystery is whether or not dinosaurs were included on Noah's ark. The Bible says that ALL living creatures with breath were brought to the ark. So He must have meant dinosaurs, too. The average dinosaur was not gigantic. Some were as small as dogs. Maybe the larger species came to the ark as young dinosaurs. If God was powerful enough to draw all the animals to the ark in pairs, He was certainly clever enough to have had room for them all. Many of the animals may have gone through a type of hibernation in order for Noah and his sons to care for them all. We cannot explain supernatural things.

Last, many people wonder what happened to the dinosaurs. No one knows exactly why or when the dinosaurs became extinct, but there are some good theories. One idea is that after the flood there was not enough vegetation to support the larger beasts. Others think that the climate itself was a problem to the dinosaurs after the flood. The Ice Age may have been too cold for the dinosaurs to survive.

Interestingly, dinosaur remains have contributed to what we call "fossil fuels" that we depend on so much today. In God's perfect timing, it is good for us that the dinosaurs lived when they did. And while we obviously don't see dinosaurs any more in populated areas, for all we know, there may be a few large beasts still roaming the planet. There have been many strange sightings that have gone unexplained, such as the Loch Ness monster. And what about "dragons"? There could have been some creatures at some time that resembled dragons since we find them repeated over and again in Old World literature.

Regardless of how the dinosaurs fit on the ark, how they coexisted with man, and why the dinosaurs "disappeared," the study of these "terrible lizards" is not so terrible. It is quite fascinating!

ACTIVITY 6

ALL STUDENTS

Make Your Memory Cards for Lessons 4–6.

6A—Younger Students

Draw a picture of Noah and the ark and include dinosaurs getting on board in pairs. I suppose you've never seen a picture of that before. Most artists don't include the dinosaurs, but they should be pictured. File your picture under "Miscellaneous."

6B—Middle Students

If you have never done a good study on dinosaurs, then this activity might be a good one. There are lots of great books about dinosaurs and pictures showing what we believe dinosaurs looked like. Take a book you can cut apart like a coloring book of dinosaurs and categorize the pictures. It will help you learn about the different types. Younger students can categorize dinosaurs by size. Older students' categories could include:

- Horned dinosaurs
- Plated and armored dinosaurs
- Bone-headed and parrot-like dinosaurs

- Meat-eating dinosaurs
- Big plant eaters
- Flying reptiles
- Marine reptiles
- Lightweights
- Clawed dinosaurs

6C—Older Students

1. Research the Loch Ness monster or other modern sightings of strange beasts. Try to identify which dinosaur may most resemble the Loch Ness creature.

2. Investigate fossil fuels. What are they? How did the dinosaurs contribute to them? On a map, show where most oil is found on the earth and explain what scientists believe to be its source.

   File your research under "Miscellaneous."

TAKE ANOTHER LOOK!

Wall of Fame

This week we will add to the timeline the people and things we have studied. Always draw or write things on your characters to help you remember them. Add dates to them, too. Put them on in this order:

1. *Noah (c. 4000–3500 b.c.)*—What else could better depict Noah than the ark itself? Make a boat with his name on it. Place a golden cross on the figure to signify the lineage of Christ. Place the figure on the undated blank bar of your timeline.

2. *Shem (c. 3500 b.c.)*—Place a baby in his arms for repopulating the earth. Also add a cross on Shem to signify the lineage of Christ.

3. *Japheth (c. 3500 b.c.)*—Place a baby in his arms also.

4. *Ham (c. 3500 b.c.)*—Place a baby in his arms also.

5. *The Ice Age (c. 3500–2500 b.c.)*—Because the Ice Age spans a long time period, try writing the words "Ice Age" in squiggly letters (like they are shivering) on a long strip of paper. Attach this strip underneath your other figures to cover about a thousand years, rather than as a one-time event.

6. *Dinosaurs (5th and 6th days of Creation)*—Scatter various pictures of dinosaurs all throughout the early years of man beginning with the fifth and sixth days of Creation.

SomeWHERE in Time

1. On an atlas or a good map, I want you to find Mt. Ararat. (It's in modern-day Turkey.) This is the mountain on which many believe the ark settled when the waters subsided. Several expeditions have gone out even in just the last 10 years to try to find the ark. Wouldn't that be a great discovery? Maybe you will grow up to be one of the men or women who finds it and helps to show the world the answer to "The Mystery of History"! Finding the ark would lead many to believe in the Bible's story of the flood, which helps to explain the age of the earth. (If you find it, let me know.)

2. On Outline Map 10, "The World," use a blue marker to color in the ice caps that extended farther south than they are today. Remember, only some parts of the earth were covered in ice sheets during the Ice Age. Warm climates still existed far away from the north pole. File this under "Miscellaneous: World" in your Student Notebook.

WHAT DID YOU LEARN?

Week 2: Quiz

This is your first cumulative quiz. These quizzes will cover **all** previously studied information. Keep a running grade average on these! This one is short, but they will get longer.

True or False? Circle your answer.

1. The firmament, or "heaven," was created on the second day.　　　　T　F

2. Adam and Eve were created on the fifth day of creation.　　　　T　F

3. Adam lived to be about 120 years old.　　　　T　F

4. Jubal was a musician with the harp and flute.　　　　T　F

5. Tubal-Cain was a mapmaker.　　　　T　F

6. Ironmaking is a simple task.　　　　T　F

7. Noah had never seen rain before the flood.　　　　T　F

8. Shem was a direct ancestor to Jesus.　　　　T　F

9. The earth grew colder after the flood.　　　　T　F

10. According to the Bible, all the dinosaurs died well before the flood.　　　　T　F

☑ WHAT DO YOU KNOW?

Pretest 3

Who Am I? From the list below, choose the correct answer for each question. This is just to see what you might already know. Don't keep a recorded grade! Save those for quizzes.

1. I am an archaeologist who discovered royal tombs. Who am I?

2. I am a wedge-shaped alphabet. What am I?

3. I am a flattened-looking pyramid. What am I?

4. I am a Greek word meaning "land between the rivers." What am I?

5. I was a great tower built out of pride. What am I?

6. I am a word meaning "confusion." What am I?

7. I am a word that refers to the worship of statues, objects, nature, and man. What am I?

8. I am a term referring to a long poem, usually written about history. What am I?

WORD BANK

epic	Tower of Babel	babel	Mesopotamia
cuneiform	idolatry	ziggurat	Sir C. Leonard Woolley

The Mystery of History

THE SUMERIANS

LESSON 7

Do you know what defines a "civilization"? A "civilization" is born when you have lots of people living near one another who depend on each other to live. People typically become really good at one craft or skill so they begin to trade their expertise for that of someone else. A civilization also includes laws, government, and written language. We begin to see signs of all of this and more after the flood in a group of people called the Sumerians.

The Sumerians lived in the "Fertile Crescent." It was named that for being very good, lush farmland that looks like the shape of a crescent roll on a map. This land is located where the Garden of Eden might have been between the Tigris and Euphrates Rivers in Iraq. In fact, the Greeks called this area "Mesopotamia," which means "land between the rivers." Others call this spot the "Cradle of Civilization" because signs of early man exist there. These terms all refer to the same area in Iraq.

The Sumerians were quite an amazing group of people in regard to the things they accomplished. You see, after the flood, much of man's achievements and skills would have been lost. But, the Sumerians show us again that early man seemed to have genuine intelligence as these people rebuilt society all over again in a relatively short amount of time.

For example, the cities of Sumeria apparently had laws, irrigation systems, flushing toilets, and even hot and cold running water in some homes! (They were more advanced than some countries are even today.) As for art, the Sumerians crafted small but ornate terra-cotta statues of people with overly exaggerated eyes. They also had calendars, poetry, libraries, and may have invented the wheel. Not bad for such an ancient people group.

The Sumerians are best known for a written language called "cuneiform." In Latin the word "cuneus" means "wedge." The shape of a wedge best describes the 600 symbols the Sumerians invented to represent sounds. They were pressed into clay tablets with a reed stylus that had a triangular point. That point allowed them to create different wedge shapes. Can you imagine having to learn 600 letters of the alphabet? These early people created schools just for that purpose. They called them "edubba," or "tablet houses."

We know about the Sumerians' way of life primarily from the great discovery by Sir C. Leonard Woolley who found the "Royal Tombs" in the city of Ur. His discovery was in the early 1900s, and it greatly helped to support the idea that man had been far more than a cave dweller in the beginning.

This is a replica of a stone Sumerian idol originally made about 2250 b.c. The large eyes are common to Sumerian sculptures.

Part of the findings in Ur included a large and elaborate ziggurat. That's the name for a structure that looks like a flattened pyramid. Unfortunately, the purpose for the buildings was to worship idols, which the people created to help them understand life. Religion was important to the Sumerians, but their knowledge of the one and only God was limited. They believed in many gods and were unsure of life after death. In the burial chambers of the wealthy, Woolley found people buried with their earthly treasures and even with their best attendants. They must have thought that they "needed" these things for the next life.

Do you know any famous Sumerians by name? You just may. Abraham, the father of the Jews, came from Sumeria. According to the Bible, God called him to leave the city of Ur and to seek the one true God. Knowing what you know now about Sumeria, you may better appreciate how brave Abraham must have been to leave so much behind for the sake of his faith.

ACTIVITY 7

7A—Younger Students

Make your own cuneiform tablet.

Materials: Clay, rolling pin, craft stick or butter knife

Shape the clay into a rectangle. Roll it out thin and flat with a rolling pin or glass from the kitchen. Use a stick or butter knife to make indentations that represent cuneiform writings. Leave your tablet in the sun to harden. Take a picture and file it in the "Asia: Iraq (Mesopotamia)" section of your Student Notebook.

How hard might it be to erase your mistakes if you wrote your schoolwork on a clay tablet?

7B—Middle Students

Build your own ziggurat.

Materials: Picture of a ziggurat for a model, Lego plastic construction toys or sugar cubes

Use these or other similar materials to build your ziggurat. Don't forget ramps, plants, and towers in the center. A real ziggurat was built out of sun-baked clay bricks.

If you like how it looks, take a photo of it and file it under "Asia: Iraq (Mesopotamia)" in your Student Notebook.

7C—Older Students

Research the archaeological findings of Sir C. Leonard Woolley when he discovered the Royal Tombs of Ur. In defense of our belief in early man's intelligence, what might be the significance of Woolley's findings? Contrast the relics he found with common portrayals of man in the Stone Age. File it under "Asia: Iraq (Mesopotamia)."

THE TOWER OF BABEL

LESSON 8

To fully understand the story of the Tower of Babel, we will need to examine the early family of Noah. The Bible says that Noah had three sons. They were Shem, Ham, and Japheth (JAY feth). When the flood occurred, it was only Noah, his wife, Noah's three sons, and each of their wives who were spared. That means that the entire human race started over again from these couples. That also means that *you* are directly related to one of these three sons of Noah!

The descendants of Noah through Shem, Ham, and Japheth probably stayed in the area of Mcsopotamia for about one hundred years. Because of the flood event, many of Noah's family might have worshiped one God. But, as man quickly repopulated and began to move around, people got away from the teachings of one god. The Sumerians, for example, worshiped idols. Idolatry, which is the worship of statues, objects, nature, or man himself, became a way of life for many.

It's in this spiritual climate that we find the story of the Tower of Babel. It says in Genesis 11:4, "And they said, 'Come, let us build ourselves a city, and a tower whose top is in the heavens; let us make a name for ourselves, lest we be scattered abroad over the face of the whole earth.'" A "tower" back then more than likely resembled a ziggurat like those built in Sumer.

It apparently bothered the Lord that people were growing self-sufficient in their attitudes. They seemed to want to take care of themselves and not depend on having a relationship with God. The people wanted their own city, their own name, and a huge tower to demonstrate their strength. We also could call that pride.

It says in the Bible that the Lord decided to put an end to this pride and rebellion by confusing their language. Up until this time everyone probably spoke the language that Noah and his sons spoke. Any other languages, had they existed before the flood, would have been lost.

Genesis 11:7 says, "Come, let Us go down and there confuse their language, that they may not understand one another's speech." ("Us" in that passage refers to the Trinity. We find the same term used in Creation.) The people then dispersed and quit building that particular city.

This act of dispersion and the confusion of different languages was critical to the way mankind would forever relate to one another. No longer could men freely communicate! No longer would they be able to trade easily or travel about the land. No longer would men and women be likely to marry someone from another land. (They wouldn't be able to talk!) In fact, in the world today there exist about 5,000 languages!

With groups of people now isolating themselves from others, some distinct genetic differences would begin to appear. Skin color, eye shape, jaw lines, and noses would become more and more pronounced and unique to each group. Before long, whole races of people would develop. Many scholars believe that the different races we see today began to develop as far back as the Tower of Babel.

Interestingly, the word "babel" in Hebrew means "confusion." Have you ever heard a toddler try to talk? We often call it "babbling." We also use "babbling" to refer to the gurgling sound a brook makes as it runs downstream. It is intriguing how some words hang around for a long time.

Even more interesting is the city of "Babylon," which springs up later in history in the same place where the Tower of Babel stood. From there, man also rebelled against God. Today an ancient tower remains in Babylon that many believe to be the Tower of Babel. Seeing that would be a great field trip!

ACTIVITY 8

8A—Younger and Middle Students

Experience your own Tower of Babel!

Materials: Obtain one or more foreign language tapes from the library

Just for fun, listen to a tape of a language completely foreign to you. Our ears can't help us to understand even though we can hear the language. The problem is in our brains, which cannot make sense of the different sounds.

Think of how odd it might have been to be one of the children at the building of the great Tower of Babel. Could you talk to your sister, father, or friends? We don't know if families were given the same language or not. What do you think?

Try putting all the tapes you have on at the same time. It should sound very confusing!

8B—Middle Students

Try this foreign language challenge.

Materials: Directions or instructions from a game or appliance printed out in a language other than English, colored pencils

Obtain instructions printed out in more than one language. With different-colored pencils, circle a word in English with its corresponding word in the other language. See how many words you can guess or really translate from English to the other language. One of the challenges is that not all languages put their adjectives before their nouns like we do in English. There are other challenges to translation. What do you find the most difficult?

8C—Middle and Older Students

Investigate who Nimrod was in the Bible. Find out what his name meant and what his association was with The Tower of Babel. File your findings under the section "Asia: Iraq (Mesopotamia)."

2750 B.C.

THE EPIC OF GILGAMESH

LESSON 9

Remember the Sumerians who had invented cuneiform writing? They were so advanced in their language skills that they even had libraries and schools. But, what do people who lived so long ago put in their libraries? Were books written about gardening, animals, marriage, or the stars? Did they write fiction stories to read just for fun?

Believe it or not, we have a record of one of the oldest books ever written other than the Bible. It comes from the Sumerians but was later copied by the Babylonians. The author of this book, which is called *The Epic of Gilgamesh,* wrote about things he had heard from other generations. An "epic" is a long poem written about something factual or fictional in the past. I think you'll find it fascinating to learn the content of this poem.

The story centers on a legendary hero named Gilgamesh, a king of Uruk, who falls asleep under a tree and wakes up to a snake who has robbed him of eternal life. Gilgamesh searches for eternal life for the sake of a dead friend, Enkidu, but doesn't find it. Does that story sound familiar? It should somewhat remind you of the story of Adam and Eve when they were deceived by the serpent in the Garden of Eden.

Another part of the story tells us of a man named Utnapishtim who was told by a god to build a great ship. It was covered with pitch inside and out. Utnapishtim loaded his family and animals on the boat when it rained for six days and nights. After some time, Utnapishtim sent out a dove, a swallow, and a raven. The last bird didn't come back because it found enough dead meat to live on. Utnapishtim gave an offering to the gods and was made into a god himself with his wife.

Now, that story should really sound familiar. Its similarity to that of Noah and the ark is incredible. The author of *The Epic of Gilgamesh* may have heard these stories after they had been passed down for hundreds of years by word of mouth. That could explain the differences between this poem and the Genesis account of Creation and the Great Flood.

Just to clarify, most Christians believe that God helped to write the book of Genesis through men like Moses. Because God was the true author, I would believe His version of the story of the flood to be the accurate one. *The Epic of Gilgamesh,* on the other hand, was written by a man or woman and copied by others over many, many years. From what I know of mankind, people make mistakes sometimes. So, I will stick with believing the Creation and Great Flood stories from the Bible. What do you think?

ACTIVITY 9

ALL STUDENTS

Make your Memory Cards for Lessons 7–9.

9A—Younger and Middle Students

Play the game of "Telephone." A group of people sits in a circle. One person whispers a secret message to the person next to him. The secret is passed on to the next person and so on until it reaches the starting place. The last person says the secret out loud to see how close it is to the original message.

Some rules might include that no one is allowed to repeat the secret. It can only be whispered once to each person. Rarely will a message get around the circle without some changes.

Imagine playing the game of "Telephone" for a couple of hundred years! How well might the original message be retained? How about a couple of thousand years? The Creation story was about 2,000 years old to the Sumerians and the flood story was a few hundred years old. Considering those figures, *The Epic of Gilgamesh* is rather incredible in how closely it resembles the stories from the Bible.

9B—Middle Students

The next time you are shopping at a grocery store, notice the headlines of some of the tabloid newspapers. These sources of information have a reputation for "sensationalizing" the truth. Talk about what that means and how important it is to heed accurate sources of news. Just as with *The Epic of Gilgamesh* versus the Bible, one must "consider the source" of the writer's information.

9C—Older Students

With parental permission, obtain a copy of *The Epic of Gilgamesh* at your local library. (Some copies in existence contain inappropriate artwork for younger children.) Reading it in its entirety may be difficult, but try to find the significant Creation and flood accounts in the story. Contrast the similarities and the differences with the biblical accounts of Creation and the flood.

TAKE ANOTHER LOOK!

Review 3: Lessons 7–9

Wall of Fame

Add these figures to your timeline.

1. *The Sumerians (c. 3500–2500 B.C.)*—Be sure your figure has big eyes like the Sumerian sculptures did.

2. *The Tower of Babel (c. 3500–3000 B.C.)*—Draw a tower stretching high into the sky.

3. *The Epic of Gilgamesh (2750 B.C.)*—Sketch what looks like an open book with the picture of a tree on one page.

SomeWHERE in Time

On Outline Map 6, "Turkey," write in the following items using the suggested colored pencils or markers. File this map under "Asia: Iraq (Mesopotamia)" in your Student Notebook.

Mesopotamia	Black
Sumer	Orange
Tigris River	Light blue
Euphrates River	Dark blue
City of Babylon	Purple
City of Ur	Green
Persian Gulf	Turquoise

WHAT DID YOU MISS?

Week 3: Exercise

Play "Millionaire Multiple Choice" using pennies, nickels, dimes, quarters and a one-dollar bill.

For a right answer on questions 1 and 2, receive a penny; for questions 3 and 4, a nickel; for questions 5 and 6, a dime; for questions 7 to 9, a quarter. And, for the final question, receive one dollar for the correct answer! (Use your book as a "lifeline.")

Circle the correct answer for each question.

1. On the fourth day of Creation, God made
   a. day and night.
   b. sea creatures and birds.
   c. the sun, moon, and stars.
   d. the firmament.

2. Tubal-Cain was known for
   a. leather work.
   b. musical work.
   c. bronze- and ironmaking.
   d. killing Abel.

3. There were how many people on the ark?
   a. 10
   b. 8
   c. 6
   d. Unknown

4. The Ice Age
   a. exposed land bridges for man to travel on.
   b. covered the entire earth with glaciers.
   c. was not a real event..
   d. occurred over a million years ago.

5. The word "dinosaur" means
   a. great beast.
   b. ancient mammal.
   c. terrible reptile.
   d. terrible lizard.

6. The Sumerians were advanced enough to have
   a. running water.
   b. schools.
   c. a written language.
   d. All of the above.

7. The story of the Tower of Babel is found in the Book of
   a. Numbers.
   b. Genesis.
   c. Deuteronomy.
   d. Leviticus.

8. "Mesopotamia" means
   a. terrible lizard.
   b. flattened pyramid.
   c. land between the rivers.
   d. huge rocks.

9. In *The Epic of Gilgamesh,* _____ was the man who built a great ship covered with pitch inside and out.
   a. Uzbekistan.
   b. Gilgamesh.
   c. Tutankhamen.
   d. Utnapishtim.

10. The Latin term "Anno Domini" means*
   a. after death.
   b. after the life of the Lord.
   c. in the year of the Lord.
   d. year of dominion.

*(The answer is in your book, but it is not in a lesson.)

The Mystery of History

☑ WHAT DO YOU KNOW?

Pretest 4

Unscramble the words to fill in the blanks. A word bank is provided at the bottom of the page.

1. Stonehenge is located in present-day (agEdnln) _____ .

2. The term "megalith" means "huge (rkco)" _____ .

3. Some pyramids were as large as ten (lablofot) _____ fields.

4. Ancient Egyptians thought that people used their (rathe) _____ to think.

5. Pharaohs were sometimes buried with their mummified (epts) _____ .

6. Most of the pyramids were built along the (elNi) _____ River.

7. The Minoan civilization flourished on the island of (erCet) _____ near Greece.

8. King Minos kept a legendary Minotaur that was part man and part (lulb) _____ .

WORD BANK

football	England	Nile	rock
bull	heart	pets	Crete

STONEHENGE
LESSON 10

Have you ever seen pictures of Stonehenge and wondered who built it, and why? Stonehenge is the name of a unique man-made monument in Wiltshire, England. It is worth our study because it displays the genius of early men and women. Besides that, it's just a cool site!

Stonehenge is made of several huge rock slabs weighing about 28 tons each. The 18-foot slabs of sandstone originally stood upright in a perfect circle that was about 100 feet in diameter. On the inside of that circle were some smaller blue rocks also standing in a circle. And inside that circle were even more rocks. These inner rocks were placed in the shape of horseshoes.

The amazing thing about the structure is the mystery of how men could have moved rocks of that size without modern-day equipment. It is believed that some of the rocks were carried from as far away as 300 miles! Others came from just 17 miles away. They may have been carried by sleds or even glaciers to get them there. The enormous rocks were not only set upright but they were capped off by other rock slabs on the top. It was quite an achievement by whoever built it. Because of the difficulty involved, scientists believe Stonehenge was built over several centuries.

In recent years, Stonehenge "fans" have attempted to re-enact the movement of the massive stones. Volunteers have actually taken the blue rocks from miles away and hitched them up to man-made sleds. In the experiment, it took at least 25 people to pull one stone. The stones were also floated on remakes of ancient boats. In transit, one of the huge blue slabs plunged right into the sea. The workers suspect the builders of Stonehenge may have experienced some of the very same problems.[1]

The puzzling but majestic Stonehenge in Wiltshire, England, was made of rock slabs weighing at least 28 tons each.

Another astounding feature of Stonehenge is the position of the stones. Though many have been moved or have fallen down over the years, it is evident that the original placement of the rocks was in connection to the rising and setting of the sun. The rocks are also positioned accurately to measure the moon and seasons. Certainly some very intelligent minds were involved in the layout of these huge rocks.

We call monuments like this "megaliths," which is just another name for "huge rocks." There are many megalithic structures around the world. In France there are the Standing Stones of Carnac. There you will find about 3,000 stones lined up for nearly 5 miles across the countryside. There are also stone structures in Asia, Africa, India, and on islands in the Pacific Ocean. Though built at different times and

---

1. Information on recent stone project obtained from Kevin Whitelaw, "Ancient Riddles: The sorcery of the stones or Elvis meets Merlin in Y2K," *U.S. News and World Report* 129, no. 4 (July 24–31, 2000): 36.

in different formations, the megaliths are hauntingly similar. Some may have been used as places of worship, burial grounds, or meeting places, whereas others seem to be set up to study the stars. All of them reflect that early man wanted to be remembered and that he was pretty smart.

If you were to visit England today, you could still see parts of Stonehenge. The government has worked to restore the site to look somewhat like it did nearly 4,000 years ago. It would be a neat experience to touch something almost as old as Noah's ark and to see the work of people who wanted us to remember them.

ACTIVITY 10

10A—Younger Students

Create a miniature version of Stonehenge.

Materials: A dozen or more small rocks about the same size, a paper plate, glue

Collect several rocks of similar size. Put them in a circle on the edge of a paper plate. Try to stack some of the rocks on top of each other. They probably won't stay up. This should make you realize how amazing it was that people once built Stonehenge. If you really like your structure, glue the rocks onto the plate and write the word "Stonehenge" on the plate. Show it to your family. Take a picture and file it under "Europe: England."

10B—Younger and Middle Students

1. If the weather is nice, go out into your backyard and try to make a huge circle in the grass. There is a secret to making it easy. Have one person stand in the "middle" with a long rope or tape measure. Have another person hold the other end and walk in a circle. The middle person must stay in one place while the other walks around. The person walking should mark the trail with birdseed, rocks, or some other markers. Imagine people doing something like this thousands of years ago when they built Stonehenge in much larger areas than your backyard.

2. If the weather is bad, try to draw perfect circles on paper without the help of any stencil or guide. It's not very easy to do.

10C—Older Students

Do you know the definition of a "solstice" or "equinox"? These are terms dealing with the position of the earth in relation to the sun at different seasons. In fact, the spring equinox is used every year to determine the date of Easter—which explains why the date changes from year to year.

We rely on experts today to calculate the position of the sun relative to the earth because it is a complicated matter. However, the builders of Stonehenge apparently understood these terms and built their stones in accordance with them. How is that for early man's display of intelligence?

Using an encyclopedia, look up solstice, equinox, and Stonehenge. Write down a good definition of each and file it in your Student Notebook under "Europe: England."

EARLY EGYPTIANS

LESSON 11

When you think about ancient Egypt, you probably picture pyramids and mummies and mysterious things like that. It's hard to imagine Egypt without these eerie phenomena. But of course there was *something* going on in Egypt before the pyramids were ever built. We'll peek into that part of history today and then we'll look at why the giant pyramids were erected to begin with.

In the early days of Egypt, the land was divided between what was called Upper Egypt and Lower Egypt. If you looked at a map of Egypt right now, it would help you to understand. You see, the Upper area of Egypt was actually far down south into Egypt along the Nile River. The Lower area of Egypt was north where the Nile spills into the Mediterranean Sea.

From our perspective the names are in the wrong place! We would probably think of north as being "upper" and south as being "lower." But you know what? The Egyptians weren't looking at the area from a map. They were describing the makeup of their land. The Upper area of Egypt is where the land was higher. At the Lower end, the land was closer to sea level. That is also why the Nile appears to run "up" when we look at it from a map. It runs from the high plains of central Egypt to the low-lying land at the sea.

Anyway, the two areas were different at first. The Upper Egyptians were very artistic and grew grain. Their symbol was that of the sedge plant, and they worshiped a vulture goddess. The Lower Egyptians were good with tools and building. They had the symbol of a bee and worshiped the cobra goddess.

By about 3100 B.C., there was one king who wanted to unite these two areas. His name was Menes (sometimes called Narmar). Uniting kingdoms was a big deal back then. As a result, ancient Egypt then became one of the first true nations to be established.

Menes created a capital city at Memphis where he could easily rule over his large kingdom. It has been estimated that it took two weeks in a boat for the king to visit both ends of his kingdom. Fortunately, hieroglyphics had been created and calendars were made to help with communication. Hieroglyphics were picture words of their language. They were used for thousands of years.

About 500 years later, another king came along with an idea that has burned an image of Egypt into the minds of us all. A king named Khufu decided he wanted to be buried in a pyramid. He oversaw the

This is an Egyptian coffin designed for a child's mummified body. The small child probably died sometime during the twenty-seventh dynasty of Egypt.

The Mystery of History

building of the first enormous pyramid known as the Great Pyramid at Giza. (Khufu also went by the name Cheops.) He started a trend that dozens of pharaohs after him copied.

The size of the pyramids is staggering. Picture the base of one of them stretching as far as 10 football fields and being as tall as a 40-story building. That would be much taller than the Statue of Liberty but not as tall as the Eiffel Tower. How heavy are these structures? We don't know for sure, but just one average stone of a pyramid could weigh 2½ tons. Some were larger and weighed up to 15 tons, or the equivalent of five elephants! More than 80 pyramids still stand today. Most are along the Nile River.

Some think it's a mystery as to how these huge stones were moved. The Nile River probably helped men transport the raw materials. But by now you are probably already convinced that man was pretty smart even a long time ago. Perhaps it is because we were created in the image of God!

The accomplishment of something as monumental as the building of the first Great Pyramid shows us, too, that quite a civilization was thriving in Egypt in 2600 B.C. For a king to accomplish that great of a feat, he must have had lots of help and money. Khufu apparently had both. The ancient pyramids of Egypt have even been remembered as one of the Seven Wonders of the Ancient World. (You'll want to remember that! We're going to learn about all seven.)

But, why did kings and queens have these huge pyramids built? Unfortunately, they did it in part because of their misunderstanding of life and death. The kings, or pharaohs, of that day believed that they needed to preserve themselves as best as possible at death in order to experience an afterlife. They also "took" their important possessions with them, which sometimes included slaves or other people. Some mummified their favorite pets. So, the pyramids were mainly built to serve as burial chambers for the great kings, queens, and their treasures. Inside the pyramids were small chambers for their bodies to rest in.

Pyramids were designed with numerous secret passages to hide mummified kings and their treasures for the afterlife.

Secret passages led there to reduce the chance of robbery.

The way the kings and queens were preserved was through a method called "mummification." The process was long and somewhat gruesome to perform. Once they were dead, their insides would have to be removed. The organs were placed in special containers and preserved. (Strangely, the Egyptians often threw out the brain because they thought the heart did all the thinking!) After the bodies dried out, they were embalmed or filled with special resins and oils. Last, the bodies were wrapped with linen cloths and sealed in elaborate coffins.

The priests and embalmers took their jobs very seriously. Perhaps their sense of duty was from respect for their dead king or queen or from fear of the afterlife for themselves. Regardless, these ancient practices have given us a great picture of the life of the ancient Egyptians. Their magnificent treasures tell us a lot about their beliefs and their ways of life.

We will learn more about the ancient Egyptians, but there is more to them than I will ever have room to write about. Be sure and get some good library books on this fascinating culture. It's pretty neat stuff.

ACTIVITY 11

ALL STUDENTS

Check the Activity Supplement in the Appendix to see if there is a museum in your area with an Egyptian display. Make a field trip to see a real mummy.

11A—Younger Students

Make a mummy!

Materials: One roll of toilet paper

With toilet paper, wrap up one of your favorite stuffed animals as if you were a king or queen who wanted to take a special item with you to the next life.

Then, have a brother or sister or friend wrap YOU up like a mummy. Don't let them cover your mouth or nose! If it works well, have someone take your picture for a keepsake.

Place the photo in the "Africa: Egypt" section in your Student Notebook.

11B—Middle Students

Construct your own pyramid.

Materials: Poster board, scissors, pencils, yardstick, tape

This activity will help you comprehend the mammoth size of the pyramids.

1. On a poster board, mark off five equal squares that are 9 by 9 inches each. Cut these out.
2. Take four of the squares and cut them into four triangles, keeping a 9-inch base on each.
3. With tape (and someone helping you hold the structure), attach the four sides to one another over the base. Tape the sides to the base as well.
4. The real pyramid at Giza, named the Great Pyramid, is about 2,000 times the size of what you just built.

11C—Older Students

The library will probably have numerous resources about ancient Egypt. Don't miss the opportunity to choose any one of a number of topics for further reading, research, or a report. Consider these items for your study:

- Book of the Dead
- Hyksos
- Queen Hatshepsut (perhaps the woman who raised Moses)
- Saite Period
- Suez Canal
- Anwar al-Sadat.

File your research under "Africa: Egypt" in your Student Notebook.

THE MINOAN CIVILIZATION

LESSON 12

Would you like to live on an island in the middle of the beautiful Mediterranean Sea? It would be nice! The Minoans were one group of people who thought so, too. They lived on the large island of Crete near southern Greece. If you find it on a map, you'll know why it was called the "land bridge between Asia and Europe." It sits right between the two continents in the middle of the enchanting Mediterranean.

Like the Sumerians, the Minoans were quite advanced. Roads connected their cities, and each city had a beautiful palace. They are considered the first important civilization in Europe after the Great Flood. (The Sumerians were closer to Asia.)

The Minoans' (sometimes called the Cretans) greatest palace was in the capital of Knossos. It was so huge that it covered 6 acres! The palace had ivory bathtubs, running water for the toilets, and beautifully detailed "frescoes." A fresco is a special painting on a wall, made by applying paint to wet plaster. These frescoes have survived far longer than ordinary paintings would have. It is evident from this spectacular palace (which has parts still standing today) that the Minoans were excellent artists, builders, craftsmen, and sailors.

The people were named "Minoans" after one of their rulers, King Minos. Legend says that King Minos built a huge labyrinth, or maze, in which he housed a monster named a Minotaur. This creature was supposedly part man and part bull. The story of this fanciful creature probably grew from the fact that Minoans enjoyed the sport of "bull leaping." Murals of this sport have been left behind on some of the great palace walls. Paintings depict men catapulting over bulls as if they were doing headstands on the bulls' backs! Imagine doing that for fun!

The Minoans were fond of elaborate artworks, or frescoes, painted on the walls of their many palaces.

As for the religion of the Minoans, it appears from the remains of their homes that special rooms were set aside for worship. They worshiped the Mistress of the Animals, the Mistress of the Crops, and a goddess who could protect the home. The last goddess was often depicted, in statue form, bare breasted, holding snakes just above her head. Snakes were a sacred symbol to the Minoans. Outdoor altars were also used as a place for priests and priestesses to offer the gods milk, wine, or blood. And like the ancient Egyptians, the Minoans believed in some form of afterlife and were buried with their earthly possessions.

Strangely though, the Minoan civilization was unknown until the 1900s when an Englishman named Sir Arthur Evans uncovered the remains of their culture. The Minoans didn't flourish longer than about 800 years. Their civilization then came to a sudden halt. So, until Evans's discovery, these people were lost in time.

Coincidentally, there was a terrible volcano on a nearby island that might explain why the Cretans seemed to vanish from history. The fall of volcanic ash can be deadly for many, many miles. No one knows for sure, however, if this was the fate of the Minoans.

But the mystery seemed to give Plato a basis for the story of the sunken city of Atlantis. Have you ever heard of the mysterious Atlantis? The Greek philosopher Plato claimed the city of Atlantis sank because the people were so wicked. He wrote an entire story about it. For centuries people have searched for Atlantis to prove Plato's story true once and for all. The city has never been found.

The Minoans might have suddenly disappeared, but their influence on the world certainly did not. Many of their ideas were borrowed by the Mycenaeans who were neighbors on the nearby shores of Greece. The Mycenaeans and other Greeks later developed a great civilization that shaped much of the Mediterranean world through art, culture, education, government, and architecture. Imagine all that influence originating from the people who created the sport of bull leaping!

ACTIVITY 12

ALL STUDENTS

Make your Memory Cards for Lessons 10–12.

12A—Younger Students

Play "bull leaping" like you would leap frog. The Minoans were known for this sport. A bull would be a lot harder to jump over than a frog!

12B—Middle Students

Toilets are strange but wonderful things, aren't they? I find it surprising that the Minoans had running water for their toilets. We use the word "plumbing" to describe the use of water in handling human waste. The word "plumbing" comes from Roman times when *lead* pipes were used to carry water to and from the houses. The word "lead" in Latin is "plumbum."

Now that you know that, look up "plumbing" in the encyclopedia and see what you can find out about the history of the profession. It's been around a long time.

12C—Older Students

Research the theories on the "Lost City of Atlantis." Discover what you can about Plato's writings and the Greek island of Thira. Be familiar with the legend because it is often referred to even today. Write a one-page synopsis of your findings. File it in your Student Notebook under "Europe: Greece."

TAKE ANOTHER LOOK!

Review 4: Lessons 10–12

Wall of Fame

On your timeline, place these figures in this order.

1. *Stonehenge (c. 2700 b.c.)*—Glue a small stone to a piece of sturdy paper. Label and date it.

2. *First pyramids and mummies (c. 2575-2500 b.c.)*—Put a triangle on the timeline for the pyramid. Write the date on this figure. For the mummy, cut out the figure of a man and wrap it up with some cloth or tissue. You probably can't write on it now, but it will sure look neat.

3. *The Minoans (2200 b.c.)*—Draw a bull with a man's head. Label and date it.

SomeWHERE in Time

1. Find Egypt in a historical atlas. Do you know which way the Nile River flows? On Outline Map 3, "Egypt," trace the Nile River in blue pencil. The Nile runs north and feeds into the Mediterranean Sea. Label Upper and Lower Egypt. Label Memphis (in Lower Egypt) and Thebes (in Upper Egypt). File your map under "Africa: Egypt" in your Student Notebook.

2. Adult supervision is required for the following project. Make a map of ancient Crete where the Minoans lived.

   Materials: Paper and pencil; Outline Map 2, "Greece"; historical atlas for reference; four tea bags; water; pan; matches or candle

   a. Using a pencil, write on the island Crete the name of the capital, Knossos; also label the Mediterranean Sea and the Aegean Sea.

   b. Find Mycenae in Greece and include it, too.

   c. Just above Crete was the tiny island of Thera (now Thira) where there was a terrible volcano. Mark this as well.

   d. Now that your map is marked, prepare the tea solution. Take about four tea bags. Boil them in a small pan of water. Remove them from the heat and let them steep, or sit, for at least 20 minutes.

   e. Now, crumple your map slightly and dip the whole thing into the tea solution. Let it drip dry. It should look aged.

   f. To make it even neater, after the paper has dried, burn the edges slightly. (Do this outside over the sidewalk or driveway.) Now it will really look like an ancient map.

   g. To preserve your map, keep it in a clear plastic sleeve that can go into your Student Notebook. File it under "Asia: Crete."

WHAT DID YOU LEARN?

Week 4: *Quiz*

Match the following items by placing the correct letter next to the number.

____1. Seventh day of Creation

a. The first two people

____2. Adam and Eve

b. An advanced civilization on the island of Crete

____3. Tubal-Cain

c. A wedge-shaped alphabet created by the Sumerians

____4. Noah

d. Means "terrible lizard"

____5. 40 days and nights

e. Place where God confused man's language

____6. Dinosaur

f. A long poem

____7. Cuneiform writing

g. Length of the Great Flood

____8. Tower of Babel

h. Helped to save the human race and all the animals

____9. Epic

i. Maker of bronze and iron

____10. Stonehenge

j. Built the first great pyramids

____11. Khufu

k. The day God rested

____12. Minoans

l. marks the summer and winter solstice

The Mystery of History

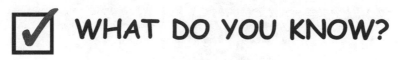

WHAT DO YOU KNOW?

Pretest 5

True or False? Circle your answer.

1. Abraham was the first patriarch of Israel.   T   F

2. The story of Abraham is found in the Book of Exodus in the Bible.   T   F

3. Esau traded his birthright for a bowl of stew.   T   F

4. Jacob loved Leah more than Rachel.   T   F

5. Jacob was given the name "Israel" by God.   T   F

6. Joseph was one of 15 sons of Jacob.   T   F

7. Joseph had a coat of many colors from Jacob.   T   F

8. The tribes of Israel moved to Egypt by the invitation of Joseph.   T   F

ABRAHAM

LESSON 13

Do you know someone who is Jewish? The Jewish people trace their heritage back to one man who lived 2,000 years before Christ. His name was Abraham.

Abraham was what we call a founding father of the Jewish faith. For that reason, he is sometimes called a "patriarch." God did many mighty things in Abraham's life when He chose to reveal Himself and His plans to the people of that era through the life of this great man.

Abraham lived in the city of Ur in about 2000 B.C. He was a descendant of Shem. As you may recall, Ur was in the country of Sumer and was a very advanced civilization. But it had its problems. The cities were full of those who worshiped idols and practiced ungodly living. It was this environment that God called Abraham to leave!

Genesis 12:1–3 is the command that God gave to Abram to flee from Ur. He promised to make him a great nation, to bless him, and to make his name great. Abram, as he was first named, meant "exalted father." God later gave him the name of Abraham, meaning "father of a great nation." And that is just what he became. Isn't it neat that the world today *does* know who Abraham was? God's word proves to be true.

The highlights of Abraham's life would certainly include his move away from Ur as well as away from his father's idols. He and his nephew Lot both left Ur following God's command but not really knowing where they were going. It must have been hard to leave the comfort of their way of life in Ur for the harsh life of traveling in tents and living off the land.

When Abraham and Lot did settle, they were not far from the cities of Sodom and Gomorrah. The wickedness of Sodom was even worse than that of Ur, and God told them to leave there also. As the story goes, Lot's wife had a hard time leaving without looking back, which they were told *not* to do. As a result, she was turned into a pillar of salt. Wow! What a tragic consequence for disobedience.

In time the Lord revealed to Abraham specifically what land he was going to inherit. It is important to be familiar with these passages in the Bible because the Jews still fight for the promise God made to Abraham. It is the promise of the land of Canaan that is the basis for war in the Middle East! God said in Genesis 13:14–15, "LIFT YOUR EYES NOW AND LOOK FROM THE PLACE WHERE YOU ARE NORTHWARD, SOUTHWARD, EASTWARD, AND WESTWARD; FOR ALL THE LAND WHICH YOU SEE I GIVE TO YOU AND YOUR DESCENDANTS FOREVER."

There are several other places where God gives the same promise but in different words. He says, "I give to you and your descendants after you the land in which you are a stranger, all the land of Canaan, as an everlasting possession; and I will be their God." (Gen. 17:8)

All of this sounded great to Abraham. But he and his wife Sarah did not understand the part of the promise that had to do with their descendants! You see, Abraham was very old (like 100) and had no children. Sarah was 90. How were they going to start a nation at their age with no kids?

Sarah wanted so badly to have children. In fact, Sarah had been so desperate to give her husband a child that she gave Abraham another woman named Hagar to have children with. This act ultimately caused a lot of jealousy and strife between the women.

Hagar did give Abraham a son. He was named Ishmael. Ishmael became the father of the Arab people, who have always been enemies to the Jews. The lineage of Ishmael is listed in the Bible in Genesis 25:12–18. But that is another story in itself.

God, though, in His faithfulness did finally give Abraham and Sarah a son. As always, God fulfilled His promise—He made Abraham the father of a great nation. Abraham named his special son Isaac. What a joy and delight he must have been for the elderly couple who had to wait so long to have children together.

It is the specialness of this one and only son of Abraham that makes the next part of the story so amazing. You see, when Isaac grew to be a young boy, God tested Abraham's faith and asked him to sacrifice his only son in worship! In other words, God asked Abraham to kill his beloved son. Can you imagine the agony Abraham must have felt as he proceeded to obey God? When Abraham showed that he totally believed in God no matter what the cost, God spared Isaac from the sacrifice. A ram appeared in a nearby thicket for Abraham to sacrifice instead.

This bronze, two-edged dagger resembles an anchor. A wooden handle would have filled the spaces you see to make it a powerful tool or weapon. This dagger was probably made in Palestine during Abraham's lifetime.

This story is profound and even relates to us. You see, the Lord later sends His only son, Jesus, as a sacrifice for us. The entire story of Abraham and Isaac is a foreshadowing of the future salvation of the world. In fact, if you were to visit Israel today and stand in the place where Abraham nearly sacrificed Isaac, you would be able to see in the distance Golgotha, the very place where Jesus WAS sacrificed. Again, we see God using parallels in history to help us understand the more difficult things of life. He wants us to know that He is the answer to the mystery of history.

ACTIVITY 13

13A—Younger Students

Sing the song "Father Abraham." The song says he had many sons. Did he have them all at once or did they come later as descendants? (Go to www.kididdles.com/mouseum/f033.html for the words to "Father Abraham" and a fun activity to go with them!)

13B—Middle Students

Do you like camping? It can be lots of fun. But for Abraham, sleeping in a tent was probably a great sacrifice. If your parents approve, spend the night in the backyard in a tent. Consider the conveniences that you miss in just one night. Imagine tent dwelling for years and years.

13C—Older Students

If your parents are comfortable with it, investigate what the Bible has to say about homosexuality. The city of Sodom in the region where Lot lived had a reputation for the practice of homosexuality. The term "sodomy," which we use today, means to engage in homosexual practice and comes from the name of the city. Familiarize yourself with at least five scriptures that address the issue. We live in a society that is very confused about the matter. Know what God says about it.

JACOB AND ESAU
LESSON 14

In our last lesson we learned that God promised to make Abraham a great nation. To understand how that promise is fulfilled, you will want to understand the lives of Abraham's grandsons, Jacob and Esau. Like many brothers, they often didn't get along.

To back up the story, Isaac (Abraham's son) grew up to marry Rebekah. Isaac and Rebekah had twin sons named Jacob and Esau. We know a lot about these grandsons of Abraham. Their stories in the Bible give us some detailed insights into the way of life of the people back then.

We know from the scriptures, for example, that Esau was redheaded and very hairy. He was born first, he loved to hunt, and he was his father's favorite. Jacob, on the other hand, was born holding his brother's foot. (This implies that they would struggle over who was firstborn.) Jacob was a mild man, and was favored by his mother.

One important story of these brothers is that of their squabble over a bowl of stew. Stew may not sound so important, but Esau once wanted Jacob's bowl of stew so badly that he flippantly traded his birthright for it. A birthright back then was as official as a legal transaction is today. It meant that the holder of the birthright, usually the older son, got a greater inheritance.

Though it may have seemed harmless at the time, the swapping of birthrights became a huge issue later when Isaac was near death. To ensure that Jacob would receive Isaac's final blessing, Jacob pretended to be Esau before his father, whose eyesight was poor. He actually laid animal skins on his arms to pretend they were Esau's hairy arms! The trick worked, too, and Jacob received a greater blessing than his brother Esau.

Jacob later paid for his deceit. For one, his brother Esau hated him, and he had to move away. Then, when he went to marry Rachel, a woman he deeply loved, she was replaced by her older sister Leah on their wedding night! The swap was as deceitful as when Jacob pretended to be Esau. Laban (the father of Rachel and Leah) was responsible for that trick. Laban didn't want his younger daughter Rachel to marry before her older sister Leah. Eventually Jacob did marry Rachel, but he had to work many more years for Laban.

The difference between Jacob's relationships with the two sisters becomes very important to Jewish history. Leah, whom he didn't really love, gave him many fine sons. But the sons that Rachel gave him were always his favorites. He had 12 sons in all. These sons, or their descendants, later became the heads of the 12 tribes of Israel. (Jacob was given the name "Israel" in Genesis 35:10.)

Jacob's sons were Reuben, Simeon, Levi, Judah, Issachar, and Zebulun, who were all born of Leah. From Rachel he had Joseph and Benjamin. From Rachel's maidservant he had Dan and Naphtali. From Leah's maidservant he fathered Gad and Asher. These 12 names become very important later in Jewish history.

There are many more wonderful stories about Jacob and Esau in the Book of Genesis. Read to find out how Jacob makes up with his brother Esau, how Jacob wrestles an angel, and the story of Jacob's ladder. The Bible is full of great stories like these.

ACTIVITY 14

14A—Younger Students

1. View one of the beautiful children's versions of the story of Jacob on video. I recommend Hanna-Barbera's "The Greatest Adventure" Series or Nest Entertainment.
2. According to the Bible, the stew that Esau wanted so badly was "lentil stew." Have you ever had lentils? I think they are delicious. Eat some for dinner tonight! (They are really good served over rice and topped with a little salsa.)

14B—Middle and Older Students

Make a family tree of the patriarchal fathers. Start with the name of Abraham at the top of the page. Next to him write Sarah. Across from her, write in Hagar. Using lines, draw arrows to point to the children the couples gave birth to. Continue in this fashion down the page to include the people in the list below. Title the page "The Patriarchs of Israel," and file it in your Student Notebook under "Asia: Israel."

Abraham

Sarah

Hagar

Ishmael

Isaac

Jacob

Rachel

Leah

Bilhah, Rachel's maidservant

Zilpah, Leah's maidservant

Reuben

Simeon

Levi

Judah

Issachar

Zebulun

Joseph

Benjamin

Dan

Naphtali

Gad

Asher

14C—Middle and Older Students

I encourage you to take time this week to read the Book of Job from the Old Testament. Job probably lived near the time of Jacob and Joseph. (Some scholars, however, place him as late as Moses.) Job is a literary classic and still a story of great comfort for those who suffer.

With Job's story in mind, please take any time you might have used to work on a history project today and use it instead to pray for any persons you or your family know who are suffering.

- Pray that they might understand God's love for them.
- Pray that they will not turn away from God even though life might be hard right now.
- Pray that they will find some relief from their problems or pain.
- Pray that if there is something you can do to comfort them that God will make it easy for you to do that. (Maybe a card, some babysitting, or a meal would be nice.)
- If you can't think of anyone close by who needs this kind of prayer or help, then pray for other Christians in the world who are persecuted for their faith. They would appreciate your prayers for them and for their families.

Write down what you did for someone and file it in your Student Notebook under "Asia: Israel."

1914 B.C.

JOSEPH

LESSON 15

Joseph is one of my favorite characters in the entire Bible. We know a lot about his life from the Book of Genesis. His life story demonstrates that he was truly a remarkable man.

First of all, Joseph was one of the 12 sons of Jacob (or Israel). He was favored greatly by his father because he was one of Rachel's sons. Remember that Jacob really loved his wife Rachel. Naturally, her children were extra precious to him. (Benjamin was Rachel's only other son, and Rachel died in giving birth to him.) Jacob so loved Joseph that he made him a special coat of many colors.

This favoritism led to serious problems between Joseph and his brothers. To make matters worse, Joseph told his brothers that he had dreams where he saw himself ruling over them. You can imagine their disgust. Things got so bad that they almost killed him and threw him into a well. But, being afraid of having his blood on their hands, the brothers instead sold Joseph into slavery. They lied to their father about the whole incident and said that wild animals had attacked Joseph.

This "selling" of Joseph into slavery is a huge part of history! It was because of Joseph's move to Egypt as a slave that the Hebrews later resided in Egypt and became slaves themselves. The brothers really didn't get away with selling Joseph.

The life that Joseph led in Egypt was astonishing. He was bought by one of the pharaoh's officers named Potiphar. It says in Genesis 39:2, "The Lord was with Joseph, and he was a successful man." He was regarded so highly by his master that he was given complete rule over the house. I believe that that feat tells us something about the good character of Joseph. He could have been a bitter and angry man because of what his brothers had done to him. But we can speculate that he must have dealt well with his misfortune or he might not have been so blessed.

In Potiphar's house, Joseph passed one of the hardest tests a man can undergo. He was tempted by Potiphar's wife to commit adultery with her. Remember that Joseph was a single man and may not even have kissed a girl yet. He was a slave without much of a social life. But his relationship with the Lord was so strong that he withstood the taunting. Potiphar's wife, though, was wicked and persistent. She set Joseph up to look as if he had attacked her. As a result, he was thrown in prison.

Again, Joseph had reason to be a bitter man. But even in prison he was a good guy. He wound up interpreting dreams, as God worked through him, and it eventually led to his promotion to the palace of the pharaoh himself. Joseph was then in a position of greatness beyond his wildest dreams. As a new prime minister, he was asked to lead a program to store up grain against a famine. God had warned Joseph that the famine was coming, and He revealed to him how to store grain. This supernatural arrangement spared the deaths of thousands to hunger.

This is where the story of Joseph really gets juicy. Guess who needed grain and came bowing to Joseph to get it? His brothers, of course—the same ones who threw him into the well and sold him off as a slave. What would you have done to your brothers in that situation? Most men would have sought revenge. Joseph, though, forgave them. This is an incredible story. I believe it is another parallel in history. We, like Joseph's brothers, are guilty and don't deserve forgiveness. But we receive it as grace from God. Joseph's brothers received it too.

The happy story ends with all the brothers and Jacob moving to where Joseph lived in Egypt. Can you even imagine the joy of Jacob in seeing Joseph again? I wonder who spoke first and what was said. What would Jacob say to the son who for years and years was believed to be dead? Did he have to choke back tears when he saw that Joseph was really and truly alive? Just imagine how the Lord feels when even one sinner who is spiritually "dead" is made "alive" through Christ. It must be a joy even greater than Jacob's!

ACTIVITY 15

ALL STUDENTS

Make your Memory Cards for Lessons 13–15. I recommend that students memorize 12 specific dates in this volume. The first one is Abraham in 2100 B.C. On your Memory Card, highlight his name and the date in yellow so that it might stand out from the other cards.

15A—Younger Students

There are many aspects of Joseph's life worth remembering. But, just for fun, these activities will focus on the coat of many colors.

1. Frost cookies with different colors of icing: Using a recipe for sugar cookies, shape dough into little coats. Bake as directed. Divide a can of white frosting into several containers and add food coloring of different shades to the containers. Frost the cookies with stripes of different colors.

2. Instead of cookies, make a "cone" of many colors. Buy vanilla ice cream. Scoop it into cones. Sprinkle with toppings of different colors.

3. Or, try to tie-dye a white T-shirt with many different colors.

15B—Younger, Middle, and Older Students

Is it easy to practice forgiveness? I think the story of Joseph is a great demonstration of some of the most difficult forgiveness to give—that is, to our own family members! Take time today and discuss the need to forgive those right in our own homes. If any unforgiveness exists, clear it up today!

If a discussion isn't feasible today, write a special note to anyone you know from whom you need to ask for forgiveness. The New Testament contains some great guidelines on the subject.

15C—Older Students

Research modern-day famine in Africa. What parts of that continent are in the greatest need? What relief efforts exist today? What does the Bible say in Proverbs about caring for the poor? Consider the responsibility Joseph undertook in preventing starvation. File it under "Africa: Egypt."

TAKE ANOTHER LOOK!

Review 5: Lessons 13–15

Wall of Fame

1. *Abraham (2100 B.C.)*— Write the name "patriarch" on him. Place a golden cross on him to signify the lineage of Christ. Near him, place a small boy with the name "Isaac." He, too, needs a golden cross to signify the lineage of Christ.

   To help in memorizing the date for Abraham, make a special page in the "Miscellaneous" section of your Student Notebook. Keep a running list of the 12 special characters and events that I recommend you memorize. I will point them out when you make your Memory Cards and when you are on timeline work.

2. *Jacob and Esau (2005 B.C.)*— Place them together like twins. Cross out the name "Jacob" and write above it "Israel." On Jacob, place a golden cross to signify the lineage of Christ. Color red hair on Esau and glue cotton balls on his arms. A red marker will make this "hair" the right color!

3. *Joseph (1914 B.C.)*—Place this figure inside a triangle (the shape of a pyramid) to signify his move to Egypt.

SomeWHERE in Time

1. Younger Students: On a present-day map or globe, find Israel and Egypt. Trace with your finger the distance Joseph, his father, and his brothers traveled to reach Egypt.

2. Middle and Older Students: On Outline Map 9, "Eastern Mediterranean," draw a line to mark the journey of Joseph and his brothers. What are the modern-day countries they traveled through? Mark these as well. File this under "Asia: Middle East" in your Student Notebook.

WHAT DID YOU MISS?

Week 5: Exercise

Using your book for a reference, renumber these people and events in chronological order. Put the correct number on the line at right, followed by the approximate date in parentheses.

1. The construction of Stonehenge began.   _____

2. Noah built the ark.   _____

3. *The Epic of Gilgamesh* was written.   _____

4. God created the heavens and the earth.   _____

5. Jubal mastered the harp.   _____

6. The Ice Age began.   _____

7. Abraham moved away from Ur.   _____

8. Men built a great tower at Babel.   _____

9. The Minoans built the Palace of Knossos.   _____

10. Joseph forgave his brothers.   _____

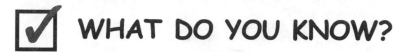 WHAT DO YOU KNOW?

Pretest 6

Fill in the blanks using one of the words provided at the bottom of the page.

1. Hammurabi was a king of _____.

2. Hammurabi is best remembered for writing _____ that helped to set standards for living.

3. Despite the success of Joseph, the Israelites eventually became _____ in Egypt.

4. While in bondage, the Israelites (or Hebrews) still _____.

5. The _____ of Egypt ordered that all the Hebrew babies be thrown into the Nile River.

6. The country of _____ is naturally isolated by mountains, oceans, and deserts.

7. A _____ is the term for a family that rules a country.

8. The _____ was a very important secret that greatly helped the Chinese economy.

WORD BANK

laws	silkworm	China	Babylonia
slaves	flourished	dynasty	pharaoh

HAMMURABI

LESSON 16

The Sumerians, as you may remember, ruled Mesopotamia, or the Fertile Crescent. Over time, other empires invaded and new rulers were put in place. A new civilization began to flourish there under the name of Babylonia. You have probably heard of the Babylonians in the Old Testament. (They are also called the Chaldeans.)

One of the more famous leaders of the old Babylonian Empire was Hammurabi (Ham-uh-RAH-bee). He lived from about 1792 to 1750 B.C. We know a lot about him because in 1901 a great discovery was made. In Susa, an ancient Babylonian city, archaeologists unearthed a 7-foot-high stone monument; written on the monument was Hammurabi's code of 300 laws. The code itself explains that these laws were written "to cause justice to prevail in the land, to destroy the wicked and the evil, to prevent the strong from oppressing the weak, and to further the welfare of the people."

What all of this means is that quite a civilization had been established under Hammurabi's leadership. One of the ways that men live alongside one another in peace is to have laws that everyone agrees upon and lives by. Before Hammurabi's laws were discovered, historians thought that there must not have been any laws in existence that early in history. Hammurabi proved them wrong.

In the code, this king of Babylon addressed many practical things. He set standards for land deals, trading, military service, loans and debts, wages, family disputes, and even dealings with witchcraft. As a king, Hammurabi also worked on fair taxation and minimum wage. We still use the concept of minimum wage today. (That is the lowest amount of money a person can be paid for a job.)

The significance of these laws becomes clearer when you stop to think about Moses. Though we have not studied him yet, we are near the time period when God gave the Israelites His laws to live by. You can find them in Exodus 20. Though there are some similarities in the laws of Moses and Hammurabi, there really exist more differences.

The Ten Commandments and the other laws God gave Moses had to do with worship of one God as well as with relationships between men. Hammurabi does not address the worship of one God. Moses gave God all the glory in the laws he recorded. Hammurabi gave glory only to himself. According to historians, some of Hammurabi's penalties were harsh, unfair, and inconsistent. On the other hand, we find God's laws and consequences to sin to be fair and just.

Still, as you can tell, Hammurabi was a remarkable king for his time. The magnificent stone that he left behind is just one indication of the impact he made in early Babylonia.

ACTIVITY 16

16A—Younger Students

A family is really a small society. During a family meeting or mealtime, discuss what rules your family has. You may discover that family rules are designed to do one of these things:

1. To keep peace
2. To keep order

3. To protect valuable things
4. To keep people safe
5. To keep people healthy

Think of examples for each item above. Talk about why they are necessary even though some are not fun to abide by. Can you come up with other reasons for family rules? Does your family have consequences for breaking the rules? What are the consequences in our society for breaking the law? Think of the similarities between families and societies.

16B—Middle Students

All societies have rules and laws to follow. Even in our language, we have rules to make sense of what we read, write, and speak. In the following paragraph on Hammurabi, some rules of English have been left out. See if you can make sense of the paragraph by adding some punctuation. Rewrite it on another piece of paper.

thepurposeofhammurabisnearly300lawswas"tocausejusticetoprevailinthelandtodestroythewicked

andtheeviltopreventthestrongfromoppressingtheweakandtofurtherthewelfareofthepeople."

Hint: To solve the problem of the paragraph, just add commas, spaces between words, and two capitals. Aren't you glad we have grammar rules?

16C—Older Students

Research the details of the "harsh consequences" to some of Hammurabi's laws. Utilize the library or Internet to find a copy of the laws. Summarize your findings and give examples of penalties. File your results under "Asia: Iraq (Mesopotamia)."

Began c. 1875–1730 B.C.

THE ISRAELITES IN SLAVERY

LESSON 17

The last we read about the Israelites, things were going well. Jacob was reunited with Joseph, and all the brothers moved their families near the palace of the pharaoh. They were spared from the devastation of famine and were prospering in the land of Egypt. The Book of Genesis ends with the story of the death of Joseph, who had lived a victorious life.

Something happened though. Exodus 1:8 says, "there arose a new king over Egypt, who did not know Joseph." This new king just did not appreciate the faith and heritage of the Israelite people. He instead saw them as a threat because they were so blessed and so numerous. He may have thought that, as foreigners, the Israelites would not be loyal to him.

The pharaoh first began to oppress the Israelites by setting harsh taskmasters, or bosses, over them. This led to more and more loss of freedom and eventually to total slavery. Through most of their captivity, the slaves were used to help build some of the magnificent structures of the Egyptians. That kind of hard labor should have slowed down the prosperity of the Israelites. But it didn't. The Lord fulfilled His promise to Abraham that He would make him a great nation. And the Israelites multiplied even more despite the harsh circumstances.

The pharaoh over Egypt was so wicked that he asked the Egyptian midwives (ladies who assist a woman in childbirth) to kill the Hebrew baby boys as they were born. (Hebrew is another term for Israelite.[1]) He thought he could stop the growth of the Hebrews.

Here's what the midwives did though. Exodus 1:17 tells us, "but the midwives feared God, and did not do as the king of Egypt commanded them, but saved the male children alive." Isn't that neat? I wonder what made these midwives fear a god that they did not know? Maybe they saw the love of God in these special people. Maybe they didn't. Regardless, the midwives risked their own lives to save the Hebrew babies, and the people flourished despite their slavery.

Finally, the pharaoh was so upset over the strong population of the Hebrews that he ordered all male babies to be thrown into the river. Does that story sound familiar to you? One very well-known baby was spared from this kind of death. His name was Moses. After 400 years of captivity in Egypt, the Hebrews were soon going to experience deliverance through the leadership of Moses. It's a remarkable story that we'll get to soon.

This bronze Egyptian dagger was made between 1787 and 1582 B.C. The stone pommel next to it was used to hold its wooden handle together. (It is rare to find a pommel with a dagger because the two are usually separated after the wooden handle weathers and deteriorates.)

ACTIVITY 17

17A—Younger Students

Make miniature "bricks." Use part Play-Doh modeling compound or clay with part grass or straw. Blend the two ingredients together with your hands. Form into little bricks. Let them harden in the sun. Think about having to make thousands of bricks for someone else. That is what the Israelites had to do under the pharaoh of Egypt. Take a picture of your bricks and file it under "Africa: Egypt" in your Student Notebook. (This is very fun and easy, just a little messy if you use real clay!)

17B—Middle Students

Investigate the field of midwifery. Are there any midwives listed in your local phone book? How are they different from doctors? Do you know of anyone in your family or among your family's friends who

---

1. The Israelites may have renamed themselves the Hebrews while in captivity because the word "Habiru" had been used to describe nomadic people of the region. The Habiru people were generally lowly and sometimes gave themselves over to slavery to survive. The downcast Israelites may have identified themselves with these people.

Incidentally, the Israelites continued to call themselves "Hebrews" until about the time of the Judges. Even later they call themselves "Jews." Don't let this confuse you! The Hebrews, the Israelites, and the Jews are all really the same people.

From *The Living Bible Encyclopedia in Story and Pictures,* Art Treasure ed., Vol. 6, s.v. "Hebrews." New York: H. S. Stuttman Co., Inc., 1968.

The Mystery of History

has used a midwife? It is a growing profession in our society today. Interview a midwife or someone who has used one. Find out why this practice from long ago is popular again.

17C—Older Students

Find current statistics on the number of abortions performed in America today. Who are the people who fight against abortion? What does "civil disobedience" mean, and how does it relate to what the Egyptian midwives did? What would you do to help save a life?

CHINA AND THE SHANG DYNASTY

LESSON 18

Do you like Chinese food? I love it! If you like it or not, we might all agree that it is unique, with a style and flavor of its very own. Well, much like its food, the vast country of China is unique, too, because of its distinct geography, culture, and government.

High mountains, deserts, and oceans guard the land where China is today. Get out a globe or atlas now and find the borders. Because of these natural barriers, China did not attract very many outside visitors long, long ago. The difficulty of the journey likely meant that when people did travel or migrate to China, they stayed there.

We find, then, that there was much interbreeding among the early settlers to China. That means the same kind of people kept marrying the same kind of people. This may account for the distinct difference in physical features of the Asian people still seen today—features such as almond-shaped eyes and jet-black hair.

The Chinese culture is thought to be the oldest pure remnant of an ancient civilization that exists. The word "culture" refers to the art, music, writings, and drama of a particular people. Because of China's longtime isolation from the rest of the world, its culture has remained very distinguishable. That means it is very easy to recognize Chinese things because they are very different from the Western world. In contrast, the cultures of the Babylonians, the Greeks, and the Romans have somewhat blended together with neighboring countries over time.

As for government, the Chinese have almost always been ruled by dynasties. A dynasty is a family that obtains power and keeps it, sometimes for centuries at a time, by passing it on to their children when they grow up. There have been 10 or more dynasties to rule China in this fashion.

One of the first dynasties we know of is the Xia. They probably ruled for four or five hundred years somewhere between the twenty-first and sixteenth centuries before Christ. Not very much is known about the people of the Xia dynasty and for a long time it wasn't clear whether they existed at all. But, in the 1960s and 1970s, archaeologists found lots of things which support the fact that these people were real. They found parts of cities, bronze tools, and burial grounds, all pointing to the lives of these ancient people.

The next ruling family of China was the Shang dynasty. A lot more is known about them except exactly when they ruled. Some historians think they lived as far back as 1760 B.C. Others say they ruled from about 1600 B.C. to 1066 B.C.

No matter when the Shang lived and ruled, they're still remembered for some neat things. For one, they started a written language, but it was very different from ours. The early Chinese used 50,000 characters to express themselves. Imagine learning their ABC song in kindergarten! They also were making bronze early on and using horses to drive chariots.

One of the unusual things the Shang knew how to do was to grow silkworms and use them to make silk fabric. A very special worm has to be cultivated, one that eats only mulberry leaves. The worm spins threads into silk around its cocoon. It requires a lot of human skill and patience to unwind these delicate threads.

Legends say there was an empress named His-Ling Shi who lived long before the Shang dynasty. She was the first to have mulberry groves planted specifically to feed the precious silkworm. Over time, silk became so valuable to people that it was sometimes used like money. In later years, silk cloth became a serious item for trading to other countries. The Chinese kept the method of making silk a secret for about 3,000 years! That's a long time for keeping a secret.

We will study the other dynasties of China as they emerge over history. Some were quite short, but most lasted hundreds of years at a time, giving China some of its unique characteristics.

ACTIVITY 18

ALL STUDENTS

Make your Memory Cards for Lessons 16–18.

18A—Younger Students

One way to remember the ancient Chinese would be to obtain some silk fabric. Many fabrics today are soft and flowing like silk but are man-made. See if you can find anything in your home that is 100 percent silk. Compare silk to polyester, cotton, and linen. How do they feel? What is one of your favorite materials for clothes? Why would silk fabric be nice to sleep in?

18B—Middle and Older Students

1. Do you like insects? Research the amazing little silkworm. How does it really make silk?
2. Research the ancient Chinese alphabet. Photocopy samples of it to file in your Student Notebook under "Asia: China." What alphabet is being used in China today?

18C—Middle and Older Students

Use the format below to begin a running list of the dynasties of China. We will add to it along the way. File it in your Student Notebook under "Asia: China."

The Dynasties of China

Date of power (years ruling)	Name of dynasty	Special notes
c. 2000–1600 B.C. (c. 400 yrs.)	Xia	Evidence of cities, bronze
c. 1600–1066 B.C. (c. 534 yrs.)	Shang	Developed writing
		Harvested silkworms

TAKE ANOTHER LOOK!

Review 6: Lessons 16–18

Wall of Fame

1. *Hammurabi (1792 B.C.)*—Draw a big black stone next to Hammurabi with scribbles on it.

2. *The Israelites in slavery (exact date unknown; it began c. 1875–1730 B.C.)*—Draw a set of chains.

3. *Shang dynasty (exact date unknown; c. 1600–1066 B.C.)*—Attach a silky scrap of fabric to your paper with the title and dates of the Shang dynasty.

SomeWHERE in Time

1. Find a map of ancient Mesopotamia with Babylon on it. Compare it to a modern-day map of Iraq. Babylon is just south of present-day Baghdad. Do you know who the ruler there was in the year 2000? Unscramble his name to find out. (Dmdsaa ensuHis)

2. Using an atlas, identify the mountains in southwest China, the oceans on the south and east sides, and the deserts to the north.
   Middle and Older Students: Transfer this information to Outline Map 4, "East Asia." Title your map "Natural Boundaries of China."

3. Middle and Older Students: Add to your map the names of these three large rivers.

   The Huang He (Yellow River)

   The Chang Jiang (Yangtze River)

   The Xi Jiang (West River)

   To help you remember which is which, consider that the river names in English are in alphabetical order on your map from bottom to top. Look and see for yourself. These rivers helped to give the people water for crops and a means of transporting things. So, we find the early civilizations were nearby.

4. Also on your map, write in the city of Anyang. It is south and slightly west of Beijing. The Shang dynasty probably ruled from here. File your map under "Asia: China."

WHAT DID YOU LEARN?

Week 6: *Quiz*

Multiple Choice. Circle one answer for each question.

1. The Bible says that on Day 1 of Creation God made
   a. day and night.
   b. the firmament, or heavens.
   c. seas and earth.
   d. cattle and creeping things.

2. According to the Bible, when Adam and Eve sinned
   a. they were ashamed.
   b. sin and death entered the world.
   c. man was cursed to work, woman was cursed with birth pains.
   d. All of the above.

3. Jubal was the father of
   a. Cain.
   b. bronzemaking.
   c. all who play harp and flute.
   d. the Jewish nation.

4. How many people were on board of Noah's ark?
   a. 6
   b. 8
   c. 10
   d. 12

5. Which of these statements about the Ice Age is false?
   a. The Ice Age ended slowly.
   b. Man lived through the Ice Age.
   c. Scientists have determined the exact dates of the Ice Age.
   d. During the Ice Age, only parts of the earth were covered by glaciers.

6. The Sumerian civilization was located
   a. on the island of Crete.
   b. in the Fertile Crescent.
   c. in China.
   d. in Egypt.

7. The word "babel" means
   a. wedge-shaped.
   b. land between the rivers.
   c. confusion.
   d. huge rocks.

8. In *The Epic of Gilgamesh,* Gilgamesh is
   a. the name of a king in the story.
   b. the name of a country.
   c. the name of the author of the poem.
   d. the name of the archaeologist who found the poem.

9. The pyramids were primarily built to be used as
   a. temples.
   b. tombs.
   c. palaces.
   d. tourist attractions.

10. According to legend, King Minos of Crete supposedly kept a half-bull, half-man creature called
    a. a megalith.
    b. a Mesopotamia.
    c. a Minotaur.
    d. a terrible lizard.

11. The name "Abraham" means
    a. father of a great nation.
    b. my beloved.
    c. the redeemed.
    d. father of Isaac.

12. Jacob had
    a. twin sons.
    b. 12 sons.
    c. 3 sons.
    d. only one son.

13. Hammurabi was a Babylonian king best remembered for
    a. building a labyrinth.
    b. writing a code of 300 laws.
    c. creating cuneiform writing.
    d. building the Tower of Babel.

14. While in slavery, the Israelites
    a. made bricks.
    b. grew in size.
    c. called themselves "Hebrews."
    d. All of the above.

15. Early China was ruled by
    a. monarchs.
    b. pharaohs.
    c. dynasties.
    d. pirates.

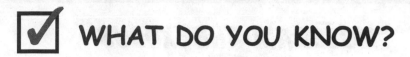

✓ WHAT DO YOU KNOW?

Pretest 7

In the following sentences, circle the word that you think makes the sentence correct.

1. After being rescued from the Nile, Moses was raised as an (Egyptian, Hebrew).

2. At the first Passover, Hebrews were told to paint the blood of a (cow, lamb) over their doorposts.

3. To demonstrate His power, God sent (5, 10) plagues against the Egyptians.

4. The Tabernacle in the wilderness was a place for the Israelites to (worship, hold banquets).

5. The Tabernacle was divided into (3, 4) segments to symbolize the Trinity.

6. In the Holy of Holies, the innermost court of the Tabernacle, only the high (judge, priest) was allowed to enter on the Day of Atonement.

7. Moses helped lead the Israelites out of Egypt, but (Aaron, Joshua) helped to lead the people into Canaan.

8. At the Battle of Jericho, the Israelites marched around the city for six days blowing horns; they marched and (cried, shouted) on the seventh day.

MOSES AND THE EXODUS

LESSON 19

The story of Moses is a fascinating one because we see God having a plan and purpose for someone's life even as an infant. While other Hebrew babies were being thrown to their death in the Nile by orders of the pharaoh, Moses was protected. His mother laid him in a safe basket and set him adrift in the river's water.

In Hebrew, the name Moses means "to draw out." This is, of course, what happened to him as a baby when the pharaoh's daughter drew him out of the Nile River. She adopted this baby in a floating basket to be her very own. But, on a deeper level, the name Moses reflects what became his life's mission: "to draw" the Hebrews out of slavery.

The amazing part of Moses' life is that he grew up in the palace of the Egyptian pharaoh. But he was a Hebrew! Despite his upbringing, God laid it upon him as an adult to set the Hebrews free. He was to completely defy his heritage as an Egyptian for his true identity as a Hebrew slave.

Placing a date on the life of Moses is difficult. The main reason is that the Egyptians had a habit of erasing or forgetting their "bad" history. The episode of Moses would not have been a good one for the existing pharaoh because in the end, the Hebrews win, and the pharaoh loses! Therefore, the written records are unclear. Some think that Moses grew up in the pharaoh's palace alongside Ramses the Great. We see this scenario portrayed in the movie *The Prince of Egypt*.

However, some believe that Moses was up against a different pharaoh when seeking the freedom of his true people. This pharaoh was named Amenhotep II. One possibility pointing to him is that the eldest son of Amenhotep II did NOT reign after him, as he should have. Maybe the son died during the plagues that killed all the firstborn of the Egyptians! We also know that one of Amenhotep's later descendants, Amenhotep IV, abandoned the worship of the Egyptian gods altogether for ONE god instead! Maybe Amenhotep IV got the idea of "one God" from Moses and the dramatic events around the Exodus. Nobody knows for sure.

This terra-cotta flask or canteen was used to carry water or wine. It was made between 1550 and 1200 B.C., which is about the time Moses traveled across the desert. He probably carried something similar to this to survive.

What was so dramatic about the story of Moses? As I said before, when Moses was an adult God led him to ask the pharaoh to set the Hebrews free. That request didn't go over very well. The pharaoh had good reason to want to keep the Hebrews. They were his greatest source of labor.

But the Lord had plans for His people. To encourage the pharaoh to listen to Moses, God sent 10 plagues, or terrible troubles, against the Egyptians. Oddly enough, it seems that the whole story of Moses may be more than that of saving the Hebrews. If you consider the specific plagues God sent, it appears that He must have been trying to speak to the Egyptians as well. Each of the 10 plagues seemed to defy one of the false gods of Egypt.

The first plague, the Nile turning into blood, demonstrated God's power over the river that brought the Egyptians so much wealth. The people actually honored the river as a god named "Hapy." Frogs, lice, and locusts all were considered gods in Egypt. The Lord used these very creatures to bring devastation. Another of Egypt's gods was a bull. It was the chief of the animal gods. The Lord struck the cattle of Egypt with sores to show His power over the bull gods.

Several days of darkness showed that God was superior to the sun god, Ra, who was greatly worshiped. The onset of hail, fire, and thunder was an answer to the false nature gods the Egyptians believed in. But the last plague was the worst. The Lord took the life of every firstborn son of the Egyptians. That included the pharaoh's son, whom the people held up as a future god.

To protect the Hebrews themselves from this final plague, the Hebrews were instructed to paint their doorposts with the blood of a lamb. Then the death angel of the Lord would "pass over" their homes. This has been commemorated ever since then in the feast of "Passover." It is a beautiful illustration of what was yet to come through the blood of Christ, which was shed so that death might pass over us!

With the last plague, the pharaoh of Egypt begged the Hebrews to leave. In haste and desperation, he sent them away only to chase after them again. But the miracles of God didn't stop. The story of the crossing of the Red Sea reveals that God supernaturally was paving a way for His children to return home.

We cannot even imagine the scene of those thousands and thousands of people who packed up for their long-awaited journey. With their goats, their oxen, their donkeys, and their wagons, they fled with their most important possessions. Perhaps a little girl carried her favorite doll, or a boy, his favorite stick. But where were the people going to go? How were they going to get there? They were headed back to where Jacob, or Israel, started his family—the land of Canaan. And Moses was going to lead them.

This great migration of people has been called the Exodus. One whole book in the Bible bears the name of this event. Though the Hebrews' journey to Canaan should have taken just a few years, the wandering of the people lasted 40 years! They had several problems along the way. But, in that time, we see God miraculously demonstrate His power. He provides "manna" and quail in the desert; He gives Moses the Ten Commandments; and He teaches the people lessons on idolatry.

God used Moses, one special man, to save a nation,

"Then Moses stretched out his hand over the sea; and the Lord caused the sea to go back....So the children of Israel went into the midst of the sea on the dry ground." Exodus 14:21-22

much like he used Noah and later Jesus Christ. Moses is clearly another parallel in history. In the next lesson, we will learn how God used the Tabernacle to show Himself even more clearly to His chosen people.

ACTIVITY 19

19A—Younger Students

With parental approval, watch the video *The Prince of Egypt.*

19B—Middle and Older Students

Consider watching both movies—*The Prince of Egypt* and *The Ten Commandments.* (Not all at the same time!) Note the similarities and the differences between the stories. *The Prince of Egypt* does an outstanding job of depicting the agony Moses might have first felt to learn of his true heritage. I wish, however, that they had shown him to be a greater man of prayer as we assume he was.

I think the pharaoh in *The Ten Commandments* does a great job in showing the rage of a king. Pick YOUR favorite character.

19C—Middle and Older Students

Make a chart for your Student Notebook that clearly explains the 10 plagues of Egypt in relation to their false gods. Set up your paper to look something like the one below. Use your Bible and the text to complete it. File it under "Africa: Egypt."

Plague (verse reference)	Egyptian god	Warning given	Pharaoh's response
1. Nile into blood (Exod. 7:14–25)	Hapy	Fish will die River will stink People will hate to drink	Heart grew hard Went into his house

---

c. 1500 B.C.

THE ARK OF THE COVENANT AND THE TABERNACLE

LESSON 20

As you know from our last lesson, during the Exodus the Lord used Moses to lead the Hebrews out of slavery in Egypt. Through horrific plagues, the crossing of the Red Sea, and other miracles, the story of the Exodus is a gripping account of the power of God to save. But on a more intimate level, while the Israelites were in the wilderness God showed His great love for them by His very presence among them. We see evidence of this in the Ark of the Covenant and the Tabernacle.

To back up a bit, the Hebrews left Egypt to head for the Promised Land. That would be the land of Canaan, or Israel, as we know it today. But as I mentioned in the last lesson, what should have been a trip that would last a few years, became a journey of 40 years. And most of it was through a desert.

So, how do thousands and thousands of people survive a desert experience for 40 years? That is a great question with a neat answer. The Lord miraculously provided food and water for them as they needed it. The Bible says that for 40 years the Hebrews would wake up to find just enough "manna" on the ground for them to eat. This manna was nourishing like bread and sweet like honey. It literally "fell" from heaven to feed the people as they needed. The Israelites were also sent an abundance of quail (a kind of bird) for food. To provide water, the Lord instructed Moses to strike a rock with his rod. And water miraculously poured forth!

As incredible as this provision of food and water was, the next act of God, recorded in the Book of Exodus, is even more amazing. The Bible says that the Lord Himself went down to meet with the Israelites at Mount Sinai!

> "Now Mount Sinai was completely in smoke, because the Lord descended upon it in fire. Its smoke ascended like the smoke of a furnace, and the whole mountain quaked greatly. And when the blast of the trumpet sounded long and became louder and louder, Moses spoke, and God answered him by voice. Then the Lord came down upon Mount Sinai, on the top of the mountain. And the Lord called Moses to the top of the mountain, and Moses went up." (Exod. 19:18–20)

It was then that the Lord gave Moses the Ten Commandments. Do you know and follow the Ten Commandments? These became the religious and moral foundation of the nation of Israel and are the basis for many laws even today. The first five commandments are directly related to man's relationship with God whereas the last five are related to how people ought to treat one another. One of the more amazing things about the Ten Commandments is that, according to the Bible, God Himself inscribed them on tablets of stone with His finger. For this reason alone I think they should be considered important!

As for the story of Moses, the Bible says that he remained on Mount Sinai, where he received the Ten Commandments, for 40 days and 40 nights. It was during this time that the Lord gave Moses some other very special instructions. For one, Moses was told how to construct the Ark of the Covenant, a sacred holding place for the Ten Commandments. Secondly, he was informed how to build a Tabernacle as a place for God to dwell and the people to worship. We will examine both of these items more closely.

The Ark of the Covenant (sometimes called the Ark of the Testimony) was designed as a holding place for at least three things. The Lord wanted the Israelites to remember all that He had provided for them in the desert wilderness. Primarily, the stone tablets containing the Ten Commandments were stored in the Ark. But for some time there was also placed in the Ark a sample of manna and Aaron's rod. (Aaron was Moses' brother. His rod or staff was used many times to perform miracles.) These items were all examples of how God cared for the Israelites.

As for the construction of the Ark of the Covenant, it was very special, too. The Lord instructed Moses to build it of acacia wood in the shape of a large box and overlay it with pure gold inside and out. The Ark was to be carried by special golden poles and rings. It was decorated on top with a "mercy seat" of pure gold. The mercy seat was made of two winged cherubim also in pure gold. It was there that God promised to meet and talk with Moses.

Throughout the Old Testament, there are stories about the Ark of the Covenant as it was literally carried before the Israelites as a symbol of God's presence with them. There were even times when the enemies of the Israelites tried to steal the Ark only to find themselves swarmed by plagues for their act of theft.

As meaningful as the Ark of the Covenant was, the second structure that Moses was told to build was even more special. Moses was instructed to build a tent-like structure called a Tabernacle, which would become the very dwelling place of God in the wilderness with His people! The Lord, in Exodus 25:8, said, "And let them make Me a sanctuary, that I may dwell among them." So you see, the Tabernacle was no ordinary tent. The Lord gave Moses very detailed instructions as to exactly how He wanted the Tabernacle erected. It was to contain very specific pieces of furniture, so to speak, that would be used in worship. One of these furniture items to be placed in the tent was the sacred Ark of the Covenant containing the Ten Commandments.

The details of the Tabernacle are staggering. Several chapters in the Book of Exodus are dedicated to describing this unique dwelling place for God. It was made with special curtains, rods, threads, boards, rings, veils, and pillars. In structure, it was to be divided into three main sections: the Court, the Holy Place, and the Holy of Holies. The most sacred section was the Holy of Holies where the Ark of the Covenant was placed behind a veil. "The veil shall be a divider for you between the holy place and the Most Holy." (Exod. 26:33) Only once a year a high priest was allowed entrance into this sacred chamber to pray for the people. This event was called the "Day of Atonement."

The furniture items placed in the Tabernacle in addition to the Ark of the Covenant included an altar of incense, a golden lampstand, a table of shewbread, a laver (bowl), and an altar of sacrifice. The priests used each of these items for specific worship rituals. Then strangely enough, the entire tent, or Tabernacle, and all of its belongings were transported to the next campground for the Israelites as they journeyed through the desert wilderness for years and years.

The Lord even gave special instruction as to where each of the 12 tribes of Israel was to camp around the Tabernacle. Basically, three tribes (which were made up of thousands of people) were to camp on each of the four sides of the Tabernacle so that it was always in the center of their view. From the Tabernacle, sacrifices were dedicated, worship took place, and the Lord directed the journey of the Israelites.

Remember that all of this activity was taking place in the desert of present-day Saudi Arabia. Why did God choose to "dwell" in the Tabernacle? I believe one reason is that He wanted the people to literally "see" that He was with them through their years of journeying to the Promised Land. The people *could* see His presence through a spectacular cloud in the day and through a bright fire at night. In the closing verses of the Book of Exodus it says that:

> "the cloud covered the tabernacle of meeting, and the glory of the Lord filled the tabernacle ... When the cloud was taken up from above the tabernacle, the children of Israel went onward in all their journeys. But if the cloud was not taken up, then they did not journey till the day that it was taken up. For the cloud of the Lord was above the tabernacle by day, and fire was over it by night in the sight of all the house of Israel, throughout all their journeys." (Exod. 40:34–38)

What an amazing sight this must have been for young and old to behold. But even more spectacular is the fact that the Tabernacle continues to have great meaning to the Christian as each and every aspect of it pointed to Christ! In God's great and glorious plan, He was dwelling in the Tabernacle as a foreshadowing of his physical dwelling in the Lord Jesus Christ. Though the Israelites were unable to grasp this revelation in full, we as believers can.

The Book of Revelation as well as many other New Testament scriptures refers to the Tabernacle. In fact, the Tabernacle is written about in 50 chapters of the Bible. That is 13 chapters in Exodus, 18 chapters in Leviticus, 13 chapters in Numbers, 2 chapters in Deuteronomy, and 4 chapters in Hebrews. (In the Book of Hebrews alone there are 131 verses about the tabernacle!) In comparison, the Creation story is told in only 2 chapters of the Bible. I think we can conclude that the concept of the Tabernacle, which is where God dwelled with His people, is very important. It ultimately symbolizes our own salvation through Christ's blood.

I think that Hebrews 9:11–14a says it best,

> "But Christ came as High Priest of the good things to come, with the greater and more perfect tabernacle not made with hands, that is, not of this creation. Not with the blood of goats and calves, but with His own blood He entered the Most Holy Place once for all, having obtained eternal redemption. For if the blood of bulls and goats and the ashes of a heifer, sprinkling the unclean, sanctifies for the purifying of the flesh, how much more shall the blood of Christ."

ACTIVITY 20

20A—Younger Students

1. Build a tent! Need I say more? Children and tents are usually pretty compatible. Think of the tent as a sacred place for prayer. Read your Bible or sing hymns in your "tabernacle."
2. Practice reciting the Ten Commandments from memory.

20B—Younger and Middle Students

Using the dimensions given in the Bible, many artists have sketched what they believe the Ark of the Covenant and the Tabernacle would have looked like. Using a Bible encyclopedia or other resource, find sketches and photocopy them for your Student Notebook. File them under "Asia: Saudi Arabia."

20C—Middle and Older Students

The symbolism of the Tabernacle to the Gospel of Jesus Christ is profound. In the list below, I have given you some examples of the correlations in parentheses. Use an outside resource to find the placement of some of the furnishings in the Tabernacle. On a sheet of paper, draw a large rectangle to represent the Tabernacle. Try to place the following items in their proper location. Label them.

- The Court
- The Holy Place
- The Holy of Holies

(These three places represent the Trinity of God: the Father, the Son, and the Holy Spirit. They also represent the three dimensions of man: the soul, the spirit, and the body.)

- The Mercy Seat

(As a gold plate "covering" the ark of the Covenant, it was symbolic of Christ "covering" our sins.)

- The Ark of the Covenant

(In holding God's laws, it represented the presence of God, which later came through Jesus Christ.)

- The Altar of Incense

(This symbolized Christ as intercessor for us.)

- The Golden Lampstand

(This represented Christ as the Light of the world.)

- The Table of Shewbread

(This symbolized Christ as the "Bread of Life.")

- The Laver

(This represented the washing away of sin through Christ and the Holy Spirit.)

- The Altar of Sacrifice

(This symbolized the great sacrifice of Christ for our sin.)

File this diagram in your Student Notebook under "Asia: Saudi Arabia."

JOSHUA, JERICHO, AND RAHAB

LESSON 21

Moses was such a significant person in history that we find the books of Exodus, Leviticus, Numbers, and Deuteronomy all dedicated to telling his story. The Israelites went through many ups and downs in their wanderings before they finally reached the Promised Land, also known as Canaan. But, upon Moses' death, God spoke to a new man to give guidance to the Hebrews. His name was Joshua. The Bible contains a whole book named after him to give us his story. Moses helped to lead the Israelites UP to Canaan; Joshua helped to get them IN to Canaan.

Though we see the Israelites go through many struggles with unbelief while following Moses, we finally see them experience victory under Joshua. It may not have been because Joshua was a better leader, but the people were learning to trust in God after all their hardships.

Canaan was the land that God had promised to His people. It is present-day Israel. But, long ago, there were other people living there. It may seem harsh that the Lord was promoting bloodshed over this land, but the people living in Canaan were evil in His sight.

One of the main cities to conquer in Canaan was Jericho. Two spies were sent to scope out the land. A great story of faith emerges here. Apparently, the reputation of the Israelites had gone before them. There was a woman living in Jericho named Rahab, who believed in the cause of the Israelites. She had heard the miraculous stories of them crossing the Red Sea and surviving in the desert. And she believed! Rahab helped the two Israelite spies and hid them in her house while the authorities were searching for them. Because of Rahab's great faith, she and her family were promised protection from any harm done to their city.

This is a rock from the ruins of the city of Jericho that are still scattered there today.

How exactly was Jericho brought down? Any military man would have laughed at the strategy God gave to Joshua to accomplish this. That seems to be God's point. He makes it clear that HE would help the Israelites to conquer their enemies. Oddly enough, the people were told to march around the city for six days bearing the Ark of the Covenant and blowing trumpets. On the seventh day they were to march around Jericho seven times and to shout on their last time around. They did exactly what Joshua commanded and, sure enough, the walls around Jericho fell down flat!

If that's not strange enough, we later read in Joshua that the sun stood still for a whole day in order for the Israelites to conquer other people. Joshua, Chapter 12, gives us a list of all the kings who were defeated to enable the Hebrews to live in Canaan. There were many.

In time, the land was divided among the 12 tribes of Israel just as the Lord foretold. The tribes were, of course, the descendants of the 12 sons of Jacob. I told you before that their names would become very important. You'll find them all mentioned in the last chapters of Joshua along with the land that each tribe was allotted.

These final verses sum up the significance of the story. Joshua 21:43–45 says, "So the Lord gave to Israel all the land of which He had sworn to give to their fathers . . . not a word failed of any good thing which the Lord had spoken to the house of Israel. All came to pass."

And what about Rahab and her family? Did they get out of Jericho as promised? Yes, they did. While the city was under attack, Rahab dangled a red cord out of her window to signal which was her home. She lived right along the wall of Jericho itself, as did many people. She and her family not only escaped, but according to Jewish tradition, Rahab later married Joshua! They became the parents of Boaz, who married Ruth. Ruth was of the lineage of David and Jesus Christ. But I'm getting way ahead of myself here.

The point of the genealogies is simply that God uses all kinds of people to bring about His plans. By profession, Rahab most likely was a harlot. But by faith, she became part of the bloodline of Jesus Christ. In fact, the Book of Hebrews in the New Testament mentions her in the list of great keepers of the faith. (Heb. 11:31) It's a neat story.

ACTIVITY 21

ALL STUDENTS

Make your Memory Cards for Lessons 19–21.

21A—Younger and Middle Students

1. Obtain a "Joshua Basket" to remember the things the Lord has done in your life. A "Joshua Basket" can be purchased at Christian bookstores. It is a beautiful family tradition created by Randy and Lisa Wilson with Cook Publishing.
2. Build a city out of blocks with a wall around it. March around the town six times to depict six days. Blow party horns as you march. Then march seven more times around the town blowing horns. On the last trip around, shout! Take turns knocking down the walls of the town just as Jericho's walls fell flat.

21B—Middle Students

Read in Joshua, Chapter 2, the story of Rahab. It is inspiring to know that a harlot from a wicked city like Jericho had faith in the God of Israel. Read the chapter carefully and try to figure out what convinced this woman to believe. (The answer lies in verses 10 and 11.)

Consider what miracles have occurred in your life that would lead others to believe in God. If you have never kept a personal journal before, perhaps this would be a good time to begin one. Keep a small notebook with your Bible to record thoughts that spring from your devotions and prayers, from answers to prayers, and from sermons you hear. Our thoughts and prayers are precious to the Lord.

21C—Older Students

Read Joshua 5:13–15 about the Commander of the Army of the Lord. He was some kind of "super angel." Research how various Bible commentaries interpret this unusual passage. How in-depth is your knowledge of spiritual warfare? Consider further research on the topic. File it under "Asia: Israel."

TAKE ANOTHER LOOK!

Wall of Fame

On your timeline, record these people in the following order. Add the dates to the figures.

1. *Moses and the Exodus (exact date unknown; sometime between 1525 and 1270 B.C.)*—On a small paper, draw lots and lots of small circles or dots to represent the thousands of Israelites who "exited" with Moses. Attach this right next to Moses. It's no wonder the pharaoh was upset; he was losing a huge workforce when the Israelites left his country.

2. *The Ark of the Covenant and the Tabernacle (c. 1500 B.C. if we correspond it to the earlier date above)*—You will probably need to make your own sketches of these.

3. *Joshua (c. 1470 B.C.)*—Try to draw some fallen bricks at his feet to represent the walls of Jericho.

4. *Rahab (exact date unknown)*—Place her next to Joshua. She should have a gold cross to symbolize the lineage of Christ.

SomeWHERE in Time

1. In a Bible atlas, find a map showing the route of Moses and the Israelites. Find Mount Sinai. That is where Moses received the Ten Commandments. Compare the Bible map to a modern-day globe. If the Exodus happened today, what countries would the people have to travel through? Answer this orally.

2. On Outline Map 7, "Israel," write in these places:

   Canaan, the Jordan River, Jericho, the Dead Sea, Jerusalem

3. Find and label the 12 tribes of Israel. Color each as directed below. You will notice that some of the names of the tribes are different from the 12 sons of Jacob, or Israel. A brief explanation is given below. File in your Student Notebook under "Asia: Holy Land."

Tribe of Gad	Pink	Tribe of Zebulun	Turquoise
Tribe of Asher	Purple	Tribe of Benjamin	Dark green
Tribe of Reuben	Red	Tribe of Dan	Dark blue
Tribe of Judah	Blue	Tribe of Issachar	Brown
Tribe of Simeon	Orange	Tribe of Manasseh	Light green
Tribe of Naphtali	Gray	Tribe of Ephraim	Yellow

The tribe of Dan was allotted two locations. The tribes of Manasseh and Ephraim were named and led by two sons of Joseph rather than Joseph leading his own tribe. Manasseh was also allotted two locations.

Note that although Levi was Jacob's son, the tribe of Levi was never granted their own territory. They were chosen to serve as priests and given 48 specific cities throughout Israel as places to live. The number of tribes remained at 12, however, because of the addition of Joseph's sons, Manasseh and Ephraim. (One son replaced Joseph and one replaced Levi.)

WHAT DID YOU MISS?

Week 7: Exercise

Complete the crossword puzzle. You may look in your book for the answers.

ACROSS
1. Walls of _____
4. Created on Day 6
5. Symbol of God's promise
6. One of the Seven Wonders
9. Mary Mantell discovered the _____ of a dinosaur
10. First dynasty in China
11. Abraham's home city
12. Hammurabi set a minimum _____
15. Mother of Ishmael
17. Hairy redhead

DOWN
1. First son of Rachel
2. Jesus descended from _____
3. False worship
6. _____ lamb
7. Jubal played the _____
8. A flattened pyramid
9. Worship tent
13. Long poem
14. A land bridge between Asia and Europe
16. _____ leaping

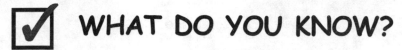

✓ WHAT DO YOU KNOW?

Pretest 8

Today's pretest isn't really a test at all. But, to familiarize yourself with the lessons to come, alphabetize these big Egyptian names and terms. After you have done that, circle the words or names you aleady know. Put a box around those that you haven't a clue about. Even your teacher may not know a few of these!

Amenhotep   1. _____

Nefertiti   2. _____

Akhenaten   3. _____

Tutankhamen   4._____

Cairo   5._____

Carter   6._____

Ramses   7._____

Abu Simbel   8. _____

The Mystery of History

AMENHOTEP IV AND NEFERTITI

LESSON 22

The ancient Egyptian people are intriguing to study. We have already looked at their approach to life after death as we studied their astonishing pyramids and the grueling process of mummification. Today, though, we will look at just one pharaoh and his wife who were quite different from the previous kings and queens of ancient Egypt. It was their beliefs that make them stand out in history.

It was during the eighteenth dynasty of Egyptian history that we find a king named Amenhotep IV and his wife Nefertiti. He was the son of another pharaoh and lived perhaps only two generations after Moses and the Exodus. Nefertiti was considered one of the more beautiful women of Egyptian history. Eloquent statues were made of her pretty face, so we have some idea of her looks.

Amenhotep IV was considered very unusual compared to all of Egypt's other rulers because he chose to worship one god. He actually abolished the other Egyptian gods! Think for a minute as to why people sometimes change an old belief system. We don't know for sure, but many wonder if the miracles during Moses' time were the reason that Amenhotep IV changed his faith. Some believe that Amenhotep II, who ruled earlier, was the actual pharaoh during the Exodus. That would make Amenhotep IV perhaps a descendant of his. If so, he might have witnessed or heard stories of the Hebrews and their God. (Please note that many scholars think the Exodus occurred during the reign of Ramses II.)

It's also interesting to know that Nefertiti, Amenhotep's wife, may not have even been an Egyptian. We don't know her race. Imagine, though, if she were maybe of Hebrew descent or some other nationality that had been exposed to "one" god. Perhaps HER beliefs influenced the pharaoh.

One thing particularly different about Amenhotep IV and his wife was that they seemed to have a genuine loving relationship. Wall murals of the couple show them giving one another tender affection. That was something unseen before in the royalty of Egypt. Most kings' marriages were arranged. Since Nefertiti might not even have been Egyptian, the chances are that the couple married out of love and not for political reasons. We don't know for sure.

Wall murals also depict the couple caressing their daughters in loving ways and playing with them. They sound kind of nice and happy to me. But some sources say that the couple had a difficult time having any *boy* babies. Supposedly, Amenhotep married again to try to have sons. To keep Nefertiti happy, he then gave her the position of co-regent. That was a huge title for a wife to have.

Though Amenhotep and Nefertiti may not have had any sons of their own, they did pretty well with "sons-in-law." You just won't believe who one of their daughters married. It was none other than the famous "King Tut"! That fact you probably won't forget.

In my opinion, the only thing controversial about this royal couple is that the one god they chose to worship was what they believed to be a "sun" god named Aten. They must not have understood the God of the Hebrews. We are not sure what their exact beliefs were, but they were strong. Amenhotep had an elaborate temple built for worship to Aten and even moved the capital of Egypt to the same location.

With his new faith, Amenhotep IV changed his name. He became Akhenaten, which meant "pious servant of Aten." Maybe he was hoping to not be associated with his ancestors who worshiped so many gods. He even had the names of the other gods chiseled off the city walls. Although as pharaoh he was powerful in changing the faith of the country on the outside, the Egyptian people returned to their old gods soon after his death. Even the capital was moved back to where it had been before.

Archaeologists are always discovering new things. Perhaps someone will find more relics to help us better understand this unique couple. Maybe it will be you!

ACTIVITY 22

22A—Younger and Middle Students

Much of what we know today about the Egyptians comes from their own record keeping. The Egyptians are famous for their wall murals, drawings, and writings. The written records were in the form of hieroglyphics, or picture writing.

The names of important people were often inscribed in a special picture box called a "cartouche." Try to make one for your name using the Egyptian alphabet located in the Activity Supplement in the Appendix.

Imagine how much room it would have taken to draw pictures for letter sounds. We can appreciate our alphabet and how easy it is to use in comparison. File your cartouche name in your Student Notebook under "Africa: Egypt."

22B—Middle and Older Students

Research in further detail the gods of the Egyptians and their names. This will help you to better understand the ramifications of Amenhotep's radical changes in religion. Write a list of the gods and sketch the symbols of each. Record your findings in your Student Notebook under "Africa: Egypt."

22C—Middle and Older Students

There is always more to history than can be captured in any one textbook. This week, research one of the following:

- The Old Kingdom (building of the Sphinx)
- Queen Hatshepsut, who portrayed herself as a man
- Temple of Tuthmosis III—excavated in 1996

1333 B.C.

TUTANKHAMEN (KING TUT)

LESSON 23

Of all the fascinating pharaohs who once ruled over Egypt, probably none is more well known than King Tut. King Tut's real name was Tutankhamen, and he lived from about 1342 to 13237 B.C. Several years ago a singer named Steve Martin wrote a funny song about this pharaoh using the name "King Tut." People still know him by this nickname. I will call him Tutankhamen out of respect, but you should know him by both names.

The story of Tutankhamen's life is, unfortunately, a very short one. He only lived to be about 18. He began to rule at age 8 or 9. But we almost know more about his short life than we know about any of the other pharaohs. Why? Because in 1922 an archaeologist named Howard Carter discovered Tutankhamen's tomb completely untouched!

That was a big deal in 1922. You see, almost all the pyramids had great wealth and gold in them because of the Egyptian belief system. Kings and queens wanted to take things with them to the afterlife. But buried treasure of that magnitude was far too appealing to thieves. So, over the years, most of the known pyramids were wiped clean by robbers.

Somehow, Tutankhamen's elaborate tomb had remained buried for over 3,000 years without anyone stealing a thing out of it! The items that Carter found in the tomb were absolutely incredible. Several rooms were found piled to the ceiling with thousands of Tutankhamen's things. You have probably already in your lifetime seen pictures from the tomb and not even realized it.

One of the most famous pieces was the actual coffin of Tutankhamen. It had four layers, but the third was made of 2,500 pounds of pure gold! This and a beautiful gold mask of the young king are pictured almost anywhere that ancient Egypt is written about. Begin to keep an eye out for how often you see them.

Other relics found in the tomb include models of typical life in Egypt. There were carved wooden boats showing us their transportation; statues of women grinding grain; models of homes and their gardens. Much information is now known about the Egyptians' way of life because of this remarkable archaeological discovery.

One thing no one knows for sure, though, is just how or why Tutankhamen died so very young. There are many speculations. Some think he was murdered by Ay (eye), his co-regent, who wanted to rule. Others believe he was murdered because of his belief system. Remember that he was married to the daughter of Amenhotep IV and Nefertiti. They had

The beautiful gold mask of young King Tutankhamen is one of many incredible treasures preserved in his tomb.

worshiped only one god, Aten. In fact, Tutankhamen's original name was Tutankhaten, which means "Beautiful in life is Aten." The priests of the old Egyptian religion forced him to change his name and abandon the religion of Akhenaten, his father-in-law.

One last interesting twist to the story is that Tutankhamen's widow was later overthrown, too. She was going to marry a prince from another country after Tutankhamen's death. The prince, however, never made it to the wedding! He was killed along the way by some Egyptians. After that, a whole new dynasty ruled the throne of Egypt under Ay. Sounds suspicious to me!

If you ever make it to Cairo, the treasures of Tutankhamen can be found in a museum there. His body and part of his coffin, however, were reverently returned to their original tomb, which was along the Nile River in a stretch called the Valley of the Kings. Maybe one day more of the mystery of "King Tut's" death will be solved.

ACTIVITY 23

ALL STUDENTS

Memorize the date of King Tutankhamen (1333 B.C..).

23A—Younger Students

1. Find a picture of King Tut's famous gold mask. Trace it, with your teacher's help if needed, on a piece of paper. Color it gold (or use glue and some gold glitter) and blue. File your mask under "Africa: Egypt" in your Student Notebook.

2. Have your teacher create a treasure hunt for you. Just like Carter, "uncover" precious and rare jewels and treasures.

23B—Middle Students

Books abound at the library on the treasures and mysteries of King Tut. With books in hand, make a list of all the different kinds of things found in the tomb. Pretend to be a news reporter at the time of the discovery. Make a startling headline for a newspaper and go on to list the items found. Carter's discovery is still considered one of the greatest archaelogical finds of all time.

23C—Middle and Older Students

1. Research the discovery of King Tut's tomb by Howard Carter. Find the answers to the questions below or make up your own questions to answer. File your research under "Africa: Egypt" in your Student Notebook.

   a. Where was Carter from?

   b. How was Carter educated? (Some would say he was "homeschooled." If so, why?)

   c. Was Carter specifically looking for King Tut's tomb or did he discover it by accident?

   d. How long did it take Carter and his men to excavate the site?

   e. What important items were found?

   f. When was King Tut's body returned to its original site?

2. As a look at what the media can do for profit, find the recording of Steve Martin's "King Tut" song. What parts of the song are accurate? What things were completely made up for the sake of comedy? Do you find the recording offensive, funny, or a little of both? What are other examples of how the media can distort facts?

1304–1237 B.C.

RAMSES II (THE GREAT)

LESSON 24

The study of history can sometimes be tedious in trying to remember dates and places. That's why I have tried instead to teach you through the lives of real people. People are far more interesting than dates and places. However, once in awhile it is helpful to examine time periods of a country to better understand the people who lived there. So, before we learn about one more ruler of Egypt, let's review the kingdoms of this intriguing land of pyramids.

Egypt divides its ancient history into groups of kingdoms. At least 12 have been identified. The four main ones are the **Old Kingdom**, the **Middle Kingdom**, the **Early New Kingdom**, and the **Later**

New Kingdom. We have already learned about some people and events that took place during these first three kingdoms. Let's stop and review them.

Kingdom	Dates	Rulers/Events
The Old Kingdom, also called the Age of the Pyramids	2700–2200 B.C.	King Khufu (Cheops) built the great pyramids at Giza.
The Middle Kingdom	2050–1800 B.C.	This was a time of weak Egyptian rulers; Joseph became prime minister in Egypt, and Jacob and his sons moved to Egypt.
The Early Kingdom	1570–1300 B.C.	During this time Amenhotep IV and Nefertiti ruled and worshiped one god. Their son-in-law, Tutankhamen, died after a short reign.

Today we're going to look at a ruler from the **Later New Kingdom,** also called the Golden Age. This kingdom was from 1300–1090 B.C. Its most famous pharaoh was Ramses II (RAM seez). He was also called Ramses the Great. He lived from about 1304 to 1237 B.C. Many scholars believe he was the pharaoh in power during the Exodus of Moses and the Hebrews, but nobody knows for sure.

Ramses the Great came to power at a time when Egypt was weak. The country had become fragile from problems within the royal families. Problems at home often make a country lose power against its neighbors. That's what happened to Egypt after the reign of Tutankhamen and others.

This authentic hieroglyphic carving contains the royal name of Ramses II. The oval surrounding his name is called a "cartouche."

Ramses the Great came to the throne at a young age and served as co-regent for a time with his father. By the time Ramses was the sole pharaoh of Egypt, his strong leadership was evident. He fought a powerful people in Asia called the Hittites and made a treaty with them to divide Syria. He also fought the Philistines, whom we know from the Bible.

While the country was growing strong and expanding its borders, Ramses the Great started a massive building campaign, which he is most famous for today. In fact, Ramses constructed a temple or building in almost every important city in Egypt. He is credited with building the largest columned hall ever built by man. It's suitably called "The Great Hall" because its columns were up to 78 feet high!

Ramses the Great also built a mortuary on the West Bank at Thebes and had a temple erected in the city of Abu Simbel. Four massive figures bearing the resemblance of Ramses II guard the entrance to the temple of Abu Simbel. Like many of the pharaohs, Ramses seemed to like monuments of himself.

Though some of Ramses' buildings were sturdy enough to still stand today, his kingdom wasn't. The great empire of ancient Egypt began to dwindle after the reign of Ramses the Great and it never again rose to the height it had known. In fact, Ramses II may have been one of Egypt's last strong pharaohs.

What was the reason for the decline of this great and mysterious power? There are several things that led to the downfall of Egypt, but one surely was the lack of iron. Many countries, including Egypt's neighbors and enemies, were using iron to build their weapons. The Egyptians didn't have their own iron and had to get this valuable resource from Asia. In the long run, they just couldn't compete.

Do you happen to remember the name of a man just eight generations from Adam who was a master in ironworking? His name was Tubal-Cain. I think it is interesting that something like iron can be so important to the success of a civilization. Despite the strong reign of Ramses II and the great temples he built, Egypt dwindled in time from lording over the ancient world.

ACTIVITY 24

ALL STUDENTS

Make your Memory Cards for Lessons 22–24. Remember to mark King Tutankhamen's card with a bright-colored highlighter on his name and date. He is one of the 12 to memorize this year.

24A—Younger and Middle Students

Make a "Kingdom Folder." (Younger students will need assistance with this.)

Materials: Paper (8½ by 11 inches), pencils, markers, ribbon

1. Fold a sheet of paper like this.

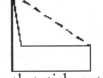

2. Cut off the bottom of the paper that sticks out.

3. Open the paper and refold it the opposite way to make an "X" pattern.

4. Take one corner of the square you have created and fold it to meet the center of the "X."

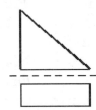

5. Repeat this with each corner and you should have four pyramid shapes on the front of your folder. Punch a hole in the tip of each for later use.

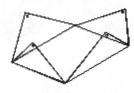

6. On the outside of each pyramid, write the name of one of the four major kingdoms. If you are young, let your teacher help you to put the names of some of the pharaohs on the inside under the right kingdom. Older Students: Record more information about each kingdom under the corresponding flaps. Include dates.

The Mystery of History

7. To seal the Kingdom Folder, run a flat ribbon through each of the holes you punched out. Tie the ribbon.

8. In big letters, write "Pharaohs and Kingdoms of Ancient Egypt" on the back of the folder. Add your name and grade on the bottom.

24B—Younger and Middle Students

Make a collage. Find as many interesting pictures of Egypt as you can. Photocopy them in color or hand-color them yourself. Cut them out nicely, and glue them to cover a notebook-sized piece of paper that can go in your own Student Notebook. Middle Students: On the back of your collage, identify the photos, where possible.

24C—Middle and Older Students

Using outside reference material, research significant time periods and rulers of the Egyptians. Expand on the chart presented in the lesson. Fill it in more completely to include these periods[1]:

1. Early Period

2. Old Kingdom

3. First Intermediate Period

4. Middle Kingdom

5. Second Intermediate Period

6. Early New Kingdom

7. Later New Kingdom

8. Post-Empire Period

9. Libyan Period

10. Sudanese Period

11. Saite Period

12. Persian Period

File this chart in your Student Notebook under "Africa: Egypt."

---

1. My resource for the names of these periods was the *World Book Encyclopedia.*, 50th Anniversary ed., s.v. "Egypt." Chicago: Field Enterprises Educational Corp., 1966.

TAKE ANOTHER LOOK!

Wall of Fame

1. *Amenhotep IV and Nefertiti (1353 b.c.)*—Include the name Akhenaten in parentheses under Amenhotep's name to avoid confusing them in the future. If you can find a picture of the famous statue of Nefertiti's face, use this on the timeline.

2. *Tutankhamen (King Tut) (1333 b.c.)*—Use all gold paper to depict King Tut. **Remember, this is a date to memorize.**

3. *Ramses II (the Great) (c. 1304–1237 b.c.)*—Make four small identical pharaohs to resemble the entrance of Abu Simbel.

SomeWHERE in Time

The geography of Egypt is pertinent to its history. Make a cake model of the land!

Materials: Vanilla sheet cake, white frosting, food coloring, paper flags, toothpicks, tape, map of ancient Egypt

1. To do this project, first bake a flat vanilla sheet cake and let it cool.
2. Divide one can of frosting into two bowls, making one smaller than the other.
3. Add blue food coloring to the smaller batch and orange or peach to the larger batch.
4. Turn the cake vertically. Using a toothpick and a map of Egypt for a guide, scrape the shape of the Nile down the center of the cake leaving room at the top for the Mediterranean Sea.
5. Carefully apply blue frosting to the river and the sea.
6. Add orange or peach frosting around the Nile to depict the land. If you are very talented, build up the icing to appear as mountains on the east side of the Nile.
7. Depending on your age and ability, make flags for the names of the places listed below. Tape the flags to toothpicks.
8. Mark the locations of major cities and building sites by placing the toothpicks carefully into the cake. Most places will be found right up and down the Nile.

Nile, Upper Egypt, Lower Egypt, Abu Simbel, Cairo
Giza, Memphis, Karnak (Great Hall), Thebes, Valley of the Kings

Take a picture of your cake before you eat it. File the photo under "Africa: Egypt" in your Student Notebook.

WHAT DID YOU LEARN?

Week 8: *Quiz*

Fill in the blanks using the word bank at the bottom of the page.

1. Early man was capable of learning and teaching _____, which is a very complicated process.

2. There are as many as _____ flood stories that exist around the world in various cultures giving evidence of the Bible account.

3. According to the Bible, _____ would have been created on the fifth and sixth days of Creation.

4. In *The Epic of Gilgamesh*, Gilgamesh supposedly fell asleep under a tree, then awoke to find that _____ had been stolen by a snake.

5. In the process of mummification, the ancient Egyptians "threw out" the brain and preserved the _____ in the belief that it was the organ man thought with.

6. Potiphar's wife falsely accused _____ of attacking her. It resulted in his being sent to prison.

7. _____ was a great king of early Babylonia and known for writing a code of 300 laws.

8. The Chinese, during the Shang dynasty, created a character alphabet that contained more than _____ figures.

9. The name _____ means "to draw out."

10. While in the wilderness, the high priest was allowed into the Holy of Holies only once—on the _____.

11. With his new faith, Amenhotep IV gave himself a new name, Akhenaten, which meant "pious_____ of Aten."

12. King Tutankhamen's coffin had four layers. The third was made of 2,500 pounds of pure _____.

13. King Tutankhamen's tomb was discovered in 1922 by _____.

14. Ramses II is best known as a great builder, with the temple at _____ and the Great Hall at Karnak.

15. One of the reasons for the decline of Egypt was its lack of _____ used in weapon building.

WORD BANK

dinosaurs	Hammurabi	Day of Atonement	gold	iron
270	Joseph	ironmaking	50,000	servant
Moses	eternal life	Howard Carter	heart	Abu Simbel

☑ WHAT DO YOU KNOW?

Pretest 9

Who Am I? From the word bank below, choose the correct answer for each question.

1. According to Greek mythology, I was considered the most beautiful woman in Greece around 1250 B.C. Who am I?

2. I was built as a secret way for the Greeks to enter Troy. What am I?

3. I was smuggled out of Turkey by archaeologists. What am I?

4. I was an old and bitter woman who lost husband and sons in the war. Who am I?

5. Though I was from Moab, I was a faithful daughter-in-law and believer in the God of the Israelites. Who am I?

6. I was a kinsman redeemer and great grandparent of David. Who am I?

7. I was a good judge over Israel before there were kings. Who am I?

8. We are the army that Gideon defeated with only broken pots, horns, and torches. Who are we?

WORD BANK

Gideon	Ruth	Boaz	Helen
Priam's treasure	Naomi	Midianites	Trojan Horse

LEGEND OF THE TROJAN HORSE

LESSON 25

Have you ever heard of the Trojan Horse? The legend of the Trojan Horse makes a great story and may very well be true. It would have occurred about 1250 B.C. Today we will look at what the captivating story was all about and who wrote it.

In the southern part of Greece lived a group of people called the Mycenaeans. They are the ones who borrowed the ways of the Minoans, or the people of Crete. (Remember them? They had a great palace at Knossos.) The Mycenaeans had a real civilization in Greece, but no one knows for sure if the story of one of their wars is true.

It seems that a prince named Paris lived in the city of Troy, which is across the sea from Greece. Troy was on the coast of modern-day Turkey. Legend says that Paris was asked to judge a beauty contest between three goddesses. He chose Aphrodite. As a reward, Aphrodite promised Paris the most beautiful woman in the world. Not long after that, he traveled over to Greece and indeed met the woman of his dreams. Her name was Helen. Supposedly Paris and Helen fell in love, eloped, and moved back to Troy.

There was a terrible problem, though, with this love story. Helen was already the wife of Menelaus, a king in Sparta (a city-state in Greece). Menelaus was furious and humiliated at the capture of his lovely wife. But he had some powerful connections to help him get Helen back. His brother, Agamemnon, was the king of Mycenae. To help out Menelaus, Agamemnon decided to go to war against the Trojans to retrieve the beloved Helen. Thus we have the story of the Trojan War, as told by the Mycenaeans. As the story goes, the Trojan War lasted for 10 years over the capture and return of Helen.

Supposedly, Odysseus, another Greek king, came up with a magnificent plan. He thought of building a giant horse and presenting it as a peace offering to the Trojans. In the legend, this huge wooden horse was delivered to the Trojans, right up to the gates of the city. Though skeptical at first, the Trojans eventually opened the city gates to roll in this incredible gift. They had a great celebration to usher in this victory, as it appeared the Greeks had given up.

It was a scam though. After the party was over, in the middle of the night dozens of daring Greek soldiers who had been hiding in the wooden horse climbed out through a trap door. Once out, they flung open the city gates for more Greek soldiers to storm through. The Greeks slaughtered the men of Troy and even burned down their city!

But what about Helen? What became of her or of Paris (the Trojan man who first captured her) or of Menelaus (her rightful Greek husband)? According to the legend, Paris was killed in battle. Helen married his brother, who would also have been a Trojan. But the Greeks soon killed him too. Eventually, Menelaus did successfully recapture his lovely bride and take her back to Sparta in Greece. They supposedly lived in peace for many years together.

A Greek man named Homer, who lived hundreds of years after the Trojan War, wrote this story for us. The story he composed was called the *Iliad*. For years most historians thought it to be pure fiction. However, a German named Heinrich Schliemann believed it to be true. He set off in the 1800s to the coast of modern-day Turkey and found exactly what he was hoping for and more. He found several layers of cities all on top of one another where Troy would have once stood. And some of the ruins showed that at least one city in the pile had been burned, just as legend says of Troy.

Interestingly, Schliemann also found great treasures in what he excavated. He believed the treasure of shields, vases, plates, and jewelry had belonged to King Priam of Troy. Thus he named them Priam's treasure. But Schliemann wasn't very generous with his findings. He deceitfully smuggled the treasures out of Turkey and took them to Germany.

For years the treasure was missing, and the Turkish government was furious. Some people believed the treasure was melted down by the Nazis during World War II. Others believed it was hidden away in a museum in Russia.

Well, sure enough, just in 1996 Priam's treasures were found and put on display in Moscow! There is even a picture of Schliemann's own beautiful wife modeling the elaborate jewelry that was discovered.

The legend of the Trojan Horse is a masterpiece—either of Homer's great imagination or of a true story. Parts of the *Iliad* are based on Greek mythology. Therefore it is hard to know which segments are true and which are fictitious. But at least Schliemann unearthed something tangible from the time period that does make you wonder. Maybe Helen of Troy herself once wore the beautiful gold jewelry that can now be seen on display in Russia.

ACTIVITY 25

25A—Younger Students

Recreate the Trojan Horse.

Materials: Toy horse, elastic bandage, toy army men

Take a toy horse, plastic or stuffed, and set it upright. Take an elastic bandage and loosely wrap it around the belly of the horse. Next, take the army men and slide them under the bandage as if they're hiding.

Act out the story of the Trojan horse. Once the horse has entered "Troy," unwrap it for all the army men to fall out.

25B—Middle Students

In the *Iliad*, Homer wove into his story the lives of some Greek gods and goddesses. In a reference book or encyclopedia, obtain information on the names of some Greek gods and goddesses. They were a very important part of Greek culture. Discuss these questions.

1. Which names of Greek gods and goddesses do you still hear today?
2. Do the Greeks still believe in ancient mythology?
3. What is a myth?
4. Why do you think people used mythology to explain things?

25C—Older Students

1. Create a chart to describe the gods and goddesses of ancient Greece. File it in your Student Notebook under "Europe: Ancient Greece."
2. Through discussion, answer one or more of these questions.
   a. What does the word "apologetics" mean?
   b. Unlike mythology, how can Christianity be defended as "truth"?

c. The apostle Paul taught the truths of Christ to many people who had been influenced by Greek and Roman mythology. Find examples in the New Testament of Paul explaining the Gospel to the Greeks.

c. 1200 B.C.

RUTH AND NAOMI

LESSON 26

The Book of Ruth is different than most other books of the Bible in that it is dedicated to a woman. Only one other book in the Bible even has the name of a woman. Can you guess it? (It's Esther, of course.) But special to Ruth is the fact that she was not even a Hebrew. She, though, as an outsider to the Israelites, became significant to the nation of Israel.

When we last studied the Israelites, they were settling into the land of Canaan. During that time period, the tribes of Israel were ruled by "judges." The Israelites didn't have a single king. The Hebrew people were having their ups and downs with faith. Many had gone astray because of the pagan influence of their neighbors. It is therefore comforting to find this story of Ruth's faith, courage, and love in the midst of this era.

Here is the noble story. During a time of famine in Canaan, we meet a Hebrew woman named Naomi whose husband has died. Naomi's sons married Moabite women, which was forbidden. The Moabites were outside of the tribes of Israel. After about 10 years, the sons die. Naomi is understandably quite distressed. She has no husband or sons. She advises her two daughters-in-law to just go back home to their families as she attempts to return to Judah.

One daughter-in-law agrees that is best. But the other, Ruth, defies all odds and refuses to leave. Something special had happened to Ruth, the Moabite woman. In marrying an Israelite man, she had been introduced to his God and adopted his faith. So, rather than go back to her old life, she insists on staying by the side of Naomi and following her wherever God would lead. In Ruth 1:16 we have record of her devotion, "Wherever you go, I will go, and wherever you lodge, I will lodge; your people shall be my people, and your God, my God." It is so cool that we have a true testimony of a converted Moabite!

As the story goes, Ruth and Naomi travel to Bethlehem where Naomi happens to have relatives. One is called a "kinsman." In those times, women had few rights and little property. They needed a husband or son for security. But, if they were widowed, it was Hebrew tradition that the nearest male relative, or kinsman, would assume responsibility for the widow. The kinsman in Naomi's family was a man named Boaz, who just happened to be rich.

Perhaps by divine appointment, Ruth goes to the fields owned by Boaz to pick up leftover grain. It was customary back then to let the poor do this. But it's a humbling job. Ruth, in her humility, is noticed by Boaz, and he is kind to her. Apparently, Ruth's conversion had become town gossip. Good gossip, that is. Boaz had heard of Ruth and Naomi's plight. He was touched by Ruth's change of faith, and he was especially impressed by her goodness to Naomi.

One thing to know about Boaz is that he was probably quite old. Ruth, on the other hand, was probably still young. His kindness to her must have been like a father to a daughter. That is why the next scene of the story is special. Ruth actually makes a wedding proposal to Boaz. Why? Because it would save the only family heritage she has, the name of Naomi's husband and sons. This is real devotion to her mother-in-law. Rather than leave Naomi and seek a young husband, Ruth feels led to be the wife of this older man. As a kinsman redeemer, Boaz can take care of her and Naomi.

Boaz, of course, is flattered by this young woman's request, and they do marry. His thoughts for her are best described in Ruth 3:10–11. "Blessed are you of the Lord my daughter. For you have shown more kindness at the end than at the beginning, in that you did not go after young men, whether poor or rich. And now my daughter, do not fear. I will do for you all that you request, for all the people of my town know that you are a virtuous woman."

This story gets even better. If you read the last few paragraphs of the Book of Ruth, you will discover who the great-grandson of Boaz and Ruth is. It's amazing. Boaz and Ruth have a son named Obed; he has a son named Jesse; and Jesse has a son named David. That is none other than the famous King David; we will study more about him later. What we see is that God used the changed faith of a Moabite to extend the lineage of Jesus Christ who was to be born of the house of David. The marriage of Ruth is far more than a sweet story.

ACTIVITY 26

26A—Younger Students

Do you think kindness is powerful? Do a kind deed for a family member. Boaz was kind to Ruth, and it blessed an entire nation!

26B—Middle and Older Students

For reasons we don't fully understand, there are many significant number patterns in Bible history. For example there are seven days of Creation, and the number "7" is used repeatedly in the Book of Revelation. We also see a pattern in the Bible with 40 or 400. The Great Flood was 40 days; the Israelites were in bondage for 400 years; they wandered 40 years in the desert; and Jesus fasted for 40 days in the wilderness. It's interesting.

Another pattern appears to us in the lineage of Adam to Boaz. See if you can find a pattern in the number of names between these significant men of the Bible who helped to sustain the Hebrew people through the generations.

Adam

Seth

Enos

Cainan

Mahalaleel

Jared

Enoch

Methuselah

Lamech

Noah

Shem

Arphaxad

Salah

Eber

Peleg

Reu

Serug

Nahor

Terah

Abraham

Isaac

Jacob

Judah

Pharez

Hezron

Ram

Amminadab

Nahshon

Salma

Boaz

(Hint: Circle Noah, Abraham, and Boaz.)

1199 B.C.

GIDEON

LESSON 27

Did you remember that Ruth and Naomi lived during the period of the judges? Well, the story of Gideon comes straight from the Book of Judges in the Bible. He lived around 1199 B.C. and served as a judge for 40 years. During this time the Hebrews were still settling into the area of Canaan and battling their neighbors for land. Elsewhere, this is about the time of the Later New Kingdom in Egypt, and in China, the Shang dynasty was still ruling.

Not all was well in Canaan. The Israelites were trying to settle in a land that was not their own. Though God promised them the land through a covenant with Abraham, not all of the Israelites' enemies had been defeated. So, the Israelites lived among people like the Canaanites and the Midianites who resented their presence.

The Israelites were also beginning to forget the great miracles that had helped them escape from slavery and reach the Promised Land. Many Hebrews were influenced by the pagan culture around them and even began to worship the false gods of that area.

We find out from the story in Judges, Chapter 6, that Gideon was one Israelite who was being bullied by the Midianites. We reach this conclusion because in the story we find him threshing grain in a winepress. Why was he doing that? It appears that he was hiding what he was really doing (threshing grain) by working in a winepress. He was probably hiding the grain from the bands of Midianites who were around looting. God chose to use this "weak man," as Gideon called himself, and amazing things began to happen.

Gideon on several occasions asked God for very specific guidance. He wanted there to be "signs" or miracles to prove that he was dealing with God. The Lord was gracious and understanding to Gideon. He answered him every time with a miracle.

This clay pot and small oil lamp were made between 1200 and 800 B.C. The pot may be very similar to those smashed by Gideon's army, and the oil lamp like those used to light the army's torches.

In one instance, God set on fire meat that was covered with broth. That miracle gave Gideon the courage to tear down the false idols of Baal. Then Gideon asked God for more "evidence" that God wanted him to be a leader. Gideon set out a dry fleece and asked that God make it wet overnight. He then asked God to take a wet fleece and make it dry. Each time God answered, and Gideon was strengthened to do as he was commanded.

Gideon's greatest mission from the Lord was to overthrow the Midianite army. Just as with Joshua at the battle of Jericho, the Lord didn't want Gideon and the Israelites to have too much confidence in their own strength. He asked them to take a small army of only 300 men and do an unusual thing. They were to take horns, torches, and clay pots and surround the Midianites in the middle of the night. Then, all at the same time, they were to blow the horns, break their pots, and raise their bright torches. They did just as instructed.

In the dark of night, the great noise of all those clay pots breaking and horns blasting was enough to scare the Midianites to pieces. And the mass number of torches made the small Israelite army look huge. In despair and confusion, some of the Midianites slaughtered themselves, and the rest fled!

As God had promised Gideon, He led the Israelites to victory once more. Gideon continued to lead the Israelites as a good judge for 40 years. It would have been great if Gideon's success could have kept the Israelites from ever wavering in their faith again. But unfortunately, we are going to see them fall away from God many more times before God deals with them once and for all.

ACTIVITY 27

ALL STUDENTS

Make your Memory Cards for Lessons 25–27.

27A—Younger Students

Make a pot out of clay!

Materials: Modeling clay or Play-Doh modeling compound

With your clay, make one long rope that looks like a snake. Coil it around and around until it forms a small pot. Let it harden. Take a picture of it for your Student Notebook. File it under "Asia: Israel."

The Mystery of History

27B—Middle Students

Adult supervision is required for this activity.

Get an old clay pot. Go outside and take turns smashing it with a hammer. (Cover your eyes!) Listen carefully to the sounds it makes and just try to imagine 300 of these pots being smashed all at the same time in the middle of the night. (Note: Save your larger clay pot pieces for a future activity. The ancient Greeks used pieces of clay pots to write on when casting a vote for the person they would "ostracize." You will want the pieces for that lesson.)

27C—Older Students

Most of the men and women listed as judges in the Old Testament are obscure figures. But a few of them have familiar names; these are the ones in bold type in the list below. The judges were in this order:

Othniel

Ehud

Shamgar

Deborah and Barak

Gideon

Abimelech (Gideon's evil son who became an outlaw)

Tola

Jair

Jephthah

Ibzan

Elon

Abdon

Samson

(**Eli** and **Samuel** are sometimes referred to as the last two judges, but Eli is better described as a priest and Samuel, as a prophet.)

Read the story of Deborah as found in Judges, Chapters 4 and 5, paying close attention to what is called "Deborah's song." Write your own "lesson" in a fashion similar to the lessons I have written. I would describe my writing as an "expository essay." It is a blend of fact with personal opinion. Research Deborah and add her to the history pages yourself.

TAKE ANOTHER LOOK!

Review 9: Lessons 25–27

Wall of Fame

1. *The Trojan Horse (1250 B.C.)*—Draw a horse of course.

2. *Ruth and Naomi (exact date unknown; place them together, holding hands, near 1200 B.C.)*—Place a golden cross on the front of Ruth because she carried the lineage of Christ.

3. *Gideon (1199 B.C.)*—Tape the remains of a burnt match to him to resemble the torches used to fight the Midianites. (Ask your teacher for the burnt matches.)

SomeWHERE in Time

1. On a historical map, locate the southern part of Greece. Follow with your finger across the sea to the city of Troy. Troy is on the coast of modern-day Turkey. Imagine how long it took Paris and Helen to make this daring voyage. Some believe Helen was taken by force!

2. On a biblical map of Canaan, find Moab, the region that Ruth was from. Moab was not considered a part of Israel because it was not settled by one of the 12 sons of Jacob. This is why Ruth was considered a "foreigner" to the Israelites.

3. On a map of Canaan that indicates the tribes of Israel, find the western tribe of Manasseh. (The Manasseh tribe was divided between an eastern and a western location.) It was in a city named Ophrah in Western Manasseh that the Lord called Gideon to pursue the Midianites. Ophrah was a small town located 6 miles southwest of Shechem, west of the Jordan river, and just north of the border of Ephraim.

The Mystery of History

PUT IT ALL TOGETHER
Worksheet 1: Lessons 1–27

You have studied 27 different lessons in the first nine weeks of this history course. Using your textbook, maps or timeline, go through this worksheet and answer the questions below. This is not a test. This is an exercise in remembering. Just like muscles have to be worked into shape, our memory has to be worked too.

I—Dates to Memorize.

I don't expect you to memorize the date of every person we learned, but I do want you to remember 12 of them. Two are from this first quarter.

Write the name and corresponding date I've asked you to memorize for both Abraham and Tutankhamen five times each in the blanks below.

Abraham   2100 B.C.

1. _____

2. _____

3. _____

4. _____

5. _____

Tutankhamen   1333 B.C.

1. _____

2. _____

3. _____

4. _____

5. _____

II—Matching. Match the following items by placing the correct letter next to the number.

_____ 1. Day 3 of Creation   a.   Roamed the earth before and after the flood

_____ 2. Adam and Eve   b.   A time when the Earth was partially covered with ice after the flood

_____ 3. Jubal and Tubal-Cain   c.   God created the seas and earth

_____ 4. Noah   d.   One of the first advanced civilizations after the flood

_____ 5. Ice Age   e.   Parents of Cain and Abel

_____ 6. Dinosaurs   f.   Character from _The Epic of Gilgamesh_ who built a boat for a flood

_____ 7. Sumerians   g.   The place where God confused man's language

_____ 8. Tower of Babel   h.   Early men skilled in music and ironmaking

_____ 9. Stonehenge   i.   One righteous man who God spared from death

_____ 10. Utnapishtim   j.   An ancient megalith

III—True or False? Circle your answer.

11. _The Epic of Gilgamesh_ contained a story about a legendary king who lost immortal life.   T   F

12. The Minoans lived in present-day Turkey.   T   F

13. The pyramids of Egypt are taller than the Eiffel Tower.   T   F

14. Abraham was from the city of Ur in the country of Sumer.   T   F

15. Jacob was favored by his father, Isaac.   T   F

16. Rachel, the wife of Jacob, died in childbirth with Dan.   T   F

17. Hammurabi worshiped the sun god, Aten.   T   F

18. Upon Joseph's request, Jacob and his sons moved to Egypt.   T   F

19. The Shang dynasty lasted for 2,000 years.   T   F

20. The story of Moses is found in the Book of Genesis.   T   F

IV—Multiple Choice. Circle one answer for each question.

21. The name Moses means
    a. to exit.
    b. to draw out.
    c. to lead.
    d. from the river.

22. The Tabernacle of God in the wilderness
    a. contained symbols that represent Christ to us today.
    b. had three main divisions.
    c. was a dwelling place for God.
    d. All of the above.

23. At the Battle of Jericho, Joshua and his men marched
    a. with spears and torches.
    b. with clay pots and horns.
    c. around Jericho for six days and shouted on the seventh.
    d. around Jericho 15 times.

24. Amenhotep IV and Nefertiti lived during the
    a. Old Kingdom.
    b. Middle Kingdom.
    c. Early New Kingdom.
    d. Later New Kingdom.

25. Tutankhamen's tomb was discovered by
    a. Howard Carter.
    b. Sir C. Leonard Woolley.
    c. Sir Raleigh.
    d. Walter Gilgamesh.

V—Before or After? Circle the word that makes the sentence correct.

26. Ramses II lived (before, after) Hammurabi in Babylon.
27. Joshua conquered Jericho (before, after) the events of the legend of the Trojan Horse.
28. Ruth and Naomi were redeemed by Boaz (before, after) the Minoans flourished in Crete.
29. Gideon was a judge over Israel (before, after) Tutankhamen was pharaoh in Egypt.
30. B.C. is (before, after) A.D.

VI—People and Places. Draw a line to connect a name listed in the second grouping to each place listed in the first grouping. Use a different-colored pencil or crayon for each line.

Potiphar's house   City of Ur   England   Giza   Crete

China   Jericho   Sodom and Gomorrah   Great Hall

Mary Mantell   Shang dynasty   Khufu   Minoans

Lot   Ramses II   Abraham   Joseph   Joshua

VII—Answer These Questions. You may refer to the lesson suggested in parentheses. Write your answers in complete sentences and use a separate sheet of paper if necessary.

1. What is the significance of men like Jubal and Tubal-Cain? (Lesson 3)

2. What was different about the earth before the flood that made it possible for plants to grow without rain? (Lesson 5)

3. Why did the ancient Egyptians bury so many things with them? (Lesson 11)

4. What three natural barriers exist around China that made travel, trade, and widespread marriage difficult? (Lesson 18)

5. What made Amenhotep IV and Nefertiti so different from other Egyptian pharaohs? (Lesson 22)

THE MYSTERY EXPANDS:
1175 B.C. to 627 B.C.

Are you beginning to like history? Are you finding it sort of interesting? Though the people we have studied lived thousands of years ago, I find them absolutely fascinating. I love the Egyptians like Nefertiti and King Tut. I like, too, the Greeks who surprised the Trojans with a horse full of soldiers! And I am in awe over the deliverance of the Hebrews through Moses with the first miraculous Passover and the parting of the Red Sea. It's just neat history, and it's full of meaning for us even today.

This next quarter you are going to learn even more about the Israelites. You will see how they go from being ruled by judges to being ruled by kings. Some were great kings like David, who killed a giant with just a slingshot, and some were foolish kings like Saul, who went nearly insane with jealousy. And even wise King Solomon, you will learn, made mistakes that led to the breakup of Israel as one nation.

Over and over we will learn of how often and how easily the Israelites lost their faith in God and the price they paid for it. Even after the great prophets warned them of their future, they refused to listen and obey God's commands. In time, some of the Israelites were removed from the Promised Land forever and taken as refugees into Assyria, a foreign country.

Though powerful and known for their military strength, the mighty Assyrians did not rule Mesopotamia easily. They had to contend with their neighbors, the Babylonians. These two nations struggled against one another for centuries over control of Mesopotamia.

And you will learn that in Greece, also, there were some neighbors who didn't get along well either. They were the Spartans and the Athenians. Though both are considered "Greek," they battled with one another like two small nations. Yet, in the midst of their hard times, the Greeks sponsored the very first Olympics in 776 B.C. As a fan of the Olympic games today, I'm so glad they did.

In this quarter we will look for the first time at the North American continent and some of the ancient people who lived there. Some may have lived right in my own backyard! Many of the ancient Native Americans left very interesting designs in the earth for us to remember them by.

In South America the earliest permanent settlements were around the modern country of Peru. A rather advanced people by the name of the Chavins built elaborate stone carvings and a three-story castle. From the carvings it is evident the people worshiped a puma or jaguar. They also fished, farmed, and wove cloth on looms.

Have you ever heard of Rome? It's a city in Italy now, but long ago it was far more than a city. It was an empire. But even the Roman Empire had to start somewhere. We will look at the very beginnings of Rome this quarter to begin to understand how it rose to power.

More than ever before, the ancient European cultures began to expand and discover more about each other through the very time period we'll be studying these next few weeks. Through great sailors like the Phoenicians, men and women began to trade their products to lands all over the Mediterranean Sea. What did they trade? People traded just about anything they found that someone else wanted. Trade items included rare spices, jewelry, dyes for making cloth, glassware, and other natural resources.

In poor communities, life remained simple because people spent a large amount of time just keeping food on the table. In other communities where wealth was abundant, we have evidence of art, cosmetics, and even games that have been preserved throughout the years.

We will also study in this quarter that in faraway China, the Zhou dynasty overtook the Shang and ruled for the next 800 years! The Chinese believed that a "Mandate of Heaven" contributed to their well-being, and this belief greatly influenced the moral climate. At the same time, we'll learn of the roots of Hinduism in India and how the caste system was developed.

The study of ancient religions and belief systems will be recurrent throughout this study of history as we seek to understand God's hand in it all. According to the Bible, God's plans remain perfect and He orchestrates the rise and fall of all the great powers we'll study. Enjoy learning about them!

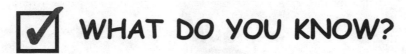

WHAT DO YOU KNOW?

Pretest 10

Let's again follow a *Jeopardy* game show format. I have provided an answer; you come up with the right question from the bottom of the page.

1. In his hair.

2. Delilah, a Philistine woman.

3. He knocked over pillars with his bare hands.

4. The Zhou dynasty.

5. The East and the West.

6. A belief that inspired the Chinese to live moral lives.

7. Samuel.

8. Hannah.

What followed the Shang dynasty in China?
Whom did Samson love?
What was the "Mandate of Heaven"?
Who was the last judge over Israel?
How was the Zhou dynasty divided?
How did Samson beat the Philistines?
Who was the mother of Samuel?
Where was Samson's strength?

SAMSON
LESSON 28

Samson was a man of great passion. He served the Lord as a judge over Israel for about 20 years. But, throughout his life, he struggled with self-control and rage. Despite Samson's weaknesses, we'll learn that God still used him to accomplish His purposes. The famous story of Samson is found in the Book of Judges, Chapters 13–16.

It is evident that God had a special plan for Samson's life. Before he was even born, an angel of the Lord told Samson's mother about him. The angel declared that her son would be set apart for God as a "Nazirite" and deliver Israel from the Philistines. (The Philistines had been ruling over the Israelites for about 40 years.) But how Samson would deliver the Israelites was not revealed to her—and probably for the better.

Just as the angel said, Samson grew up as a Nazirite. In those days in Israel, a faithful Nazirite would set himself apart from others by keeping three vows: never to drink alcohol, never to touch something dead, and never to cut one's hair. (John the Baptist was also a Nazirite.) But Samson was set apart in another way. He was given supernatural strength. And because of it, he performed some amazing feats during his life.

One time Samson killed a wild lion with his bare hands. This was certainly a brave thing to do. But later, Samson touched the bones of the lion he killed. In doing so he broke one of the Nazirite vows. (The one about touching something dead.) He also broke the Nazirite vow not to drink wine because he was known to carouse and drink with the Philistines, the very people he was born to conquer.

If Samson's actions weren't disappointing enough as a young man, he decided to marry a Philistine woman! His parents must have been brokenhearted. They had been told that Samson would begin to deliver the Israelites from the Philistines. Instead, he was marrying one! The forbidden relationship became a disaster. Samson provoked his own wedding guests with such a perplexing riddle that they rose up against him. Samson lost his precious bride in the process. She

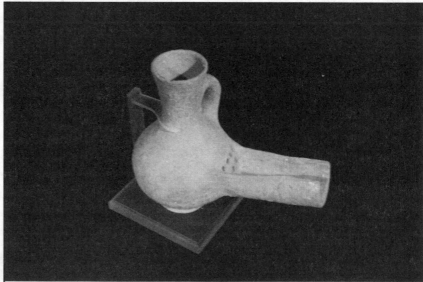

This is a beer, wine, or olive oil strainer made around 1000 B.C. Samson may have used a similar piece to drink with the Philistines.

was carried back to her homeland by the Philistine guests.

Samson tried to retrieve his wife a year later but failed. This sent him into quite a jealous rage. In an act of complete revenge, he tied flaming torches to the tails of foxes and chased them into the fields of the Philistines. In an unconventional way, Samson was beginning to fulfill his calling of weakening the stronghold of the Philistines over Israel.

On another occasion, Samson displayed his superior strength by single-handedly slaying a thousand Philistines with just the jawbone of a donkey. His personal victory won him the respect of Philistines and Israelites alike. Because no one dared to challenge this champion of supernatural strength, the Philistines left him alone for awhile. For years, Samson was able to serve the Lord as a true judge over Israel though he was mostly admired for his physical capabilities.

In Samson's later years, however, the secret to his strength became a serious problem. The problem began when he fell in love with another Philistine woman. Her name was Delilah. You might have heard of her. Unfortunately, she was bribed by her own people, the Philistines, to discover once and for all what made Samson so unusually strong. Day after day Delilah pestered Samson until he could take it no more.

As the story goes, Samson finally revealed his secret. He told Delilah that his strength was in his hair having never been cut, which was the one vow he had kept as a Nazirite. For reasons we don't understand, God had set Samson apart in this way. Sadly, Delilah didn't respect the Lord that Samson served. With her heart racing and fingers trembling, Delilah deceitfully cut off Samson's hair in the night! It was an act of complete betrayal.

As a weakened man, Samson was easily taken captive by the Philistines. I wonder if Delilah realized Samson's fate when she cut his long, long hair. We don't know how she felt after the deed. To add to Samson's humiliation in losing his strength, his captors gouged out his eyes before they threw him in prison. It was an act of utter cruelty.

But, while Samson was in prison, one thing certainly happened. His hair grew back. I suppose haircuts were not a high priority for prisoners, and in time Samson's enemies forgot where his strength came from. That was their last mistake!

At a huge party, Samson was led out of prison to be taunted before some Philistines. Samson asked a young boy to direct him to two massive pillars centered in the room. Expecting some kind of show, the crowd watched Samson with great expectation. What happened next is, well, history. Samson placed his bare hands against the stone-cold marble pillars. Then, with all the strength he had left and his last breath of life, Samson pushed the pillars down, forcing the entire building to collapse. In doing so he lost his own life and killed thousands of Philistines who were present. Through this solitary act, Samson probably eliminated more Philistines than he ever had before. This fulfilled what the angel of the Lord had said about Samson. He did indeed help to deliver the Israelites from the Philistines.

Many believe that the physical strength of Samson was both "figuratively" and "literally" in his hair. His true strength seemed to have come from the Lord for His own purposes. Through both Samson's bodily strength and his moral weaknesses, God used him in an unforgettable way.

ACTIVITY 28

28A—Younger Students

With lightweight building blocks, construct two mighty pillars. Close your eyes and knock them down on top of yourself. Remember that Samson fulfilled God's calling for his life by being so brave.

28B—Middle Students

Have an arm-wrestling contest with your family members or friends to determine who is strongest.

Have a discussion with your family on what you think is the message of professional wrestlers today. To whom do they give credit for their strength? Do they use their strength for good or to promote evil? What would you do if you were incredibly strong?

c. 1122 B.C.

ZHOU DYNASTY (CHOU)

LESSON 29

To understand China, you need to understand the dynasties that ruled this vast country. We have already studied the Shang dynasty. Today we look at the next dynasty, one that lasted for almost 800 years.

In about 1122 B.C. (historians don't agree on the exact date), a king named Wen founded the Zhou dynasty. In some books, the Zhou dynasty is written as "Chou." Both are pronounced JOE. (The Zhou dynasty started about the same time that Boaz and Ruth were getting married.) But King Wen couldn't completely beat out all the people who were loyal to the Shang dynasty. If you remember, a dynasty is really a family. People rose to power because they were born into it.

King Wen's son, King Wu, was more successful in overthrowing the Shang family, and he conquered the last Shang king in battle. But it still took three to five years after Wu's death for the Zhou dynasty to really be in charge of China.

The Zhou dynasty has been defined by two different regions. One was called the Western Zhou and the other was the Eastern. The Western Zhou dynasty didn't last so long. Problems existed because family members kept dividing up the land. One prince named Bing finally fled east and started a new capital. That was the beginning of the Eastern Zhou dynasty and Prince Bing became King Bing. (In our language it rhymes, but it might not have rhymed in their language.)

The Eastern Zhou was never as strong militarily as the Western Zhou dynasty, but it lasted a lot longer. One reason for its success is that eventually people were picked to rule areas because of their expertise, not because they were born into the position. That change in leadership made a big difference in the way things were run.

What was life like, then, in the Eastern Zhou dynasty? It was busy! Some Chinese cities back then had as many as 100,000 people in them. Many people were farmers. They mainly grew millet, a grain. (Millet is a seed grain we often find in bird food today.) There were roads leading from state to state, coins were made, irrigation (a method of watering crops) was used, and ironmaking was big. Remember how important iron was to the Egyptians? Better weapons could be made from iron. The Chinese had enough to sell and trade with other countries.

The hard part of life during this time in China was the huge gap that existed between the rich and the poor. The rich lived luxuriously in palaces, while the poor lived quite simply in huts. There were also many years of civil war between the states during which thousands of men fought and died at a time. It was often the poor who made up the armies.

Morally, the Zhou believed that a "Mandate of Heaven" had made them victorious over the earlier Shang dynasty. They felt that heaven had rewarded them. But this Mandate could be taken away if the people were bad! As a result, people lived up to very high standards of behavior. Although fear may have motivated them to lead good lives, this belief made the Chinese strong and stable. The Zhou dynasty lasted about 800 years overall! That is an incredibly long time for any line of rulers to maintain power.

ACTIVITY 29

29A—Younger Students

The next time you are near a pet store, look for millet that is sold there for birds. It is a good grain for people too. The ancient Chinese were skilled at farming this grain. You may not want to sample the bird food, but you can sample millet that you buy at the health food store. Try it!

29B—Middle Students

There were a lot of new words and names in this lesson. To help you review them, unscramble these words from the lesson. Then, orally, tell your teacher one thing about the word, using the lesson for help. The answers can be found in the Pretest Answer Key in the Appendix.

1. lelitm	6. Kgin uW	11. hCuo
2. ghnaS	7. giKn gniB	12. stiiec
3. uhoZ	8. niarigtori	13. roop
4. onri	9. Etasrne	14. ichr
5. nigK Wne	10. rnWtese	

29C—Middle and Older Students

1. Update your list of Chinese dynasties with the following information on the Zhou dynasty. For the "Special notes" column, review the lesson and list what you consider the most significant achievements of this dynasty. Keep your list filed under "Asia: China."

The Dynasties of China

Date of power (years ruling)	Name of dynasty	Special notes
c. 1122–256 B.C. (c. 866 yrs.)	Zhou	

2. Older Students: How much do you know about modern China? Research the form of government there today. Write a few paragraphs to describe the leadership of China, particularly the names of current rulers.

   Then cut out current newspaper articles on China. With a highlighter, mark the names of the people that you discovered in your research as they appear in the news.

   It's a good feeling to be informed about current events! File your summary and articles under "Asia: China."

SAMUEL

LESSON 30

Not long after Samson crushed the Philistines, Israel's final judge came to power. Some consider him more of a prophet. His name? Samuel. Although he didn't push over buildings with his bare hands, his CHARACTER appeared to be far stronger than that of Samson. In his honor, there are two books of the Old Testament named after him.

One neat thing about studying Samuel is that we have stories about him as a baby, a boy, and a grown man. Before Samuel was even born, his mother, Hannah, prayed over him. She loved the Lord dearly but had no children. She prayed to God and said that if He would just give her a baby, she would dedicate the baby back to God for a lifetime of service. That is exactly what she did.

Samuel had only a few years to live with his mother before he went to live with the priest and serve in the Temple. He remained home until he was weaned. We can probably assume that those years were significant ones under his mother's teachings. For you see, Samuel was very godly even as a young boy. Eli, the priest, had unruly sons who worked at the Temple, too. But Samuel never appeared to be influenced by their bad behavior.

In fact, Samuel was so sensitive to the Lord, that he heard Him speak out loud when just a young boy. The voice was so strong that Samuel at first thought it must be Eli talking to him. "Samuel, Samuel," he heard one night. It was the Lord. God spoke to Samuel directly to tell him of the fate of Eli and his wicked sons. From that point on, Samuel became a real prophet of God and continued to have a strong relationship with Him the rest of his life.

Exciting stories are found in the books of Samuel, such as when the Philistines tried to steal the Ark of the Covenant. For years, other nations attempted to keep the Ark of the Covenant for themselves but were never successful. Instead, for their wickedness they were plagued with terrible tumors. You might want to read more about it in I Samuel 4–7.

Although Samuel was a good judge, the people of Israel struggled with faithfulness to God. Over and over they were brought to repentance under the leadership of Samuel. Even then, though, the people complained about one main thing. They wanted a king. The Israelites' neighbors had kings who ruled their lands. They wanted to be like them.

The Israelites' desire for a king saddened God's heart because He considered Himself to be their king. Samuel warned the people that having an earthly king would bring its own set of problems. They refused to listen.

In I Samuel 8 it is recorded that God heard the people's request. He told Samuel to anoint a king after all. They had been warned by God of the difficulties that a king would bring them. Of course, the Lord was accurate. In our next lesson we will study the first king of Israel and the events that followed. With a king, a whole new era began in the history of the Israelites and the period of the judges was over.

ACTIVITY 30

ALL STUDENTS

Make your Memory Cards for Lessons 28–30.

30A—Younger Students

From I Samuel 3 in the Bible, read the story of Samuel as a little boy when he heard the voice of God calling him. Act out the scene. You will need someone to be Eli, Samuel, and the voice of the Lord.

30B—Middle Students

Make a Mini-Timeline. Using the life of Samuel, make a small timeline book.

1. Take a piece of paper (8½ by 11 inches) and fold it in half twice. It should like like a small book.

2. On the outside, write Samuel's name and the years he lived.

3. On the inside, draw a horizontal line all the way across both pages as they are opened up.

4. Starting on the left, begin to insert information about Samuel. Include these segments:

   Hannah's prayer.

   Samuel serves under Eli in the Temple.

   Samuel hears God's voice.

   Samuel becomes God's prophet.

   The Ark of the Covenant is stolen by the Philistines.

   Samuel judges Israel.

   Samuel anoints the first king.

   Samuel anoints David the second king.

30C—Older Students

The stories around the Ark of the Covenant are fascinating. So much so that one of the Indiana Jones movies is based on it. Do your own research on the Ark of the Covenant. What was kept in it? How did it help the Israelites in battle? What happened to people who accidentally touched it?

You can find all these answers in your Bible. Use a concordance to help you. Write a one-page summary of the Ark of the Covenant and include a photocopy of what artists believe it looked like. File it in your Student Notebook under "Asia: Israel."

Wall of Fame

1. *Samson (c. 1175 B.C.)*—Draw a pillar on either side of him. Put small X's over his eyes.

2. *Zhou dynasty (c. 1122 B.C.)*—Write the word "Zhou" on a small piece of paper. Then draw a jagged line down it to divide it into the East and the West. In smaller letters, write "East" on one side and "West" on the other.

3. *Samuel (c. 1113 B.C.)*—Give him big ears for "hearing God."

SomeWHERE in Time

1. Color and label Outline Map 4, "East Asia," as directed below. Then file this map in your Student Notebook under "Asia: China."

   a. Color the boundaries of the Zhou dynasty in orange. It was much smaller than China is today.

   b. In green, shade the modern border of China.

   c. Label and color as you wish the countries surrounding present-day China.

2. In a Bible atlas, find Philistia, the land of the Philistines. What was advantageous about their location? (See answer at the bottom of this page.)

(**Answer:** The Philistines were on the coast of the Mediterranean Sea, which is ideal for trading.)

WHAT DID YOU MISS?

Week 10: Exercise

Today's exercise is a word search. But it is not the ordinary kind. Using colored pencils or markers, circle the words in the color indicated for each group. To help you get started, the first letter of the first word in each group is set bold. There are no "backward" words!

1. Find and circle in red the names of Noah's three sons.
   Shem
   Ham
   Japheth

2. Find and circle in blue three things the Sumerians are known for.
   ziggurats
   cuneiform
   Fertile Crescent

3. Find and circle in pink three things the Minoans are known for.
   bull leaping
   Knossos
   Minotaur

4. Find and circle in black three things about Hammurabi.
   king
   Babylonia
   laws

5. Find and circle in gold these three things found in the Tabernacle.
   mercy seat
   incense
   lampstand

6. Find and circle in turquoise these three Egyptians.
   Amenhotep
   Tutankhamen
   Ramses

7. Find and circle in orange three things about the Trojan Horse.
   Helen
   Odysseus
   Schliemann

8. Find and circle in gray these three things about Samson.
   hair
   Delilah
   Philistines

9. Find and circle in brown these three things about the Zhou dynasty.
   King Wen
   Eastern
   Mandate

10. Find and circle in purple these three things about Samuel.
    Hannah
    Eli
    prophet

"What Did You Miss?" Word Search

T	O	**S**	C	H	L	I	E	M	A	N	N	W	K	**K**	H	P	**B**
D	F	F	H	L	H	V	B	A	B	Y	L	O	N	I	A	T	U
R	E	P	B	E	A	T	P	W	X	O	L	P	O	N	G	D	L
S	R	R	J	H	M	I	N	O	T	A	U	R	S	G	R	Y	L
Y	T	L	A	W	S	N	O	V	D	R	C	S	S	R	S	W	L
L	I	V	P	N	R	C	B	N	M	Y	G	D	O	T	P	Z	E
A	L	W	H	M	G	E	C	S	N	T	S	T	S	Z	H	R	A
M	E	V	E	M	A	N	D	A	T	E	W	S	M	Q	I	T	P
P	C	P	T	W	H	S	F	O	Q	H	N	Q	E	O	L	U	I
S	R	Q	H	X	**M**	E	R	C	Y	S	E	**A**	T	U	I	T	N
T	E	A	S	T	E	R	N	W	Z	G	M	M	P	P	S	A	G
A	S	J	R	C	B	S	P	R	O	P	H	E	T	M	T	N	M
N	C	U	N	E	I	F	O	R	M	W	H	N	Q	B	I	K	G
D	E	L	I	L	A	H	**H**	A	N	N	A	H	S	V	N	H	B
K	N	**H**	A	I	R	L	G	M	Q	P	B	O	T	W	E	A	T
S	T	D	Z	F	T	M	W	S	T	Z	P	T	R	N	S	M	S
K	I	N	G	W	E	N	H	E	**H**	E	L	E	N	P	R	E	Q
Z	I	G	G	U	R	A	T	S	P	B	Z	P	W	S	R	N	P

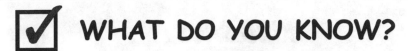

WHAT DO YOU KNOW?

Pretest 11

Matching. Here are the names of three kings we will study this week. See if you can properly match their names to the statements given below. Use a colored pencil to draw lines to each. Use a different color for each king, and make a decorative box around each king's name with "his" color.

SAUL	DAVID	SOLOMON

I was the first king of Israel.   I loved Bathsheba.   I built the Temple.

I was the wealthiest man in the world.   I ended my own life.

I killed Goliath.   I hated David.

I wrote many of the Psalms.   I had 700 wives.

I wrote many of the Proverbs.

My son was Jonathan.   I played the harp for Saul.

KING SAUL

LESSON 31

King Saul is a tragic figure in the story of the Old Testament. On the one hand, he's a great guy; on the other hand, he's awful. Why do we see these two extremes? We'll study his life today and figure that out.

As you already learned, the Israelites begged Samuel, a judge and a prophet, to give them a king. After consulting with the Lord, Samuel anointed Saul to be the first king of Israel. The practice of "anointing by oil" had many different uses in that era. Here it is symbolic of Saul's being "set apart as king."

When Saul was first chosen to be king, he was more than qualified. He was humble, generous, pure, and even tall and handsome. What a great guy! All these qualities are attributed to him in the Book of I Samuel. Most importantly, he had God's spirit upon him. I Samuel 10:9–10 says that "God gave him another heart . . . then the Spirit of God came upon him and he prophesied among them." There we have evidence of the source of Saul's greatness. It was the Lord.

However, by Chapter 13 in I Samuel, we begin to see some problems develop. At one time, Saul grew impatient waiting for Samuel to bless the troops before battle. He began to take action on his own rather than wait on God. On another occasion he cut short the counsel of the priests and rushed his men off to battle without eating. They didn't do well because of their hunger. Saul was not listening to the wise counsel God provided him through the priests or the prophets.

One final act of foolishness was when Saul disobeyed God's command to kill the evil king of the Amalakites. In a state of pride, Saul spared the king and greedily kept some of the best livestock that had been captured. He had been told not to. I suppose the Lord wanted Saul to trust in Him for provision, not in his army.

To make matters worse, Saul then had the nerve to blame his poor decision on his own men. This disobedience and arrogance were apparently too much for God. I Samuel 16:14 says, "The Spirit of the Lord departed from Saul, and a distressing spirit from the Lord troubled him."

Saul's distressing spirit seemed to last the rest of his life. Some time later he also had to deal with the rising fame of David, who eventually succeeded him as king. Saul practically went mad with jealousy and spent his last years on a manhunt for David. Tragically, Saul ended his own life, defeated in every way.

It is sad that a man of such promise could fail so dramatically. This first king of Israel proved to be disappointing, just as the Lord had warned through Samuel. It is a reminder to us to heed God's word, to not take God's blessings for granted, and to not allow pride and impatience to rule us.

ACTIVITY 31

31A—Younger and Middle Students

Play charades.

Use these words from the story of King Saul to play charades. Write these words on small pieces of paper and select one at a time. Try to act out the word without using any sounds or talking. (Younger students can have this list of words to choose from when guessing.)

Handsome	Disobedient
Tall	Arrogant
Anointing	Distressed
King	Jealous
Impatient	Suicide

31B—Middle Students

Notice that the 10 words listed above summarize the story of King Saul's life in the order they are written. If you made slips of paper already for charades, take the papers and try to arrange them in order without looking at the list above. If you didn't play charades, stop and make small cards with the words on them. Then proceed with arranging them in order.

31C—Older Students

Toward the end of Saul's life, he committed a sin against God by consulting a "medium" to know his future. Where do we see this prevalent today? (Psychic hotlines on TV?) What New Testament scriptures warn us of the use of witchcraft? Use a concordance to familiarize yourself with these passages. Write them down and add them to your Student Notebook under "Asia: Israel."

c. 1055 B.C.

DAVID

LESSON 32

David is probably one of the most beloved characters of the entire Bible. Interestingly, he was not always "good." Why then is he so popular to those who study the Bible? It could be that we feel we know him so well. He poured out his soul in the writing of at least 73 of the 150 Psalms in the Old Testament. And though he had some flaws, he was said to be "a man after God's own heart." That probably explains our being drawn to him. Let's look at his intriguing life, as found in I and II Samuel.

We first learn of David when the prophet Samuel went to anoint him as the second king of Israel. David was a boy at the time. Samuel anointed David in secret because Saul was still reigning as the first king of Israel. Jesse, David's father, and all his brothers were a bit shocked to learn that the youngest boy of the family would be the future king.

Not long after the anointing, David received his first "assignment," so to speak. He was to leave the shepherd's life temporarily to visit the king's palace. You see, King Saul couldn't sleep at night. (He was struggling with the "distressing spirit" we learned about earlier.) David, who was a gifted singer, was sent to help soothe the restless spirit of Saul through songs and music. It is so ironic that the unusual relationship

Michelangelo, a famous Italian artist, created this beautiful statue of David out of solid marble. It stands 12 feet high in a museum in Paris.

between Saul and David began there at the palace through such calming circumstances. For later, this same soothing shepherd boy drove Saul practically insane.

Upon completing the task of singing for the king, David returned to his shepherd's work for a time. That is, until his well-known encounter with Goliath, the giant. In case you don't know the story, it goes roughly like this. Not one soldier in Israel was willing to fight against a Philistine "giant" by the name of Goliath. David was just checking up on his brothers when he heard about the standstill. He was shocked that none of the soldiers had confidence in God for a victory. So, with just a simple slingshot, he showed them all what a powerful God he served. He slung a stone right to the head of Goliath that sent him crashing to the ground! As David was still a young man, it was incredible that he had the faith to fight Goliath with just a slingshot and without any armor! From this act of courage and confidence in God, we begin to see how different David was from ordinary men.

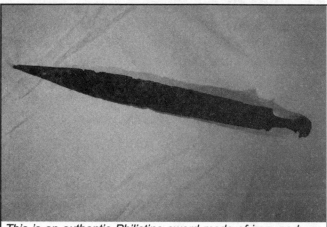

This is an authentic Philistine sword made of iron, perhaps like Goliath's.

With the story of the victory over Goliath circulating all over Israel, David gained more praise and honor than King Saul could handle. David became loved by the people of Israel; he earned a lifetime friendship with Saul's son Jonathan; Saul's daughter Michal fell in love with him. Not bad for a former shepherd boy. David married Michal and for awhile enjoyed his great success. Most importantly, I Samuel 18:14 tells us that "David behaved wisely in all his ways and the Lord was with him."

However, things soon changed dramatically for David. King Saul's rage and jealousy over David's popularity with the people of Israel and with Saul's own children was enough to drive Saul to madness. For years, Saul stalked David, who had to flee the palace that had become his home and at times go so far as to live in caves. Some of the Psalms of David were written from this dark time of his life while being hunted like an animal. He wrote, "O Lord . . . You are my refuge, My portion in the land of the living. Attend to my cry, For I am brought very low. Deliver me from my persecutors, For they are stronger than I. Bring my soul out of prison that I may praise Your name." (Ps. 142:7. See also Psalm 57.) David knew he was the next rightful king of Israel, but he had to hide to save his own life.

More than once David had the opportunity to attack Saul and kill him. But in his valor, David chose to spare Saul's life. David never meant to be Saul's enemy. During those years on the run, David's character was greatly developed through hardship.

The final day came, however, when Saul and Jonathan both died in battle. Even in Saul's death, which should have been a relief and a victory for the next king, David remained respectful of him. He had a special song written in Saul's memory. He wrote, "Saul and Jonathan were beloved and pleasant in their lives, and in their death they were not divided; they were swifter than eagles, they were stronger than lions . . . how the mighty have fallen." (II Sam. 1:23, 25) With the loss of Jonathan, David's closest friend, his grief at the time was more than doubled.

The entire Book of II Samuel tells the rest of the story of David's life and his reign as one of the greatest kings of Israel. The stories are magnificent. David conquered the city of Jerusalem and made it the capital of Israel. That is why Jerusalem is sometimes called the "city of David." (Bethlehem is also referred to as the "city of David" because he was from there.)

In the process of moving to Jerusalem, David orchestrated a great parade to have the Ark of the Covenant transported there. Knowing what you know about the sacred Ark, you can imagine how meaningful it was to the Israelites to give it a real "home." For the joyous occasion, David assembled

30,000 men and all kinds of instruments to bring the Ark into Jerusalem. Then he stripped down to just a simple cloth and "danced before the Lord with all his might." (II Sam. 6:14a) David wanted to go so far as to build an elaborate temple for the Lord, but God told him that task was reserved for David's son, Solomon. However, God did make a special covenant with David to assure him that his *throne* would last forever. (This came true through the bloodline of Jesus, the King who does reign forever.)

We also see in II Samuel the amazing story of Mephibosheth, a crippled man who was the last of the descendants of Saul. Rather than be threatened by this man and want to do away with him, David brought Mephibosheth right into his own palace and gave him a place of honor. This act of kindness, as well as many others, demonstrated just how extraordinary David was. He was loved by his people, he was victorious in battle, and he walked closely with the Lord.

Unfortunately, even good kings make mistakes. A day came when David's greatness was tarnished. Though he had seven wives, he desired to have one more woman—a woman who was already married to another man! Her name was Bathsheba.

When it came to this matter of the heart, David went to the extent of murder to get what he wanted. By David's orders, Bathsheba's husband was sent to the front line of battle where he would surely be killed. David's plan worked, as he wanted it to. In doing away with Bathsheba's husband through death, David freed Bathsheba to become the king's wife. But David's sins of lusting, lying, and murder were seen by God. David and Bathsheba paid a great price for their sin. Their firstborn child was stricken by the Lord and died.

This act of God could have made David a bitter man. But it didn't. The first thing David did upon hearing of his child's death was to go and worship the Lord. David was a man who accepted God's punishment for his sin. He understood that he had done something seriously wrong and penned the beautiful Prayer of Repentance in Psalm 51.

David's reign as king of Israel lasted for 40 years. His later years proved to be challenging and heartbreaking because one of his own sons, Absalom, rebelled against him. Just as King Saul once rose up against David, Absalom did the same. You can read Psalm 3 to better understand David's pain from the situation. But as only a good father would, David loved his son Absalom still! When Absalom was eventually killed in battle, David mourned and grieved deeply over the loss of his son who had made himself to be an enemy. According to II Samuel 18:33, David said, "O my son Absalom—my son, my son Absalom—if only I had died in your place! O Absalom my son, my son!"

Perhaps it is passionate scriptures like these that help make David such a favorite Bible character. We have a clear view into his soul through Old Testament stories and through his very own writings in the Psalms. We know of his love for the Lord, the mistakes he made, and the pain he harbored through so many of his relationships. Read Psalm 145, the last one he wrote, to catch a glimpse of his unwavering faith. Always seeking peace and reconciliation, David was as the scripture says, "a man after God's own heart."

ACTIVITY 32

ALL STUDENTS

Memorize when David lived, c. 1055 B.C.

32A—Younger Students

Obtain a slingshot or make one using a rubber band and a strong stick (shaped like a "Y"). Have your teacher help you use it carefully outside. Imagine facing a giant with just a slingshot. David's confidence was in God, not in his own ability.

32B—Middle Students

Create and illustrate an accordion-style timeline booklet on the major events of David's life.

1. Using the lesson or your Bible, choose 10 events to illustrate or write about in one sentence. (i.e., Samuel anoints David, David plays the harp for Saul, etc.)
2. To set up your booklet, tape two pieces of blank paper (8½ by 11 inches) end to end.
3. Fold this long paper in accordion fashion, creating 10 segments of equal size.
4. Open the paper and number each segment from 1 to 10.
5. Enter your facts for each segment—either by sentence form, sketch, or both.
6. Tie a ribbon around your finished product to seal it. Tuck it into your Student Notebook.

32C—Middle and Older Students

Knowing the situation under which David wrote will make the Psalms far more meaningful to you. There are 14 Psalms that give exact historical settings in their introductions. For example, if you look at Psalm 3, it contains a subtitle stating "A Psalm of David when he fled from Absalom his son." These types of subtitles were not added by the publishers of our English Bibles as a commentary note; rather, they are an actual part of the original text.

Look up the 14 Psalms listed below, which include historical references, to learn the circumstances in which David wrote. Create a list of these Psalms that includes the number of the Psalm and the actual subtitle. Some of the events will be familiar from the lesson, such as when David fled from Saul. (You will soon discover that the Psalms are not in chronological order.)

During difficult times in your own life, you can reflect on these Psalms. Underline some of your favorite verses. (I really like Psalm 59:16-17). File your list under "Asia: Israel."

Look up: Psalm 3, 7, 18, 30, 34, 51, 52, 54, 56, 57, 59, 60, 63, and 142.

---

c. 1015 B.C.

SOLOMON

LESSON 33

If you were granted just one wish in your life, what would it be? Would you ask for great wealth and treasures, to rule the world, or to live a long, healthy life? Well, Solomon, when given the chance, asked for neither wealth, nor power, nor a long life. Let's learn what Solomon requested that made him one of the greatest men who ever lived.

According to I Kings 3:5, the Lord appeared to Solomon in a dream. In it He said, "Ask! What shall I give you?" Solomon's answer was very pleasing to God. Here is what he said,

> "Now, O Lord my God, You have made Your servant king . . . but I am a little child; I do not know how to go out or come in. And Your servant is in the midst of Your people who You have chosen, a great people, too numerous to be numbered or counted. Therefore give to Your servant an understanding heart to judge Your people, that I may discern between good and evil. For who is able to judge this great people of Yours?" (I Kings 3:7–9)

The Lord's response is so significant to the outcome of Solomon's life that I'm going to write it out word for word here. God said,

"Because you have asked this then, and have not asked long life for yourself, nor have asked riches for yourself, nor have asked the life of your enemies, but have asked for yourself understanding to discern justice, behold, I have done according to your words; see, I have given you a wise and understanding heart, so that there has not been anyone like you before you, nor shall any like you arise after you. And I have also given you what you have not asked: both riches and honor, so that there shall not be anyone like you among the kings all your days." (I Kings 3:11–13)

Wow! To think that Solomon had enough wisdom to ask God for more wisdom! That's pretty incredible. But to think about all that God granted him in return, like riches and long life, is even more incredible. I hope you're beginning to see what an extraordinary man Solomon was. According to the Bible, he *was* one of the wisest men who ever lived because of his great understanding.

Solomon's reputation for wisdom went far beyond the land of Israel. I Kings 4:34 says, "And men of all nations, from all the kings of the earth who had heard of his wisdom, came to hear the wisdom of Solomon." When men and women (such as the Queen of Sheba) visited, they usually brought gifts of huge proportion to demonstrate their appreciation to Solomon. This made the king even wealthier, making God's promises come true.

One of Solomon's greatest achievements was in how he used his wealth. Much of it was used to build a beautiful Temple for the Lord as God had told David he would. The dimensions and furnishings of the Temple were staggering. It was built of all kinds of special woods, like cedar from Phoenicia, and overlaid with pure gold. Much like the Tabernacle (that was used for worship in the wilderness), the Temple contained an inner sanctuary, or Most Holy Place. This became the sacred resting place for the Ark of the Covenant. After about 400 years, the Ark of the Covenant had a permanent home. Also like the Tabernacle, each and every item or furnishing in the Temple had great spiritual meaning.

The significance of the new Temple for the Lord was tremendous. For the Jew, it became the most sacred and valued building ever to exist. It wasn't special because of who built it; it was special because of *who* lived there. The Bible says,

"And it came to pass, when the priests came out of the holy place, that the cloud filled the house of the Lord, so that the priests could not continue ministering because of the cloud; for the glory of the Lord filled the house of the Lord. Then Solomon spoke: 'The Lord said He would dwell in the dark cloud. I have surely built You an exalted house, and a place for You to dwell in forever.' " (I Kings 8:10–13)

Otherwise, Solomon's great wisdom is made evident in the books he wrote. From the Old Testament, Solomon wrote the Book of Ecclesiastes, the Song of Solomon, and most of the Book of Proverbs. In particular, Solomon wrote a lot concerning his own discovery that wealth and fame are *not* everything. He would know because he owned just about everything a man could own back then. (He is still known as one of the wealthiest men who ever lived.) Yet, for most of his life he was wise enough to know that the Lord was the best source of fulfillment over riches or fame.

Unfortunately, Solomon reached a point later in his life when he failed to practice what he preached. He began to accumulate far more horses, riches, and women than were necessary for one king. His abundance violated an

The pomegranate was a sacred emblem to the Jews. This solid gold one may have survived from Solomon's Temple.

instruction for kings as given in Deuteronomy 17:16. It states, "He shall not multiply horses for himself, neither shall he multiply wives for himself, lest his heart turn away, nor shall he greatly multiply silver and gold for himself."

Solomon became guilty of all these indulgences. He had horses, riches, silver, and gold. But his greatest downfall was probably his love for women. Especially foreign women. Solomon had as many as 700 wives and 300 concubines! Many of these women were probably gifts to the king, as was the custom back then. Nonetheless, they were his.

But the true problem was that Solomon began to cater to the false gods of all his wives. Many of them worshiped Baal. I Kings 11:4 says, "For it was so, when Solomon was old, that his wives turned his heart after other gods; and his heart was not loyal to the Lord his God, as was the heart of his father David."

It is sad that Solomon failed to remain faithful to the Lord who had given him so much. Even with all the wisdom he possessed, Solomon strayed from the God he loved! The Lord was angry. He told Solomon that after his death, his kingdom would be torn in two because of his disobedience. And it was. Israel remained a split nation, divided in two, for centuries to come as a result of the king's actions.

If you remember, in the last days of the judges, the Lord warned the people through Samuel that an earthly king would bring hardship. It was happening. Very few of Israel's later kings ever honored the Lord again as had David and Solomon in their early years. Though Solomon's later reign was flawed by sin, he left us a great legacy of wisdom in the books he wrote while walking close to God. We would be wise to heed Solomon's sayings better than he did himself.

ACTIVITY 33

ALL STUDENTS

Make your Memory Cards for Lessons 31–33. Highlight the name and date of David (c. 1055 B.C.) on his card; his is the third date for you to memorize! (Quick, what were the first and second dates?)

33A—Younger and Middle Students

A close friend of mine, Lisa Wilson,[1] created the idea of making Proverbs notebooks. She felt that even before children could read, their spirit could discern the things of God. So, by the time her children were 3, she had them begin to write and illustrate the Proverbs so that the word of God would begin to be a rich part of their lives.

You can do the same. In a special notebook or journal, write out some of the Proverbs of Solomon as found in the Bible. Illustrate them. (If you are very young, have your teacher write out the verses.) Whenever you come across a Proverb with a contrast, write one sentence at the top of the page and the contrasting sentence in the middle of the page. Make a little drawing under each sentence. Make this a regular practice and save this collection of Proverbs and drawings for your own children one day.

Here is an example, contrasting "the wicked" and "the righteous."

Proverbs 10:25

When the whirlwind passes by, the wicked is no more,

But the righteous has an everlasting foundation.

---

1. For more creative ideas from Lisa and Randy Wilson, look for the book *Celebrations of Faith* by Cook Communications. It is a treasury of inspirational activities for the whole family.

The Mystery of History

33B—Middle and Older Students

Research the special features of the Temple of Solomon. It contained much of the same symbolism as the Tabernacle. What was it built with? Who could enter it? Photocopy pictures you come across in your research that depict what scholars believe the Temple looked like. It is no longer standing today. Write your findings and file them under "Asia: Israel" in your Student Notebook.

33C—Older Students

Read the Book of Ecclesiastes. In your own words, write a few paragraphs to summarize the conclusion found in Ecclesiastes 12:11–14. Find out what a "goad" is. What is the word picture Solomon is creating here? File this short paper under "Asia: Israel."

TAKE ANOTHER LOOK!

Review 11: Lessons 31–33

Wall of Fame

1. *King Saul (c. 1100 B.C.)*—Give Saul an angry face.

2. *David (c. 1055 B.C.)*—David needs a cross on him to signify the lineage of Christ. Otherwise, give him the symbol of your choice (for example, a harp, slingshot, crown, pen and book of the Psalms). **Remember, this is a date to memorize.**

3. *Solomon (c. 1015 B.C.)*—He could be depicted with a dollar sign for his riches, books for his wisdom, or hearts for his many wives. Include all of these if you have room. He also needs to have a golden cross on him to signify the lineage of Christ.

SomeWHERE in Time

1. In a Bible atlas, find Mt. Gilboa in Israel where Saul and Jonathan were killed in battle.

2. We will look at Jerusalem from two different angles today. From a distance and close up.
   a. In an atlas, find the modern city of Jerusalem in Israel. This is where David moved his capital and where Solomon later built the Temple. What other countries border Israel today?
   b. On a close-up map of the city of Jerusalem, locate the Temple. Do you know what is standing in the same place today? (The Dome of the Rock, the most sacred site of the Islamic faith)

3. Older Students: Using a Bible atlas as a resource, on Outline Map 7, "Israel," shade the extent of David's kingdom in one color and the extent of Solomon's kingdom in another color. Label it "The Early Kings of Israel." File it under "Asia: Israel."

WHAT DID YOU LEARN?

Week 11: *Quiz*

True or False? Circle your answer.

1.	The sons of Noah were Jubal and Tubal-Cain.	T F
2.	The Sumerians developed cuneiform writing.	T F
3.	At the Palace of Knossos, the Lord confused man's language.	T F
4.	The pyramids in Egypt are considered one of the Seven Wonders of the Ancient World.	T F
5.	Abraham had 12 sons, who became the 12 tribes of Israel.	T F
6.	China is naturally isolated by mountains, oceans, and deserts.	T F
7.	After Moses, Joshua led the Israelites into the land of Canaan.	T F
8.	Amenhotep IV and Nefertiti worshiped all the gods of Egypt.	T F
9.	Tutankhamen's tomb was found intact by archaeologist Sir George Gilgamesh.	T F
10.	Ruth, who was not an Israelite, was from the land of Philistia.	T F
11.	Gideon hid from the Midianites in a winepress while threshing grain.	T F
12.	King Wen was first to overthrow the Shang dynasty of China and start the Zhou dynasty.	T F
13.	The prophet Samuel was dedicated by Ruth as a baby to serve in the temple.	T F
14.	As a young man, Saul was highly talented and had the makings of a great king.	T F
15.	Eventually, Saul was killed by David in battle.	T F
16.	David moved his capital to Jerusalem, which has been called the city of David ever since.	T F
17.	David wrote most of the Book of Proverbs.	T F
18.	Solomon was one of the wealthiest men who ever lived.	T F

Bonus: What does the letter "c." stand for before a date in history?

✓ WHAT DO YOU KNOW?

Pretest 12

Who Am I? From the list below, choose the word that you think best answers the question.

1. I am used to make a stinky but beautiful dye. Who am I?

2. We developed the first "phonetic" alphabet. Who are we?

3. I am a country divided in half. Who am I?

4. I am the son of Solomon who was not so wise. Who am I?

5. I was formed by Jeroboam as something to worship. What am I?

6. I am called "the fiery prophet" of God. Who am I?

7. We brought Elijah food in the wilderness. What are we?

8. I took Elijah up into heaven. What am I?

WORD BANK

Israel	Elijah	ravens
murex snail	Rehoboam	Phoenicians
chariot of fire	golden calf	

THE PHOENICIANS
LESSON 34

At the same time that Israel was adjusting to its new kings, the Phoenician people were climbing to the height of their civilization. We practically know more about the products of the Phoenician people than about the people themselves. They were known for their goods.

The Phoenicians were originally the Canaanites and lived on the coast of the Mediterranean near Israel. Their capital was Sidon, a name that meant to "catch fish." Living on the coast probably led to a lot of fishing. (The Philistines were further south on the same coast.) The Phoenicians maintained their place on the map at least through the days of Paul's missionary journeys. Now the countries of Lebanon, Syria, and Israel occupy the land.

Since the Phoenicians lived by the Mediterranean, they had a lot of experience with the sea. They became well known as the greatest seafarers and traders of the ancient age. Because they could sail well, they traveled all over the Mediterranean world trading their goods and colonizing new cities. They went as far west as Spain and colonized many parts of northern Africa. (You might want to remember that they settled a city named Carthage in Northern Africa. It becomes fairly important later on in history.)

One of the Phoenicians' most famous goods was a beautiful purple-red dye. It came from the gland of a sea snail called a murex snail. Expensive cloth was made from this dye and was cherished by the Greeks and Romans. But it was a smelly job to make it. The snails were collected in huge nets and then left to rot. Eventually workers could skim a liquid off the top to make the dye. The city of Tyre, near the capital, became rich from this trade but was also known for

This unusual plate or strainer was made by the Phoenicians between 1000 and 500 B.C. Its exact use is unknown.

the stinky garlic-like odor. The Phoenicians might have derived their name from this reddish dye because the word "phoinos" means "red" in Greek.

Another trade item of the Phoenicians was transparent glass. The art of glass blowing is very complicated. We can hardly imagine life without it. But before the Phoenicians, few people in that region could make it. (The Egyptians were already pretty good at it.)

Even more importantly, the Phoenicians had a 30-letter alphabet that is the basis of our language today! Up until this time, other cultures used symbols to represent whole words or parts of words. People would have to learn hundreds of symbols to communicate in writing.

The Phoenicians along with the Hebrews began to make symbols to represent just *one* sound. Their first alphabet had only 22 characters, but thousands of words could be made by combining them. Did you learn to read using "phonics"? You can thank the Phoenicians for their contribution to this system. In fact, even the word Bible comes from "Byblos," which was a Phoenician port. The Greeks used this word for "book."

There are two Phoenician people who we know about from stories in the Bible. One is King Hiram of Tyre. He sold cedar wood to Solomon when he built the Temple of Jerusalem. Have you ever heard of the "cedars of Lebanon"? That country has always been famous for its trees. Remember that Phoenicia was where Lebanon is today.

The other well-known Phoenician we know of was the evil Jezebel. King Ahab of Israel, whom we will study later, married this princess of Tyre. It wasn't a good situation. Jezebel became responsible for the death of many of Israel's prophets. She even tried to kill Elijah.

Overall, the Phoenicians failed to adopt a faith that would bring them blessings. Though they were neighbors to the Hebrews, they worshiped their own false gods. In Ezekiel 26, the Lord foretold the future of this nation through His prophets. He said, "they will plunder your riches and pillage your merchandise . . . I will make you like the top of a rock; you shall be a place for spreading nets, and you shall never be rebuilt, for I the Lord have spoken . . . How you have perished, O one inhabited by seafaring men." (Ezek. 26:12, 14, 17) Now that we understand the way of life of the Phoenicians, it makes this prophecy more meaningful.

The Bible forbids the worship of false idols. This terra-cotta idol of Baal, a Phoenician fertility god, dates back to 1000-700 B.C.

The Phoenicians did not leave behind a great legacy of religion or philosophy, and their civilization did disappear as God prophesied. But they left their mark by the goods they invented and traded. When you see the Bible or study phonics, remember the Phoenicians and the city of Byblos on the coast of the Mediterranean.

ACTIVITY 34

34A—Younger Students

Visit a glass blower. What is glass made out of? Why do they heat it? Isn't glass neat? Count the number of ways it is used around your home.

34B—Younger and Middle Students

You will need to have adult supervision for this activity.
Make a stinky dye.

Materials: Blender, strawberries, blueberries, garlic cloves, strainer, old cloth

In a blender, add a handful of each fruit. Blend thoroughly. Note the good aroma. Now, add a few garlic cloves just for odor. Blend and smell again. If it's not stinky enough, add more garlic. Strain the mixture, and try to dye an old piece of cloth. It may have to sit for awhile.

Imagine a city that kept an odor like that. Can you think of any cities near you that have an odor due to industry?

Copy by hand or photocopy the early Phoenician alphabet. Compare the letters to our letters. Send a short note to a friend with the Phoenician alphabet. Include the code for them to translate. File the alphabet (or copy of your note) under "Asia: Israel."

a	⋉	b	ꓹ	g	ꓶ	d	△	h	ꓴ
w	Y	z	I	ḥ	⊞	t	⊗	y	ꓜ
k	ꓤ	l	ꓡ	m	ꕽ	n	ꕾ	s	ꓫ
o	○	s	ꕀ	P	ꓶ	q	φ	r	ꓯ
š	W	t	+						

---

c. 925 B.C.

THE KINGDOM OF ISRAEL DIVIDES

LESSON 35

When we last studied the life of Solomon, we knew he had made Israel the greatest nation in the world at that time. Why then do we find the Kingdom of Israel divided after just 100 years or so? In part it had to do with Solomon's own sin at the end of his reign, but it also had to do with the mistakes made by his own son. Here is that story.

Upon Solomon's death, his son Rehoboam took charge as king. He wasn't wise at all like his father had been. Early in his reign he was harsh to his own people. He became so after consulting with the wrong men. It says in I Kings 12:8, "But he [Rehoboam] rejected the counsel which the elders gave him, and consulted the young men who had grown up with him." Their counsel was disastrous. Rehoboam declared, "My father laid a heavy yoke on you, I will add to your yoke; my father chastised you with whips, but I will chastise you with scourges!" (I Kings 12:11)

Understandably, 10 tribes of Israel rebelled against Rehoboam and his terrible attitude. They kept the name of Israel but were often referred to as the Northern Kingdom. They selected Jeroboam as their own king.

I wish I could write that the new Israel remained a faithful nation. But unfortunately, Jeroboam was not a wise *spiritual* leader. He made golden calves for the people to worship since the Temple was far away in Jerusalem. (Jerusalem was located south and still under Rehoboam's rule.) What was Jeroboam thinking to lead his people to worship golden calves instead of the living God? I don't know, but he ruled for 22 years in this manner.

And what about the other two tribes of Israel? They remained under the rule of Rehoboam. They were the tribes of Judah and Benjamin. They called themselves Judah for short. (That's where the name "Jew" comes from that we hear today to refer to the Israelites!) We also refer to them as the Southern Kingdom.

Rehoboam reigned over Judah for 17 years, and unfortunately his kingdom did no better in honoring God than the Northern Kingdom. I Kings 14:22 says, "Judah did evil in the sight of the Lord, and they provoked Him to jealousy with their sins which they committed, more than all that their fathers had done."

We will see this pattern over and over again in the history of Israel and Judah. It is important to keep straight which kingdom is which if you want to understand the rest of the Old Testament, especially the prophets. You see God sent prophets to *both* kingdoms to try to turn the people from their sins. God loved these people. We have amazing insight into the Creator of the Universe because His words, spoken through the prophets, have been recorded.

ACTIVITY 35

ALL STUDENTS

Memorize this date: c. 925 B.C., the Kingdom of Israel divides.

35A—Younger and Middle Students

Memorize some facts about the two kingdoms of Israel that will help you keep them straight. Here is a simple pattern that will help. Each word in the columns below is in alphabetical order! The "I" in Israel comes before the "J" in Judah; "N" comes before "S" in Northern and Southern; and "A" comes before "B" in the words Assyrians and Babylonians.* Everything works except the capital cities, so we'll keep them in parentheses. Younger students need only write out the lines with bold words following the instructions below.

1. Take a piece of paper and fold it lengthwise like a hot dog. On the outside, write the words, "The Kingdom of Israel Divides" (c. 925 B.C.)
2. Open the paper. On the upper piece (above the crease), write out the first two lines of the information below. (Younger students need only write out the first line.)
3. On the lower half (below the crease), write out the next two lines. (Younger students write only the third line.)
4. Go back and circle the first letter in each word to accent it.
5. Punch three holes in the top and file this in your Student Notebook under "Europe: Israel."

Israel	**Northern Kingdom**	**Assyrians** Conquer
(Samaria, the capital)	(10 tribes)	
Judah	**Southern Kingdom**	**Babylonians** Conquer
(Jerusalem, the capital)	(2 tribes)	

*(We haven't studied Assyria and Babylon yet in relation to Israel, but we will see them over and over again later. It will benefit you now to memorize these.)

35B—Middle and Older Students

I believe it is absolutely essential to know the kings and prophets of the two different kingdoms of Israel in order to understand the fascinating stories of the Old Testament. Therefore, I want you to begin two pages in your Student Notebook on the kings and prophets of Israel and Judah. (File under "Asia: Israel.") Set them up like the samples in the Activity Supplement in the Appendix. We will add more names to these pages over time. The above exercise may be helpful to students of any age.

ELIJAH, THE FIERY PROPHET

LESSON 36

The Bible is full of extraordinary people. The prophet Elijah is certainly one of them. Let's get to know him and how he developed the reputation of being a fiery prophet.

First, Elijah was no city boy. He was brought up in the rugged country and his personality reflected it. As such, Elijah was not the kind of prophet who wrote things down—he just spoke. And very boldly at that. That is why Elijah is written about in the Bible, but he doesn't have his own book like some of the other prophets do.

Elijah lived during the reigns of Ahab, Ahaziah, and Jehoram. These were all kings of Israel, the Northern Kingdom. (There had been lots of kings since Jeroboam, but we won't study them all.) Ahab "did evil in the sight of the Lord, more than all who were before him." (I Kings 16:30) That's a pretty bad track record. One of Ahab's mistakes was marrying Jezebel the princess from Tyre in Phoenicia. Remember the Phoenicians? Many of them, including Jezebel, worshiped Baal. As a result, Ahab, a king over Israel, became a worshiper of Baal, too.

Because of Ahab's sin, Elijah proclaimed under God's instruction that it wouldn't rain until he said so. After giving Ahab this bad news, Elijah had to flee for his life. Ahab and Jezebel both wanted to kill Elijah.

But God took care of Elijah, even in the wilderness where he hid from Ahab. The Lord sent ravens to feed Elijah bread and meat every day for years. God also led an old widow to care for and feed Elijah. In gratitude to the widow and to show he was a true man of God, Elijah miraculously kept food in the widow's house. If that wasn't enough, Elijah even raised the widow's son from the dead!

After years of hiding, Elijah finally met up with Ahab again at a place called Mt. Carmel. Here they had a showdown of the power of the gods, and it involved FIRE. Elijah's motives were purely to demonstrate who God was. He prayed, "Hear me, O Lord, hear me, that this people may know that You are the Lord God, and that You have turned their hearts back to You again." (I Kings 18:37) And that is what happened on Mt. Carmel. God sent down a great fire and consumed the sacrifice that had been drenched with water. Many people believed in God that day. The prophets of Baal were executed.

When Ahab returned to his wife Jezebel and told her all that he had seen, she plotted to kill Elijah just as she had slaughtered the other prophets. Elijah found out and was so distressed by this woman that he pleaded in humility for God to take his life! The Lord had much for Elijah to do yet. So, He sent an angel to bake a cake over hot coals to nourish Elijah. Twice the Lord did that because He was preparing Elijah for 40 days without food.

God's next instruction to Elijah was to anoint Jehu as the future king over Israel and to anoint Elisha as the prophet to take Elijah's place. But before either Jehu or Elisha ruled, Elijah had some last business with Ahab. He confronted Ahab one more time about his sin.

This time it had to do with a vineyard. Ahab and Jezebel had worked a shady deal to obtain an innocent man's property. Elijah exposed this wrongdoing, and he also prophesied a gruesome death for Jezebel. (Which later came true when she fell to her death and her body was eaten by dogs!)

The last miracle of Elijah before he was taken away was to prove once and for all that he was the prophet of God to the next king, Ahaziah. Ahaziah was an evil king of Israel who had called upon a false god to try to know his future. Through Elijah, God sent FIRE down from heaven and consumed Ahaziah's men three different times to show who was God! Then Ahaziah died just as Elijah prophesied he would. Jehoram ruled next and then Jehu, whom Elijah anointed as king.

Elijah never died a natural death. It is written in II Kings 2:11 that "suddenly a chariot of FIRE appeared with horses of FIRE, and separated the two of them [Elisha was watching nearby; caps mine]; and Elijah went up by a whirlwind into heaven." When you consider the boldness of this prophet and the difficult life he lived in order to speak the truth, his glorious departure was only fitting. His life's message was clear. The Lord abhors evil and the worship of other gods, but He is merciful to those who will turn toward Him.

It says in the last words of Malachi in the Old Testament that Elijah will come again. That is why we hear his name many times in the New Testament. People were always looking for him. He did appear at the transfiguration of Jesus. And, on one occasion, Jesus implies that John the Baptist is Elijah. (Matt. 11:14) Bible scholars don't agree on the interpretation of this passage. So, no one knows for sure if Elijah has already appeared, or if he still will. Read Malachi 4:5–6 and Matthew 11 for yourself. What do you think?

ACTIVITY 36

ALL STUDENTS

Make your Memory Cards for Lessons 34–36. Mark "The Kingdom of Israel Divides" (c. 925 B.C.) with a special highlighter as a date to memorize.

36A—Younger Students

Read out loud I Kings 19:4–8. Act out the scene of Elijah as he was ministered to by angels. Take some food, such as a rice cake, and pretend to bake it over coals. Provide water, too, as the story says. (These verses make a good script for two young people to act out because there are two short speaking parts.)

36B—Middle and Older Students

Add the names of these kings to your list of Israel's kings. Highlight the five we have mentioned in our study so far. Across from the kings, add the following prophets' names.

ISRAEL

Kings	Prophets
1. JEROBOAM	Ahijah
2. Nadab	
3. Baasha	Jehu (the prophet)
4. Ela	
5. Zimri	
6. Omri	
7. AHAB	ELIJAH and Micaiah
8. AHAZIAH	
9. JEHORAM	
10. JEHU (the king)	

36C—Older Students

1. From what you already know, consider the comparison of Elijah to John the Baptist. List Biblical examples of each of their ministries.

2. Consider the last words of Malachi in the Old Testament about the return of Elijah. Investigate the notes of different authors in Bible commentaries as to what they believe the coming of Elijah to mean. File your comparison under "Asia: Israel" in your Student Notebook.

TAKE ANOTHER LOOK!

Review 12: Lessons 34–36

Wall of Fame

1. *The Phoenicians (c. 1000 B.C.)*—Make a snail to help you remember the Phoenicians. (Sprinkle a little garlic powder on it, and it will smell, too!)

2. *Israel divides (c. 925 B.C.)*—Create a small picture of a palace and cut it in two with jagged edges. On one half, write "Israel (Northern Kingdom)" and on the other half, "Judah (Southern Kingdom)." **Remember, this is a date to memorize.**

   Now that Israel has been divided, create a split in your timeline. Make two horizontal strips of paper run parallel to one another. Mark the top one as the Northern Kingdom and the bottom as the Southern Kingdom. Place the kings and the prophets we study in the proper kingdoms as we get to them.

3. *Elijah (c. 859 B.C.)*—Place Elijah in a chariot of flames in the Northern Kingdom.

SomeWHERE in Time

1. In a historical atlas, find the Phoenician cities of Sidon, Tyre, and Byblos. (On some maps, Byblos is named Gebal.) On the northern coast of Africa, find the city of Carthage, a Phoenician colony.

2. Because the division of Israel is so important to understanding the Old Testament, this is a good time to make a salt map of the area.

   Materials: Cardboard, glue, toothpicks, and a copy of Outline Map 7, "Israel," for each student; one physical map of Israel for all students to view; blue, orange, and green food coloring; salt dough. (To make salt dough, mix 1 cup salt, 1 cup white flour, and water to thicken like mud.)

   a. Divide the dough into three clumps. With food coloring, make one clump blue, one orange, and one green.

   b. Glue the map of Israel to the cardboard. Shape the dough onto the map to make these places as listed. Use a physical map to know where there may be some mountains you can create with the stiff dough.

   • Shape Judah out of the orange dough.

   • Shape Israel out of the green dough.

   • With the blue dough, shape the Mediterranean, the Dead Sea, and the Jordan River.

   • With toothpicks, flag the capital city of each country—Jerusalem for Judah and Samaria for Israel.

   If the salt map is too much for this week's schedule, draw in the two kingdoms on Outline Map 7, "Israel." Include the capitals of Jerusalem and Samaria using a Bible atlas for reference. File this map under "Asia: Israel."

The Mystery of History

WHAT DID YOU MISS?

Week 12: Exercise

Beat the Clock. To play this game, you will need a timer, your timeline (or Contents page), and copies of this exercise. You will need one for every participant (including the teacher!).

See how fast each of you can list these events, people, or places in the proper chronological order. I recommend using pencil and having an eraser handy.

Hint: First write down the date of each item next to it in the first column; *then,* in the second column, list the items in the order in which they occurred. The first two have been done to help you get started.

_____1. Ramses II	1. Jubal and Tubal-Cain
_____2. Jubal and Tubal-Cain	2. Noah and the flood
_____3.Kingdom of Israel divides	3. _____
_____4. Noah and the flood	4. _____
_____5. King Saul	5. _____
_____6. King Tutankhamen	6. _____
_____7. Hammurabi	7. _____
_____8. Zhou dynasty begins	8. _____
_____9. Elijah	9. _____
_____10. Stonehenge is started	10. _____
_____11. Tower of Babel	11. _____
_____12. Solomon	12. _____
_____13. Abraham	13. _____
_____14. Gideon	14. _____

Final Time:_____

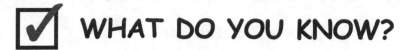

☑ WHAT DO YOU KNOW?

Pretest 13

Unscramble the words to fill in the blanks. (There is a word bank for younger spellers at the bottom of the page. Older students should cover it up!)

1. Elisha witnessed (jhliaE) _____ being swept up into a chariot of fire.

2. The Old Testament records that Elisha performed at least 17 (lesircam) _____.

3. The prophet Joel is considered a (omnir) _____ prophet because his book is short, not because it is less important.

4. Joel wrote about a devastating (stcolu) _____ plague to communicate to the Judeans their fate.

5. Like Joel, Obadiah was also considered a minor (rohppet) _____.

6. Obadiah spoke prophesy to the descendants of (ausE) _____, the twin of Jacob and son of Isaac.

7. Homer, who wrote the *Iliad* and the *Odyssey,* was probably (inbld) _____.

8. Homer included a lot of Greek (thymgyloo) _____ in his stories.

The Mystery of History

ELISHA
(ISRAEL'S PROPHET)
LESSON 37

The last we saw of Elisha, he was standing next to Elijah as God swept Elijah away in a chariot of fire. Can you even imagine such a sight? It would be life changing. And to Elisha it was. It is recorded that he performed at least 17 miracles in his lifetime. They range from supernatural feedings to complete healings. Elisha was truly a wonderful man!

Already in our study of history, I have mentioned "parallels"—that is, when God uses two similar stories to make a point. The lives and relationship of Elijah and Elisha are somewhat like John the Baptist and Jesus. Elijah, like John, spent a lot of time away from the crowds of people living off the land and boldly speaking for God. Remember that Elijah was fed by ravens in the wilderness. John the Baptist spent time in the wilderness, too, preaching of repentance and eating wild locusts.

Elisha, we will learn, spent more time with the people of Israel, performing gentle life-giving miracles, much as Jesus did. Let's look at a few close-up examples so that you may remember them. Miracles can show us the greatness of God and lead others to believe in Him.

On one occasion, three kings asked Elisha for help in fighting the Moabites. (Do you remember who was a Moabite? It was Ruth.) There had been no rain in Israel, and the troops were parched. Elisha told the soldiers to dig pools in the dry earth, and the pools would be filled. They *were* miraculously filled with water, but to the Moabites it appeared to be blood! A large pool of blood would fool any army into thinking their enemies were dead. But they were not. Unprepared for battle, the Moabites rushed into the camp of the Israelites only to find them alive and well. The Israelites easily defeated them that day.

Another miracle to remember is the healing of Naaman. Naaman lived as far away as the country of Syria, which is north of Israel. Even that far away, Naaman had heard of the amazing miracles of Elisha and his God. You see, Naaman had leprosy and sought out Elisha for healing. And, he wasn't even a Hebrew! Elisha told Naaman to wash in the Jordan River seven times, and he would be healed. Though skeptical at first, Naaman did it. And, he was healed! No one was ever cured of leprosy in those days. Naaman's response was what we might hope for. He said, "Indeed, now I know that there is no God in all the earth, except in Israel." (II Kings 5:15)

One last story to remember about Elisha would be the miracles for the Shunammite woman. This woman had given Elisha a place to stay, but she had no son and her husband was old. For her hospitality, Elisha promised her she would have a son. And she did. Later, however, this boy was very ill and died in his mother's arms. This woman of great faith believed that Elisha could heal her son since he was a "gift" from this man of God. Miraculously, Elisha did revive the boy and gave him life.

Elisha performed miracles for individual citizens as well as for kings and their troops. Even in his death he touched others. When Elisha was buried, another dead man was placed close enough to his bones to make contact. The dead man came back to life! Some theologians see this miracle as a foreshadowing of Jesus' ministry to come: giving life to the dead. What an amazing life we see in Elisha.

ACTIVITY 37

37A—Younger Students

Do some cool experiments with oil and water.

Materials: Cooking oil, water, food coloring

Elisha performed many miracles. One of them was to supernaturally keep a woman's supply of oil from running out. (I Kings 17:8–16) With your mom's help, find some cooking oil in your kitchen. What happens when you try to mix it with water? Add food coloring to some water. Add it drop by drop to a cup of oil. What does your family use oil for? How important might oil have been to the woman Elisha helped?

37B—Middle and Older Students

Add these names to your list of Israel's kings and prophets. Highlight Elisha to indicate our study of him.

ISRAEL

Kings	Prophets
10. Jehu (the king)	ELISHA
11. Jehoahaz	
12. Joash	

37C—Older Students

Compare and contrast the miracles of Elisha with those of Jesus. Make a list of all the miracles you can find that Elisha performed. To the right of your list, write down examples of Jesus' ministry that were similar. For example, consider the miraculous feedings. File your comparisons under "Asia: Israel" in your Student Notebook.

835 B.C.

JOEL AND OBADIAH

LESSON 38

Up until now, almost all the Bible characters we have studied appear in the order they were written about in the books of Genesis and II Kings. Today, though, we will have to flip toward the end of the Old Testament to find the next two people we will study, Joel and Obadiah.

You will notice that the "minor prophets," as Joel and Obadiah are considered to be, are all placed in the back of the Old Testament. That's not because they happened later in history. It's only because they are all short books. And though they are called "minor," they are not any less important than the "major" prophets. "Major" is the name given to the longer books of prophesy such as Jeremiah, Daniel, and Ezekiel, to name a few.

Joel was a prophet to the people of Judah, not to Israel as Elijah and Elisha were. However, Joel was probably alive about the same time as Elisha. Joel and Elisha may or may not have ever known one another because they lived far away from each other. But they did know the same God. The Lord spoke through Joel as He did through Elisha to reveal Himself to His people.

At the time that Joel was a prophet to Judah, Joash (sometimes written as Jehoash) was king. He became king when he was only 7 years old. Even though he was just a child, the Bible says, "Jehoash did what was right in the sight of the Lord all the days in which Jehoida the priest instructed him." (II Kings 12: 2) Finally we see a good king ruling for awhile. Unfortunately, his goodness did not change the ways of all the people of Judah. Some were still sacrificing and burning incense in the high places, which means they were not worshiping the one true God.

The Lord had a message then for these people, and He used Joel to speak it. It was unique in that Joel wrote during the time of a locust plague so terrible that crops were being eaten up, cattle were dying, and people were starving from famine. The Lord used this calamity as a word picture for the people. He told the Judeans that just as the land was wasted by the locusts, so their homeland would be wasted in the future by other countries unless they repented and worshiped the Lord.

Sometimes in reading the Book of Joel, it's hard to tell when he is talking about locusts and when he is talking about soldiers. He describes the locusts like armies that climb walls and march in formation. Joel is also prophesying about some things that may not have happened yet! It says in Joel 2:30–31, "And I will show wonders in the heavens and in the earth: blood and fire and pillars of smoke. The sun shall be turned into darkness, and the moon into blood, before the coming of the great and terrible day of the Lord." These passages are interesting to people who study the end times.

The main point of the Book of Joel was for the people to turn to the Lord. He wanted them to be restored after the famine, both physically and spiritually. "So I will restore to you the years that the swarming locust has eaten…You shall eat in plenty and be satisfied, and praise the name of the Lord your God who has dealt wondrously with you." (Joel 2:25–26)

The prophet Obadiah had a message to another group of people. He spoke to the Edomites. Edom goes way back. Remember Jacob and Esau? Esau was the rough and hairy brother who sold his birthright. Edom means "red" and was used as the name to describe the redheaded Esau and his descendants. They settled in a mountainous region and were rather rugged people.

Obadiah preached to these mountain people and warned them of their future. They apparently were not worshipers of the One true God. They were prideful. Obadiah wrote, "Though you exalt yourself as high as the eagle, and though you set your nest among the stars, from there I will bring you down, says the Lord . . . Will I not in that day, says the Lord, even destroy the wise men from Edom, and understanding from the mountains of Esau?" (Obad. 1:4, 8)

The Lord was serious. The Edomites don't exist any longer, but the descendants of Jacob, the Jews, are still here today. Theologically, Edom represents the fleshly side of man that depends on himself. God really wants us to depend on Him.

ACTIVITY 38

38A—Younger Students

Go on a locust hunt.

If you live in an area where there are locusts, try to catch one and study it for a day. (Then set it free.) If you can, find the shell of a locust stuck on the side of a tree. They climb out of these shells when they grow. If you can't find real ones, look them up in an encyclopedia or library book.

Locusts can be very loud on a summer day. Imagine thousands and thousands of them during the time that Joel wrote.

38B—Middle and Older Students

Research the devastation done by locusts. If you can, obtain a *National Geographic* magazine from December 1915. Your local library may have it archived. This can be fun to look up on microfilm. The magazine contains photos of another locust plague that happened in Jerusalem in 1915.

Write a few paragraphs on the harm that locusts can do. Include photocopies if you can. File this under "Asia: Israel."

38C—Middle and Older Students

Add these names to your list of **Judah's** kings and prophets. Highlight the four we have studied.

JUDAH

Kings	Prophets
1. REHOBOAM	Shemaiah
2. Abijam	
3. Asa	Azariah and Hanani
4. Jehoshaphat	
5. Jehoram	
6. Ahaziah	OBADIAH (exact date unknown)
7. Athaliah (a queen)	
8. JOASH	JOEL

c. 800 B.C.

HOMER

LESSON 39

About the same time that Joel was prophesying to Judah during the terrible locust plague, a man named Homer was living in the area we now know as Greece. We have already studied one of the stories that Homer is remembered for. Do you know what it was? It was the legend of the Trojan Horse.

We don't have a lot of personal information about Homer. Historians think he lived around 800 B.C. and that he was probably blind. That means that Homer may not have actually written down the stories he told. He just "composed them."

If you remember, writing back then was very difficult. Paper had not yet been invented. People were using symbols for words rather than an alphabet. Homer's stories were probably actually written down years after he lived when the language of the Greeks had been refined. They adopted many of their ideas for an alphabet from the Phoenicians.

Homer was what we call a "bard." That was a person who wrote long epics or poems and retold them over and over. That is probably how Homer made a

The early Greeks typically decorated their vases with geometric shapes and patterns.

Homer never wrote down his stories, but as a bard, he recited them over and over to his audiences.

living. A bard was very valuable to people who couldn't read or write themselves. And since there was no TV or radio, a bard could have provided great entertainment to people as well as educating them on some history.

Homer is credited with composing what is called the *Iliad* and the *Odyssey*. They are two long epic poems. The *Iliad* tells the story of the siege of Troy using the giant wooden horse. The *Odyssey* tells of a hero named Odysseus who traveled back to Ithaca after the Trojan War. The original events would have taken place about 1250 B.C. Homer incorporated his belief system into the stories by adding Greek gods and goddesses into the plot.

If you remember, for years historians thought that Homer's tales were just made up because of all the mythology involved. But, as we learned earlier, Heinrich Schliemann excavated the ancient city of Troy and found much evidence to support the possibility that the main events of the stories were real. True or not, Homer's tales were so popular that generations of Greeks memorized them to recite over and over until they were printed. You can still read them today!

Just as a note of interest, there are more original copies of Homer's *Iliad* than there are of most historical documents, like those of Plato or Aristotle. There are, in fact, about 700 of them. That's pretty good for an old book. Did you know, though, that there are about 24,000 handwritten originals of the New Testament? And, about 5,000 of those are in the original Greek language, as was the *Iliad*. There is no comparison between the two figures.

Even more amazing is that the *Iliad* was written anywhere from 700 to 1,500 years after the events of the story took place. The New Testament, on the other hand, was recorded just 15 to 60 years after its events took place. It just goes to show that you can be confident that the Bible is a very historically accurate document when stacked up against other old books. And that's good to know!

ACTIVITY 39

ALL STUDENTS

Make your Memory Cards for Lessons 37–39.

39A—Younger Students

Practice a recitation.

Listen to a short poem as someone else reads it. Memorize what you can and recite it back. Practice over and over again until you can recite the poem perfectly. This is what a bard had to do in the days of ancient Greece. Poems or epics were taught mostly by listening and reciting.

To make it even more interesting, be blindfolded while you listen and recite. Most likely, Homer was blind. Do you think it was harder or easier for Homer to recite without his vision?

39B—Middle Students

Take the time to read *The Children's Homer* and write a short book report on it. Try this approach: Keep a running list of the characters as they are introduced in the story. Keep a separate list of the gods and goddesses mentioned. In your book report, try to explain what happened to the MAIN characters.

Just for your information, the term "mentor" comes from the name of one of the characters of the *Odyssey*. Mentor is the name of someone who cared for and educated Odyssey's son in his absence. A "mentor" today is a caring and influential teacher.

39C—Older Students and Adults

1. Obtain a full translation of the *Iliad* or the *Odyssey*. Read as much of it as you can. It is very difficult in the English prose version by Lang, Leaf and Myers, which is recommended for advanced readers only.

2. I mentioned the validity of the New Testament briefly in the lesson. Turn to the Activity Supplement in the Appendix for more information regarding the subject of the Bible's authenticity.

TAKE ANOTHER LOOK!

Review 13: Lessons 37–39

Wall of Fame

1. *Elisha (c. 840 B.C.)*—He performed so many miracles! Make a symbol of one of your favorites to put with him. Place him just next to Elijah in the Northern Kingdom of Israel.

2. *Joel (835 B.C.)*—Place Joel in the Southern Kingdom with a swarm of locusts around his head.

3. *Obadiah (exact date unknown; place him near Joel to remember the lesson on both prophets)*—Place Obadiah between the Northern and Southern kingdoms on your timeline because he spoke to the Edomites, not the Israelites or the Judeans. Place these words coming out of his mouth, "Woe to Edom."

4. *Homer (c. 800 B.C.)*—Make it appear that he is speaking with a comic strip bubble over his head. Put small X's over his eyes.

SomeWHERE in Time

1. Review the kingdoms of Israel and Judah. Which was the capital city of each? Which of the 12 tribes made up the kingdom of Judah?

2. In a Bible atlas, find the region of Edom. What were the names of the mountains found there?

3. On a map of ancient Greece, find Ithaca where Odysseus was from. Retrace with your finger the story line of the capture of Helen of Troy, according to the legend of the Trojan Horse. Who captured Helen? Where was she taken?

WHAT DID YOU LEARN?

Week 13: *Quiz*

Match the following items by placing the letter next to the number.

_____ 1. Day 1 of Creation

_____ 2. Adam

_____ 3. Canopy

_____ 4. Stonehenge

_____ 5. Jacob

_____ 6. Shang dynasty

_____ 7. Tutankhamen

_____ 8. Samson

_____ 9. Phoenicians

_____ 10. David

_____ 11. Elisha

_____ 12. Joel

_____ 13. Homer

_____ 14. "Anno Domini"

a. The pharaoh whose tomb was found intact

b. A megalithic structure in England

c. A blind bard from Greece

d. The people known for purple-red dye

e. A judge to Israel whose strength was in his hair

f. The making of day and night

g. A great king of Israel before it was divided

h. Lived to be over 900 years old

i. A prophet of Judah during a locust swarm

j. A twin who tricked his father for a blessing

k. "In the year of the Lord"

l. a water vapor covering the Earth

m. the prophet who followed Elijah

n. One of the earliest ruling families of China

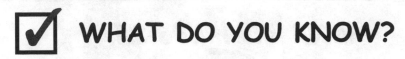

WHAT DO YOU KNOW?

Pretest 14

True or False? Circle your answer.

1. The name of the country of India comes from the Indus River.   T F

2. Hinduism is still a prominent religion in India today.   'T F

3. The caste system of India treats people of all classes equally.   T F

4. The first Olympics were started by the ancient Romans.   T F

5. Men competed in the early Olympics in the nude.   T F

6. Winners of the first Olympics were given medals of gold,
   silver, and bronze.   T F

7. The prophet Jonah was sent to preach to the Egyptian people.   T F

8. Before he was called to preach, the prophet Amos was a fig farmer.   T F

INDIA AND HINDUISM

LESSON 40

In our study of history so far, we have not yet looked at the mysterious country of India. But she has obviously been there, patiently waiting for us to notice her. Today we will study the ancient people of India, the roots of Hinduism (their largest religion), and the "caste system." Each of these contributes to the unique makeup of India today.

In present-day Pakistan, there runs a river called the Indus. Look for it now in a world atlas. As far back as 2500 B.C., a great civilization thrived there with well-planned streets and brick-lined sewers. The country of India gets its name from the Indus Valley. Like the Sumerians we studied earlier, the people of the Indus Valley were quite advanced. But they disappeared. No one knows for sure why they vanished.

Later in history, a group of people who lived in India were the Dravidians. They were dark-skinned and possibly descendants of Ham. Northern India was their home until bands of warriors invaded them around 1500 B.C. These were the mighty Aryans. Their name means "lord of the land." The Aryans left central Asia and poured into India by crossing the great Himalaya Mountains. (Mt. Everest, the highest mountain in the world, is in the Himalayas.) The Aryans were possibly descendants of Japheth and were light-skinned people. Racial tensions developed immediately between the lighter Aryans and the darker Dravidians. As a result, the Dravidians were pushed deep into the south of India.

Much like the Greeks, the Aryans had the tradition of passing on their history by word of mouth. Instead of "epics" they were called "Vedas." It is the collection of these Vedas that forms the basis of the Hindu religion. The oldest written record of the Vedas is the Rig-Veda, which contains over 1,000 hymns recorded in Sanskrit, the language of the Aryans.

Unlike most religions, there is not one man or woman alone who is credited with founding Hinduism. Neither is there one special holy book or event that defines it. Therefore, it is difficult to put a date on the very beginnings of this faith. We do know that its teachings were well established by 800 B.C., which is the same time that Homer was a bard in Greece.

The Hindu religion is difficult to define. The Hindus call it "sanatan dharma," which means "eternal religion." Hindus believe that "Brahman" is the Supreme Spirit who is everywhere and in everything. Strangely to us, the Hindus don't congregate regularly as Christians do to worship their one god. Instead, the Hindu believes there are hundreds of gods to worship as stepping-stones to Brahman. Much like Greek and Roman mythology, the Hindus "see" Brahman in all these different gods and goddesses. Because of this belief, Hindus celebrate the stories of their favorite gods and goddesses at colorful, elaborate festivals and set up shrines of worship in their homes. Their holidays include time spent with family, the giving of gifts, and sharing treats.

Hinduism is greatly based on these kinds of traditions rather than on strict doctrines. That makes the Hindus most often a peaceful people who tolerate other religions. For centuries it was believed that you could only be "born" a Hindu. However, in recent years, people all over the world, including in the United States, are adopting forms of this religion, whether they were born into Hinduism or not.

In Hinduism, people believe that a soul can be "reincarnated," or given another chance to live a good life. They think a person may reincarnate hundreds of times before becoming good enough to reunite with Brahman. People's deeds in this life then determine how they will live their next life. If they lived a bad life, they may even come back as an animal. This belief is so widespread that even if a Hindu was starving, he or she wouldn't kill an animal to eat it. Cows, in particular, have become a sacred animal to the Hindus and are known to walk the streets of even the busiest cities. This belief of rebirth into other people and animals is also called the "law of Karma."

The law of Karma, along with the prejudices between the Aryans and the Dravidians, led the country of India thousands of years ago to develop what is called a "caste system." The Aryans used this system to separate themselves from the Dravidians. They created four major ranks that people lived in. The highest rank was the "Brahmans," or the priests. Next to these were the "Kshatriyas," who were warriors and rulers. Next were the "Vaisyuas," the farmers and craftsmen. Last were the "Sudras." They were the unskilled laborers.

Unfortunately, some people were so low in society that they were beneath the Sudras. These people were labeled the outcastes or "untouchables." In 1947, the government of India outlawed the class of "untouchables" to help these people have a better way of life.

The caste system is very foreign to the Western world. In the United States, a person can be born into poverty but rise up to success through many forms of achievement. For example, Abraham Lincoln was born into a poor family but rose to become president of the United States. But in ancient India, the castes that people were born into were permanent. Even today, there are about 3,000 castes that exist among the Hindus of India. They are subcultures based on one's birthplace and occupation.

It is very important to understand the Hindu belief system in order to grasp the history of India itself. The poverty that is in India today is complicated. But, more than likely, some of the problems come from the caste system that was started thousands of years ago as part of Hinduism and prejudice. Later, we will learn that another major religion, Buddhism, came from a man who wanted to change the unfair caste system of the Hindus.

ACTIVITY 40

40A—Younger and Middle Students

Make a diagram of the caste system.

1. Take an 8½-by-11-inch piece of paper and cut it into a pyramid-shaped triangle.
2. Divide the triangle horizontally into four sections.
3. Write the names of the four castes on the levels you created.
4. Glue this pyramid onto a regular piece of notebook paper. Title it "Social Classes of India." File this activity in the "Asia: India" portion of your Student Notebook.

40B—Middle Students

1. Using books from the library, look at the people and places of India. Find out what you can about the "untouchables" and how difficult their lives were. If you choose to write about it, file it under "Asia: India."
2. Research the Taj Mahal. It is a beautiful palace known throughout the world as a landmark of India. Who built it and why? Write a one-paragraph summary with a photocopy of the site. File it under "Asia: India."

40C—Older Students and Adults

We will be studying several of the major world religions. Beginning with Hinduism, develop a format to compare and contrast these religions to Christianity. There are several methods but try to include the main points listed below. File your paper under "Asia: India" in your Student Notebook.

1. The founder of the religion and date of origination.

2. The source of authority (written works of the religion, visions, prophecy).

3. The doctrine of God (believing there is one God or many gods).

4. The doctrine of Jesus Christ (believing Jesus was God in the flesh or just a prophet).

5. The belief in sin.

6. The doctrine of salvation. (On what basis is sin forgiven or accounted for?)

7. The doctrine of things to come. (Is there a belief in life after death or in a coming judgment of the world?)

8. What draws people to this religion (lifestyle, ritual, heritage, etc.)?

776 B.C.

THE OLYMPIC GAMES

LESSON 41

Do you like to watch the Olympics? I love to watch ice-skating in the winter games and gymnastics in the summer games. Most people have their own favorites. Well, believe it or not, the very first recorded Olympics dates as far back as 776 B.C.! The Greeks started the competitive events that are still enjoyed so much today.

The concept of athletics in Greece was most likely started as a means of keeping soldiers in shape for battle. When not in war, men would train to run fast, throw hard, and wrestle. These training times developed into intense competition.

The first Olympic races were held on the plains of Olympia in Elis, Greece. The Eleans started the games with just foot races in honor of Zeus, the king of their gods. As the event caught on to surrounding city-states, the sports grew to include jumping, discus throwing, javelin throwing, and wrestling. They later added boxing and chariot racing.

A flaming torch was passed from one runner to another at the early Olympics—the start of a tradition that continues today.

Women were not allowed to compete in the games, and in fact they couldn't even watch them. That may have been for the best since the athletes competed in the nude! Women did have their own running events in a festival called Heraia. It was named after the goddess Hera.

One of the more demanding Olympic games was the pentathlon. It was the combination of five different events—running, wrestling, jumping, discus and javelin throwing. This concept of multiple events is still used today to find the most well-rounded athletes.

The Olympics lasted only five days and was held every four years. Winners were given olive wreaths, palm branches, and woolen ribbons. Just like today, some of the athletes became favorites, and people would flock to see them. Some men became "professionals" and made their living by representing their city-state.

The grounds for the games were quite elaborate. Just like today, huge buildings and stadiums were erected specifically for the Olympics. As many as 40,000 spectators could view a track event at one time.

The ancient Olympics lasted until A.D. 395 when Olympia was destroyed by earthquakes. A Frenchman resurrected the tradition of the games in the late 1800s. Many things have remained true to the early Olympic games. The famous lighting of the Olympic flame comes from an ancient relay race in which a flaming torch was passed from runner to runner. The winner lit a fire up on an altar. Doesn't that sound familiar?

Athletics have been a part of most cultures around the world. But we can thank the ancient Greeks for starting the spectacular tradition of the Olympics that we still enjoy today.

ACTIVITY 41

41A—Younger and Middle Students

With your family or school group, create a mini-Olympics and hold five events similar to a pentathlon.

1. Running: If outdoors, have a real race, like a 50-yard dash. If you must be indoors, race on your knees and see who can "run" the fastest down a short stretch.
2. Wrestling: Compete in arm wrestling.
3. Jumping: See who can jump the highest by taping a piece of paper on a wall and jumping with a light-colored marker in your hand. Let the highest mark be the winner.
4. Discus throwing: If the weather permits, see who can launch a Frisbee flying disc the farthest. If you are limited to the indoors, try flicking coins across a room.
5. Javelin throwing: If outdoors, see who can throw a long stick the farthest with a running start. If indoors, resort to flicking toothpicks across a table.

Indoors or out, this can be fun if you like competition. One of the Olympic rules was for good sportsmanship to be followed. Keep up the tradition!

41B—Younger and Middle Students

Create a wreath for the winner of the mini-Olympic games.

Materials: Bay leaves, pipe cleaners, glue

Using pipe cleaners, shape a wreath to fit on someone's head. Glue on leaves. Have a ceremony to "crown" the winner!

41C—Older Students

Research more on the history of the Olympics. What years were the Olympics canceled or boycotted and why? File your findings under "Europe: Greece."

JONAH AND AMOS

LESSON 42

Can a man really live in the belly of a big fish? According to the Bible, it can happen. Today we will study Jonah, the prophet who tried to hide from God. We will also look at Amos because Jonah and Amos were prophets at about the same time. Because the story of Jonah is quite familiar, we will begin with it.

Most of us can relate to the character of Jonah. He struggled with obedience to God. He was bitter toward the people of Nineveh because they were so evil. That is why he fled from the Lord after receiving instructions to preach to the Ninevites to repent. He tried to avoid his mission by jumping on a boat headed to Tarshish. As the story goes, he didn't get very far.

The Bible says that a great storm came up. Realizing his disobedience to God, Jonah believed the storm to be his fault. With great courage Jonah allowed himself to be thrown overboard. I think he fully expected to die! But God, in His great sovereignty, had more interesting plans for him. Jonah was swallowed by a big fish and remained there for three days. I suppose he learned to pray like never before during those damp, dark days. The fish spit him out as the Bible says, and Jonah was given a second chance.

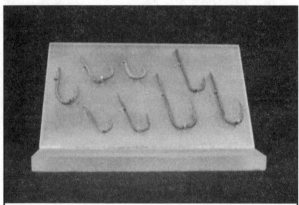

It would have taken hooks much bigger than these to catch the fish that swallowed Jonah! These are real Assyrian fishhooks.

Why didn't Jonah go to Nineveh in the first place? Who were these people that he so despised? Nineveh was in the land of Assyria. They were brutal enemies to the Israelites and known for horrendous acts of cruelty. They had a reputation for skinning their prisoners alive! It is no wonder Jonah was hesitant to go there.

The story of Jonah is significant in many ways. For one, when Jonah was swallowed by a big fish for three days, we see another one of those "parallels" in history. Jesus Himself said that Jonah's three days of darkness are symbolic of the three days Christ was dead before he rose from the grave. (Matt. 12:40)

We also learn from this story that the Lord was concerned for people other than the Israelites. Just as He sent Jesus to save the Gentiles and the Jews, He sent Jonah to preach a powerful message to the Ninevites. Jonah just didn't understand the big picture. The story ends well, as the Ninevites he despised *did* repent. The very enemies of Israel listened to a foreign prophet! The story is quite amazing. Unfortunately, the revival in Nineveh didn't last long enough. Eventually the Assyrians went to war against the Israelites.

Amos, on the other hand, was a different kind of prophet. Though he lived in Judah, he was told by God to go to Israel. Unlike Jonah, he immediately did what he was told. Amos was actually from a small town near Jerusalem in Judah. Like Jonah, he went to a place practically foreign to him. He was a small-town herdsman and a fig farmer asked to move to the big city of Samaria in Israel.

The Book of Amos in the Bible is a short one, but it is strong. The words of Amos are passionate and stern. He says of himself, "A lion has roared! Who will not fear? The Lord God has spoken! Who can but prophesy?" (Amos 3:8) Amos saw powerful visions, too. He saw the Lord threaten Judah with locusts and fire unless repentant. And he saw the Lord measure the sins of Judah against a "plumb line" to find her guilty. A plumb line is a measuring device used by builders to see if their walls are going up straight. I think the Lord was using this as a symbol that the Judeans were not living right.

The people of Israel had begun to enjoy prosperity. They were at peace with their neighbors and were getting wealthier. This led to their spirit of independence from God. Amos rebuked them for their careless living and accused them of using rituals to replace true righteousness. Unlike the people of Nineveh who listened to the prophet Jonah, the Israelites ignored the preaching of Amos. The high priest, Amaziah, even had Amos thrown out of the city for preaching such a strong message in such powerful language.

Both Jonah and Amos lived just decades before the Israelites fell to Assyria as punishment for their sins. They, along with many other prophets, spoke words of truth from a God who really loved his people but hated sin.

ACTIVITY 42

ALL STUDENTS

Make your Memory Cards for Lessons 40–42.

42A—Younger and Middle Students

Make a soap carving.

Materials: Two bars of Ivory soap per student, dull knives

1. Take a bar of Ivory soap. Lay it down flat. With a pencil, make a silhouette of a big fish, or ask your teacher to make it for you.
2. Using a dull knife, and with your teacher's help, slowly carve away the soap outside the lines. Repeat these steps and carve a man out of the other bar of soap. Play with these in the bathtub or just use them up during your shower. For as long as the soap bars last, you'll be reminded of the story of Jonah.

42B—Younger and Middle Students

1. In honor of Amos, the fig farmer, eat some cookies that have a fig filling. There are several kinds at the grocery store.
2. Make a "plumb line." Take a long piece of string (about 3 feet). Tie a heavy weight, such as a washer or other piece of metal hardware, to the bottom of the string. Hold the string against the wall and allow it to stop swinging. No matter where you hold it, notice how gravity makes the string hang completely straight at a right angle to the floor. It is an accurate measure. In the same way, the Lord wanted Israel to live "straight" and holy lives.

42C—Middle and Older Students

Add these names to your running list of kings and prophets of Israel. Highlight the ones in capital letters.

12. JOASH   JONAH
13. Jeroboam II   AMOS

TAKE ANOTHER LOOK!

Review 14: Lessons 40–42

Wall of Fame

1. *Hinduism in India (exact date unknown)*—Try to draw the shape of India on a small piece of paper and write the word "Hinduism" in it.

2. *Olympics (776 B.C.)*—Draw the five Olympic rings with the date underneath.

3. *Jonah (760 B.C.)*—Place his name and face on a big fish. Jonah was from the Northern Kingdom, but he preached to the Ninevites of Assyria. So, place Jonah right between the kingdom strips as you did Obadiah. Coming out of his mouth write the words "Woe to Nineveh."

4. *Amos (760 B.C.)*—Place him in the Northern Kingdom because this is where he preached. Put him in overalls to depict him as a farmer.

SomeWHERE in Time

1. On Outline Map 4, "East Asia," label the following. Use a modern atlas for reference. Color the features as suggested.

Countries:	India	(light green)
	Nepal	(light purple)
	Pakistan	(light orange)
	China	(pink)
Cities:	Calcutta, Delhi, Bombay	
Mountains:	Himalayas	(brown, shape like teepees)
Rivers:	Indus, Ganges	(dark blue)

2. On a map of ancient Greece, find the plain of Olympia. It's in the southern portion of Greece.

3. Using a historical atlas, find the ancient city of Nineveh in Assyria with your finger. Find Tarshish. Scholars believe it may be the ancient city of Tartessus, located on the Atlantic coast of Spain. Look at how far away from Nineveh Jonah was planning to travel to hide from his calling.

The Mystery of History

WHAT DID YOU MISS?

Week 14: Exercise

The Chocolate Candy Game. I'm in the mood for fun today—how about you? To make this exercise more enjoyable, I recommend that you receive a small piece of chocolate candy for every right answer! Since I'm not there with you, however, your teacher will have to provide the treats. (If sugar is off-limits, consider nickels instead!)

I have provided the questions in a quick "Who was _____?" format. If you can give your teacher a reasonable answer in less than 10 seconds, you get your treat. Fair enough? If you struggle for an answer, no treat! Some of these are easy, some are not. Good luck!

1. Who was Eve?
2. Who was Tubal-Cain?
3. Who was Japheth?
4. Who were the Sumerians?
5. Who was Gilgamesh?
6. Who was King Minos?
7. Who was Khufu?
8. Who was Hagar?
9. Who was Isaac?
10. Who was Hammurabi?
11. Who was Joshua?
12. Who was Nefertiti?
13. Who was Ramses II?
14. Who was Helen?
15. Who was Gideon?
16. Who was Boaz?
17. Who was Delilah?
18. Who was King Wen?
19. Who was Saul?
20. Who was Solomon?
21. Who was Rehoboam?
22. Who was Jeroboam?
23. Who was Elijah?
24. Who was Elisha?
25. Who was Joel?
26. Who was Obadiah?
27. Who was Homer?
28. Who were the Aryans?
29. Who was Jonah?
30. Who was Amos?

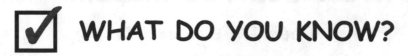

☑ WHAT DO YOU KNOW?

Pretest 15

Fill in the blanks using the word bank provided at the bottom of the page.

1. The _____ of early Rome used a language that is still studied today but not spoken.

2. Legend says that Romulus and Remus were twin boys raised by a _____.

3. Because of their eloquence and style, the writings of Isaiah the prophet have been compared to the writings of _____.

4. In Isaiah 53, the prophet wrote about the coming of _____ as a "suffering servant."

5. Like Amos, Micah was a simple _____ but a powerful prophet.

6. Micah proclaimed that Jesus would be born in _____ hundreds of years before it happened.

7. Israel was finally taken captive by _____.

8. The _____ took over the land of the Israelites and were despised for it.

WORD BANK

Samaritans	Christ	Shakespeare	wolf
Latins	Assyria	Bethlehem	farmer

The Mystery of History

THE CITY OF ROME

LESSON 43

Less than 10 years after Jonah learned his difficult lesson in the belly of a big fish, some people in Europe were establishing a civilization in Rome that would greatly influence the rest of the world. It influences us even now.

Rome today is a city on the west side of the country of Italy. Rome has gone through many changes and many rulers since it was originally founded. At first it was just a city, as we will learn today. Later, though, the name "Rome" came to describe an entire empire that covered the Mediterranean world. Sometimes the terms are confusing. For example, you will learn that the Roman "Empire" was quite different from the Roman "Republic." Try to pay close attention to the different names for the Roman world, which were used at different times.

More than a thousand years before the time of Christ, tribes of people by the name of the Italiis (I TAHL ee eez) lived in Southern Italy. That is where the country of Italy got its name. One of the strongest tribes was the Latin tribe. They really liked the land on the West Coast of Italy because it was good for farming and the coast was dotted with many natural ports for ships. They called this area the "Latium Plain." There was also one great river, the Tiber (TY bur), that was deep enough for ships to sail far into the mainland. By about 753 B.C., the Latins named their new settlement "Roma."

The language of the Latin people is the same Latin that many study today. However, there are no countries today that speak Latin as their everyday language. It is studied because many of our modern languages came from Latin. English is one of them. Latin became the common language of the lands the Romans conquered and remained so for hundreds of years while they were in power. Eventually, Romans became very unpopular with the rest of the world. As a result, many countries that had learned Latin went back to their own languages when the Roman Empire fell.

According to legend, the name "Roma" came from a story of twin brothers named Romulus and Remus. They were supposedly abandoned by a wicked king. A she-wolf found the babies and kept them alive. They were reunited with their grandfather, but they quarreled with one another. Romulus was said to have killed Remus and thus became the first king.

Other legends tell of seven hills and of seven kings who ruled early Rome. No one knows for sure the truth behind these legends, though it seems likely that Rome was settled in the midst of hills. But the Romans were not alone on the peninsula of Italy. To the north lived a tribe of Etruscans in the area of Etruria (I TROOR ee uh). They greatly dominated the Latin people and brought with them many new things.

The Etruscans had learned some trades—such as crafts, leather working, and paving streets—from the Greeks. They also were good at creating sewer systems, weapons, and metal. All these skills advanced the Romans far beyond their other neighbors.

Have you ever made a wish on a wishbone? This custom actually comes from the ancient Etruscans of Italy. They believed that hens were prophetic and could tell the future just because they cackled *before* they laid their eggs. This belief eventually led to the Etruscan custom of wishing on the bone of the chicken. Two people would pull on the wishbone at the same time. Whoever was able to break off the larger segment was the winner of his wish. This was sometimes referred to as a "lucky break."

Though the Etruscans had much to offer the Latins in skills and crafts, for centuries to come there were struggles between these two groups. Eventually the cultures blended to become the powerful Romans. We will be learning much more about Rome in the future. The rise and fall of this once great empire is worth our study because many of our American ideas of government come from the Romans. For now, remember the Latins for their language and the Etruscans for the wishbone. Together, they made up "Rome."

ACTIVITY 43

43A—Younger Students

1. Take a United States penny, dime, nickel, and quarter. Look closely at the tiny words printed on them. Each coin will have the same words, "E Pluribus Unum." Did you know that these words were in Latin? They mean "one from many" and refer to the fact that one nation, the United States, was formed from many states. While you have the coins out, find another phrase our founding fathers put on each coin. What is it?

2. The next time you have a big holiday with a turkey for dinner, save the wishbone. Wash it well, and let it dry. Then have two people grab either end, make a wish, and pull. The winner is the one with the larger piece. (Personally, I believe prayer is more powerful; this wishing stuff is just for fun.)

43B—Younger and Middle Students

The study of Latin is very interesting because we use it so often and don't even realize it. For example, the Latin word "aqua" means water. We have the word "aquarium" in our language to mean something that holds water. Look at these Latin words. Think of English words we use that sound almost the same.

agricola

athleta

familia

machina

persona

rosa

schola

Some English words are straight from the Latin language and never changed their form. Here are a few. Which ones do you know the meaning of?

campus

cancer

chorus

circus

discus

genius

minister

The Mystery of History

Investigate which fields of study still use Latin today. There are at least four of them. Consider the benefits of knowing some of the Latin language.

740 B.C. and 735 B.C.

ISAIAH AND MICAH
(JUDAH'S PROPHETS)
LESSON 44

The prophet Isaiah is an extraordinary character of the Old Testament. As Shakespeare is to theater and Beethoven is to music, so Isaiah is said to be to prophecy. His writings stand above all the other prophets in their grandeur and eloquence.

Who was this remarkable man? We know he was well educated by the style in which he wrote. We also know from the scriptures that he was married and had two sons. Can you imagine receiving a lecture from a dad who was a full-time prophet?

The profound things that Isaiah wrote about we should assume were inspired by God. For just as there are 66 books of the Bible, there are 66 chapters of Isaiah. There are 39 books of the Old Testament and, similarly, the first 39 chapters of Isaiah are about the Law and the Covenant. The likenesses get even better! Just as there are 27 books of the New Testament, there are 27 remaining chapters of Isaiah that tell mainly of the coming of Jesus Christ.

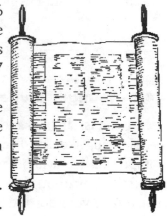

So, the Book of Isaiah is like a small Bible itself. But Isaiah could not have known about this pattern of books and chapters because the events of the New Testament had not even happened yet! The format of the Book of Isaiah is really amazing.

The things that Isaiah wrote about were both harsh and compassionate. He scolded the people for their sins and explained God's love to them as well. For example, in Isaiah 8:9 the people are rebuked. The passage says, "Be shattered, O you peoples, and be broken in pieces!" Then Isaiah writes "even them [meaning foreigners such as the Phoenicians] I will bring to My holy mountain, and make them joyful in My house of prayer . . . for My house shall be called a house of prayer of all nations." (Isa. 56:7–8).

Most incredible of Isaiah is his writing on the coming Messiah whom he had not yet met. Isaiah 53:3–5 says, "He is despised and rejected by men, a man of sorrows and acquainted with grief . . . surely He has borne our griefs and carried our sorrows; yet we esteemed Him stricken, smitten by God, and afflicted. But he was wounded for our transgressions, He was bruised for our iniquities; the chastisement for our peace was upon Him, and by His stripes we are healed." Isaiah was writing prophecy about the stripes Jesus would receive when He was whipped and crucified for our sins. This is a beautiful passage to any believer who recognizes the sacrifice of Christ.

Isaiah was eloquent in writing, but his boldness cost him his life. Jewish tradition says that Isaiah lived under a wicked king named Manasseh who had Isaiah killed by sawing him in half inside a hollow tree. What a sad and gruesome ending for such a marvelous man.

At the same time that Isaiah so profoundly wrote the truth, God was using another man to prophesy in simpler terms. His name was Micah. Both men were prophets to Judah. Unlike Isaiah, Micah was a farmer, a man of the fields. He probably wrote to an audience of people more like himself.

The first chapters of Micah display God's disgust with the sins of His people in Jerusalem. They read, "Therefore I will wail and howl, I will go stripped and naked: I will make a wailing like the jackals and a mourning like the ostriches, for her wounds are incurable. For it has come to Judah; it has come to the gate of My people, even to Jerusalem." (Mic. 1:8-9)

However, like many of the prophets, Micah ends with assurance that God does love His people. He wrote, "Who is a God like You, pardoning iniquity and passing over the transgression of the remnant of His heritage? He does not retain His anger forever because He delights in mercy." (Mic. 7:18) These have been words of comfort to many generations.

Last, Micah is known for the prophecy of where Jesus would be born. Micah 5:2 reads, "But you, Bethlehem Ephrathah, though you are little among the thousands of Judah, yet out of you shall come forth to Me the One to be ruler in Israel." We don't know if Micah fully understood the significance of the little town of Bethlehem, but we still sing of it every Christmas.

I have referred to this before, but I will write it again as we close on these two prophets. The mystery of the scriptures, the mystery of the ages, and the mystery of history itself is God revealing Himself through Jesus Christ. Isn't it neat that without really knowing who Jesus was, both Isaiah and Micah wrote about His glorious coming?

ACTIVITY 44

44A—Younger Students

Read Isaiah 64:8 and Romans 9:20–21. These verses talk about God being like a potter and His people being like clay. Today, you pretend to be a potter and make a pot out of clay or Play-Doh modeling compound. Think about who is in charge of the shape of your pot. Does the pot tell you how it wants to look? Of course not. You decide. In much the same way, God designs us the way He wants us to be. Take a picture of your pot and file it under "Asia: Israel" in your Student Notebook.

44B—Middle Students

Following the theme of the potter and the clay found in Isaiah 64:8, visit a ceramic shop if there is one in your area. Try to find a vase to paint and finish. Maybe there is one available that looks somewhat rustic and old like a relic from the Old Testament. Perhaps you could write the words of Isaiah the prophet on the vase or at least the reference on the bottom. Keep it to remember this profound man of God.

44C—Older Students

Outline the Book of Isaiah by writing out the chapter titles as suggested in your Bible. Pay close attention to the divisions of the chapters and how they parallel with the breakdown of the Bible as described in the lesson. File your outline under "Asia: Israel" in your Student Notebook.

ISRAEL FALLS TO ASSYRIA

LESSON 45

In the last few weeks, we have learned about several of the Old Testament prophets. The prophets were special men of God who preached to the Israelites after the period of the Judges and when the earthly kings began to rule. What we will learn today is that these prophets of old spoke the truth.

II Kings 17:13 tells us that through the prophets God had warned His people not to sin. It reads, "Yet the Lord testified against Israel and against Judah, by all of His prophets, namely every seer, saying, 'Turn from your evil ways and keep My commandments and My statutes according to all the law which I commanded your fathers, and which I sent to you by My servants the prophets.'"

The Lord specifically told the people of the Northern Kingdom that they would fall to a neighboring nation for their sins. The prophet Hosea wrote, "The idol also shall be carried to Assyria as a present for King Jareb." (Hos. 10:6) Hosea probably lived to witness his own prophecy. He was the last major prophet to Israel before the Assyrians came.

What were the Israelites doing that was so bad? In II Kings 17 we find a summary of the sins they were guilty of. It includes that they walked in the statutes of other nations; that they secretly did against the Lord things that were not right; that they set up sacred pillars and wooden images; that they did wicked things; that they served idols; that they caused their sons and daughters to pass through the fire; that they practiced witchcraft; and that they sold themselves to do evil in the sight of the Lord. Wow, that's a heavy list of sins!

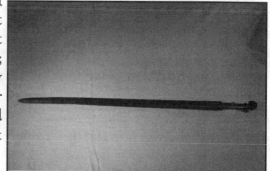

The Assyrians were known for their fierce weapons. This Assyrian bronze dagger, for use in battle, was made somewhere between the eighth and sixth centuries B.C.

In II Kings 17 we also find God's response. "Therefore, the Lord was very angry with Israel, and removed them from His sight; there was none left but the tribe of Judah alone." The Assyrians may have thought that they were finally victorious over their neighbors the Israelites. But, according to scripture, God allowed Assyria to take down His people. "The Lord removed Israel out of His sight, as He had said by all His servants the prophets. So Israel was carried away from their own land to Assyria." (II Kings 17:23)

What actually happened in 722 B.C. was that 27,290 Israelites were deported to Assyria and replaced by foreigners. We know the exact number because the king of Assyria (his name was Sargon) inscribed on his palace walls what he had done. The Israelite people were not just conquered and given a new ruler; they were moved like refugees from their Promised Land. It must have been a very sad journey for them.

To make matters worse for the Israelites, other people moved into their land by request of King Sargon. You may have heard of these people. Over time they were called the Samaritans. They might have gotten their name from the former capital of Israel, which is Samaria. It is understandable that the Israelites didn't care for the people who took over their houses and fields. But it wasn't all that easy on the Samaritans either.

You see, the Samaritans encountered some tough times in their new land after the Israelites left. The Bible says that great numbers of lions attacked them! The problem was so bad that the Samaritans asked the king of Assyria to send back some Jewish priests who could help them understand the religion and god of that land. They suspected that the God of the Israelites had sent the beasts. According to II Kings 17:25, they were right. "And it was so, at the beginning of their dwelling there, that they did not fear the Lord; therefore the Lord sent lions among them, which killed some of them."

As a result of this judgment on them, the Samaritans began to mix the religion of the Jewish priests with their own religion. They sort of picked the parts of the Jewish religion that they liked but not all of it. The Samaritans were greatly looked down on by the Israelites for their confused and mixed beliefs, and they were despised for having moved into the Israelites' old land. (This prejudice is seen in the New Testament parable of "The Good Samaritan.")

As for the Israelites, they remained refugees in Assyria for a long time. In fact, they never were freed. They have been nicknamed the "lost tribes of Israel" because they disappeared over time. (The Jews of today are descended from the Southern Kingdom.)

The story of Israel, the Northern Kingdom, is summed up best in this passage, "Then the king of Assyria carried Israel away captive to Assyria . . . because they did not obey the voice of the Lord their God, but transgressed His covenant and all that Moses the servant of the Lord had commanded; and they would neither hear nor do them." (II Kings 18:11–12) Can you imagine how the Lord felt about this? Was He sad? Was He angry? Did He still love the people that He judged? In our next lesson, we will learn from the Scriptures exactly how God felt.

ACTIVITY 45

ALL STUDENTS

Make your Memory Cards for Lessons 43–45

45A—Younger Students

Visualize thousands and thousands.

Materials: 100 small objects such as pennies, toothpicks, matchsticks

The number of Israelites who were deported to Assyria was 27,290. Today, try to visualize a number that large. Make one group of 100 things such as pennies, toothpicks, or matchsticks. It will take awhile to count this much. Then imagine that it would take 2,790 groups just like the one you made to equal 27,290. Hopefully this will help you realize that that is a very large number. It was a sad time for the people of Israel because it was their own sin that put them in the hard situation.

45B—Middle and Older Students

Look into the headlines of a current newspaper to follow any story of refugees. If you are unable to investigate any at the present time, look into researching the events of Kosovo. Middle students may need only to familiarize themselves with the events through photos and news stories. Older students may go further and write about the horrific tragedy of the Kosovo refugees.

If you have refugee people living in your community, consider a service project to minister to their specific needs.

45C—Older Students

Do you like challenging research? Try to find more information of the "lost tribes of Israel." I found very little information on it in my own research, but I believe there are theories out there. See what you can find!

The Mystery of History

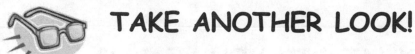

TAKE ANOTHER LOOK!

Review 15: Lessons 43–45

Wall of Fame

1. *Rome founded (753 b.c.)*—Draw a little wolf to remember Romulus and Remus.

2. *Isaiah (740 b.c.)*—Place him in the Southern Kingdom of Judah. Place a pen in his hand.

3. *Micah (735 b.c.)*—Place him also in the Southern Kingdom. Make him look like a farmer. (A pitchfork perhaps?)

4. *Israel falls to Assyria (722 b.c.)*—The Assyrians were known for the symbol of a winged lion/man statue. If you can find a picture of this, sketch it, trace it, or photocopy it and use it on the timeline.

SomeWHERE in Time

1. On Outline Map 5, "Europe," find Italy and Rome and write them in. To the north of Rome, write in the Etruscans. To the south, write in the Latins. Many people are confused as to the name of the Latin language because "Latinos" are people living in Central and South America. File your map under "Europe: Italy."

2. In a Bible atlas, find the country of Assyria. Note its closeness to Israel. Find with your finger the capital of Israel, Samaria. Compare Biblical maps to notice when the area of Israel is renamed Samaria. (Bible maps will usually name former Israel as Samaria during Christ's time. Now you know why!) The name of the country of Israel will not appear on a map again for a long time (not until 1948).

WHAT DID YOU LEARN?

Week 15: *Quiz*

Circle the correct answer for each question.

1. Adam and Eve were created on the _____ day of Creation.
   a. second
   b. fourth
   c. fifth
   d. sixth

2. During the Ice Age, natural land _____ were formed from one continent to another.
   a. caverns
   b. bridges
   c. holes
   d. arches

3. The Sumerians were considered a "civilization" because they had
   a. laws.
   b. government.
   c. a written language.
   d. All of the above.

4. *The Epic of Gilgamesh* was written about a _____ named Gilgamesh.
   a. town
   b. man
   c. country
   d. woman

5. Abraham's wife was
   a. Rebekah.
   b. Rachel.
   c. Sarah.
   d. Nefertiti.

6. The Israelites were named after
   a. Abraham.
   b. Isaac.
   c. Jacob.
   d. Moses.

7. Joseph was a servant in _____ house.
   a. Amenhotep's
   b. Potiphar's
   c. Sargon's
   d. Hammurabi's

8. The Tabernacle in the wilderness was
   a. portable.
   b. used for worship.
   c. a dwelling place for God.
   d. All of the above.

9. Ramses the Great built
   a. the palace of Knossos.
   b. the Sphinx.
   c. a temple at Abu Simbel.
   d. the Parthenon.

10. During the Zhou dynasty, the people upheld high morals because of their belief in
    a. a Mandate of Heaven.
    b. the caste system.
    c. the sun god, Aten.
    d. Baal worship.

11. King Saul, who grew to despise David, first met him as
    a. a prophet.
    b. a singer.
    c. a victor over Goliath.
    d. a Temple servant.

12. The Kingdom of Israel split **after** the reign of
    a. Jeroboam.
    b. David.
    c. Solomon.
    d. Rehoboam.

13. The Phoenicians were skilled at
    a. making dye.
    b. making glass.
    c. using phonics.
    d. All of the above.

14. Elijah the prophet was nearly killed by
    a. Jezebel.
    b. King Minos.
    c. Ramses II.
    d. Howard Carter.

15. The prophet Joel
    a. was a fig farmer.
    b. had an unfaithful wife.
    c. lived during a locust plague.
    d. was run out of the city by a priest.

16. In the religion of Hinduism, _____ teaches that people come back to life over and over according to how they lived their lives.
    a. the Mandate of Heaven
    b. reincarnation
    c. Aten, the sun god
    d. Hammurabi

17. In the early Olympics, a pentathlon was an event featuring _____ skills.
    a. 15
    b. 3
    c. 6
    d. 5

18. Jonah fled to _____ to avoid preaching to the Ninevites.
    a. Tarshish
    b. Crete
    c. Ur
    d. Rome

19. The city of Rome was first settled by
    a. the Cretans, or Minoans.
    b. the Etruscans and the Latins.
    c. the Italians and the Greeks.
    d. the Phoenicians.

20. Isaiah and Micah were both prophets to
    a. Edom.
    b. Assyria.
    c. Judah.
    d. Israel.

Bonus question:
    What language did the early Romans speak? _____

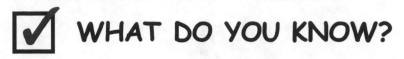

✓ WHAT DO YOU KNOW?

Pretest 16

In the following sentences, circle the answer that makes the sentence correct.

1. Hosea was a prophet to (China, Israel).

2. Hosea's wife (Gomer, Cleopatra) was an unfaithful woman.

3. Hezekiah was a very (humble, wicked) king over Judah.

4. Sennacherib, the king of Assyria, was extremely (proud, shy).

5. Miraculously, an army of 185,000 Assyrians fell (asleep, dead).

6. The earliest people to live in America were probably (miners, hunters).

7. The Hopewell Indians in America created earth structures in the shape of (animals, trees).

8. The ancient Native Americans buried their (trash, dead) in huge mounds.

HOSEA
(ISRAEL'S PROPHET)

LESSON 46

Have you ever had your feelings hurt by someone you love? It doesn't feel very good. It hurts a lot when someone you really care about is unkind, ignores you, or loves someone else instead of you. In the Book of Hosea in the Old Testament, we catch a glimpse of how the Lord felt when the Israelites, the people He loved so much, were unfaithful to Him, ignored His commandments, and loved the world more than they loved Him.

Hosea was a prophet to the Northern Kingdom before and during its destruction. It was, of course, a very sad time because of the great sin of the Israelites. Like the prophets before him, Hosea spoke for God, telling people not to sin and that God loved them. But besides that, the Lord used Hosea's life in a unique way to show the Israelites, and to show us, something about God's tender heart and how it can hurt from our sins.

What we come to know of Hosea is that the Lord told him to marry a woman named Gomer who was a "harlot." Hosea was told to marry a harlot and have children with her. A harlot is a sinful woman who commits adultery. In the Ten Commandments, God forbids adultery because it is a form of unfaithfulness. Why would God ask Hosea to marry this kind of woman? He did so to make Hosea's life an example of pain and true love.

The Lord used Hosea's marriage to symbolize how He felt about Israel. Just as Gomer was an unfaithful wife, the nation of Israel was unfaithful to God. The Lord said to Hosea, "Go again, love a woman who is loved by a lover and is committing adultery, just like the love of the Lord for the children of Israel, who look to other gods and love the raisin cakes of the pagans." (Hos. 3:1)

While married to Hosea, Gomer had three children. Each was given a specific name to represent the children of Israel. The first son was named Jezreel. This name means "God scatters." He was given that name to indicate how God was going to scatter the Israelites for their sins. Second, Gomer gave birth to a daughter whom the Lord said to name Lo-Rumhamah. The name means "not pitied," which is how God felt toward the nation of Israel. He said, "I will no longer have mercy on the house of Israel, but I will utterly take them away." (Hos. 1:6) As you already learned, the Northern Kingdom was literally taken away and scattered by the Assyrians just as Hosea prophesied because they did not repent of their evil ways.

The third child Gomer gave birth to was a son named Lo-Ammi, which means "not My people." This name reflected the fact that the Israelites were going to be sent away for abandoning their love for God and worshiping false idols. In the personal life of Hosea, Israel's actions were demonstrated by Gomer's leaving her husband and children to go back to a life of harlotry. She hurt her husband by loving other men.

Did Hosea ever quit loving his unfaithful wife? Apparently not. The Bible says that after Gomer left Hosea he went looking for her. He found her at a slave market and brought her back home. The reason for all this detail about Hosea's marriage is again because it was symbolic. Though the nation of Israel was judged harshly for its sins, God never quit loving His people just as Hosea never quit loving his wife.

The Mystery of History

What made the Israelites like an unfaithful wife? How were they so bad? The Book of Hosea confirms what we have learned before. The Israelites were guilty of swearing, lying, killing, stealing, acts of adultery, and bloodshed. They were also worshiping wooden idols and making sacrifices to Baal, a false god. All these sins were painful to the Lord. But like a good parent, God loved His children. His tender feelings, like those of a father, show clearly in these verses:

> "When Israel was a child I loved him, and out of Egypt I called My son. As they called them so they went from them; they sacrificed to the Baals, and burned incense to carved images. I taught Ephraim to walk, [sometimes the 10 tribes of Israel were called "Ephraim"] taking them by their arms; but they did not know that I healed them. I drew them with gentle cords, with bands of love, and I was to them as those who take the yoke from their neck. I stooped and fed them." (Hos. 11:1–4)

This is a small window into the very heart of God who cares for His people the way a father cares for his young child.

So, how did God feel about the Israelites after all their disobedience? Just as a man would hurt after his wife was unfaithful to him, God hurt from the sins of His people. But, just as a father loves his children, so the Lord loves his people. Hosea's words were written long ago, but they still hold true today.

ACTIVITY 46

46A—Younger Students

Have you ever had someone break a promise to you? Maybe it was just a little thing. Still, big or small, it is usually hurtful when someone fails to do something they promised. Hosea's wife broke her marriage promise to be faithful. The people of Israel broke their relationship with God by all kinds of sin.

Today, just talk about broken promises. Discuss how God feels when we disappoint Him with sin in our lives.

46B—Middle and Older Students

Add these names to your lists of kings and prophets.

ISRAEL

Kings	Prophets
13. Jeroboam II	AMOS and HOSEA
14. Zechariah	
15. Shallum	
16. Menahem	
17. Pekahiah	
18. Pekah	
19. Hoshea	

JUDAH

Kings	Prophets
9. Amaziah	
10. Azariah (Uzziah)	ISAIAH and MICAH
11. Jotham	
12. Ahaz	
13. Hezekiah	

Using a Bible concordance, do a word study on "faithfulness." It is a powerful word with many implications for our lives whether we are married or not. Look up the word and list on paper several verses that represent the benefits of faithfulness. In contrast, what does the Bible say about "adultery"? What are the consequences, as listed in Proverbs? File your word study under "Asia: Israel."

701 B.C.

HEZEKIAH AND SENNACHERIB
LESSON 47

You have learned in our other lessons that many of the kings of Israel were wicked. And, because of the sins of the people, the Lord allowed Israel to be conquered by the fearsome Assyrians. Today we will see that pattern broken. You will learn that there was one good king in Judah who, through his noble character, prevented his kingdom from destruction by the Assyrians. This story is refreshing!

The name of the good king who ruled in Judah was Hezekiah. The eighteenth chapter of II Kings has many verses about his godly character. Verses 5–6 say, "He trusted in the Lord God of Israel, so that after him was none like him among all the kings of Judah, nor any who were before him. For he held fast to the Lord; he did not depart from following Him, but kept His commandments, which the Lord had commanded Moses." What a tremendous guy!

At age 25, Hezekiah inherited the throne from his father. The years that Hezekiah served as king were not easy. The new king of Assyria, named Sennacherib, was quite anxious to conquer Judah just as his ancestors had conquered Israel. Sennacherib was a very proud man. In II Kings 18:17–37, we find a record of how he boasted that surely he was supreme over Hezekiah and "his god." Sennacherib stated in complete arrogance, "Has any of the gods of the nations at all delivered its land from the hand of the king of Assyria? . . . Look! You have heard what the kings of Assyria have done to all lands by utterly destroying them; and shall you be delivered?" (II Kings 18:33, 19:11)

Hezekiah's humble response to Sennacherib's threat is quite admirable. He prayed these words, "O Lord God of Israel, the One who dwells between the cherubim, You are God, You alone, of all the kingdoms of the earth. You have made heaven and earth . . . Now I pray, save us from his [Sennacherib's] hand, **that all the kingdoms of the earth may know that You are the Lord God, You alone.**" (II Kings 19:15, 19)

I love the way Hezekiah approached the Lord. He acknowledged God first as the one who "dwells between the cherubim." He is referring to the cherubim on the Ark of the Covenant in the Most Holy Place. It is a beautiful reminder of God's closeness to His people. Then

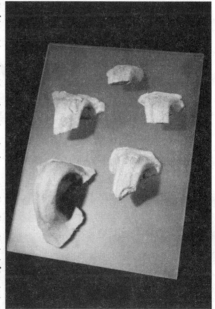

These five broken handles were once attached to large storage jars belonging to King Hezekiah. The handles are stamped in Hebrew as "belonging to the king."

Hezekiah appealed to the Lord for the sake of the whole world knowing who He was. Isn't that just what the "mystery of history" is all about? It is God revealing Himself to man.

The Lord answered Hezekiah's prayer in a very dramatic way. It says in II Kings 19:35, "And it came to pass on a certain night that the angel of the Lord went out, and killed in the camp of the Assyrians 185,000; and when people arose early in the morning, there were the corpses—all dead." Wow! The army of Judah never even had to fight the Assyrians to keep them away. The Assyrian army was completely wiped out by God's death angel in just one night. It was an awesome display of His power to shape history.

As for Sennacherib, he went home only to face assassination by his own sons. Hezekiah became sick and very near death. But he had learned about the power of God from the incident with the Assyrian army. So, Hezekiah humbled himself again to God. He prayed and wept to God over the matter of his dying. As before, the Lord listened to his pleas and healed Hezekiah. In fact, Hezekiah lived another 15 years.

Hezekiah used his extra years wisely. The Bible says, "Hezekiah prospered in all his works." (II Chron. 32:30b) Among many great things, he rebuilt some very significant waterways for the city of Jerusalem. The great prophet Isaiah, whom we studied earlier, witnessed the events of Hezekiah's life and helped guide him along with words from the Lord. What fitting company these two godly men must have been to one another as each sought to serve the God they loved.

ACTIVITY 47

47A—Younger Students

With your teacher, look up the word "proud" in a dictionary. What does it mean? Sometimes we say the word proud in a good way, like "I'm so proud of you!" But sometimes we use proud as a bad word, like when a man is too proud of himself.

Also, look up the word "humble." What is the difference between proud and humble? These words were used in the lesson about Hezekiah and Sennacherib. Which man best fits the definition of each word? What was the difference in their lives?

47B—Middle Students

Pretend you are Hezekiah and write a letter to Isaiah describing what the Lord did in wiping out Sennacherib's army. He certainly would have given God the credit for the protection. After writing your letter, crumple it and stain it in "tea" water to make it appear aged. File it under "Asia: Israel."

47C—Middle and Older Students

In the story of Hezekiah and Sennacherib, we learn of the angel of the Lord fighting for the Judeans. What other Bible stories come to your mind in which the angel of the Lord appears? The theology of angels can be very interesting. Do your own Bible search using a concordance to find other examples of the activities of angels. Pay particular attention to the terminology of "angel of the Lord." Write down your findings and file them under "Miscellaneous."

ANCIENT NATIVE AMERICANS

LESSON 48

For some time now we have been studying ancient people on the other side of the world from us. Well, we're bringing it home today. We are going to look at ancient people who lived right here on land that is now the United States at about the same time that Hezekiah was being a good king over Judah. And that was a long time ago.

If you were to back up in time, you would find that people traveled to North and South America as far back as the Ice Age. That's when the oceans were shallower and land was exposed to connect continents that are now separated. Geologists believe that at one time people were able to cross from Alaska to Russia without a boat. They could have walked!

That means that brave and daring people migrated and settled in the Americas a long time ago. Putting an exact date on these people is difficult to do. We don't have written records of them at all. But anthropologists have labeled the early people of North America into these four groups: the Paleo Indians, the Archaic Indians, the Adena Indians, and the Hopewells. Let's take a quick look at each. Maybe some of them used to live in your backyard!

The Paleo Indians would be the ones we know the least about. They roamed North America as far back as 5000 B.C. It appears that they had only lightweight tools and few belongings because they traveled around a lot. They followed herds of animals for food and skins.

The Archaic Indians seemed to be more settled. By staying in a place for awhile, they would have changed their eating and cooking habits. They dried their meat for storage and harvested grain to keep. They also had tools for sculpting things and made decorative masks out of wolf heads. These items suggest some development of traditions.

Built by Native Americans over 2,000 years ago, these mounds still stand at Fort Ancient in Lebanon, Ohio.

The Adena Indians get a little more interesting. They actually farmed their land and fertilized it with ashes. They made pottery to store the things they grew and made. Better yet, the Adenas left something behind for us to remember them by. They built huge burial mounds—as high as 65 feet—that are still standing today.

Archaeologists believe that when someone in a tribe died, they might have been buried in their own home. Then layers of other bodies were buried over them as time went on. Some mounds held as many as a thousand bodies! That's a lot of bones.

Although I'm jumping ahead in history, I really want to tell you about the next culture because they practically did live in my backyard. By 150 B.C. the Hopewell Indians were centered in Ohio. These people took the idea of mounds from the Adenas and really went crazy with them. The Hopewell mounds not only served to bury the dead, they also became works of art. In fact, these mounds are so impressive that anthropologists often refer to these people as "the Mound Builders." Not a creative name, but it helps us remember them. Besides, the Hopewells left no written records, so we have no idea what they called themselves.

This hollow stone pipe was carved by Native Americans around 800 B.C. The mouth of the pipe is at the top of its head. (A replica is pictured here.)

In the state of Ohio alone, the Hopewells built more than 10,000 mounds. Most of the mounds are just cone-shaped. But some are shaped like huge animals and are as long as 1,600 feet. The largest mound in Ohio is in the shape of a snake. It's called the Great Serpent Mound. One mound in Wisconsin is in the shape of a turtle.

One of the amazing things about these earthen sculptures is just how they were built without an aerial view. That means that from way overhead, say in an airplane, you could clearly see the animal shapes. But, up close, it is hard to tell what they are. From what we have already learned about early man, we know he was somehow smart enough to figure this out. We just don't know how.

Items that archaeologists have found near the mounds tell us a little about these people. The Hopewells were farmers of corn, and they raised tobacco for smoking in pipes. They made the coolest pipes out of the shapes of animals. They also must have liked to travel and trade because relics that could only be from other areas of the present-day United States have been found near the mound sites. For example, in Ohio they have found grizzly-bear teeth from Colorado, copper from Lake Superior, shells from the coast of Texas, and mica from New England.

The mounds that stand today are also incredible because they withstood the weather for more than 2,000 years. Unlike the pyramids of Egypt that are made of brick, these mounds are made of just earth. The Mound Builders may have hoped to be remembered by their structures. They definitely accomplished that! It's amazing to me that we have any knowledge of these ancient Native Americans who lived right here. It was just so long ago!

ACTIVITY 48

ALL STUDENTS

Make your Memory Cards for Lessons 46–48.

Field Trip Possibility

If you live near any of the Mound Builder sites, make a visit to see them for yourself.

48A—Younger Students

Build your own mound.

Materials: A shoe box, enough dirt to fill it, some water

Fill a shoebox with dirt. Add just enough water to help make the dirt clump together. Shape the dirt into an animal shape like the Hopewell Indians did. Choose something simple, for instance, a snake or turtle. Or, if you have left over chicken bones from dinner, you could bury them under a cone-shaped hill in your shoebox. If you like what you've created, take a picture and place it in your Student Notebook under "North America: United States."

48B—Younger and Middle Students

Using reference materials from the library, find pictures of the animal pipes discovered from the Hopewell Indians. They are pretty neat. Using clay or Play-Doh modeling compound, try to sculpt your own animals around a short straw to make it look like a pipe. It's not that easy. Take a photo and file it under "North America: United States."

48C—Older Students

Using the library or Internet, research more on the Hopewell or Mississippian Indians. Try to find a site that will mail you a brochure on the mounds. File your information under "North America: United States."

TAKE ANOTHER LOOK!

Review 16: Lessons 46–48

Wall of Fame

1. *Hosea (c. 701 B.C.)*—Place him in the Northern Kingdom of Israel. Add tears to his eyes and face.

2. *Hezekiah (701 B.C.)*—Place him in the Southern Kingdom and give him a halo for being a good king. Place a golden cross on him to signify the lineage of Christ.

3. *Sennacherib (701 B.C.)*—Write the word "proud" on him.

4. *Ancient Native Americans (we can't place one date on these groups of peoples; place them near 700 B.C. to remind us of their presence)*—Draw the silhouette of a snake or turtle and write "Mound Builders in America" on it.

SomeWHERE in Time

With a dark pencil, trace the outline of a USA map. Next, trace and label the following states: Ohio, Arkansas, Kentucky, Tennessee, Illinois, Wisconsin, and Minnesota. Use colored pencils to make them attractive. Using a blue pencil, add the Ohio River and the Mississippi River. These are the locations of most of the Mound Builders. In brown, draw in scattered symbols of mounds along the river valleys. Label your map and file it in the "North America: United States" portion of your Student Notebook.

This is a matching exercise, but it's a little different. Follow the list of instructions for how you should "mark" each word that is listed on the right. The trick is finding the word according to the clues given.

1. Draw a musical note on the name of one of the earliest men to compose music.

    a. Moses

2. Put feet and a tail on the word referring to the animals of the ark who are now extinct.

    b. Minoans

3. Draw an oval around the people King Minos ruled.

    c. Rahab

4. Draw a staff next to the man who led the Israelites out of slavery.

    d. Amos

5. Draw a sun around the name of the pharaoh who worshiped one god.

    e. Hopewells

6. Draw a red cord around the name of the woman who harbored spies for the Hebrews.

    f. Jonah

7. Draw a box around the name of the last judge of Israel.

    g. Amenhotep IV

8. Put dollar signs on the third king of Israel.

    h. Solomon

9. Draw a line under the big thing that happened to Israel in 925 B.C.

    i. The Kingdom divided

10. Draw a flame around the fiery prophet.

    j. Joel

11. Draw bug wings around the man who was a prophet during a locust plague.

    k. dinosaurs

12. Draw five rings next to the event of 776 B.C. that was a first.

    l. Jubal

13. Draw a fish fin over the prophet to Nineveh.

    m. Samuel

14. Draw a straight line (plumb line) through the fig farmer.

    n. Elijah

15. Put a big "A" over the event of 722 B.C. that had been prophesied.

    o. Israel falls to Assyria

16. Draw a hill next to the ancient people in America.

    p. Olympics

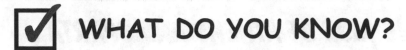

☑ WHAT DO YOU KNOW?

Pretest 17

To familiarize yourself with this week's lessons, alphabetize the following word list. Circle the items you have heard of before and discuss with your class what you know about them.

Athens   1. _____

Sparta   2. _____

Acropolis   3. _____

Achaens   4. _____

Manasseh   5. _____

Assyrians   6. _____

Catapults   7. _____

Ashurbanipal   8. _____

THE RISE OF ATHENS AND SPARTA
LESSON 49

The country of Greece is only about the size of Alabama. But the influence of this country on the world has been huge. How did it all begin? Today we will look at two city-states of Greece that were beginning to rise at about the same time the Mound Builders were in America.

First, though, we will back up and find out what happened to the Mycenaeans, the people who fought in the Trojan War. They ruled over Greece for about 500 years. But, around 1200 B.C., the Mycenaean's world broke up. They had bad harvests that led to famine and poor trade. These years in Greek history are called the Dark Ages. If people are struggling to survive, they don't usually have time for art and recreation. Some skills, such as painting and jewelry making, were completely abandoned in the Dark Ages of Greece.

Fortunately, over time, the Greeks re-established themselves. By 700 B.C., the city-states of Athens and Sparta were developed. Historians call this time of progress the Archaic period of Greece. This is near the time when Homer was retelling the tales of Troy. Homer himself referred to his people as the "Achaens." Some Greeks called themselves "Hellenes." That could be confusing, but they're the same people. We'll see the term "Hellenization" later on in this study to describe people acting like the Greeks—so remember it!

Large communities in ancient Greece were called "city-states" because they were the size of modern cities, but they acted like small nations. The city-states were spread out across the countryside of Greece and for

This Greek drinking cup was called a "kylix." Its big handles made it easier to hold while reclining on a couch.

years chose NOT to come together for peace or prosperity. Instead, they warred against one another. Imagine the tension if New York City, Chicago, and Los Angeles each had its own president instead of being part of the United States. That is exactly what happened in early Greece.

Sparta was one of the strongest city-states in Greece for a long time. It was strong because the Spartans believed in training men, women, and children for battle. The Spartans led very strict lives without much pleasure or time spent on the arts. They feared their neighbors and didn't allow people in and out of their city-state.

The people of Athens, on the other hand, were far more interested in cultural things. They loved drama, music, and all forms of art. They also believed strongly in education. Great schools of thinking were developed there.

Athens had something else that "put them on the map." They had the spectacular Acropolis, which means "High City." The Acropolis is a huge rocky hill that overlooks Athens. It had its own source of spring water and became a natural place for temples and shrines. The ruins of the Parthenon (built later, in 447 B.C.) stand there today in the great city of Athens, which remains the capital of Greece.

Athens and Sparta were the two largest city-states of ancient Greece. Both had tremendous strengths. But, because of their differences, they just never could get along. We will learn later how tragic that was.

The Mystery of History

ACTIVITY 49

49A—Younger and Middle Students

Paint a Greek pot.

Materials: Small terra-cotta clay pots, black markers

During the Dark Ages of Greece, pottery was painted in simple geometric patterns. Life was hard then, and the artwork of the people reflected it. In the Archaic period, when Athens and Sparta became strong city-states, the pottery became fancier. Artists would draw detailed scenes from everyday life or pictures of mythology on their pots. Greek pottery was distinguished by its black and red colors.

Take a reddish clay pot and draw things on it with your black marker. Decide if you want to make it simple like pottery from the Dark Ages, or fancy, like the Archaic period. (You might use a pencil first.) Take a picture of your pot and file it in your Student Notebook under "Europe: Ancient Greece."

49B—Younger and Middle Students

Olive oil was an essential product to the Greeks. It was against the law in Athens to uproot an olive tree. Use an encyclopedia to find out what olive trees look like. They are known for their unusual beauty. Make a copy of any picture you can find of an olive tree and place it in your Student Notebook under "Europe: Ancient Greece." Middle students should investigate further as to how the olives are made into oil.

49C—Middle and Older Students

Although Greek mythology is contrary to Christianity, it can be beneficial to understand the beliefs of the ancients. In classical literature, references are often made to the gods of mythology. Using outside sources, familiarize yourself with the legends of the more prominent gods and goddesses such as Zeus, Poseidon, Pluto, Aphrodite, and Apollo. Discover the differences between the Titans and the Olympian gods. To record your findings, create a family tree on paper starting with Uranus and Gaea. Try to include the 14 Titans and the 12 Olympian gods. File this in your Student Notebook under "Europe: Ancient Greece."

691 B.C.

MANASSEH

LESSON 50

The first time we hear the name "Manasseh" in the Bible, it is in reference to one of the sons of Joseph. The name is later used as one of the 12 tribes of Israel. (Joseph gave his sons Manasseh and Ephraim each a tribe to replace himself and the tribe of Levi. This kept the number of tribes to 12.) So, there is a whole tribe of Israel named after Manasseh as well as the land given over to him. But today you will learn that there was also a king by the name of Manasseh. He was one of the kings of Judah. This could be confusing. Let me tell you more about him.

First of all, Manasseh was the son of Hezekiah. Remember him? Hezekiah was the really good and humble king of Judah. He was influential in restoring Judah to the ways of the Lord. Unfortunately, as a young man, Manasseh was neither good nor humble. And rather than help restore Judah, he brought the country way down.

Manasseh came to be king of Judah when he was just 12 years old. Because of his young age, Manasseh depended on the counsel of older men to rule his country. As soon as Hezekiah died, some of Manasseh's counselors advised him to go right back to the pagan worship that Hezekiah had worked so hard to get rid of! And that was what happened.

Sadly, Manasseh was considered to be one of the worst and most evil kings that Judah ever had. His sins, listed in II Kings 21, are atrocious. He not only worshiped false gods, but he used the Temple as a place to erect his foreign idols. That is the same Temple that Solomon built as a sacred place for God to dwell in. Manasseh also took part in witchcraft and sorcery. The Bible says he even had his own son "pass through the fire," which meant that he might have sacrificed him to Moloch, an Ammonite god. Though it has never been confirmed, Manasseh may be the one who had Isaiah the prophet sawed in half!

But, in II Chronicles 33, we get a little bit more of the story. It seems that at one point the Assyrian army captured Manasseh. The Assyrians had, of course, captured the Northern Kingdom years before this time. They wanted the Southern Kingdom, too. So, the Assyrian army took Manasseh to *Babylon* with hooks and bound him with bronze fetters or chains. (More on Babylon later.) I told you once before that the Assyrians were known for cruel treatment of their prisoners. If you remember, that's why Jonah didn't want to go there!

But a serious thing happened to Manasseh under these brutal circumstances. This man who had been so evil began to pray. I mean really pray! In II Chronicles 33:12–13 it is written, "Now when he [Manasseh] was in affliction, he implored the Lord his God, and humbled himself greatly before the God of his fathers, and prayed to Him; and He received his entreaty, heard his supplication, and brought him back to Jerusalem into his kingdom. Then Manasseh knew that the Lord was God."

It appears that the Lord heard Manasseh's humble prayer. Manasseh acknowledged God, and God in turn delivered him from the Assyrians. Out of His mercy, the Lord completely restored the throne of Judah to Manasseh. It is an amazing story of God's forgiveness.

Manasseh spent the rest of his life repairing the damage he had done from his years of evil living. He restored a wall around the city of Jerusalem and tore down the false idols that he had built. He went so far as to *command* the people of Judah to serve the Lord God of Israel. Outwardly, the people did so. But inwardly, the Judeans were as rebellious as ever. So much destruction had been done earlier to their spiritual lives that they were not easily turned around. Although Manasseh had repented for his own sins, he was still responsible in part for leading the people so far from God to begin with.

I'm glad, though, that at least Manasseh personally experienced God's forgiveness. The story is encouraging for all of us. But Manasseh's life as a whole is a reminder that there is also great consequence for sin. Because of Manasseh's early years of rebellion, Judah was a mess. I suspect that he lived with some serious regrets.

ACTIVITY 50

50A—Younger, Middle, and Older Students

I think that the story of Manasseh and his turning to God is powerful. Sometimes we think that very, very evil people will never turn to God. Manasseh reminds us otherwise.

The Mystery of History

Your activity today is not typical of most. Take time to pray for any leaders in our world right now who seem to be evil. Pray for them to come to know the Lord God through Jesus Christ. Pray for them consistently and follow them in the news. As we have learned, the faith of a leader can change history!

689–612 B.C.

THE POWERS OF MESOPOTAMIA
LESSON 51

In studying the mysteries of history, you have to be a good detective. I'm wondering if any of you caught something unusual about our last lesson. Did anyone notice that the Assyrians carried Manasseh to *Babylon*? Why would they go there? *Nineveh* was the capital of Assyria. Babylon was the chief city of Babylonia, an entirely different country in Mesopotamia. (Notice the ending to the word Babylonia. The added "ia" always refers to the country.) Let's figure out this mystery.

Do you remember the differences between the Spartans and the Athenians? We learned that they were two very different cultures. The Spartans were warlike, and the Athenians were cultural. Those same differences existed in Mesopotamia between two other people groups. They were the Assyrians and the Babylonians. They were at odds with one another for years. Power went back and forth between these countries that were located near the Tigris and Euphrates Rivers.

The Assyrians were the more warlike people. They had a reputation for being terrifying. Their dictators were cruel and didn't allow freedom in their states. The Assyrians were one of the first people to put together a large organized army that used horses and chariots. They were the creators of new weapons such as battering rams and catapults that were used to besiege their enemies. The Assyrians were extremely feared by their neighbors for their military power.

These are the same people that Jonah was called to preach to. No wonder he fled! Perhaps now we get a better understanding of how incredible it was that for a time the Assyrians sought peace with Israel's God. These are also the people of Sennacherib, who boasted of the strength of his army. They were strong militarily, but God wiped out most of them overnight without using a battle at all.

The last great ruler of Assyria was Ashurbanipal. Like his ancestors, he was considered ruthless and cruel. However, unlike other Assyrian rulers he had a passion for cultural

The "Lion of Babylon," a statue in present-day Iraq, stands in memory of ancient Babylon.

things. He built a tremendous library in Ninevah that has since been uncovered. It is from his library collection that much of Assyrian history is known.

One very interesting thing about Assyria is this: Its language was Aramaic. Guess who spoke that language? Jesus did. Jesus probably spoke Hebrew, Greek, and Aramaic. But some scholars believe Aramaic was his home language.

The Babylonians, who lived in southern Mesopotamia near the Euphrates River, held control of the entire Mesopotamian region on and off in the seventh century B.C. If you remember, the Sumerians lived in the valley first. They were builders of great ziggurats and made impressive clay statuettes. Then the great Hammurabi with his strict laws ruled the area. The Babylonians were incredible mathematicians. They devised a counting system based on 60, which is where we get our number of minutes in an hour and the number of degrees in a circle. From all these achievements, we might rightfully conclude that the Babylonians were smart!

In closing, the reason that Manasseh was taken away to Babylon by the Assyrians was because at that time the Assyrians had control over *all* of Mesopotamia, which included Nineveh *and* the city of Babylon. As I said earlier, these two nations struggled for years back and forth over who was in charge of the Mesopotamian region. Things like that still happen today.

In the near future we will learn who—the Assyrians or the Babylonians—lost power forever in Mesopotamia. Maybe you already know, but it's a great story.

ACTIVITY 51

ALL STUDENTS

Make your Memory Cards for Lessons 49–51.

51A—Younger Students

Examine a clock. Count how many minutes there are in an hour. You probably already know. The number is 60, and we get it from the ancient Babylonians who counted by 60's.

Take a protractor and draw shapes with it. Inside the protractor are numbers that we call degrees. These are also counted by 60's because of the Babylonians. Isn't that neat?

Make a whole page of circles and shapes with your protractor and title the page "Contributions of the Babylonians." File it in your Student Notebook under "Asia: Iraq (Mesopotamia)."

51B—Middle Students

Using outside resources, find pictures of battering rams and catapults. Try to make your own replicas out of household items such as toilet paper rolls, rubber bands, buttons for wheels, and so forth. If it turns out, take a picture. Glue it on a page titled "Contributions of the Assyrians." File it under "Asia: Iraq (Mesopotamia)."

51C—Middle and Older Students

Here are some Aramaic words that we find used in the English New Testament. In a Bible dictionary, find out what they mean. Title your paper "Aramaic: The Language of the Assyrians." File your findings under "Asia: Iraq (Mesopotamia)" in your Student Notebook.

Talitha cumi	Eli, Eli lama sabachthani
Abba	Ephphatha
Maranatha	

TAKE ANOTHER LOOK!

Wall of Fame

1. *Athens and Sparta (700–500 B.C.)*—Make a small silhouette of a pot. Write "Athens and Sparta become city-states" on it.

2. *Manasseh (691 B.C.)*—Take the silhouette of a man and draw a line straight down it. Make one-half of him look evil and one-half of him look good. Add a golden cross on him to signify the lineage of Christ.

3. *The Powers of Mesopotamia (689–612 B.C.)*—Draw two punching gloves for this. Write "Assyria" on one and "Babylonia" on the other.

SomeWHERE in Time

1. In a modern atlas, find the cities of Athens and Sparta. Athens is now the capital of Greece. Sparta did not exist for almost 2,000 years after Rome controlled it, but it was re-established as a city in the 1800's. It now is home to about 8,000 people.

   Older students: Color Outline Map 2, "Greece," with major cities, rivers, mountains, and bordering countries. File it under "Europe: Greece."

2. Using a Bible atlas as a reference, on Outline Map 6, "Turkey," write in the countries of Assyria and Babylonia. Using pencils, lightly color Assyria orange and Babylonia green. Add the capital cities of Nineveh and Babylon. With blue pencil, write in the Tigris and Euphrates Rivers. Title this map "The Powers of Mesopotamia 689–612 B.C." File it under "Asia: Iraq (Mesopotamia)."

WHAT DID YOU LEARN?

Week 17: *Quiz*

Fill in the blanks using the word bank provided at the end of this quiz. We have learned a lot in 17 weeks. These quizzes are going to get more difficult!

1. The earliest large pyramids in ancient Egypt were built under the direction of _____.

2. Joseph, one of the 12 sons of Jacob, was born from Jacob's favorite wife, _____.

3. The Tabernacle of God was a sacred _____ built to worship God while the Israelites were wandering in the desert.

4. After Moses died, God worked through _____ to lead the people of Israel into the land of Canaan.

5. _____ lived to be only 18 years old, but we know a lot about his short life from his tomb that was discovered untouched in 1922.

6. According to the legend of the Trojan Horse, _____ was the Greek king who thought up the plan to retrieve Helen from Troy. Homer wrote a separate book on the adventures of this king on his way home from the war.

7. The _____ lived on the coast of the Mediterranean and were known for their trading and production of a purple-red dye derived from snails.

8. _____, the second king of Israel, extended great kindness when he brought Mephibosheth, a crippled relative of Saul, into his kingdom.

9. The prophet _____ warned the mountain people of Edom of their end to come. The Edomites were descendants of Esau.

10. _____ was a blind bard from Greece who wrote the *Iliad*.

The Mystery of History

11. Hindus believe in _____, or the law of Karma, which to them is a continuous rebirth, or another chance to live a good life.

12. The Book of Isaiah is patterned in a fashion similar to the _____ itself by the number of chapters and the content of them.

13. The _____ took over the land of Israel and were attacked by lions.

14. The death angel of the Lord killed 185,000 _____ soldiers to protect Hezekiah from Sennacherib.

15. Some ancient Native Americans buried their dead in huge earthen _____.

16. In the city of Athens, the _____ looked out over the city-state. Many shrines and temples were built there.

17. The Assyrians used _____ and chains to haul Manasseh away.

18. As different as the Spartans were from the Athenians, so the Assyrians were from the _____.

WORD BANK

Tutankhamen	David	Samaritans
Khufu (Cheops)	Phoenicians	mounds
Babylonians	Rachel	Homer
Bible	Acropolis	Joshua
Obadiah	tent	Odysseus
reincarnation	Assyrian	hooks

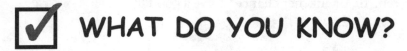

WHAT DO YOU KNOW?

Pretest 18

Guess the right number. All of today's questions are number-related. I doubt you'll know most of the answers, but you have a 50/50 chance of guessing the right one! Circle the answer you think is right. See how well you do.

1. The massive walls of Nincvch were wide enough to hold (3, 13) chariots on top of them, side by side.

2. The towers of Nineveh were as high as (70, 200) feet.

3. King Josiah became a king at the age of (8, 18).

4. By age (16, 76), King Josiah sought to clean Judah of its false idols and images.

5. King Josiah was killed suddenly at the age of (18, 39).

6. Jeremiah, the prophet, lived during the reign of the last (5, 12) kings of Judah.

7. Jeremiah was so unpopular in his day that he was "silenced" at least (2, 10) times.

8. The number of Memory Cards you "should" have made so far is about (32, 51). Hope you're not too far behind!

The Mystery of History

KING JOSIAH

LESSON 52

The last king over Judah that we studied was Manasseh. He was incredibly wicked as a young man but repented of his evil ways when he grew older. Do you remember him? Today we will learn about his grandson Josiah. He was sincerely a great man from the beginning of his reign to the end.

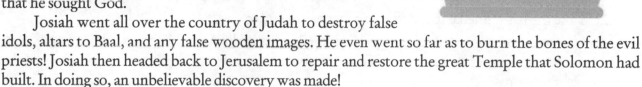

Josiah was only 8 years old when he became king. That is even younger than Hezekiah was. The Bible says that by the time he was 16, "while he was still young, he began to seek the god of his father David." (II Chron. 34:3) This one young man, you will learn, had a powerful impact on the nation of Judah by the fact that he sought God.

Josiah went all over the country of Judah to destroy false idols, altars to Baal, and any false wooden images. He even went so far as to burn the bones of the evil priests! Josiah then headed back to Jerusalem to repair and restore the great Temple that Solomon had built. In doing so, an unbelievable discovery was made!

As craftsmen were working on the walls of the Temple, someone came across the Book of the Law (the first five books of the Old Testament). It was as if they had found the only Bible left in the land of Judah! When it was presented to Josiah, he humbly tore his clothes and wept before the Lord. (Tearing one's clothes was a custom to demonstrate great sorrow.) He must have felt a mixed blessing. There was joy to have the Law again, but there was sorrow to learn how much the people had fallen away from the rediscovered Law.

It would have taken a scribe years back then to copy the book for others to read. So instead, Josiah assembled all the people together, "the great and the small," and had the book read out loud to the gathered crowd. As a result, quite a revival took place. It says in II Chronicles 34:33 that "in all his [Josiah's] days, they did not depart from following the Lord God of their fathers."

To add to the joy, Josiah held a Passover feast like none that had ever been held before. They prepared as many as 30,000 offerings and sacrifices. The Judeans followed the exact instructions of the Lord in their ceremony. The priests were lined up, the singers were in place, and even the gatekeepers followed protocol. The people of Judah followed the Passover with the Feast of Unleavened Bread that lasted for seven days. It must have been an awesome experience of worship and fellowship.

Sadly though, Josiah did not live much longer. In a battle between Egypt and Carchemish, Josiah was fatally wounded by archers. That means he died from a shot by an arrow. The country was stunned! Josiah was only 39 years old when this happened. That's about my age! That is also about how old Princess Diana of England was when she died suddenly. You may remember how shocked the world was at her death. Judah must have felt the same shock about Josiah. The Bible says that all of Judah and Jerusalem mourned for Josiah and "to this day all the singing men and the singing women speak of Josiah in their lamentations. They made it a custom in Israel." (II Chron. 35:24–25).

What a great loss to the people who were just beginning to "get it." True worship had just been restored when Josiah died. The reign of Josiah was like the last breath of fresh air before a storm. And believe me, a big "storm" was yet to come over Judah.

ACTIVITY 52

52A—Younger and Middle Students

Make an ancient scroll.

Materials: Two empty paper towel rolls, several sheets of paper, tea bags, black marker, tape, yarn or raffia ribbon

This project may take more than one day.

1. First, make a strong brew of tea in a large pot on the stove. Remove from heat. Crumple several pieces of paper and set in the tea water. Leave until darkened. Remove and allow to dry.
2. Take the tea-stained paper and tape a few pieces end to end.
3. Using the Hebrew words in the Activity Supplement in the Appendix, copy some phrases onto the paper using a black marker. (Younger students may prefer to glue on a photocopy of the Hebrew words.)
4. Tape the end of one sheet to an empty paper towel roll. Roll the paper onto the towel roll and tape the other end to the other roll.
5. Roll up your scroll and tie it with yarn or raffia.

Younger students may pretend to read the Book of the Law to any audience you can assemble. Maybe even to a gathering of your dolls and stuffed animals.

52B—Middle Students

How well do you know the layout of the Old Testament books of the Bible? Create an outline of the major divisions of the OT books. Using a study Bible for reference, divide the books by these categories:

Pentateuch (5)
Historical Books (12)
Poetic Books (5)
Prophetic Books
    Major prophets (5)
    Minor prophets (12)

File your paper under "Miscellaneous" in your Student Notebook.

52C—Middle and Older Students

The story of Josiah is a reminder of the power of God's word. How are you doing on scripture memory? Many times we memorize verses but lose them from lack of review. Take time today to review verses you may have already memorized as a child or to learn new ones if this is not already a spiritual discipline you have been doing. Test your parents on this! You may know more verses than they do!

The Mystery of History

NAHUM AND ZEPHANIAH

LESSON 53

The Book of Nahum is a short one, but it is very powerful. Nahum, the prophet, lived during the reign of Josiah, but he had a message of doom for the ferocious Assyrians. They were going to pay for their cruelties. Just as the Book of Jonah was dedicated solely to the Ninevites of Assyria, so the Book of Nahum was written to the Assyrians as well.

What again was so terrifying about the Assyrians? Besides being great warriors with new, strong weapons, the Assyrians were known for atrocities to their prisoners. Their own pictures depict captives being hung on stakes and even skinned alive! They were known, too, for handling people with hooks pierced in their bodies. The Assyrians were terribly savage and brutal.

The strength of Nineveh, the capital, was unsurpassed. It had walls 100 feet high with 1,500 towers that stood 200 feet high. The city walls were wide enough that three chariots could be driven on top of them, side by side. The population of Nineveh may have been more than a million.

This is the massive city that Nahum had some strong words for. Interestingly, the name Nahum means, "comfort." That is an odd name for a man who was going to tell the Assyrians about their coming destruction. The comfort of Nahum's message, then, is to the godly. It is a reminder that the wicked will be taken care of by God.

So, what did Nahum have to say exactly? In the form of a poem, he scorned the Ninevites for their wickedness. "Your name shall be perpetuated no longer. Out of the house of your gods I will cut off the carved image and molded image. I will dig your grave, for you are vile." (Nah. 1:14) He told them of their destruction to come, "Your shepherds slumber, O king of Assyria; your nobles rest in the dust. Your people are scattered on the mountains, and no one gathers them." (Nah. 3:18)

Finally, Nahum prophesied *exactly* how Nineveh would be destroyed. He said it would be by a flood. In a few lessons, you will see just how accurate Nahum was and that once again the prophets of God always spoke the truth.

Zephaniah was also a prophet during the reign of Josiah. But his message was to Jerusalem itself and surrounding nations. You see, under Josiah, reforms and revival had sincerely taken place in Judah. But there are always some who don't join in. Zephaniah preached to those people who only *outwardly* gave tribute to the Lord but who inwardly were still lost.

Zephaniah wrote only a short prophecy, but it would have been highly regarded. It seems that he was the great-great-grandson of Hezekiah. That also made him cousin to King Josiah. Those are pretty serious credentials for a prophet. Perhaps it was Zephaniah's relationship to the royalty of Judah itself that helped Josiah make the reforms he made.

Zephaniah wrote to give the people of Jerusalem hope, hope in things yet to come. Like many of the prophets, he wrote of future things that would demonstrate God's ultimate love for his people. "Do not fear; Zion, let not your hands be weak. The Lord your God in your midst, the Mighty One, will save; He will rejoice over you with gladness, He will quiet you in His love, He will rejoice over you with singing." (Zeph. 3:16–17).

Just like Nahum, Zephaniah also predicted the future of Nineveh. He said, in Zephaniah 2:13, "He will stretch out His hand against the north, destroy Assyria, and make Nineveh a desolation." Do you suppose that really happened? Just wait and see!

53A—Younger Students

What size city do you live in? The city of Nineveh was as large as London is today. It may have covered 60 miles from one end to the other. The next time you are traveling by car over a long distance, ask your parents to tell you when you have driven 60 miles. It will take you about an hour. That is how big the city of Nineveh was (but they didn't have cars to get them from one side to the other)!

53B—Younger and Middle Students

Use building blocks to construct a massive city wall that, like Nineveh, has towers that are twice the height of the wall. Make the walls wide enough for three small toy cars to drive on them, side by side. (Just pretend they're chariots.) You may not have enough building blocks for such a feat! If not, attempt one wall instead of a closed wall. Take a picture and title it "The Walls of Nineveh." File it under "Asia: Iraq (Assyria)."

53C—Middle and Older Students

What countries in the world are known now for atrocities as wicked as those of Assyria? Research places where Christians are currently under persecution. Use "The Voice of the Martyrs" as a resource. They are on the Internet at www.persecution.com.

Or write for materials at: The Voice of the Martyrs
P.O. Box 443
Bartlesville, OK 74005
(You may request a special "Link Homeschooler" subscription.)

---

627 B.C.

JEREMIAH
(JUDAH'S PROPHET)

LESSON 54

There are some prophets who just seem more "real" than others. Jeremiah is one of those. As one of the last prophets before the fall of Judah, Jeremiah wrote during horrific times. Like the other prophets, Jeremiah preached with great conviction. But from his writings, we learn that he is a man with great depth of heart. It was as if he had God's own heart, which was broken.

Jeremiah lived during the reign of the last five kings of Judah before the nation finally collapsed. Jeremiah was fortunate to have served first under Josiah, the young godly king who died suddenly. The next four kings were disappointing ones.

After Josiah, the kings of Judah wouldn't listen to Jeremiah or heed his counsel. In fact, few of the Judeans would listen to him either. Instead they mocked and ridiculed him. In an attempt to bring the people to an understanding of God's ways, Jeremiah tried at times to communicate with visual objects. He once took a tattered and mildewed waistcloth that had been hidden behind a rock and showed the people that they were like the worthless cloth when they lived behind false religions. On another occasion, Jeremiah smashed wine bottles together and threw pots to the ground. Smash! Bang! He warned them they would be just like these objects, broken by the Lord for their sins. His warnings were ignored.

Twice in his ministry, Jeremiah was "silenced" by the law for preaching the truth. No one wanted to hear of the destruction that was coming. When he was forbidden to preach, Jeremiah used a scribe by the name of Baruch to write down the words of the Lord. Even then, King Jehoiakim was callous to Jeremiah's preaching and had his sacred scrolls burned. Despite the setbacks, Jeremiah remained a faithful voice of God. He endured many trying times that included prison, exile, and being locked in the stocks.

Though we haven't studied the end of Judah yet, you probably know by now that it's coming. Jeremiah lived through this painful event. It is during this heartbreaking time of Judah's destruction that we get a glimpse not just of Jeremiah, but of God Himself. The Lord seemed to pour His emotions out through this tender prophet so that we might understand how He loves His people.

Jeremiah wrote, "O my soul, my soul! I am pained in my very heart! My heart makes a noise in me; I cannot hold my peace, because you have heard, O my soul, the sound of the trumpet, the alarm of war." (Jer. 4:19)

Jeremiah also left us with an entire book expressing the sorrow of Jerusalem's fall to Babylon. It is the Book of Lamentations. In it he writes,

"For these things I weep; my eye, my eye overflows with water; because the comforter, who should restore my life, is far from me. My children are desolate because the enemy prevailed . . . My eyes fail with tears, my heart is troubled; my bile is poured on the ground because of the destruction of the daughter of my people, because the children and the infants faint in the streets of the city." (Lam. 1:16, 2:11)

It is from passages like these that Jeremiah is remembered as the "weeping prophet." Though he endured much pain, he also wrote, "This I recall to my mind, therefore I have hope. Through the Lord's mercies we are not consumed, because His compassions fail not. They are new every morning; great is Your faithfulness." (Lam. 3:21–23)

By God's mercy, Jeremiah himself was not taken into captivity to Babylon as the majority of Jews were. He moved to Egypt with other Jews who were forced to leave Jerusalem. It was there in Egypt that Jeremiah died. He had seen a lot in his lifetime, both of God's wrath and of His love. We are fortunate to have his heartfelt writings recorded as part of the Old Testament.

ACTIVITY 54

ALL STUDENTS

Make your Memory Cards for Lessons 52–54.

54A—Younger and Middle Students

Jeremiah used an old garment to make a word picture for the people of Judah. With your teacher's approval, take an old, small T-shirt. Cut off the sleeves and neck opening. You should have a round piece of fabric left that is like a waistcloth. Cut some jagged holes in the waistcloth you've made. Then take it outside and roll it around in some dirt. You may need to add water.

This cloth should look pretty bad now. Imagine Jeremiah holding this up to a crowd and showing them that they were worthless like the cloth. He was not a very popular prophet. Tape a sample of your cloth onto a piece of paper and title it "The Prophet Jeremiah Speaks of Sin." File it under "Asia: Israel."

54B—Middle and Older Students

Update the list of kings and prophets over Judah. Highlight the ones that are in capital letters, meaning we have already studied them or will study them in coming lessons.

JUDAH

Kings	Prophets
13. HEZEKIAH	
14. MANASSEH	NAHUM
15. Amon	ZEPHANIAH
16. JOSIAH	JEREMIAH
17. Jehoahaz	
18. JEHOIAKIM	
19. Jehoiachin	
20. ZEDEKIAH	

54C—Older Students

1. Read the Book of Lamentations. Underline every reference to "weeping" or "lamenting."
2. Or, analyze Lamentations 3. Make a contrasting list of the sorrows the writer experienced versus the goodness of the Lord. For example:

Sorrows	Goodness of God
Seeing affliction (Vs. 1)	His compassions fail not (Vs. 22)
Aged my flesh (Vs. 4)	Great is Your faithfulness (Vs. 23)
Broken my bones (Vs. 4)	I hope in Him (Vs. 24)
(continue list)	

_____   _____

_____   _____

_____   _____

_____   _____

Wall of Fame

1. *King Josiah (640 B.C.)*—Show him holding the Book of the Law and place him in the Southern Kingdom. Place a golden cross on him to signify the lineage of Christ.

2. *Nahum (630 B.C.)*—In a cartoon bubble, write the words, "to the Ninevites."

3. *Zephaniah (630 B.C.)*—Write on him "Cousin of King Josiah" and give him a happy face. Place him in the Southern Kingdom.

4. *Jeremiah (627 B.C.)*—Add tears to his face. Have him holding the Book of Lamentations. Place him in the Southern Kingdom.

SomeWHERE in Time

1. On a globe or map of the ancient world, follow with your finger a journey from Assyria to Egypt. What countries must you pass through? The Egyptians were often at war with Assyria and Babylonia. As you can tell from the map, Judah was caught in the middle. For this reason, it is not surprising that King Josiah died in a battle that involved the Egyptians.

2. Look at a scale on a map to determine how many miles it might have been from Jerusalem to the border of Egypt. We know that somehow Jeremiah made this painful journey. What is the greatest distance you have ever traveled? Use the scale of a map to roughly determine it.

PUT IT ALL TOGETHER

Worksheet 2: Lessons 28–54

Since the last worksheet, you have learned 27 more lessons. That is a lot of people to keep straight. Complete this worksheet using your book, timeline, or Memory Cards.

I—Dates to Memorize. In this quarter, there were two significant dates I wanted you to memorize. Recopy them here five times each.

David   c.1055 B.C.

1. _____

2. _____

3. _____

4. _____

5. _____

The Kingdom of Israel Divides   c. 925 B.C.

1. _____

2. _____

3. _____

4. _____

5. _____

II—What Came First? Write the order in which these things happened in history. (Renumber each group separately from 1 to 5.)

1. _____ King Saul ruled over Israel.

2. _____ Samson was a judge.

3. _____ David ruled as king of Israel.

4. _____ The Zhou dynasty overthrew the Shang.

5. _____ Solomon ruled as king of Israel.

1. _____ Homer composed the *Iliad* and the *Odyssey*.

2. _____ The Kingdom of Israel divided.

3. _____ The city of Rome was founded.

4. _____ The first Olympics were held.

5. _____ Elijah prophesied to Israel.

            The Mystery of History

1. _____ Hezekiah ruled in Judah.

2. _____ Isaiah was a prophet to Judah.

3. _____ Manasseh was a king in Judah.

4. _____ Israel fell to Assyria.

5. _____ Jeremiah prophesied to Judah.

III—Where Is It? Match these cities with their countries by placing the correct letter next to the number.

_____1. Samaria   a. Babylonia

_____2. Nineveh   b. Italy

_____3. Athens and Sparta   c. Assyria

_____4. Babylon   d. Israel

_____5. Rome   e. Greece

_____6. Jerusalem   f. Judah

IV—What Goes Where? Match these two columns the same way.

_____1. Homer   a. India

_____2. Jonah and Nahum   b. North America

_____3. Mound Builders   c. Judah

_____4. Jeremiah   d. Nineveh

_____5. Hinduism   e. Greece

V—Fill in the Dates. Use your timeline or the Contents page in your textbook for the answers.

1. The Kingdom of Israel divided in_____.

2. Homer composed the *Iliad* and the *Odyssey* in about _____.

3. The first Olympic games were held in _____.

4. The city of Rome was founded in _____.

5. Israel fell to the Assyrians in _____.

VI—Who Was It? Use different-colored pencils to connect the statement in column 1 to its "match" in column 2.

1. A prophet who wrote about locusts   a. Amos

2. A prophet related to a king of Israel   b. Hosea

3. A prophet who was a fig farmer   c. Manasseh

4. A prophet with an unfaithful wife   d. Joel

5. An evil king who repented   e. Zephaniah

6. The Powers of Mesopotamia   f. Assyrians and Babylonians

VII—Answer These Questions. Refer to the lesson given in parentheses. Write your answers in one or more complete sentences and use a separate sheet of paper if necessary.

1. What were some of the wrongs done by King Saul that led to his downfall? (31)

2. If you were a Phoenician, what kind of skills might you have? (34)

3. How were Elijah and Elisha similar to John the Baptist and Jesus? (37)

4. In what ways were the Spartans and Athenians so different? (49)

5. What was Jeremiah "weeping" about? (54)

Bonus: What kind of snail did the Phoenicians use to make their stinky dye?

SEMESTER I TEST

Lessons 1–54

You should be well prepared for a test like this covering so much back information because every quiz this year has reviewed old lessons. The difference in this test is that it is longer and will cover almost every topic we have studied so far. So, you might want to study first! Use your two worksheets as study guides.

I—True or False? Circle your answer.

1. According to the Bible, God created man and woman on the sixth day.   T   F

2. Adam lived only 39 years because of his sin.   T   F

3. Jubal and Tubal-Cain were explorers and mathematicians.   T   F

4. Noah didn't have room for the dinosaurs on the ark.   T   F

5. During the Ice Age, land bridges were exposed that allowed people to travel more easily from continent to continent.   T   F

6. The Sumerians were known for building Stonehenge.   T   F

7. At the Tower of Babel, people saw rain for the first time.   T   F

II—Multiple Choice. Circle one answer for each question.

1. The Minoans, who built the great Palace of Knossos, lived on the island of
   a. Patmos.
   b. Crete.
   c. Hawaii.
   d. Salamis.

2. The first pyramids in Egypt were built by
   a. King Tut.
   b. Ramses.
   c. Khufu (Cheops).
   d. Aliens.

3. Abraham of the Old Testament was called by God to leave the city of
   a. Sumer.
   b. Ur.
   c. Babylon.
   d. Sodom.

4. Joseph of the Old Testament was one of the 12 sons of

   a. Judah.

   b. Potiphar.

   c. Abraham.

   d. Jacob.

5. Hammurabi's laws were written for the people of

   a. Babylon.

   b. China.

   c. Crete.

   d. Israel.

6. Even before the Shang dynasty of China, the Chinese had discovered how to make

   a. sugar.

   b. silk.

   c. a simple alphabet.

   d. a labyrinth.

7. The _____ were kept in slavery in Egypt after the time of Joseph.

   a. Minoans

   b. Babylonians

   c. Sumerians

   d. Hebrews

III—Fill in the Blanks. Use the word bank at the bottom of this section.

1. As an infant, Moses was placed in a basket to float down the _____ River.

2. The _____ was a sacred tent used for worship by the Hebrews.

3. Nefertiti's husband was the Pharaoh _____, who worshiped a sun god.

4. After the strong reign of Ramses the Great, Egypt began to dwindle as a world power because it lacked the natural resource of _____ for weapons.

5. According to the legend of the Trojan Horse, the _____ were eventually victorious through the cleverness of King Odysseus.

6. Through _____, the Lord helped the Israelites defeat the Midianites using only 300 men with torches, pots, and loud shouts.

7. In the story of Ruth, _____ was her "kinsman redeemer."

8. King Wen of the _____ dynasty was not completely successful at overthrowing the Shang, but his son King Wu was able to do so.

WORD BANK

Tabernacle	iron	Nile	Zhou
Amenhotep IV	Gideon	Greeks	Boaz

The Mystery of History

IV—Who Was It? Use different-colored pencils to connect the statement in column 1 to its "match" in column 2.

1. A strong man with long hair	a. Saul
2. The judge who anointed Saul as king	b. Elijah
3. Jonathan's crazy father	c. Phoenicians
4. The people who helped develop phonics	d. Samson
5. Author of many psalms	e. Samuel
6. Author of Ecclesiastes	f. Obadiah
7. The prophet fed by ravens and hated by Jezebel	g. David
8. The prophet to Esau's descendants	h. Solomon

V—What Came First? Try to number the events in each group in the order that they occurred in history.

1. _____ Noah's sons get off the ark.
2. _____ Dinosaurs were created.
3. _____ Adam and Eve disobeyed God.
4. _____ The Sumerians settled Mesopotamia.
5. _____ Jubal made musical instruments.

1. _____ Ramses II built great structures.
2. _____ King Tutankhamen died.
3. _____ Khufu built the first great pyramids of Egypt.
4. _____ Nefertiti and Amenhotep IV worshiped one god.

1. _____ The Hebrews worshiped in the Tabernacle.
2. _____ Abraham was called by God to move from his home.
3. _____ Moses led the Hebrews out of Egypt.
4. _____ Joseph was sold by his brothers.
5. _____ Gideon served as a judge to Israel.

VI—Sentence Completion. Circle the word that makes the sentence correct.

1. Homer wrote (*The Epic of Gilgamesh*, the *Iliad*).
2. The roots of Hinduism can be traced back to the writings of (the Vedas, Hammurabi's laws).
3. The first Olympics were held by the (Latins, Greeks).
4. The city of Rome was occupied by the (Latins, Edomites) and the Etruscans.
5. Isaiah and Micah were both prophets to (Judah, Israel).
6. The prophet Hosea experienced an unfaithful (son, wife).
7. When the Israelites were deported to Assyria, the (Minoans, Samaritans) moved into their old land.
8. Hezekiah was a (good, bad) king over Judah.

VII—Who Am I? From the word bank below, choose the correct answer for each statement.

1. We lived in North America. _____

2. I am known as the weeping prophet. _____

3. I was a huge city with great towers and walls. _____

4. I was a very godly king who destroyed idols in Judah. _____

5. We are two city-states that fought a lot. _____

6. I was a wicked king over Judah who later repented. _____

WORD BANK

Mound Builders	Athens and Sparta	Manasseh
Josiah	Jeremiah	Nineveh

VIII—Bonus Essay.

In a few sentences, give some examples of how we know that early man was intelligent. For example, "Men built huge pyramids without modern machinery." You may earn one bonus point for every example you can give. Use a separate sheet of paper if necessary.

SEMESTER II

THE CLASSICAL WORLD

CONTENTS

THE MYSTERY BUILDS:
612 B.C. to 404 B.C.

AROUND THE WORLD

Congratulations! You've made it through the first semester of this history course, which is the halfway mark. By this point you have learned a lot! We have studied the rise of most of the great ancient civilizations around the world from Creation through about 600 B.C. From Israel and Assyria to China and India, we have covered a lot of ground. And we've seen just the beginnings of ancient Greece and Rome.

I hope you've made your Memory Cards along the way in the color I recommended. I suggested that the first semester cards be in DARK GREEN. I've referred to that semester as "Creation and Early Civilizations" because that is exactly what we studied.

The second semester of this course is subtitled "The Classical World." What do you think of when you hear the word "classic"? We sometimes use it to describe movies, music, or books that are old but well loved. It refers to things that withstand the test of time because they are deeply appreciated.

In history, the term "classical" really means the same thing. But what you'll find in "The Classical World" in this semester are *ideas* that have stood the test of time. Ideas like democracy, higher education, and equal representation. There was also the development of arts, theater, science, and medicine that greatly improved from 600 B.C. to the time of Christ. Both the Greeks and the Romans were instrumental in laying the foundation for what we call "the classical world." Their ideas and thinking still greatly influence us today. So, when you begin to make your Memory Cards for the second semester (quarters 3 and 4), use a RED marker to set them apart from the others. I'll remind you again when it's time to make them.

You'll also learn in this quarter about the roots of two major religions, Buddhism and Confucianism. One comes from India and the other from China, but both religions are prevalent in all parts of Asia today.

In Judah, we'll see the reign of the last "good" kings before the Babylonians take over. You'll probably recognize some familiar Bible stories, such as that of Daniel in the lions' den and Shadrach, Meshach, and Abed-Nego surviving the fiery furnace. At the same time, you'll begin to learn more about the Medes and the Persians, who unite and emerge to become a prominent nation in history.

As for other places around the world, we know that in Mexico there was a group of people we refer to as the Olmecs who had an established civilization. They built pyramids like the Egyptians did, but their pyramids were made of earth instead of stone. Like the builders of Stonehenge, the Olmecs constructed huge stone figures but their figures were shaped like heads.

In case you noticed, we have briefly mentioned every one of the seven continents so far except one. Do you know which one it is? How about Antarctica? For the record, it is so cold there that man didn't really explore this frozen land until the early 1900s. The "race to the South Pole" is a great story in and of itself—but we're getting way ahead in history here.

For now, continue to think B.C., the years "before Christ." This quarter actually covers only about 200 years of history. But a lot happened in that short period of time that I think is worth learning about. And, as I've said before, I believe you will see God's great hand in the process of orchestrating the events of time.

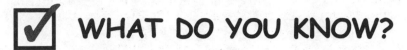

☑ WHAT DO YOU KNOW?

Pretest 19

Jeopardy. I have given you eight answers. Match them to the eight questions below.

1. The Tigris River

2. Nimrod, the great-grandson of Noah

3. Habakkuk

4. Jeremiah the prophet

5. Huldah the prophetess

6. Nebuchadnezzar II of Babylon

7. Three

8. A water tunnel built by Hezekiah

> What minor prophet wrote *to* God?
> What helped the Judeans stay alive during the takeover by Babylon?
> What king first invaded Jerusalem?
> Which major prophet lived at the time of Habakkuk?
> What female helped Josiah interpret the Book of the Law?
> How many tries did it take Nebuchadnezzar to defeat Judah?
> What is a major river in Mesopotamia?
> Who originally founded Nineveh?

NINEVEH DESTROYED

LESSON 55

Nineveh. Most of us know this city from the familiar story of Jonah. Because of Jonah's fear and dislike of the Ninevites, he jumped on a ship to Tarshish rather than heed God's instruction to go there. Of course, after spending three thought-provoking days and nights in the belly of a big fish, Jonah went to Nineveh after all, and the people repented of their wickedness. But then what happened to Nineveh? Have you ever wondered if it's still around today? Let's look now at a brief history of Nineveh and learn of its ultimate fate.

You may find it interesting that Nineveh was originally founded after the Great Flood by one of the great-grandsons of Noah. His name was Nimrod. You can read about him in Genesis 10:8. The Bible indicates that he was "a mighty hunter before the Lord," and that he settled several cities including Babylon. What we can gather from this information is that Nineveh was a very old city—one of the oldest cities of the ancient world.

Besides being old, Nineveh was huge! Much like many large cities today, Nineveh was really a group of small cities clustered together. They stretched as far as 30 miles in length. At least a million people lived in the vicinity. A 100-foot wall with high towers surrounded the city as well as three water-filled moats. The city wall was so wide that three chariots could ride on top of it, side by side.

As for the people of Nineveh, they were fierce. Or at least their army was. The Assyrians were known for developing massive weapons of war such as catapults and battering rams. Worse than that, the Assyrians were known for how cruelly they tortured their prisoners of war by skinning them alive and removing body parts. Remember, too, that Assyria was home to the ever-prideful Sennacherib, the king who tried to take over the Southern Kingdom of Israel but was stopped by God's death angel.

Trilobe arrowheads, such as these, have three sides instead of two, creating a deadly weapon. These date back to Israel, somewhere between the seventh and fourth centuries B.C.

However, there was a time of spiritual revival for Nineveh before Sennacherib ever ruled. For decades after Jonah preached to them, the Assyrians changed their evil ways and made drastic political reforms. Why the change didn't last, no one really knows. But it didn't. That's why, years later, Nahum and Zephaniah prophesied to the Ninevites as well. They had some serious words of warning for these people.

For example, Zephaniah wrote to the Ninevites, "And He will stretch out His hand against the north, destroy Assyria, and make Nineveh a desolation, as dry as the wilderness . . . This is the rejoicing city that dwelt securely, that said in her heart, 'I am it, and there is none besides me.' How has she become a desolation, a place of beasts to lie down! Everyone who passes by her shall hiss and shake his fist." (Zeph. 2:13, 15)

Nahum warned, too, about the destruction of Nineveh. "Your name shall be perpetuated no longer. Out of the house of your gods I will cut off the carved image and the molded image. I will dig your grave, for you are vile." (Nah. 1:14) Nahum then gave detail as to how bloody and gory the end would be for Nineveh. He wrote, "She is empty, desolate, and waste! The heart melts, and the knees shake; much pain is in every side, and all their faces are drained of color . . . Woe to the bloody city! . . . Horsemen charge with bright sword and glittering spear. There is a multitude of slain, a great number of bodies, countless corpses—they stumble over the corpses." (Nah. 2:10, 3:1, 3.)

With amazing accuracy, Nahum even predicted how Nineveh would be destroyed—he said it would be by a flood. "But with an overflowing flood He will make an utter end of its place . . . The gates of the rivers are opened, and the palace is dissolved." (Nah. 1:8, 2:6)

Sure enough, in about 612 B.C., there was such a bad flood from a nearby river that it caused some of the huge walls surrounding Nineveh to erode and collapse. This greatly weakened the defenses of Nineveh against neighboring countries that she had been fighting for almost two years. With the walls washed out, the once powerful city was finally taken advantage of and destroyed altogether by nearby enemies. Their enemies included the Medes, the Sythians, and, of course, the Babylonians.

Nineveh never recovered. This ancient city, which had been home to millions since the Great Flood, was completely laid to waste. With the loss of Nineveh, the country of Assyria lost control of the Mesopotamian region once and for all, just as Nahum and Zephaniah had prophesied.

In fact, for nearly 2,000 years Nineveh laid hidden under the earth as if it had disappeared from time. Archaeologists uncovered it in the mid-1800s. It was quite an amazing discovery about 200 years ago to find this city that some believed was only a tale from the Bible. In the ruins were found Sennacherib's elaborate palace and the library of Ashurbanipal. One-third of this magnificent library, which held 100,000 volumes of writings, has been restored and is on display in England.

Though hidden for hundreds of years, both the ruins of the palace and the documents of the library give great tribute to the power of the ancient Assyrian kingdom. The unearthing of Nineveh also verifies just how accurate the Bible really is. It proves itself over and over again to be a great history book.

ACTIVITY 55

55A—Younger Students

If you have a sandbox outside, build a sand castle in it. Then, with a garden hose, wash the walls of the castle away. This is what the Lord allowed to happen to Nineveh. He is a Holy God who hates sin. We are fortunate to know Jesus Christ who died for our sins! Discuss this with your family if it is something you don't yet understand.

55B—Middle Students

In the Bible there are some occasions where sin is "washed away." Can you think of examples? (A list is provided in the footnote[1] on this page, but don't look until you need to!) Talk with your teacher about the power of the blood of Christ in washing away OUR sins.

55C—Older Students

Dig deeper into the topic of the founding of the city of Nineveh by Nimrod. Obtain a copy of *The Works of Josephus.* (Josephus was a Jewish historian who lived after the time of Christ. Most scholars accept his works as being extremely accurate.)

Look up Nimrod in the index of *The Works of Josephus.* Read what Josephus had to say about Nimrod's attitude toward building his great cities. The eventual destruction of Nineveh takes on a deeper meaning if Josephus was accurate in the description of Nimrod.

Write a one-page essay on your discovery. File it under "Asia: Iraq (Mesopotamia)."

---

1. Examples: the Great Flood, blood of sacrificed animals, the Passover, the blood of Christ on the cross, baptism

HABAKKUK AND HULDAH

LESSON 56

Each of the prophets of the Old Testament that we have studied so far has had his own special message. Obadiah wrote to the people of Edom, who were Esau's descendants. Jonah and Nahum preached to the people of Nineveh. Joel used locusts to describe devastation to the people of Judah. Hosea wrote of his unfaithful wife to describe the Israelites. Can you name some of the others we've studied and what their special message was?

Unlike any of the other prophets, Habakkuk didn't write to any people at all. He wrote to God Himself! In the Book of Habakkuk, we find a conversation between Habakkuk and God that is quite amazing.

Apparently Habakkuk, who lived in Judah about the same time as Jeremiah, was quite bothered by the sins of the Jewish people. In the opening chapters of the book, Habakkuk asks God, "Why do You show me iniquity, and cause me to see trouble? For plundering and violence are before me; there is strife, and contention arises." (Hab. 1:3)

The Lord explains to Habakkuk that He has a plan. "For indeed I am raising up the Chaldeans, a bitter and hasty nation which marches through the breadth of the earth, to possess dwelling places that are not theirs. They are terrible and dreadful . . . " (Hab. 1:6–7) In case you are confused, let me explain something. "Chaldeans" is just another name for the Babylonians. You should remember that they are now the "powerhouse" of Mesopotamia because the Assyrians of Nineveh had been destroyed.

So, we now see the Lord telling Habakkuk ahead of time that the Babylonians, though "terrible and dreadful," will be used by God Himself to end the evil of His chosen people. In Habakkuk 2:18–19, God specifically warns Habakkuk against the man-made idols that the people were still trusting in. You will soon learn that the Babylonians did take over Judah for a time, just as Habakkuk prophesied. I imagine you're not surprised!

I also want to write about Huldah today. Huldah was a woman who was a prophet so we refer to her as a "prophetess." Just to let you know, there were many Old Testament prophets and prophetesses who didn't have books named after them in the Bible—one of them being Huldah. In fact, God may have spoken through hundreds of different men and women as prophets and prophetesses, though not all are recorded in the Bible.

Because we don't have a book written about Huldah, we don't know much about her. Her brief story is in II Chronicles 34:22–28 as well as II Kings 22:14–20. We do know she lived at the time of both Habakkuk and Jeremiah. Do you remember good King Josiah? One of his men found the old translation of the Book of the Law in the Temple. Josiah used Huldah as one of the people to verify that the book was real. Huldah was influential in helping the people understand the book. She must have been well respected because the people *did* listen, and they tried to make reforms according to the Book of the Law.

Through both the private life of Habakkuk and the public ministry of Huldah, the Lord continued to reveal Himself and His laws to the people He loved. Through the Bible, we have record of it even today.

56A—Younger Students

Habakkuk was a man who felt he could ask God questions. Do you feel like you know God well enough to talk to Him? We talk to God through prayer. With your teacher, pray to God about questions you might have. God is always pleased when we come to Him in prayer about anything.

56B—Middle and Older Students

At the close of the Book of Habakkuk, the prophet prays a hymn of faith. Read it yourself in Habakkuk 3:17–19. The prophet basically declares that even though things may not go well, he will still trust in the Lord. Because of the times in which Habakkuk lived, he used examples of failures in nature.

In modern-day words, rewrite the hymn of faith that Habakkuk wrote but use examples of problems we encounter today. For example, "Though the car won't start, or my math doesn't make sense . . . yet I will rejoice in the Lord." Give as many examples as Habakkuk did, just modernize them.

Remember that Habakkuk had an attitude of trust and confidence in God even though his world was falling apart. His country was about to be taken over. Some of our stress is mild compared to his. File your hymn under "Asia: Israel."

56C—Middle and Older Students

1. Habakkuk wrote to God. Do you keep a journal of prayers or thoughts to God? I especially like to write my thoughts to God when going through difficult or special times. Keep a journal for such occasions if you don't already do so.

2. Using a Bible encyclopedia, research the role of women in the Old Testament. What was their primary position in society? Were women allowed to vote, own property, receive an education, divorce, or speak in court? How special might it have been for a woman to be a prophetess? Write a short paper on the role of women in the Old Testament. File it under "Asia: Israel."

605, 597, 586 B.C.

THE BABYLONIAN CAPTIVITY

LESSON 57

You might have known this was coming. Almost one hundred years after the Lord allowed the Assyrians to conquer Israel, Judah herself was going down. However, it wasn't going to be the Assyrians who would take over Judah; it was going to be the Babylonians. Despite the warnings of all the prophets like Isaiah, Micah, Zephaniah, and Jeremiah, the people of Judah were still entrenched in sin. And the Lord wasn't going to tolerate it anymore. Beginning in 605 B.C., the people of Judah were going to learn a very hard lesson.

The invasion of Judah began first with the city of Jerusalem. The man behind the campaign was Nebuchadnezzar II, the king of Babylon. (There are a lot of fascinating things to know from the Bible about Nebuchadnezzar II, so the next lesson focuses on him alone.) In 605 B.C., Nebuchadnezzar II and his army captured the king of Judah, named Jehoikim, and made him a prisoner! This was just the beginning of the downfall of Judah. At the same time, Nebuchadnezzar "took captive" some of the youth of Jerusalem. He took them back home to Babylon where he hoped he could use them to benefit his own country. One of those young men was Daniel of the Old Testament. (We will learn *much* more about him later, too.)

This terra-cotta, Persian horseman was crafted between 586 and 300 B.C.

The conquest of Jerusalem was not an overnight success. Nebuchadnezzar had to return two more times over the course of several years to finally conquer Jerusalem once and for all. In reading the Old Testament, you might find this time period confusing. It is difficult to follow because even though Jehoikim had been captured by the Babylonians, there were two additional kings who ruled Judah after him. This is because Nebuchadnezzar II appointed two men as "puppet" kings over Judah. In the same way that a puppet is directed by a puppeteer, these kings were really ruled by Nebuchadnezzar II.

By name, the two kings appointed by Nebuchadnezzar were Jehoiachin and Zedekiah. Lacking real kings with any authority of their own, the Kingdom of Judah was in a terrible position of weakness for several years. (You will notice that Jehoikim and Jehoiachin are very similar names. To remember who came first, notice that Jehoikim ends with an "m" and Jehoiachin ends with an "n." The last letters of their names happen to be in alphabetical order according to who was first.)

As a result of Babylon's slow and steady takeover, Judah slipped into complete despair and chaos. As more and more people were taken prisoner, families were divided. Marketplaces, businesses, and farms were lost or abandoned. Food became scarce. There was nowhere to turn for help. Eventually most of the people of Judah were driven out of the cities and taken prisoner to Babylonia! It was awful.

There were three main dates when most of the Judeans were taken into captivity. They were 605, 597, and 586 B.C. If you understand that some people were taken away and some were left behind, it will give you a better understanding of what life was like then in Judah. It would have been a terrible time. No one knew for sure who was going to be taken prisoner to Babylon or left in Jerusalem to try to survive. Some people lived in denial that the takeover was happening at all though devastation surrounded them. These were the horrific times that Jeremiah wrote about and wept over in the Book of Lamentations.

One interesting thing that helped the city of Jerusalem resist Nebuchadnezzar II for a time was its water supply. You see, when an enemy wanted to take a city, it usually tried to cut off the food and water supply to the city. This didn't happen easily in Jerusalem, which may be one reason it took three sieges to capture the city for good.

The city of Jerusalem had a water source, called the Spring of Gihon, that was located just outside the city gates. This location wasn't good for the people in wartime because an enemy could easily steal their water. Without water, the people would eventually die. But King Hezekiah, who lived years before this time, had secretly built a tunnel for this water. His tunnel was 1,700 feet long and built through solid rock! It pointed downhill into the city to a place called the Pool of Siloam. This water source helped to keep the people of Jerusalem alive for at least the last few years that they fought off the Babylonians.

The final invasion by the Babylonians was the worst. When Zedekiah, the last "appointed" king of Judah, was taken prisoner the guards killed his sons right in front of him and then blinded him. It was an extremely cruel act. The Babylonians then stripped Jerusalem of any valuables that had been left behind and burned the city to the ground. For the next 70 years, Jerusalem, the once great city of God, lay in complete ruin. Only the very poor, old, or crippled remained there to till what was left of the soil and try to survive.

The words of Jeremiah, the prophet, were completely accurate. "I will send and take all the families of the north, says the Lord, and Nebuchadnezzar the king of Babylon, My servant, and will bring them against this land, against its inhabitants, and against these nations all around, and will utterly destroy them, and make them an astonishment, a hissing, and perpetual desolations . . . And this whole land shall be a desolation and an astonishment, and these nations shall serve the king of Babylon seventy years." (Jer. 25:9, 11)

It is a sad story about sin and its consequences. The Judeans had been warned over and over again of their fate if they failed to repent. They were learning again that the prophets of God always spoke the truth.

ACTIVITY 57

ALL STUDENTS

Make your Memory Cards for Lessons 55–57. Use a RED MARKER now for the new semester and time period, "The Classical World." The Babylonian Captivity (605 B.C.) is a date to memorize. Highlight the card.

57A—Younger Students

Make two puppet kings.

Materials: Two lunch-size brown paper bags, crayons or markers

In today's lesson I wrote about two kings who were "puppet" kings of Judah. That means that someone else really ruled over them. That made them like puppets. You can make your own puppets today. Take your paper bag and turn it upside down. Draw a face on each bag to represent Jehoiachin and Zedekiah. Insert your hand into the bag and have them act out being kings. Because they are puppets, you are really telling them what to do. That is how Nebuchadnezzar ruled over the last two kings of Judah.

57B—Middle Students

Where is the water source for your community? How important is water to human survival? Find out in an encyclopedia or some other resource, how long people can live without water. Hezekiah was brilliant to have had the foresight to reroute water into the city of Jerusalem. Write a few paragraphs on your findings and file them under "Asia: Israel."

57C—Older Students

Use a concordance such as *Strong's Exhaustive Concordance of the Bible* to look up the Pool of Siloam. There are references to the Pool of Siloam in the New Testament. We can conclude then that the aqueduct built by Hezekiah remained intact for years after the Babylonian Captivity. Can you find more information on this topic? In one of my resources I was able to find a modern picture of the tunnel, which still stands today. See what you can find!

TAKE ANOTHER LOOK!

Wall of Fame

1. *Nineveh destroyed (612 B.C.)*—Using pencil, write the words "Nineveh Destroyed" on a small piece of paper along with the date. Then, hold this piece of paper under running water for a few seconds and crumple it up with your hands. After it dries, attach it to the timeline. It should appear damaged by water, just like Nineveh!

2. *Habakkuk (607 B.C.)*—Draw the silhouette of a man on his knees with his head looking up. This will depict how Habakkuk spoke directly to God.

3. *Huldah (exact date unknown)*—Place her next to Josiah. Depict her holding a book.

4. *The Babylonian Captivity (605, 597, 586 B.C.)*—On a piece of paper, draw chains and include the three dates of deportation. **Remember, this is a date to memorize. (You only have to remember the date of 605 B.C.)**

SomeWHERE in Time

1. Compare a historical map of Assyria with a modern map of Iraq. What modern city do you think is located closest to the ancient city of Nineveh?

2. On Outline Map 6, "Turkey," use chalks or pastels to draw in the three different trips taken by the captives. Make a key on the page that explains the time frame of each deportation.

3. Older Students: Using the same color as the one you chose for the second deportation, make a trail from Palestine to Egypt. It was during the second deportation that many of the Jews escaped to Egypt. Jeremiah was one of those who escaped.

   Clearly label your map "The Babylonian Captivity" and file it under "Asia: Israel."

WHAT DID YOU MISS?

Week 19: Exercise

Before learning about more prophets, let's review those we've studied so far. You may use your book if necessary, and you will also need highlighters, markers, or crayons.

1. Circle (or highlight) in dark green the prophet who was also the last judge over Israel.

   a. Nahum

2. Circle in orange the prophet who was carried away in a chariot of fire.

   b. Joel

3. Circle in light blue the prophet who performed miracles most like Jesus.

   c. Isaiah

4. Circle in black the prophet who used a locust plague as an analogy.

   d. Jeremiah

5. Circle in light purple the prophet to the Edomites.

   e. Obadiah

6. Circle in gray the first prophet to Nineveh.

   f. Samuel

7. Circle in red the prophet who was kicked out of the city by the priest.

   g. Micah

8. Circle in light pink the "well-educated" prophet.

   h. Elisha

9. Circle in yellow the prophet who foretold Jesus' birthplace.

   i. Zephaniah

10. Circle in turquoise the prophet whose name means "comfort."

    j. Habakkuk

11. Circle in light green the prophet who was the great-great-grandson of Hezekiah and cousin to Josiah.

    k. Hosea

12. Circle in hot pink the prophet who used a filthy waistcloth to display the sin of Judah.

    l. Jonah

13. Circle in dark blue the prophet who wrote to God.

    m. Elijah

14. Circle in brown the prophetess we studied.

    n. Huldah

15. Circle in dark purple the prophet who married Gomer.

    o. Amos

Now, do these four things: Place a star over every prophet to Israel (5 in all). Place a box around every prophet to Judah (6). Put squiggles around the prophets to Nineveh and Assyria (2). Place a check mark over the prophets who preached outside of Israel, Judah, or Assyria (2).

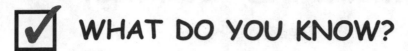

WHAT DO YOU KNOW?

Pretest 20

There are three names listed here and nine facts below. With a pink highlighter or marker, highlight "Nebuchadnezzar II" and the three facts below that you think belong to him. Do the same with "Daniel" in green and "Aesop" in yellow.

Nebuchadnezzar II   **Daniel**   **Aesop**

Had bad dreams

Ate only veggies

Was once a Greek slave

Wrote stories

Sat before lions

Built the Hanging Gardens

Was murdered

Went "mad"

Saw the future

NEBUCHADNEZZAR II AND THE HANGING GARDENS

LESSON 58

You have already been introduced to Nebuchadnezzar II in our last lesson as the Babylonian king who took over Judah. There is much more about his life that is fascinating to me. He learned about the God of Israel the hard way.

Besides being strong militarily, Nebuchadnezzar was a great builder. One thing he is remembered for is the building of the beautiful Ishtar Gate. The gate was a huge archway that led to a temple outside the city. It was made of blue, glazed brick and had pictures of lions and dragons on it. Ishtar was the name of an ancient goddess that the people worshiped. The Ishtar Gate was recovered by German archaeologists and reconstructed in a museum in Berlin. You could see it there today.

Another really amazing structure built by Nebuchadnezzar was the Hanging Gardens of Babylon. Supposedly Nebuchadnezzar's wife was from Media and she missed the lush mountains of her homeland. So, Nebuchadnezzar built for her what was basically a huge ziggurat with plants and trees covering it. The gardens didn't really hang but only appeared to as they stretched way up into the sky and surrounded the structure. The Hanging Gardens of Babylon is considered to be one of the Seven Wonders of the Ancient World. Of course, we don't have photos of this ancient spectacle, but from all historic accounts, the Hanging Gardens was an incredible sight to see.

The Hanging Gardens of Babylon, built by Nebuchadnezzar for his homesick wife, is one of the Seven Wonders of the Ancient World.

These feats are interesting to read about. But Nebuchadnezzar had some serious problems. For one thing, he had a lot of pride over his accomplishments. He also had dreams that frightened him. Nebuchadnezzar asked all his wise men to interpret one of his dreams, but he wouldn't tell them what the dream was.

Only one man was capable of interpreting the king's dream, and he was not even a Babylonian. He was Daniel, who had been taken captive from Jerusalem as a young man. With God's help, Daniel revealed to Nebuchadnezzar what the dream was and what it meant. The prophecies of Daniel are a topic we will study later. What is important to remember is that Daniel was a godly man who spoke the truth to Nebuchadnezzar.

Many times Nebuchadnezzar acknowledged the God of Daniel. Still, he apparently held on to some of his own beliefs and to his pride until near the end of his life. At one point he was walking about the royal palace of Babylon and said, "Is not this great Babylon, that I have built for a royal dwelling by my mighty power and for the honor of my majesty?" God's answer to him was, "the kingdom has departed from you! And they shall drive you from men, and your dwelling shall be with the beasts of the field. They shall make you eat grass like oxen; and seven times shall pass over you, until you know that the Most High rules in the kingdom of men, and gives it to whomever He chooses." (Dan. 4:30–32)

And that is exactly what happened to Nebuchadnezzar. He went "mad" and lived like an animal for seven years, eating grass. The Bible says his hair grew like eagles' feathers and his nails like birds' claws. That is quite a step down for such a successful conqueror.

The Lord used it for good though. At the end of the seven years, Nebuchadnezzar regained his sanity and actually praised the God of Israel. He said, "Now I, Nebuchadnezzar, praise and extol and honor the King of heaven, all of whose works are truth, and His ways justice. And those who walk in pride He is able to abase." (Dan. 4:37)

Just as I wrote in the opening of this lesson, Nebuchadnezzar learned about the Lord the hard way. It took seven years of living like a wild animal for this king to be humbled and to call upon the Lord. We don't know if he ever abandoned his own false gods, but he certainly had close encounters with the One true God.

ACTIVITY 58

58A—Younger Students

In a book from the library or from a computer encyclopedia, obtain a photocopy of the Ishtar Gate. Color the gate blue. If the shapes of lions and dragons are clear, color those white. The Ishtar Gate was beautiful because of the blue tile covering it. File this picture in your Student Notebook under "Asia: Iraq (Babylonia)."

58B—Middle Students

At the library or on the computer, find more information on the Hanging Gardens of Babylon. Many artists have drawn what they think it looked like but nobody knows for sure. Try to sketch what you think the structure would have looked like. File your drawing under "Asia: Iraq (Babylonia)."

58C—Older Students

Using outside resources, research the false gods of the Babylonians. Because the names are frequently used in the Old Testament, they are worth our understanding. Begin with Marduk and Ninmah. There were approximately 50 temples built for the gods in the city of Babylon alone. Another lead is to read Isaiah 46:1. There are references to "Bel" and "Nebo." The names of these gods became prefixes for the kings! In a short paper, write down all the information you can find. File it under "Asia: Iraq (Babylonia)."

635–536 B.C.

DANIEL

LESSON 59

You have probably heard the story of Daniel in the lions' den. It's a great testimony to God's faithfulness. But do you know the life story of Daniel? The Bible tells us a lot about him. Like David, he is one of my favorite Bible characters.

We first learn of Daniel during the reign of Nebuchadnezzar. Remember how the people of Judah were carried off to Babylon on three different occasions? Daniel and some of his friends were taken as prisoners in the very first deportation. Daniel would have been only a young man or a teenager. This means that he was probably about 14 or 16 years old when King Josiah died. Daniel would also have been alive when Jeremiah gave his prophecies. Both of these godly men may have influenced Daniel because he had an unusually strong faith in God.

Can you imagine how scary it would be to be taken away from your home in ropes and chains? It may have terrified Daniel and his friends. But we learn in the Bible that Daniel was very brave by the time they reached Babylon.

You see King Nebuchadnezzar wanted Daniel and his friends to eat his "good" food so that they would become strong men and work for him. Daniel boldly said no! He asked to be given all "natural" foods instead of the king's. The king's food would probably have been more refined and some may have been used for sacrifices to heathen idols. By refusing the special food, Daniel and his friends put their trust in God's provisions (the natural foods) instead of man's.

Do you know what happened? In just a short time, Daniel and his friends were far stronger and healthier than any of the other men in training. That took a lot of courage and faith. But, for Daniel, it was only the beginning of a lifetime of trusting God.

Years later, Daniel was brave enough to face death in a lions' den rather than worship King Darius. It is a story most of us know from childhood. Darius was really fond of Daniel but was tricked into trying to put him to death for praying to God instead of to him. By God's absolute grace, Daniel was spared from the hungry lions. They didn't eat him! To Darius and many others who witnessed the miracle, it was a great demonstration of God's power to save. It continues to be a powerful story.

Those are just a few reasons why I like Daniel. But you should also know how much God loved him. Several times, the Lord refers to Daniel as His "beloved." Some people say that Daniel in the Old Testament is a lot like John in the New Testament. Both were greatly loved by God, both were faithful to God all their lives, and both received supernatural visions of future events.

These visions seen by Daniel are not easy to explain. You should be familiar with them, though, because Daniel foretold the future very clearly. That miracle is a testimony to the authenticity of the Bible. "Authenticity" just means that the Bible is absolutely true.

One of the things Daniel foretold was that four great empires were going to rule in the future. He saw visions of beasts that represented the empires. King Nebuchadnezzar had dreams of them, too. Daniel had been the only man who could interpret the dreams for Nebuchadnezzar. The four empires were the Babylonians, the Medes-Persians, the Greeks, and the Romans. You may not realize it now, but Daniel's prophecies about the empires all came true and for a good reason. Christians believe that God used the Roman world to usher in the time of Christ. Under the Romans, the Gospel spread easily because transportation and communication were strong. So, Daniel's prophecy of the Roman rule to come was very meaningful. He saw God's marvelous hand in history.

Daniel also made claims to know of a special date. He prophesied that there would be "seventy weeks" between the time of rebuilding Jerusalem and the Messiah. (Dan. 9:24) By now you ought not to be surprised to know that the prophecy was fulfilled to the exact date! (In case you are confused about the 70 weeks, it meant 490 years in prophetic terms.) There was that much time between the rebuilding of Jerusalem and when Jesus rode through Jerusalem on a donkey. God's word is incredible!

There are more fascinating stories about Daniel that we will study in the future. In the meantime, you can read more about him in the Book of Daniel in the Bible. And by the way, Daniel wrote the book in two languages, Aramaic and Hebrew. Can you remember where Aramaic was spoken? Think about it.

ACTIVITY 59

59A—Younger Students

Make a "pasta" picture of a lion.

Materials: Macaroni noodles, linguini or spaghetti noodles, glue, construction paper, pencils

Trace or draw a simple picture of a lion on construction paper. Glue macaroni noodles over the part of the lion that is his mane. Glue the spaghetti or linguini noodles in other places on the lion, like his tail or legs. Leave room to draw a picture of Daniel nearby. He was in the lions' den praying for God to protect him. Of course, God did.

59B—Middle Students

Read in Daniel, Chapter 1, how Daniel and his friends ate for 10 days. They turned down the king's delicacies for vegetables and water. Do your own experiment. Cut out sugary foods for 10 days and see if you notice any difference in how you feel. This could be a great challenge for some families. Sugar is found in many of our commercial foods. Read the labels of the foods you eat and do your best. Like Daniel, we might all do better to stick to foods that God created, not man.

59C—Older Students

The portion of Daniel regarding prophecy is far too rich to pass up. Do a deeper study on one of his three main prophecies:

The Four Empires
The Seventy Years
The End Times

Using Bible encyclopedias and/or commentaries, write a two-page explanation of the prophecy you chose to study. File your study under "Asia: Iraq."

---

600 B.C.

AESOP'S FABLES

LESSON 60

In the last few weeks we have studied pages and pages of the history of Israel. I think it's important to know how the Old Testament Bible figures fit into world history. But, of course, there were other things going on in the world besides the Babylonian Captivity that were not mentioned in the Bible.

So today we are going to move over to Greece and learn about a man named Aesop. More than likely you have already heard of him.

Aesop (E sahp) lived about 600 B.C. During this time, Greece was still in the Archaic period and organized into city-states. Like many people in Greece, Aesop was actually a slave for some part of his life. But unlike most slaves, Aesop possessed a skill that eventually bought him his freedom. What was his valuable skill? Aesop was a master storyteller.

The stories that Aesop told were called fables. This means that they had a moral to them. Most often Aesop used animals to make a point in his stories. In much the same way, Jesus used parables to explain spiritual truths to people because it made these truths easier to understand.

Aesop probably used animals to represent people in different positions in society. A powerful lion could depict a king, a clever wolf could portray a cruel nobleman, and a small grasshopper could represent a person of lesser importance. In using these symbols, Aesop could safely make a point in his stories without directly offending these people and possibly winding up in jail.

Some scholars think that many of Aesop's fables were written by other people. They may have been folktales passed down for generations. Indeed, many of his stories may have been just that. Others think that Aesop himself actually wrote a majority of the fables he is credited with writing.

We don't know a lot about Aesop's personal life. But, supposedly, Aesop was a slave who was set free by one of his masters because his stories were so clever. His master saw more value in him as a free man and storyteller than as a slave. Once free, Aesop became so popular that even the kings invited him to their courts for entertainment.

Legend says that a king named Croesus asked Aesop to go to the city of Delphi and distribute some money to the people there. Aesop thought the people were not worthy of the money because they were dishonest. Without their money from the king, the people of Delphi became so angry with Aesop that they threw him over a cliff!

Supposedly, terrible plagues came over the people of Delphi as a result of this violent act. From that incident came the expression the "blood of Aesop." It refers to the payback the people of Delphi received for having killed an innocent man.

Despite the tragic ending of Aesop's life, there is a true beauty to the fables he left behind. His stories are timeless because the morals still hold true today.

For example, the popular story of the tortoise and the hare can be retold over and over and still make a point about the perseverance of the humble. The slow, steady tortoise won a race over the quick, proud hare because he remained focused and on track. The hare lost the race against the tortoise for being a careless show-off.

Be like the tortoise yourself in focusing on your schoolwork! Good, steady studying will pay off in the long run!

ACTIVITY 60

ALL STUDENTS

Make your Memory Cards for Lessons 58–60.

60A—Younger Students

Obtain a copy of *Aesop's Fables* and read them with your teacher. Pick one of your favorites and bring it to life with puppets. Make your puppets out of paper sacks or socks. Re-enact the fable with your puppets for the whole family. Take pictures and file it under "Europe: Greece."

60B—Middle Students

From a copy of *Aesop's Fables*, find the story of "The Wolf and the House Dog." After reading it, consider why Aesop would have written a fable like this. (He had been a slave himself.) Do you agree with the moral that "It is better to starve and be free than to eat well and be a slave"? Discuss this with your teacher.

60C—Middle and Older Students

Complete a creative writing project. Write your own fable. Be sure to include a moral and use animals to depict a truth. Aesop was a master at this. He made it look simple when it really isn't all that easy! File your fable under "Europe: Greece."

TAKE ANOTHER LOOK!

Wall of Fame

1. *Nebuchadnezzar II (605 B.C.)*—Draw him with feathers and long nails to depict his later years.

2. *The Hanging Gardens of Babylon (c. 605 B.C.)*—Because this spectacle was one of the Seven Wonders of the World, recreate a "Hanging Garden" picture and place it next to Nebuchadnezzar.

3. *Daniel (635–536 B.C.)*—Draw a carrot in his hand to symbolize his special diet at the palace. If there is room on your timeline, add a lion at his feet. You can place Daniel anywhere between the above dates. Your timeline will already be crowded at around 605 B.C.

4. *Aesop (600 B.C.)*—Put a pen and book in his hands.

SomeWHERE in Time

Find Greece on a map. We are not sure what city Aesop was from. What are the modern-day major cities of this country? What is the capital? Who is the present ruler of Greece? Answer these questions orally if you are young. If you are older, record the answers on Outline Map 2, "Greece," and file it in your Student Notebook under "Europe: Greece." (You may have separate divisions for "Ancient Greece" and "Greece.")

WHAT DID YOU LEARN?

Week 20: Quiz

I. True or False? Circle your answer.

1. According to the Bible, man and woman were created on the fourth day of Creation. T F

2. During the Ice Age, the ENTIRE earth was covered by ice. T F

3. The Minoans are named after King Minos and lived on the island of Crete. T F

4. Abraham was the father of Jacob. T F

5. The Israelites were in slavery in Egypt for about 200 years. T F

6. Tutankhamen married the daughter of Nefertiti. T F

7. Solomon's greatest downfall was the love of gold. T F

8. Homer composed the *Iliad* and the *Odyssey*. T F

9. The city of Rome was founded by the Mycenaeans. T F

10. When Israel fell, the people were deported to Assyria. T F

II. Fill in the Blanks. Use the word bank below.

11. Hezekiah's son _____ was both a good and a wicked king over Judah.

12. Compared to the Babylonians, the _____ were a more warlike people known for their cruelty.

13. King Josiah held a huge _____ after finding the Book of the Law in the Temple.

14. The prophet _____ was related to Hezekiah and Josiah. He wrote to caution the people who were only outwardly living right.

15. _____, a major prophet over Judah, lived through the Babylonian Captivity and wrote the Book of Lamentations.

16. As predicted by the prophets, the city of Nineveh was destroyed by a _____.

17. The prophet _____ wrote a book to God Himself.

18. It was _____ of Babylon who first invaded Jerusalem, later built the Hanging Gardens, and eventually went "mad."

19. Through visions from God, _____ was able to foresee the future of four upcoming empires.

20. _____ was at one time a Greek slave but was released because of his clever ability to tell stories or fables.

WORD BANK

Passover feast	Manasseh	Daniel	Assyrians	Habakkuk
Jeremiah	Zephaniah	Aesop	flood	Nebuchadnezzar

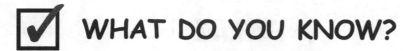

WHAT DO YOU KNOW?

Pretest 21

Who Am I? Choose one of the names from the word bank below to answer each question.

1. Once I ate a scroll. Who am I?

2. We came back to life to symbolize hope for Judah. Who are we?

3. I was thrown into a fiery furnace. My Hebrew name is Hananiah. Who am I?

4. I was also thrown into a fiery furnace. My Hebrew name is Mishael. Who am I?

5. I, too, was thrown into a fiery furnace. My Hebrew name is Azariah? Who am I?

6. My real name is Siddhartha Gautama. But I am better known as "the enlightened one." Who am I?

7. I am considered "a peaceful state of mind." What am I?

8. I am the country where Buddhism originated. Who am I?

WORD BANK

nirvana	Shadrach	Ezekiel
Meshach	India	Abed-Nego
Buddha	dry bones	

EZEKIEL

LESSON 61

I think Ezekiel was a pretty interesting guy. He wrote the Book of Ezekiel in the Old Testament and lived through a hard time in the history of Israel. Just like Daniel, Ezekiel was carried into captivity in Babylonia as a young man. It was about five years after that that he became a prophet for God.

Ezekiel didn't live in the big city of Babylon like Daniel did. He lived along the River Chebar, north of Babylon. There was a large community of Judeans there who were actually allowed to worship as they pleased and resume somewhat of a normal life. Ezekiel was a priest and a prophet to these people.

God called Ezekiel to prophesy in a very unusual way. He first gave Ezekiel visions of heavenly things that are difficult for us to understand. Ezekiel wrote that he saw fiery clouds and strange creatures right before his eyes. The creatures had four faces and four wings and moved like a "wheel in the middle of a wheel."

Ezekiel then saw "the appearance of a rainbow in a cloud on a rainy day, ... This was the appearance of the likeness of the glory of the Lord." (Ezek. 1:28) The sight was so awesome to Ezekiel that he fell on his face in humility before God.

Then, strangest of all, the Lord gave Ezekiel a scroll to eat! God said to him, "Son of man, feed your belly, and fill your stomach with this scroll that I give you ... go to the House of Israel and speak My words to them." (Ezek. 3:3–4) After all he had seen, Ezekiel eagerly obliged and ate the scroll.

When Ezekiel first began speaking prophecy, the city of Jerusalem had not yet been completely taken captive. (Remember that it took Nebuchadnezzar three times to overtake Judah.) So a large part of Ezekiel's message was to warn the people of Jerusalem's coming doom. Some believed that Jerusalem would never fall, but of course you already know that it did. (It was at the same time that Zedekiah was taken away and blinded.)

Ezekiel used some odd word pictures to speak to the Judeans. God told him to shave his hair and scatter it in different directions. Ezekiel proclaimed that this scattering was symbolic of the ways in which the Israelites would be dispersed.

Sadly enough, on the day of the last attack on Jerusalem, Ezekiel's wife suddenly became ill and died. He was so distraught that he lost his ability to speak, and he withdrew from the public. Ezekiel's grieving over the loss of his wife was symbolic of God's own grief over losing His beloved Jerusalem.

After the fall of Jerusalem, Ezekiel remained a prophet for years to come to give the people hope for the future. On one occasion, God used dry bones to represent the people of Israel. He asked Ezekiel to prophesy to a valley full of old, dry bones and watch as they came back to life. Can you imagine the sight of dead bones coming to life? God said that in the same way the bones were resurrected, Israel would one day be restored.

Unfortunately, Ezekiel did not live to see that prophecy come true. He lived the rest of his life in Babylonia in captivity. Some think that Ezekiel was killed by a fellow Hebrew who didn't like the truths he spoke. But the majority of the Hebrews that Ezekiel lived with abandoned their idolatry and worshiped the One true God. After all they had been through, the Judeans were finally learning to listen to the prophets.

ACTIVITY 61

61A—Younger Students

Make an edible scroll!

Materials: One piece of bread per student, a dull knife, rolling pin, honey in a drizzle bottle

Take a piece of bread and use a dull knife to cut off the crust. Then, press the bread down with a rolling pen. The Bible says that the scroll handed to Ezekiel had written on it "lamentations and mournings." Those are sad words for what was happening to Jerusalem. With a drizzle bottle of honey, try to write the words "Oh Israel" on the bread. (It won't be very easy.) Now, roll up the bread like a scroll. Then eat the scroll of bread as Ezekiel did. Of course, his wasn't really made of bread, but I don't think your teacher would want you to eat paper!

61B—Middle and Older Students

It has been awhile since we caught up on our list of prophets and kings. Of course there are no more kings to list after Zedekiah because he was the last king over Judah. But there were several prophets during what is called the "Post-Exile." We have yet to study three more prophets and then we will have covered the story of every major and minor prophet in the Old Testament.

Post-Exile Prophets

DANIEL
EZEKIEL

61C—Older Students

The Book of Ezekiel is filled with fascinating descriptions of God and the heavens. Take time to read this book using a Bible commentary along with your reading to understand the symbolism behind it. As you read, keep an outline of the main chapter titles to help you sort through it all. File your outline under "Asia: Israel." Title the outline "The Book of Ezekiel."

575 B.C.

SHADRACH, MESHACH, AND ABED-NEGO

LESSON 62

Do you remember the king who went mad for seven years and then believed in the God of Israel? That was Nebuchadnezzar II. He was also the king of Babylon who was responsible for the Babylonian Captivity. Well, there was one unusual incident that happened before he went mad that may have added to his believing in God. He witnessed a powerful miracle that you might be familiar with.

The miracle was the protection of Shadrach, Meshach, and Abed-Nego in the fiery furnace. It's an amazing story from the Bible. But before we examine the story closely, let's review what you already may know about these men.

When we studied Daniel earlier, I mentioned that he and some of his "friends" were taken captive together. Shadrach, Meshach, and Abed-Nego were the friends I was referring to. The Bible says, in Daniel 1:4, that the king wanted "young men in whom there was no blemish, but good-looking, gifted in all wisdom, possessing knowledge and quick to understand, who had ability to serve in the king's palace, and who they might teach the language and literature of the Chaldeans [Babylonians]." That was no small list of qualifications! These young men would have been any mother's dream.

Many were chosen and taken as prisoners, but we know best the story of Belteshazzar, Shadrach, Meshach, and Abed-Nego. Wait, are you wondering who Belteshazzar was? He was Daniel. That was his Hebrew name. All four boys had Hebrew names that were changed when taken as prisoners. Shadrach was really Hananiah, Meshach was Mishael, and Abed-Nego was Azariah.

If I had been a Hebrew prisoner, I would not have appreciated being renamed after a Babylonian god. In Hebrew, the syllable "el" at the end of a name meant "God" and "iah" meant "Jehovah." These young men had been named by their parents with meaningful, godly names. In contrast, "Abed-Nego" meant "servant of Nego," a Babylonian god. The renaming was probably done to try to reshape the identity of the young men so they would be loyal to their new country and new king. Evidently, the plan didn't really work.

The first thing we learn of these four young men is that they wouldn't eat the king's food. I already told you that story in our lesson about Daniel. Shadrach, Meshach, and Abed-Nego were the "friends" of Daniel that I mentioned who wouldn't defile themselves with the delicacies of the king. The end result was that they all grew stronger and were promoted to a high place of service under Nebuchadnezzar.

Daniel was promoted a step closer to the king after interpreting his disturbing dreams. When he went up in the ranks of the palace, he remembered his three Hebrew friends. He "petitioned the king, and he set Shadrach, Meshach, and Abed-Nego over the affairs of the province of Babylon; but Daniel sat in the gate of the king." (Dan. 2:49)

These events all led to the real test of faith endured by Shadrach, Meshach, and Abed-Nego. They were required by Nebuchadnezzar to bow down to a huge gold image he had built. Being faithful Hebrews, they refused. This so angered the king that he asked his guards to heat up a fiery furnace seven times hotter than normal and throw in the three Hebrews. The furnace was so hot that it killed the guards who got close to it! Why would a guard die this way? He would probably rather die a quick death in the fire than disobey the king and have to go through torture.

Despite the intense heat, not one hair was singed on Shadrach, Meshach, or Abed-Nego! As Nebuchadnezzar himself peered into the flames, he witnessed a most amazing miracle. The men were completely unharmed and there was even someone else in the fire with them! It could only have been the Lord protecting them Himself.

This event rocked the belief of the Babylonian king. He declared, "Blessed be the God of Shadrach, Meshach, and Abed-Nego, who sent His Angel and delivered His servants who trusted in Him, and they have frustrated the king's word, and yielded their bodies, that they should not serve nor worship any god except their own God!" (Dan. 3:28) He further declared that anyone who spoke against the God of these men would be cut into pieces and their houses burned. No doubt, people respected these three Hebrews for awhile!

ACTIVITY 62

62A—Younger and Middle Students

Note: This project can be done only under adult supervision and may not be suitable for some children.

Run a fire experiment.

Materials: Candle, metal tongs or long-handled barbecue fork, several small items to burn (e.g., small piece of cloth, hair, penny, leaf, paper clip, chalk, sponge, toothpick), bowl of water

Your teacher will light a small candle in a sturdy candleholder. Using tongs or a long fork, pass various household objects through the flame of the candle to see what will burn and what won't burn. (Be sure to quickly put out the things that will burn by dropping them in the bowl of water!) Guess which objects are flammable. What did the cloth do? What about the hair? If your teacher agrees that it's okay, pass your own finger over the flame quickly.

Discuss what a miracle it was that the Hebrews didn't burn and that their hair was not even singed. Define the word "singe." Think about the astonishment of Nebuchadnezzar over the marvelous way these Hebrew men were protected!

62B—Middle and Older Students

The library should have books on the meaning of names. Research the meaning of the names of your own family. Does your last name indicate the profession of your ancestors? Are you named after a Bible character? In the Old Testament, names were extremely significant in shaping a person's identity.

Find out as much as you can about your own name and record it on paper. Do you live up to your name? File your written information under the "North America: United States" divider in your Student Notebook.

Imagine someone giving you another name based on a religion totally contrary to your faith. Stop and thank God now for the freedom we have in this country.

c. 563 B.C.

BUDDHA (SIDDHARTHA GAUTAMA)

LESSON 63

Do you remember learning about India? I told you then that you would learn about a man who was bothered by the unfairness of the caste system, which was a big part of India's culture. Today we will look at this man, Siddhartha Gautama, or Buddha, and discover what he thought about life. His beliefs grew into one of the world's major religions.

In about 560 B.C., Siddhartha Gautama was born in India in a place that is now the country of Nepal. He was born a wealthy son of a rajah, or ruler. He had a very pampered childhood spending most of his life in the comforts of a palace. When he was old enough to get out and see the world around him, he found it very disturbing. He was upset at seeing poverty, disease, and death. These things are a part of life that is hard for all of us to understand.

Siddhartha left his life of comfort and wandered as a holy man for about six years. With just the bare necessities of life, he searched for truth. Supposedly, Siddhartha sat under a tree, determined not to get up until he found the truth he was looking for. He sat for seven days! During that time, he felt he had become "enlightened" through his thinking. He changed his name to "Buddha," which means "enlightened one."

Unlike Jesus, Buddha never claimed to be God or asked to be worshiped. He just wanted to make the world a better place. He began to teach people things that were different from the way of life he saw in India. One of his teachings was that of "nirvana," which is similar to a state of "being at peace." It is not a place to go to, like heaven, but a mind-set of what perfection is. Buddha thought people would be happy if they never had any desires to battle with. He liked to live apart from the things of this world that were tempting. He also thought that to have peace in one's life, a person must have self-control and be humble, generous, and loving.

The primary teaching of Buddha is called the Eightfold Path. These are eight principles that Buddha believed would help people end their worldly desires and reach nirvana. They are:

1. Right opinion
2. Right intentions
3. Right speech
4. Right conduct
5. Right livelihood
6. Right effort
7. Right mindfulness
8. Right concentration

At first glance, these are great principles to live by. But a deeper examination reveals that they are difficult to achieve on one's own merit. That is why the Buddhist must continually strive for perfection, particularly through meditation. Buddha stressed that anyone, regardless of his or her caste, could achieve nirvana by following the Eightfold Path.

Buddha lived to be 80 years old. Understandably, the peaceful way of life he taught was very comforting to the people around him. His dislike of the caste system gave great hope to his disciples. It was after his death that his followers began to make him out to be a god. But remember, he never claimed to be God! He in fact disagreed with the teachers of Hinduism that there is a "Brahman," or one true god.

Where are the majority of Buddhists today? Although the religion started in India, it moved to China and some of the neighboring countries. You can recognize a Buddhist temple by the large figure of a man sitting with his hands on his lap in meditation. That is a statue of Buddha. Devout followers, or monks, are sometimes seen in yellow robes with their heads cleanly shaven. They now practice their religion all over the world but are found mostly in China. Over the years, Buddhism and Hinduism have largely blended together in many cultures.

Siddhartha Gautama renamed himself Buddha, meaning "enlightened one." Thousands of statues or shrines have been built in his honor.

Let's stop and look at Buddhism compared to Christianity. There are many great differences. For one, a Buddhist doesn't believe in one God, especially in a personal God. Second, Buddhists don't believe in salvation by grace. They think that good works and kind deeds will save them from their sins. Like the Hindus, the Buddhists cling to the idea of reincarnation though it differs somewhat in their interpretation of it. (Reincarnation, again, is the belief that people die but can come back to life in a better or worse form depending on how they lived their life while here.)

Christianity has so much hope to offer this religion! Christians do believe in a personal God who has revealed Himself to man since the Garden of Eden. Christians believe that provision for sin has been made through the death and resurrection of Jesus. And Christians believe that there is eternal life in heaven for those who confess Jesus as Lord. That is great news!

The study of other religions in the world should not make the Christian uncomfortable. It should remind us that people are desperate to find peace in their lives. So much so that they would follow a man who claims to be "enlightened" but not a god. Though Buddha was a great and compassionate teacher, he performed no lifesaving miracles, he didn't die for the sins of the world, and he didn't rise from the dead. Many people probably worship Buddha because they don't know about Jesus. Maybe someday you will be one who will tell them the Gospel.

ACTIVITY 63

ALL STUDENTS

Make your Memory Cards for Lessons 61–63. Buddha (c. 563 B.C.) is a date to memorize. Mark your Memory Card accordingly.

63A—Younger Students

When studying other religions, it is wise to know more about your own beliefs. With your teacher, find John 10:9, 31 and 14:6 in the Bible. Talk about what these passages mean. Jesus told us He was the one way to the Father. If you have your own Bible, underline these verses to help you remember where they are.

63B—Middle Students

Unlike Buddha, Jesus claimed to be the Son of God. It was considered "blasphemy" to the Jews to call yourself God. Read John 10:30–33. Think about the crime for which Jesus was going to be stoned. Also read Mark 2:5–12 and John 8:56–58. Try to identify for yourself exactly what Jesus was doing or saying that made Him guilty of blasphemy before the people. On a separate piece of paper, write your findings as shown here, then file this under "Miscellaneous."

Jesus' Claims to Be God

1. John 10:30–33	Jesus said "I and My Father are One"; the people wanted to stone Him for blasphemy
2. Mark 2:5–12	Jesus . . .
3. John 8:56–58	Jesus . . .

63C—Older Students and Adults

As an older student, you should have some understanding of the world's major religions. They would include Hinduism, Buddhism, Islam, Judaism, and Christianity. Of course there are hundreds of other belief systems besides these. Many are variations of one of the main religions I just listed.

If you didn't research Hinduism during our earlier study of India, consider doing it now, using the suggested format from Activity 40. If you have already researched it, take the same outline and apply it to the study of Buddhism. File the study of Buddhism under "Asia: India" or "Asia: China" in your Student Notebook. It started in one place and spread to the other.

TAKE ANOTHER LOOK!

Wall of Fame

1. *Ezekiel (593–571 B.C.)*—Put a scroll at his mouth.

2. *Shadrach, Meshach, and Abed-Nego (575 B.C.)*—If you write small enough, put the Hebrew names of these men under their Babylonian names. Cluster the men together and place them over a piece of orange construction paper that is cut to look like a flame.

3. *Buddha (c. 563 B.C.)*—Depict a little man with a big belly in a sitting position. There are numerous images of Buddha. Or photocopy a small picture of a Buddha shrine. **Remember, this is a date to memorize.**

SomeWHERE in Time

1. In a world atlas, find Jerusalem and Babylon. With your finger, trace the path that Daniel, Shadrach, Meshach, and Abed-Nego might have taken when they became prisoners.

2. Middle and Older Students: Using a map key, estimate how many miles it is between Jerusalem and Babylon.

WHAT DID YOU MISS?

Week 21: Exercise

It's time again for "Millionaire Multiple Choice." Follow the same instructions as last time except there are more questions for this round.

For a right answer on questions 1 to 4, receive a penny. For questions 5 to 9, receive a nickel. For questions 10 to 14, receive a dime. For questions 15 to 19, receive a quarter. And, for the final question, receive one dollar for the correct answer. You may use your book as a "lifeline."

Circle the correct answer for each question.

1. The Tower of Babel was located in
   a. India.
   b. Mesopotamia.
   c. China.
   d. England.

2. Jacob was also named
   a. Josiah.
   b. Joseph.
   c. Israel.
   d. Isaac.

3. The pharaoh who worshiped one sun god was
   a. Khufu.
   b. Amenhotep IV.
   c. Ramses II.
   d. Hammurabi.

4. The legend of the Trojan Horse was told by
   a. Aesop.
   b. Homer.
   c. Herodotus.
   d. Hippocrates.

5. King Saul was anointed by the last judge of Israel, who was
   a. Gideon.
   b. Boaz.
   c. Moses.
   d. Samuel.

6. The Phoenicians were well known for making
   a. purple-red dye.
   b. silk cloth.
   c. porcelain.
   d. slaves.

7. When the Kingdom of Israel divided, _____ took the Northern Kingdom, leaving two tribes in the Southern Kingdom.

   a. Rehoboam

   b. Solomon

   c. Jeroboam

   d. Samuel

8. The primary religion of India is

   a. Hinduism.

   b. Judaism.

   c. Buddhism.

   d. Confucianism.

9. When good King Hezekiah ruled over Judah, God sent a death angel to wipe out the army of the proud

   a. Ramses.

   b. Xerxes I.

   c. Sennacherib.

   d. Nebuchadnezzar.

10. The two greatest powers in Mesopotamia between 700 and 600 B.C. were

   a. the Minoans and the Mycenaeans.

   b. the Spartans and the Athenians.

   c. the Greeks and the Romans.

   d. the Assyrians and the Babylonians.

11. When he was killed in battle, King Josiah was only

   a. 18.

   b. 29.

   c. 39.

   d. 49.

12. The city of Nineveh was located near the _____ River.

   a. Tigris

   b. Euphrates

   c. Nile

   d. Chebar

13. The Book of _____ depicts a conversation between a prophet and God.

   a. Huldah

   b. Hezekiah

   c. Hagar

   d. Habakkuk

14. The last king of Judah before the complete takeover by Babylon was
    a. Zedekiah.
    b. Zephaniah.
    c. Zechariah.
    d. Zebullum.

15. Nebuchadnezzar built one of the Seven Wonders of the Ancient World. It was
    a. the ziggurats of Ur.
    b. the Ishtar Gate.
    c. the Hanging Gardens of Babylon.
    d. the pyramids at Giza.

16. Aesop was most likely murdered by the people of
    a. Athens.
    b. Tyre.
    c. Sparta.
    d. Delphi.

17. After the Judeans were taken into captivity, Ezekiel lived
    a. in the city of Babylon.
    b. along the River Chebar.
    c. in Nineveh.
    d. in Egypt.

18. Daniel's Hebrew name was
    a. Hananiah.
    b. Mishael.
    c. Azariah.
    d. Belteshazzar.

19. Buddha's original name was
    a. Sennacherib.
    b. Hammurabi.
    c. Siddhartha Gautama.
    d. Veda.

20. Buddha was born in
    a. 1525 B.C.
    b. c.1055 B.C.
    c. 605 B.C.
    d. 563 B.C.

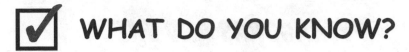

☑ WHAT DO YOU KNOW?

Pretest 22

Unscramble the words to fill in the blanks. A word bank is provided at the bottom of the page.

1. Pythagoras was a great Greek mathematician. He helped develop the idea of odd, even, and (mperi) _____ numbers.

2. Pythagoras, too, thought that just maybe the world was (duron) _____.

3. Confucius was a wise man who wanted to make (aCnhi) _____ a better place.

4. Confucius taught that people should (ptserce) _____ their elders.

5. Though Confucius was not a particularly religious man, Confucianism has become one of the world's major (liernsgio)_____.

6. According to the Bible, Belshazzar had a big (yrpat) _____ before he died.

7. Daniel was able to interpret the (ndtirgawhin) _____ on the wall that predicted Belshazzar's death.

8. Cyrus the Great granted the Jews the (ecmrfdo) _____ to go home after 70 years of captivity in Babylonia.

> **WORD BANK**
>
> | handwriting | religions | prime |
> |---|---|---|
> | party | China | round |
> | freedom | respect | |

PYTHAGORAS AND THE
TEMPLE OF DIANA

LESSON 64

So far in history, we have studied *many* people, countries, and religions. I hope you are not getting dizzy by our jumping from one culture to another. Remember, we are approaching this study of history from a chronological standpoint: we are looking at events happening around the world near the same time. I think it shows us that, as God allows, individuals affect history through their choices and beliefs.

Today, we are going back to Greece to learn of a man named Pythagoras (pih THAG oh rus). The last Greek personality we studied was Aesop. I hope you haven't forgotten Homer, the first Olympics, or the rise of Athens and Sparta. All of these are a buildup to understanding the ancient Greek world, which still influences us today.

Pythagoras is a man most remembered for his mathematical discoveries. Have you ever heard of the Pythagorean theorem? It is a famous idea in geometry about triangles. I won't try to explain it here; just trust me that it was big and important. (Middle and older students can examine it more closely in your activity.)

Pythagoras also helped people understand odd, even, and prime numbers. In the field of astronomy, Pythagoras believed the world was round. That was a big deal 500 years before Christ. It was more than a thousand years before people agreed that the earth wasn't flat! And it was some of the pupils of Pythagoras who later thought that the earth might revolve around the sun. Needless to say, Pythagoras and his students were very smart and way ahead of their time.

However, Pythagoras was more than a mathematician—he was also a "philosopher." There were many Greek philosophers who tried to understand life from their own experiences. Because Pythagoras was a mathematician, he naturally relied on his knowledge of numbers to explain life. He thought there might be mystical numbers behind everything.

Like the Hindus, Pythagoras also believed that people were born over and over again as different beings. He had such strong ideas that he started his own school to teach his theories. Some of his ideas even influenced Plato, who we will learn more about later. The school, or brotherhood, of Pythagoras was eventually destroyed because people became suspicious of him and his followers.

What does the Bible say about knowledge and wisdom? It says, "the fear of the Lord is the beginning of knowledge." (Prov. 1:7) And "the fear of the Lord is the beginning of wisdom, and the knowledge of the Holy One is understanding." (Prov. 9:10) I think that the philosophies of man can't fully explain life and are ultimately disappointing. I believe that God alone gives us the answers to the "mysteries" of life.

While we are in this time period, I want to introduce to you yet another one of the Seven Wonders of the Ancient World. This one was called the Temple of Diana (or Artemis). It was extremely beautiful and ornate. The temple was made completely of marble except for the roof. It took more than 120 years to built this incredible structure that had more than 100 columns standing 60 feet high. It was built as a monument to the goddess Diana. The Greeks built it in 550 B.C., but it was burned down in 356 B.C. Interestingly, this temple to Diana was built in the city of Ephesus, the same city to which the Apostle Paul later wrote an epistle. The next time you read Ephesians, remember the type of worship and the culture that once existed there.

ACTIVITY 64

64A—Younger Students

To help remember Pythagoras's contribution to math, look at a number line. Use a yardstick if necessary. Name the even numbers up to 20. Name the odd numbers. Do you understand the difference between them?

One easy way to understand them is to use small objects like pennies and match them in pairs. If they match up evenly, you have an **even** number of objects. If the pairs don't match up evenly and you have an extra object, you have an **odd** number. Play with this idea until you can name the odd and even numbers up to 20 or higher.

64B—Middle Students

Do you understand prime numbers? A prime number is one that can only be divided by itself and the number 1. For example, 13. There are no numbers besides 1 and 13 that can be multiplied together to equal 13. So, 13 is a prime number. What is the highest prime number you can think of? Mathematicians have found a number with thousands of digits that is prime. That's a big number!

On a piece of paper, write out all the prime numbers up to 100. Title your paper "Pythagoras Helps Explain Prime Numbers" and file it under "Europe: Ancient Greece" in your Student Notebook.

64C—Middle and Older Students

Do you know the Pythagorean theorem? As a simple formula, it would read $c^2 = a^2 + b^2$.

Using a math textbook, an encyclopedia, or a dictionary, expand the definition of the Pythagorean theorem. Write it down with an example if possible. Title it "Pythagoras" and file it under "Europe: Greece." Include the date the theorem was created.

---

551 B.C.

CONFUCIUS

LESSON 65

Learning about the roots of the world's major religions can be so fascinating! There are millions of people who would call "Confucianism" a religion though it is more of a philosophy. But did Confucius, the man for whom the religion is named, mean to start a religion? Let's look at the facts.

Confucius was a Chinese man born in about 551 B.C. In Chinese he is called "Kung Fu-tzu." He was born in the state of Lu as part of a noble family and the youngest of 11 children! However, his father died when he was very young. This left his family poor. Confucius observed the life around him, which at that time was a struggle. This was during the second half of the Zhou dynasty. The government was not in good shape. Many cruelties were used to torture enemies of the country.

Confucius worked hard at his education; by age 21 he had formulated some of his own ideas for what might make life better in China. He thought that people ought to live more kindly and treat others with dignity and respect. He especially thought that older people and ancestors ought to be respected, as had once been the tradition in China.

Confucius's ideas made others see him as a *sage*, or wise man. He spoke with great wisdom at a time when it was badly needed. One of his teachings was that men in government should be allowed to rule only if they were honest and well educated. He also believed it a great honor and a high calling to serve the government because it could influence so many people for the better. At one point he was able to live out his teachings as he himself was appointed a high government official. His term did not last long, though, because a jealous ruler forced him out.

Confucius still traveled and spoke about his ideas for improving China, and many people listened. He taught his disciples, or followers, to be gentlemen. He believed that the virtues of courtesy, good faith, diligence, and kindness ought to shape one's behavior and could eventually shape a whole nation. But it is hard to change a large government. Though Confucius taught for nearly 50 years, he died as a man hardly recognized for his teachings in comparison to how he is remembered today.

Confucius—the most famous sage, or wise man, of China—taught the importance of honest government.

Toward the end of his life, Confucius compiled his notes into books called the *Five Classics*. Years after his death, his followers created more books from the teachings and sayings of Confucius. All the books emphasize the belief that people are basically good; that people can solve their problems themselves through proper living; and that there ought to be harmony in all human relationships. The popular "yin-yang" symbol is an example of the belief that there is ultimately harmony in all things.

Interestingly, Confucius himself was not a "religious" man. He didn't teach much on life after death, on sin, or on God. His teachings centered instead on people in relationship to other people. That is why his teachings were not really "religious." However, over the years, the memory of Confucius has grown to supernatural proportions. After his death, people began to present sacrifices at his grave and celebrate his birthday. He was, and is, practically worshiped as a god though he never claimed to be one.

As a wise teacher, Confucius continues to strongly influence the world today. In China he is considered one of the greatest men that ever lived. For centuries his teachings were elevated to a sacred level. Indeed, Confucius was a great teacher, and the things he taught helped bring much-needed stability to China.

As Christians, though, we should recognize that the wisdom of Confucius was limited to man's definition of what is good and right. He did not claim to be inspired by God. And unfortunately, his respect for the elderly and for one's ancestors became the basis for the actual worship of dead ancestors. That aspect of Confucianism is quite widespread. (A good example of this thinking is found in the Disney movie *Mulan*.)

What does God say about worshiping anything or anyone besides Him? He makes it clear in the Ten Commandments and in many places in the New Testament that He alone is worthy of our worship. The Bible also teaches that man is sinful and cannot be saved apart from Christ, no matter how wise or peaceful a person may be. Pray for the people of China that they would gain knowledge of the living God who provides salvation and awaits our worship.

ACTIVITY 65

ALL STUDENTS

The date of Confucius (551 B.C.) is one to memorize.

65A—Younger and Middle Students

Make a "bamboo" tablet. In the days of Confucius, paper had not been invented. Confucius wrote on bamboo tablets that were tied together with string. The Chinese write their words up and down instead of left to right as we do.

1. Take about 10 craft sticks. Lay them side by side with a tiny space between them.

2. Lay string or shoelaces over the sticks with extra length at the end.

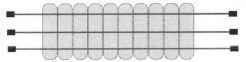

3. Glue the string in place and let it sit until dry.
4. Using a black marker, copy what would look like Chinese writing on the side of the sticks without the string. A writer back then would have used a fine paintbrush. I think that would be hard.
5. When the marker is dry, practice rolling up your tablet, as a scribe would have done in the time of Confucius.
6. Take a picture of your tablet and file it under "Asia: Ancient China."

65B—Younger and Middle Students

The Chinese have long had a custom of respecting older people, even before Confucius developed the belief of ancestral worship. The Bible also teaches that we should respect the elderly as in I Timothy 5:1, "Do not rebuke an older man, but exhort him as a father."

If you have grandparents, take time to write them a special note or card. Tell them what you appreciate about them. If your grandparents are not living, choose an older person from your church or community to reach out to. You could make a real difference in that person's day.

65C—Middle and Older Students

Just as you outlined the beliefs of Hinduism and Buddhism, examine the beliefs of Confucianism. Though it is a way of thinking more than it is a religion, Confucianism is regarded as one of the world's major religions according to the *World Book Encyclopedia*. Write a one-page paper on the beliefs and practices of Confucianism and file in under "Asia: China."

BELSHAZZAR AND CYRUS THE GREAT

LESSON 66

In our last three lessons, we have learned about men from three very different parts of the world. Buddha was from India, Pythagoras was from Greece, and Confucius was from China. Today we will go back to a familiar corner of the world. We will look at ancient Babylon one last time before its predestined destruction.

Near the end of Daniel's life, a rather weak king by the name of Belshazzar reigned over the city of Babylon. (Don't confuse Belshazzar's name with the Babylonian name given to Daniel. There is only one syllable's difference between their two names.) Belshazzar was a descendant of Nebuchadnezzar. At this time, the people of Judah were still in Babylonia in captivity since they were forcefully driven out of Jerusalem.

Belshazzar's father, the rightful king of Babylon, preferred the study of archaeology over the duties of being a king. So he put his son Belshazzar on the throne in his place. This probably wasn't a great decision. Belshazzar didn't last too long.

According to the Bible, Belshazzar had a wild party and feast one October night. As part of the festivity, he and his guests defiantly drank wine from the actual gold and silver goblets that were stolen from Solomon's Temple! Then, right in the middle of the party, something supernatural happened. The Bible says that a hand mysteriously appeared and wrote these words on the wall: MENE, MENE, TEKEL, UPHARSIN. We would pronounce that as MEE nee, MEE nee, TEE kuhl, yu FAHR sin.

I imagine everyone freaked to see such an odd sight! The worst part was that they didn't understand the meaning of these strange words. But there was at least one Hebrew still living who could understand the things of God. It was none other than Daniel. Now an old man, Daniel interpreted the writing as meaning this: "God has numbered your kingdom [Belshazzar's kingdom] and finished it; you have been weighed in the balances, and found wanting; your kingdom has been divided and given to the Medes and Persians." (Dan. 5:26–28) Media and Persia were countries just to the north and east of Babylonia where present-day Iran is.

Though the words were frightening, Belshazzar was impressed with Daniel's wisdom. For this incredible insight, Belshazzar offered Daniel the third highest position in the kingdom along with a purple robe and a gold chain for his neck. (It was the "third" position that Belshazzar offered because his father was still "first" in the kingdom, and Belshazzar was "second" to him.)

Belshazzar really didn't need to bother with all that formality. For just as Daniel had prophesied, Belshazzar was killed the very night of the wild feast! And as foretold, it was the Medes and Persians who attacked Belshazzar and took over Babylon. Just like the handwriting on the wall announced,

Shown here is an ancient set of weights and balances used for measuring trade items. Daniel said to Belshazzar, "You have been weighed in the balances, and found wanting." (Dan. 5:27)

The Mystery of History

Babylonian rule was destroyed and it never recovered! But this story isn't over. It gets even better for the Jews.

The Medo-Persian king who conquered Babylon was Cyrus the Great. Upon his victory, Cyrus the Great appointed Darius the Mede to rule over Babylon.[1] Cyrus became a real instrument of God in the whole event. For you see, it was prophesied that Cyrus, a Persian, would be used to actually free the Jews of the Babylonian rule. And he did!

Interestingly, Isaiah the prophet wrote about this event years before it ever happened. He wrote, "Who says of Cyrus, 'he is My shepherd, and he shall perform all My pleasure' . . . thus says the Lord to His anointed, to Cyrus, whose right hand I have held . . . to loose the armor of kings, to open before him the double doors so that the gates will not be shut." (Isa. 44:28–45:1)

The story of Cyrus the Great is amazing. Cyrus was quite different from the Babylonian rulers who had held the Jews captive. He promptly issued a decree that the Jews could go back to their homeland! He actually freed them. And Cyrus did this in the precise time that the Bible said he would! It was the prophet Jeremiah who predicted that the Jews would be captive for 70 years. And they were.

Can you imagine the commotion and rejoicing Cyrus started when the decree was sent out? What a clatter of hustling and bustling the Jews must have made as they planned and packed for their long-awaited journey. Did they all go back, though? No, they didn't. Understandably, there were some Jews who were so settled in their businesses and farms that they chose to stay in Babylonia, at least for awhile. But 42,360 Jews headed back to Palestine with all the belongings they could carry. Women, children, grandmas, and grandpas—all would have helped out.

Are you wondering where Palestine is? "Palestine" was the name given to Judah when the Jews left the region. (Some people living in the Middle East are still called "Palestinians" from the name "Palestine.") Many things, such as the names of places, were different 70 years later. Life was not necessarily going to be easy back "home." But at least the Jews were free. With renewed spirit, they were more than willing to travel the dangerous 500-mile trip back to Jerusalem and Palestine.

ACTIVITY 66

ALL STUDENTS

Make your Memory Cards for Lessons 64–66. Remember to indicate that Confucius (551 B.C.) is a date to memorize.

66A—Younger Students

1. Re-enact the mysterious handwriting on the wall at the feast of Belshazzar. Take large pieces of paper, like butcher paper, and tape them next to each other on a wall in your dining area. Have your teacher lightly sketch some bricks on the background of them. Paint or color the outline of the bricks. Then, using a marker, copy the words found in Daniel 5:25, "Mene, Mene, Tekel, Upharsin." If you can remember, explain the meaning of the words to your teacher or to family members at dinner tonight.

---

1. *Note to Teacher:* Although Cyrus the Great appointed Darius the Mede to rule over the city of Babylon, this point can be confusing because both men are referred to as "kings" within biblical literature. A better explanation might be to consider Cyrus the Great as king and Darius as a type of governor. Though Darius the Mede is not important now, I will be teaching more about him later. (*The Living Bible Encyclopedia in Story and Pictures,* Art Treasure ed., Vol. 4. New York: H.S. Stuttman Co., Inc., 1968; p. 500.)

2. Dress up like a Persian king. It may sound funny to us, but Cyrus the Great believed it was all right for men to wear shoes that made them taller and makeup to make them handsomer. The following is a quote from the historian Xenophon about Cyrus the Great.

"[Cyrus the Great] chose to wear the Median dress himself . . . and thought that if anyone had any personal defect, that dress would help to conceal it, and that it made the wearer look very tall and very handsome. For they have shoes of such a form that without being detected the wearer can easily put something into the soles so as to make him look taller than he is. He encouraged also the fashion of penciling the eyes, that they might seem more lustrous than they are, and of using cosmetics to make the complexion look better than nature made it."[2]

Using a robe, some high-heeled boots, and a little makeup, dress up as Cyrus the Great might have. Take a photo and file it under "Asia: Iran (Persia)" in your Student Notebook.

66B—Middle Students

Daniel told Belshazzar that he had been "weighed in the balances and found wanting." Do you understand the use of weights and measures before there was standard currency? Most things were weighed to determine their value. Daniel was telling Belshazzar that he had little value.

Create a weight-and-measure set. Use string, small paper cups, sticky poster putty, tape, pencil, and a wooden ruler. Set two small paper cups (like bathroom-size cups) at even intervals at the ends of the ruler. Adhere them to the ruler using poster putty. Tie string tightly around each end of the ruler. Use the tape to secure the string. Tie the two strings together about 10 inches up. With tape, secure the knot over a pencil and test the reliability of your scales by adding coins to each side. Count the number on each side and see if they are equal in weight so that they "balance out" each other. You might have to fiddle around with it, but it does work!

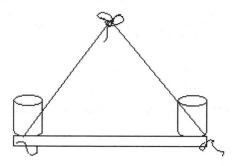

66C—Older Students

We have only briefly touched on the Medes and the Persians. Persia is the ancient name for Iran. Trace back the history of the Medes and the Persians as separate countries. What brought these two cultures together as allies? Were they brought together under peaceful conditions or by means of force? Who was the ruler most responsible for the union? Write out your findings and file them under "Asia: Iran (Persia)."

---

2. Don Nardo, *The Persian Empire.* San Diego: Lucent Books, 1998; p. 52.

TAKE ANOTHER LOOK!

Review 22: Lessons 64–66

Wall of Fame

1. *Pythagoras (566 B.C.)*—Draw a triangle on him.

2. *Temple of Diana (550 B.C.)*—Make a sketch of a building with great columns. Add to it the name of the city of Ephesus.

3. *Confucius (551 B.C.)*—If you have seen any drawings of Confucius, he is usually shown holding his hands together in front of him under the big sleeves of his garment. Try to depict this or photocopy a small drawing of him. **Remember, this is a date to memorize.**

4. *Belshazzar (c. 538 B.C.)*—Instead of a man, put a hand on a piece of paper with a pen in it as if it were writing on a wall.

5. *Cyrus the Great (c. 538 B.C.)*—I'm stumped on this guy. All I can think of is a smiley face. ☺ What can you think of to depict this Persian ruler?

SomeWHERE in Time

1. On a map of ancient Greece, see if you can find the island of Samos. That is where Pythagoras was born. However, he eventually resettled in a Greek colony named Crotona, which was located in southern Italy. Look for it on a map of Italy. Consider how a person back then would go about "moving."

2. In a Bible atlas, locate the city of Ephesus where the Temple of Diana was built.

3. On a modern map of China, try to locate the Shandong province (sometimes written Shantung). On Outline Map 4, "East Asia," outline the Shandong province of China and rename it "Lu." That was the name of the area when Confucius lived there.

4. Middle and Older Students: Make a map overlay.

   a. First take Outline Map 1, "Persia," and use colored pencils to write in these places: Media, Persia, Elam, Babylon, Ur, Tigris River, Euphrates River, Moab, Judah, Jerusalem, Jordan River, Samaria, Dead Sea, Phoenicia, Mediterranean Sea.

   b. Lay a clear overhead transparency over the map you just made. Using a wet-erase marker, indicate the modern names of the countries of the area. They would include: Syria, Jordan, Israel, Saudi Arabia, Iraq, Iran, and Lebanon. If you can, outline the modern boundaries of these countries.

   c. Title your maps "The Middle East When the Jews Returned Home: 538 B.C." and "Modern-Day Middle East."

   d. File both maps together in your Student Notebook under "Asia: Iraq (Mesopotamia)."

WHAT DID YOU LEARN?

Week 22: Quiz

I. Matching. Match the descriptions on the left with the words on the right by placing the correct letter next to the number.

___1. An early civilization that appeared after the Great Flood.

a. Samson

___2. A fictional story about creation and a flood.

b. Jonah

___3. The son of Jacob who was sold into slavery by his brothers.

c. The Sumerians

___4. The pharaoh most known for great buildings.

d. Athens/Sparta

___5. The Hebrew judge betrayed to the Philistines by his wife.

e. Aesop

___6. The prophet who used the word picture of locusts in his writings.

f. King Josiah

___7. The prophet to Nineveh who fled to Tarshish out of disobedience.

g. Joseph

___8. Two city-states in Greece that were constantly at odds.

h. *The Epic of Gilgamesh*

___9. The godly king over Judah who found an old copy of the law hidden in the walls of the Temple.

i. Ramses II

___10. A Greek storyteller who used animals to make a point.

j. Joel

II. Multiple Choice. Circle the correct answer for each question.

11. Which of these things did NOT happen to Ezekiel?

a. He saw a "wheel within a wheel."

b. He ate a scroll.

c. He saw handwriting on the wall.

d. He saw dry bones come to life.

12. Which of these things DID happen to Ezekiel?

a. He was taken into captivity as a young man.

b. His mother died.

c. He wrote the Book of Lamentations.

d. He was freed from captivity at the age of 70.

13. Buddha

a. claimed to be god.

b. was killed at just 39 years old.

c. started the Hindu faith.

d. was born into a wealthy family in India.

The Mystery of History

14. The name "Buddha" means
    a. happy one.
    b. enlightened one.
    c. royal one.
    d. wise one.

15. Pythagoras is most remembered for
    a. his school.
    b. starting a new religion.
    c. teaching ironmaking.
    d. his mathematical contributions.

16. Pythagoras believed
    a. the world is round.
    b. in reincarnation.
    c. numbers could explain everything.
    d. All of the above.

17. Confucius was born in
    a. China.
    b. India.
    c. Nepal.
    d. Egypt.

18. Confucius wrote what is called
    a. *The Epic of Gilgamesh.*
    b. the *Five Classics.*
    c. the *Iliad.*
    d. the Vedas of China.

19. Belshazzar was "second in the kingdom" because
    a. his brother was first.
    b. his father was the true king, but he liked archaeology better.
    c. he gave Daniel first place.
    d. he was a governor under Cyrus the Great.

20. Cyrus the Great was used by God to
    a. free the Hebrews from slavery in Egypt.
    b. destroy Nineveh.
    c. set the Jews free from the Babylonian Captivity.
    d. start a new religion.

Bonus: Name at least one supernatural event that helped to change the heart of Nebuchadnezzar.

✓ WHAT DO YOU KNOW?

Pretest 23

True or False? Circle your answer.

1. Darius the Mede was tricked into throwing Daniel into the lions' den.　　　　T　F

2. The first postal system was developed by the Jews.　　　　T　F

3. Darius I was the father-in-law of Esther from the Old Testament.　　　　T　F

4. Zerubbabel was appointed governor of Judah by Cyrus the Great.　　　　T　F

5. Zerubbabel and his men immediately rebuilt the Temple in in just four months.　　　　T　F

6. The Jews had a huge party to celebrate the laying of the Temple foundation.　　　　T　F

7. The Book of Haggai in the Old Testament is longer than most.　　　　T　F

8. The prophet Zechariah was a farmer by trade.　　　　T　F

DARIUS I

LESSON 67

Darius the Mede was mentioned briefly in our last lesson on Belshazzar and Cyrus the Great. Darius was given Babylon to rule by Cyrus and called a "king" although he was more of a governor. It's a little confusing to understand because both Cyrus the Great and Darius were called "kings" of Persia at the same time. I would guess, though, that you have remembered Darius the Mede for another reason. He is the one in the familiar Bible story who threw Daniel into the lions' den. He only ruled for a short time.

Today, though, we will look at yet another Darius who ruled over all the Medo-Persian Empire some time after Cyrus the Great. He was Darius I. Unlike Darius the Mede, there is a lot to know about Darius I.

Darius I's official title was "Shahanshah," which means "king of kings." Have you ever heard of the Shah of Iran? He was one of many rulers in Iran who carried the title "shah" as started by Darius I. The last Shah of Iran ruled only decades ago, up until 1979 when he was overthrown by Ayatollah Khomeini. Your teacher may remember that incident.

But back to Darius I. He apparently had a big ego. He, like many of the ancient Egyptian rulers, thought he was appointed by the gods to be ruler. He had a stone carved with these words about himself, "Progeny of Amun, living image of Re [a god], who placed him upon the throne in order to bring to a good end that which he [Re] had begun on Earth." Though overly proud, Darius I did a lot of good for Persia during his reign.

One thing Darius I did was to organize his large empire into 20 provinces called "satrapies." This made his kingdom run much more efficiently. He introduced the use of silver and gold coins throughout Persia, and he had better roads built.

The roads were improved so that messages could more easily be sent from the king to anywhere in Persia. In fact, Darius I may have started the first serious postal service. A Greek historian named Herodotus said this of the system: "Not snow, no, nor rain, nor heat, nor night keeps them from accomplishing their appointed course with all speed." (Hdt. 8.98) Does that sound familiar to you? Our postal service has a similar motto.

Darius I was a smart thinker in another way. Darius had words and pictures inscribed on a giant carving called the Behistun (bay hihs TOON) Rock. This 10-by-18-foot rock towered 500 feet above the ground. The significance of the words is that they were in three different languages. That meant that once one of the languages was understood, archaeologists could unlock the meaning of the other two. That's what happened in 1839. A man named Rawlinson dangerously climbed a tall ladder and for years copied the lettering the sculptors had left. His work gave historians the ability to understand cuneiform writing for the first time! (Quick, do you remember who developed cuneiform writing? It was the Sumerians.)

The Behistun Rock also gave us a picture, so to speak, of what Darius looked like. One historian, A. T. Olmstead in *History of the Persian Empire*, describes Darius looking this way, "Darius, a fine Aryan type with high brow and straight nose, stands his natural height, five feet ten inches. On his head is the war crown, and . . . gold band studded with oval jewels and rosettes. His front hair is carefully frizzed, and his drooping mustache is neatly twirled at the tip . . . The square beard is arranged in four rows of curls alternating with straight strands, quite in the manner of those of his Assyrian predecessors."[1]

As for the character of Darius I, we might assume he valued honesty and fairness. He had these words carved about his attitude. "To that which is just I am a friend, to that which is unjust I am no friend. I do not wish that the weak should suffer harm at the hands of the powerful, nor that the powerful should suffer harm at the hands of the weak . . . The follower after falsehood do I detest."[2]

I have one last thing that I think is neat to know about Darius I. He had a son named Xerxes (ZURK seez) who had a very well-known wife. Any guesses? Here is a hint: Xerxes' name in Hebrew is Ahasuerus (uh haz you EE rus). Does that name "ring any bells"? He is the king who married Esther. Her whole story is in the Old Testament. We'll get to that. I just thought you might want to associate Darius I as the father-in-law of Esther, though the two may or may not ever have met. Ahasuerus didn't take the throne and become king until Darius I died.

When we study more on the Greeks and the Jews, you will hear about Darius I again. For now, you can remember him as one of the more significant Medo-Persian rulers.

ACTIVITY 67

67A—Younger Students

To remember one of Darius's good ideas for Persia, play a game of Post Office. Make up some notes as if you were a messenger in the Persian army. Send them to Darius I. Make a mailbox out of an old tissue box. Make a mail-carrier bag out of a paper sack (it will need a shoulder strap attached with staples). Be a loyal post office worker and pretend to work through rain, flood, snow, and hail. File your "letter" under "Asia: Iran (Persia)."

67B—Middle Students

Darius introduced the use of silver and gold coins to Persia. Using an encyclopedia or book from the library, research the history of the use of coins. Write a short report on coins. Who used them first? What was put on the coins? Add some drawings to your report. File it under "Asia: Iran (Persia)."

67C—Older Students

The political struggles of the Middle East can be very confusing. The more you understand the history of the region, the less complicated the issues may be to you. Research the overthrow of the Shah of Iran in 1979. Summarize the political leadership and the religion of Iran since 1979. This will help greatly in understanding news headlines today. File your report under "Asia: Iran."

---

1. Don Nardo, *The Persian Empire.* San Diego: Lucent Books, 1998; p. 41.
2. Ibid., p. 53.

ZERUBBABEL
LESSON 68

Think back with me to the kings of Judah just before the Babylonian Captivity. The last three were Jehoiakim, Jehoiachin, and Zedekiah. None of them was a very admirable king. Jehoiachin however, had a grandson named Zerubbabel, who was a true servant of God.

Zerubbabel, because of his royal lineage, was appointed by Cyrus the Great to be the governor of Judah when Cyrus said the Jews could go back there. That must have felt great after having been a captive for most of his life. Zerubbabel, the rightful heir to the throne of Judah, was finally getting to fulfill some position of leadership.

We can speculate that Zerubbabel was a reverent man because one of the first things he did when returning to Jerusalem was to build an offering to God. More importantly, he and his men made it a priority to rebuild the Temple as soon as the people were settled in. They really had come home to a mess of ruins.

Cyrus himself helped the Jewish men begin the rebuilding. He helped by giving them back the possessions that had been stolen out of the Temple. The Book of Ezra says that 5,400 articles were given back to the Jews. Still, the task of rebuilding the Temple was enormous. Solomon, who built the original Temple, had been the wealthiest man alive and had used his numerous resources to build it spectacularly. Zerubbabel was returning to a land without much to offer in comparison.

The Jewish people pulled together, though, and brought what wealth they had to help in the rebuilding. After what they had been through in captivity, their hearts were turned to God. They wanted to see the Temple restored. When the foundation was finally laid, the priests and Zerubbabel held a great dedication ceremony. They brought out the trumpets and the cymbals and raised their voices in singing and shouting to the Lord.

Can you imagine this sight? Some of the people there were those who had actually lived in Judah before the Babylonian Captivity. They were fairly old now because the captivity had lasted for 70 years. The Bible says that these people did not sing, but, rather, cried out loud at the ceremony. For what their eyes saw was so much less majestic and beautiful than Solomon's Temple had been. Of course, they were only looking at the foundation that had been laid, but I suppose their hearts ached because it was the sin of their generation that had led the people to captivity in the first place. The very need to rebuild must have been disturbing.

Despite the great ceremony and enthusiasm shown over the rebuilding of the temple, the project was tough. It took much more time than planned. The local people who had stayed in Judah were not real friendly to all these Jews returning home. The Jews who were left behind had lost their identity and intermarried with the nonbelievers of the area. Some of those were the Samaritans who settled the country of Israel after the people were deported to Assyria. Remember that story? (Lions had attacked them!)

Incense shovels like these were used in the Temple to carry coals from the altar of sacrifice to the altar of incense in front of the Holy of Holies.

After years of fighting between the local people and the returning Jews, King Darius I was called upon to settle the situation. He did something pretty neat. He looked back at the history books of Cyrus the Great to figure out just what to do. He discovered the written decree of Cyrus that had given the Jews the right to rebuild. He then took unbelievable action.

Darius I made a decree that not only could the Jews finish the building of the Temple, but they could also use the king's money to do it! And the builders were to be supplied with anything at all they needed. Darius I further said that anyone who got in the way of the building campaign would be hanged and his house made a refuse heap. Wow!

The key to Darius's kindness might be found in Ezra 6:10. Darius says, "that they [the Jews] may offer sacrifices of sweet aroma to the God of heaven, and pray for the life of the king and his sons." Darius must have heard enough about the God of Israel over the years that he wanted to be in good standing with Him. He wanted to be blessed himself.

Fortunately for Zerubbabel, he lived long enough to see the completion of the second Temple. With the help of the king of Persia, it probably turned out nice after all.

ACTIVITY 68

68A—Younger Students

1. Have you ever been so happy that you shouted, jumped, or sang with excitement? At times of celebration, the Jews, like many other people, rejoiced with dancing and music. The Bible says they used trumpets and cymbals at the dedication celebration of the Temple.

    Reenact their joyful occasion. Use your imagination and create trumpets out of paper-towel tubes and cymbals out of pot lids. As long as you are acting, one of you ought to cry as some of the older people did. They were missing the original Temple.

2. If there is a building site near you, take time to watch the laying of the foundation.

68B—Middle Students

King Darius made the effort to have someone research the history of the Jews before he made a decision about the rebuilding of the Temple. How comfortable are you with your library?

Have your teacher create a scavenger hunt for you at the library. Have her list 5 to 10 books of interest to your family and you find them without her assistance. (*Note to Teacher*: You can make this as challenging as needed by requiring more difficult discoveries such as the name of a specific work, the author, the year of a publication, or information about a periodical, or a media piece. Work on whatever research skills are lacking but keep it fun so the student leaves feeling confident, not overwhelmed.)

68C—Older Students

Darius was dependent on the research skills of trained men to search the archives for one scroll of information. How are your research skills? Can you differentiate between primary and secondary resources? Do you know how to accurately document any source you have used? As an older student, you should be quite comfortable with these skills and with the library itself. Assess with your teacher your knowledge of the library system and documentation procedures. Have her create an appropriate assignment to test your familiarity with various resources such as periodicals and media pieces and the ability to document them properly. This will look a little different for each student. Take this assignment seriously while you're still at home. The first time you hit a college library with a huge assignment in hand, you will wish you knew more!

HAGGAI AND ZECHARIAH

LESSON 69

Before we leave the story of Zerubbabel and the Temple too far behind us, I want you to know the story of two more prophets. The prophets Haggai and Zechariah were both used by God to help Zerubbabel with the huge task of rebuilding the Temple. They may or may not have laid real bricks with their own hands to help with the rebuilding, but these prophets definitely helped to lay the spiritual foundation of the structure.

The Book of Haggai is a short one found right near the end of the Old Testament. It only covers a four-month time period and tells us very little about Haggai himself. What we do learn is more about the heart of God.

Apparently, Zerubbabel allowed way too much time to pass between that great dedication party for the foundation of the Temple and the actual rebuilding. In fact, it was about 14 years. In that much time, the ground began to grow weeds and the foundation looked terrible. Through the prophet Haggai, the Lord displayed how he felt about the neglect the people had shown to their priorities.

As I told you in the last lesson, the Samaritans were making the building program a nightmare for the Jews. Rather than fight, the Jews were being too accepting of their circumstances. The Lord wanted to show the people He could still work miracles. That must be when Darius appeared, ready and willing to help the Jews rebuild.

The main thing we learn from the Book of Haggai was that God was ready to bless the people again. He states through the prophet, "From this day forward, I will bless you." (Hag. 2:19b) The period of "desolation" was over for them. This must have been hard to grasp after all the years they suffered in captivity.

Zechariah, the other prophet of the same time period, had even more to say to the Jews. He was both a prophet and a priest, which was not common. The priests had become important leaders to the Jews, much like the judges had once been. This dual role of priest and prophet made Zechariah a very important man.

(By the way, there are 28 men in the Old Testament bearing the name Zechariah. It meant "Jehovah remembers" and was apparently a common Jewish name. Don't be confused; only one Zechariah was a prophet and a priest.)

The Book of Zechariah is a fascinating one that ought not to be overlooked. The prophet first tells of seven visions that reveal how much God loved His people. The Lord says, "I am zealous [again] for Jerusalem and for Zion with great zeal . . . I am returning to Jerusalem with mercy. My house shall be built in it." (Zech. 1:14, 16). Just to let you know, the term "Zion" is used a lot for the name of Jerusalem *after* the Jews returned there. Zion was originally the name given to a rocky ridge west of Jerusalem. Over time, people used it to mean the whole city. In the Book of Revelation, it is used to describe the New Jerusalem yet to be seen.

Think with me a minute about what it meant for God to be returning His house to Jerusalem. Remember when God dwelt among His people in the Tabernacle? He was so close to them then. Eventually the Temple was built by Solomon where God could freely receive the worship of His people. He allowed it to be destroyed when the people went into captivity, but do you think He missed it? I suppose He did.

I suspect that He was thrilled to be having His people return home and to meet Him again in worship. They had learned their lesson. God's joy, love, and even zeal for His people all come out in the Book of Zechariah.

The book becomes even more meaningful at the end. The last few chapters begin to give clues to the people that an even better thing is going to happen: The Lord Himself is going to come to earth through the Messiah! What could be more incredible? The Temple was a place to worship God, but He was going to come to meet them face to face through Jesus! Zechariah wrote, "Behold your King is coming to you; He is just and having salvation, lowly and riding on a donkey, a colt, the foal of a donkey." (Zech. 9:9). Doesn't that passage remind you of just what we celebrate on Palm Sunday? Jesus rode right into the city of Jerusalem, the city He loved so much, on a donkey.

In closing, Zechariah prophesied even further into the future. He described the "day of the Lord" which is even yet to come. He says, "And the Lord shall be King over all the earth. In that day it shall be the Lord is one . . . In that day 'HOLINESS TO THE LORD' shall be engraved on the bells of the horses." He adds that terrible things will be for those who don't call on the Lord. His message is pretty clear to me. For those who believe in Him, the future is good.

ACTIVITY 69

ALL STUDENTS

Make your Memory Cards for Lessons 67–69.

69A—Younger Students

With your teacher, read Zechariah 3:1–5. In this passage, God uses the analogy of filthy garments and clean ones to describe the difference between the old sins of the people and the new blessings that were coming. Dress yourself in the dirtiest old clothes that you have and take a picture. Then, put on the newest and fanciest outfit that you own. Wrap your head in a towel or cloth like a clean turban. Now, take your picture again.

Take a piece of notebook paper and fold it in half. On one half, write Verse 3:3 about the filthy garments. On the other half, write Verse 4b–5, which says, "I have removed your iniquity from you, and I will clothe you with rich robes. Let them put a clean turban on his head." When you get your photos developed, glue them on the paper under the right verses. File this under "Asia: Israel."

69B—All Students

Read Haggai 2:20–23. The prophet says that Zerubbabel will be like a "signet ring." A signet ring was common but very valuable in the Old Testament. It was like a personalized stamp worn around the arm, neck, or finger. It was used to "sign" a document and make it official. God was saying that Zerubbabel and his rebuilding of the Temple was an official statement of his blessings on the people.

At a craft store, purchase a rubber stamp with your favorite symbol or your initials on it. Use this stamp on your family notes, school papers, or letters to represent yourself. On a piece of paper, write out Haggai 2:20–23. Add your stamp mark. File this under "Asia: Israel."

The scriptures say that God's favorite "stamp," or seal, is ultimately that of the Holy Spirit. See Ephesians 1:13 and 4:30 and I Corinthians 1:22.

69C—All Students

Read Zechariah 5:5–11. In the vision, the woman (or Wickedness) was thrust into a basket and carried away to another land. (It was Babylon, as a matter of fact.) God was showing that the wickedness that had been in the land would be removed far away. Are you ever "wicked"? All of us are guilty of sin at times, especially toward our family members. Take a small basket and keep it in a prominent place in your home. At family devotions, write down any offenses that you are guilty of toward your parents or siblings. Place the paper in the basket and allow your parents to take it far away! Make it a regular practice. Of course, in any offense we should apologize to the person we have hurt and ask their forgiveness. Because of the blood of Christ, we can all be forgiven. Use the basket just as a symbol of where wickedness belongs—far, far away!

 # TAKE ANOTHER LOOK!

Review 23: Lessons 67–69

Wall of Fame

1. *Darius I (521 B.C.)*—Stick a real stamp on the body of Darius I.

2. *Zerubbabel (520 B.C.)*—Put a hammer in his hand. Place a golden cross on him to signify the lineage of Christ.

3. *Haggai and Zechariah (520 B.C.)*—Place these guys together near Zerubbabel. Out of their mouths, give them the words, "God bless you, God love you!"

SomeWHERE in Time

1. On a globe, find with your finger the country of Iran. At the time of Darius I, the Persian Empire included Iran and many surrounding nations.

2. Middle and Older Students: Using a historical map, locate the Persian Empire around 500 B.C. It may be called the Achaemenid Empire in some resources. On Outline Map 1, "Persia," try to color in the boundaries of the empire. Mark Persepolis, the capital city under Darius I.

3. The story of Zerubbabel, when he rebuilt the Temple, occurred in Jerusalem. By looking at a map we have already done of Israel, make sure you know where the city is. Do you remember how far the journey was for the Jews from Babylonia to Palestine? Look it up!

The Mystery of History

WHAT DID YOU MISS?

For weeks now I have had you absorbing new facts and information. Today, I want to take you to a higher level of thinking. You see, anyone can memorize a date. But I would like to know if you could analyze the significance of some dates of history.

Here is an example of what I would like you to discuss and write down with your teacher for each date you have memorized so far. There are no "wrong" answers, and you can use your book to help. (In my example below, I gave you seven possible answers. Try to come up with at least three for each.) Write your answers in complete sentences on a separate sheet of paper.

1. Example: Abraham lived in 2100 B.C. What was the most significant thing about this time period?
   - It was after the flood, when life was "starting over."
   - People were beginning to live independently of God (for example, the Tower of Babel).
   - God used Abraham to begin a new nation.
   - God showed His power through the miracle of Isaac's birth.
   - Isaac was almost given as a sacrifice the same way Jesus was given later.
   - God made known His covenant with Abraham to give him the Promised Land. That is still an issue in the Middle East today.

2. King Tutankhamen lived in 1333 B.C. Besides being famous for his tomb, what else is significant about his early death?

3. David became the king of Israel in about 1055 B.C. What was going on in Israel that was important then?

4. The Kingdom of Israel divided in about 925 B.C. Why did it split, and what difference did it make? (What can we better understand by knowing about the different kingdoms?)

5. The Judeans were taken into captivity by the Babylonians beginning in 605 B.C. Why did God allow it, and what difference did it make in the long run?

6. Buddha was born in India about 563 B.C. What is so significant about his life?

7. Not long after Buddha lived, Confucius lived in China (551 B.C.). How are his teachings still important today?

☑ WHAT DO YOU KNOW?

Pretest 24

Circle the correct word to complete each sentence, then write it in the blank.

1. Tarquin the Proud was the last Etruscan _____ to rule over Rome before it became a republic.

   queen   king   child

2. The Romans wanted to have _____ rulers, or consuls, to govern the new Roman Republic. This helped prevent any one person from having too much power.

   three   ten   two

3. In Rome, the _____ were the ruling upper class and the plebeians were the lower working class.

   patricians   Caesars   mothers

4. In a modern-day marathon race, men and women run about 26 _____.

   days   yards   miles

5. The name for a marathon came from a battle fought on the plain of Marathon in _____.

   Turkey   Greece   Egypt

6. A runner by the name of _____ ran about 25 miles from Marathon to Athens to tell of the Greek victory.

   Pheidippides   Hercules   Aesop

7. Herodotus is known as the _____ of history.

   sister   father   son

8. Herodotus was particularly fascinated with the _____ and wrote extensively about their wars.

   Italians   Chinese   Persians

The Mystery of History

THE ROMAN REPUBLIC

LESSON 70

Several lessons back, we studied the founding of the city of Rome. I told you then that you would be hearing a lot more about Rome. It is because of their great influence on our own country that we will continue to learn about the Romans.

In review, the Romans were a blend of Latins and Etruscans. The Latins had come from the east of Italy and the Etruscans from the north. At one point, three different Etruscan kings ruled over the city of Rome in a row. The last Etruscan king to rule in Rome was named Tarquin the Proud. He was very cruel.

A Roman king had a lot of power back then. He was the leader of the army, the highest judge, the priest, the head of the nation, and the father of the state. That is a lot of responsibility for just one man. The people decided to change the way things were in Rome. They didn't like the idea that one person alone could be so powerful. So, in 509 B.C., Tarquin the Proud (the Etruscan king) was driven off the throne.

To ensure that no single ruler would ever dominate Rome again, the people formed the Roman Republic. A republic is a type of government where people are allowed to vote. The Romans also decided to have two rulers instead of one. They were called "consuls." One consul could override the decision of the other one. That meant that they had to agree on big decisions in order for them to pass. This protected the Romans from one ruler who might become greedy or evil.

The Romans controlled the decisions of the consuls by appointing men to a Senate. These senators were supposed to represent all the people. They gave advice to the consuls as to how Rome ought to be managed.

This all sounds like a nice way to run a country, but there were some problems. Years before, the Romans, like the people of India, had developed a class system based on one's birth. It had only two divisions though—the patricians (puh TRISH unz) and the plebeians (pli BEE unz). The patricians were the upper class and involved themselves with religion, politics, and society. The plebeians were the lower class and represented those who worked hard at farming and other basic trades.

Though now in ruins, the Forum was home to 10 or more governmental buildings and temples in the heart of Rome. For hundreds of years the Forum was the most powerful political center of the world.

In the early days of the Senate, only patricians served as senators. As the only senators, the patricians just weren't capable of fairly representing the plebeians. It took about 300 years for the plebeians to finally gain equal representation. Once they did, Rome was stronger for it. (Unfairness still existed, though, because slavery was rampant in early Rome.)

This lesson covers events that happened more than 2,000 years ago. However, the mind-set of the Romans still influences us today. Our government is built on the idea of people having a vote for who their ruler will be. We also try to equally represent people through the election of senators and representatives. We don't have two rulers like the Roman Republic, but we do have a system of checks and balances because of our three separate branches of government.

You will learn that the Roman Republic had a strong foundation that lasted for centuries. Eventually, the Romans, with their well-organized government, paved the way for the spread of the Gospel of Christ. Little did they realize the significance they would have on the world to come.

ACTIVITY 70

70A—Younger Students

Do you know the Pledge of Allegiance? Say it with your teacher. Notice that you use the word "republic" in the pledge. Now that you have studied the Roman Republic, I hope you better understand why we call our government a republic. If you want, copy the words of the Pledge of Allegiance and file them in your Student Notebook under "North America: United States."

Do you know any patriotic songs? Practice them today to remember that we live in a free country based on the right to vote for our leaders. That is a good thing!

70B—Middle Students

On a piece of paper, diagram the three main branches of our government in the shape of a triangle. If you don't already know them, they are the President (the executive branch), the Congress (the legislative branch), and the Supreme Court (the judicial branch). They make up what we consider our system of checks and balances. On the bottom of your paper, write in the definition of each of these branches using a dictionary or library text.

Do you know the two divisions of our Congress? Add the Senate and the House of Representatives to your list of definitions. With your teacher's help, find out the names of your senators and representatives. It is an incredible freedom in our country to be able to vote for our leaders. Know who your leaders are. File this under "North America: United States."

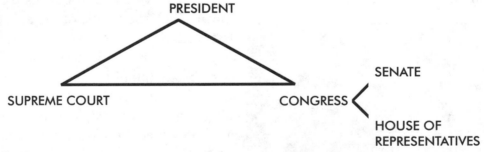

PRESIDENT

SUPREME COURT   CONGRESS

SENATE

HOUSE OF REPRESENTATIVES

70C—Older Students

More than likely you will study government as a formal course before you graduate from high school. In preparation, define the following terms and be familiar with the basic function of each. Many men have died for our freedom—we should not take for granted the system that has been established. Know it well. File your definitions under "North America: United States."

- Executive branch
- Legislative branch
- Judicial branch
- Separation of powers
- Judicial review

- Two-party system
- National elections
- Constitutional amendment
- Bill
- Veto

The Mystery of History

THE BATTLE OF MARATHON

LESSON 71

Have you ever heard of a "marathon"? It refers to a foot race of about 26 miles. That's a long way to run. In this lesson we are going to learn where the name of the race came from. It's a neat but sad story.

First we have to go back to the Medo-Persian king we studied earlier, King Darius I. (Not Darius the Mede, king of Babylon, who threw Daniel in the lions' den, but the other Darius. The one who started the postal service and divided Persia into satrapies.) Darius I had his eye on many of the countries surrounding Persia. One of those was Ionia. That country was on the coast of Turkey (or Asia Minor).

Darius I managed to conquer Ionia but not without a difficult fight. The nearby Greeks from Athens tried to help the Ionians fight Darius. Darius was naturally quite threatened by this. The Greek historian Herodotus says this of Darius's reaction to the Athenians.

> "The Great King asked who the Athenians were, and then on being told, called for his bow. He took it, set an arrow on the string, shot it up into the air and cried: 'Grant, O God, that I may punish the Athenians.' Then he commanded one of his servants to repeat to him the words, 'Master, remember the Athenians,' three times, whenever he sat down to dinner."[1]

So this is where the trouble started between the Persians and the Greeks. With some careful planning, Darius marched over to Greece to try to fight them, too. The two armies met on the plain of Marathon, which is about 25 miles from Athens. It's important to remember that distance.

The Persian army under Darius I was not prepared for the fight they found in Greece. Though the Persians greatly outnumbered the Greeks, the Greek army charged on them aggressively. In fact, they ran the Persians right back to their ships! Darius actually withdrew from the fight. The Persians lost as many as 6,000 men while the Athenians lost only about 200. It was an incredible victory for the Athenians, and it showed the world that the mighty Persians could be defeated. They had been on a real winning streak up until then.

While there was great reason to celebrate in the Greek army camp, it occurred to the leader that the Persians who sailed off in their ships might try to sneak to the actual city of Athens. Since there were no telephones or news networks back then, the Athenians in the city wouldn't even know that the Greek army had won the Battle of Marathon. The Persians might act as if they had won and try to sack the city of Athens itself.

The leader of the Greek camp came up with a great idea. He would send one man as a messenger on foot all the way to Athens to tell the people there of the victory. He chose the fastest runner around, whose name was Pheidippides (fiy DIP uh dees). Pheidippides had already been running messages to Sparta and back and was undoubtedly tired. Nonetheless, Pheidippides took off running for 25 long miles to Athens.

When Pheidippides got there, he bravely shared the news of the victory at Marathon. Exhausted and breathless, he stated, "Rejoice, we conquer!" And with those last words, he fell down dead from exhaustion!

---

1. As quoted in Don Nardo, *The Persian Empire.* San Diego: Lucent Books, 1998; p. 63.

In honor of the long run that Pheidippides made, which cost him his life, the term "marathon" came to mean a long race of 26 miles. Sometimes we use the term to refer to anything that is long and difficult. Now you know just how serious the first marathon was and can really appreciate the term.

The Athenians themselves had an interesting way to remember the Battle of Marathon. The Athenians wanted their countrymen and those they traded with to never forget who won and who fled. So they decided to add a crescent moon to one of their favorite coins that was used far and wide in the region.

The coin was called a tetradrachma. It was already decorated with an owl on it as a symbol of the goddess Athena and some olive branches to represent their wealth. Why then did they choose to add a moon shape to the coin to remember the Battle of Marathon? The reason for the crescent was that Darius was defeated on a night when the moon was "waning." A waning moon is in the shape of a crescent! What a clever way for the Greeks to keep the memory of their victory alive.

ACTIVITY 71

71A—Younger Students

Do you like to run? Hold a race today and see who is the fastest runner in your family or school group. Good marathon runners learn to pace themselves and not run too fast in the beginning. Sprinters run as fast as they can through a whole race because it is for a shorter distance. With your teacher, talk about what it means to "pace yourself."

71B—Younger and Middle Students

1. The Athenians remembered their victory over the Persians by adding a crescent moon to one of their coins. Can you think of ways that we commemorate battle victories in our country?

   Obtain a copy of the lyrics to our national anthem. Sing it! Learn the meaning behind the words to this familiar song if you don't already know them. What famous battle is remembered in the song?

2. Do you know the phases of the moon? Find and write out definitions for the following terms: new moon, crescent moon, first-quarter moon, gibbous moon, last-quarter moon, and full moon. A moon is called "waxing" as it progresses from a new moon to a full moon, and it is called "waning" as it moves from a full moon back to a new moon. Though the Battle of Marathon happened thousands of years ago, we know from their records what the moon was doing on that significant night.

71C—Older Students

Pheidippides was a person who showed incredible sacrifice. For the sake of the Athenians, he ran until it killed him. Do we see such acts of patriotism today? Report on a current event in which you see heroism displayed. Sometimes we hear of stories of heroes during natural disasters. See what you come up with in just one day's newspaper.

HERODOTUS

LESSON 72

My reason for liking Herodotus is personal. He loved history, just as I do! He contributed so much to the study of history that he is called the "father of history." He was one of the first men to seriously study and write about the events of the past as well as to document the things happening right around him.

We don't know a lot about the personal life of Herodotus (he ROD oh tus). We do know he was born in Ionia in a Greek colony. Ionia is also Asia Minor, or Turkey, where Troy was. Herodotus traveled to Egypt, the Middle East, and North Africa. At one time he lived in Athens, but he eventually settled in Southern Italy. It was a Greek colony at that time.

All that traveling gave Herodotus a perspective, or view, on life that many people back then didn't get. Most people were unable to travel very far. It was much more difficult than it is now. Because of his experiences, Herodotus saw many different customs, manners, foods, and religions. He must have wanted to share it with others because that is exactly what he did.

Herodotus wrote things in a very enjoyable manner. He took events in history and retold them in entertaining ways. Unfortunately, some of his writings are said to not be completely accurate. In his effort to be interesting, he may sometimes have written things that weren't true.

Apart from that, Herodotus's writings have been very beneficial to scholars. He wrote nine books just on the Persians and the Persian Wars. This was a breakthrough for his time. Few historians would ever write about people other than their own. Herodotus wrote extensively on the Persians in order that his own people would better understand them.

For example, from Herodotus we have descriptions of what the Persians wore in battle, what their values were toward education, and what a rich man would do for his birthday. And in case you're wondering, the following paragraph is what Herodotus wrote about birthdays.

"A rich Persian on his birthday will have an ox or a horse or a camel or a donkey baked whole in the oven and served up at table, and the poor some smaller beast. The main dishes at their meals are few, but they have many sorts of dessert, the various courses being served separately. It is this custom that has made them say that the Greeks leave the table hungry, because we never have anything worth mentioning after the first course."[2]

I hope you picked up on the humor of Herodotus in that excerpt. He threw in his opinion of Greek food and the lack of great desserts compared to the Persians.

Remember when we studied Darius I? I told you that he started a postal system. It was Herodotus who wrote the famous words to describe the dedicated Persians. ("Not snow, no, nor rain, nor heat, nor night keeps them from accomplishing their appointed course with all speed." Hdt. 8.98) Similar words are inscribed today at the General Post Office in New York City. Maybe you'll see them yourself someday.

Herodotus had ambitious reasons for writing as he did. These are his own words about why history was important to him:

"These are the researches of Herodotus of Halicarnassus, which he publishes, in the hope of thereby preserving from decay the remembrance of what men have done, and of preventing the great and

---

2. As quoted in Don Pardo, *The Persian Empire*. San Diego: Lucent Books, 1998; p. 54.

wonderful actions of the Greeks and the Barbarians from losing their due meed of glory; and withal to put on record what were their grounds of feuds."[3]

I like the fact that Herodotus wrote about cultures other than his own. He gave us a wealth of information about the Persians, the Greeks, and others. I think he was accurate, too, in that much of history is studying the conflicts between different people groups. What do you think about history? I hope you are finding it to be fascinating!

ACTIVITY 72

ALL STUDENTS

Make your Memory Cards for Lessons 70–72.

72A—Younger Students

Be a historian. Using a tape recorder, tell a story about something that has happened in your family. You might report on a favorite vacation or the birth of a brother or sister. Maybe you just have a funny story to tell. Be like Herodotus and try to make it interesting. Interview people in your family if you need to. History is just the stories of real people like you put into words. Allow the whole family to listen to your tape later.

72B—Middle Students

One of the reasons for the success of Herodotus was his perspective on the events he wrote about. He was known to actually interview or gather the stories of people who were involved in that which he was writing about.

In your head, think of a family event or special memory. Using a tape recorder, interview family members who were there for the same event. Don't let them hear one another's accounts. Gather these different perspectives and see how closely they tell the exact same story. Write down the final story with all the facts. File this under "North America: United States" in your Student Notebook. (Historians are often at the mercy of the memory of others.)

72C—Older Students

Obtain the original works of Herodotus. If you have access to the Internet, there is a free site that offers his nine books on the Persians. Go to http://classics.mit.edu to find Herodotus and many other original classics.

I found parts of Herodotus hard to understand because of the names of the people groups he uses that we are not familiar with. Otherwise, I could hardly quit reading the material. Some of his stories are *very* interesting. Just in Book I, if you scroll halfway down the text, you will find an incredible story of the childhood of Cyrus. It's full of suspense, mistaken identity, and murder. Also, if you keep scrolling, you will find a neat story about the Persian queen named Nitocris who left unusual instructions about her tomb for other kings to ponder. Darius fell prey to her trap! Still in Book I you will find Herodotus's account of Cyrus the Great taking over Babylon. It's difficult reading, but fascinating. Try it!

---

3. From http://classics.mit.edu/Herodotus/history.1.i.html; transl. by George Rawlinson.

The Mystery of History

TAKE ANOTHER LOOK!

Review 24: Lessons 70–72

Wall of Fame

1. *The Roman Republic (509 B.C.)*—Make a banner type of sign that says, "Vote Today." Underneath, write "The Roman Republic" with the date.

2. *The Battle of Marathon (490 B.C.)*—Draw the silhouette of a tennis shoe. Write your information on it.

3. *Herodotus (c. 484 B.C.)*—Draw a book in one hand and a pen in the other. Include on him the title, "Father of History."

SomeWHERE in Time

1. Using a historical atlas, find the ancient boundaries of the Roman Republic anytime between 509 and 31 B.C. The boundaries of Rome will change many times over the course of our study.

   On Outline Map 5, "Europe," sketch with dotted lines of any color the boundaries of the Roman Republic. Make a key in the corner to signify what the color and line mean.

   Write in these features: Gaul (France), Spain, Italy, Africa, Judaea (Judea), Asia Minor (Turkey), Greece, Macedonia, Thrace.

   For the waters, include: the Mediterranean Sea, the Aegean Sea, the Adriatic Sea, the Ionian Sea, the Black Sea, the Red Sea.

   Also include the islands of Corsica, Sardinia, Sicily, Crete, and Cyprus. Keep this map under "Europe: Rome." We will use it again.

2. Using a historical atlas, find Athens and the plain of Marathon. On Outline Map 2, "Greece," label both of these places. With a colored pencil, draw the route that Pheidippides would have run to tell the news of the victory.

   In your atlas, trace with your finger the path from Iran to Turkey (Ionia) and then over to Greece. Do you see how far away from Persia Darius and his men were fighting?

   On the same outline map of Greece, color and write in these places: the plain of Marathon, Athens, Ionia, Troy, Sparta, Aegean Sea, Crete, Knossos, Peloponnese Peninsula, Macedonia. (Some of these places we have not studied yet. We will though, so I want you to begin to be familiar with them.)

3. On the same map, label and color the land of Ionia in light green. In nice handwriting, include the names "Asia Minor" and "Turkey" under the name "Ionia." In another colored pencil, write the words, "Birthplace of Herodotus" in Ionia.

WHAT DID YOU LEARN?

Week 24: *Quiz*

Stump the Teacher. I'm tired of the same old quiz, how about you? Here's something new. I want *you* to create a 20-question quiz for YOUR TEACHER to take! Let's see how well your teacher is learning and remembering the material. This will require you to look back at all the lessons and be creative. (That is the part where you'll learn something, which is the whole point of these quizzes anyway.)

Take this assignment seriously. You may still be graded on the questions you ask. Let's say you get one point for every "good" and legitimate question you come up with. You have a potential for 20 points. (Your teacher's score won't affect yours.) It's up to you whether your teacher is allowed to consult the book.

Each student should create a test. Start here and continue on another sheet. Have fun trying to "stump the teacher"!

1.

2.

3.

4.

5.

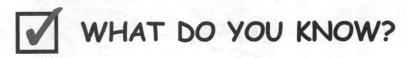

WHAT DO YOU KNOW?

Pretest 25

Circle the choice that makes the sentence correct.

1. Xerxes brilliantly created the plan to march to Greece over the Hellespont on a (suspended, floating) bridge.

2. Xerxes' defeat against the Greeks was prophesied by (Moses, Daniel) in the Old Testament.

3. Xerxes was forced to fight in the (sea, swamp) and lost.

4. Esther was a Jewish (prophetess, orphan) before she became the queen.

5. Mordecai was Esther's (cousin, brother). He refused to bow to Haman.

6. During the (Golden, Silver) Age of Athens, the Greeks were generally at peace with Persia and with one another.

7. At the theater, Greeks wore huge (shoes, masks) to make themselves appear to be different characters.

8. The Greeks are well remembered for the building of the (Lincoln Memorial, Parthenon), which overlooks the city of Athens.

XERXES I

LESSON 73

Do you remember Darius I? He was a Persian king with a vengeance against the Greeks. He was so determined to remember them that he had his servant state three times at each meal, "Remember the Athenians." Despite his passion against them, Darius was badly defeated at the Battle of Marathon. Our lesson today is about Darius's son Xerxes I. Like his father, he carried a grudge against the Greeks that resulted in a war. Besides that, Xerxes I was married to someone rather special as I mentioned in a previous lesson. Do you remember who it was? I'll tell you at the end of the story.

Xerxes took the throne of Persia when Darius died. He had these strong words to say about his father and his desire to finish what Darius had started against the Greeks:

> "I have found a way to win for Persia not glory only but a country as large and as rich as our own . . . and at the same time to get satisfaction and revenge . . . I will march an army . . . into Greece, and punish the Athenians for the outrage they committed upon my father and upon us."[1]

With fury in his heart, Xerxes set out in 480 B.C., just 10 years after the Battle of Marathon, to see what damage he could do to the Greeks. One of the problems Xerxes faced was getting to Greece without being noticed. Xerxes came up with a most unusual but brilliant plan. To understand it, you'll have to get a map right now and follow along with me.

Find the Black Sea and the Aegean Sea. They are connected by a long strait of water. This place on the map was called the Hellespont. It was difficult to cross. The Greeks would never expect the Persians to come from that direction. But they did.

In order to cross the Hellespont, Xerxes had a huge fleet of ships line up side by side, and a bridge was laid over them. It was a floating bridge that was so long it took Xerxes' huge army seven days to cross over it! What a great sight that would have been! (Details of the bridge are listed on the Activity page.)

Xerxes' army was massive! He recruited people of many different nations and even some women to fight for him. His conglomerate army of nearly 200,000 soldiers may have been the largest one ever assembled up until then. The Greek historian Herodotus joked about the size of this army, saying that when "Xerxes' army drank water, whole rivers ran dry."[2] Xerxes really wanted to conquer Greece this time.

In the beginning of the war, Xerxes was successful. His first victory was at the Battle of Thermopylae. He had only to conquer a small army of Spartans. With great confidence, Xerxes then moved south to Athens, where he successfully sacked and burned the magnificent capital city. He must have felt great delight in turning Athens to ashes.

Xerxes' luck eventually ran out, though. He was forced to fight at sea against the Greeks at the Bay of Salamis. The Battle of Salamis may have been the first major sea battle ever fought. Supposedly, Xerxes witnessed the whole event from a seat high up on a hill. Although the Persians had some great ships, the Greek navy cleverly backed them into a corner where they were unable to turn around easily. The smaller, faster Greek vessels were able to completely overtake the Persians. It was a crushing blow to Xerxes. How upsetting it must have been to watch his huge navy defeated.

---

1. As quoted in Don Nardo, *The Persian Empire.* San Diego: Lucent Books, 1998; p. 70.
2. As quoted in Will Durant, *The Life of Greece.* New York: Simon and Schuster, 1939; p. 238.

The Mystery of History

For the non-Persian countries, it was something to celebrate. This one battle at sea stopped the Persians from ruling over the entire Mediterranean world. And the Persian loss fulfilled Daniel's prophecy that another ruler would take over who would be far more powerful. (That was going to be Alexander the Great!)

There is one other story, though, that I'll mention briefly now because it portrays God's hand on Xerxes' life. Xerxes is also the figure in the Bible who is given the name Ahasuerus (uh haz you EE rus). Ahasuerus, or Xerxes, is the one who married Esther of the Old Testament. By doing so, Xerxes actually helped to preserve the lineage of the Jews. The story is so good that we'll have a whole lesson on it next.

ACTIVITY 73

73A—Younger and Middle Students

Make a Greek battleship.
Adult supervision is needed for this project.

Materials: Rectangular piece of floral Styrofoam plastic foam about 6 inches long, toothpicks; optional: spray paint, stick, and paper for sail

The Greeks were known for creating great battleships. One was called a "trireme" because it held three levels of oars. (The prefix "tri" means three of something, like in the word "tricycle.")

1. With a dull knife or scissors, try to "whittle" the ends of the Styrofoam into points.
2. Now take toothpicks and poke them into the sides of the boat for oars. Try to put them in three levels. It will take a lot of toothpicks.
3. If you want to get fancy, create a mast and sail out of paper and sticks. You could even spray paint the boat if it turned out well and draw eyes on it like the Greeks did.

At your next bath, see how well your vessel floats! Make a couple of these and have a sea battle. Take a picture of them and file it under "Europe: Greece."

73B—Middle Students

Recreate the floating bridge at Hellespont. Using pieces of Styrofoam plastic foam, cardboard, and army men, creatively assemble a "bridge" of boats. Try it out in the bathtub! If it works or not, take a picture of it and file it under "Europe: Iran (Persia)." Imagine the magnitude of the bridge built by Xerxes. The following paragraph is a summary by Herodotus of the bridge of boats.

"Galleys and Triremes were lashed together to support the bridges . . . they were moored slantwise to the Black Sea and at right angles to the Hellespont, in order to lessen the strain on the cables. Specially heavy anchors were laid out both upstream and downstream . . . Once the vessels were in position, the cables were hauled taut by wooden winches ashore...The next operation was to cut planks equal in length to the width of the floats, lay them edge to edge over the taut cables, and then bind them together on their upper surface. That done, brushwood was put on top and spread evenly, with a layer of soil, trodden hard, over all. Finally a paling (fence) was constructed along each side, high enough to prevent horses and mules from seeing over and taking fright at the water."[3]

---

3. As quoted in Will Durant, *The Life of Greece.* New York: Simon and Schuster, 1939; p. 71.

We have only skimmed over the history of the Persian Empire. Under Darius I it was really quite vast. Do additional research on the Persians. Include in your report the origin of the name "Persia," the Achaemenid dynasty, the borders of the empire under Darius, Zoroastrian (the religion of the Persians), and the end of the empire. File this under "Europe: Iran (Persia)."

Unknown

ESTHER

LESSON 74

The story of Esther is absolutely beautiful. It is a "rags-to-riches" fairy tale come true. Let me tell you what makes the story so special.

Esther was a Jewish orphan girl living in Susa. The city of Susa was east of the Tigris River in what had been Babylonia. Now, the Persians ruled it.

Think of what you already know of the Jews. They were deported to Babylonia under Nebuchadnezzar. Then Cyrus the Great, a Persian, gave them the freedom to go home to Judah. Many, though, stayed where they were.

Esther was one of the Jews who remained in Babylonia. She lived with her cousin Mordecai. They were probably ordinary people making a living there and participating in the social life around them.

One year, Xerxes, the Persian king (also called Ahasuerus), gave an incredible party. It was so huge that it lasted for 180 days. That is about six months! Toward the end, the king must have been getting bored with it all. He asked his queen, named Vashti, to come and dance before his men. That was unheard of then. In fact, it was against the law. In Persia, women of good reputation kept themselves separate from the men at parties.

Vashti refused the king's request to dance, which greatly insulted him in front of all his friends. It cost Vashti her position as queen. She was banished! To fill her spot, Xerxes put out a letter that every girl of marrying age in the region had to come before him so he could choose a new queen.

Even if you didn't know the story, you could probably already guess the plot. Esther was one of the girls who had to go. Can you imagine being her? An ordinary Jewish orphan girl was being asked to come to the king's palace for a beauty contest. And the winner got to be queen!

This is an ancient cosmetic applicator and mirror, much like that used by Esther to prepare herself for the king.

It so happened that Esther was a real beauty. Even so, for months Esther and the other young women were groomed to be even more beautiful, as was the custom. Of all the women the king looked over, Xerxes chose her. It is truly a Cinderella story to become a queen overnight. However, the king didn't know that Esther was a Jew.

The plot thickens in this story because Xerxes' top aide had a vengeance against the Jews. He went so far as to devise a scheme to have them all killed. His name was Haman. One of the reasons Haman disliked the Jews was because Mordecai, Esther's relative, refused to bow down to him. Even though he was living in a foreign land, Mordecai was a faithful Jew who would never bow to anyone other than God.

Xerxes, unaware of his beautiful wife's Jewish heritage, agreed to Haman's plan. Xerxes used his own signet ring to place his approval on a document that went out to the whole land and declared the fate of the Jews.

The news was devastating to the Jews. They prayed, fasted and wept. Mordecai pleaded with Esther that she was going to have to beg the king for the lives of her people. He said to her, "Do you think in your heart that you will escape in the king's palace any more than all the other Jews. For if you remain completely silent at this time . . . you and your father's house will perish. Yet who knows whether you have come to the kingdom for such a time as this?" (Esther 4:13–14)

There was just one small problem with Mordecai's idea. The king could have Esther killed for making such a request. No one approached the king without his asking. No one. Death was the outcome unless the king extended his favor using his gold scepter. Esther would have to risk her own life to plead for the lives of her fellow Jews.

What would you have done? In God's sovereignty, He gave Esther the wisdom and courage to face Xerxes with her petition. When the king saw Esther standing in the court, she found favor in his sight, and he held out to her the golden scepter. Before making her bold request, she buttered him up with a great feast to which she even invited Haman. She wanted Haman right there to explain to the king what he had schemed.

The dinner apparently was a hit. The king listened to Esther and learned of her fate and the fate of her people, the Jews. Xerxes told Esther she could certainly have anything she requested; additionally, he had Haman executed for coming up with the plot.

Still, there was a big problem. Xerxes had already sent out his men with the orders to kill the Jews on the thirteenth day of March! Haman chose the date by chance (or by "pur" in the Persian language). What could be done now? To try to stop the crusade, Esther was given the authority by Xerxes to warn the Jews of the date and to equip them to fight. They did exactly that and successfully protected themselves. The Jews were spared from mass destruction as a result of Esther's involvement.

To this very day, the Jews celebrate the festival of "Purim" in remembrance of the Lord's intervention against the day of chance, or "pur," chosen by Haman. Some people will fast on the day before Purim to remember that Esther prayed and fasted before she approached the king. The beautiful story of Esther is a reminder of the power of prayer and the sovereignty of God.

ACTIVITY 74

74A—Younger Students

If you are a girl, ask your mother, older sister, or a friend to do a "makeover" on you. (Be sure you have your parent's permission.) Esther prepared for 12 months before she went in to see the king. That is a long time to work on beauty! Like Esther, see what you can do with your hair, clothes, perfume, and makeup.

If you are a boy, make a gold scepter out of a wrapping paper tube. Spray paint it gold and decorate it. Demonstrate how you think a king may have extended a scepter to show approval.

74B—Middle Students

The signet ring was an important custom in ancient days. It gave official meaning to documents. One way we do that today is through a "notary public." Make a mock decree of some sort. Now, seek out a real notary. They are usually at your family's bank, and their services may be free. See if your notary might be willing, for educational reasons, to notarize your document or at least to explain the procedure. It is an interesting process. File the document under "Asia: Iran (Persia)."

74C—Older Students

1. If you are female and have a younger sister, please enjoy the makeover activity listed above. (Be sure you have your parent's approval to do this.) Emphasize to your sibling that inner beauty is far more important than outward appearance.

2. Research the customs of the Jewish feast of Purim. Discover what some Jews practice today on *Taanit Esther*, the day before Purim, to honor the actions of Esther. File your findings under "Asia: Israel" in your Student Notebook.

479–431 B.C.

THE GOLDEN AGE OF ATHENS

LESSON 75

Together, we have already studied many famous Greeks and Greek events. Can you name some of them? There have been nine lessons so far dealing with ancient Greece. In this order, we learned about the Trojan Horse, Homer, the first Olympics, the rise of Athens and Sparta, Aesop, Pythagoras, the Battle of Marathon, and Herodotus. All of these have contributed to the rich culture of ancient Greece.

There was one period of time, though, that historians call the Golden Age of Athens (or the Golden Age of Greece), which was the most outstanding era in all of Greece's history. Surprisingly, it was a short time period—it lasted only about 50 years, from 479 B.C. through 431 B.C.

One of the main reasons that life was so good during the Golden Age was that the big wars with Persia were over. Tension still existed with Sparta, but a 30-year peace treaty was helping to keep things somewhat calm.

It is during times of peace and when money is abundant, that people are freer to be creative. When people are not so concerned with survival, they have more time for entertainment, the arts, and deeper thinking. This is what happened in Athens during its Golden Age.

As for entertainment, the Greeks loved the theater. They were the first we know of to introduce actors to a stage. At an annual event called the "Dionysia," men competed in performing tragedies, comedies, and "satyr plays." A satyr play incorporated the use of men dressed like part horse or goat to make fun of serious things. It would be like what we call a "satire" today.

An entire play back then may have used only two or three actors. To make them look like different characters, the actors wore big masks. The masks could make them look young, old, happy, sad, or even part animal. The masks usually had large, exaggerated eyes and mouths to help the audience see the actors, even from far away.

When it came to art, the Greeks had discovered how to create very real-looking, three-dimensional statues. Unlike the Egyptians before them whose art was simple and one-dimensional, the Greeks created art that dramatically came to life. They painted and sculpted their subjects with greater facial expression and with clothes that appeared to flow with movement. The Greeks also made beautiful black and red pottery of intricate design. It is common to find pictures of these in books on Greece.

As for deep thinking, Athens attracted great mathematicians, philosophers, scholars and doctors, all of whom contributed to the growth of the society. We soon will devote some lesson time to the three most well-known Greek philosophers: Socrates, Plato, and Aristotle.

Besides everything I've already written about, there was still more to the Golden Age. There was the development of music, poetry, toys, games, and sports. But my list of the Greeks' achievements wouldn't be complete if I didn't include their architecture. The everyday houses were often simple, but when it came to their temples and other public buildings, they were extravagant. They erected huge buildings with beautiful columns. The columns were sometimes simple (called "Doric" columns) or more ornate (called "Ionic" and "Corinthian" columns).

The greatest of ancient Athens's buildings was probably the Parthenon. It was huge, very ornate, and towered over the city because it was built right on top

The Parthenon, one of four magnificent structures on the Acropolis, was built to honor Athena Parthenos, the goddess of Athens.

of the Acropolis. Its basic structure still stands today despite suffering great damage over the years. Structurally, it is one of the most perfect buildings ever built. It contained no straight lines but only the illusion of them. The Greeks understood the optical illusions our eyes will create. The Lincoln Memorial in Washington, D.C., is patterned after this magnificent structure.

However, the Parthenon was built as a temple for the goddess Athena. Unfortunately the Greek culture was steeped in false religions and superstitions about the gods. Mythology was a huge part of life in ancient Greece.

As you know, though, this incredible growth spurt of the lovely city-state of Athens didn't last too long. The jealous and war-loving Spartans were going to slow down these great advancements. War isn't very nice, is it? But in history we see a lot of it.

ACTIVITY 75

ALL STUDENTS

Make your Memory Cards for Lessons 73–75. The Golden Age of Athens (479 B.C.) is a date to memorize.

75A—Younger Students

Make a Greek theater mask.

Materials: Paper plate, pencils, crayons, markers, scissors, yarn, glue, elastic, stapler

On a paper plate, lightly draw a face using pencil, and give it a strong expression, happy or sad, by how you draw the large eyes and mouth. Cut out just the eyes and mouth. Color in the background with bright crayons like yellow or orange. Use markers to outline the eyes and mouth. Glue strands of yarn to the top for hair. Attach elastic with a stapler so the mask will fit your head. If you make several masks with different expressions, you—alone—could perform a short play by changing characters.

75B—Younger and Middle Students

Learn the differences between the columns that the Greeks were famous for (Doric, Ionic, and Corinthian). Using library books on ancient Greece, trace or sketch the three styles. Remember this simple clue: The more syllables in the word, the fancier the column. Place your columns under "Europe: Ancient Greece."

Drive around your town or city and try to identify Doric, Ionic, and Corinthian columns.

75C—Middle and Older Students

Using resources at the library, obtain pictures of both the Parthenon and the U.S. Capitol. Note the architectural similarities. Write a short paper on the Parthenon, including who built it, what size it was, what materials were used, and what its purpose was. Find pictures of the Parthenon as it stands today. Photocopy them and include them in your report. If you're older, add to your research the religious practices of the ancient Greeks. You may particularly want to investigate the "mystery cults." File your report under "Europe: Greece."

The Mystery of History

TAKE ANOTHER LOOK!

Review 25: Lessons 73–75

Wall of Fame

1. *Xerxes I (480 B.C.)*—Put his other name (Ahasuerus) in parentheses under his name.

2. *Esther (exact date unknown)*—Make her very pretty, with long eyelashes and a crown of glitter.

3. *The Golden Age of Athens (479–431 B.C.)*—Make a small collage of Greek-looking things, such as black and red pottery, columns, statues, Greek letters, and so forth. **Remember, this is a date to memorize. (You only have to remember the date of 479 B.C.)**

SomeWHERE in Time

1. On Outline Map 2, "Greece," find what would be called the Hellespont and label it. Also label the Black Sea and the Aegean Sea. Color the seas in blue. File this map under "Europe: Greece."

2. Using a Bible atlas, find the city of Susa where Esther was from. Notice the great distance that Xerxes was from his Persian homeland when he was fighting over in Greece.

3. The ancient Greeks developed a system of imaginary, intersecting lines that form a geographic (or global) grid around the Earth. This grid uses lines of latitude and longitude, and it helps us to correctly find any location in the world. Think of it as a worldwide "address book"! Let me explain.

   Lines of latitude (also called parallels because they run parallel to the Equator) run east and west around the globe and measure location north or south of the Equator. The Equator is 0° latitude.

   Lines of longitude (also called meridians) run between the North Pole and the South Pole and measure location east or west of the prime meridian. The prime meridian runs through Greenwich, England, and is 0° longitude.

   The latitude or longitude of a point on the earth is called its coordinate. If you know both coordinates, you can locate any point on our planet. When giving coordinates, list the latitude first, followed by the longitude.

4. Looking on a good atlas or globe, what city would you find at these locations: (a) 38°N, 23°E; (b) 30°N, 31°E? The answer is given below.

   Can you find the approximate coordinates for your hometown?

Answer: (a) Athens, Greece; (b) Cairo, Egypt

Complete the crossword puzzle on the next page. You may look in your book for the answers. (The lesson number is in parentheses.)

ACROSS
1. Ate a scroll (61)
5. Five-sport event (41)
8. Destroyed by a flood (55)
9. Greek mathematician (64)
11. The Ishtar _____ (58)
13. The Behistun _____ (67)
14. Roman lower class (70)
17. Celebration to remember Esther (74)
18. Created on the third day (1)
20. "Father of History" (72)
22. "Enlightened one" (63)
23. "To draw out" (19)
24. Half bull/half man (12)

DOWN
2. Third Chinese dynasty (29)
3. Roman language (43)
4. "Between the rivers" (7)
6. Son of Hezekiah (50)
7. Discovered Tut's tomb (23)
10. Location of floating bridge (73)
12. "Huge rocks" (10)
15. "Father of a Great Nation" (13)
16. Capital of Northern Kingdom (35)
19. Prophetess (56)
21. Annual Greek theater event (75)

✓ WHAT DO YOU KNOW?

Pretest 26

To familiarize yourself with this week's lessons, alphabetize the following word list. Circle the ones you have heard of before and discuss what you know about them.

Socrates

1. _____

philosopher

2. _____

poison hemlock

3. _____

Hippocratic Oath

4. _____

Asclepius

5. _____

Persia

6. _____

Ezra

7. _____

Longimanus

8. _____

The Mystery of History

SOCRATES

LESSON 76

The life of Socrates is a sad one to me. It is sad because of how it ends. But I won't start there. Let's first learn who Socrates was and what he believed.

Socrates (SAHK ruh teez) was one of the greatest Greek philosophers who lived during the Golden Age of Athens. The word "philosopher" means "lover of wisdom." And that describes Socrates well. However, Socrates never wrote down any of his teachings but rather spoke his thoughts out loud to anyone who would listen. We know his teachings today because his students wrote them down for him.

Socrates enjoyed life and talking to people. He was popular because of his wit and humor, and he made it his career to talk to others. He was not so much into politics or religion as he was into trying to understand man's behavior.

What were the profound thoughts of Socrates? He believed that men were "good" if they had wisdom and knowledge, and that men were "bad" if they were ignorant. So he challenged the Athenians to think wisely about things that they did in order to be better people.

One example of the humor of Socrates would be his attitude toward his wife. Apparently he was married to a difficult woman named Xanthippe. He was known to say that living with

With friends mourning around him, Socrates showed no fear in drinking the poison hemlock.

her made the rest of life easier. She must been a pretty tough person to live with.

Another of Socrates' sayings, although he didn't originate it, was "Know thyself." He thought that closely examining one's heart would lead to improvement. He also challenged people to see the difference between opinions and knowledge. This began to get him in trouble because there were many "opinions" floating around the city of Athens in those days.

Although he was still popular with most Athenians, not all the people found him charming. Some of the leaders thought Socrates was a threat to the idea of democracy. As you know, democracy was very important to the Athenians. Some leaders feared that his ideas would make young people break away from the government or call upon new gods.

The threat became so real that Socrates was actually arrested for his teachings. Being the amazing man that he was, he defended himself at his own trial. Though he gave a tremendous speech (that was recorded by his pupil Plato), he was found guilty and given the death sentence!

It has been written that the friends of Socrates tried to sneak him out of prison, but Socrates preferred to submit to the law rather than flee—even if it cost him his life. He felt that he would do more good for Athens, the city he loved, by dying. He believed that strongly in his philosophies and the right to free speech.

In his final hours in prison, Socrates was visited by family and his closest students without apparent fear of death. As he stroked his young son's hair for the last time, he said, "Tomorrow, Phaedo, I suppose that these fair locks will be cut." It was the custom then for a person's hair to be cut when mourning the loss of a loved one. Socrates then said farewell to his tearful wife, Xanthippe, and had her escorted home.

Finally the last hour came. At sunset, a trembling jailer gave Socrates a cup of poison hemlock to drink. Onlookers claim that Socrates drank the poison without a struggle. According to Plato, Phaedo said of his father, "Without the least fear of change of color or feature, he quite readily and happily drank the poison."[1] Socrates was confident in his cause and died a courageous death.

In Socrates, I think we see a good person who really tried to understand mankind. Much like Confucius, he looked for goodness *in* people. In my opinion, his only shortcoming was expecting to find true goodness in people based on man's knowledge and wisdom rather than on God's.

Even in death, Socrates was optimistic. In his last hours he said, "Wherefore O Judges, be of good cheer about death, and be sure of this—that no evil can happen to a good man either in life or after death. He and his are not neglected by the gods. The hour of departure has come; and we go our ways; I to die, you to live. Which way is the better, God alone knows."[2]

ACTIVITY 76

76A—Younger Students

Dress up like a Greek philosopher.

Materials: Twin-size flat bed sheet, sandals, ribbon for a headband

Wrap the sheet horizontally around your waist. Tuck in the short end. Throw the extra length over your shoulder and drape the tail over your arm. Add sandals and a ribbon around your forehead. There were many different styles for men and women, but one of the more common was the "himation" that draped over the shoulder and arm. Take a photo and file it under "Europe: Greece." (Don't confuse this with the toga, a Roman garment.)

76B—Middle Students

1. Socrates was administered the death sentence through a poison cup of hemlock. Look up the poisonous hemlock in the encyclopedia. What can you learn about the herb? What about the hemlock tree?

2. What safety precautions can you take in your home to prevent poisoning? Do you know the number for the poison control center? Or should you just dial 911? Find out the answers to these questions. If you have younger siblings in your home, are dangerous products out of their reach? Run a safety inspection by pretending to be a toddler. Crawl around your house and see what things you can reach that are dangerous. Make it a goal to fix the problems!

76C—Older Students

Socrates didn't write down his own words, but his famous pupil, Plato, recorded many of his teachings. Obtain the works of Plato that give accounts of Socrates' conversations. In particular, hunt for *The Last Days of Socrates* by Plato, which gives an account of the trial of Socrates. Some works can be found in *The Book of Virtues* by William J. Bennett. Other sources would be the Internet or library.

---

1. As quoted in Don Nardo, *The Trial of Socrates.* San Diego: Lucent Books, 1947; p. 79.
2. As quoted in Don Nardo, *The Trial of Socrates.* San Diego: Lucent Books, 1947; p. 67.

The Mystery of History

HIPPOCRATES AND THE
STATUE OF ZEUS

LESSON 77

Hippocrates (hi PAHK ruh tee) has been named the "father of medicine." It's not that he invented medicine—it was probably used around the world long before his time. But in Greece, where Hippocrates lived, the world of medicine was greatly changed by his ideas. His ideas were good ones, too.

Up until the time of Hippocrates, the Greeks were practicing medicine alongside their religion. Because of their superstitions, they assumed that every disease was related to their gods. If a person was ill, family and friends thought it might be a punishment of the gods and took the patient to the priests of the temples for healing. The priests might do some practical things to make the people feel better, but then they would turn to their gods for a miracle.

The Greek god of healing was named Asclepius. People sometimes slept in the temple overnight by the statue of the healing god in hopes that they would be cured. The sick would also perform sacrifice to the gods and go through ceremonies of purifying themselves. This Greek mind-set had been around for a long time. The Egyptians had many of the same ideas.

Hippocrates wasn't so sure about this whole system. He believed that diet, rest, and exercise affected people's health, not the temper of the gods. He began to approach medicine more scientifically than religiously. Hippocrates started examining people who were ill and searching for causes of disease. He would then prescribe herbs, fresh air, diet changes, and exercise. He believed that surgery should be used only as a last resort. That was good because there was no anesthesia back then. Surgery would have really hurt!

One of Hippocrates' theories was that doctors should be trustworthy men. He believed that if a man had been trained in the knowledge of being a doctor, he was obligated to use his skills wisely and for the better of mankind. This was a very important safeguard for the common people. This belief helped to prevent doctors from taking advantage of the sick.

Some time after Hippocrates, a document was written that was named the Hippocratic Oath. It reflected the very beliefs that Hippocrates held to about the obligation of doctors to care for the sick. This oath became a standard for doctors to live by. Still today, the American Medical Association uses an adapted form of the Hippocratic Oath as a pledge for doctors graduating from medical school. Oftentimes you will see the oath framed and hanging in the waiting rooms of doctors' offices.

Interestingly, the original Hippocratic Oath includes a statement that says, "I will not give to a woman an instrument to produce abortion." (Abortion is the killing of an unborn baby.) Though it is a legal practice in the United States and much of the world, abortion is still a controversial issue. That means that not everyone agrees as to whether or not this practice is a right thing to do. We might gather from the original Hippocratic Oath that abortion was a controversial issue back in ancient Greece, too. The writers of the Hippocratic Oath were obviously against it.

Before we leave this time frame, I want to mention that in 450 B.C. one of the other Seven Wonders of the Ancient World was built. It was a huge statue of Zeus, the "king" of Greek gods, built by Phidias in Olympia. It stood 40 feet high and was laid with jewels, gold, and ivory. Zeus was sitting on a throne with sparkling stones set in his eyes. It would have been quite a sight! The giant statue lasted about 800 years but was burned in A.D. 476. There is no trace of it now.

Do you remember the other three ancient wonders we have studied so far? Only the pyramids of Egypt are still standing.

ACTIVITY 77

77A—Younger Students

Pretend to be Hippocrates and make an herbal remedy for a patient. Obtain a mortar and pestle (or use a bowl and the back of a big spoon). Gather spices from your kitchen—bay leaves, basil, cinnamon, and the like. Add water and a touch of honey or similar *edible* kitchen liquid. Grind the spices together like an old-fashioned pharmacist would do.

Discuss how the doctors of long ago might have come up with cures. I suppose somebody had to sample the trial medicines! If your teacher approves, try the concoction you made up. Do you think it could help anyone who was ill?

77B—Middle Students

1. Research the ancient practice of bloodletting. Physicians used to believe that a person's blood was the source of disease and so would drain a patient's blood to cure him. Even Hippocrates followed this practice. Find out how long this technique lasted. You might be surprised! File your findings under "Europe: Ancient Greece."

2. Using the encyclopedia or a library book, find a picture of what historians believe the Statue of Zeus looked like. It was written about by Pliny the Elder in about A.D. 70. It was built at the site of the original Olympics.

77C—Middle and Older Students

1. Read a modern version of the Hippocratic Oath as found in the Activity Supplement in the Appendix. Discuss the content with your teacher.

2. Hippocrates promoted natural medicines when possible over the use of drugs and surgery. Research the field of natural and alternative medicines. Find out the difference between herbal medicine, homeopathic medicine, and chiropractic care. Write a few paragraphs on each as if they were in a brochure for a doctor's office. File this under the "Miscellaneous" section of your Student Notebook.

EZRA AND ARTAXERXES
LESSON 78

Do you remember Zerubbabel? He was the one who led about 50,000 Jews back to Jerusalem and rebuilt the old temple. He was greatly helped in the long process by the prophets Haggai and Zechariah. The story of Zerubbabel is found in the first half of the Book of Ezra in the Old Testament. But the second half of the book is all about Ezra. This lesson focuses on Ezra's story and on a very influential king by the name of Artaxerxes.

It was about 80 years after Zerubbabel lived in Jerusalem that Ezra lived in Persia. He was a Jewish priest and a scribe. A scribe was a person who had been well educated in the scriptures. Remember that not all the Jews returned to Judah. Some people, like Esther and Mordecai, stayed in Babylonia under Persian rule.

While in the land of Persia, Ezra heard that the religious life of the Jews wasn't so great back in Judah. It had been 80 years since the Jews returned home. The rebuilt Temple there was being used for worship, but the spiritual life of the people was weak. Ezra felt led by God to go back to Jerusalem to teach the people about living right.

Before Ezra could just pick up and move, he had to ask the king of Persia for permission to leave. You see, even though the Jews were "freed" by Cyrus to go home and set up their Temple for worship, they were still being ruled by the Persians. Do you know whom Ezra had to talk to about leaving Persia? It was the son of Xerxes I named Artaxerxes I (ar tuh ZERK seez). His nickname was "Longimanus," or "Longhanded." He apparently developed this nickname from a deformity in his right hand.

Now we don't know for sure, but Artaxerxes just might have been the son of Esther! We do know he was the second son of Xerxes, and we do know that Esther was one of Xerxes' wives. If Artaxerxes was not Esther's son, she still may have influenced him as a stepmother and a queen. I wonder about this fact because Artaxerxes was unusually gracious to the request of Ezra. Perhaps it was the testimony and life of Esther that made a difference.

You see, the Bible tells us that Artaxerxes not only gave Ezra complete permission to go to Judah, but he offered to fund the entire trip! That means he paid for it. The letter of authorization is found in Ezra 7:11–28. You should stop and read it now. Artaxerxes decreed that silver, gold, wheat, offerings, and whatever else Ezra needed was his. He added that taxes should be lifted from the priests and that Ezra ought to teach the people all about the Law if they didn't know it already. It is an amazing letter!

Ezra did travel back to Jerusalem and several thousand Jews went with him. This was the last great exodus of Jews to leave Babylonia. Even on the trip we see evidence of a strong spiritual life in the people. At one point along the four-month journey of 900 miles, the Jews stopped for three days just to fast and pray for safety. They certainly needed God's protection because they were carrying back loads of treasure from Artaxerxes.

It says in Ezra 8:21, "I proclaimed a fast there at the river of Ahava, that we might humble ourselves before our God, to seek from Him the right way for us and our little ones and all our possessions." It goes on to say that Ezra didn't even request soldiers or guards from the king for the trip because he had already said that God would protect them. And Ezra adds, "He answered our prayer."

Upon their arrival, Ezra found the spiritual lives of the people very upsetting. Many of the men had married foreign wives who practiced other religions. Do you remember the downfall of Solomon, the wisest man who ever lived? His foreign wives had led him away from God. Ezra feared the same would happen to the people of Israel.

It seems harsh to us, but Ezra declared that the men who had broken the laws of God in marriage had to leave these women and their children. It was that important for them to be a "pure" race. It took several months for all of this to take place. Slowly though, the people returned to proper worship and religious practices.

All in all, we see in Ezra a man who was knowledgeable in the Word of God and was faithful in reforming the Jews to abide by it. We'll learn a little bit more about him in the next lesson, on Nehemiah. The two men were probably good friends.

ACTIVITY 78

ALL STUDENTS

Make your Memory Cards for Lessons 76–78

78A—Younger and Middle Students

1. In the story of Ezra, you learned that Artaxerxes had a nickname. Do you have a nickname? Discuss how people sometimes get their nicknames. Some names are cute and some are mean. Be careful what you call people. A nickname might hurt someone's feelings.

2. In Ezra 8:21 we see that the people prayed for protection on their long journey for "us, our little ones and all our possessions." Do you pray for protection when you travel? On a small card, write out, or ask your teacher to write out, the verses from Ezra 8:21 and 8:22b. Tape this card in a prominent spot in your family car. The next time you get in for a trip, remember the story of Ezra. Pray for the safety of your family and your belongings. God really does care for you!

78B—Middle Students

Ezra was a scribe and a priest. A scribe was skilled in writing and copying documents. That is why Ezra was so knowledgeable on the scriptures. Obtain or borrow a calligraphy pen. Using a guide to calligraphy, copy the Ten Commandments in your best handwriting. Imagine copying books and books of the Bible as Ezra may have done. Title your page "Ezra, the Scribe and Priest" and file it under "Asia: Israel."

78C—Middle and Older Students

Through the study of the Israelites, we have become acquainted with three different empires: the Assyrians, the Babylonians, and the Persians. Just in the Book of Ezra alone, there are seven kings mentioned from these empires. To help keep them straight, make three separate lists of these kings under the appropriate titles. Highlight the kings we have specifically studied. (I found seven of them.) The list is located in the Activity Supplement in the Appendix. File all three lists in your Student Notebook under "Asia: Iran (Mesopotamia)."

TAKE ANOTHER LOOK!

Review 26: Lessons 76–78

Wall of Fame

1. *Socrates (c. 469–399 B.C.)*—Show him holding a cup and smiling as he willingly drank the poison.

2. *Hippocrates (c. 460–377 B.C.)*—Put a document in his hand with a small title on it, "The Hippocratic Oath."

3. *The Statue of Zeus (450 B.C.)*—Photocopy a sketch of it if you can or draw him. Zeus was sitting down on a throne. Write the words "One of the Seven Wonders of the Ancient World" above your photocopy or sketch.

4. *Ezra (457 B.C.)*—Draw a scroll and pen in his hands because he was a scribe and brought the Law back to the people of Israel.

5. *Artaxerxes (457 B.C.)*—His nickname was Longimanus because of a deformity on his right hand. Give him an unusual-looking hand and a smiley face for granting favor to Ezra.

SomeWHERE in Time

Using a historical or biblical map, find the country of Persia and the city of Jerusalem. On Outline Map 6, "Turkey," color in Persia and label the city of Jerusalem. Mark the 900-mile route that Ezra would have followed in about four months. Find the River of Ahava where the people stopped for prayer and fasting. Add it to your map in blue. Remember that God protected the massive caravan of people without the use of soldiers, even though they carried great amounts of treasure with them. Title this map "Ezra's Journey to Jerusalem" and file it under "Asia: Israel."

Name_____ Date_____

 # WHAT DID YOU LEARN?

Week 26: *Quiz*

I. Fill in the Blanks. Use the word bank provided below.

1. At the _____, God confused man's language.

2. The _____ civilization was advanced in many ways and located on the island of Crete.

3. _____ was told by God to leave the city of Ur.

4. At the Battle of _____, Joshua and his men obeyed God's command and marched around the city seven times.

5. Ruth married a kinsman redeemer by the name of _____ and preserved the family line of Jesus.

6. _____ was the second king over Israel and authored many of the Psalms.

7. Obadiah was a minor prophet who preached to the _____, who were descendants of Esau and did not worship the One true God.

8. _____ was the minor prophet who had been a fig farmer in Judah before God called him to preach to the Israelites.

9. The great city of _____, which was destroyed by a flood, was uncovered by archaeologists in the 1800s.

10. _____ was a prophetess and helped to determine the authenticity of the books found buried in the Temple.

> **WORD BANK**
>
> | | | | |
> |---|---|---|---|
> | Abraham | David | Nineveh | Huldah |
> | Minoan | Tower of Babel | Boaz | Amos |
> | Jericho | Edomites | | |

II. Matching. Place the correct letter next to the number.

_____ 1. Went mad for seven years   a. Esther

_____ 2. Siddhartha Gautama   b. Zerubbabel

_____ 3. Born in Lu, China   c. Herodotus

_____ 4. Rebuilt the Temple   d. Ezra

_____ 5. Lost the Battle of Marathon   e. Buddha

_____ 6. Father of history   f. Nebuchadnezzar

_____ 7. Jewish orphan girl   g. Darius I

_____ 8. Poisoned by hemlock   h. Socrates

_____ 9. Father of medicine   i. Confucius

_____ 10. Given permission to return to   j. Hippocrates
         Judah by Artaxerxes

Bonus: Name a concept from the Roman Republic that exists in our nation today. (Each concept is worth one additional point.)

           The Mystery of History

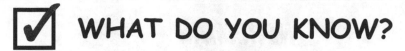

✓ WHAT DO YOU KNOW?

Pretest 27

Who Am I? From the word bank below, choose the correct answer for each question.

1. I am a cupbearer to King Artaxerxes. Who am I?

2. I was rebuilt in just 52 days. What am I?

3. I was a great speaker and politician of Greece, but I died from the disease of a plague. Who am I?

4. I am a term referring to "Greek military commanders." What am I?

5. I am the name given to the southernmost peninsula of Greece. What am I?

6. I am a structure that helped Athens stay connected to a port. What am I?

7. I was a war between Athens and Sparta that lasted a long time. What am I?

8. We lost the Peloponnesian War. Who are we?

WORD BANK

Peloponnesian War	Pericles	Nehemiah	Athenians
Peloponnese	Long Walls	walls of Jerusalem	strategoi

NEHEMIAH

LESSON 79

Nehemiah of the Old Testament was a pretty impressive guy. Many adults enjoy studying the Book of Nehemiah for that very reason. He showed great leadership skills in accomplishing a major task in a short amount of time. Through him, Jerusalem was made a different place.

Let's back up a bit before we get into the story. Like Ezra, Nehemiah was a Jew living in Persia. Even when Ezra went back to Jerusalem with thousands of Jews, Nehemiah stayed behind. He had a good reason to—he had a great career as a cupbearer to King Artaxerxes.

A cupbearer was more than just a waiter. A cupbearer had the position of tasting all the food and drink that was presented to a king and queen. If the food was spoiled or had been poisoned, it would kill the cupbearer and not the king or queen. The position was one that could only be filled by a person the king greatly trusted. It was common that cupbearers were also chosen for their attractiveness or good personality because they were so frequently in the presence of the king and queen.

While serving in this role, Nehemiah got word from Jerusalem that the city was still having trouble with its neighbors. One reason was that the old wall around the city had been destroyed years before and never rebuilt. The gates had been burned, and the stones were in ruins. Before the days of police and the National Guard, the people depended greatly on physical walls to protect them from intruders.

When Nehemiah heard the bad news, his spirit was in such sorrow that even King Artaxerxes wanted to know what was bothering him. Nehemiah was a wise and godly man. After much prayer and planning, he shared with Artaxerxes the problems back in Jerusalem and asked for a 12-year leave of absence! Though he was not a wall builder himself, he felt led by God to accomplish the task. It is an awesome story of trusting God.

If you remember, Artaxerxes had already sent Ezra off with his generous blessing. Now, about 12 years later, he agreed to let Nehemiah go, too. With letters in place and supplies in hand, Nehemiah set out to rebuild the walls of Jerusalem. The Book of Nehemiah tells us that it was no easy task at all. The Jews had many enemies, such as the Samaritans, looking for ways to stop their progress.

Besides the enemies, there was so much rubbish, or debris, in the way that it was hard to build. At times the Jews were just flat-out afraid of outsiders attacking them as they rebuilt. Workers laid bricks with one hand and held weapons with the other—the opposition to their rebuilding plan was that serious!

Despite all of this, in the remarkable time of just 52 days, the walls of Jerusalem were rebuilt. It was not that Nehemiah did all the rebuilding by himself, but he carefully organized small groups to each do a part. It was an incredible job of delegating the task, and it worked.

Nehemiah accomplished his goal of rebuilding the wall, and I suppose he could have left it at that. But he saw other needs in the people. Because of Nehemiah and his tremendous leadership, a census was taken, guards were put in place, the walls were dedicated, and most importantly, the Word of God was restored. In fact, as part of the restoration, the Book of the Law was read publicly. The host of ceremonies for the big event was none other than Ezra, the devout scribe.

This time, the Jews truly listened and realized all that God had done in preserving them as a nation. They celebrated at what was called the "Feast of Tabernacles." As part of the celebration, they built small booths out of large palm trees to remember the days of their wandering in the desert. The Bible says that at the dedication, "they offered great sacrifices and rejoiced, for God had made them rejoice with great joy; the women and the children also rejoiced, so that the joy of Jerusalem was heard afar off." (Neh. 12:43) I would love to have heard the singing and shouting.

By the way, Nehemiah kept his commitment to King Artaxerxes, and after 12 years, he returned to Persia to serve in the king's palace. What an interesting leave of absence he had experienced!

ACTIVITY 79

79A—Younger Students

With your teacher, read Nehemiah 8:13–18 about how the children of Israel built booths to celebrate the Feast of Tabernacles. Build your own! Drape a blanket between two chairs to make a little place where you can sit. Have your teacher place all around the house large "leaves" made out of construction paper. Collect these as the Israelites did and lay them on top of the blanket you have set up to make it look like a leaf booth. Once it is all made, have your teacher read parts of the first five books of the Old Testament like Ezra did. Take a photo and put it in your Student Notebook under "Asia: Israel." Title the page "The Feast of Tabernacles." Include the reference to the verses in Nehemiah.

79B—Middle Students

In the books of Ezra, Nehemiah, and Esther, there are many references to the Jewish months. Make a calendar out of 13 small sheets of paper stapled together. On the top of each, write the name of the Jewish month and then write the English equivalent in parentheses beneath it. The information you need is in the Activity Supplement in the Appendix. Glue the calendar on a sheet of paper to file in your Student Notebook under "Asia: Israel."

79C—Older Students

Read a book on leadership skills. Whether you feel like a leader or not, as a Christian you will always be a leader to someone. I recommend *Hand Me Another Brick* by Charles R. Swindoll or *Nehemiah and the Dynamics of Effective Leadership* by Cyril J. Barber. I'm sure there are others.

443–429 B.C.

PERICLES

LESSON 80

This lesson is on a Greek man named Pericles (PEHR ih kleez). I really like this guy. Historians say that he was a great speaker. It's not easy to communicate well, but Pericles was a master at it. Though he was *not* a king, Pericles was so loved by the people of Athens that he was treated like royalty. Pericles lived during "The Golden Age of Athens." Remember how great that time was for Greece? Pericles was the strongest politician or statesman during this time period.

Athens was only one city-state in Greece, but it was the most significant. It was there, under Pericles and others, that "direct democracy" was tried for about 50 years. In this type of democracy, citizens vote for their leaders and have a direct say in government affairs. The word "democracy" comes from the

Greek word "demos," meaning "people," and "kratos," meaning "rule." The people themselves tried to rule.

A republic on the other hand (as was Rome) is a representative government. People in a republic vote for special men or women to represent them in making decisions. Both systems give people the right to vote.

As a politician, Pericles was successful in allowing even the poor the right to serve in the government. He also started the idea of paying salaries to people who work in the government.

At that time in Athens, there were 9 "archons" who had ceremonial duties, and there were 10 "strategoi" who were elected as military commanders. Pericles himself was just one of the strategos, but he was so popular that he was looked to as greater than that.

Under Pericles, the Acropolis of Athens was restored. If you remember, the Persians under Xerxes' command had invaded Athens and burned the buildings on the Acropolis. Pericles helped to put the Parthenon and other significant buildings back together.

Pericles was the most beloved and eloquent statesman of ancient Athens.

Pericles was gifted at creating strong patriotism among the Athenians. His strong speeches made the people glad to be who they were. In one famous oration at a funeral for soldiers, he is quoted as saying, "I would have you day by day fix your eyes upon the greatness of Athens, until you become filled with the love of her; and when you are impressed by the spectacle of her glory, reflect that this empire has been acquired by men who knew their duty and had the courage to do it, who . . . freely gave their lives to her as the fairest offering which they could present at her feast."[1]

There came a time in Greece when the patriotism and strength of Athens became a threat to Sparta. Spartans were jealous of the Athenians and feared they would rule over all of Greece. War broke out between these two great powers.

Ugly things happen in war. One of Sparta's tactics against Athens was to cut the city off from the outside. Disease can spread easily when people are trapped without fresh food and water. A plague broke out inside Athens that killed many, including the beloved Pericles. Though he was a great statesman, he was not resistant to the deadly disease.

Athens never quite recovered from the loss of Pericles. There was no one ever like him again to bring the city-state together. There was no one like him to speak words of encouragement or hope to the Athenians. It goes to remind us that our hope ought to be in more than a man but in God instead.

Nonetheless, Pericles once said, "Future ages will wonder at us, as the present age wonders at us now." He was quite right in his prediction. The ancient Greeks and their belief in democracy have not been forgotten.

ACTIVITY 80

80A—Younger Students

1. Part of being a good citizen in Greece included serving on a jury. On juries, people vote as to whether a person is innocent or guilty of a crime. The way Greeks "voted" was to turn in a special token that looked like a top. If the center of the token was solid, it meant the person was innocent. If it was hollow, the person was guilty.

---

1. Quoted in Charles Alexander Robinson, Jr., *Athens in the Age of Pericles*. Norman, OK: University of Oklahoma Press, 1959; p. 45.

The Mystery of History

Make your own tokens. Take two quarters and tape small pieces of paper over them. On one quarter, draw a filled-in circle. On the other quarter, draw an open circle. Pretend to vote using the tokens. Each juror should have his or her own set.

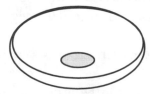 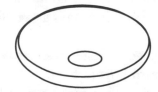

2. Another thing that citizens got involved in was the practice of "ostracism." If there was a man in the community who was unpopular, people could write down his name on a piece of pottery and lay it in a pile at the marketplace. After at least 6,000 "ostrakons" were marked, the man with the most votes had to leave for 10 years! From this practice we have the word "ostracize."

On pieces of flattened clay, make your own ostrakons. Banish someone to "time out" for bad behavior in the family! (Use the broken pieces of clay pottery from the lesson on Gideon.)

80B—Middle Students

Pericles began the concept of paying salaries to government workers. Our government officials today receive a salary for their work. Research and find out what salary the President of the United States earns in one year. Also, look up congressmen and Supreme Court judges so you have knowledge about all three branches of the government. File your information under "North America: United States."

80C—Older Students

1. Try to find original works of Pericles.

2. In studying the Roman Republic and Athens, we have so far addressed both the republican and democratic forms of government. In the United States, we have retained the titles "Republican" and "Democratic" to describe the two major political parties. On paper, define the two parties and make a list of the differences in philosophies. File this under "North America: United States."

431–404 B.C.

PELOPONNESIAN WAR
LESSON 81

Before you can understand the Peloponnesian War, you need to know what the "Peloponnese" is. Get out a globe or map right now. When you find Greece, notice how the lower, or southern, portion of it is almost a separate island. That peninsula is called the Peloponnese. The main city-state in that area was Sparta. And just 100 miles to the northwest is Athens. You already know that these two city-states did *not* get along. The struggle between them finally erupted into what has been called the Peloponnesian War.

Let's look again at the two cultures in this war. Though both people groups were Greek, the Athenians and the Spartans were very different. The Spartans were the harsh, war-loving people who believed that military strength was the only sure way to survive. They so deeply believed this that Spartan men were known to leave their infants in the mountains to die if the babies appeared weak or small.

The Spartans would also put their boys into military training by age 7. They grew up in dormitories away from their families where they were taught to survive. Part of their training consisted of learning how to steal and kill. Failure would result in severe beatings. Women and girls were not exempt, but they usually stayed at home to learn how to fight.

Spartan men were required to marry by age 30 but rarely for the reason of love. They married to make more Spartan soldiers out of their children! Like the young boys, the men lived away from their wives and children.

In contrast, the Athenians, as we have already learned, were fond of the arts and deep thinking. War to them was good only if it helped to protect their beloved democracy. In anticipation of war, the Athenians built a brilliant structure called the "Long Walls" at Port Piraeus. This was a stretch of fortified brick walls that went from the heart of Athens to the sea. They built the walls because the city of Athens was landlocked. The walls gave them a way to get goods in and out of the city and to be connected to their navy.

At war or peace, the Greeks used oil lamps and fillers like these to see at night.

Unfortunately, the Long Walls weren't foolproof in keeping unwanted things out. Just one year after the Peloponnesian War started, a plague broke out in Athens. Because the Athenians were "locked" in their city, it was difficult to treat the victims properly. One-fourth of the people died from the illness. (That's when Athens lost Pericles.) The war raged on for years.

If that wasn't bad enough for Athens, 15 years later one of their leaders fled to Sparta as a traitor and helped the Spartans fight against them. By 411 B.C. the Athenian government had been taken over by a council of 400 men. By 405 B.C., the Spartans completely wiped out the Athenian navy in a surprise attack. Without the navy, the Athenians who were left in the city behind the Long Walls were starved out and forced to surrender. In humiliation, the Athenians were forced to tear down the Long Walls with their own hands while musicians played music to celebrate their defeat.

The victorious Spartans installed a group of 30 men to rule Athens for awhile. These 30 men were soon known as the "Thirty Tyrants" for their murderous reign of terror. The Thirty Tyrants killed or drove away any democrats or free thinkers in Athens. With the reign of these vicious men, democracy itself was defeated, not just the people of Athens.

It is a shame that these two city-states could never bring their powers together. One group was so strong and one group was so culturally advanced. Though the Spartans officially won the Peloponnesian War, they never ruled over Greece successfully. Without any perspective on family, love, or God, the Spartans failed as lasting conquerors. They lived to survive, but knowing not what they were surviving for. While sidetracked over the war, the Spartans also failed to notice a great power rising just north. The empire of Alexander the Great was soon to change the short term of victory they were experiencing.

ACTIVITY 81

ALL STUDENTS

Make your Memory Cards for Lessons 79–81.

81A—Younger and Middle Students

In Sparta, both girls and boys trained to be strong fighters. It was shocking to other Greek communities to see girls in short dresses running and exercising. Run your own training camp by doing some vigorous exercises around the house. Practice marching in lines as the Greek soldiers did. There was often a flute player in the battle line to keep the soldiers marching in rhythm.

81B—Younger and Middle Students

The Greek soldiers were called "hoplites." Using library books, find pictures of the hoplite armor and helmet. Make a hoplite helmet following these directions.

1. Get an old bike helmet. (You could use a good one—you will only temporarily be making it into a Hoplite helmet.)
2. Stick a narrow strip of Play-Doh modeling compound right down the middle of the helmet. The strip needs to be about 1 inch deep and 2 inches wide.
3. Insert right into the Play-Doh compound about 100 of either toothpicks, broken spaghetti noodles, or bristles from an old broom. It ought to resemble a "Mohawk" haircut.

Try your helmet out for awhile. Is it a bit intimidating? It was meant to be. Take a photo and file it under "Europe: "Ancient Greece."

81C—Middle and Older Students

The "helots" were a huge portion of the population of the Spartans. Research the helots to find out their origin. Also, find out their status in Sparta and what they nearly accomplished in 460 B.C. It's rather interesting. File your information under "Europe: Ancient Greece."

TAKE ANOTHER LOOK!

Review 27: Lessons 79–81

Wall of Fame

1. *Nehemiah (444 B.C.)*—Draw a brick wall behind him.

2. *Pericles (443–429 B.C.)*—Draw a cartoon box coming from his mouth and write the words "My fellow Athenians . . ." in the box.

3. *Peloponnesian War (431–404 B.C.)*—Draw a round shield and write the name and dates of the war on the front of it.

SomeWHERE in Time

1. Obtain a biblical map of the city of Jerusalem. Notice the walls surrounding it. It was a huge undertaking by Nehemiah and his workers to repair the damaged walls.

2. On Outline Map 2, "Greece," write in the city-states of Athens and Sparta. As best as you can, draw in the Long Walls that connected Athens to the sea. These were very strategic in the Peloponnesian War.

   On the same map color the oceans and seas blue and label them as follows: Adriatic Sea, Ionian Sea, Aegean Sea, Mediterranean Sea, Sea of Crete, Gulf of Corinth, Saronic Gulf.

   File your map under "Europe: Greece."

The Mystery of History

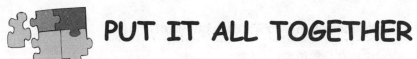 # PUT IT ALL TOGETHER

Worksheet 3: Lessons 55–81

Remember, you may use your book, timeline, or Memory Cards to help you complete this worksheet.

I—Dates to Memorize. In this quarter there were four dates I wanted you to memorize. Recopy them here five times each.

Babylonian Captivity   605 B.C.

1. _____
2. _____
3. _____
4. _____
5. _____

Buddha   c. 563 B.C.

1. _____
2. _____
3. _____
4. _____
5. _____

Confucius   551 B.C.

1. _____
2. _____
3. _____
4. _____
5. _____

The Golden Age of Athens   479 B.C.

1. _____
2. _____
3. _____
4. _____
5. _____

II—People and Places. Draw a line from the people to the nations they lived in. Some nations will be used more than once. Use crayons or markers to make each line a different color.

1. Habakkuk	India
2. Nebuchadnezzar	Greece
3. Daniel	China
4. Aesop	Judah
5. Buddha	Babylonia
6. Pythagoras	Persia
7. Confucius	
8. Cyrus the Great	

III—Multiple Choice. Circle the correct answer for each question.

1. The prophet Zechariah was by profession a
   a. scribe.
   b. priest.
   c. shepherd.
   d. cupbearer.

2. At the Battle of Marathon, Pheidippides ran all the way to _____ to announce the victory.
   a. Sparta
   b. Rome
   c. Carthage
   d. Athens

3. Herodotus is considered the
   a. father of history.
   b. father of Alexander the Great.
   c. father of theater.
   d. father of the bride.

4. Xerxes I built a floating bridge at a place called
   a. Marathon.
   b. Thermopylae.
   c. the Hellespont.
   d. the Roman Republic.

5. In the story of Esther, Haman and Mordecai were
   a. brothers.
   b. enemies.
   c. uncle and nephew.
   d. good friends.

IV—True or False? Circle your answer.

1. Pythagoras developed great mathematical theorems.   T F
2. Cyrus the Great was gracious to the Jewish people and ended the Babylonian Captivity.   T F
3. During the Roman Republic, the plebeians had to fight for the same rights as the patricians. T F
4. Xerxes was the kinsman redeemer to Esther.   T F
5. Socrates tried to escape from prison but failed.   T F
6. Hippocrates was against abortion for women.   T F
7. Ezra's request to return to Jerusalem found favor with King Artaxerxes.   T F
8. Pericles died of a spear wound in the Peloponnesian war.   T F

V—Compare/Contrast. Write three distinctive beliefs of each religion listed.

1. Judaism

   a.

   b.

   c.

2. Buddhism

   a.

   b.

   c.

3. Confucianism

   a.

   b.

   c.

VI—Describe. We have studied several Greek people this quarter. Give a one-sentence explanation of what each is remembered for.

1. Aesop

2. Pythagoras

3. Herodotus

4. Socrates

5. Hippocrates

6. Pericles

VII—Writing. In one paragraph, summarize the major events of Judah that occurred within this semester of study. Use a separate sheet of paper.

   Older Students: In one additional paragraph, explain the *significance* of the Babylonian Captivity. What was the end result?

QUARTER 4

THE MYSTERY IS REVEALED:
347 B.C. TO A.D. 29

Of all the quarters I've written about so far, I think this is my favorite. From about 400 B.C. to the coming of Jesus Christ, there were some very colorful people woven into the tapestry of history.

We're going to learn about such legends as Alexander the Great, who "conquered the world" while in his twenties, and Hannibal, who nearly conquered all of Rome with an army of elephants. I will introduce you to Shi Huang Ti of China, who built the Great Wall of China and later buried himself with thousands of terra-cotta soldiers.

In Israel you will meet the brave Judas Maccabee who, in defeating an enemy, experienced a true miracle. This "miracle" has since been remembered as the celebration of Hanukkah.

Another man of great courage was Spartacus, a Roman slave who led as many as 90,000 slaves in revolt against slavery. His is a sad story.

This quarter gets even more interesting as the dramatic story of Julius Caesar, Cleopatra, and Mark Antony unfolds. Their love stories are mingled right into the history of Rome itself.

I include in this time period the final three of the Seven Wonders of the Ancient World. Have you wondered yet though who officially selected these? Apparently there was a man by the name of Antipater who lived around 100 B.C. He compiled the list of the Seven Wonders. At the time he selected them, he couldn't have known how many were going to be destroyed through earthquakes or other disasters. The only structure that stands today is the Great Pyramid at Giza. We are fortunate that Antipater gave us a look into the world he admired and documented it for us.

However none of these stories or monuments can compare with the coming of Jesus Christ Himself. His birth changes the way history is forever recorded because we use it to distinguish B.C. from A.D. As you know, B.C. stands for "Before Christ" and A.D. stands for "Anno Domini"—"in the year of the Lord"—in Latin.

It would seem then that Jesus' birth would be in the year zero. However, several years after Christ died, the calendar was changed because of an error. That change actually placed Jesus' birth at about 4 B.C. He died on the cross at the age of 33, which is counted as A.D. 29. Discuss this with your teacher if it is still a little confusing.

We will end this quarter and Volume I of *The Mystery of History* with the death, resurrection, and ascension of Jesus Christ. Believe me, you have packed a lot of history into this year of study. I hope it has been easy to keep straight. I still believe that the life of every man, woman, and child has been ordained in time by God Himself. Make the most of your life and study hard! You don't know what impact you may have on future generations by passing on the knowledge you have acquired in just this year.

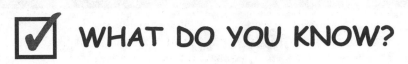

☑ WHAT DO YOU KNOW?

Pretest 28

Unscramble the words to fill in the blanks. A word bank is provided at the bottom of the page.

1. The last book of the Old Testament is named after the prophet (aalhciM)_____.

2. After the last prophet, there was a span of (rufo) _____ hundred years of silence.

3. Plato was one of the greatest (ippuls) _____ of Socrates.

4. Plato started a school called the (deymcaA)_____, which was basically the first university ever established.

5. (sirtoletA) _____ was a famous Greek philosopher who tutored Alexander the Great.

6. The Macedonians get their name from a Greek god called Macedon who they believed was the son of (sZue)_____.

7. Philip II of Macedonia was the father of (anAldeexr) _____ the Great.

8. A "mausoleum" is another name for an aboveground (mtob) _____.

WORD BANK

tomb	Zeus	pupils	four
Aristotle	Malachi	Alexander	Academy

MALACHI
LESSON 82

Finally, after months of learning about the prophets of Israel, our study is coming to an end. Malachi is the last of the Old Testament prophets. Can you guess how many we have studied? There have been 20 in all. The Book of Malachi is not only the last of the prophets, but it is also the last writing of the Old Testament. Four hundred years will go by before another prophet speaks for God and before the events of the New Testament take place. That is a rather long period of time.

If you had been God, what would you want to tell your people before a 400-year span of silence? Do you realize that it was also 400 years that the Hebrews were in slavery before Moses delivered them? I don't believe these numbers are coincidental. Though the Israelites are not under physical bondage at the time of Malachi, they are under the bondage of the Law. Just as they needed Moses to deliver them from Egyptian slavery, they needed a Savior to deliver them from the slavery of sin. Let's look closer at the Book of Malachi and see just what the Lord had to say before signing off on the Old Testament.

First, God seemed to do some fussing. He rebuked the Israelites for the way they gave their offerings. The presentation of offerings had become a formality to the Israelites and was not representing true sacrifice. This was evident by the fact that some of the animals given for sacrifice were blemished. Some were even blind. By giving damaged animals as sacrifices, the people weren't giving anything special to God or trusting in Him.

Second, the Lord scolded the priests for not being true to God and for leading others astray. He felt that the priests had broken the sacred covenant of Levi. The Levites had always been a special tribe set apart for service to God. They were losing their reverence for holy things.

Last, the Lord mentioned his hatred for divorce and for the way Israelite men treated their wives. If you recall, Ezra had made great reforms in the area of marriages. Apparently the changes weren't lasting ones.

After the fuming, the Lord explained through Malachi that He was sending a messenger. He said, "Behold, I send My messenger, and he will prepare the way before Me. And the Lord, who you seek, will suddenly come to His temple, even the Messenger of the covenant, in who you delight. Behold, He is coming." (Mal. 3:1) This first "messenger" was going to be John the Baptist, the next prophet of God to come. The one following after him was, of course, Jesus Christ. I doubt the people realized just how long it would be before all of this would happen.

As we see with so many of the other prophets, in the Book of Malachi God also had encouraging words to share with the people. God reminded them that there was eternal blessing for those who loved Him and were faithful to Him. In fact, through Malachi the Lord used a beautiful word picture of a book to explain His feelings. He said a "Book of Remembrance" would be written in front of Him that would list all those who have really loved Him. (Mal. 3:16) I wonder if that would be like God's own personal diary? It's a neat thought.

The Lord also said there would be punishment for those who never really served Him. He was referring to the Jew and the Gentile. He knows there are always some people who act religious but who don't have sincere hearts.

So, these are the words of our Lord at the close of the Old Testament. Do you remember when we learned about Elijah? At that time we read the last passages of Malachi, which say that Elijah will return before the day of the Lord. Some people think that John the Baptist was the fulfillment of this prophecy, but others believe that Elijah himself will come back. I don't know which is true, but it would be an awesome sight if Elijah would return in a chariot of fire just the way he left. As believers, we have many great things to anticipate about the Lord's return, just as the Jews waited for the coming Messiah.

ACTIVITY 82

82A—Younger Students

In honor of God's Book of Remembrance, make your own.

Materials: Inexpensive, pocket-sized address book; felt or contact paper; fake jewels with flat sides; rickrack or gold ribbon; glue

Purchase a small, inexpensive address book. Cover it with contact paper or felt. Decorate your book with fake jewels that are flat on one side and can be glued on. Add gold ribbon or rickrack. On the inside, cover the first page with paper. In pretty letters write on it "The Book of Remembrance: Malachi 3:16–18."

On the inside under the appropriate alphabetical tabs, list the names of friends and family who you know are believers. If you have friends who are not Christians yet, put their names in a special place as a reminder to pray for them so you can add their names when they are saved!

82B—Middle Students

We have covered many prophets in our study so far. Take all the Memory Cards that have prophets on them and use them to create a game to help you remember them. It may be as simple as flashcards, Bingo, or Go Fish. Or you may create a board game. Make the game on an easy level if you have younger brothers or sisters. If not, make it hard enough for your parents! Many adults cannot identify the very things you have already learned about the prophets. I encourage you to know the prophets well! They reveal a lot to us about God Himself.

82C—Middle and Older Students

We need to update your list of the prophets in your Student Notebook. Under "Post-Exile Prophets," which refers to all the prophets we have studied since the Babylonian Captivity, you should have the names listed below. Use the text to add the dates of the prophets. Because there are only a few, write a short synopsis as well.

> **Post-Exile Prophets**
>
> Daniel
>
> Ezekiel
>
> Haggai
>
> Zechariah
>
> Malachi

PLATO AND ARISTOTLE

LESSON 83

I have included Plato and Aristotle together in this lesson because there is a strong relationship between these two legendary Greeks. You see, Aristotle was a pupil of Plato. And Plato had been one of the top students of Socrates. All three men are closely linked.

What do you remember about Socrates? He was the Greek philosopher who didn't write much down but talked all the time with students and others. Some of his ideas were so strong that he was put to death with poison for threatening the stability of Athens. It was a tragic ending to the life of a great thinker.

I told you in the lesson on Socrates that his pupils had recorded his ideas after his death. His number-one student to help do that was Plato. Plato was actually a nickname that meant "broad shouldered." Plato's real name was Aristocles. That sounds too much like Aristotle, so I'll call him Plato, too.

Plato was from a well-to-do family in Athens. As part of his education he was sent to study under Socrates. It was from Socrates that many of Plato's ideas were developed. Probably his greatest accomplishment was starting a school, which was basically the first university ever established.

Plato called his school the Academy because it was in the grove of Academus. Of course we still use this Greek word to refer to a place of learning. The ideas that Plato taught are hard to explain. He thought that life, like music, should fit some pattern. He was interested in the inner man apart from the external man. I think he was really searching for meaning in life.

As a philosopher, he also tried to figure out what inspired men to be truly good. I believe that apart from the Lord, man cannot make sense of good and bad. But Plato concluded, as best as he could, that the virtues of "temperance, courage, and wisdom" would make a man "just."

One year Plato received a new student who was just 17 years old. His name was Aristotle. He stayed in Plato's school for about 20 years. How little did Plato know of the influence his pupil would have on the world!

Beautifully decorated with laurel leaves and ivy, this hydra vase was most likely used to collect water from a fountain.

Aristotle had a great impact on the world for many reasons. His brilliant mind furthered the teachings of both Socrates and Plato. Aristotle took the field of philosophy into the field of logic. In this short text I can't begin to explain just what all his philosophies were. He was more systematic than either Plato or Socrates. He studied more natural sciences and wrote many books on them. He also wrote about things that we would call psychology. He even started the idea of analyzing literature and drama. These were all new fields to the Greeks.

Most importantly though, Aristotle was asked to privately tutor one special young man. Who could be so important as to have a great philosopher like Aristotle all to himself? The king of Macedonia believed that his son was worthy of such a request. His name was Alexander the Great. Have you ever heard of him? If not, don't worry. We will definitely study him later.

At the end of Aristotle's life he followed the path of Plato and started a school. It was called the Lyceum. His students there were called "peripatetics," which means "to walk around." Just as Socrates and Plato used to stroll and discuss great things at length, so the students of Aristotle were taught to walk and think out loud. I guess talking and especially listening can be great ways of learning!

Last, as a tip to remember who came first of the three philosophers, think of the word "SPA." Each letter represents the first letter of the names Socrates, Plato, and Aristotle. That ought to help you keep them straight.

ACTIVITY 83

83A—Younger Students

Both Plato and Aristotle had names for their schools. Do you have a name for your homeschool? If not, try to come up with a special name that you can use on important documents that ask where you go to school. Our homeschool is named Wimberly Hills Homeschool because Wimberly is the name of the town where my husband and I went on our honeymoon. So, our school name has a special meaning to us.

If you already have a name for your school, use this time to make a banner with the name on it. Make it as attractive as you can and hang it on a wall in your home. I hope you are proud of your homeschool!

83B—Middle Students

Did you know that the Greeks didn't always write left to right as we do? At one time, the people wrote in a style called "boustrophedon," which meant "ox turning." That means that one sentence would be written from left to right, and the next would be written from right to left. This pattern would repeat itself with sentences going in different directions. That is the way an ox would plow a field.

If that doesn't sound difficult enough to read, the Greeks didn't always use spaces between their words! Study the sample in the Activity Supplement in the Appendix. Then, try to copy a paragraph from the lesson on Plato and Aristotle using the boustrophedon method. (Or you could write me a letter telling me about your family!) File a copy of your letter or your boustrophedon sampler under "Europe: Greece."

83C—Older Students

Do your best to obtain some original works by Plato or Aristotle. *The Book of Virtues* by William J. Bennett contains samples of both philosophers. My favorite has been "Aristotle on Self-Discipline" from the *The Nicomachean Ethics* (found in *The Book of Virtues*). Sort through what you can of their works. What is your impression of their philosophies?

Summarize the distinct teachings or philosophies of each man and file your summaries under "Europe: Ancient Greece."

PHILIP II OF MACEDONIA AND THE MAUSOLEUM OF HALICARNASSUS

LESSON 84

In the last lesson I told you that Aristotle was hired to personally tutor Alexander the Great. Before we get to him, I want to tell you about his father, Philip II, because he was pretty incredible, too.

When Philip II was just a young boy, his brother was the king of Macedonia. That was the name of the region in northern Greece. The Macedonians believed they were descended from the Greek god Macedon, the supposed son of Zeus. The people were somewhat rugged and to the Greeks of Athens, they had a strange dialect. The Macedonians were looked down on for these differences. That was soon going to change!

It seems that the king of Macedonia was attacked by the Thebians, a neighboring country, and he was forced to give his brother, young Philip II, as a hostage to the enemy! We don't know how long Philip lived as a prisoner of war in Thebes, but it would have made for a very unusual childhood.

Eventually, the leadership in Macedonia changed hands and Philip was returned home. As a young man, he became regent and then king in just a short time. Philip II ruled over Macedonia for about 25 years. In that time, he did some amazing things.

Philip II was said to have been a great organizer, a great soldier, a great speaker, a great diplomat, and to have a charming personality. What does a leader do with all these qualities? He probably would expand his kingdom. That is exactly what Philip did.

Philip II completely reorganized the Macedonian army and made it stronger than any other Greek army. His name meant "horse lover" and he truly was. Unlike other kings, Philip II himself would ride with his troops straight into battle. Maybe that is how one of his eyes was gouged out by an arrow!

One of Philip's best ideas for his army was the creation of a "phalanx." A phalanx was a group of soldiers lined up in a marching rectangle 8 or 10 rows deep. The soldiers would overlap their round shields and hold extra-long spears and swords straight out in front of them. If one man became injured, the next man behind him would move up to take his place. This mass of manpower was very intimidating to an enemy!

All the fighting under Philip II made the Macedonian empire quite large. Philip II managed to take in almost all of Greece and the land as far north as the Danube River. No one had ever united the city-states of Greece before. If you remember, the city-states usually fought against one another. Sadly, in uniting Greece, Philip II had no problem with killing fellow Greeks either. It was a bloody reign.

Just when Philip II probably thought things were going well, his life was abruptly ended by assassination. An assassination is a sudden murder done in secret. No one knows for sure who was behind Philip's death. Philip had just married a new wife even though he already had a queen. Some suspect that the old queen or maybe even Alexander was behind the plot! It was only in 1977 that the grave of Philip II was found. That was not long ago. Perhaps one day the mystery of his death will be solved.

While we are in this time period, I want to mention one more of the Seven Wonders of the Ancient World. The Mausoleum at Halicarnassus was built about 353 B.C. It was built under orders of Queen

Artemisia as a tomb for King Mausolus. He was the king of Caria in Asia Minor. The tomb was so tall and beautiful that all tall tombs became known as "mausoleums" after that.

ACTIVITY 84

ALL STUDENTS

Make your Memory Cards for Lessons 82–84.

84A—Younger Students

The next time you are driving near a cemetery, have your parents point out a mausoleum to you. Remember that the name for these raised tombs came from a king named Mausolus.

84B—Younger and Middle Students

Make your own phalanx.

Materials: Lids for canning, inexpensive bag of plastic army men, permanent markers, glue, poster putty, shoebox lid, toothpicks, straws, tape

1. Take lids for home canning and decorate them with permanent markers to look like bronze shields. They were often marked with family or city emblems.

2. On the inside lid of a shoebox, line about 20–24 army men into rows to make a rectangle. (Don't glue the men in yet because you may have to reposition them several times.) Put a small dab of poster putty in front of each man and vertically place the shield in front of him, pushing the shield into the putty. Have the shields just overlap one another to protect the men.

3. Depending on the number of men in your front and back rows, make that many long spears by taping toothpicks to jut out of the straws. Along the front row, lay the straws to extend as far as they can from behind the shields. The back row of men should have spears pointing straight up. There should be one spear between every two men.

4. The middle men should each get a plain toothpick as a sword. Set the toothpicks upright just to the side of each man, using a small dab of putty to make them stick. Glue the men down. You should now have an "army" resembling a hoplite phalanx. Take a picture and put it under "Europe: Greece."

84C—Older Students

Macedonia is mentioned in the New Testament. Using a concordance, find the reference. Read the context of the passage. Familiarize yourself with the borders of Macedonia under Philip II. We will soon see this empire grow under his son Alexander the Great.

TAKE ANOTHER LOOK!

Review 28: Lessons 82–84

Wall of Fame

1. *Malachi (exact date unknown; near the end of the 5th century B.C.)*—Have him holding a small book titled the "Book of Remembrance."

2. *Plato (429–347 B.C.)*—Give him big shoulders and place a school named "The Academy" in his background.

3. *Aristotle (384–322 B.C.)*—Place a small boy named "Alexander" next to him because Aristotle tutored Alexander.

4. *Philip II (382–336 B.C.)*—Place an X over one of his eyes and show a dagger in his chest.

5. *Mausoleum of Halicarnassus (353 B.C.)*—Draw a rectangular building that is tall and skinny. (Unlike some mausoleums today, it would not have had a cross on it. Do you know why? Jesus had not died and risen.)

SomeWHERE in Time

1. On Outline Map 2, "Greece," use an orange pencil to outline the borders of Macedonia before Philip II ruled. With green pencil, outline the new border of Macedonia after the reign of Philip II.

2. Begin a map of the Seven Wonders of the Ancient World. (You will complete the map at a later date, so keep it in a safe place.) On Outline Map 6, "Turkey," mark these places.

   a. Pyramids at Giza, along the Nile in Egypt

   b. Hanging Gardens of Babylon, in Babylon of course

   c. Statue of Zeus, in Olympia, Greece

   d. Temple of Diana, Ephesus, Greece

   e. Mausoleum of Halicarnassus, Asia Minor

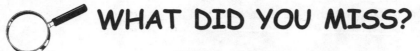

WHAT DID YOU MISS?

Week 28: Exercise

True or False? Circle your answer. Then use the blank space provided after each question to change false statements into true ones! I have given you an example. You may use your books, timeline, or Memory Cards.

1. According to the Bible, seeds were created on the same day as man.   T ⓕ
   Seeds were created on the third day of Creation and man on the sixth.

2. The first pyramids of Egypt are still standing today.   T F

3. The Shang dynasty started a written language in China.   T F

4. During the Zhou dynasty, iron was scarce in China.   T F

5. The Northern Kingdom (Israel) was defeated by the
   Babylonians in 722 B.C.   T F

6. King Josiah lived through the Babylonian Captivity.   T F

7. Daniel was a young man of 14 or 15 when taken into captivity.   T F

8. Belshazzar's father was an archaeologist and the true king of Babylon.   T F

9. Artaxerxes was nicknamed Longimanus for having a deformed foot.   T F

10. The Golden Age of Athens lasted only about 50 years.   T F

11. Socrates wrote the book titled *Know Thyself.*   T F

12. Hippocrates inspired an oath to ensure that doctors would be trustworthy.   T F

13. For the trip back to Judah, Ezra took 100 of the king's bodyguards to protect the riches he was carrying.   T F

14. Nehemiah served as a cupbearer to King Artaxerxes.   T F

15. Though Pericles was only a military commander (one of the strategoi), he was treated and loved as a king.   T F

16. In the Peloponnesian War, the Spartans completely wiped out the navy of Athens in a surprise attack.   T F

17. Malachi is the eighth book of the Old Testament.   T F

18. Plato started a school named the Lyceum.   T F

19. Socrates privately tutored the young Alexander the Great.   T F

20. Philip II of Macedonia had been a prisoner in Egypt as a child.   T F

☑ WHAT DO YOU KNOW?

Pretest 29

Match these quotes to the person most likely to have said them. Choose from one of the five possibilities below and write each answer below the quote.

1. "No one can ride the spirited Bucephalus but me!"

2. "As for the broken horn . . ., four kingdoms shall arise out of that nation."

3. "Eureka, eureka!" while running nude.   **Alexander the Great**

4. "Look here, Alexander. You are in our holy book, so don't hurt us!"   **Jewish priests**

5. "If you give me something to stand on, I could move the world!"   **Archimedes**

6. In tears: "There is no more of the world to conquer."   **Daniel**

7. "I'll take Egypt, please."   **General Ptolemy**

8. "The circumference of a circle is equal to pi times the diameter."

ALEXANDER THE GREAT

LESSON 85

When I think of some of the heroes of the Bible like Moses, David, and Daniel, I think of the term "great." But the world often defines "greatness" differently. Such is the case, in my opinion, with Alexander the "Great." Let's see how he earned his reputation.

I'm sure you remember that Philip II of Macedonia had his son Alexander personally tutored by Aristotle. (Maybe it was like being homeschooled!) The private tutor must have been worthwhile, for young Alexander was a very well trained student.

Alexander developed a real love for Greek ideas as well as a taste for the world. Guess what his favorite story was? It was the *Iliad* by Homer. He was said to have carried a copy of it with him and to have chosen the character Achilles as his role model.

Like his father, Alexander had a love for horses and supposedly was able to tame one incredibly ferocious horse that no one else could ride. The beautiful horse's name was Bucephalus. Alexander named a city in India after Bucephalus when it died. When Philip II heard of Alexander's ability to tame this wild horse he said, "Oh my son, seek out a kingdom worthy of thyself, for Macedonia is too little for thee."

Apparently Alexander thought so too. Upon his father's death, he became king although he was only 20, and he set out to conquer more land than had ever been ruled by one person before. His mother certainly had confidence in him. She told him that he was descended from the Greek god Hercules. The Egyptians told him he was a descendant of their "sun god." It is no wonder he claimed to be a god to his own men.

Even in legend, Alexander was "great." According to Greek mythology, a man named Gordius once tied a knot so difficult to untie that whoever could do it would be the ruler over all of Asia. Many had tried and failed to untie the special knot. Alexander, however, decided to just cut it with his sword! When he did, Alexander declared that he had fulfilled the prophecy.

With so much power and confidence working for him, Alexander was able to conquer the "world," as it was known back then. His kingdom included Greece, Egypt, Asia Minor, Mesopotamia, Persia, and part of India. He even made Babylon his capital. The entire empire was huge! One place he took was Thebes where his father had grown up as a hostage. Alexander destroyed almost the entire city and took 30,000 people as prisoners! Sounds like revenge to me.

Alexander was said to have wept at the thought of there not being any other lands to conquer!

The Mystery of History

Another place that Alexander captured was the city of Tyre in Phoenicia. Remember that "stinky" city famous for its purple-red dye? Part of the city was actually on an island almost one mile off the coast. In order to conquer it, Alexander "floated" some of his catapults into position along with 120 warships. His army then built a causeway, or highway, to connect the city to the mainland for his attack! It was quite an achievement. The causeway still stands today.

Though sometimes clever, Alexander's war tactics were also ruthless, and many thousands of men were slaughtered or taken prisoner when he marched eastward. He named many of the cities he conquered after himself. Alexandria, Egypt, still carries his name. In almost every city he conquered, he placed Greek men into positions of leadership. It was this tactic that spread the ideas of Greece all over the Mediterranean world.

Alexander tried to unify his large kingdom by introducing one kind of money and encouraging trade. He also promoted the marrying of people from one country to another. He hoped it would bring people together under his leadership. He himself married two foreign women.

Some of his policies may have been good, but Alexander also left behind the fear of crossing him. In a drunken fight, he killed one of his closest friends. This caused some men to question his leadership. Anyone who threatened Alexander's authority was put to death. Some of his own army abandoned him, but foreigners were available to replace them. Had he lived long, there is no telling where Alexander's power would have gone. He was said to have wept once at the thought that there might not be any other lands to conquer!

Alexander the Great did not live long though. He died suddenly when he was just 33 years old. Some historians believe he became ill with malaria contracted from a mosquito bite. If so, it is ironic that the "Great" Alexander was stopped by a tiny, infected bug! Others believe his poor health and death resulted from drinking too much alcohol. It is believed that he drank excessively, but whether or not that killed him is yet to be known. His body was placed in a golden coffin and sent to Memphis, Egypt. It was later moved to Alexandria, Egypt, the city that bore his name.

Now that you have heard his story, you may understand why he's been remembered as Alexander the "Great." He did manage to conquer a huge part of the world in just a few short years as a young king. However, in light of his cruelty, drunkenness, and belief that he was a god, I prefer to remember some of the truly godly men we have studied as the world's "greatest."

ACTIVITY 85

ALL STUDENTS

Memorize the date of Alexander the Great (336 B.C.).

85A—Younger Students

1. Do you remember Bucephalus, the spirited horse? I read that it was one of the world's most famous horses. Get some books from the library on horses and find out names of other famous horses. Copy or trace your favorite picture of a horse that looks wild. Name it Bucephalus and put it in your notebook under "Europe: Macedonia."

2. If at all possible, tour a real horse stable. Ask questions about training wild horses. Ask to see the most spirited horse they have. Find out how they handle this one horse compared to the others. Take a picture of this horse. Pretend it is Bucephalus. File your picture under "Europe: Macedonia."

85B—Younger and Middle Students

Research the coinage of the Mediterranean World. It may surprise you to find that Alexander himself never put his picture on the new coins he made. He had the profile of Hercules placed on one side and an image of Zeus on the other side. Zeus is holding a scepter and an eagle. The eagle was supposed to symbolize the soul of a dead king watching over his kingdom.

However, many coins were made with Alexander's profile on them. Find out who made them and when. Write a few paragraphs about it and include a sketch or photocopy of the coin. File it under "Europe: Macedonia."

85C—Older Students

Due to limited space in the lesson, I wasn't able to elaborate on Alexander's military brilliance. Research what is called the Battle of Gaugamela. *World Book Encyclopedia* calls it "one of the 15 decisive battles of history." (It may also be listed as the Battle of Arbela.) You'll discover in this battle that the Greeks had not yet forgotten the time the Persians burned Athens. Write a one-page report on the battle. File it under "Asia: Iran (Persia)."

---

323 B.C.

THE SPLIT OF ALEXANDER'S EMPIRE

LESSON 86

It may seem odd to have an entire lesson covering the end of someone's career. But trust me that the breakup of Alexander the Great's empire is interesting. Let's first back up to the Israelites, of all people, who are part of the story.

Our last lesson on Israel was about the prophet Malachi. I told you then that it would be 400 years before the events of the New Testament would take place. That time span is sometimes called the "intertestamental period"—the period "between" ("inter") the testaments. Alexander the Great's empire was at its height during this time period.

Alexander's success was no "new" news to the Israelites. It seems that Daniel of the Old Testament prophesied about Alexander's rise and fall about 300 years before it ever happened! Here is a neat story of how God used His word to protect the Jews.

According to Josephus, a Jewish historian, Alexander planned to march on Jerusalem just like he did on all the surrounding countries. However, upon his arrival outside Jerusalem, some priests went out to greet him all dressed in white. The priests simply showed Alexander the passages in the Book of Daniel that described him.

The verses read, "...three more kings will arise in Persia, and the fourth shall be far richer than them all; by his strength, through his riches, he shall stir up all against the realm of Greece. Then a mighty king shall arise, who shall rule with great dominion, and do according to his will." (Dan. 11:2–3)

Who wouldn't be flattered to find themselves written about in a holy book? In fact, Alexander was so impressed by the passage that he peacefully departed from the Jews and their blessed Jerusalem that they had worked so hard to restore. I'm sure Nehemiah would have been happy had he still been living.

I wonder, though, if the priests explained to Alexander the "rest of the story." In the next verse of Daniel, the prophet foretold the end of Alexander's empire. Daniel 11:4 says, "And when he [Alexander] has arisen, his kingdom shall be broken up and divided toward the *four* [italics mine] winds of heaven, but not among his posterity nor according to this dominion with which he ruled; for his kingdom shall be uprooted, even for others besides these."

Daniel also described Alexander's kingdom and its breakup in the vision recorded in Daniel 8:20–22. It says, "The ram which you saw, having the two horns—they are the kings of Media and Persia. And the male goat is the kingdom of Greece. The large horn that is between its eyes is the first king. As for the broken horn and the four that stood up in its place, four kingdoms shall arise out of that nation, but not with its power."

As you certainly have learned by now, God's prophets always spoke the truth. After the unexpected death of Alexander, his generals fought over who would rule next and decided to break the kingdom up into four "more manageable" portions! They didn't know it but they were fulfilling Daniel's words to the last detail. They settled on this arrangement. The general named Ptolemy gained Egypt; the general named Lysimachus ruled Thrace and Asia Minor; Seleucus got Syria, Mesopotamia, and Persia; and Cassander took Macedonia and Greece.

Over time, three dynasties remained strong from the four kingdoms. They were the Ptolemies in Egypt; the Seleucids in Syria, Mesopotamia, and Persia; and the Antigonids in Macedonia and Greece. You will hear of some of these again, at least until the mighty Romans swallow them all up to fulfill the rest of Daniel's prophecy.

One important thing about Alexander's achievements is that his unification of so many countries helped to set up the world for the future spread of the Gospel. Everywhere Alexander went, he took the Greek language, which eventually was the language used in the New Tesament to tell the Good News of Christ.

One other neat thing about Alexander's whole story is the reminder that God has a plan for the world. The strange-sounding prophecy Daniel gave about goats, rams, and horns is not so strange when you see it fulfilled. In the same way, the Book of Revelation contains many things we don't fully understand yet. In time though, the world will know and understand everything the Lord has foretold to us.

ACTIVITY 86

86A—Younger Students

In the lesson on Alexander, I talked about the Greek language being spread all over the empire. Did you know that our word "alphabet" comes straight from the Greek language? The first letter of their alphabet is "alpha" and the second letter is "beta." So, when the Greeks wanted to talk about learning the ABCs, they would have called it the "alpha-beta." We use the term "alphabet" to refer to all our letters.

In the Bible, Jesus used the Greek alphabet to tell us how He ruled over everything. He said, "I am the Alpha and the Omega, the Beginning and the End, the First and the Last." (Rev. 22:13) Look at the Greek alphabet in the Activity Supplement in the Appendix. Find out which letter "omega" is to better understand what Christ meant.

Write your own name as best as you can using the Greek alphabet. File it under "Europe: Greece."

86B—Middle Students

Do you remember how Alexander died? It was most likely from malaria. (No one knows for sure.) Read in an encyclopedia what the symptoms of malaria are and how a person can get it. With that information, pretend you are a newspaper writer for the *Macedonian Times*. On a blank sheet of white paper, create a large headline telling of the death of Alexander the Great. Write a short article on what Alexander died from. You would be able to describe only the symptoms of malaria in your article because in ancient days, doctors did not realize the role that the mosquito played in passing the disease. That was discovered hundreds of years later. End the article by reporting who would be taking over the empire. (In real life, these events were many years apart.)

86C—Older Students

Personally, I find the study of prophecy to be intriguing. Every time I reread about prophecies fulfilled, it gives me chills. For the sake of defending your faith, focus on studying the prophecies of Daniel alone. Practice verbally articulating what you know about the fulfillment of Daniel's prophecies. It will take some work. Create a written outline, but present it as if it were for a speech class. File your outline under "Asia: Israel."

c. 287–212 B.C.

ARCHIMEDES AND THE LIGHTHOUSE OF ALEXANDRIA

LESSON 87

I really like Archimedes. He would have been an interesting man to know. He was a brilliant Greek mathematician and inventor whose ideas are still in use today.

Archimedes was born in Syracuse, Sicily, which was a Greek colony. He went all the way to Alexandria, Egypt, to go to school. Remember that Alexandria had become a great city that was possibly even more impressive than Athens. Archimedes must have received a great education there because he went back to Syracuse and invented many amazing and practical things.

One thing Archimedes understood was the power of the lever and pulley. He created devices that could raise and lower great ships in and out of the water. He once said if you gave him a place to stand, he could move the world! He was referring to the ability to move great things with the use of pulleys.

Also helpful to the navy would have been Archimedes' idea of using large mirrors on a ship to reflect the sun's rays and burn down other ships! I guess it would take a pretty big mirror to do that.

Archimedes also figured out a great way to move water. He invented what is known as the Archimedes screw. Imagine placing a giant screw (like the size of a man) in a pond of water. As you would turn the screw, water would catch in the grooves and move right up out of the pond. This system of irrigation has been used at the Nile River for centuries, as well as in the Netherlands.

As for mathematics, Archimedes calculated the meaning of "pi," which is used to help determine the dimensions of circles. He came close to inventing calculus itself, which is an upper-level approach to mathematics.

But more than any of these, I find this next invention to be the most interesting. Apparently, the king where Archimedes lived was suspicious that the gold crown he ordered to be made was not of pure gold. He asked Archimedes how he could know if the crown were of solid gold or if some of the gold had been replaced with less expensive metal.

Archimedes pondered over this question for a long time. At last, one day as he was lowering himself into a bathtub, he noticed the amount of water that splashed out. It gave him the idea of *displacement*. He realized that the displacement of water for the weight of the gold crown would be different from the displacement of water from a crown of cheap metal.

Archimedes had stumbled onto a great theory, but in doing so, something funny happened. He was so excited about his observation of the water that he jumped out of the tub and went running to tell the king without any of his clothes on! Along the way he yelled "Eureka, eureka!" which means "I have found it" in Greek.

Unfortunately, this same kind of absentmindedness might have contributed to his death. It seems that many years later, the Romans were attacking his city. The Roman general who was overseeing the attack had forbidden his soldiers to harm Archimedes because he was a respected and valuable man. The stories differ, but some say Archimedes remained working in his study with some special instruments and was completely unaware of what was going on. A Roman soldier found him and killed him in hopes that the tools he was using were made of gold. Other sources say a Roman soldier killed Archimedes while he was walking down the street carrying an important invention. The stories are close to one another. Both imply that Archimedes wasn't paying much attention to the battle.

Either way, the brilliant life of Archimedes ended tragically. The Roman general who had hoped to spare the life of Archimedes had a special tomb built for him. The death of Archimedes was a great loss to both the Greeks and the Romans.

It was during the lifetime of Archimedes that builders in Alexandria, Egypt, were erecting what became another of the Seven Wonders of the Ancient World. It was the Pharos, or lighthouse, of Alexandria. Pharos was a small island at the harbor of Alexandria. I'm referring to the Alexandria that Alexander the Great built right at the mouth of the Nile.

This 400-foot lighthouse was extraordinary. To give you a perspective of how large it was, the Statue of Liberty is only 150 feet high. The lighthouse was built by the Greek architect Sostratos somewhere between 283 and 246 B.C. It had a square base, an eight-sided middle cylinder, and a round top. A huge fire surrounded by mirrors blazed on top of it to warn sailors of the land for miles and miles. After standing nearly 1,500 years, an earthquake brought it down. Were it not for historians, writers, and artists of long ago, we would never have known the Pharos existed. I wonder if Archimedes ever saw it completed? I think he would have been impressed with it.

ACTIVITY 87

ALL STUDENTS

Make your Memory Cards for Lessons 85–87. Remember to highlight Alexander the Great (336 B.C.) as a date to memorize.

87A—Younger and Middle Students

This is a fun one. Get a one-foot length of masking tape and a permanent marker. Adhere the tape vertically in your bathtub. Fill the bathtub about the usual amount for a bath. When the water is done filling up, mark the water line with the marker. Now, climb in the tub and be very still. When the water has finished sloshing around, mark the new water line. It should be higher than the last line.

To make this more interesting, mark different lines for other people in your family (for whoever is willing to participate in your experiment). The heaviest people in the family should have the highest watermark. That means they would "displace" more water than the lighter people would.

If you feel like making this more fun, don't forget to yell "Eureka, eureka!" when you get out. (Nudity is optional!)

87B—Younger and Middle Students

1. With adult supervision, see what you can do with a small mirror and the sun. (Be careful not to reflect the light to anyone's eyes!) See how warm you can make a piece of paper by reflecting direct sun rays onto it. Archimedes was able to start a fire with this method. You probably won't have the same success, but work over concrete just in case!

2. Prove Archimedes' idea that the circumference of a circle (the measure AROUND a circle) is just a little more than three times the diameter (the measure ACROSS a circle). This is what he called "pi."

   Take a tape measure and several circular objects such as a plate, the top of a stool, a lampshade, and the like. First, measure across the circle (its diameter). Remember the number and mark it with a paper clip on the tape. Then, measure the outside edge of the circular object. As you measure, stop at the place where the paper clip is and start over. It should take you just a little over three times the length of your diameter to get around the entire circle. That is why pi is equal to 3.1416. Kind of neat, isn't it?

87C—Older Students

Archimedes was a great mathematician. When he formulized a value for pi, decimals had not yet been developed. He found the value of pi in a fraction instead. Decimals were introduced in the 1600s. Pi was then calculated at about 3.1416. For the sake of discussion, why do you think that the value of pi cannot be put into an exact decimal? It is said to be impossible!

I know the younger students usually have the fun, edible activities in this curriculum. For a change, why don't you have a real "pie" today. Before you eat it, measure the circumference and the area of the pie using these formulas. (Pi is represented by the π symbol.)

Circumference = π(diameter) or 2πradius   Area = π(radius) squared

TAKE ANOTHER LOOK!

Review 29: Lessons 85–87

Wall of Fame

1. *Alexander the Great (356–323 B.C.)*—Put him on top of a great big horse. **Remember, this is a date to memorize. (You only have to remember the date of 336 B.C.)**

2. *Alexander's empire splits (323 B.C.)*—Fold a square piece of paper twice to make a "windowpane" type of fold. In each of the four quadrants, write the name of the four generals who divided the empire.

3. *Archimedes (c. 287–212 B.C.)*—Draw an old-fashioned-looking bathtub. Write his name on the outside with "Eureka!" printed on it.

4. *The Lighthouse of Alexandria (c. 283 B.C.)*—Try to find a small picture of a lighthouse in a magazine or make one yourself. Cut out a small piece of foil and glue it on top to give the impression that it reflects light.

SomeWHERE in Time

For this project you will need a historical map of Greece and Outline Map 1, "Persia."

1. Using a reference book, you now need to find the boundaries of Alexander the Great's empire at its height. Shade it a light green. It should cover Greece to the far west, India in the far east, Egypt in the south, and go as far north as the Jaxartes River.

2. Still using a reference book, you will now need to find the four divisions of Alexander's empire after his death. This may take some work. The lesson I wrote gives the names of the country or countries each general took as his own. Use a colored pencil to outline each country. Then use the patterns shown in the legend box below to represent each division that you can draw OVER the green shaded areas. (Add a legend box like the one below to the corner of your map.) File this project under "Europe: Macedonia" because that is where Alexander started.

Seleucid Dynasty	///////
Ptolemy Dynasty	^^^^^^
Lysimachus Dynasty	:::::::::::
Cassander Dynasty	\\\\\\\\\

3. On a map of the Mediterranean, find the island of Sicily. It is the one that looks like it's getting "kicked" by Italy. Archimedes was born in Syracuse, Sicily. It was a Greek colony then, but Italy now governs it.

Name _____ Date _____

 WHAT DID YOU LEARN?

Week 29: *Quiz*

I. Multiple Choice. Circle the correct answer for each question.

1. More than likely, the Ice Age lasted about
   a. 10 years.
   b. 100 years.
   c. 1,000 years.
   d. one million years.

2. The Sumerians were distinctive for creating
   a. large-eyed statues.
   b. ziggurats.
   c. an advanced civilization.
   d. cuneiform writing.
   e. All of the above.

3. Jacob had a brother named
   a. Enoch.
   b. Shem.
   c. Esau.
   d. Harry.

4. Joseph of the Old Testament was thrown into
   a. a fiery furnace.
   b. a well.
   c. a den of lions.
   d. the sea.

5. The Tabernacle built in the wilderness was used as a place of worship
   a. for 40 days.
   b. for 40 years.
   c. for 400 years.
   d. forever.

The Mystery of History

II. True or False? Circle your answer.

1. Samson was the third king of Israel.   T F
2. The first Olympics were held on the plain of Olympia in Greece.   T F
3. Ancient Native Americans were responsible for the building of
   the Great Serpent Mound in Ohio.   T F
4. Manasseh was an evil king over Judah all his life.   T F
5. Because of King Josiah's humility, the Lord gave him 15 more
   years to live after Sennacherib was defeated.   T F

III. Who Am I?

Guess who the speaker is. Choose one of these five names.

Darius I   Zerubbabel   Xerxes   Pythagoras   Buddha

1. I am from India. My name means "enlightened one." Who am I?

2. I am the grandson of Jehoiachin and helped to rebuild the temple. Who am I?

3. I'm a Persian king who helped to start the first organized postal system. Who am I?

4. By marriage, I am related to Queen Esther of the Bible. Who am I?

5. I was a Greek mathematician and philosopher. Who am I?

IV. Matching. Match the following items by placing the correct letter next to the number.

_____1. Fifty great years in the history of Greece   a. Statue of Zeus

_____2. A beautiful temple built on the Acropolis   b. Hippocrates

_____3. A Greek philosopher   c. Golden Age of Athens

_____4. The "Father of Medicine"   d. Socrates

_____5. One of the Seven Wonders of the Ancient World   e. Parthenon

V. Answer in a complete sentence: What happened to the empire of Alexander the Great that fulfilled prophecy?

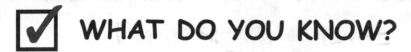

☑ WHAT DO YOU KNOW?

Pretest 30

Who Am I? From the word bank below, choose the correct answer for each question.

1. I was the strongest emperor of India during the Mauryan Empire. Who am I?

2. I am large enough to provide shelter for people. Who am I?

3. I am a book named after 70 men. Who am I?

4. I am a great city in Egypt with a huge library. Who am I?

5. We had no Bible other than the Septuagint until the New Testament was written. Who are we?

6. I straddled over the harbor of a small island. Who am I?

7. We were buried with thousands of other clay replicas with Shi Huang Ti. Who are we?

8. I was the one who started the Great Wall of China. Who am I?

WORD BANK

Colossus of Rhodes	banyan tree	Emperor Asoka
7,500 clay soldiers	Alexandria	Septuagint
Early Christians	Emperor Qin	

The Mystery of History

EMPEROR ASOKA OF INDIA

LESSON 88

It has been several lessons now since we learned about the land of India. The reason we study so much more about Israel, Greece, and Rome is that those cultures have had more influence on us. Still, I want you to know a great deal more about India than what we've already learned.

When Alexander the Great was out conquering nations, he took over part of India, too. His takeover didn't last too long, however, because he died unexpectedly. The governors he left behind eventually blended in with the Indian government.

But, in about 321 B.C., there was one dynasty in India that was very strong and rose to be a large power. The dynasty was started by Chandragupta Maurya. We don't know a lot about this man, but we do know something about his grandson. His name was Asoka. (a SHO ka)

Emperor Asoka is the most famous of the Mauryan rulers. He made almost all of the present country of India his territory by fighting against his neighbors. His capital was Patna in the state of Bihar.

Asoka made many contributions to India by improving water supplies and creating the first "rest stops" for travelers. He had the giant banyan tree planted along major roads to provide shelter for people. Banyan trees are peculiar in that one tree can look like a small forest. As its large branches grow, they develop supports the size of tree trunks. These new trunks in turn grow down and root themselves in the soil. Banyan trees are an incredible sight and would be welcoming to any weary traveler.

But Asoka did far more to influence India than plant beautiful trees. He changed the major religion of India—at least for a time. As the story goes, Asoka had a war experience that was horrifying. The blood and gore he saw challenged the way he viewed life and death. In searching for answers to the reasons behind war, Asoka discovered the peaceful teachings of Buddha.

If you recall, Buddha strongly believed that others should be treated with dignity and respect. That kind of thinking was contrary to the ambitions of being a warring king. Asoka converted to Buddhism and never fought another battle.

With his new religion, Asoka used his position as emperor to influence the nation of India toward Buddhism. Though India had been primarily Hindu, Asoka spread his new faith far and wide. Within India alone he established 84,000 Buddhist monasteries and built hospitals for both people and animals. To spread Buddhism outside of India, Asoka sent hundreds of missionaries to neighboring lands such as Syria, Egypt, and Greece.

On a more unique note, Asoka was responsible for building multitudes of rock pillars to promote Buddhism and peace. The pillars were inscribed with moral "edicts," or instructions on how to live, written in the common language of the Hindu people. One pillar kindly states that all the people of India, no matter their beliefs, were like children to Asoka. At least 10 of these pillars remain standing today. The country of India still uses as its state emblem a picture of one of the shrines Asoka built.[1]

Asoka hoped to unify India with one major religion. However, it proved only to divide people against one another. Shortly after his death, the Mauryan Empire broke up, and most of India went back to practicing Hinduism.

---

1. Will Durant, *Our Oriental Heritage.* New York: Simon and Schuster, 1954; pp. 446–450.

Like many others, Asoka had good intentions for his people in converting to Buddhism. I believe, though, that Buddha's teachings fail to deal with man's sin and God's forgiveness. Instead, Buddhists look to themselves to control their desires and be free from evil. They believe that "nirvana" is a state of peace that can only be found in the mind. Remember to pray for the people around the world who still need to know the Good News of the Gospel.

ACTIVITY 88

88A—Younger Students

1. Do you travel often? If you take long trips by car, you have probably stopped at a "rest stop" before. What would you find at a typical rest stop along the interstate? Make a list of these things. Now pretend you are in ancient India. If you were a traveler and stopped at a banyan tree along the road, what might you find there? Make a list of those things and compare your two lists. File your lists under "Asia: India."

2. Hindi is the name of the most common language in India. Turn to the Activity Supplement in the Appendix to learn how to count to 10 in Hindi.

88B—Younger and Middle Students

1. Look in the encyclopedia for information on the banyan tree. Discover what is so unique about these trees, where they grow, and how old they may get. They're pretty incredible. Photocopy a picture of a banyan tree and file it under "Asia: India."

2. India has a wide variety of animals because there is a wide range of habitats. There are mountains, plains, rain forests, and deserts. Even as early as 300 B.C., there were laws in place to help protect the unique wildlife of India. Research the animals of interest to you:

King cobra	Bengal tiger
Himalayan black bear	Indian lion
Red panda	Common kingfisher
Asian elephant	Gibbon ape
Rare, one-horned Indian rhinoceros	

88C—Middle and Older Students

According to Gospel for Asia, a missionary group committed to reaching Asia, "over 80% of the Asian nations are restricted or closed to Western missionaries. Yet, most of the 12.7 billion people in the world who have never once heard the gospel live in these closed countries."[2]

Write to Gospel for Asia and request the video *Glad Sacrifice* to learn about one strategy that is helping to reach Asians. K.P. Yohannan, the founder of the agency, gives very good insights to the problems of India and includes footage of India on the tape. Here is the address:

Gospel for Asia
1800 Golden Trail Ct.
Carrollton, TX 75010-9907
1-800-WIN-ASIA
Web site: www.gfa.org

---

2. From jacket cover of *Glad Sacrifice*, video of Gospel for Asia.

The Mystery of History

THE SEPTUAGINT AND THE COLOSSUS OF RHODES

LESSON 89

The Septuagint is a group of ancient manuscripts that still exist today. They are no ordinary books though. They are the oldest Greek translation of the Old Testament. Let's look closer at them to find out why they are so special.

Do you remember the name Ptolemy? He was one of the four generals who took over Alexander the Great's empire. The Ptolemy family was a Greek family that ruled over Egypt. (The famous Cleopatra was from this family!) One of the kings from that family was named Ptolemy II, or Philadelphus. He ruled over Egypt from 285–247 B.C. and lived in the city of Alexandria.

Let me tell you some things about Alexandria, Egypt. Nearly one-quarter of the city was designated for the Jews to live in. If you recall, the Greeks became friendly with the Jews after the incident with Alexander the Great. I'm referring to the time he went to conquer Jerusalem but was stopped by the priests. He was flattered by what the Old Testament had to say about him, and he left the Jews alone. Other Greeks became fond of the Jews as well and welcomed them into their cities.

Picture, though, what happens to people when they live away from "home" for awhile. After years and years of living in Alexandria, Egypt, the Jews lost their understanding of Hebrew. They began to speak Greek instead. As a result, the Jews could no longer read and understand the scriptures.

No one knows for sure who had the original idea for the Hebrew Old Testament to be translated to Greek, but it was agreed to by Ptolemy II. Some people think it was Ptolemy's own idea for the Hebrews to write the Septuagint. This would make sense if you knew the size of his library. Ptolemy II had a library in Alexandria that was probably bigger than any had ever been in the world. He naturally would have welcomed the addition of more books.

Other people believe the Septuagint translation was the idea of the faithful Jews who wanted to understand and teach the Old Testament but were unable to understand it anymore in Hebrew. The books were translated then out of a true need.

Regardless of who began the project, it is said that 70 to 72 men translated the first five books of the Old Testament in just 70 to 72 days. That is where the term "septuagint" came from. It means "seventy" in Latin. The book title is sometimes abreviated in Roman numerals as LXX.

Scholars disagree as to whether these books could really be translated in that time period. They do think that it took the next 200 years to translate the rest of the Old Testament. Keep in mind that this entire rewriting would have been the first major translation of its kind. I think it is neat that the Bible holds this record.

How did it help the Jews? It helped greatly that the Greek-speaking Jews were able to read about the coming Messiah. They needed to be looking for the Savior. Even after the time of Christ, the Septuagint was important. For the first Greek Christians, it was the only Bible text they had before the writing of the New Testament. Some authors still like to use the Greek translation because in some places it is easier to understand than the Hebrew Old Testament.

All in all, the Septuagint translation of the Hebrew Old Testament was and still is an important piece for both Christians and Jews alike. I believe God sovereignly makes Himself known through the powerful written word.

And finally, we are going to learn about the last of the Seven Wonders of the Ancient World—"The Colossus at Rhodes," built sometime in the 200s B.C. Rhodes was a small island in the Aegean Sea, but it had a huge statue to set it apart from all the others. A Greek sculptor named Chares built the 105-foot bronze statue of Helios, the Greek sun god, right at a harbor entrance.

No one knows exactly what the Colossus of Rhodes looked like because it failed to survive after an earthquake c. 225 B.C. Some artists depict the statue as straddling the land from one side of the bank to the other. A ship would have to sail right under the legs of the statue to pass through the harbor.

The word "colossal," which means "big," is derived from the name of this statue. The "Colossus" certainly helped to put the tiny island of Rhodes "on the map."

ACTIVITY 89

89A—Younger and Middle Students

1. Do you know your Roman numerals yet? They were made up a long time ago, but we still use them today for many things such as page numbers and hours on a clock. There is a page in the Activity Supplement in the Appendix with Roman numerals, and the Latin pronunciation of them is listed for you. If you are a younger student, copy the actual Roman numerals with one of our numbers next to it. If you are a middle student, also write out the Latin pronunciation of the Roman numerals. You will recognize some as sounding very much like our months of the year. File your numerals under "Europe: Rome."

2. There are still many people around the world who don't yet have the Bible in their own language. For more information on this, pick up the colorful children's book *From Arapesh to Zuni: A Book of Bibleless People* by Karen Lewis. It is a Wycliffe Bible Translators publication.

89B—Middle Students

Bible translation is a challenging field. Obtain as many different versions of the Bible as you can from around your home or from the library. Look up Psalm 1:1–2 in each of the Bibles and write out the passages on paper. With a red pen, circle the words that are different. I want you to notice that the meaning usually doesn't change even though different words are used. Imagine the task of translating a book from one language to another! That is what the 70 men did. Title your paper "The Septuagint" and file it under "Africa: Egypt."

89C—All Students

Have you ever heard of Wycliffe Bible Translators? They are a missionary group committed to translating the Bible into different languages. Contact Wycliffe and request information on their ministry. They can be reached at:

Wycliffe Bible Translators
P.O. Box 628200
Orlando, FL 32862-8200
1-800-WYCLIFFE or visit their Web site at www.wycliffe.org for some great activities for all ages.

THE QIN DYNASTY (CH'IN)

LESSON 90

If you were up in outer space today looking down on the earth, do you know what you would see? Well, besides the continents and oceans, there is one man-made image that astronauts have told us they can actually see. It is the Great Wall of China. By the end of this lesson you will know who was behind the building of that wall and why.

In quick review, what do you last remember studying about China? In this order we learned about the Shang dynasty, the Zhou dynasty, and Confucius. Well, obviously there is a lot more to know about China than that.

After the Zhou dynasty and Confucius, states continued to war with one another. The fighting was referred to as the "feudal system." It lasted years until one man stepped up with enough power to unite the feuding states into one government. His name was Qin. It is pronounced "chin" and sometimes written as "Ch'in." From this came the name "China."

Qin was so powerful that he named himself "Shi Huang Ti," which means "First Emperor of China." He was by no means the first ruler of China, but he was the first man to unify all the states that had been fighting one another. His brilliant leadership greatly influenced China forever.

Shi Huang Ti had canals built to better water the crops; he created one type of money for all the Chinese people; he made one standard system of weights and measures; and he standardized the size of chariots and wagons. Qin was an elaborate builder of palaces. His palace tomb contained a

Qin, or Shi Huang Ti, was buried with 7,500 terra-cotta soldiers—each with individually created features.

model of heaven on the ceiling and a map of his empire on the floor. And like Emperor Asoka of India, Qin made sure that trees were planted along the roads that radiated from the capital city.

Before I make this guy sound too good, let it be known that Shi Huang Ti was also known for imposing high taxes on his people and being cruel toward those whose beliefs were threatening to him. He executed more than 400 scholars. Many were men who held to the teachings of Confucius. He agreed to the burning of thousands of history books that were written before his reign. That way, "history" would begin with the story of him!

Shi Huang Ti must also have been a proud man because he boasted that his dynasty would last 10,000 years. He was only off by 9,986 years! His dynasty, lasting only 14 to 15 years, was actually one of China's shortest.

The reason behind much of Shi Huang Ti's confidence was in the building of the Great Wall of China. Apparently, China was often under attack by her neighbors. As a result, small villages had built walls around their territories. Shi Huang Ti decided to connect these existing walls. The end result was bigger than anyone dreamed!

Here are the facts on the Great Wall. It runs 1,500 miles; it is about 25 feet high; it has 35- to 40-foot towers every 200 to 300 yards; it is 25 feet thick at the base; and it is 15 feet wide across the top where chariots can ride.

To build this massive barrier, Shi Huang Ti used soldiers, prisoners, and peasants. Supposedly thousands died in the process of working for years and years in all kinds of extreme weather. What's worse, if a man left a crack in the bricks big enough for a nail to sink into, he was immediately executed! Some who died were buried right into the structure of the wall itself!

Oddly, the Great Wall did not ultimately accomplish for China what it was designed for. Within time, raiders from Mongolia managed to cross over it anyway.

Shi Huang Ti has become even better known to the world in recent years. In 1974, some diggers came across the unbelievable tomb of this emperor. It seems that he had himself buried with 7,500 life-sized clay soldiers! Each soldier was individually carved with his own facial expression. There were also replicas of horses, chariots, and weapons. I don't mean little horses either. Some of them were full size.

Though the size of this collection of relics may make Shi Huang Ti look a bit eccentric, the clay soldiers may indicate that the Chinese were at least abandoning the practice of burying real people with their ruler. Seventy-five hundred terra-cotta soldiers are better than the sacrifice of 7,500 men.

Shi Huang Ti did not leave a dynasty that lasted 10,000 years as he had hoped, but China, the Great Wall, and Shi Huang Ti's tomb are still well known 2,000 years later. I wonder how many *more* years the Great Wall will stand to remind us of ancient China?

ACTIVITY 90

ALL STUDENTS

Make your memory Cards for Lessons 88–90.

90A—Younger Students

1. On a map of the United States, find the cities of New York, New York, and Omaha, Nebraska. Can you see how far away the two cities are? That is about the length of the Great Wall of China if it were all stretched out. Be sure to get some library books to find pictures of the Great Wall.

2. Using clay or Play-Doh modeling compound, try to make a replica of yourself like the soldiers did for Shi Huang Ti. Use toothpicks to create detail for your hair, eyes, and mouth. And/or you could sculpt horses and chariots. Take a photo of your creation. File it under "Asia: China."

90B—Middle Students

It is easy to find more information on the Great Wall of China. Because it is the longest structure man has ever built, it is worth your time to know the details. Write a one-page report on the Great Wall. Photocopy pictures to include in your report. File it under "Asia: China."

90C—Middle and Older Students

Research the archaeological finds from Shi Huang Ti's tomb. The excavation work continues to be a great challenge because the tomb is under a modern village. If you enjoy art, try to sketch the facial expressions of some of the soldiers. They appear quite lifelike. File your sketch or a photocopy of the soldiers under "Asia: China."

TAKE ANOTHER LOOK!

Review 30: Lessons 88–90

Wall of Fame

1. *Emperor Asoka (273–232 B.C.)*—Depict a small Buddha to represent this converted king.

2. *The Septuagint (250 B.C.)*—Make a small book with the title "Septuagint" on it.

3. *The Colossus of Rhodes (exact date unknown; sometime in the 200s B.C.)*—Use the description in the lesson to draw what you think it might have looked like.

4. *Qin dynasty (221–206 B.C.)*—Photocopy a small picture of the Great Wall of China. (Pictures are numerous and easy to find.)

SomeWHERE in Time

1. Map the boundaries of the Mauryan Empire on Outline Map 4, "East Asia." Label the surrounding neighbors of India.

   Nepal   (light purple)
   Pakistan   (light orange)
   China   (pink)

2. What is the latitude and longitude of Alexandria, Egypt? We have studied several significant things about this city. What were they? (Hint: Think of Alexander the Great, Archimedes, the Pharos of Alexandria, and the Septuagint. What connection did each of these have with Alexandria? See the answers below.)

3. On an ancient map of China, find the boundaries of the Qin dynasty. Transfer this to Outline Map 4, "East Asia." Zigzag the approximate location of the Great Wall of China.

   Search on a modern-day map of China for the province of Shaanxi. Within this province, look for the city Xi'an (or Lintong). This is the site of the tomb of Qin, still under excavation today.

4. On Outline Map 6, "Turkey," continue plotting every one of the Seven Wonders of the Ancient World. You may have to go back to some former lessons to get the exact location of each. But here is a list of the wonders in the order in which they were built. On your map, label the wonder and write the date next to it. File this map under "Miscellaneous."

The Pyramids at Giza	2575 B.C.
The Hanging Gardens of Babylon	605 B.C.
The Temple of Diana (or Artemis) at Ephesus	550 B.C.
The Statue of Zeus at Olympia	450 B.C.
The Mausoleum of Halicarnassus	353 B.C.
The Pharos, or Lighthouse, of Alexandria	280 B.C.
The Colossus of Rhodes	280 B.C.

(*Answers: Alexander the Great was buried there; Archimedes went to school there; the Pharos of Alexandria was built there; the Septuagint was translated there.*)

WHAT DID YOU MISS?

Week 30: Exercise

Much like you did in Quarter 2, play Beat the Clock!

To play this game, you will need a timer, your timeline (or Contents page), and copies of this exercise. You will need one for every participant (including the teacher!).

See how fast each of you can list these events, people, or places in the proper chronological order. I recommend using pencil and having an eraser handy.

Hint: First write down the date of each item next to it in the first column; *then*, in the second column, list the items in the order in which they occurred. The first one has been done to help you get started.

_____1. Plato   1. Noah

_____2. The first Olympics   2. _____

_____3. Noah   3. _____

_____4. David   4. _____

_____5. Confucius   5. _____

_____6. Israel divides   6. _____

_____7. Abraham   7. _____

_____8. Golden Age of Athens   8. _____

_____9. Tutankhamen   9. _____

_____10. Buddha   10. _____

_____11. Babylonian Captivity   11. _____

_____12. Alexander the Great   12. _____

Final Time:_____

The Mystery of History

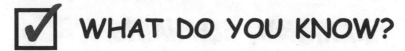

☑ WHAT DO YOU KNOW?

Pretest 31

Jeopardy. I provide the answers, you give me the right question for each from the list below. Draw neat lines in different colors to connect them.

1. Elephants	5. Paper
2. The Alps	6. Antiochus Epiphanes
3. Salt	7. Oil
4. Silk	8. Dedication

What Seleucid ruler sacrificed a pig on the Jewish altar?

What was the greatest trade item made by the Chinese?

What animal did Hannibal use to fight against the Romans?

What was miraculously provided at Hanukkah?

What mountains did Hannibal cross with his war elephants?

What substance was scattered across Carthage to ruin it?

What does the word "Hanukkah" mean?

What did the Chinese invent during the Han dynasty?

HANNIBAL, ELEPHANTS, AND THE PUNIC WARS

LESSON 91

Far away from China at about the same time that Qin started the Great Wall, trouble was stirring between two important cities. The city of Rome was determined to rule over all the Mediterranean. However, one city, Carthage, wasn't going to let this happen very easily.

Carthage, an ancient city and state located in northern Africa, was a threat to Rome because it was a great trading city. Look on a historical map now and find both Carthage and Rome. They are really quite close to one another although they are on two different continents. Only the beautiful Mediterranean Sea separated them.

The fighting between these cities became known as the Punic Wars. It was called that because the Romans used the word "Punic" for "Phoenicians." What do the Phoenicians have to do with it? Glad you asked that question. It was the Phoenicians of long ago who first settled the city of Carthage in the Mediterranean. It was what we call a "colony" of Phoenicia for many years.

During the First Punic War, the Carthaginians fought with the Romans over the island of Sicily. That is the small island that looks like it is being "kicked" by the peninsula of Italy. (Archimedes was from there.) Carthage lost that battle.

Twenty years later, though, a brilliant general named Hannibal rose to power in Carthage. He would greatly challenge the Roman rule. While just a boy, Hannibal developed an intense hatred for Rome. His father once asked him to make an oath that he would never be friends with a Roman. Hannibal kept that oath all his life.

The most amazing thing Hannibal ever did was to completely surprise the Romans in an attack. You will have to look at a map to appreciate this strategy. Rather than trying to attack Rome from the south where Carthage was, Hannibal marched to

In an incredible effort to attack Rome, Hannibal crossed rivers and scaled the Alps with 37 war elephants!

Rome by heading west through Africa, north at the Strait of Gibraltar, and east across the perilous Alps mountains! This man and his army, who lived south of Rome and across a sea, attacked Rome from the northwest. It was a brilliant idea.

To make the endeavor even more astounding, Hannibal took 37 war elephants with him! Can you imagine elephants climbing the Alps? To be honest, they didn't do a very good job. On the way, all but one died from either the freezing conditions or from falling to their deaths. One-third of Hannibal's men died for the same reasons, along with the fact that some men just starved to death.

Still, Hannibal was very courageous. It is said that he himself often hiked or rode his horse to the next highest peak, yelling back to the men that it was safe for passage. I can picture him shouting and waving. Both he and his men were subject to slippery ice, deep snow, and freezing weather. It is incredible that they made it at all.

Over the next 15 years, the mighty Hannibal managed to defeat the Romans at three different battles within Italy, but he was yet to meet up with the best that Rome had to offer in generals. His name was Scipio (SIP ee oh).

While Hannibal was in Italy far from home, Scipio took his men straight to Carthage to attack by way of the sea. News of that forced Hannibal to head back to Carthage the same way he came. In 202 B.C., Scipio and Hannibal finally met face to face to fight at the Battle of Zama. The fate of the rule of the Mediterranean was at stake. The result of this battle was to shape the rest of history!

Since you've probably never heard of Carthage before this lesson, you can probably guess who won this decisive battle. Hannibal and his men were unable to win this time. The powerful Romans claimed the final victory over the Second Punic War, which was just the beginning of showing how strong they could be.

Hannibal, on the other hand, left the army of Carthage and worked on rebuilding his city instead. He was so successful that he again posed a threat to the Romans. They set out to have Hannibal ousted from Carthage once and for all. He had to flee far from his own country to save his life.

After 10 years, the Romans finally caught up to Hannibal while he was in hiding on the island of Crete. That is the same island where the Minoans once lived. Rather than suffer the humiliation of being captured, Hannibal ended his own life. He supposedly drank poison that he kept stored in a secret ring on his finger.

Some of Hannibal's last words were "Let us now put an end to the great anxiety of the Romans, who have thought it too lengthy, and too heavy a task, to wait for the death of a hated old man."[1] Ironically, Hannibal's old enemy Scipio died that same year.

Both men died without the knowledge that Carthage was later obliterated by the Romans in the Third Punic War. The destruction was one of the worst in all of history as the entire city was burned over two weeks and any survivors were carried away into slavery.

As a final act of cruelty and to ensure that Carthage wouldn't rise again, the Romans contaminated the burned city with salt. The strategy behind this was to ruin the town's farmland. The salt in the soil would have made the land incapable of growing food crops. Without anything to eat, no one could live there. This obliteration of the great trade city of Carthage certainly would have broken Hannibal's heart.

ACTIVITY 91

91A—Younger Students

Write a story about what it would be like to have a pet elephant. What would you want him to do for you? Where could he take your family? Where would he sleep, and how much would he eat? To make your story believable, read some information about elephants in the encyclopedia and weave these facts into your story. Dictate the story to your teacher and include it in your Student Notebook under "Africa: Tunisia." (Tunisia is the modern country in Africa where Carthage used to be.)

---

1. As quoted in Don Nardo, *The Punic Wars.* San Diego: Lucent Books, 1996; p. 82.

91B—Middle Students

Pretend you are a soldier with Hannibal's army. Write a diary page of what it is like to travel with the elephants. Although it was not a funny expedition, you could write your diary page in a humorous fashion. Use your imagination. File your page under "Africa: Tunisia."

91C—Older Students

1. Write a synopsis of each of the three Punic Wars. These wars were considered pivotal to history, and the tactics of Hannibal are ingenious. Pay attention to the name Scipio. There was more than one. File your research under "Africa: Tunisia."

2. Are you a war buff? If you like battle scenes, research the details on the Battle of Zama, Scipio versus Hannibal. It was quite a showdown.

---

202 B.C.–A.D. 220

THE HAN DYNASTY

LESSON 92

When you think of images of ancient China, what comes to your mind? Do you picture bustling streets, ornate palaces, and beautiful works of art? I hope so because all of these are part of China's rich past.

Much like the Greeks in Athens, the Chinese had a time period during which their cultural achievements began to blossom. The Han dynasty marks the beginning of China's more creative side.

In review, the Qin dynasty was rather short. It basically lasted the lifetime of Shi Huang Ti, who started the Great Wall of China. After his death, the Han dynasty ruled over China from 202 B.C. to A.D. 220. That is more than 400 years!

If you remember, the Qin dynasty unified the warring states of China into one big country. This is the land that the Han dynasty inherited. They made it even bigger under Emperor Wu Ti. He added parts of central Asia, the southeast coast of China, and conquered the Mekong Valley.

Even with all this new land, China remained somewhat isolated from the rest of the world. The Chinese didn't really need anything from the Western world except for horses. These animals didn't breed well in China and had to be imported. Otherwise, the Chinese had their own natural resources and plenty of farmland for food. But the Western world sure wanted something that China had. And that was silk!

Remember learning about the simple little silkworm that the Chinese learned to harvest? I told you that they kept the worm a secret for about 3,000 years. They were very smart to do that. The art of silk-making was a mystery to the people of Rome, Greece, and other countries. That made the demand for silk quite great and the price of it exorbitant.

The desire for silk was so great that a group of roads from China to Syria was later nicknamed the "Silk Road." These trade routes stretched for 2,500 miles and basically connected the East with the West. It has been said that the value of silk was so high in Rome that it was equal to gold. No wonder men were willing to travel over mountains and through deserts to trade this fine cloth.

Within China itself, travel became more interesting during the Han dynasty as many villages were connected by long canals or waterways. Some families even lived on houseboats to make a way of life out of moving goods from village to village. It was common to see babies who lived on the houseboats wearing bamboo floats to protect them from drowning before they learned to swim!

Culturally, many beautiful things were built during the Han dynasty, though few remain intact. Art was becoming more appreciated for its beauty. The Chinese became famous for their delicate pottery that we still call "fine china" today. It refers to a type of porcelain made from fine white clay.

As for inventions, it was during the later Han dynasty that paper was invented by the Chinese. It is hard for us to believe that paper, as we know it, didn't come into existence until about A.D. 100!

The Chinese are also responsible for inventing the first seismograph, a device that measures and helps to detect earthquakes. Though the first seismograph looked like an ornate toy in comparison to today's version, the Chinese were thinking way ahead of themselves.

The Han dynasty was not known only for silk trading, porcelain, and inventions. The emperors of this era took China back to some of its former roots. Remember when Shi Huang Ti burned the ancient history books and teachings of Confucius? He couldn't really burn them all. The writings of Confucius were rediscovered under the Han rule and brought back into the politics of the country.

One of the principles of Confucianism was the idea that men should be appointed to rule based on their abilities, not on their birth. So people who wanted to serve in the government in China, had to take a test that showed they understood politics. Unfortunately, this rule did not apply to the emperor. Sometimes even babies inherited the throne. In that case, their mothers were sometimes the real rulers. This wasn't always good.

Overall though, the Han dynasty was good for the people of China. For 400 years the Chinese were prosperous and stable. In the course of history, that is a long time. When we get to the study of Jesus Christ and the early church, remember that the Han dynasty would still have been ruling over China.

ACTIVITY 92

92A—Younger Students

Does your family have any dishes that are made of fine china? If so, compare them to regular dishes. Of course you will need to handle the china carefully! Fine china can break very easily. With permission, eat a snack or your lunch on the china dishes. Talk about how you think these dishes are made and what makes them so easy to break.

92B—Middle and Older Students

1. Update your list of Chinese dynasties with the following information on the Qin and Han dynasties. For the "Special notes" column, review the lesson for each dynasty and list what you consider the most significant achievements of each. Keep your list filed under "Asia: China."

Date of power (years ruling)	Name of dynasty	Special notes
221–206 B.C. (15 yrs.)	Qin	
202 B.C.–A.D. 220 (422 yrs.)	Han	

2. The Chinese traders depended on camels for the long journeys across the Silk Road. Research the interesting characteristics of these animals that make them perfect for such travel.

1. Investigate the short-lived Hsin dynasty. It is based on one man who overthrew an infant on the throne of China to fight for the peasants' rights. Find out who the "Red Eyebrows" were in the story. Record your findings under "Asia: China."

2. Research the recent discovery (1972) of the tomb of Lady Dai. She had lived sometime during the Han dynasty and probably died about 150 B.C.

167–143 B.C.

THE MACCABEAN REVOLT
LESSON 93

At about the time the Han dynasty was being established in China, the Lord was at work protecting His people in Israel from a very cruel man. The history of the Jews never ceases to amaze me. Over and over again, God kept His hand on the Jews in order to bring about His plan to send Jesus Christ.

In Israel, the Jews were being seriously oppressed by a man named Antiochus Epiphanes, or Antiochus IV (An tee OCK us e PI fu nees). He was the eighth ruler of the Seleucid dynasty. The Seleucids were one of the four families we studied earlier who gained part of Alexander the Great's empire after he died.

Antiochus Epiphanes was a ruthless man. He had no respect for the beliefs of the Jews. He wanted them to adopt the Greek way of life. This is called "Hellenization," the term given to the practice of the many nations who adopted the Greek style of living after Alexander's empire.

Antiochus Epiphanes was so cruel that at one point he took over the Jewish Temple and sacrificed a pig on the altar to mock the Jews. He also put up a statue of the Greek god Zeus right there in the Temple. You can imagine the rage and the hurt of the Jews to have the house of the Lord defiled in that way. This was the same Temple that Zerubbabel had worked so hard to restore.

In remembrance of the miracle in the Temple, people of the Jewish faith still light candles on a menorah at Hanukkah.

Furthermore, Antiochus IV forbade the custom of circumcision, and he destroyed as many copies of the Old Testament writings as he could find. The Jews who opposed him were killed.

God was watching though. He raised up a man named Judas Maccabee who was able to stop the tyranny of Antiochus IV, but it wasn't easy.

Judas Maccabee was the son of a priest named Mattathias. It was Mattathias who first led a rebellion against Antiochus. Mattathias refused to give sacrifice to a pagan god and was forced to flee for his life to the hills. He died shortly after that, so Judas, his son, took his place in leading an all-out revolt against Antiochus Epiphanes. This has become known as the Maccabean Revolt.

Interestingly, Judas had far fewer men and probably fewer weapons than his enemy, yet time and time again he was victorious in defeating Antiochus. In fact, Judas earned the name Maccabee, which means "hammerer," from this series of victories. It is apparent to me that the Lord was on their side for the three years they fought.

Finally, in 165 B.C., Judas Maccabee regained control of the sacred Temple. The Jews immediately went to the task of cleaning up the mess the intruders had made. The Apocrypha books (which are special writings that were not included in the Bible) tell an amazing story that happened during the cleanup.

The books say that during the Temple rededication, the Jews found only one small bottle of oil left in the Temple with which to light their holy lamps. Miraculously though, the oil lasted for eight days! It was as if the Lord extended the life of the oil just long enough for the people to complete their time of worship and dedication of the Temple.

It is from this small but meaningful miracle that the custom of Hanukkah was started. The word Hanukkah means "dedication." To this day the Jewish people remember the eight days of worship and the burning of the oil lamps. In the Book of John in the New Testament, it is called the "Feast of Dedication." (John 10:22)

In the celebration of Hanukkah, the Jews light one additional candle each night on a lampstand called a "menorah." By the eighth night, all the candles are lit together, and this scripture is recited: " 'Not by might, nor by power, but by My Spirit,' says the Lord." (Zech. 4:6) The Jews also give gifts to one another and to the poor on this special holiday that falls near Christmas.

Judas Maccabee himself died in battle just a few years after the Temple rededication. His brothers, however, carried on the tradition of fighting for the Jews' independence. How little did they know Who was soon to come to bring His message of peace to the whole world!

ACTIVITY 93

ALL STUDENTS

Make your Memory Cards for Lessons 91–93.

93A—Younger Students

1. Obtain a real menorah as used by the Jews on Hanukkah (or make one out of eight candleholders). With adult supervision, light the eight candles from left to right. It is a tradition to recite these words in addition:

   "We kindle these lights because of the wondrous deliverance You performed for our ancestors."

   Take a picture of your candles and place it in your Student Notebook under "Asia: Israel." Title the page "The First Hanukkah."
2. Plan the Hanukkah game of dreidel. Directions are in the Activity Supplement in the Appendix.

93B—Middle Students

Make a traditional Hanukkah dish. A recipe can be found in the Activity Supplement.

93C—Older Students

Obtain a copy of the Apocrypha. Familiarize yourself with the various books. Look up I Maccabees 4:52–59 and II Maccabees 10:6 to follow the story of Hanukkah.

TAKE ANOTHER LOOK!

Review 31: Lessons 91–93

Wall of Fame

1. *Hannibal and his elephants (218–146 B.C.)*—Find a picture of an elephant. Of course, write Hannibal's name and the date on it.

2. *Han dynasty (202 B.C.–A.D. 220)*—Tape a small sample of silk (or imitation silk) on a card marked "Han Dynasty."

3. *The Maccabean Revolt (167–143 B.C.)*—Sketch or photocopy a small menorah, the eight-candle lampstand used by the Jews to celebrate Hanukkah. Or tape eight small birthday candles to the timeline.

SomeWHERE in Time

1. (a) Using a historical map of the Mediterranean region, find Carthage in northern Africa.

    Trace the route with your finger from Carthage to Rome, heading west, going across the Strait of Gibraltar, and then going east across the Alps. On Outline Map 8, Mediterranean Lands," mark the major points of interest such as Carthage, the Strait of Gibraltar, the Pyrenees mountains, the Alps, and Rome. Mark the route of Hannibal and his elephants using a dotted red line.

    (b) Middle and Older Students: Do you know what a "physical map" is? It is one that depicts the terrain of the land. Using reference maps from encyclopedias, shade the route you just created; use four different colors according to the physical terrain. Shade the higher mountains in light purple, the lower mountains in dark green, average land in light green, and deserts in light brown. Focus on the mountain ranges and the lowlands covered by Hannibal.

    Title the map "Hannibal—the Second Punic War." File these maps under "Africa: Tunisia" because that is the modern country where the ruins of Carthage were found.

2. (a) Using a reference book or historical map of China, find the boundaries of the Qin dynasty and the Han dynasty. On Outline Map 4, "East Asia," mark the boundary of the Qin dynasty in purple. Mark the Han dynasty in green. Label each accordingly.

    (b) Use a zigzag line to depict the Great Wall of China.

    (c) Mark as best as possible the route of the Silk Road. One popular stop for caravans was the city of Kashgar in Central Asia. Hunt for this city on both historical and modern maps. File this map under "Asia: China."

The Mystery of History

WHAT DID YOU LEARN?

Week 31: *Quiz*

I. True or False? Circle your answer.

1. Sir Richard Owen first used the term "dinosaur," which
    means "megalithic lizard."   T F

2. According to the Bible, man's language was confused at Stonehenge.   T F

3. Ancient Egyptians built pyramids as tombs.   T F

4. Hammurabi, who wrote a code of 300 laws, was the king of Crete.   T F

5. The Tabernacle was a worship tent used for about 40 years in
    the Wilderness.   T F

6. Rahab protected the Hebrew spies in the city of Jericho.   T F

II. Multiple Choice. Circle the correct answer for each question.

1. Samson delivered Israel from the _____ just as an angel foretold his mother.
    a. Phoenicians
    b. Midianites
    c. Philistines
    d. Egyptians

2. When the kingdom of Israel divided, how many tribes became known as Judah?
    a. 12
    b. 10
    c. 2
    d. 14

3. In the Old Testament, Elisha helped to cure Naaman of
    a. blindness.
    b. leprosy.
    c. bone disease.
    d. mental illness.

4. The prophet Hosea was brokenhearted over the unfaithfulness of his wife,
    a. Bathsheba.
    b. Jezebel.
    c. Delilah.
    d. Gomer.

5. Sennacherib of Assyria tried to defeat Judah under the reign of
   a. David.
   b. Gideon.
   c. Hezekiah.
   d. Daniel.

6. The prophet Jeremiah suffered being
   a. silenced.
   b. imprisoned.
   c. exiled.
   d. placed in "stocks."
   e. All of the above.

III. Matching. Match the following people and places by putting the correct letter next to the number.

_____1. Nebuchadnezzar   a. Israel

_____2. Aesop   b. India

_____3. Buddha   c. Babylonia

_____4. Confucius   d. Greece

_____5. Artaxerxes   e. Persia

_____6. Haggai   f. China

IV. Fill in the Blanks. Use the word bank provided below.

1. Alexander the Great had a beautiful and spirited horse named _____.

2. _____ was an intelligent Greek scientist who discovered the principle of displacement while soaking in the tub.

3. Emperor Asoka of India planted _____ across his country for travelers.

4. Shi Huang Ti, the emperor of the Qin dynasty, was responsible for building the _____ of China.

5. To try to defend the city of _____ from Rome, Hannibal marched across the Alps with elephants.

6. Judas Maccabee was successful in ridding the Jews of the ruthless rule of _____.

> **WORD BANK**
>
> banyan trees   Archimedes   Carthage   Bucephalus
> Great Wall   Antiochus Epiphanes

V. Answer these questions in complete sentences. Use a separate sheet of paper.

1. Why did the Egyptians believe it to be so important to mummify the human body at death? What did this reflect of their understanding of life after death?

2. What features of the Septuagint make it such a special book?

                                                         The Mystery of History

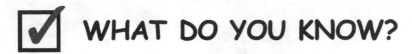 **WHAT DO YOU KNOW?**

Pretest 32

Circle the word that makes the sentence true.

1. Spartacus was the name of a Roman (slave, king).

2. The word "gladiator" in Latin means ("happy," "sword").

3. The Roman (Republic, Empire) came first in history.

4. The word "triumvirate" means rule by (two, three) persons.

5. Pompey was a famous Roman general known for getting rid of (sharks, pirates) in the Mediterranean Sea.

6. Crassus, a Roman consul, put down a rebellion of (slaves, students).

7. Caesar fell in love with the queen of Egypt named (Cleopatra, Sheba).

8. Julius Caesar created the new month of (February, July) to add to the calendar.

SPARTACUS

LESSON 94

If from time to time I were able to rewrite parts of history to give it a happier ending, this lesson would be one of those times. The story is about a Roman slave named Spartacus who was courageous enough to try to change the miserable life that he was forced to live.

Let's back up first and review what life was like during the Roman Republic. If you remember, there were two main classes of people, the patricians and the plebeians. The patricians were the upper class and the plebeians were the lower class. But besides these two groups, there were thousands and thousands of people who were slaves.

In the early days of the Roman Republic, only a few of the rich people kept slaves. However, over the years, the Romans defeated more and more countries around them. With each victory, the Roman soldiers carried back men, women, and children as prisoners of war who were sold as slaves. The number of slaves in Italy grew to be as much as one-fifth of the population! In the city of Rome alone there were 200,000 slaves out of the one million people who lived there.

The life of a slave was quite horrendous for most. It was common to be beaten and treated like an animal. Many of the slaves were used as gladiators who provided entertainment for the Romans. The term "gladiator" comes from the Latin word "gladios," which means "sword." A gladiator was trained with swords and other weapons to fight until death against other gladiators. It was a gruesome way to live or to die!

Because of this terrible treatment, the slaves tried over and over to revolt against the Romans. The largest uprising that ever took place was led by Spartacus, a slave from Thrace.

Spartacus had once been a free man. He became a slave as a result of war with the Romans.

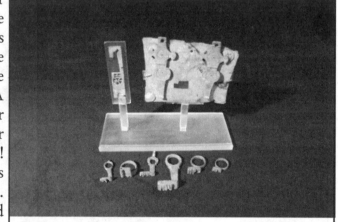

Not even Roman locks and keys like these could hold Spartacus back from trying to lead thousands of slaves to freedom.

It was probably the memory of living "free" that motivated Spartacus to fight against his captors. A famous historian named Plutarch said of him, "Spartacus . . . was a man not only of high spirit and valiant, but in understanding, also, and in gentleness superior to his condition."[1] He sounds like an incredible man to me. And he proved to be a real threat to the Romans.

It was while Spartacus was in gladiator school near Rome that he first managed to escape from slavery. After setting thousands of other slaves free, Spartacus formed a huge army of freed slaves! These men acquired their own weapons and trained for full war. For almost two years, Spartacus and his men fought off the Romans in what was called the Servile War. Roman armies large and small were unable to bring these daring men, women, and children back into submission.

1.Plutarch quote from Will Durant, *Caesar and Christ.* New York: Simon and Schuster, 1944; p. 137

The Mystery of History

Unfortunately, there were some powerful men in Rome who began to get pretty nervous over the conquests of Spartacus and his men. The Roman leaders feared that all the slaves in Italy would be made free and attack Rome itself. It was time for serious war. A man named Crassus stepped up to fight.

The year was 71 B.C. when Crassus and his army met up face to face with Spartacus and his army of 90,000. Plutarch wrote that in full view of all his men, Spartacus stood bravely next to his own horse and killed it with his sword. He claimed that if they won that day, he would pick a new horse from the Romans. But, if they lost that day, he wouldn't need a horse anymore. With that, he fought his last fight. The Roman army killed nearly the entire group of slaves including the determined Spartacus.

To make matters even more gruesome, the 6,000 slaves who managed to survive the battle were put to death through crucifixion. That is the same excruciating way that Jesus died. The slaves who were hung this way were lined up for miles and miles along the Appian Way, a famous road in Rome. This cruel death sentence was meant to scare the other slaves from the idea of ever rebelling again. I suppose it worked, too, as there was never again an uprising of Roman slaves to this degree.

I told you ahead of time that this was a sad story. Perhaps we would all do well to think about the incredible bravery and courage of Spartacus and his men rather than dwell on their final defeat.

ACTIVITY 94

94A—Younger Students

Slavery is not a humorous matter at all. But, in order to somewhat feel the bondage that the Roman slaves felt, make yourself "a slave for an hour" for your family. For example, over a one-hour time period, do for your parents or siblings *whatever* they request of you. Do it without questioning them. (They should keep it to menial tasks around the house!) How does it feel to be told what to do over and over again?

94B—Younger and Middle Students

One of the practices of keeping slaves in the days of Rome was to hang a sign around a slave's neck with a list of his or her qualifications on it during a slave trade. That way, slave masters could barter for slaves with specific qualities or skills that they were looking for. Out of paper and string, design for yourself a sign that would describe your strengths. For example, "strong hands, good teeth, works well with numbers." Or, "sings well, obedient, likes to cook." On your sign, use the letter "v" to replace the letter "u" because there was no letter "u" in Latin. It will make the sign look more authentic.

Thanks be to God that our "value" is not dependent on what skills or talents we possess but on the fact that a loving Lord created us.

94C—Older Students

With parental approval, watch the video entitled *Spartacus* starring Kirk Douglas. It is a gripping drama of the life Spartacus led. Some parts of the movie are dramatized for effect rather than based on historical accuracy. Still, I think it's a must-see FOR OLDER STUDENTS. (One scene in the movie clearly shows a slave wearing a sign like the one described in the above activity. Watch for the sign when Tony Curtis, playing the part of a slave, is sent to Crassus.)

THE FIRST TRIUMVIRATE

LESSON 95

Sit back and hold on tight because we are about to launch deep into the complex history of Rome. You have already learned quite a few things about the *Roman Republic*. But our next six or seven lessons will be key to understanding the founding of the more powerful *Roman Empire*.

The interesting part of the rise of Rome really begins with three men. The men were Marcus Licinius Crassus, Pompey the Great, and Julius Caesar. Crassus you have already learned about. He was the rich and powerful Roman who managed to stop Spartacus and the other slaves from their rebellion. Crassus served Rome as a consul and a censor. A consul was like a president who was voted to serve for one year with another consul. A censor was a person who watched the conduct of the Roman Senate. We still use the word "censor" today to refer to those who examine public materials (such as books and the like) and remove any objectionable or forbidden content.

Like Crassus, Pompey the Great also served as a consul to Rome. Pompey (POM pee) became well admired by the Romans for fighting against pirates in the Mediterranean Sea. Pirates had been a serious threat to sailors and traders in the sea until Pompey came along. In just 40 days, Pompey destroyed 1,300 pirate ships without losing any Roman ships! He was also a war hero for conquering the country of Syria in the east.

Before I go on to introduce Julius Caesar, the third man in this lesson, we have to do a little review. If you remember from earlier in our study, the Romans decided a long time ago that they didn't like having one king rule over them. So, they appointed *two* consuls to rule at the same time. That was when they founded the Roman Republic. A "republic" refers to a country without a king. This was the kind of government still found in Rome in the first century before Christ.

The two strongest leaders in Rome about 60 B.C. were Crassus and Pompey. Each was struggling to gain ultimate power. However, there was one guy who just wasn't patient enough to wait for Pompey or Crassus to settle their disputes. That man was Julius Caesar. Through bribes and violence, Caesar cunningly swayed Pompey and Crassus to join a coalition with him. One plus two equals three. So the Roman Republic was then ruled by three men instead of two, making up what has become known in Roman history as the "First Triumvirate." The word "triumvirate" means "rule by three persons or parties."

Three is an odd number, of course, and that just about describes the arrangement of these three men. Each leader was powerful in his own way and probably not one of them completely trusted the other two. To add to the complexity of the situation, Caesar's daughter was married to Pompey! So Caesar and Pompey were "in-laws."

Julius Caesar was a brilliant man on many different levels. He was born in Rome but went to Greece to study philosophy and speech. Before he was elected consul, Caesar served Rome as the director of public works and games. Julius Caesar became very popular in this role because he was willing to spend a lot of money on spectacular entertainment and recreation for the people. He spent so much on entertainment that he went into debt, but the people didn't care.

To further his career even more, Caesar chose to serve Rome as a military general. He went to the land northwest of Italy called Gaul. That is where France is now. For nine years, Caesar fought practically undefeated through Gaul, Germany, and even into Great Britain. Caesar was hungry for land and power. Though he was a military genius, he was also cruel. He attacked village after village across Europe and swallowed them up under his control. Thousands upon thousands lost their lives in trying to stand up against Caesar and his army.

What you will soon learn is that the power of Julius Caesar became frightening. He scared not only the non-Romans that he conquered, but some of the Romans as well. In our next lesson, we will see just how far Julius Caesar got in gaining complete control of the Roman world.

ACTIVITY 95

95A—Younger Students

Pompey was known for dealing with the problem of pirates in the Mediterranean Sea. Did you know that pirates were real? Dress up today like a pirate by rubbing dark makeup on your face for a beard and wrapping a bandana around your head. Add a gold-hoop earring if you can. Hide some "gold" around your house and then make a treasure map to lead someone to it. "Wrinkle" the map a little to make it look old. In the process of hunting for buried treasure, bump into Pompey and pretend to fight him. (Don't hurt each other though!)

95B—Younger and Middle Students

Much of the strength of Rome came from its well-organized army. Turn to the Activity Supplement in the Appendix to find out more information about the structure of the army. Copy and color the chart provided and file it under "Europe: Italy (Ancient Rome)."

95C—Older Students

William Shakespeare loved history. Many of his plays were based on real history. At the library, obtain a copy of Shakespeare's play on Julius Caesar. Read as much of it as possible. Another option would be to view the 1953 video entitled *Julius Caesar*, starring Marlon Brando.

100?–44 B.C.

JULIUS CAESAR

LESSON 96

I have already introduced you to Julius Caesar. But because he was such an incredible man, I want you to learn much more about him. Some people would say he was one of the greatest men who ever lived! It depends on how you define greatness.

You already know that Julius Caesar was one of the three men who made up the First Triumvirate. That was a new system of leadership for Rome. I told you, too, that Caesar had moved to Gaul and other parts of Europe to fight as a general for the Roman army. He was extremely successful although his tactics were nothing to be proud of. A lot of blood was shed for Caesar to be so victorious.

In the last lesson, I told you that even the Romans were beginning to fear Caesar. In fact, when Caesar was ready to return home to Rome, he was told by the Roman Senate not to show up with his army. They told him he could return to Rome only as a private citizen, not as a general or ruler.

At the time of this mandate, Julius Caesar was near the Rubicon. The Rubicon was a stream that ran as a border between Gaul and Italy. If Caesar crossed over the stream with his army, he would essentially be declaring war against Rome itself! What do you think he did? Historians say that Caesar crossed over the water without a second thought. Within minutes he was well on his way toward Rome with the ambition of taking complete control of it. To this day, the expression, "crossing the Rubicon" refers to someone making a strong decision that can't be reversed.

Caesar's defiant act was so threatening to Pompey that he ran right out of Rome. Pompey's wife, who happened to be Caesar's own daughter, had died earlier in childbirth. So the two men, Caesar and Pompey, were no longer willing to pretend to get along. Pompey actually fled to Egypt where he was murdered! Crassus had already died in 53 B.C. This "vacancy" in the Roman government left the

Once Julius Caesar crossed the Rubicon, there was no turning back from his plan to be sole ruler of Rome.

position wide open for Julius Caesar. In 49 B.C. he single-handedly took over as ruler of Rome. It was quite a turning point in the Roman Republic that had never wanted a "king."

Once Caesar was in Rome, he did do some amazing things. Being the brilliant man that he was, Julius Caesar oversaw many improvements in Rome. For one, he saw to it that the calendar, which had been in confusion for awhile, was updated. In the process, Caesar had two more months inserted into the year and renamed another month after himself. (That would be "July," of course. It replaced the month called "Quintiles.")

Even though Caesar had a reputation for being ruthless toward his enemies, he provided good care for the citizens of Rome. He tried to replace dishonest politicians with respectable ones. He also worked hard for the poor people of Rome. He established a system for them to receive free grain. As a speaker and writer, Caesar had few equals. He wrote extensively about his war experiences in Gaul. Most Latin students today are familiar with his works, titled *Seven Commentaries on the Gallic War*.

One of Caesar's downfalls, however, was in the matter of romance. His life story really gets interesting here. It seems that while he was in pursuit of Pompey, who had fled to Egypt, Julius Caesar met the enchanting Cleopatra. Though he was already married, Caesar fell in love with Cleopatra and helped her to secure her throne as queen of Egypt. Even with all their faults, these two made an incredible pair! Cleopatra was rich, powerful, intelligent, and ruthless in her efforts to become queen. Caesar was equally smart, strong, and ambitious. Together they dreamed of ruling the entire world as it was known back then.

One problem, though, was that Caesar began to spend more time in Egypt than in Rome. The mighty leader was failing to be such a great ruler from so far away. You will learn in the next lesson that the Romans had some very mixed feelings about Caesar. Though Caesar had still never called himself a "king," he was acting like one. He arrogantly gave himself the title of "dictator for life." Caesar most enjoyed the term "Imperator," which is how the Roman army addressed him. From that term came the word "emperor." Though Caesar may have had the title of dictator for life, he couldn't have known just what little "life" he had left!

ACTIVITY 96

ALL STUDENTS

Make your Memory Cards for Lessons 94–96. Julius Caesar (49 B.C.) is a date to memorize; highlight the Memory Card.

96A—Younger Students

Re-enact the crossing of the Rubicon. Create a "stream" out of a blue blanket or sheet. Lay it in a doorway between two rooms. Along with some "army men" (toy action figures) and play horses, stand by the stream. Have a messenger inform you of the situation in Rome. If you and your men cross the river instead of turning back, you will be declaring war against Rome! Decide you are willing to fight against Rome itself and cross over the stream. Once you have crossed, though, you cannot go back over the stream and into the room you left. (At least for an hour or so.)

96B—Younger and Middle Students

1. Copy on paper the variations of the name of "Caesar," which are "czar," "tsar," and "kaiser." Using a dictionary, find out which countries use these names to signify a dictator or king.

2. Julius Caesar saw to it that the Roman calendar was updated to be more accurate. Turn to the Activity Supplement in the Appendix for more information on the calendar that you can copy and place in your Student Notebook under "Europe: Italy (Ancient Rome)."

96C—Older Students

1. Have you ever heard of a "c-section" birth? The "c" stands for "cesarean." Supposedly, Julius Caesar was born by surgical rather than natural delivery, hence the name cesarean birth. Research the accuracy of this legend.

2. Investigate for yourself the original works of Julius Caesar. Even Napoleon Bonaparte studied Caesar's *Commentaries*, believing that all great generals should be required to know it.

3. If you like research, try to find out what the famous phrase "Veni, Vidi, Vici" means. Caesar once wrote this in a letter to a friend. Write about it in a few paragraphs and file it under "Europe: Italy (Ancient Rome)."

Wall of Fame

1. *Spartacus (Unknown–71 B.C.)*—Draw chains between his feet and a sword in his hand.

2. *The First Triumvirate (60 B.C.)*—Draw a three-headed "monster" with the names of Crassus, Pompey, and Julius Caesar on each of the heads. Label it underneath as the First Triumvirate.

3. *Julius Caesar (100?–44 B.C.)*—Put a wreath of leaves on his head. **Remember, this is a date to memorize. (You only have to remember the date of 49 B.C.)**

SomeWHERE in Time

One map will cover all three of our lessons this week. On Outline Map 5, "Europe," label and color as suggested:

- Countries: Gaul (green), Italy (red), Spain (orange), Thrace (pink), Africa (brown), Egypt (purple), and Britain (gray)
- Cities: Carthage, Alexandria, Athens, and Rome
- Rivers: Po, Tiber, (the Rubicon is just a stream; find it if you can!)
- Bodies of water (in various shades of blue): Mediterranean Sea, Adriatic Sea, Black Sea, and Aegean Sea

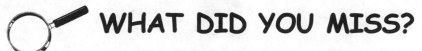

WHAT DID YOU MISS?

Week 32: Exercise

The Chocolate Candy Game. We have played this game before. But I'm changing the rules. You have learned so much more since the last time we tried this quiz.

This time, you get two pieces of candy for every answer you can give within 10 seconds without looking in your notes. If you look in your notes, you only get one piece, but you can take your time to find the answer. If you answer incorrectly or don't even try to look it up, no treat. Pretty simple. (As before, if sugar is off-limits, consider nickels instead.)

I have provided the questions in a quick "Who was _____?" format. Your teacher will have to determine if the answer is reasonable. She may have to look in the book to decide!

1. Who was Tubal-Cain?

2. Who was Gilgamesh?

3. Who was Jacob?

4. Who was Hammurabi?

5. Who was Moses?

6. Who was Amenhotep IV?

7. Who was Ruth?

8. Who was Gideon?

9. Who was Delilah?

10. Who was Eli?

11. Who was Obadiah?

12. Who was Homer?

13. Who was Jonah?

14. Who was Micah?

15. Who was Manasseh?

16. Who was Jeremiah?

17. Who was Habakkuk?

18. Who was Daniel?

19. Who was Abed-Nego?

20. Who was Pythagoras?

21. Who was Confucius?

22. Who was Darius I?

23. Who was Socrates?

24. Who was Ezra?

25. Who was Malachi?

26. Who was Archimedes?

27. Who was Emperor Asoka?

28. Who was Shi Huang Ti?

29. Who was Hannibal?

30. Who was Judas Maccabee?

31. Who was Spartacus?

32. Who was Crassus?

33. Who was Pompey?

34. Who was Julius Caesar?

✓ WHAT DO YOU KNOW?

Pretest 33

Fill in the blanks using the word bank provided below.

1. Julius Caesar was assassinated on the Ides of _____ .

2. Even Caesar's friend _____ was part of the mob that stabbed him to death.

3. The _____ Triumvirate was made up of Octavian, Lepidus, and Mark Antony.

4. Cleopatra was the last of the _____ rulers over Egypt.

5. While in hiding, Cleopatra met Julius Caesar rolled up in a _____ .

6. After Caesar died, Cleopatra married _____ to again unite Egypt and Rome.

7. Herod the _____ was responsible for the killing of many of his own family to keep the throne.

8. Herod remodeled the _____ in Jerusalem to make it even more incredible than Solomon's was.

WORD BANK

Temple	Brutus	carpet	Ptolemy
Second	March	Great	Mark Antony

The Mystery of History

THE SECOND TRIUMVIRATE

LESSON 97

You would think that the Romans would have learned from the First Triumvirate that three men in power can lead to trouble. But it happened again. It is remembered as the Second Triumvirate. First, though, let's look at what happened to Julius Caesar, the one man left from the First Triumvirate.

As you will recall, Caesar was beginning to act a lot like a king. The Romans were still opposed to the idea of one man having ultimate control of their country. But Caesar was really the one person in charge of Rome. He called himself a "dictator for life," and he wasn't cooperating with the Senate. He began to use the senators as more of an advisory board than as the decision-makers they were appointed to be. Though Caesar made some good contributions to Rome, his power was just too threatening to many of the other leaders.

On March 15, 44 B.C., on a windy night called the "Ides of March," Julius Caesar was assassinated. As he nonchalantly strolled into the Senate that evening for a meeting, Caesar was stabbed to death by a group of senators. Sadly, some were his closest friends! One man in particular was named Brutus. In the dramatic play by William Shakespeare on the life of Caesar, Caesar is portrayed as seeing that his friend was part of the killing mob. He uttered, "You, too, Brutus?" before he fell to his death. This phrase has come to refer to a person who betrays a friend.

With the death of Julius Caesar came the birth of the Second Triumvirate. The three men to fill the position were Gaius Octavian, Marcus Lepidus, and Mark Antony. Gaius Octavian, who was just 18 at the time, was actually the great-nephew of Julius Caesar and his adopted son. As revenge for Caesar's death, Octavian had the two men killed who were behind the plot to assassinate Caesar. Octavian then tried to restore order to the Roman world with the help of Antony and Lepidus. These three men became the Second Triumvirate. It was a short-lived union.

Octavian and Mark Antony did not see eye to eye on how to govern Rome. This was awkward considering the fact that Mark Antony had married Octavian's sister. Just as Julius Caesar and Pompey had become "in-laws" by marriage, Antony and Octavian had become in-laws, too. These marriages were probably for political reasons, but they sound more like a soap opera.

Lepidus, the third person in the triumvirate, retired from his position early on, leaving Octavian and Mark Antony to fight over their differences. At one point, the two men simply divided the huge Roman Republic. Octavian took the Western portion of the Republic, and Mark Antony took the East. Antony's division included Egypt, which you will later learn to be quite an important fact.

I do think that war is an ugly thing, but in this case the showdown between Octavian and Mark Antony makes a great story. Before I can tell you how it ends though, you have to learn more about Cleopatra. This daunting queen of Egypt became a big part of the story of Rome—again.

ACTIVITY 97

97A—Younger Students

Make a mosaic.

Materials: One piece of construction paper, tissue paper cut in small pieces, glue

One of the beautiful ways that Romans decorated things was by making mosaics. They skillfully used thousands of little pieces of tile or stone to make pictures. Using block letters, draw your initials on a piece of construction paper. (Your teacher may need to help you.) Create a mosaic by gluing bits of cut tissue paper to cover the letters. Title this paper "Roman Mosaics" and file it in your Student Notebook under "Europe: Italy (Ancient Rome)."

97B—Middle Students

After the assassination of Julius Caesar, the next ruler, Augustus Caesar, decided it would be wise to have well-trained bodyguards. In fact, he wanted them to be more like a small army. He named them the Praetorian Guard. Research these elite soldiers. If it interests you, add to your research the role and qualifications of the bodyguards who protect the president of the United States. When in history have they failed to protect a president from death?

97C—Older Students

Assassinations have long been a part of history. How familiar are you with the assassination stories of Abraham Lincoln and John F. Kennedy? This would be a good time to become acquainted with the names and stories behind these famous murders. They are frequently referred to in literature and the media. If you are lacking in research papers this year, this could be a good one. Include it in your Student Notebook under "North America: United States."

69–30 B.C.

CLEOPATRA

LESSON 98

 Of all the women in history, I find Cleopatra to be one of the most fascinating. It is not that she was a particularly good person. On the contrary, Cleopatra was quite possibly one of the most manipulative women ever to be a queen! Nonetheless, I find her life story quite intriguing.

First of all, Cleopatra lived in Alexandria, Egypt, but wasn't an Egyptian at all. Her father was one of the last rulers from the line of Ptolemy. If you remember, the Ptolemies were one of the four ruling families to take over the empire of Alexander the Great after his sudden death. The Ptolemies were of Macedonian descent, so Cleopatra might have been light-skinned with blue eyes. No one knows for sure what she looked like. Some say she was not particularly beautiful, but, according to Plutarch, an ancient historian, "the contact of her presence was irresistible."

Living in a busy port like Alexandria, Cleopatra was exposed to many things as a young princess. She was able to speak several languages. Plutarch also wrote this about her.

The Mystery of History

"It was a pleasure merely to hear the sound of her voice, with which, like an instrument of many strings, she could pass from one language to another; so that there were few of the barbarian nations that she answered by an interpreter; to most of them she spoke herself, as to the Ethiopians, Troglodytes, Hebrews, Arabians, Syrians, Medes, Parthians, and many others, whose language she had learnt."[1]

The family life of Cleopatra was somewhat unusual. Being a princess must have led to a very different way of life. Her relationships to her brothers and sisters were spoiled by the fear of who might kill the other one for the sake of one day having the throne. Cleopatra's mother died when she was young and her father was not a strong king. The siblings were right in knowing that one day, one of them would probably be king or queen.

However, the people of Egypt were tired of having an outside family rule over them. Plots and schemes to assassinate Cleopatra's father, Ptolemy XI Auletes, were rampant around the kingdom. At one point, Auletes decided to call upon the powers of Rome to protect him against his own kingdom of Egyptians. The leading "power of Rome" at the time was none other than Julius Caesar. (I told you this story was interesting!) Though the Egyptians weren't eager for Rome to take any control over them at all, the Ptolemies were desperate to have the protection and power of Rome behind them.

Amidst all the turmoil of the kingdom, Cleopatra must have been watching for her opportunity. At age 18 she managed to become queen by marrying one of her brothers! He was murdered, and she married her other brother. He also died suspiciously. It was a fragile situation, and she recognized that the best way for her to keep the position would be to use the Romans. She did exactly that. After much strife between her and her siblings, Cleopatra at age 21 pulled off a very unusual introduction to Julius Caesar. (He was in his early fifties.) As the story goes, Cleopatra had herself delivered to Caesar in a rolled-up carpet! Still in fear for her life, she smuggled her way into this meeting with Caesar in the carpet to ask for his help. Can you imagine the face of Julius Caesar as she rolled out in front of him and landed on the floor?

I guess Julius Caesar was rather impressed with this lively demonstration of her determination to be queen. Caesar not only helped Cleopatra secure the throne of Egypt for good, he also fell in love with her. They never married but maintained a relationship for years while living in Egypt. Just imagine the union of ambition they created together. Egypt had wealth, and Rome had power. Side by side, Julius Caesar and Cleopatra must have believed they were invincible. They even had a child together who, Cleopatra hoped, would be an heir to their joined kingdoms.

When Julius Caesar was suddenly assassinated, the dream of world power for

Cleopatra was well known for her extravagance, even in the way she traveled. This drawing depicts one of her luxurious barges.

Cleopatra died too. What would become of her without the Romans? Would her son be accepted as an

---

1. Plutarch quotes from Kristiana Gregory, *The Royal Diaries: Cleopatra VII, Daughter of the Nile.* New York: Scholastic, Inc., 1999; p. 182.

heir to the throne of Rome or Egypt? And what about the Second Triumvirate that had formed after Caesar's death? These were the questions facing the queen of Egypt. But not for long.

It so happened that when Octavian and Mark Antony split the Roman Republic into the East and West, Mark Antony became overseer of Egypt. This gave him the opportunity to visit Cleopatra himself. Whatever it was that Cleopatra did to bring Julius Caesar under her spell, she also did to Mark Antony. He fell desperately in love with her. By all appearances, it was true love between Antony and Cleopatra, but it is hard not to assume there were some other motives on Cleopatra's part. She now had another Roman man in her life with whom to pursue the dream of ruling the world.

Cleopatra and Mark Antony married in Egyptian fashion and had three children, including a set of twins. However, their ambitions were short-lived as well. I'll explain their fate in the lesson after next. We need to check in on Israel first. Very important things were developing there.

ACTIVITY 98

98A—Younger Students

I think it is humorous that Cleopatra met Julius Caesar in a rolled-up carpet. Using a beach towel as a carpet, re-enact the scene if you have some brothers or someone else who can carry you into the room all "rolled up." Be sure you can breathe! While you are at it, you might want to research what kind of clothes Egyptian queens would have worn. Do your best to make up a costume.

98B—Middle Students

For supplemental reading, obtain a copy of the book referred to in the footnote earlier—*The Royal Diaries: Cleopatra VII, Daughter of the Nile* by Kristiana Gregory.

The book covers Cleopatra's life as a young woman before she met Julius Caesar. If you are a girl, pretend you are adding a page or chapter to the diary of Cleopatra and describe what it was like to meet Julius Caesar. Since it is fictitious, it will be up to you to decide if she really loved Caesar or if she saw him as a way to become powerful.

If you are a boy, write a page from the diary of Julius Caesar as if you just met Cleopatra for the first time when she rolled out of the carpet. Do you think he laughed or was shocked? You decide how to write the diary page.

98C—Middle and Older Students

1. With parental approval and discretion, watch the video version of *Cleopatra*, starring Elizabeth Taylor. I found the movie to be historically very accurate, though obviously some leeway was taken in Hollywood fashion to add to the drama.

   Please note, however, that we have not yet studied the events that encompass the second half of the movie. You may choose to save the last part of the movie until our lesson on the Battle of Actium. It is almost a four-hour movie anyway.

   Either way, watch the movie with a critical eye for historical accuracy. On paper, jot down at least eight things you observe that were based on indisputable fact. For example, the movie opens with Julius Caesar grieving over the death of Pompey. That is a fact! Pompey was indeed beheaded in Egypt as portrayed.

2. Research the palace of Cleopatra that has recently been excavated. Interestingly, most of it is now underwater because the city of Alexandria is located right on the edge of the sea. Find out all you can about how the queen might have lived. Write about it and file it under "Africa: Egypt."

37 B.C.

HEROD THE GREAT

LESSON 99

I know I've left you hanging from our last lesson with the story of Cleopatra and Mark Antony. But remember that in this history course I'm trying to give you a broad view of people and events in the exact order that they happened. I believe it helps us to better see the hand of God at work through the lives of individuals. We now look more closely at Herod the Great who was taking over Judah in 37 B.C. Let's see just how he fits into *The Mystery of History*.

In review, the last time we looked at Judah, Judas Maccabee had bravely defended his country against the evil Antiochus Epiphanes. Remember that guy? He had defiantly placed Greek idols and a pig in the Temple of Jerusalem. Then the miracle of Hanukkah occurred when the Jews restored the Temple for worship. Well, after all of that the Maccabeans managed to keep Judah free from the rule of other countries for about 100 years. They enjoyed the freedom to worship God in the way they had been taught.

Eventually, however, the aggressive Romans began to look at Judah, or "Palestine," as another place for them to conquer. ("Palestine" is the term most used to describe Judah after the Babylonian Captivity. I will call Judah by that name from now on.) By 63 B.C., the Romans were successful in conquering Palestine in much the same way that they captured the rest of the Mediterranean world. The Romans were cruel and harsh in their style of leadership and remained unwelcome in Palestine for several hundred years.

God had a plan though. He was quite aware of the Roman rule over His beloved city of Jerusalem. He has always been in control of the rise of leaders, both good and evil. In order to fulfill the prophecies of the birth of Jesus, I believe certain men were "put in place" in history. One of those men was Herod the Great.

Herod the Great had an interesting upbringing because his mother was an Arabian princess and yet his father was from Judea. In fact, in recent years archaeologists have discovered the ancient city of Petra where Herod's mother was from. As a young man, Herod was well educated in the classic Greek style. In time he rose to be a governor over Galilee. He inherited the position from his family.

Herod the Great went to great lengths to expand and renovate the Temple, which later was visited by Jesus Himself.

By 37 B.C., Herod the Great wanted more. With permission from Octavian and Mark Antony, Herod the Great took over all of Palestine after a three-year struggle with the ruling family of the area, the Hasmonians. Herod even acquired the title "King of the Jews." Though the Jews hated him, Herod managed to rule over Palestine for the next 34 years.

Herod was so evil that he killed off nearly every member of his family one by one. You see, he had married a Hasmonian princess to try to keep peace with the family he had overthrown. However, his marriage drove him toward near madness! Though he loved his wife, he couldn't trust her or the children he had with her. That is why they were eventually all murdered. He also killed the mother and the brother of his own wife. His acts of cruelty added to his horrible reputation.

The Wailing Wall (or Western Wall) in Jerusalem is all that's left of the Temple. It is still a sacred spot to the Jews who visit there to pray.

In order to find some favor with the Jews, Herod ordered that the Temple in Jerusalem be remodeled to be even more spectacular than Solomon's was. And that it was. Sprawling over 35 acres, the new Temple was magnificent. Stones as large as 60 to 80 tons were laid to precisely fit into one another. Even the high priests themselves were trained in the skills of carpentry and masonry so that they could go into the Holy of Holies and remodel without upsetting the worship that went on there. (According to custom, only high priests were allowed in these special places.)

By my own speculation, it gives me chills that the most glorious temple site ever built for the Jews was the one that God Himself would visit through Jesus Christ. He was dedicated there as a baby; He taught there as a boy; and He preached there as a grown man. I'm glad it was remodeled for His visit.

This one gesture of refurbishing the Temple was probably the only "nice" thing Herod ever did for the Jews. And it *still* impacts them. On the news, have you ever seen the place called the Wailing Wall? It is a sacred place where thousands and thousands of Jews to this day go to pray. This wall is the last that remains of the Temple that Herod rebuilt. It is no wonder why it is so meaningful to the devout Jew today.

Besides the Temple, Herod the Great orchestrated some other incredible building sites. He was the mastermind behind the building of Caesarea, a port city he named after Augustus Caesar. Jesus Himself spent time in this city. It was an incredible place because Herod had to outsmart nature to keep the ocean from tearing it apart. He found a way to pour concrete underwater to fortify the city. Concrete had been used in Rome by this time period, but underwater concrete was very new to the Middle East.

Now think for a minute of what you might already know about Herod the Great. He was the same evil Herod who in the New Testament set up the three wise men to help him find the baby Jesus. The Bible says that Herod wanted to destroy Jesus because he heard that He was going to be a "king." It was because of Herod's fear of this child that the angel of the Lord told Mary and Joseph to flee to Egypt to hide. And they did.

The Mystery of History

But guess what? God was in control of all these events. Hundreds of years before Mary and Joseph took Jesus to Egypt to hide from Herod, the prophet Hosea said, "Out of Egypt I called My son." (Matt. 2:15; Hos. 11:1) God knew long before then that Jesus, His Son, would be there in Egypt because of Herod's paranoia. That is a fancy word for fear.

It was just sometime later that Herod the Great proceeded to show his cruelest side yet. When he realized that the wise men were not going to lead him to Jesus as he had hoped, Herod ordered that all the Jewish baby boys in Bethlehem were to be killed! It was a horrendous tragedy. Every boy in Bethlehem two years and younger was murdered. The act has been referred to as the "Massacre of the Innocents."

Herod was desperate to do anything to prevent the Christ child from growing up and being a king. But even those actions were a fulfillment of prophecy! Jeremiah said, "A voice was heard in Ramah, lamentation, weeping, and great mourning, Rachel weeping for her children, refusing to be comforted because they were no more." (Matt. 2:18; Jer. 31:15) Look for it yourself in your Bible. It is another reminder that the words of the prophets of God always come true!

Herod's last days were not exactly peaceful ones. Before he died, he often retreated to an incredible palace named Masada. It was a beautiful rock fortress built atop a mesa that rose up in the middle of the desert. Much like Herod's own desolate character, his palace was isolated. He probably retreated there out of his own paranoia that he would be killed anywhere else.

Strange diseases finally overcame Herod. He experienced fever, intense itching, tumors in his feet, worms in his organs, and pains all over his body. However, despite the elaborate funeral he had, his tomb has never been found. Even in death, he seemed to be fearful of others and had his body hidden.

In closing, note that there were other men named Herod in the New Testament. But there never was another in Judea as power crazed as Herod the Great. The Romans may have thought they were powerful on their own accord, but I believe that God was working through them to prepare the world for His coming. How could anyone back then even dream that the Lord Himself was about to visit?

ACTIVITY 99

ALL STUDENTS

Make your Memory Cards for Lessons 97–99.

99A—Younger and Middle Students

Read together Matthew 2:1–12. Herod the Great is well known from the story of the three wise men who sought to worship Jesus. Can you name the kinds of gifts that the three wise men brought to Jesus? Did you know there are special meanings to these gifts? The gold would symbolize a gift fit for a king. Gold was also symbolic of righteousness. Frankincense was used by the Israelites as something to burn when they gave sacrifices to God. Jesus became a great sacrifice when He died for our sins. Myrrh was used as an ingredient in embalming people after they died. It helped to preserve the body from decaying. We know that the body of Jesus never decayed because He rose from the dead! All these gifts were symbols of what would happen to Jesus.

In the Activity Supplement in the Appendix, find directions for how to make three Christmas tree ornaments to symbolize the gold, frankincense, and myrrh from the wise men.

99B—Middle Students

In the story of Herod, angels were involved in warning Joseph and Mary about the plan to kill Jesus. Angels are fascinating beings to study. Using a Bible concordance, investigate other angel stories in the Bible. Look specifically for situations when they were used by God to warn people of danger. Write down on paper your findings of at least three angel accounts that are worth remembering. I think it is great to be reminded of the role angels play in helping us.

99C—Middle and Older Students

Research the practice of modern Jews in their pilgrimage to the Wailing Wall and their worship there. It is also referred to as the Western Wall. It was actually part of the Temple mount wall as rebuilt by Herod. Look for television footage of this location. Add pictures to your research if possible.

TAKE ANOTHER LOOK!

Review 33: Lessons 97–99

Wall of Fame

1. *The Second Triumvirate (44 B.C.)*—Create another three-headed "monster" and write in the names of Lepidus, Antony, and Octavian.

2. *Cleopatra (69–30 B.C.)*—Color her in gold. Add glitter to her dress. (I would not put her on the timeline at the time of her birth but rather toward the end of her life.)

3. *Herod the Great (37 B.C.)*—Put a knife in his hand as unfortunately he is probably best remembered for the Massacre of the Innocents and the killing of his own family members.

SomeWHERE in Time

1. Younger and Middle Students: On a map of the Mediterranean, look for the city of Rome and the city of Alexandria in Egypt. Notice the distance between the two. With your finger, trace the sea route that Julius Caesar or Mark Antony would have taken to visit Cleopatra. Her palace was in Alexandria.

2. What are the latitude and longitude of Jerusalem? What is the climate of this important city? Familiarize yourself with the city and the location of the Western Wall. Many current events revolve around this historic city.

WHAT DID YOU LEARN?

Week 33: *Quiz*

I. Matching. Match the following items by placing the correct letter next to the number.

_____ 1. First day of Creation   a. Xia

_____ 2. Creators of cuneiform writing   b. Crete

_____ 3. Means "confusion"   c. Babel

_____ 4. Where the Minoans lived   d. Sumerians

_____ 5. First recorded dynasty of China e. Day and night

_____ 6. Protected Hebrew spies   f. Ramses II

_____ 7. Pharaoh of Later New Kingdom   g. Rahab

II. Fill in the Blanks. (There is no word bank this time!)

1. During the Zhou dynasty, the Chinese believed that a _____ of Heaven had made them prosperous and that it should be honored with right living.

2. As a young boy, _____ went to work in the temple with Eli, as his mother Hannah had promised he would.

3. Solomon wrote _____ different books of the Old Testament.

4. The Phoenicians had mastered the ability to make a beautiful dye from a _____.

5. _____ has been nicknamed the fiery prophet for the miracles God worked through him.

6. Obadiah preached to the descendants of _____, who were called the Edomites.

7. The Book of _____ in the Old Testament is a literary masterpiece and closely resembles the Bible itself by its chapter divisions and content.

III. Multiple Choice. Circle the correct answer for each question.

1. The strong city of Nineveh was destroyed by _____ as the prophets foretold.
   a. an earthquake
   b. a flood
   c. fire
   d. famine

2. _____ of Babylonia first invaded Jerusalem in 605 B.C. It took three times to completely subdue the country.
   a. Belshazzar
   b. Sennacherib
   c. Ashurbanipal
   d. Nebuchadnezzar

3. _____ of the Old Testament had visions that predicted the four great empires of the Babylonians, the Medes-Persians, the Greeks, and the Romans.
   a. Jeremiah
   b. Isaiah
   c. Daniel
   d. Elisha

4. Shadrach, Meshach, and Abed-Nego were given the names of _____ gods.
   a. Babylonian
   b. Minoan
   c. Sumerian
   d. Egyptian

5. Darius I rediscovered and used the decree of _____ in order to help the Jews fight off their enemies and rebuild the Temple.
   a. Moses
   b. Cyrus the Great
   c. Hammurabi
   d. Gideon

6. _____ has been remembered as the "father of history" for his early efforts to document events.
   a. Hippocrates
   b. Hammurabi
   c. Herodotus
   d. Howard Carter

7. _____ was very gracious to the Jews and allowed Ezra to return to Judah with great treasures.
   a. Herod
   b. Mordecai
   c. Xerxes
   d. Artaxerxes

IV. True or False? Circle your answer.

1. Aristotle was the pupil of Plato and the teacher of Alexander the Great.   T F

2. Archimedes built the Pharos of Alexandria.   T F

3. The Septuagint was the first translation of the Old Testament
into Aramaic.   T F

4. In the First Punic War, Hannibal was killed by wild elephants.   T F

5. Spartacus led thousands of slaves in revolt against the Romans.   T F

6. Julius Caesar was part of the Second Triumvirate.   T F

7. Cleopatra was the last ruler of the Ptolemies in Egypt.   T F

V. Answer the questions in complete sentences. Use a separate sheet of paper if necessary.

1. What special secret did the Chinese keep for thousands of years and how did it help them economically?

2. What evidence is there today that people lived in North America hundreds of years before Christ?

3. If you lived during the Golden Age of Athens, what kind of things might you be good at? (I'm looking for examples of the achievements of the Greeks during this time period.)

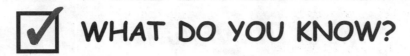 WHAT DO YOU KNOW?

Pretest 34

True or False? Circle your answer.

1. Mark Antony married Cleopatra in Egyptian fashion.   T   F

2. Cleopatra liked to dress like the goddess Isis.   T   F

3. Defeated by Octavian, Cleopatra committed suicide using a dagger.   T   F

4. Augustus Caesar was the son of Julius Caesar and Cleopatra.   T   F

5. Augustus means "exalted one."   T   F

6. John the Baptist's father was named Gabriel.   T   F

7. John had the privilege of baptizing Jesus in the Jordan River.   T   F

8. John was imprisoned and beheaded for not paying taxes.   T   F

THE BATTLE OF ACTIUM

LESSON 100

We will now go back to the complex but intriguing study of the Romans. While Herod the Great was establishing himself in Palestine, the Second Triumvirate was starting to crumble.

Our story goes back to the romance of Mark Antony and Cleopatra. If you remember, Octavian and Mark Antony had decided to split the large Roman Republic into two areas to govern. This split is where the union between Antony and Cleopatra developed since Egypt was under Antony's control. Octavian was the great-nephew of Julius Caesar, and Mark Antony had been Caesar's friend. Together, Octavian and Antony were trying to rebuild the Roman government. But they didn't really trust one another.

To make Antony look bad, Octavian led the Romans to believe that Antony had betrayed them by marrying an Egyptian queen. Octavian felt that Antony wasn't being loyal to Rome because he was spending too much time in Egypt, wining and dining like an Egyptian. At festivals, Antony was said to even dress like the Egyptians. Besides all of that, in marrying Cleopatra, Antony rejected his Roman wife who was Octavian's sister! The whole situation was a mess.

Octavian also convinced the Romans that Cleopatra was against them and was trying to become the queen over Rome. Maybe she was. Either way, Antony must have really been in love with Cleopatra to even appear to shirk his Roman responsibilities and to be so loyal to Egypt.

Over time, the arrangement between Octavian and Antony just wasn't working. In the fall of 33 B.C., Octavian declared war against Mark Antony. This would be yet another civil war because Roman would be fighting against Roman. After the violence of the First Triumvirate, the Roman people were growing weary of the bloodshed.

The ultimate battle between the two men was fought at sea. It has been remembered as the Battle of Actium. Mark Antony had, of course, the support of Cleopatra. All three of these leaders and their navies were in their warships the day of the battle. But Octavian's men were clearly fighting smarter.

History records that as Octavian's ships appeared to overtake Antony's, Cleopatra panicked. She and her fleet of 60 ships started to sail away in fear and despair. To make matters worse, Mark Antony saw or heard of her ship leaving. In a decision he probably lived to regret, Antony abandoned his own men who were fighting for him to sail after Cleopatra! This act of abandonment didn't go over well with those left behind. Antony's decision to leave the battle was really the end of Antony's power. The rumor of Mark Antony being more loyal to Cleopatra than to Rome was showing itself to be true.

Though Antony and Cleopatra survived the escape from the Battle of Actium, their lives were not to last much longer. Octavian hunted them both down. Almost like the story of Romeo and Juliet, Antony thought at one point that Cleopatra was dead and so he tried to kill himself. But, before he died, he was taken to her side. There, Mark Antony died in the arms of his beloved Cleopatra. She in turn committed suicide rather than live to face Octavian.

In much the way that Cleopatra's life was dramatic, her death was as well. In life she often portrayed and dressed herself as the Egyptian goddess Isis. It is said that she went to her tomb elaborately dressed like Isis. There in her tomb Cleopatra and her lifelong attendants allowed a snake to poison them with its deadly venom. We may not be able to imagine the great sense of hopelessness this woman must have felt to take her life at just 39 years of age. Though she had once captured the love of two of the greatest Roman leaders who ever lived, she was going to die. And though she lavishly ruled over one of the richest countries in the world, she was going to her grave by her own hand. Stooping to death seems so far from what she had dared to dream.

Though the story makes a great script, remember that it was a true and tragic event. I wish that Cleopatra could have lived longer so that she might have come to know the true King who was soon to demonstrate real power through the resurrection. I'm referring to Jesus Christ of course who was to be born just 30 years after Cleopatra's tragic death.

ACTIVITY 100

100A—Younger Students

Mark Antony was accused by his fellow Romans of beginning to eat and drink like an Egyptian. What did the Egyptians eat? Follow the list of foods in the Activity Supplement in the Appendix and create an Egyptian meal.

100B—Middle Students

Before Cleopatra committed suicide, she supposedly did some research to find out which snake would kill a person the fastest with the least amount of pain. Most historians think she died from the bite of an asp or a horned viper. Investigate the asp and the viper in an encyclopedia. Write a short report on these poisonous snakes and include pictures of them. File under "Africa: Egypt (Ancient)."

100C—Older Students

1. If you have not yet watched the video *Cleopatra* with Elizabeth Taylor or viewed its conclusion, do so over the weekend. As suggested before, list at least eight historical facts found in the film.

2. Research the Egyptian goddess named Isis. Cleopatra often portrayed herself as this goddess either because she believed she was her descendant or she wanted the people to view her as having the power of a goddess. Isis was known for three symbols—one on her head, one in her left hand, and one in her right. Try to find out what these three symbols were and include them in your report with a sketch of each. Search for drawings of Cleopatra with any of these symbols. File your report under "Africa: Egypt."

AUGUSTUS CAESAR AND THE ROMAN EMPIRE

LESSON 101

You have already been introduced to Augustus Caesar. But you learned of him by the name of Octavian. That is the same Octavian of the Second Triumvirate who defeated both Mark Antony and Cleopatra. At the end of this lesson you may be surprised to learn where else you may have heard the name of Augustus (probably many times).

In review, Augustus (Octavian) was the great-nephew of Julius Caesar. Caesar had written in his will that Octavian would be his adopted heir. Octavian was born in Rome but spent much of his youth in a Greek colony. It was against his mother's wishes that he move to Rome upon the death of Julius Caesar. He was just 18. Perhaps his mother was afraid that he would wind up murdered like many of the other Roman leaders. Regardless, Octavian was a smart, ambitious young man and jumped at the opportunity to fill the shoes of Caesar.

As you know, Octavian formed a union with Mark Antony and Lepidus called the Second Triumvirate. It came to an end at the death of Mark Antony. (Lepidus had retired earlier.) Just like Julius Caesar at the end of the First Triumvirate, Octavian suddenly found himself the lone ruler over all of Rome. He was just 32 years old. But Octavian learned from Caesar's mistakes and did some things very differently.

One of the main differences between the two men was in the way they treated the Senate. Remember that it was the senators who had murdered Caesar on the Ides of March. They didn't trust him as a dictator. Octavian, though, made friends with the senators. They welcomed his leadership. Strangely though, Octavian was, in the end, as much of a dictator as Caesar had ever hoped to be. But by 27 B.C., the Romans were ready to accept it. Octavian had the power to veto laws, to declare war without the Senate's approval, to put men in office, and to rule over the armies. He was even called the Pontifus Maximus, which meant that he was the high priest of their religion. And somehow it all worked beautifully.

In a wise and humble way, Octavian declined the title of king or dictator. The Senate decided to declare him "emperor" and gave him the name Augustus, which means "exalted one." In respect for Julius Caesar, he retained the name Caesar as well. Personally, Augustus liked to be addressed as the "princeps," or "first citizen," of the land. It sounded noble and nonthreatening. And I suppose it was because, for more than 40 years, "Augustus Caesar" (as I'll now refer to him) managed to rule over the great Roman Empire and usher in a

After winning the Battle of Actium, Augustus Caesar became the first Roman emperor. Shortly after, he declared that a census be taken. This resulted in Mary and Joseph traveling to Bethlehem, where Jesus was born.

long period of peace and prosperity. Young Augustus proved to be a brilliant leader and someone that Rome could trust.

Do you recall my earlier mention of the Roman Empire? It was under Augustus Caesar that the Roman Republic became the Roman Empire, and Augustus became the first true emperor of Rome. If you remember way back in this book, at one time Rome was only a city in Italy. In fact, Rome is still a city in Italy. But at the time of Augustus, the term "Rome" was often used to refer to the entire empire that spread over most of Europe. The Roman Empire was huge in comparison to other countries and became extremely powerful.

In fact, the time period called the Pax Romana occurred during the reign of Augustus. "Pax Romana" means the "Peace of Rome." Much like the Golden Age of Athens under Pericles, the Romans flourished during the Pax Romana. They were free to grow culturally while they were at peace. I've told you before that nations often flourish during times of peace when people are not so stressed out over survival. It just makes sense. Though the Roman Empire lasted for many hundreds of years, the 200 years of the Pax Romana stand out in history as being special. Seldom in history do we see such a long time go by without major war.

Under Augustus, many public buildings such as temples, bathhouses, and theaters were built. The boundaries of Rome were more clearly set following natural land divisions that were easy to guard. Great waterways and aqueducts were built to provide good water to the larger cities. In the whole empire there lived about 80 million people! And they were at peace, generally speaking.

So, now you have the whole story of how the Roman Empire came to be. It took several lessons to get there, but I hope you enjoyed them. The changeover from a republic to an empire was not nearly as dreadful as the people once thought it might be.

In closing, though, I need to tell you where you may have already heard of Augustus many, many times. Open your Bible to the familiar passages of Luke 2:1–7.

"And it came to pass in those days that a decree went out from Caesar Augustus that all the world should be registered . . . And Joseph also went up from Galilee, out of the city of Nazareth, into Judea, to the city of David, which is called Bethlehem, because he was of the house and lineage of David to be registered with Mary, his betrothed wife, who was with child. So it was that while they were there, the days were completed for her to be delivered. And she brought forth her firstborn Son and wrapped Him in swaddling cloths, and laid Him in a manger, because there was no room for them in the inn."

Isn't this scripture just a reminder that God is in control of every aspect of history? It was prophesied in Micah 5:2 that Jesus would be born in Bethlehem. This prophecy came to pass when Augustus wanted to count all his people. That meant that everyone had to travel back to his city of origin. In the course of that long journey by donkey, Jesus was born to Mary and laid in a manger IN THE CITY OF BETHLEHEM. The story is just incredible!

ACTIVITY 101

ALL STUDENTS

This is a date to memorize: Augustus Caesar and the Roman Empire (27 B.C.).

101A—Younger Students

The wealthier Romans like Augustus were famous for taking long, luxurious baths. They built special, beautiful buildings with lots of rooms where men could gather for bathing and talking about politics and other matters while slaves would attend to their needs. The men could bathe in cold water, hot water, get an oil massage, or just relax at swimming. They sometimes used olive oil as soap.

Pretend to be a Roman citizen tonight and take an extra long bath. Perhaps someone could first give you a back massage with olive oil. Then when you dip in the tub, have your favorite drink served to you along with some grapes. Last, have a warm towel handed to you when you're done! Throw a sheet around yourself like a toga and have your picture taken for your Student Notebook.

If you visited Rome today, you would still find the ruins of some of these bathhouses. Who could blame them for indulging in that kind of luxury!

101B—Middle Students

The health of a civilization can be measured somewhat by how well people handle clean water and wastewater. The Romans were masters at channeling water to and away from their cities. They built vast aqueducts that carried water for miles and miles. In fact, the aqueducts may have been responsible for carrying as much as 200 million gallons of water every day.[1] Some of the structures are still standing.

In a resource book, find pictures of aqueducts such as the famous Pont du Gard in France. Sketch it as best as you can or photocopy it and file it in your Student Notebook under "Europe: Italy (Ancient Rome)." Where does your water come from?

101C—Older Students

Throughout this curriculum, I have made reference to the lineage of Christ and we have attempted to trace it on the timeline. But, on paper, list the ancestors of Jesus Christ from Abraham to Joseph, as found in Matthew, Chapter 1. This may seem tedious but the lineage of Jesus was prophesied as being from the house of David. Notice too that the Bible says, in Matthew 1:17, that there was a pattern of 14 generations between certain men. Highlight these men in yellow on your list. Also, circle the men we have studied in this curriculum thus far.

Second, I want you to study and list out the genealogy in Luke 3:23–38. Luke gives us an account all the way back to Adam! It is an amazing record. *Today's Dictionary of the Bible* (Bethany House Publishers) states that the two accounts of Matthew and Luke differ somewhat because one traces the link between Joseph and Jesus and the other traces the link from Mary to Jesus. (Both Mary and Joseph are descendants of David). Isaiah clearly prophesies that Jesus would be a blood descendant of David. That proves itself to be true through Mary because Joseph was the "adopted" father of Jesus, not a blood relative.

I just thought I would explain why these seemingly boring lists are actually quite fascinating.

---

1. Don Nardo, *Life in Ancient Rome.* San Diego: Lucent Books, 1997; p. 42.

JOHN THE BAPTIST

LESSON 102

History has certainly moved along hasn't it? From creation, to the Egyptians, to the Israelites, to the Greeks, and to the Romans, we have seen God's hand at work. Now we are entering into the study of the greatest person who ever lived, Jesus Christ. God in His sovereign plan wanted to make sure that people knew who He was. So, before He entered the world, He sent a man to prepare the way before Him. That man was John the Baptist.

As you may already know, John the Baptist was no ordinary man. Jesus said of him in Matthew 11:11, "I say to you, among those born of women there has not risen one greater than John the Baptist." What an incredible endorsement from God Himself!

What we know of John is very interesting. His father was a priest named Zacharias and his mother was named Elizabeth. The Bible says that they were godly people who kept the Lord's commandments. However, at a very old age and with no children, an unusual thing happened to them. An angel named Gabriel visited Zacharias while he was in the Temple. The angel explained to Zacharias that he and Elizabeth would have a very special son who they should name John.

At first, Zacharias didn't believe it. Because of this disbelief, Gabriel said that Zacharias would become mute until his son was born. That means that he couldn't speak. What a difficult thing to live with at such an exciting time!

Just as foretold, Zacharias didn't speak a single word until John was born. But once he spoke, he became a true prophet for God. Luke 1:67–80 gives us the beautiful words Zacharias spoke when he was finally given the opportunity. You should stop and read them now.

John never let his parents down in fulfilling the mission God said he was created for. Luke 3:2 tells us that "the word of God came to John the son of Zacharias in the wilderness. And he went into all the region around the Jordan, preaching a baptism of repentance for the remission of sins."

What is just amazing is the fact that Isaiah prophesied hundreds of years before this time about John the Baptist and his message. Isaiah said, "The voice of one crying in the wilderness: Prepare the way of the Lord, make His paths straight." (Isa. 40:3–5; Luke 3:4) There it is again, another evidence of fulfilled prophecy.

As it was proclaimed, John the Baptist started his preaching right out in the desert. He spoke in a powerful style like that of the prophets in the Old Testament. It is written of John that he dressed in plain clothes made of camel hair and ate only locusts and wild honey. He must have reminded the Judeans of the rugged prophet, Elijah.

John didn't speak lightly to the crowds that would listen to him. He told them in sharp words that they needed to change their hearts and bear real fruit. John taught that the people not only needed to keep the law, but that they needed to share their possessions and not be selfish. He also explained that "One mightier than I is coming whose sandal strap I am not worthy to loose. He will baptize you with the Holy Spirit and with fire." (Luke 3:16) You already know who John was talking about. He was referring to Jesus.

John lived to see his own prophecy come true. I suppose that maybe the greatest day of John's life was the afternoon that Jesus Himself came to him at the Jordan River to be baptized. The Bible says that when Jesus rose from the water, the Holy Spirit descended on Him in the form of a dove and God spoke from heaven these beautiful words, "You are My beloved Son; in You I am well pleased." (Luke 3:22)

Though John was privileged to know Jesus the Messiah personally, he didn't have an easy life. In fact, John was thrown into prison by Herod. It was not Herod the Great though, for he was already dead. It was Herod Antipas, the son of Herod the Great, who threw John into prison.

The reason for the lockup was not particularly because of John's ministry in the wilderness, but it was because of other truths that he spoke. You see, Herod Antipas had an immoral relationship with his wife. They were related and should not have married. John preached the truth to Herod Antipas about this matter. His boldness cost him his life.

The wife of Herod Antipas, named Herodias, schemed a way for John to be executed. Sadly, Antipas made a mockery of John and had his head served on a platter at a big party. How tragic it was to end the life of God's special prophet in this horrible manner.

Remember, though, that it had been about 400 years since the last prophet of God had spoken. The people weren't used to such strong preaching. I imagine there were many people who didn't understand exactly what John's prophecy about Jesus meant. They were soon to find out that God had a more glorious plan for the world than anyone had ever imagined.

ACTIVITY 102

ALL STUDENTS

Make your Memory Cards for Lessons 100–102. Highlight and memorize the name and date of Augustus Caesar and the Roman Empire (27 B.C.).

102A—Younger Students

John's father, Zacharias, was unable to speak for a long time. We call that being "mute." Do you know anyone who cannot speak? Some people use sign language to overcome the inability to communicate. Some can't speak because they are deaf.

Pretend for an hour that you are mute. Communicate using sign language you might know or just use gestures. It won't be easy! Imagine all that Zacharias wanted to be able to say but couldn't.

If it interests you, look in an encyclopedia for a sign language alphabet. Learn your name. Photocopy the alphabet and place it in your Student Notebook under "Asia: Israel." Title it "Zacharias Becomes Mute."

102B—Younger and Middle Students

Make an edible locust!

Materials: Vienna (canned) sausages, canned potato sticks, mustard, apples, honey

1. Use the Vienna sausage for a body.
2. Take six short potato sticks and insert them into the sides of the body as if they were legs.
3. Slice two thin pieces of apple for wings. Keep them thick enough at one end to insert a toothpick.
4. Attach the wings to the body. The locust may need to lie on its side at this point.
5. Use mustard to create the look of two little eyes.
6. Drizzle honey on your plate because John ate locusts and wild honey.

7. Take a picture before you eat them! File it later under "Asia: Israel." Title the page "John the Baptist Eats Locusts and Wild Honey."

Eat and appreciate the fact that most of us don't have to eat bugs!

102C—Younger, Middle, and Older Students

Have you been baptized? If you are young and you have been baptized, photocopy your baptismal certificate and place it in your Student Notebook under the continent and country where you were baptized. That will probably be in "North America: The United States."

Middle and Older Students: Use a concordance and look up the word "baptism." Be sure that you have a biblical understanding of the significance of this ordinance. Familiarize yourself with the beliefs of your own church. If you have not been baptized, discuss the matter with your parents or pastor.

TAKE ANOTHER LOOK!

Review 34: Lessons 100–102

Wall of Fame

1. *Battle of Actium (31 B.C.)*—Sketch the silhouette of a ship. Write the name and date inside of it.

2. *Augustus Caesar and the Roman Empire (27 B.C.)*—Place a laurel wreath on his head. **Remember, this is a date to memorize.**

3. *John the Baptist (c. 4 B.C.–A.D. 26)*—Find a scrap of fuzzy fabric and glue it over the body of John.

SomeWHERE in Time

1. On an outline map of Greece that you have already made, write in "The Battle of Actium" on the west coast of Greece.

2. Using a reference book, find a map of the Roman Empire at the time of Augustus Caesar. Compare it to a map of the Roman Republic. On Outline Map 5, "Europe," create the borders for the Republic in orange, and the Empire in green. Label the significant countries if you've not done this before.

3. Open a biblical map of Palestine at the time of Christ. Find the Dead Sea and the Jordan River. Just north of where the Jordan pours into the Dead Sea is the place where John baptized Jesus.

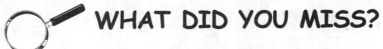

WHAT DID YOU MISS?

Week 34: Exercise

Before this year is over, I want to review the prophets one more time. Remembering something about them will greatly enhance your understanding of the Old Testament. There are 20 all together if we include Samuel who was the last of the judges and a prophet.

Using colored pencils or markers, follow the instructions for each. Then match the items by placing the correct letter next to the number. (You may use your book for answers. To make this easier, the number in parentheses after each name is the quarter where you'll find the lesson about that prophet.)

_____1. Draw an "N" over the second prophet to Nineveh.

        a. Obadiah (2)

_____2. Put an eye with long eyelashes over the prophetess who helped Josiah with the Book of the Law.

        b. Samuel (2)

_____3. Put wings on the prophet who taught during a locust plague.

        c. Zechariah (3)

_____4. Put big ears around the name of the prophet who was a judge and heard God as a boy.

        d. Nahum (2)

_____5. Put a tear over the weeping prophet.

        e. Micah (2)

_____6. Draw a carrot on the prophet who refused the king's food.

        f. Jonah (2)

_____7. Draw a big fish on the prophet who fled from God to Tarshish.

        g. Daniel (3)

_____8. Draw flames on the fiery prophet.

        h. Zephaniah (2)

_____9. Write the word "Last" over the last Old Testament prophet.

        i. Malachi (4)

_____10. Give a pen to the well-educated and articulate prophet.

        j. Elijah (2)

_____11. Draw a scroll on the prophet who
        ate one.   k. Isaiah (2)

_____12. Write an "E" over the prophet to
        the Edomites.   l. Hosea (2)

_____13. Draw bones around the prophet who,
        even in his death, brought a dead man back to life.   m. Huldah (3)

_____14. Draw a straight line on the prophet who
        was a fig farmer and saw a vision of a plumb line.   n. Haggai (3)

_____15. Draw a heart with a jagged slash through
        it for the prophet with an unfaithful wife.   o. Jeremiah (2)

_____16. Place a pitchfork by the prophet who was
        a farmer and predicted the place of Jesus' birth.   p. Habakkuk (3)

_____17. Write the word "Priest" over the prophet who was both
        priest and prophet and who prophesied the Lord's coming
        to Earth through the Messiah.   q. Amos (2)

_____18. Draw a mailbox by the prophet who
        wrote a letter to God.   r. Ezekiel (3)

_____19. Write a "T" for Temple by the prophet who
        came alongside Zerubbabel to inspire the rebuilding
        of the Temple (the prophet other than Zechariah).   s. Joel (2)

_____20. Place a crown on the prophet who was
        related to King Hezekiah and King Josiah.   t. Elisha (2)

Now do the following:

a. Highlight in yellow the five prophets to Israel (Samuel, Elijah, Elisha, Amos, and Hosea).

b. Highlight in green the six prophets to Judah (Joel, Isaiah, Micah, Zephaniah, Jeremiah, and Huldah).

c. Highlight in pink the five Post-Exile prophets (Daniel, Ezekiel, Haggai, Zechariah, and Malachi).

d. Highlight in blue the four stray prophets (Obadiah, Jonah, Nahum, and Habakkuk).

WHAT DO YOU KNOW?

Pretest 35

Today's pretest is far different from most. I want to see how familiar you are with the main events of Jesus' life. There are so many, but I will focus on just this week's lessons.

Rewrite these events in the order that they happened.

- Pilate sends Jesus to Herod Antipas.

- Augustus Caesar issues a decree for a census.

- Jesus teaches and performs miracles.

- Pontius Pilate washes his hands of the death of Jesus.

- Angels proclaim the birth of Jesus.

- Jesus is born in Bethlehem.

- Jesus lives as a carpenter in Galilee.

- Herod Antipas sends Jesus back to Pilate for sentencing.

1. _____

2. _____

3. _____

4. _____

5. _____

6. _____

7. _____

8. _____

JESUS CHRIST, HIS BIRTH
LESSON 103

Matthew 13:11 reads, "To you it has been granted to know the *mysteries* [italics mine] of the kingdom of heaven." Are you ready to know? Do you personally know the Mystery behind all of history? I hope so. There is not one man or woman we have studied yet who will change your life like Jesus Christ will. You may one day forget every lesson we have learned so far, but you don't want to forget the lesson of Jesus. I sincerely believe He wrote every page of history because He created every man, woman, and child that has ever lived in the order that He ordained. Let's look today at the presence of Jesus Christ at the beginning of all time and His humble birth about 2,000 years ago.

The miracle of Jesus Christ really starts at Creation itself. John says in his gospel in the New Testament, "In the beginning was the Word, and the Word was with God, and the Word was God. He was in the beginning with God. All things were made through Him, and without Him nothing was made that was made . . . and the Word became flesh and dwelt among us, and we beheld His glory, the glory as of the only begotten of the Father, full of grace and truth." (John 1:1–3, 14)

My friends, there are few words you will ever read that are quite as profound as the phrase from John, "And the Word became flesh and dwelt among us." The Word means "God" and to become flesh means to become a man! Think for a minute about all the things you already know about God. In six days He created everything that we know and He rested on the seventh. He revealed Himself to Adam and his kin. He spared the human race from the Great Flood through Noah. He freed the Hebrews through Moses. He dwelt in the Tabernacle in the wilderness. He gave the Hebrews the Promised Land. He sent prophets to the Israelites to warn them of their sin. He sent Cyrus the Great to free His people from captivity. He sent more prophets. He fulfilled Daniel's prophecy through Alexander the Great. And He sent John the Baptist to prepare the way for the coming of the Lord.

That is a long list of things, yet it does not even begin to tell the whole story. In fact, it takes the entire Bible to tell all the stories of how God has been working in the world since Creation.

Do you see a pattern here? I believe that God in His incredible love for us has moved through history all along to make Himself known. But the final act of coming here Himself just blows all the rest away, doesn't it? God poured Himself into the tiny form of a baby so that He could grow up to be the Savior of the World! The Bible says that "Christ Jesus who, being in the form of God, did not consider it robbery to be equal with God but made Himself of no reputation, taking the form of a servant, and coming in the likeness of men. And being found in appearance as a man, He humbled

"And the Word became flesh and dwelt among us, and we beheld His glory." (John 1:14)

Himself and became obedient to the point of death, even the death of the cross." (Phil. 2:6–8)

The actual story of the birth of Jesus is rather well known. All over the world people celebrate the Christmas holiday to remember the event. But I hope your familiarity with the story does not make it any less meaningful. On the contrary, I hope the story leaves you in awe and wonder every time you hear it.

Gabriel, the same angel who spoke to Zacharias, paid a visit to a very young woman named Mary. At first he startled her. Then Gabriel assured her, saying, "Do not be afraid, Mary, for you have found favor with God. And behold, you will conceive in your womb and bring forth a Son, and shall call His name Jesus . . . The Holy Spirit will come upon you, and the power of the Highest will overshadow you. Therefore, also, that Holy One who is to be born will be called the Son of God." (Luke 2:30–31, 35)

So Jesus was to be born of the Virgin Mary. And His earthly father would be Joseph, who was engaged to Mary. Do you realize that in just those two facts, Jesus was fulfilling prophecy? (He fulfilled about 350 prophecies altogether!) In fact, there are 13 different places in the Old Testament that say Jesus would be born of the lineage of David (for example, Ps. 89:3–4; Isa. 9:6–7; Jer. 23:5). Stop right now and read Luke 3:23–38 to better understand how Jesus came from the family of David. You will also see the names of many other Bible figures we have studied, such as Noah, Shem, and Boaz. It's kind of neat to see how every generation was planned by God to bring about His Son!

Back to the story though. Mary and Joseph were to become parents just about the time that Augustus Caesar made his decree for a census to be taken. Because of this, Joseph had to travel back to his childhood home of Bethlehem, the city of David, to be counted. Do you know why Bethlehem was called the "city of David"? That is where David grew up and tended his father's sheep. In fact, if you were to visit there today, you would still find shepherds in the business of tending flocks. Remember, too, that the prophet Micah said, "But you, Bethlehem Ephrathah, though you are little among the thousands of Judah, yet out of you shall come forth to Me the One to be ruler in Israel, whose goings forth have been from of old, from everlasting . . . And this One shall be peace." (Mic. 5:2, 5)

I can't imagine how difficult that donkey ride must have been for Mary, being so close to giving birth. She knew her time was near, but there wasn't an available inn for miles with the busy census going on. Mary and Joseph settled on a barn as their resting place on the very night that Jesus came into the world. Jesus was born and placed in a bed of hay for animals. We call it a manger. Though storybooks make it out to be a quaint setting, it was probably just an ordinary animal loft. And possibly quite smelly, too. Jesus was born of humble means rather than like a king as many expected. God had so much yet to teach the people about what His life would be like here.

The Jews, you see, were waiting for a warrior-type king to come and take care of the Romans. They certainly didn't expect the Savior to come in such meekness. But He did. I think it is one of the most beautiful parts of the story. Even the name "Jesus" was a common name back then, kind of like "Joe" would be today.

My favorite part of the story of the birth of Christ is the reaction of the angels of God. Angels are a little bit mysterious to us on this side of heaven. But on the night of Christ's humble but majestic birth, they were very visible. Luke 2:9–10 and 13–14 says this, "And behold, an angel of the Lord stood before them (the shepherds), and the glory of the Lord shone around them, and they were greatly afraid. Then the angel said to them, 'Do not be afraid, for behold, I bring you good tidings of great joy which will be to all people. For there is born to you this day in the city of David a Savior, who is Christ the Lord' . . . And suddenly there was with the angel a multitude of the heavenly host praising God and saying: 'Glory to God in the highest, and on earth peace, good will toward men!' "

So the prophets proclaimed His coming and the angels declared it with great joy. I ask you again, do you personally know this One who brings peace to the world? I hope so.

ACTIVITY 103

ALL STUDENTS

The Birth of Jesus (c. 4 B.C.) is a date to memorize.

103A—Younger Students

I love the scene of the nativity to remind us of the humble birth of Jesus who came from heaven to live with us. Just for fun, make a very unusual and creative nativity set that is "edible"!

1. Make Baby Jesus out of something like a peanut still in its shell, or a fuzzy piece of kiwi fruit. Use a marker to give it eyes. Wrap it in a small cloth and tie a string around it.
2. Create Mary and Joseph out of fruits or vegetables such as oranges, tomatoes, or bell peppers. Use a marker to make faces on them and scraps of fabric around them for robes.
3. The wise men could be brought to life out of bananas, apples, pears, or even boiled eggs. Use your imagination.
4. Take a photo of your nativity set before you eat it!

103B—Middle Students

While Jesus was still just a baby, He was recognized as the Messiah by two special people. Who were they? Read Luke 2:25–38 for the answer. Discuss with your teacher why it might have been significant for these stories to be included in the New Testament.

103C—Middle and Older Students

1. There are so many prophecies that were fulfilled through the birth of Jesus Christ. On a piece of paper, copy the Old Testament and New Testament references that are listed in the Activity Supplement in the Appendix. File it under "Asia: Israel."
2. Watch the video entitled *Jesus*, produced by Campus Crusade for Christ. It is one of the more biblically accurate film versions on the life of Christ because it follows the Book of Luke in the New Testament. Research the number of languages that the film has now been translated into. Contact Campus Crusade at 1-407-826-2000 for more information.

c. A.D. 26–29

JESUS, HIS TEACHINGS AND MIRACLES

LESSON 104

The birth of Jesus Christ that we just studied is an incredible story. It will always be amazing to think that God came to Earth in the form of a baby. "The Word became flesh and dwelt among us." But even more amazing than that are the teachings and miracles of Jesus that still influence the world to this day! Let's examine them more closely.

The Mystery of History

By profession, Jesus was a carpenter for many years. But, by age 30, He left His workshop to start a ministry that changed the world. What exactly did He teach in just three years that was so revolutionary?

To name a few things, Jesus taught about the kingdom of heaven, repentance, and loving one's enemies. He spoke of how to pray, how to fast, and how to have faith. Jesus demonstrated forgiveness, servanthood, and the blessing of children. He also taught lessons on marriage, witnessing, managing money, persecutions, and of things yet to happen in the future.

Many of Jesus' teachings were very practical and came in the form of parables, or stories. He was considered a great rabbi, or teacher, and many of his followers called him Master. But one of the most important teachings of this man had to do with Who He claimed to be. You see, unlike any of the other great teachers or the Old Testament prophets, Jesus claimed to actually be God! If you remember, neither Confucius nor Buddha ever said that he was God. But Jesus did.

For example, Jesus said, "If you had known Me, you would have known the Father also . . . I am from above, I am not of this world . . . if you do not believe that I am He, you will die in your sins." (John 8:19, 23–24) In fact, Jesus made it so clear to the Jews that He thought He was God, that the people got angry enough to stone him on several different occasions. According to Leviticus 24:16, stoning someone was a punishment for "blasphemy." That's a big word for calling yourself God. John 8:58–59 says, "Truly, truly, I say to you, before Abraham was born, I AM.' Therefore they picked up stones to throw at Him."

Unlike the former prophets, Jesus also allowed the worship of Himself while He was here on Earth. Because He taught what He called "the Truth," He never would have allowed Himself to be worshiped unless He WAS God. A touching example of worship was when Mary, the sister of Martha and Lazarus, poured oil on Jesus' feet and wiped them dry with her hair. (John 12:3) It is a beautiful act, for which Jesus commends Mary.

It is also significant to know that Jesus often spoke of His death and resurrection to come. For example, in Matthew 20:18–19 Jesus said, "the Son of Man . . . will be delivered to the Gentiles to mock and to scourge and to crucify. And the third day He will rise again." Unlike Jesus, we don't know how or when we will die. He lived with the knowledge of both, as only God could.

One of many other ways that Jesus demonstrated He was God was by forgiving sins. The people believed that only God had the authority to do that. Jesus said, though, " 'that you may know that the Son of Man has power on earth to forgive sins . . . I say to you [a paralyzed man], arise, take up your bed, and go your way to your house.' And immediately he arose, took up the bed, and went out in the presence of them all, so that all were amazed and glorified God, saying, 'We never saw anything like this!' " (Mark 2:9–12)

There were actually many things the people of Israel had never seen before that Jesus did. We refer to these as the miracles of Christ. The miracles were so important because they helped to *prove* the teachings of Jesus. It was one thing for a man to *claim* to be God. But it was an entirely different matter for a man to perform miracles *like* God. And that is what Jesus did so powerfully and dramatically.

It is recorded in the New Testament that Jesus performed at least 36 life-changing miracles. He gave sight to the blind, hearing to the deaf, and words to the mute. He healed people of diseases and gave paralyzed people the ability to walk. He cured people of leprosy and cast out demons. Most shocking, Jesus raised people from the dead! We can only imagine the story of Lazarus, who was dead for three days when Jesus asked him to come back. And I especially like the story of Jairus's daughter, who was brought back to life out of Jesus' compassion. After all, she was just a young child.

From our limited human perspective, we can't explain the events that are recorded for us in all four of the Gospels. We are not supposed to understand them but rather to just be in awe. Jesus claimed to be God, and He proved it by His miraculous powers. I suppose He knew that there would always be some of us who needed to see miracles in order to believe. Many have been worshiped as gods in this world.

But none could prove it like Jesus did. The biggest miracle of all was yet to happen. He was going to conquer death itself. And He had a great reason to do it. Do you know why He willingly died? It had something to do with all of us.

ACTIVITY 104

104A—Younger Students

What is one of your favorite miracles that Jesus performed? Talk about it with your teacher and try to act one out. If you are stuck, consider reading about one of my favorites in Matthew 9:20–21. A woman was healed by the faith she had in just touching the hem of Jesus' robe! That would be an easy one to act out. Another would be the healing of a leper. (Matt. 8:1–4) With poster putty, adhere small, torn pieces of red paper to your arms and legs. Pull them off miraculously when healed by Jesus.

104B—Middle Students

There are many stories in the Bible about the unfortunate people who had leprosy. Some were blessed to be healed by Jesus. Research this dreaded disease, which is also called Hansen's disease. Is it still around? If so, where is it found and how are these people treated? Write a short paper about it. File your paper under the country with the largest number of leprosy cases.

104C—Middle and Older Students

1. Write an essay on the teachings of Jesus. Choose five topics that He taught about and summarize what it was that Jesus said about them. Include scripture references.

2. With parental approval, read the classic story *Ben Hur* or watch the video starring Charlton Heston. It is a fictional story based on fact. Excellent in my opinion!

---

42 B.C.–A.D. 37
Unknown–A.D. 36
Unknown–A.D. 40

TIBERIUS CAESAR, PILATE, AND HEROD

LESSON 105

The birth, the life, and the death of Jesus Christ are all fascinating events. But they are much better understood if you are familiar with the government and the politics of Jesus' time. In this lesson, we look at three of the Roman rulers who lived during the life and death of Jesus.

First, you'll want to remember the structure of the Roman government. After Octavian defeated Mark Antony and Cleopatra at the Battle of Actium, he became the very first emperor of the Roman Empire. With the new name of Augustus Caesar, he had the highest authority in Rome.

As you know from the familiar Christmas story, Augustus Caesar was alive at the time of Jesus' birth. He had sent out a census to count all the people, which is why Mary and Joseph were in Bethlehem when Jesus was born. (It also fulfilled prophecy that Christ would be born there!) Augustus died when Jesus was in His teens, in about A.D. 14. They probably never met.

The next Roman emperor was named Tiberius. He was referred to as Tiberius Caesar or sometimes just Caesar. In honor of Julius Caesar, many of the emperors were given the second name of Caesar, but don't let it confuse you as to who was who. (To help remember the order of "caesars," think of the acrostic JAT for Julius, Augustus, and Tiberius.) Tiberius Caesar was a decent ruler when it came to foreign affairs, but the Romans didn't like him too much. He didn't handle money matters very well.

Ironically, it is in the context of money that we know a little bit about Tiberius Caesar. Jesus spoke about him in the Bible. You see, in Luke 20:25 Jesus said, "Render [or give] unto Caesar that which is Caesar's . . ." Jesus meant that it was all right to pay taxes to the Romans. This was an important lesson for the Jews because they were hoping that the Messiah would break them free from Roman rule and taxes. Jesus, on the other hand, was trying to teach the people how to be free from their own sin, not just free from the harsh Roman government. There is a big difference.

Tiberius Caesar ruled over Rome from about A.D. 14 to 37. Those years included the life, death, and resurrection of Jesus, but the two men may or may not have ever met. However, Tiberius would have been responsible for placing governors, or "procurators," in power who *did* get to meet Jesus. During the life of Christ, a man named Pontius Pilate was selected by Tiberius to govern Judea, or Palestine. You probably recognize the name of Pilate from the Easter story.

Like Tiberius, Pontius Pilate was not a very popular Roman. Though he ruled over the Israelites, he never really understood them or their religion. At the time of Jesus' death, Pontius Pilate's name and position became very important. You see the Romans had established a somewhat fair legal system. There were laws regarding how a person could be found guilty of a crime. The Romans had courts set up where people were given trials. Our court system today is not a great deal different from that of the Romans. Because of this, the last days of Jesus were stretched out in the legal courts while the governors of the land tried to decide what to do with Him.

The other name that we hear of in the Bible during Christ's trial was that of Herod. This was Herod Antipas, who had John the Baptist beheaded; not to be confused with Herod the Great. He was, however, the son of Herod the Great. Herod Antipas governed over Galilee. That is where Jesus grew up. During Jesus' trial, Pontius Pilate sent Jesus to Herod Antipas for another opinion as to whether or not Jesus was guilty of a crime. It only made sense for Herod to be involved because Jesus was a Galilean.

Interestingly, the gospel of Luke says that Herod was excited to finally meet Jesus. He hoped to see a miracle. But Jesus said nothing and performed no miracles for Herod. He was not there to put on a show. In disappointment, Herod mocked Jesus and returned Him to Pilate for his final sentencing.

Did you know that both these Roman men, Pilate and Herod, thought that Jesus was innocent? Though they didn't understand who He was, they really didn't want to see Jesus put to death. Pilate was probably even fearful of it. His wife was having bad dreams about the incident and warned him to have nothing to do with Jesus' death.

The Lord had a plan though. It was necessary in His plan for Jesus to die for our sins. So, despite what the governors said, a loophole was found in the system that allowed Jesus to be turned over to the crowd for crucifixion. In disagreement over the sentencing, Pilate "took water and washed his hands before the multitude, saying, 'I am innocent of the blood of this just Person. You see to it.' " (Matt. 27:24) At a later point we will study the exact events of Jesus' death. The best part of that story is how it ended after three days!

ACTIVITY 105

ALL STUDENTS

Make your Memory Cards for Lessons 103–105. Indicate with a highlighter that Jesus' birth (c. 4 B.C.) is a date to memorize.

105A—Younger Students

Make your own ancient coins. Directions are found in the Activity Supplement in the Appendix.

105B—Middle Students

The creation of the arch was a tremendous achievement for the Romans. They built arches all over the Empire in the form of bridges, aqueducts, monuments, and city gates. Many are still standing today. What's the big deal about arches? An arch is more than just a shape; it is an architectural phenomenon that uses gravity to create strength. Leonardo da Vinci said, "An arch consists of two weaknesses which, resting on each other, become a strength."[1] Use the guidelines below to report on arches and file your report under "Europe: Italy (Ancient Rome)."

1. Go to an encyclopedia to find out how an arch supports itself. Look for the meanings of these terms: keystone, skewbacks or springers, voussoirs, span.

2. Sketch an arch and label its parts.

3. Visit any famous arches in your area (such as the one in St. Louis). Don't mistake a suspension bridge for an arch. They operate on different principles. Take pictures of any arches you find, large or small, and include them in your report.

An example of arches; these are in Rome.

105C—Older Students

The Roman Forum (or "Forum Romanum," as it is written in Latin) was an incredible political site. I had a chance to visit there once, but it was long before I knew what I now know of history! I wish I could go back. Maybe you will go there one day! According to a Greek named Strabo:

> "If one should go to the Old Forum and see one forum after another ranged beside it, with their basilicas and temples, and then see the Capitol and the great works of art on it and the Palatine . . . it would be easy to forget the world outside . . . It is a spectacle from which it is hard to tear yourself away."[2]

Parts of the Forum still stand today. Research the Forum to learn about what took place there, the layout, and what remains today. Look for the Temple of Jove; the Temple of Julius Caesar; the Curia, or Senate House; the Arch of Septimius Severus; the Arch of Augustus; the Basilica Julia, Basilica Aemilia, and the Tabularium. Photocopy a sketch of what it might have looked like in the first century A.D. and a photo of it now. Include this in your report and file it under "Europe: Italy (Ancient Rome)."

---

1. As quoted in Rich Murphy, *Science With Paper: Learning About Bridge Structures Using Paper.* Schenectady, NY: Maranatha Life, 1997; p. 16.

2. As quoted in Don Nardo, *Life in Ancient Rome.* San Diego: Lucent Books, 1997; p. 43.

TAKE ANOTHER LOOK!

Review 35: Lessons 103–105

Wall of Fame

1. *The Birth of Jesus (c. 4 B.C.)*—We will place Jesus on the timeline in three places to depict different stages of his life. Place a baby in a manger at 4 B.C. It was determined later in history that the original historians who placed Jesus at A.D. 1 were off by a few years. Therefore, His birth was about four years before time was counted as A.D. **Remember, this is a date to memorize.**

2. *Jesus teaches and performs miracles (c. A.D. 26–29)*—Draw Jesus with two men. Give one man only X's for eyes to show blindness. Draw the other with wide-open eyes and a smile to depict receiving sight.

3. *Tiberius Caesar (42 B.C.–A.D. 37)*—Draw a coin with his face and name on it.

4. *Pontius Pilate (unknown–A.D. 36)*—Depict him with one thumb up and one thumb down as he asks the Jews what they want him to do with Jesus.

5. *Herod Antipas (unknown–A.D. 40)*—Make him look evil like his father, Herod the Great.

SomeWHERE in Time

1. We have looked at Israel several times. Today, find a Bible map that says "Jerusalem [or Israel or the Holy Lands] at the time of Christ." With your teacher, look for familiar places such as:

   • Bodies of water: Dead Sea, Jordan River, Mediterranean Sea, Sea of Galilee

   • Countries: Samaria, Galilee, Judea, Phoenicia

   • Cities: Jerusalem, Bethlehem, Jericho, Damascus, Caesarea

2. Middle and Older Students: Have you ever noticed that Herod Antipas and Pontius Pilate were both in Jerusalem during Jesus' trial? Yet one was the governor of Palestine and one, the governor of Galilee.

   Apparently both men were visiting. Pontius Pilate's place of residence was the city of Caesarea on the coast. He often visited Jerusalem during times of celebration—remember, it was Passover—to help keep the peace and attend to other duties.

   Luke 23:7 tells us that Herod was also in Jerusalem then, although he lived in Galilee, a region north of Palestine. Had Herod not been in Jerusalem, he might never have met Jesus.

   On Outline Map 7, "Israel," mark the cities of Caesarea and Jerusalem and the region of Galilee. Write the names of the two governors in their places of residence.

WHAT DID YOU LEARN?

Week 35: *Quiz*

I. Fill in the Blanks. See how well you can do without a word bank.

1. According to the Bible, _____ was the father of all those who play the harp and flute.

2. God sent a _____ as a symbol of His promise to never destroy the world by a flood again.

3. _____ is an ancient megalithic structure still standing in England today.

4. The _____ at Giza in Egypt were probably the first of the Seven Wonders of the Ancient World to be built.

5. The name _____ means "father of a great nation."

6. Amenhotep and Nefertiti worshiped Aten, the _____ god.

7. In the legend of the Trojan Horse, _____ was the beautiful queen who was stolen away to Troy.

8. Ruth, from the country of _____, proved to be a faithful daughter-in-law to Naomi.

II. Matching. Match the following items by placing the correct letter next to the number.

_____1. King Saul   a. a religion in India

_____2. David   b. Greek city-states

_____3. Homer   c. first king of Israel

_____4. Hinduism   d. warring countries of Mesopotamia

_____5. Rome   e. killed a giant

_____6. Athens and Sparta   f. prophet to Judah

_____7. Assyria and Babylonia   g. founded by Latins and Etruscans

_____8. Zephaniah   h. a Greek bard who wrote the *Iliad*

III. Multiple Choice. Circle the correct answer for each question.

1. At the last invasion of Babylon, Zedekiah watched his _____ be killed and then he himself was blinded.

   a. mother

   b. wife

   c. sister

   d. sons

The Mystery of History

2. The prophet Ezekiel was shown a vision from God in which dry _____ came to life.
   a. leaves
   b. bones
   c. sand
   d. figs

3. _____ died the night that he saw the handwriting on the wall predicting his fall.
   a. Sennacherib
   b. Cyrus the Great
   c. King Tut
   d. Belshazzar

4. The early Roman Republic designed a group of men called the _____ to represent the people and make decisions in governing Rome.
   a. House of Representatives
   b. Sanhedrin
   c. Senate
   d. Triumvirate

5. The name "father of _____" has been given to Hippocrates.
   a. medicine
   b. history
   c. Socrates
   d. Zeus

6. Despite the danger involved, _____ and his caravan of thousands of Jews and treasure crossed the desert from Babylon to Judah without bodyguards.
   a. Mordecai
   b. Eli
   c. Ezra
   d. Nehemiah

7. The great statesman Pericles died from _____ in Athens.
   a. a mosquito bite
   b. a spear wound
   c. assassination
   d. the plague

8. After years of fighting in the Peloponnesian Wars, the _____ were finally victorious.
   a. Assyrians
   b. Spartans
   c. Athenians
   d. Midianites

IV. True or False? Circle your answer.

1. Plato was a Greek philosopher who studied under Socrates.   T   F

2. As a young boy, Philip the II of Macedonia was kept as a
   prisoner of war in Thebes.   T   F

3. Emperor Asoka of India converted to Hinduism and spread
   the religion around his country.   T   F

4. During the Han dynasty, the ancient history books of
   Confucius were burned and his followers executed.   T   F

5. The First Triumvirate was comprised of Caesar, Antony, and
   Cleopatra.   T   F

6. At the Battle of Actium, Octavian sailed after Cleopatra
   in despair.   T   F

7. Tiberius Caesar was the second emperor of Rome and lived
   during the later lifetime of Jesus.   T   F

8. Pontius Pilate was the governor of Palestine.   T   F

V. Answer these questions in complete sentences. Use a separate sheet of paper if necessary.

1. What are some examples of great achievements by early man that teach us how intelligent he was?
   (Example: the building of Stonehenge)

2. Give examples of two prophecies we studied that came true.

3. What was the result of Queen Esther's courage in pleading for the lives of the Jews to her husband,
   Xerxes?

4. According to the Bible, what was John the Baptist's life purpose?

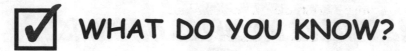

WHAT DO YOU KNOW?

Pretest 36

This is your last pretest. Answer these questions out loud with your teacher or class.

1. How many disciples did Jesus have? Name them!

2. Who were the three disciples closest to Jesus?

3. Who walked on water and then denied Jesus three times?

4. Who betrayed Jesus?

5. Who were called the "sons of thunder" and argued over who was greater?

6. At the Last Supper, Jesus was celebrating what Jewish holiday?

7. What does "Golgotha" mean?

8. How long did Jesus stay on earth after His resurrection?

THE TWELVE DISCIPLES OF CHRIST

LESSON 106

We are so near the end of the first volume of *The Mystery of History*. I can hardly believe how many different men and women we have studied. Some have been brave, some have been brilliant, and some have been just plain bad. There were 12 disciples of Christ, though, who had the privilege of being trained and taught by Jesus Himself. And to them we owe much of our Christian heritage.

By definition, a disciple is anyone who follows the teachings of another person. Many great thinkers, teachers, and philosophers had disciples. In the New Testament, there were hundreds who followed Jesus during the time of His earthly ministry. However, there were 12 who were specifically chosen by Jesus to spend more intimate time with Him. They are sometimes called apostles.

The 12 disciples were remarkable yet ordinary men. They were remarkable for what they did in spreading Christ's message after His death. They were ordinary, however, in the kind of people they were before they knew Christ. For instance, James and his brother John, the sons of Zebedee, were fishermen. Andrew and Simon Peter were also fishermen by trade, and they were brothers. All four of these men were asked by Jesus to "follow" Him. He said He would make them "fishers of men." (Matt.4:19) What a neat way to describe a disciple of Christ.

Matthew was an interesting choice for a disciple because he was a Jewish tax collector. That meant he was employed by the Roman government to collect money from his own people! Most tax collectors were hated by the Jews for being unfair and greedy. But being a tax collector probably meant that Matthew was an educated man capable of recording an accurate and believable account of Jesus' life. And that is exactly what he did. We call Matthew's book in the Bible one of the four Gospels.

Jesus said to his disciples at the Last Supper, "You may eat and drink at My table in My kingdom, and sit on thrones judging the twelve tribes of Israel." (Luke 22:30)

I've now introduced you to 5 of the 12 disciples: James, John, Andrew, Peter, and Matthew. Can you name the others? They were Philip; Bartholomew; Thomas; James, the son of Alphaeus; Lebbaeus (whose surname was Thaddaeus); Simon the Canaanite; and Judas Iscariot. One of the most familiar names on the list may be the last one. Judas Iscariot was the one who betrayed Jesus to the authorities, which led to His crucifixion.

But what do we know about these other men? Philip was probably a disciple of John the Baptist before following Christ because he lived near the region where John preached. Philip is remembered for bringing Nathaniel to Jesus just shortly after his own conversion as well as for bringing other Gentiles and Greeks to Him. Other than that, we don't know a lot about Philip. In the Book of Acts, there is another Philip that many confuse him with.

Thomas has a reputation for being the disciple who doubted that Jesus had really risen from the dead. Have you ever heard the expression, "Don't be a doubting Thomas"? We say it to refer to people who struggle with their faith because Thomas felt he needed to *touch* Jesus to believe He was risen from the dead. Jesus kindly let Thomas touch Him, too.

The other apostles—James, the son of Alphaeus; Thaddaeus; and Simon the Caananite—almost disappear in history except for their names as apostles. One of the Gospels uses the name of Jude instead of Thaddaeus, so we are not really sure who he was.

But, out of the 12, there were most certainly three disciples who were closest to Jesus. They were Peter, James, and John. These three disciples alone witnessed the miracle of Jairus's daughter rising from the dead, the Transfiguration, and the prayer of Jesus in the Garden of Gethsemane. The Transfiguration is a big word that refers to one miraculous scene in Jesus' life when His bodily form changed. The Bible says that the three disciples saw that "His face shone like the sun, and His clothes became as white as the light. And behold, Moses and Elijah appeared to them, talking with Him." (Matt. 17:2–3) I don't know why Jesus showed Himself in dazzling white the way He did for those brief moments. But it was one of many things that proved to the disciples that Jesus was indeed the Son of God.

There are many great stories of Peter, James, and John in the New Testament. Peter had the faith to walk on water, but at the end, he denied Jesus three times. John wrote the Gospel of John in the New Testament and gloated that he was the "disciple Jesus loved." James and John were nicknamed "the sons of thunder" for their boldness, yet they argued over who would be next to Jesus in Heaven. These men weren't perfect by any means, but they followed a Man who was.

And why were there 12 disciples? That's a great question. It says in Matthew 19:28 that Jesus said to His disciples, 'when the Son of Man sits on the throne of His glory, you who have followed Me will also sit on twelve thrones, *judging the twelve tribes of Israel.*' [italics mine] It appears that Jesus has a plan for the 12 disciples in heaven to judge over the 12 tribes of Israel. What an incredible connection this is between the Old Testament and the New Testament, from the sons of Jacob to the fishermen of Galilee.

In closing, remember this. The Lord not only chose John to write one of the four gospels, He also chose him to author the great Book of Revelation. As the last book in the New Testament, Revelation tells of some things YET to happen. John claims he was taken up to heaven and given a glimpse of events to come at the end of time. We would be wise to pay attention to his writings because as we have learned over and over again in the Old Testament, God's words through the prophets always come true!

ACTIVITY 106

106A—Younger Students

We all know there were 12 disciples, and we all know that there are 12 eggs in a dozen. Just for fun, make a game of naming the disciples following these directions.

1. Boil 12 eggs and save the carton.
2. Inside the carton, have your teacher write the name of one of the 12 disciples inside each of the hollows that held an egg.
3. When you can handle the eggs, write the name of one of the disciples on the bottom of each egg with a black marker.

4. Decorate each of the eggs with a face, using crayons, yarn, buttons for eyes, pipe cleaners for smiles, and so forth. Make each face unique.

5. Now place each egg in the carton where it "belongs," according to the name.

6. Create your own matching games with a brother, sister, or your teacher. For example, point to an egg and see if your opponent can guess who it is without looking. See how many names you can remember and take turns until someone gets them all.

7. Play a game yourself by looking at the eggs and seeing if you can name all 12 disciples. Peek if you get stuck!

8. Eventually you will have to eat these guys. If you liked the game, save the carton and replace the real eggs with plastic eggs.

106B—Middle Students

Create a stick-figure timeline of the life of Peter. First you will need to skim through one of the four gospels and the Book of Acts to jot down key events that took place in his life. This will be time consuming but hopefully rewarding.

Then on paper, make a stick figure diagram of his life. It might look like this:

Fishing   *Confessing Christ*   *Transfiguration*

106C—Older Students

The Book of Revelation is a fascinating study. I encourage you to be familiar with these three particular prophecies.

1. Turn to Revelation 6–8. Make a list of the seven seals as they are mentioned.

2. From Revelation 8–9, jot down the visions of the seven trumpets.

3. In Revelation 16 you will find the seven bowls of judgment. Write down those as well.

These are prophecies yet to be fulfilled. They sound terrifying for the unbeliever. Meditate on the response we should have as believers in being motivated to share the Gospel.

C. A.D. 29

JESUS, HIS DEATH AND RESURRECTION

LESSON 107

As significant as Christ's coming to Earth was, His leaving the Earth was even more so. The death of Jesus Christ was far more than a tragedy for a man just 33 years old. His death was the ultimate sacrifice for the sin of all mankind. Then, in one miraculous act of supernatural power, He rose from the dead—

ending the curse that began with Adam. I believe that today's lesson concerns the single most important event ever recorded in history!

First, let's examine what happened just before Jesus' death. At the Last Supper that Jesus had with His disciples before he was arrested, Jesus was celebrating the Passover Feast. This story is full of meaningful symbolism.

In the first Passover during the plagues of Egypt, the Hebrews placed blood on their doorways so that the death angel would "pass over" their homes. In yet another parallel in Bible history, Jesus celebrated Passover just before His own blood was going to "pass over" the sins of man! The Passover is just one more way we see a connection between the Old Testament and the New.

Jesus also used the Passover as the time to institute what we call "communion." Jesus asked the disciples to remember bread for His body that was broken for us and wine for His blood that was shed for us. This is a beautiful word picture to use in remembering His sacrificial death.

As for how Jesus was brought to the point of death, only God's providence can explain it. You see, historically it was a custom in Rome to crucify criminals. Jesus, as a teacher and a rabbi, certainly didn't appear to be a criminal to the Romans. And, obviously, the devout followers of Jesus didn't want Him to die. But there were many people who were threatened by the authority and power Jesus possessed. The teachings and miracles of Jesus were drawing thousands to follow Him, and He was speaking of the things of heaven that they didn't understand. In particular, it was the Jewish priests and members of the Sanhedrin (the Jewish council) who were most concerned with who Jesus claimed to be. He was claiming to be God.

Regardless of who understood His teachings and who did not, Jesus came with a mission to carry out. He came to take away the sin of the world. How does a man do that? An ordinary man can't. But Jesus could because He was divine. The Bible says that He lived a perfect life. He therefore could present Himself as a pure offering and an unblemished sacrifice for our sins.

Remember in the Old Testament how the people gave sacrifices to God? They were always to choose their best lamb. Jesus has been called the "Lamb of God" for this reason. He was the perfect sacrifice. And even like a lamb going for slaughter, Jesus didn't cry out to be spared from death.

Well, as Jesus' trial proceeded, the Jews who wanted Him dead sent Him first to the Sanhedrin. The Sanhedrin found Him guilty of blasphemy, but they didn't have the authority to sentence Him. That's when Jesus was sent over to Pontius Pilate who didn't know what to do with Him. Basically, the Sanhedrin pushed until they succeeded in getting the verdict they wanted. In God's sovereignty, there was enough pressure on Pontius Pilate for him to issue the death penalty. Jesus was convicted to die by crucifixion.

The place where Jesus was executed has a couple of different names. In Latin, which was the language of the Romans, the place was called "Calvary." We hear that word used often in hymns and songs.

But the place was also referred to as "Golgotha," which is Aramaic. That is one of the languages Jesus would have spoken. It means "place of the skull" because supposedly the hill resembled a skull from far away. If you remember, a long time ago when we studied Abraham, I told you then that the place where Isaac was nearly sacrificed was near Golgotha. It is an interesting fact.

While Jesus hung on the cross at Calvary, He said some very interesting things. First, Jesus remembered others around Him. He said "Father, forgive them for they know not what they do." He then pardoned one of the criminals who was hanging next to Him. He told him he would be with Him in Paradise. Jesus also remembered Mary, his own mother, while hanging in agony on the cross. He told John to take care of her.

Jesus' final three hours, though, were focused on His mission. At one point Jesus quoted scripture in Aramaic. He said, "Eli, Eli, lama sabachthani" (EE lie, EE lie, LUH mah suh BOCK thuh NIE), which means "My God, My God, why have you forsaken Me?" (Matt. 27:46) It was at that most incredible

"But God demonstrates His own love toward us in that, while we were still sinners, Christ died for us." (Rom. 5:8)

moment in history when Jesus would have literally taken on the sin of the whole world. We cannot describe His torment. In harboring every sin of mankind, He would certainly be in the greatest pain any man had ever known!

Jesus said next that He was thirsty. (John 19:28) He may have just wanted His lips and mouth moistened well enough to be able to speak a few more words. He uttered, "It is finished." (John 19:30) And with a loud voice, which would have been difficult, He proclaimed, "Father, into your hands I commend My Spirit." (Luke 23:46) With those final words, He took His last breath and died. Even His last words were prophetic. Jesus was quoting scripture from Psalm 31:5. And the time of day in which He gave His life was no coincidence either. The Bible says that Jesus died at the "ninth hour," which is what we would call 3 o'clock in the afternoon. That was the exact same time that the Jews gave their sacrificial offerings in the Temple! Again He showed Himself to be "the perfect sacrifice" for our sins.[1]

Strange and miraculous things occurred when Jesus gave up His life. A huge curtain in the Temple that separated men from the Holy of Holies was torn in half by itself! People rose from their graves and visited with loved ones. It was also recorded that an earthquake happened and the sky was as dark as night even though it was only afternoon. All those things were powerful displays of the significance of what had just happened. Jesus was no ordinary man. I believe He was and still is God!

Fortunately, Jesus' death is not the end of the story of His life. You already know what happened don't you? Just three days after Christ was buried, some women went to His sealed tomb to place spices and fragrances on His body. But thanks be to God, Jesus' body wasn't there. Though startled at first, it was these precious women who were the first to figure out the Mystery of History! Jesus was alive and had been raised from the dead. That means that He conquered death! And, not just for Himself, but for everyone who would or who will believe in Him!

The resurrection of Jesus Christ stands out above all other miracles. It redefined salvation. Instead of getting into heaven based on obedience to the Law, we were given Grace by the Lord Jesus to get into heaven based on *His* merit. What Good News for the entire world!

I hope that message is one you personally understand. And if it is, I hope that you freely share it with others. There is no greater story to tell in history than the one about Jesus. As it says in I Corinthians 2:7–8:

"but we speak God's wisdom in a *mystery* [italics mine], the hidden wisdom, which God predestined before the ages to our glory, the wisdom which none of the rulers of this age has understood; for if they had understood it, they would not have crucified the Lord of glory."

1. Notes on the last words of Christ on the cross used by permission from Dr. Jonathan Burnham of Hope Evangelical Free Church, Mason, Ohio.

The Mystery of History

ACTIVITY 107

107A—Younger Students

Make Resurrection Cookies. The recipe is in the Activity Supplement in the Appendix.

107B—Middle Students

Crucifixion was one of the most horrible means of death one could imagine. Typically a person suffered for days before death actually came. Investigate the act of crucifixion to determine the physical reason it killed a person. It might surprise you. (Further information is in the Activity Supplement in the Appendix.)

107C—Older Students

Obtain *The Resurrection Factor* by Josh McDowell. Read it and discuss it with your teacher. Write down and memorize at least five points that Josh makes on the validity of the resurrection of Christ. File this under "Asia: Israel."

Yesterday, Today, and Forever

JESUS, THE MYSTERY OF HISTORY

LESSON 108

Before the close of *The Mystery of History*, there are a few final things I want you to know. You see we live in a world in which many people do not believe as I do that Jesus was the Son of God. If you are a true believer and follower of Christ, I think it is important to remember some of the facts that make the whole story so convincing. Let's look at what the Bible says happened after Jesus rose from the dead, which may ultimately help to strengthen your own faith.

First, Jesus appeared to women at the place of His burial. They were the first to report that He was gone from the grave. This is important to note because if anyone back then was trying to lie about the incident, they never would have included a woman's testimony in the story. You see, women back in those days were not greatly respected, especially in a court of law. If the disciples had wanted to make up the story of Jesus' tomb being empty, they would NEVER have used women in the story. No one would have believed it.

Second, Jesus was said to have appeared to over 500 people after His resurrection! That fact is written in I Corinthians 15:3–6. In any court of law, 500 would be considered a great number of eyewitnesses. Also, most of these 500 or so people would have been alive when the Gospel books were written to verify the truth of them.

Third, if Jesus had not risen from the dead as His disciples and others claimed, then where *was* His body? Surely if there had been a dead body, the authorities would have found a way to produce it. The idea of the resurrection of Jesus was so disturbing to his enemies that plans were made to protect against it. The Romans placed extra guards at the tomb and put a special seal over the rock that closed it off. Still, no corpse was ever brought forward as Christ's. Only accounts of a LIVING Savior circulated in Judea and eventually throughout the world.

The Bible says that Jesus remained on Earth for 40 days after His resurrection. In that time, He of course appeared and spoke to His beloved disciples. We can only imagine the joyful reuniting of Jesus and these followers. In those 40 days, the message and ministry of Jesus must have *finally* made sense to the disciples. Jesus had told them so many times that He would die and come back to life. In the Book of Matthew alone we know of three times that Jesus foretold His death and resurrection. (Matt. 16:21, 17:22–23, and 20:18–19.) The disciples lived to see Jesus fulfill those very prophecies.

There are really many facts and arguments that support the claims of Christ. But some of the most convincing to me are the hundreds of prophecies that were fulfilled by Jesus in His birth, His life, His death, and His resurrection. One of the reasons why I placed so much emphasis on the Old Testament prophets in this curriculum was because I knew that they, along with so much else, would point to Christ.

Isaiah said that Jesus would be called the Everlasting Father. (Isa. 9:6) John quoted Jesus as saying, "I and My Father are one." (John 10:30) Zechariah prophesied that Jesus would be a priest. (Zech. 6:12–13) Hebrews 8:1 says, "We have such a high priest, who is seated at the right hand of the throne of the Majesty in the heavens." David, in his last words, said that the Rock of Israel spoke to him and that He shall be like "the light of the morning." (II Sam. 23:2–4) I Corinthians 10:4 says, "they drank of that spiritual rock that followed them, and that rock was Christ." Revelation 22:16 states, " 'I, Jesus, have sent My angel to testify to you these things in the churches. I am the root and the offspring of David, the bright and morning star.' " Daniel said that the Messiah would be killed. (Dan. 9:26) The New Testament confirms that in many places. In Hosea 13:14, the prophet claimed there would one day be victory over death. I Corinthians 15:55 declares to believers in Jesus, "O death, where is your sting? O Hades, where is your victory?"

Those are just a few of the numerous prophecies that Jesus fulfilled. Like a thread woven through a great tapestry, so is the story of Jesus Christ in history. From Genesis to Revelation, He is there between the pages. The prophets foretold Him, the Jews waited for Him, the angels sang about Him, the Wise Men worshiped Him, and the world beheld Him.

The last the disciples saw of Jesus on this Earth was when He ascended into heaven. Jesus predicted ahead of time that He would do so. The Book of Acts describes the scene. It says, "Now when He had spoken these things, while they watched, He was taken up, and a cloud received Him out of their sight." Then two angels said to them, "This same Jesus, who was taken up from you into heaven, will so come in like manner as you saw Him go into heaven." (Acts 1:9–11). That certainly gives us something to look forward to. Jesus Himself also said that He would return. And we can see that everything He ever spoke about His life was true!

I suppose I could write more and more about Jesus Christ. After all, He is my own Lord and Savior. I came to know Him in a personal relationship when I was 17 years old. He changed my life in so many ways and continues to fill it with meaning, purpose, and forgiveness. Because of His work in my life, I feel that I was inspired to write *The Mystery of History*.

Ephesians 6:19 sums up my inspiration. It says, "pray on my behalf that utterances may be given to me in the opening of my mouth to make known with boldness the *mystery* [italics mine] of the gospel." I hope the mystery has been made clear to you! That has been my desire throughout this text.

There is so much more I *could* have written, but I will close with the words of John as he wrote in the last line of his gospel, "And there are also many other things that Jesus did, which if they were written one by one, I suppose that even the world itself could not contain the books that would be written. Amen."

ACTIVITY 108

ALL STUDENTS

Make your final Memory Cards, for Lessons 106–108.

108A—Younger Students

When Christians tell the story about when they first came to know Jesus Christ personally, it is called giving their "testimony." Perhaps you have accepted Jesus as your Savior. Do you remember the details? Talk about it with your teacher.

In our family, we celebrate the day that our children accepted Christ. We give small token gifts that represent the heart. Maybe you could start the same tradition.

108B—Middle Students

If you are a believer in Christ, how did you come to know Christ personally? Practice giving your personal testimony in about three minutes. Here is a simple outline to follow.

1. My life before knowing Jesus was . . .
2. I learned the truth about Jesus from . . .
3. I made the decision to follow Christ when . . .
4. Now that I know the Lord personally, my life is . . .

108C—Older Students

If you are a believer in Christ, are you competent in sharing your faith? There are many great tools available to help you. Investigate what resources are out there through your own church. For more suggestions, consult Campus Crusade for Christ in Orlando, Florida, through their Web site at www.campuscrusade.com or call them at 1-407-826-2000.

TAKE ANOTHER LOOK!

Wall of Fame

1. *The Twelve Disciples (followed Jesus c. A.D. 27–29)*—On a piece of paper, make 11 smiley faces large enough to write the name of a disciple on each. Make one more face and give it a frown. Write the name "Judas Iscariot" on it.

2. *The Death and Resurrection of Jesus Christ (c. A.D. 29)*—On the timeline, place a cross with the words "He lives" written on it.

3. *The Ascension of Christ (c. A.D. 29)*—Make a cloud with cotton balls glued to it.

I have a final activity for you to do involving the timeline. I think it's pretty cool.

Materials: A long piece of yarn (several feet) in a color like green, purple, or gold; tape

Because I believe that God ordained the lives of men and women to bring about His purposes, I want you to connect the men and women in the lineage, or bloodline, of Christ. He literally has been a thread throughout time. So, we are going to visually run a thread from Adam to Christ to join those who preceded Him as blood relatives.

In your Bible, turn to the two genealogies of Christ listed in Matthew 1:1–17 and Luke 3:23–38. Read over these lists and pay attention to the names of some familiar characters. We studied 14 of the people who are listed. Each of these people on your timeline should have a golden cross to signify the lineage of Christ. We're now going to connect them!

Beginning with Adam and Eve, tape the end of the yarn just over their hands and then stretch the yarn over to the next person you have on your timeline who was in the lineage of Christ. (Noah and Shem for example.) Fasten the yarn with tape. Continue in this fashion, fastening the yarn from generation to generation, until you reach Christ Himself.

The figures to be connected are: Adam (Eve), Noah, Shem, Abraham, Isaac, Jacob, Rahab, Ruth, David (Bathsheba), Solomon, Hezekiah, Manasseh, Josiah, Zerubbabel—and Jesus!

Sit back and reflect on God's providence through unlikely characters such as Rahab, the foreign harlot, and Manasseh, the wicked and good king of Judah. See how the Lord works through all kinds of people to bring about His plan. It's neat!

SomeWHERE in Time

You have no new mapping assignments this week! Use the time instead to finish any map work left incomplete.

PUT IT ALL TOGETHER

As a reminder, you may use your book, timeline, and Memory Cards to help you complete this worksheet. Most questions pertain to subjects taught in this quarter only.

I—Dates to Memorize. There were four dates to memorize this quarter. Write each three times.

Alexander the Great   336 B.C.

1. _____
2. _____
3. _____

Julius Caesar   49 B.C.

1. _____
2. _____
3. _____

Augustus Caesar and the Roman Empire   27 B.C.

1. _____
2. _____
3. _____

The Birth of Jesus   c. 4 B.C.

1. _____
2. _____
3. _____

II—Who Came First? Circle the right answer.

1. Archimedes or Aristotle?
2. Judas Maccabee or the Septuagint?
3. Spartacus or Hannibal?
4. Augustus Caesar or Julius Caesar?
5. Plato or Alexander the Great?
6. Cleopatra or the Qin dynasty?
7. Jesus Christ or John the Baptist?
8. The Crucifixion or the Resurrection?

III—Who Goes Where? Below are the names of 12 men. Write their names in the appropriate lists below according to the country each is associated with.

Malachi   Plato   Judas Maccabee   Spartacus   Julius Caesar
Archimedes   Herod the Great   Aristotle   Mark Antony
Augustus Caesar   Hippocrates   John the Baptist

Greece	Rome	Israel
1._____	1._____	1._____
2._____	2._____	2._____
3._____	3._____	3._____
4._____	4._____	4._____

IV—Military Might. We studied four battles or wars this quarter (in addition to those of Alexander the Great). What are the names of these battles, who fought against whom, and who won? (Do not include Alexander's battles.) Indicate the winner by circling the name. An example from last quarter is given.

Battle	Fighters		
1. Battle of Marathon	1. (Greeks)	vs.	Persians
2.	2.	vs.	
3.	3.	vs.	
4.	4.	vs.	
5.	5.	vs.	

V—In Memoriam. In this quarter, we read about some unusual deaths. Match the names of the victims to their unfortunate fates by placing the correct letter next to the number.

_____ 1. Crucifixion

_____ 2. Possibly malaria

_____ 3. Assassinated by Senate

_____ 4. Poisoned by snake

_____ 5. Killed by a Roman soldier

_____ 6. Committed suicide using poison stored in a ring he wore

_____ 7. Beheaded

_____ 8. Died of strange diseases

a. Julius Caesar

b. Herod the Great

c. Hannibal

d. Archimedes

e. Jesus

f. Alexander the Great

g. Cleopatra

h. John the Baptist

VI—Name the Seven Wonders of the Ancient World. (You will need information from the other quarters to complete this unless you remember them!)

1._____

2._____

3._____

The Mystery of History

4. _____

5. _____

6. _____

7. _____

VII—Emperor's Legacy. The first emperor of China—Qin, or Shi Huang Ti—is remembered mostly for two things: the terra-cotta soldiers he was buried with and the building of the Great Wall of China. Fill in these facts on the Great Wall.

- It runs _____ miles;

- It is about _____ feet high;

- It has 35- to 40-foot _____ every 200 to 300 yards;

- It is 25 _____ thick at the base; and

- It is 15 feet wide across the top where _____ can ride.

VIII—True or False? Circle your answer; then correct any statement that is false by crossing out the wrong word(s) and inserting the right word(s).

1. John the Baptist's father was blinded for his disbelief until John was born.   T   F

2. The Bible contains 13 prophecies that Jesus would be born of the lineage of David.   T   F

3. While on earth, Jesus forbid anyone to worship Him.   T   F

4. In His own words, Jesus claimed to be God.   T   F

5. After the trial of Jesus, Herod claimed to "wash his hands" of Jesus' death.   T   F

6. Jesus' three closest disciples were Matthew, Mark, and Luke.   T   F

7. At the Last Supper, Jesus instituted the tradition of communion.   T   F

8. At the Ascension, the angels said that Jesus would return the same way He left.   T   F

IX—Answer These Questions. Write in complete sentences and use a separate sheet of paper.

1. What principle did Archimedes discover while in the bathtub?

2. What type of tree was planted around India for travelers to rest under?

3. How long did the Han dynasty last?

4. Who made up the First Triumvirate of Rome?

5. Who were the three main people in the Battle of Actium?

6. Which angel told Mary that she would conceive a son?

7. For what reason did the Jews want to stone Jesus?

8. Which of Jesus' disciples was a tax collector?

SEMESTER II TEST

Lessons 55–108

There are 54 questions on this test, just as there were 54 lessons in the last two quarters. Be sure you have studied your worksheets for Quarters 3 and 4.

I—Which Is It? Circle the right answer.

1. Just as predicted, the city of Nineveh was destroyed by a (plague, flood).

2. (Hammurabi, Habakkuk) expressed himself by writing directly to God.

3. Nebuchadnezzar not only built the beautiful Ishtar Gate, he also built the (Temple of Diana, Hanging Gardens) for his homesick wife.

4. Daniel was thrown into a (lions' den, fiery furnace).

5. Aesop is best remembered for writing (fables, *The Epic of Gilgamesh*).

6. The prophet (Jeremiah, Ezekiel) saw visions of a wheel within a wheel and was asked to eat a scroll.

7. Shadrach, Meshach, and Abed-Nego had their names changed to those of (Persian, Babylonian) gods.

8. Pythagoras was an intelligent Greek (statesmen, mathematician).

II—True or False? Circle your answer.

1. Belshazzar died the very night that Babylon was invaded just as Daniel said.   T F

2. Darius I organized his empire into satrapies and started a postal system.   T F

3. Amazingly, Zerubbabel rebuilt the Temple in just 52 days.   T F

4. Haggai and Zechariah were both prophets to Nineveh.   T F

5. In the Roman Republic, senators were established to represent the people of Rome.   T F

6. Pheidippides was the fast runner who delivered a message to Athens with his dying breath.   T F

7. Herodotus wrote extensively about the Chinese and their culture.   T F

8. Xerxes I, who married Esther, is also well remembered for building an incredible floating bridge at the Hellespont.   T F

III—Who Was It? Place the correct letter next to the number.

_____1. Jewish orphan   a. Hippocrates

_____2. Philosopher forced to commit suicide   b. Nehemiah

_____3. Inspired the Hippocratic Oath   c. Pericles

_____4. Jewish scribe and priest   d. Esther

_____5. Cupbearer to Artaxerxes   e. Peloponnesian

_____6. Well-loved Greek statesman   f. Malachi

_____7. War between Athens and Sparta   g. Ezra

_____8. Last Old Testament prophet   h. Socrates

IV—Multiple Choice. Circle the correct answer.

1. Plato started the first
   a. hospital.
   b. Senate.
   c. university.
   d. Olympics.

2. Philip II hired _____ to tutor his son Alexander.
   a. Aristotle
   b. Socrates
   c. Plato
   d. Pythagoras

3. Alexander the Great's empire was divided into _____ kingdoms, just as Daniel prophesied.
   a. 7
   b. 4
   c. 40
   d. 22

4. Archimedes was taking a _____ when he discovered the principle of displacement.
   a. hike
   b. break
   c. bath
   d. test

5. Emperor Asoka of India
   a. improved water systems.
   b. planted banyan trees.
   c. converted to Buddhism.
   d. All of the above.

6. The Septuagint was the original Old Testament translated into
   a. Aramaic.
   b. Hebrew.
   c. Persian.
   d. Greek.

7. Shi Huang Ti, or Qin, declared himself the first emperor of China and was responsible for
   a. building the Great Wall of China.
   b. standardizing weights, measures, and money.
   c. burning thousands of history books.
   d. being buried with thousands of terra-cotta soldiers.
   e. All of the above.

8. After running Hannibal off, the Romans completely obliterated the city of
   a. Phoenicia.
   b. Tyre.
   c. Carthage.
   d. Athens.

V—Who Am I? From the word bank below, choose the correct answer for each question.

1. I was established to improve trade between the East and the West. Who am I?

2. I successfully gained control over Jerusalem and the Temple, which had been occupied by Antiochus Epiphanes. Who am I?

3. A Roman slave and gladiator, I led a great but unsuccessful rebellion? Who am I?

4. I am the name of a union formed between Julius Caesar, Crassus, and Pompey. Who am I?

5. I was a member of the Second Triumvirate and given Egypt to rule. Who am I?

6. I captured the love of two great Roman leaders and nearly ruled the known world. Who am I?

7. I murdered just about everyone in my own family for the sake of keeping my throne over Palestine. Who am I?

8. I was a massive sea battle between Rome and Egypt that helped to shape the course of history. Who am I?

WORD BANK

Spartacus	Cleopatra	The First Triumvirate	The Silk Road
Judas Maccabee	Battle of Actium	Herod the Great	Mark Antony

VI—Fill in the Blanks. This time without a word bank.

1. _____ preached a message of repentance in the wilderness and proclaimed the coming of Jesus Christ.

2. Jesus performed many _____ that helped to demonstrate His power and deity.

3. Though _____ gave Jesus the death sentence, he thought that Jesus was innocent. He washed his hands "of the blood of this just Person."

4. _____, one of Jesus' disciples, walked on water and yet denied Jesus three times.

5. At the Last Supper, Jesus was celebrating the _____ Feast.

6. After resurrecting from the dead, Jesus first appeared to _____, who were not highly respected in a court of law.

VII—Connect the Dates. Use crayons or markers to make each line a different color.

1. Golden Age of Athens	a. 605 B.C.
2. Alexander the Great	b. c. 563 B.C.
3. Babylonian Captivity	c. 551 B.C.
4. Birth of Jesus Christ	d. 479–431 B.C.
5. Confucius	e. 336 B.C.
6. Julius Caesar	f. 49 B.C.
7. Buddha	g. 27 B.C.
8. Augustus Caesar and the Roman Empire	h. c. 4 B.C.

VIII—Bonus Essay. Answer these questions in complete sentences. Use a separate sheet of paper if necessary.

1. What have you learned about the prophets of the Old Testament?

2. According to the author, who is the Mystery of History and why?

OUTLINE MAPS

CONTENTS

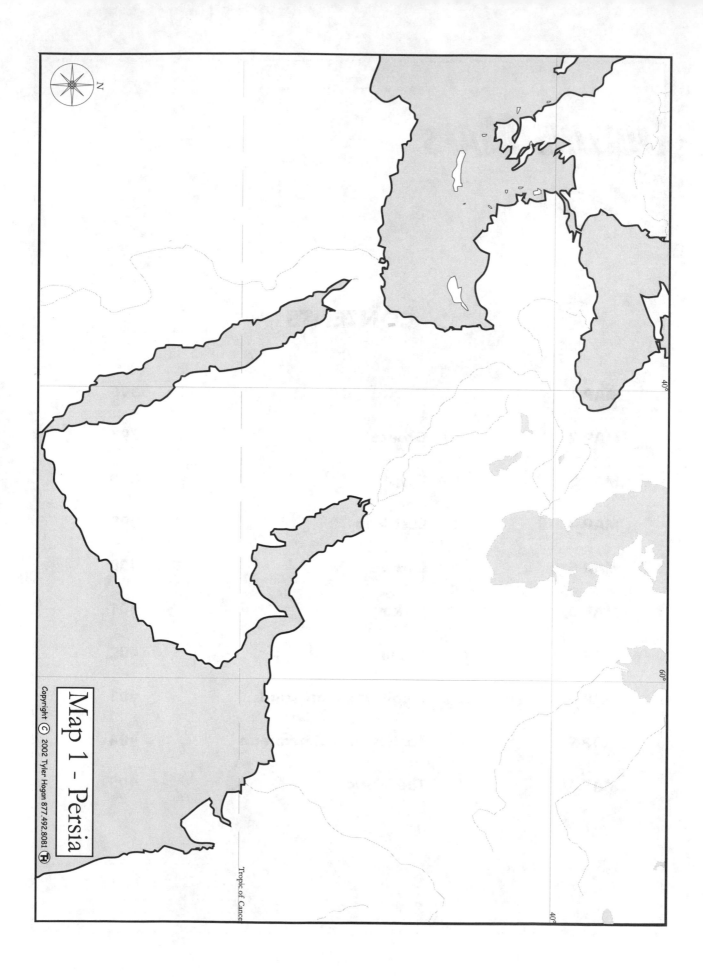

N

Map 1 - Persia

40°

60°

40°

Tropic of Cance

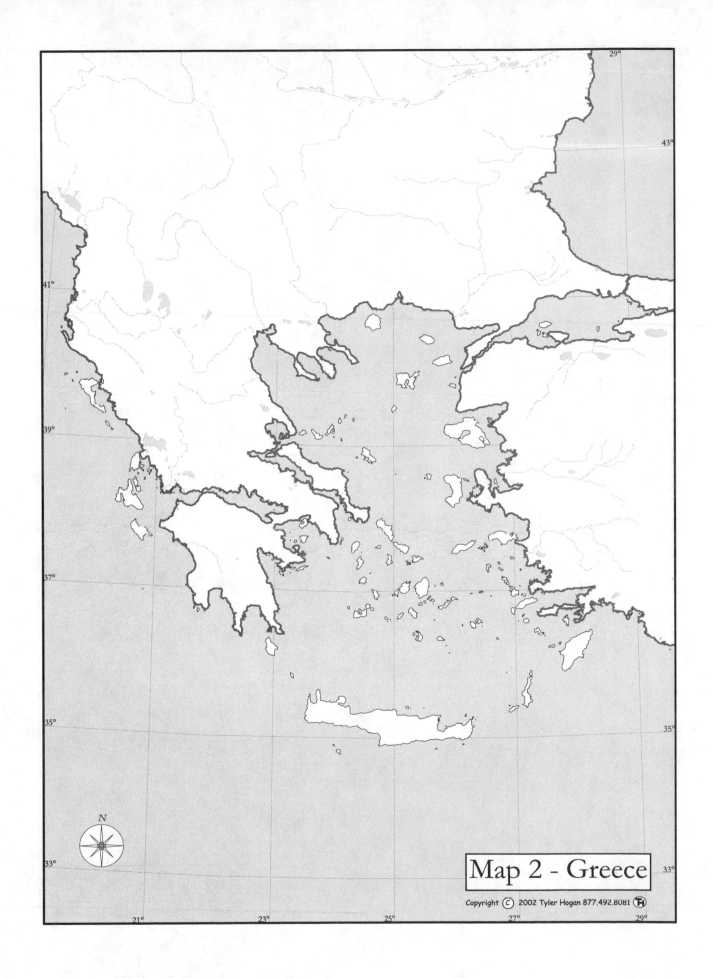

N

Map 2 - Greece

29°
43°
41°
39°
37°
35°
35°
33°
33°

21°   23°   25°   27°   29°

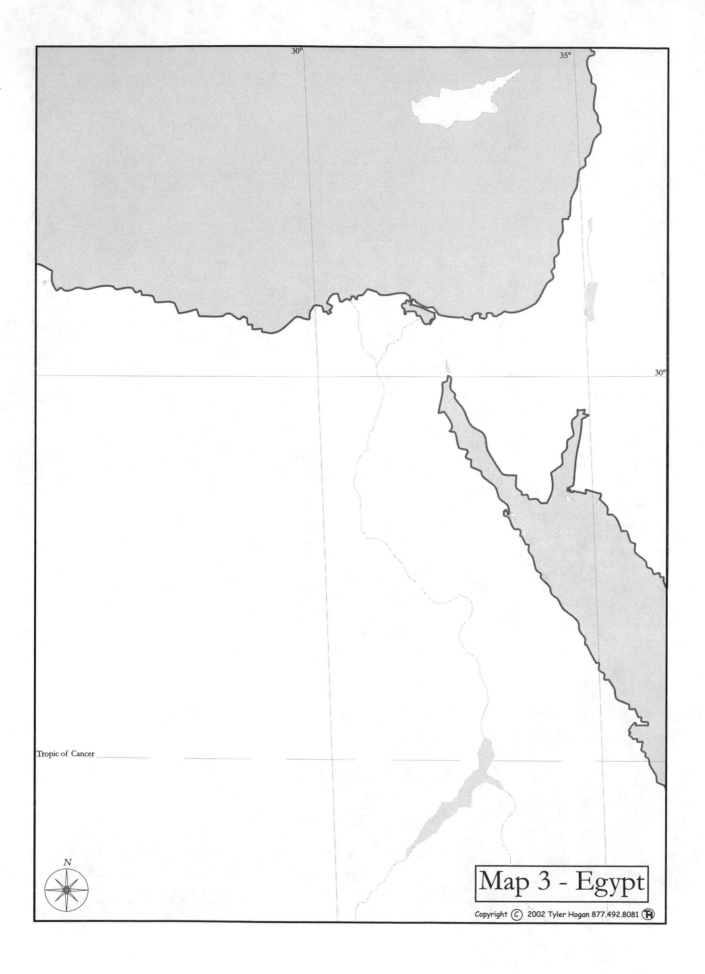

30°   35°

30°

Tropic of Cancer

N

Map 3 - Egypt

Copyright Ⓒ 2002 Tyler Hogan 877.492.8081 Ⓗ

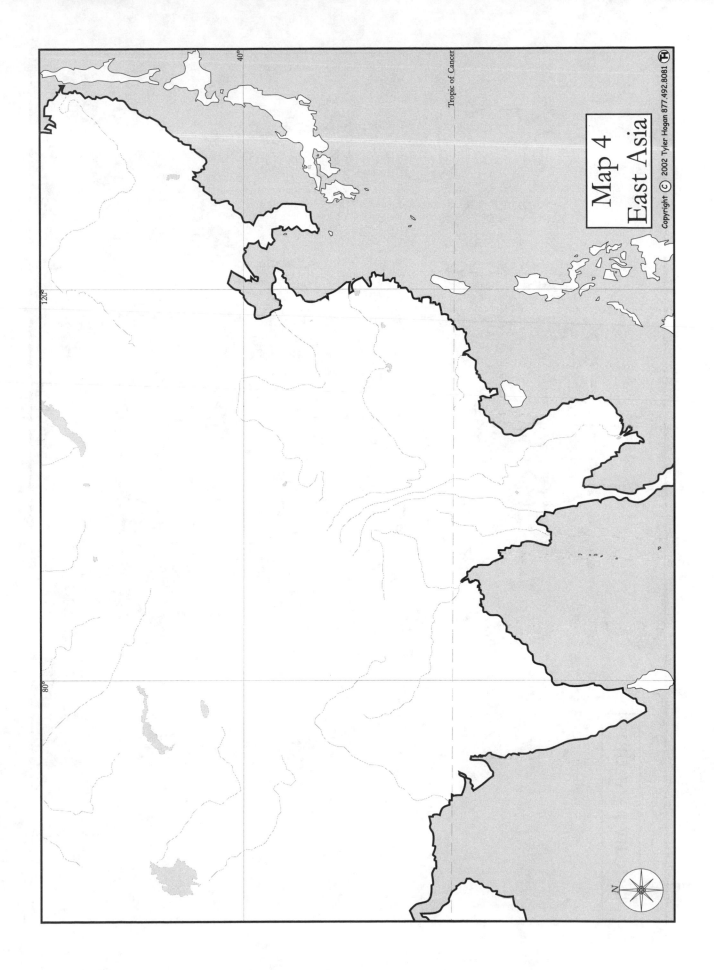

Map 4
East Asia

Tropic of Cancer

40°

120°

80°

N

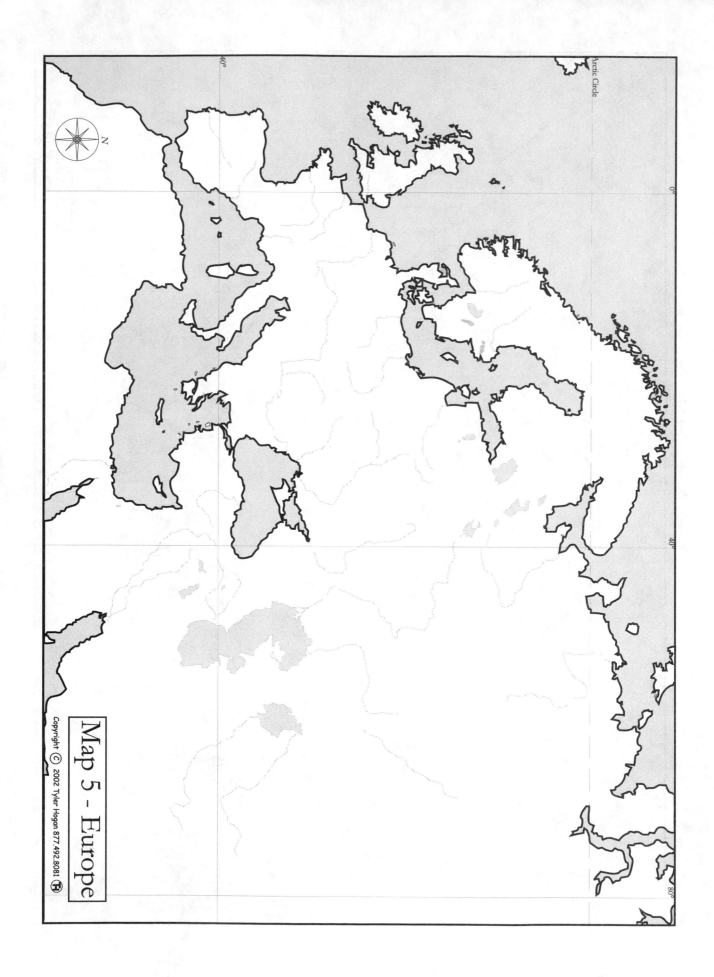

Arctic Circle

N

Map 5 - Europe

Copyright © 2002 Tyler Hogan 877.492.8081

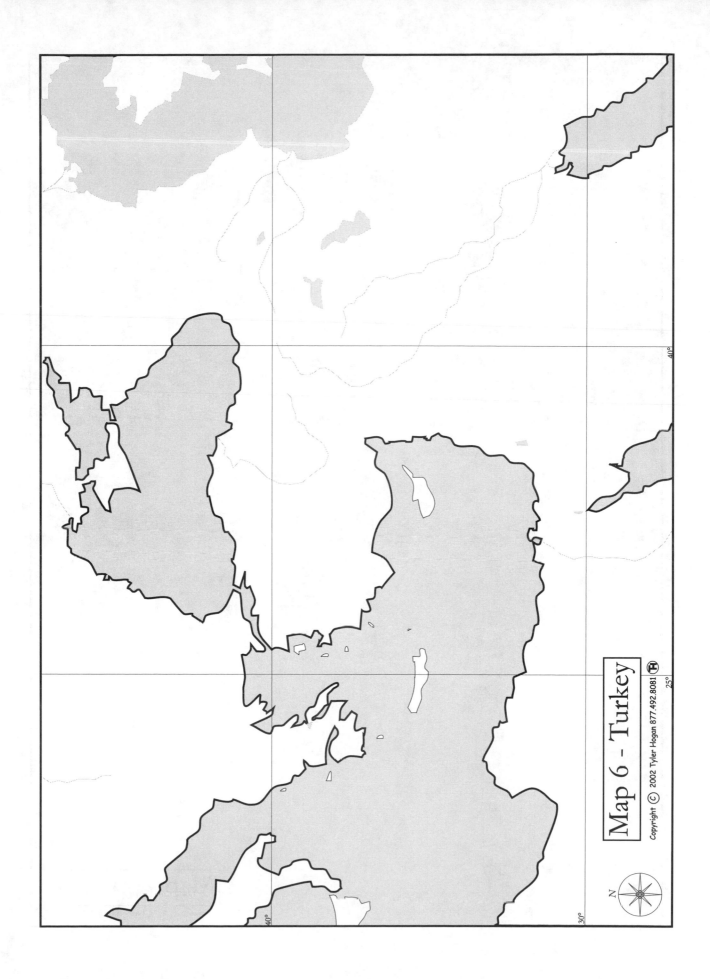

Map 6 - Turkey

Copyright © 2002 Tyler Hogan 877.492.8081 Ⓗ

N

40°

25°

40°

30°

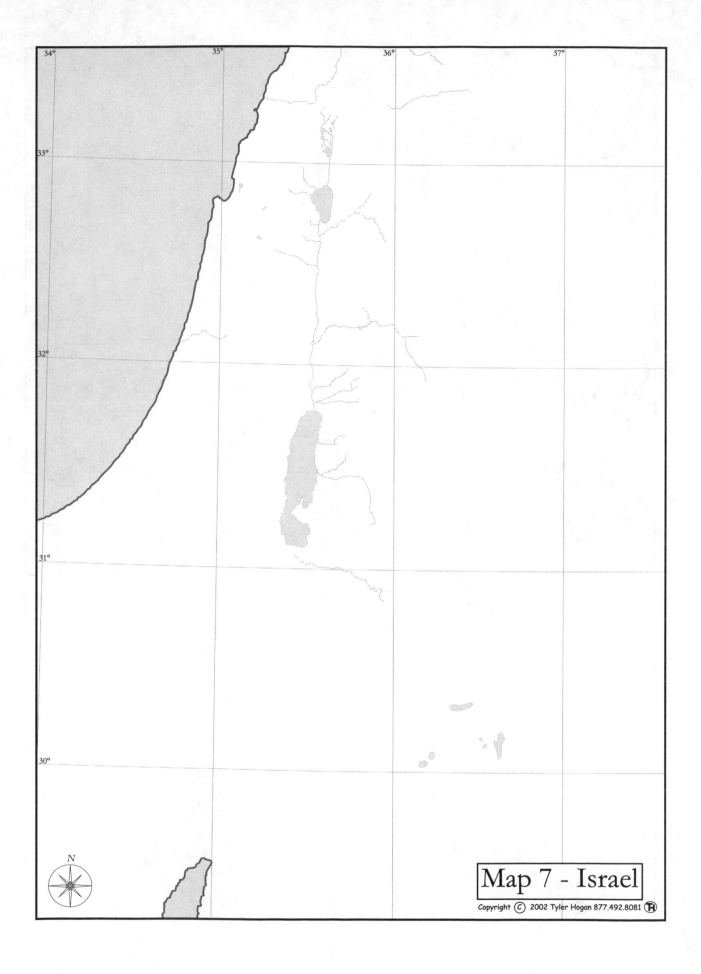

N

Map 7 - Israel

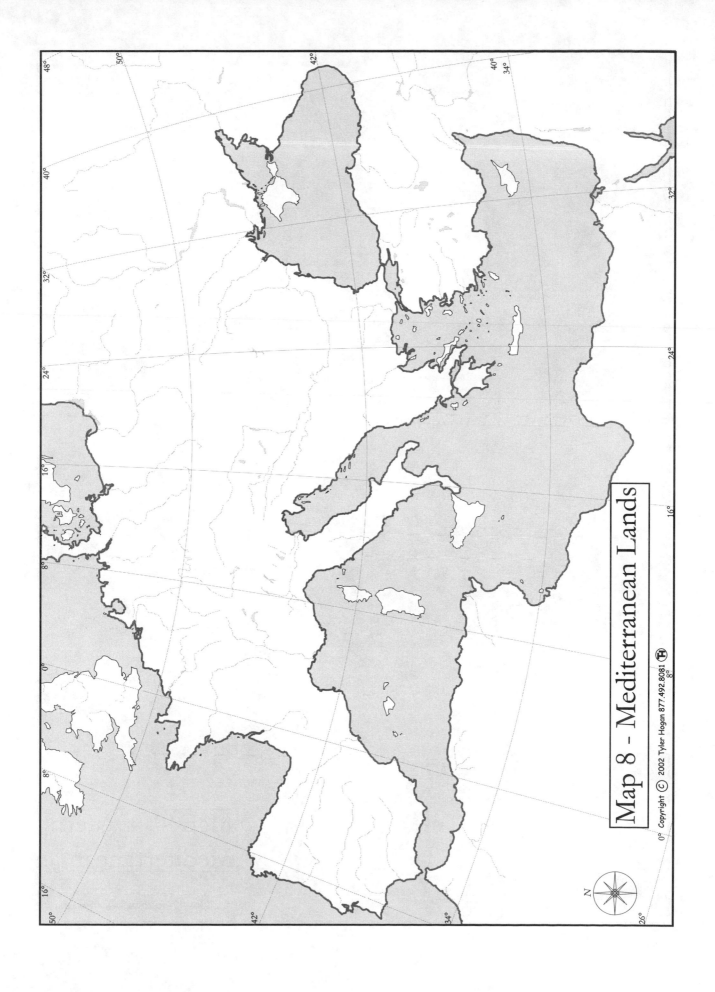

Map 8 - Mediterranean Lands

0° Copyright © 2002 Tyler Hogan 877.492.8081 Ⓗ

N

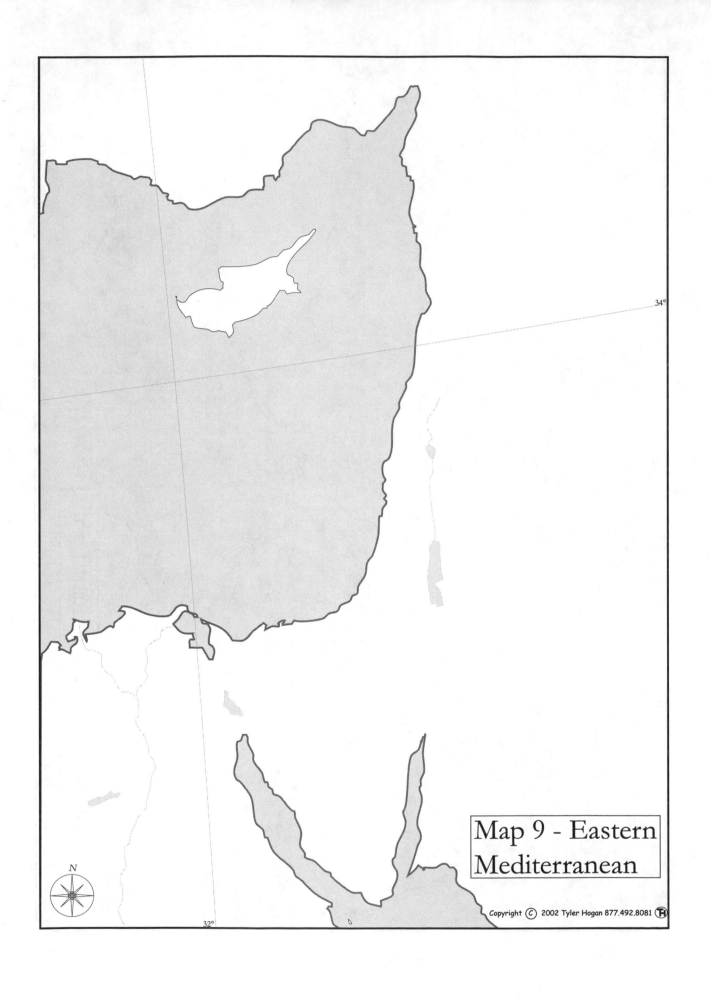

34°

Map 9 - Eastern
Mediterranean

N

32°

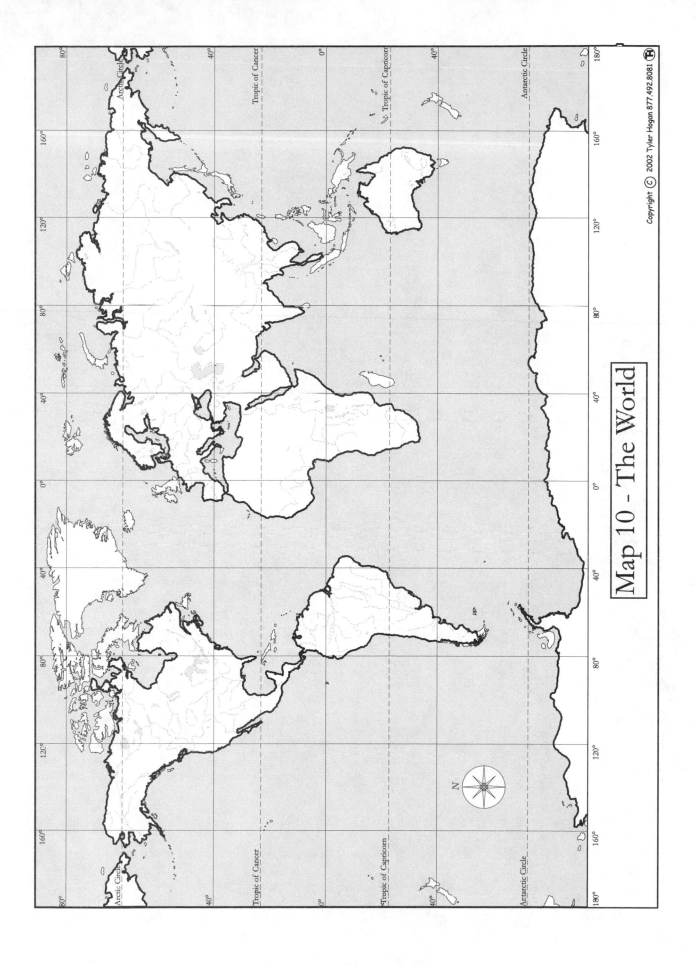

Map 10 - The World

APPENDIX

CONTENTS

We all belong to a family, but did you know that God has His own family, too? If you are a member of His family, He will always be there for you. To belong to God's family, you have to know four facts:

FACT 1: God loves *you* and has a plan to make *you* part of His family.

God's Word, the Bible, says:

God loves you.

God loved the world so much that He gave His only Son [Jesus]...so that whoever believes in Him may not be lost, but have eternal life (John 3:16).

God has a wonderful life planned for you.

(Jesus speaking) *I came to give life—life in all its fullness* (John 10:10).

But why aren't we part of God's family already?

FACT 2: Your sins keep you from being part of God's family.

What is sin?

Sin is something we do or say or think that does not please God. The Bible says that *everyone* has sinned. What are some sins? (Fighting, bad thoughts, lying, stealing, disobeying parents, bad words)

All people have sinned and are not good enough for God's glory (Romans 3:23).

Even though God made us and loves us, sin causes us to be far away from God. Because of our sin, we deserve punishment for doing wrong things. But God doesn't want to see anyone punished. He wants to give us a gift instead. That gift is a new kind of life.

When someone sins, he earns what sin pays... But God gives us a free gift—life forever in Christ Jesus (Romans 6:23).

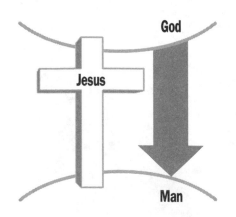

This picture shows how our sin keeps us from knowing and pleasing God. Many people try to please God by doing good things, such as going to church, praying more, and helping others. Doing these things makes you a nicer person, but they can't erase your sin or make you part of God's family.

FACT 3: Jesus is the only One who can take away your sin.

Jesus was punished in your place by dying on a cross.

[Jesus] died for us while we were still sinners. In this way God shows His great love for us (Romans 5:8).

And Jesus came back to life!

[Jesus] was buried and was raised to life on the third day (1 Corinthians 15:4).

Jesus is your way to God.

Jesus answered, "I am the way. And I am the truth and the life. The only way to the Father is through Me" (John 14:6).

Jesus made a way for us to come to God, our heavenly Father, and be a part of God's family. Jesus did this by paying for your sin when He died on the cross. But just knowing this is not enough ...

FACT 4: To become part of God's family, you must accept God's gift. Jesus is God's gift to you. When you accept Jesus, God's Son, you become God's child.

Some people did accept [Jesus]. They believed in Him. To them He gave the right to become children of God (John 1:12).

How do I accept God's gift?

You accept God's gift by asking Jesus to forgive you of your sins. Right now, Jesus is waiting to forgive your sins and come into your life.

(Jesus speaking) *Here I am! I stand at the door and knock. If anyone hears My voice and opens the door, I will come in* (Revelation 3:20).

God's book, the Bible, tells us that there are two kinds of people. Some people run their own lives. Others let Jesus control their lives.

You can accept God's gift right now by asking Jesus to forgive your sins. Talking to Jesus is called prayer. If you pray this prayer, you will belong to God's family!

Dear Jesus:

I need You. Thank You for dying on the cross for my sins. Thank You for forgiving my sins and making me part of God's family. Take control of my life and make me the kind of person You want me to be. **Amen.**

If you prayed this prayer—and really meant it—you are part of God's family **right now!**

But what happens if you sin again? Will you still be part of God's family?

Yes!

When you disobey your parents you make them unhappy. But you are still their child. To make things right, you tell them you are sorry for what you did. When you disobey God, He is not pleased, but you are still part of His family. He still loves you. But you need to tell Him you are sorry for what you did.

If we confess our sins, He will forgive our sins. We can trust God. He does what is right. He will make us clean from all the wrongs we have done (1 John 1:9).

As soon as you sin, tell God you are sorry. then God will forgive you and things will be right again between you and God.

ACTIVITY 11

Museum Listings for Egyptian Field Trip

Arkansas: Little Rock	Museum of Science and Natural History
California: San Jose	Rosicrucian Egyptian and Oriental Museum
Georgia: Atlanta	The Emory History Museum
Illinois: Urbana	University of Illinois Classical and European Culture Museum
Kentucky: Louisville	The Louisville Museum
Massachusetts: Boston	Museum of Fine Arts
Michigan: Detroit	The Detroit Institute
Missouri: Kansas City	William Rockhill Nelson Art Gallery, Atkins Museum
New York: Brooklyn	The Brooklyn Museum
New York: Buffalo	Albright-Knox Art Gallery
New York: New York	The Metropolitan Museum of Art
Ohio: Cleveland	The Cleveland Museum
Ohio: Cleveland	Western Reserve Historical Society
Ohio: Toledo	The Toledo Museum of Art
Pennsylvania: Philadelphia	The University of Pennsylvania Museum
Virginia: Richmond	The Virginia Museum of Fine Arts

From Avery Hart and Paul Mantell, *Pyramids! 50 Hands-On Activities to Experience Ancient Egypt.* Charlotte, VT: Williamson Publishing, 1997. Phone 1-800-234-8791.

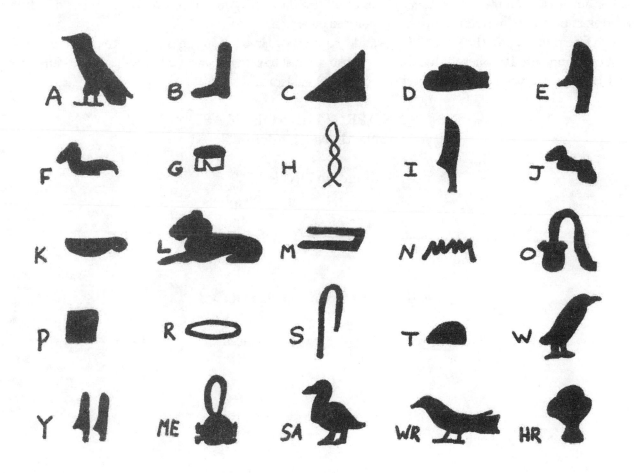

ACTIVITY 35B

Kings and Prophets of Israel and Judah

Copy the information below on two separate pieces of notebook paper. (Different-colored paper would be nice, but it is not a must.) To create lines on colored paper, you can photocopy a piece of white notebook paper with lines right onto blank colored paper.

On one piece, copy the list of "Kings and Prophets of Israel." On the other piece of paper, copy the list of "Kings and Prophets of Judah." These lists are just to get you started. We will add to them over time. Place them in your Student Notebook under "Asia: Israel."

KINGS AND PROPHETS OF ISRAEL
(The Northern Kingdom)

Before the Kingdom Divided

Kings	Prophets
King Saul	Samuel
King David	Nathan, Gad
King Solomon	Ahijah

After the Kingdom Divided in 925 B.C.

Kings	Prophets
1. Jeroboam	Ahijah
2. Nadab	

****

KINGS AND PROPHETS OF JUDAH
(The Southern Kingdom)

Before the Kingdom Divided

Kings	Prophets
King Saul	Samuel
King David	Nathan, Gad
King Solomon	Ahijah

After the Kingdom Divided in 925 B.C.

Kings	Prophets
1. Rehoboam	Shemaiah
2. Abijam	

ACTIVITY 39C

Authenticity of the Bible

The authenticity of the Bible is a rich and complex study. For now, since we just studied Homer, I want you to copy the following chart that indicates the dates written, the time span, and the number of copies of many historical documents. File this information in your Student Notebook under "Miscellaneous."

Work	Written	Earliest Mss.	Time Span	No. of Copies
Iliad (Homer)	900 B.C.	400 B.C.	500 years	643
Aristotle	350 B.C.	A.D. 1100	1,400 yrs.	49
Plato	400 B.C.	A.D. 900	1,300 yrs.	7
Caesar	50 B.C.	A.D. 900	1,000 yrs.	10
Tacitus	A.D. 100	A.D. 1100	1,100 yrs.	20
New Testament	A.D. 40–100	A.D. 125	85 yrs.	+24,000

To clarify the time span on the above chart, consider Plato for example. Plato lived and wrote things down in about 400 B.C. However, the earliest manuscript that has been found, which means a copy of it, was found in A.D. 900. That means there were 1,300 years between the original writings of Plato and the first copies of it that we have. All those years of recopying the original could have led to error or misinterpretation. And the number of copies is only 7.

The New Testament obviously has the best track record. It was written as early as A.D. 40. The oldest copies we have are from A.D. 125. That is only an 85-year time span of recopying the very first documents, such as the Gospels and letters from Paul. And look at the number of copies! It is astounding.

Chart above from a Sunday school presentation at Hope Evangelical Free Church, Mason, Ohio.

Shalom (peace)

שׁלוֹם

Psalm 33:11
"The plans of the Lord stand firm forever."

עצת יהוה לעולם תעכד

Psalm 100:3
"It is he who made us,

הוא עשׂנו

and we are his."

ולו אנחנו

ACTIVITY 77C

The Hippocratic Oath

There are a number of updated, modern versions of the classic Hippocratic Oath in use today. The American Medical Association does not recommend any particular version of the Oath. However, on its Web site, it does provide an "Oath Registry" that contains the oaths administered today in U.S. medical schools. (The registry is organized by state, then by school.)

The following is a popular modern version of the Hippocratic Oath that is used by the Duke University School of Medicine as well as by various other medical schools.

The Oath of Hippocrates

I do solemnly swear by that which I hold most sacred:

That I will be loyal to the Profession of Medicine and just and generous to its Members:

That I will lead my life and practice my Art in uprightness and honor:

That into whatsoever house I will enter, it shall be for the good of the sick and the well to the utmost of my power, and that I will hold myself aloof from wrong and from corruption, from the tempting of others to vice:

I will exercise my Art solely for the cure of my patients and will give no drug, perform no operation for a criminal purpose and far less suggest such a thing.

That whatsoever I shall see or hear in the lives of men which is not fitting to be spoken, I will keep inviolably secret. These things I do swear.

These things I do promise and in the proportion as I am faithful to this oath, may happiness and good repute be ever mine, the opposite if I shall be foresworn.

ACTIVITY 78C

Kings of Mesopotamia

Assyria

Tiglath-Pileser III (745–727 B.C.)

Shalamaneser IV (727–722 B.C.)

Sargon (722–705 B.C.)

Sennacherib (705–681 B.C.)

Esar-haddon (681–668 B.C.)

Ashurbanipal (668–626 B.C.)

Babylon

Nebuchadnezzar (606–562 B.C.)
  Hanging Gardens

Evil-Merodach (562–559 B.C.)

Nergal-sharezer (559–555 B.C.)

Labashi-Marduk (555 B.C.)

Nabonidus (552–536 B.C.) father of Belshazzar

Persia

Cyrus the Great (536–529 B.C.)

Cambyses (529–521 B.C.)

Gaumata (521 B.C.)

Darius I (521–486 B.C.) Allowed rebuilding of the Temple

Xerxes I (485–464 B.C.) Ahasuerus of Esther

Artaxerxes I (Longimanus) (465–424 B.C.)

Xerxes II (424 B.C.)

Darius II (Nothus) (424–404 B.C.)

Artaxerxes II (Mnemon) (404–359 B.C.)

Artaxerxes III (Ochus) (359-338 B.C.)

Darius III (Codomanus) (336–330 B.C.)

ACTIVITY 79B

Months of the Jewish Calendar

The Jewish calendar was traced by the cycles of the moon. It is called a lunar calendar. Our modern calendar is based on the path of the earth around the sun. It's called a solar calendar. Because of this difference, you will notice on the chart below that each of their months corresponds to half of two of our months.

Nisan	March and April
Zif	April and May
Sivan	May and June
Tammuz	June and July
Ab	July and August
Elul	August and September
Ethanim, Tisri	September and October
Marchesvan, Bul	October and November
Chisleu	November and December
Tebeth	December and January
Sebat, Sevat	January and February
Adar	(A month we don't have.)
Ve-Adar	(Time added to Adar when it was needed.)

From *Today's Dictionary of the Bible,* compiled by T. A. Bryant. Minneapolis: Bethany House Publishers, 1982; p. 430.

Boustrophedon Writing

The following is a sample of Boustrophedon writing. It went from left to right and then right to left without any spaces between the words. See if you can decipher the paragraph below. Then write one yourself.

   (The Scripture reference for this sample is given below, but see if you can decipher it on your own first. Then check your work.)

Andheshowedmeapureriverofwater oflife
ehtmorfgnideecorplatsyrcsaraelc
throneofGodandoftheLambInthemiddleof
ehtfoedisrentienodnateertssti
riverwasthetreeoflifewhichboretwelvefruits
yrevetiurfstignidleiyeerthcae
monthAndtheleavesofthetreewereforthe
llahserehtdnA snoitanehtfognilaeh
benomorecursebutthethroneofGodandofthe
llahsstnavressiHdnatiniebllahsbmaL
serveHimTheyshallseeHisfaceandHisname
sdaeherofriehtnuebllahs

(Rev. 22:1-4)

ACTIVITY 86A

Greek Alphabet

This is one version of the Greek alphabet. The name of each letter is given first, then its symbol, then its English equivalent.

Alpha	Beta	Gamma	Delta	Epsilon	Zeta
A	**B**	**Γ**	**Δ**	**E**	**Z**
A	B	G	D	E	Z

Eta	Theta	Iota	Kappa	Lambda	Mu	Nu
H	**θ**	**I**	**K**	**Λ**	**M**	**N**
AY	TH	I	K	L	M	N

Xi	Omikron	Pi	Rho	Sigma	Tau
Ξ	**O**	**Π**	**P**	**Σ**	**T**
X	AH	P	R	S	T

Upsilon	Phi	Chi	Psi	Omega
Y	**Φ**	**X**	**Ψ**	**Ω**
U	PH	CH	PS	O

From Roger L. Berry, *God's World: His Story.* Harrisonburg: Christian Light Publications, Inc., 1976; p. 190.

ACTIVITY 88A

Numbers 1–10 in Hindi

The words are listed to help you know how to pronounce the numbers.

1 ache

2 dough

3 teen

4 charr

5 paunch

6 chay

7 sot

8 art

9 now

10 duss

The Mystery of History

ACTIVITY 89A

Roman Numerals

English	Roman Numeral	Latin Pronunciation	Similar English Words
1	I	un'a	unit
2	II	du'o	dual
3	III	tri'a	tricycle
4	IV	quat' tuor	
5	V	quin'que	
6	VI	sex	
7	VII	sep'tem	September
8	VIII	oc'to	October
9	IX	no'vem	November
10	X	de'cem	December
11	XI	un'decim	
12	XII	duo'decim	
13	XIII	tre'decim	
14	XIV	quattuor'decim	
15	XV	quin'decim	
20	XX	vigin'ti	
100	C	cen'tum	centennial
1,000	M	mil'le	millennium

ACTIVITY 93A / 93B

The Maccabean Revolt

The Game of Dreidel

Materials: A dreidel top, counters (coins, bingo markers, etc.)

The spinning game of dreidel has been a popular Hanukkah game for centuries. A dreidel is a top with four sides; each side is imprinted with a Hebrew letter. The letters stand for the expression: "Neis gadol haya sham," which means, "A great miracle happened there." (Sometimes written as "here.") In the game of dreidel, the four letters are used to stand for game instructions.

Here's how to play the game: Each person begins with an equal number of counters. Every player places at least one counter (or any other agreed-upon number) in the "pot." Players take turns spinning the dreidel until it lands. Players win or lose counters based on what letter is right-side up when the top stops spinning. Use the following as a guide:

Nun "None" – the player gets nothing
Gimel "get" – the player gets the entire pot
Hei "Half" – the player gets half the pot
Shin "share" – everyone puts one counter into the pot

Continue to spin the top until either one person gains all the counters or all players agree to quit the game. If all players agree to end the game, the player with the most counters wins.

Potato Pancakes

It is a Jewish tradition at Hanukkah to make food fried in oil to remember the miracle of the oil that God provided. One favorite dish is the potato pancake. With supervision, make the following recipe.

1 large onion
½ cup matza meal
7 medium potatoes
2 eggs

Salt and pepper to taste
Vegetable oil for frying
Applesauce
Sour cream

Grate the potatoes and chop the onion. Drain excess liquid from both. Mix all ingredients together. Then heat the oil in a large frying pan. Drop the batter by tablespoons into the hot oil and fry over medium heat until crisp and golden on each side. (When the batter stops bubbling, that side is ready.) Drain on paper towels. Serve with applesauce and sour cream.

Adapted from *Haneirot Halalu: These Lights Are Holy—A Home Celebration of Chanuka*, edited by Elyse D. Frishman. New York: CCAR Press (Central Conference of American Rabbis), 1989.

The Mystery of History

ACTIVITY 95B

The Roman Army

8 men = 1 **contubernium**

These men ate together and shared a tent.

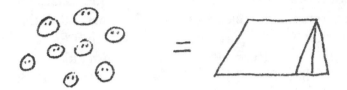

10 **contubernium** = 1 **century** (80 men)

These men were led by a *centurion*. One man carried a *standard* to identify the century. Another man, called the *tesserarius*, gave out a new password every day to keep out spies.

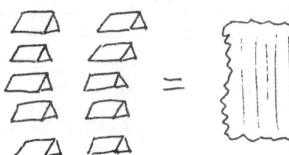

6 **centuries** = 1 **cohort** (480 men)

These men were led by the *tribunus militum*.

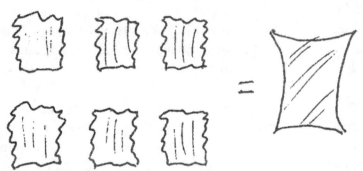

10 **cohorts** = 1 **legion** (about 5,000 men)

These men were led by the *legatus*. An *aquilifer* carried an eagle as a sign of power.

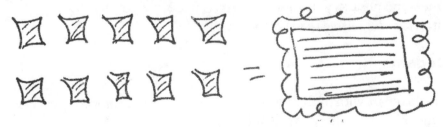

With colored pencils, shade the eight men orange. Shade the tents green. Shade the centuries blue. Shade the cohorts purple. Shade the legion red.

Section B: Activity Supplement

ACTIVITY 96B

The Roman Calendar

The calendar is an amazing device created to help us prepare for the different seasons and to track time. This is not easy though. For thousands of years man has tracked the seasons, but some did it by following the sun and others did it by tracking the moon. So, some calendars are "solar," or sun-based, whereas others are "lunar," or moon-based. To this day, some of our holidays (such as Christmas) fall on the same date every year because they follow the solar calendar, whereas other holidays (such as Easter) move around each year. That is because they follow the lunar calendar! Pretty interesting, isn't it?

Because time is so difficult to track, most of the ancient calendars were inaccurate at one point or another. The first Roman calendar had only 10 months and the year lasted 304 days. Those 10 months were Martius, Aprilis, Maius, Junius, Quintilis, Sextilis, September, October, November, and December. As you can see, the last six months were named according to their number order. They were the fifth, sixth, seventh, eighth, ninth, and tenth months in Latin.

But, there were some problems with this calendar. It was too short. So one Roman king decided to add Januarius and Februarius at the END of the year. It also helped him to collect more taxes from the people!

About 700 years later, the calendar was still inaccurate. In 46 B.C. Julius Caesar ordered a man by the name of Sosigenes to fix the problem. To him we owe much gratitude. Sosigenes figured out that the solar calendar should have 12 months with alternating days of 30 and 31 except for February, which he gave only 29. Every fourth year however, he gave February 30 days. Starting to sound familiar? Sosigenes also decided the year should START with Januarius instead of Martius. This was necessary but it made the months named after "numbers" all fall in the wrong place! And they are still wrong to this day.

It also messed up the year in which the changes had to be made. So, the year we call 46 B.C. became known as the "year of confusion." It had 445 days in it! In the midst of all the changes, the Romans renamed the month Quintilis after Julius Caesar. We know it now as July. Years later, Augustus Caesar wanted a month named after him, too. So, he renamed Sextilis and thus we have August. Augustus also wanted his month to be a longer one. So, he stole one day from February, giving August 31 days and February only 28.

That Roman calendar should sound very familiar now. It is not a great deal different from the one we use. The "Julian" calendar, as it has been called, worked for about 1,500 years. Eventually some changes had to be made that included the adding of leap year. The new calendar was called the Gregorian calendar after Pope Gregory XIII. Some countries, Russia and Turkey for example, only started using it in the early 1900s. So, a lot of dates from history differ around the world.

I hope you find it interesting to know the origin behind some of the words and numbers you use almost every day. The next time someone asks you your birthday, think of the Romans!

Following are two activities for you related to the calendar.

Younger and Middle Students

Copy by hand or machine this chart with the names of the months as they developed over time. File it in your Student Notebook under "Europe: Italy (Ancient Rome)."

	Early Rome	Julian Calendar	Our Calendar
1.	Martius	Januarius	January
2.	Aprilis	Februarius	February
3.	Maius	Martius	March
4.	Junius	Aprilis	April
5.	Quintilis	Maius	May
6.	Sextilis	Junius	June
7.	September	Julius	July
8.	October	Augustus	August
9.	November	September	September
10.	December	October	October
11.		November	November
12.		December	December

Middle Students

In an encyclopedia (under "calendar") or in some other resource book, find what is called a "perpetual calendar." It is a chart of years, months, and days. The chart gives you the ability to easily calculate what day of the week any date has fallen on.

For example, do you know what day of the week your birthday will fall on this year? Following the directions with the perpetual calendar, find out the day. Then calculate the day of the week of your birthday in a year long ago, say 1900. Pick other famous days in history such as the signing of the Declaration of Independence on July 4, 1776, or Lincoln's assassination on April 14, 1865.

ACTIVITY 99A

Wise Men Ornaments

Make Christmas ornaments to remember the gifts of the wise men.

Materials: 4-by-4-inch squares of fabric or felt (one for each ornament desired); about 10 inches of yarn, string, or raffia ribbon (one strand per ornament); a large-eyed needle

For "gifts" choose what is easiest for you to obtain from the following suggestions:

- Gold: Pieces of fool's gold; chocolate coins covered in gold foil wrap; foreign coins that are gold or bronze in color; gold-colored crayons; gold tissue paper

- Frankincense: Pieces of incense from the drug store; chips of wax from a fragrant candle; a sliver from a bar of fragrant soap

- Myrrh: An old empty perfume bottle as tiny as you can find, filled with a mix of part baby oil and part water with red food coloring added; chips of a red candle; vanilla flavoring in a tiny bottle (because myrrh smelled good but was bitter like vanilla). Myrrh in its natural form was an oily substance from a tree, but it hardened quickly. So, a liquid or solid could represent myrrh.

1. Take the square piece of fabric and fold it twice.

2. Trim the outer edge in a curve so that it opens up to be a circle.

3. On the backside of the cloth, draw a circle about 1 inch from the edge of your fabric.

4. With assistance if necessary, thread the needle with your string. Sew in and out of the fabric all the way around the drawn circle so that you have a drawstring to close your fabric "pouch."

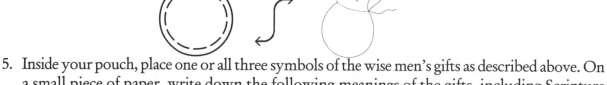

5. Inside your pouch, place one or all three symbols of the wise men's gifts as described above. On a small piece of paper, write down the following meanings of the gifts, including Scripture references, and add them to the pouch, too. (*Note to Teacher:* Abbreviate the information below for younger students.) Take time to look up the Scriptures as you work. Tie the string in a bow and use the tie as a hanger for your Christmas tree.

   - Gold represents a gift fit for a king and a life of righteousness. (I Tim. 6:15)
   - Frankincense was used by the Israelites when giving sacrifices to the Lord. Jesus was a perfect sacrifice for our sins. (Heb. 9:26)
   - Myrrh was used for anointing sacred things and for preserving the dead. Jesus' body was sacred and resurrected from the dead. (Mark 14:8, I Cor. 15:20)

The Mystery of History

ACTIVITY 100A

Egyptian Menu

Here is a list of Egyptian foods that someone like Mark Antony might have enjoyed. As a wealthy Roman, he would have already been accustomed to eating quite nicely and exotically. (The Romans even ate flamingos!)

Choose one, two, or three items from each category and throw an Egyptian feast. Keep things in bite-sized pieces because the Egyptians didn't use forks or spoons. They just ate with their hands. They usually kept small bowls of water at the eating table to dip their fingers in during the meal.

- Meats: Beef, antelope, gazelle, honeyed sweetmeats, fish, duck, geese, oxen, onyx, pig (ham or bacon), sheep, goats
- Vegetables: Onions, garlic, leeks, beans, lentils, lettuce, cucumbers
- Grains: Wheat (bread or cream of wheat), barley bread, millet, cakes
- Fruit: Grapes, dates, figs, melons, apples, raisins, pomegranates, coconut, (no citrus)
- Drinks: Beer, wine, water. (There are nonalcoholic beers and wines available that might add to the sense of an authentic feast!)

ACTIVITY 103C

Jesus Christ, His Birth: Prophecies Fulfilled

To help you retain the information about fulfilled prophecies, I would love to see you do two things. First, copy this list of the prophecies. Set your paper up as I have. List the Old Testament prophecies in the far-left column. Place the New Testament fulfillment next to it. Then, give a short explanation to the right. I have done two for you as an example. File your completed paper under "Asia: Israel."

Next, I would like you to choose five or more of these prophecies and highlight them in your Bible. At the bottom of the page in your Bible, write down where the New Testament fulfillment can be found. In the future these references may be helpful in defending what you believe to be truth.

Old Testament	New Testament	Explanation
Isa. 7:14	Luke 1:34–35	Jesus was born of a virgin.
Mic. 5:2	Matt. 2:1–2	Jesus was born in Bethlehem.
Isa. 9:6	John 7:46	
Isa. 9:6	Col. 1:20	
Isa. 28:16	I Pet. 2:4–6	
Ps. 8:2	Matt. 21:15–16	
Jer. 31:31	Matt. 26:28	
Dan. 9:26a	Heb. 2:9	
Isa. 53:11	Heb. 9:28	
Ps. 41:9	Mark 14:17–18	
Zech. 11:12–13	Matt. 26:14–15	
Isa. 53:7	Matt. 27:12–14	
Isa. 53:7	Matt. 27:27–31	
Isa. 50:6	Matt. 26:67	
Ps. 22:16	Matt. 27:38	
Ps. 22:17, 34:20	John 19:32–33	
Hos. 13:14	I Cor. 15:55–57	
Ps. 2:6–7	Acts 13:30–33	
Ps. 80:17, 110:1	Acts 5:31, Mark 16:19	

ACTIVITY 105A

Roman Coins

Make your own Roman coins

Materials: Light cardboard or poster board, foil, glue, dark marker

1. Cut circles out of the cardboard about 1 or 2 inches in diameter (the bigger they are, the easier little hands can draw on them).
2. Trace the shape of the circles onto the foil. Make two foil pieces for each cardboard shape.
3. Glue the foil onto the cardboard.
4. Using a pencil first, follow the suggested pattern and trace or sketch the words and pictures of the type of coin Jesus may have referred to when He said, "Render unto Caesar's that which is Caesar's."
5. Outline the sketch with the marker.

ACTIVITY 107A

Resurrection Cookies

1 cup whole pecans   3 egg whites   1 cup sugar
1 tsp. vinegar   pinch of salt   zipper bag and wooden spoon

1. Preheat oven to 300 degrees.

2. Place pecans in zipper bag; let children beat them into small pieces with the wooden spoon.
   Explain that after Jesus was arrested He was beaten by the Roman soldiers.
   Read John 19:1–3.

3. Let each child smell the vinegar. Put 1 tsp. vinegar into mixing bowl.
   Explain that when Jesus was thirsty on the cross He was given vinegar to drink.
   Read John 19: 28–30.

4. Add egg whites to vinegar.
   Eggs represent life. Explain that Jesus gave His life to give us life.

5. Sprinkle a little salt into each child's hand. Let them taste it and brush the rest into the bowl.
   Explain that this represents the salty tears shed by Jesus' followers and the bitterness of our own sin.

6. So far the ingredients are not very appetizing. Add 1 cup of sugar.
   Explain that the sweetest part of the story is that Jesus died because he loves us. He wants us to know and belong to Him.
   Read Psalm 34:8 and John 3:16.

7. Beat with a mixer on high speed for 12–15 minutes until stiff peaks are formed.
   Explain that the white color represents the purity in God's eyes of those whose sins have been cleansed by Jesus.
   Read Isaiah 1:18 and John 3:1–3.

8. Fold in the broken nuts. Drop by teaspoons onto cookie sheet covered with wax paper.
   Explain that each mound represents the rocky tomb where Jesus' body was laid.
   Read Matthew 27:57–60.

9. Put the cookie sheet in the oven, close the door, and turn the oven OFF.
   Give each child a piece of tape and seal the oven door. Explain that Jesus' tomb was sealed.
   Read Matthew 27:65–66.

10. Go to bed.
    Explain that they may feel sad leaving the cookies in the oven overnight. Jesus' followers were in greater despair when the tomb was sealed.
    Read John 16:20, 22.

11. In the morning, open the oven and give everyone a cookie. Notice the cracked surface and take a bite. The cookies are hollow! On the first Easter, Jesus' followers were amazed to find the tomb open and empty.
    Read Matthew 28:1–9. HE HAS RISEN!

This recipe is from a friend who circulated it over the Internet. Original source unknown.

ACTIVITY 107B

The Crucifixion

The Question: How does a person physically die from the act of crucifixion?

The Answer: When a person hangs from two hands, blood quickly sinks to the lower parts of the body. Within about 10 minutes, blood pressure drops 50 percent. At the same time, the pulse doubles. Fainting soon follows as the heart loses blood. Circulation ceases. Suffocation is one result of the havoc placed on the body. Ultimately, however, the heart fails. You could say that Jesus died of a broken heart. It is a fitting statement as He died because of our SINS, which broke His heart.

One of the cruelties of crucifixion is the fact that a board is placed at the feet of the victim that will allow the victim to push his body up. When he does so, he is better able to breathe, but it would be excruciating to do so because of the nails driven through the feet. The person would constantly be battling between the two pains. This is the reason why some victims had their legs broken. It would speed up the death process because the person would be unable to catch his breath. "But when they came to Jesus and saw that He was already dead, they did not break his legs." (John 19:33)

To add to the pain would be the fact that most victims were scourged before being placed on the cross. A "scourging" was being whipped by a rope with bits of sharp metal or bone on the end. Sometimes a scourging alone could kill a man. As a person hung on a cross, pushing himself up and down to breathe would be worsened by the pain of the open wounds on the back.

Reflect on the passages found in Isaiah 53:5, "But He was wounded for our transgressions, He was bruised for our iniquities; the chastisement for our peace was upon Him, and by His stripes we are healed." In prayer, just thank Him for what He did for us.

From *The Living Bible Encyclopedia in Story and Pictures,* Art Treasure ed., Vol. 4. New York: H. S. Stuttman Co., Inc., 1968; p. 461.

I have compiled for you this recommended list of books and videos that would nicely supplement my text. All my suggestions are optional. By "Younger Students," I am referring to those children about kindergarten through 2nd grade. "Middle Students" would mean 3rd to 5th graders, and "Older Students" refers to 6th grade through 8th (as well as high school students and adults).

I am also including what I call a "Wish List." This refers to neat educational toys, games, or activities that are commonly found at large bookstores. The Wish List may be best in the hands of grandparents needing birthday and holiday gift ideas!

Special Note: It is difficult to suggest videos according to age because all families have their own set of standards. I sometimes allow my younger children to see older videos for their historical value and significance, but NOT all of them. Please use YOUR best judgment on any of the videos I have listed. I have recommended such a large number of different videos because some may be hard to find. The more choices listed the more likely your library or video rental store will have at least one!

Caution! This list can be overwhelming! Remember that I wrote this history curriculum to be a history course, not a unit study. However, it would be natural to incorporate a student's Bible course and reading course into this study of history to make time for all this good reading. YOU select the number of books your family can manage or videos you have time to watch. These are just possibilities!

QUARTER 1

LESSON 1 Creation
• All Students: *The Illustrated Origins Answer Book*, Paul S. Taylor (Answers in Genesis).
• Younger Students: *When the World Was New*, L. J. Sattgast (Grand Rapids, MI: Zondervan).
• Middle and Older Students: Genesis 1, the Bible.
• Older Students: *The Young Earth*, John D. Morris, Ph.D. (Answers in Genesis).

LESSON 2 Adam and Eve
• Middle and Older Students: Genesis 2 and 3, the Bible.

LESSON 3 Jubal and Tubal-Cain
• All Students: *Adam and His Kin, The Lost History of Their Lives and Times*, Ruth Beechick (Arrow Press).
• Middle and Older Students: Genesis 4, the Bible.

LESSON 4 Noah and the Flood
• Middle and Older Students: Genesis 6–9, the Bible.
• Older Students:
  (1) *The Genesis Flood*, John C. Whitcomb and Henry M. Morris (Baker Books).
  (2) *Noah's Ark: A Feasibility Study*, John Woodmorappe (Answers in Genesis).
• Videos:
  (1) *Ancient Secrets of the Bible: Noah's Ark—What Happened to It?* (1997). Not Rated.
  (2) *In Search of Noah's Ark* (1970). Rated G.

LESSON 5 The Ice Age
• Younger and Middle Students: *Life in the Great Ice Age*, Michael and Beverly Oard (Anwers in Genesis). This has great illustrations and facts.
• Middle and Older Students: *Genesis: Finding Our Roots*, Ruth Beechick.

LESSON 6 Dinosaurs
• All Students: *What Really Happened to the Dinosaurs?* Ken Ham (Answers in Genesis).
• Younger Students: *D is for Dinosaur* (Answers in Genesis; available in video as well).
• Younger and Middle Students: *The Great Dinosaur Mystery and the Bible*, Paul S. Taylor (Answers in Genesis).
• Video: *Project Dinosaur*, produced by ShowForth Videos, Bob Jones University Press. This video addresses the defense of Creation and is suitable for all ages.

LESSON 8 The Tower of Babel
• Younger Students: *From Arapesh to Zuni: A Book of Bibleless People*, Karen Lewis (Wycliffe Bible Translators).
• Middle and Older Students: Genesis 9, the Bible.

- Older Students: *The Rise of Babylon*, Charles H. Dyer (Tyndale).
- Videos:
  (1) *Ancient Secrets of the Bible: Tower of Babel—Fact or Fiction?* (1997). Not Rated.
  (2) *Tower of Babel* (1979), documentary. Not Rated.

LESSON 10 Stonehenge
- All Students: *The World Heritage: Prehistoric Stone Monuments* (Chicago: Children's Press). This is a library resource with many colorful pictures.

LESSON 11 Early Egyptians
- Younger Students: *World Wise Series on Egypt* (New York: Franklin Watts).
- Younger and Middle Students: *Pyramid*, David Macaulay.
- Younger and Middle Students: *Pyramids! 50 Hands-On Activities to Experience Ancient Egypt*, Avery Hart and Paul Mantell (Williamson Publishing).
- Middle Students: *Golden Goblet*, Eloise Jarvis McGraw (Puffin Books).
- Videos:
  (1) *Ancient Mysteries: The Great Pyramids* (1995), narrated by Kathleen Turner. Not Rated. (A&E).
  (2) *Mummies and the Wonders of Ancient Egypt* (1996), four parts. Not Rated. (A&E).

LESSON 12 The Minoan Civilization
- All Students: *The Search for Lost Cities*, Nicola Barber (Raintree-Steck Vaughn, 1998). This is a beautiful and informative library book that features the city of Knossos.

LESSON 13 Abraham
- Middle and Older Students: Genesis 12–23, the Bible.
- Videos:
  (1) *Abraham* (1994), starring Richard Harris. Not Rated. (TNT).
  (2) *Ancient Secrets of the Bible: Sodom and Gomorrah—Legend or Real Event?* (1997). Not Rated.

LESSON 14 Jacob and Esau
- Middle and Older Students: Genesis 25–35 and Book of Job, the Bible.
- Video: *Jacob* (1995), starring Matthew Modine. Not Rated.

LESSON 15 Joseph
- Younger and Middle Students: Genesis 37–50, the Bible.
- Videos:
  (1) *Greatest Adventure Series: Joseph and His Brothers* (1990). (Hanna-Barbera; animated).
  (2) *Joseph* (1995), starring Paul Mercurio. Not Rated.

LESSON 17 The Israelites in Slavery
- Middle and Older Students: Exodus 1, the Bible.

LESSON 18 China and the Shang Dynasty
- Video: *Great Cultures, Great Nations—China: The History and the Mystery* (1996).

LESSON 19 Moses and the Exodus
- Middle and Older Students: Exodus 2–24, the Bible.
- Videos:
  (1) *The Prince of Egypt* (1999). Rated PG. (Dreamworks Home Entertainment; animated).
  (2) *The Ten Commandments* (1956), starring Charlton Heston.
  (3) *Moses* (1996), starring Ben Kingsley. Not Rated.

LESSON 20 The Ark of the Covenant and the Tabernacle
- See Wish List for Quarter 1!
- Middle and Older Students: Exodus 25–30, the Bible.
- Older Students: *A Dwelling Place for God*, Ruth Specter Lascelle (Rock of Israel, 1990).
- Video: *Ancient Mysteries: The Ark of the Covenant* (1994). Not Rated. (A&E).

LESSON 21 Joshua, Jericho, and Rahab
- Middle and Older Students: Joshua 1–6, the Bible.
- Video: *Ancient Secrets of the Bible: Walls of Jericho—Did They Tumble Down?* (1997). Not Rated.

LESSON 22 Amenhotep IV and Nefertiti
• Younger and Middle Students:
  (1) *Nefertiti, the Mystery Queen*, Burnham Holmes (Raintree-Steck Vaughn, 1992). This is a great library book I stumbled across that is easy to read and very informative. Great pictures, too.
  (2) *See-Through History: Ancient Egypt*, Judith Crosher. A neat book with see-through layovers to depict the inside and outside of Egyptian structures.

LESSON 23 Tutankhamen (King Tut)
• Younger and Middle Students:
  (1) *Tut's Mummy: Lost . . . and Found*, Judy Donnelly. (Random House, *Step Into Reading* series, 1988).
  (2) *Hieroglyphs from A to Z: A Rhyming Book with Ancient Egyptian Stencils for Kids*, Peter Der Manuelian (Scholastic, 1991). This is both a beautiful and a practical book I found at the library.
• Older Students: *The Murder of Tutankhamen A True Story*, Bob Brier (Putnam, 1998). This is an excellent defense of who the author, Bob Brier, believes to have killed King Tut. Bob Brier was the historian responsible for the A&E documentary. Great reading for older students and adults.
• Video: *King Tut*, Vols. 1–4 (1992). (A&E).

LESSON 24 Ramses II (The Great)
• Middle Students: *Mara, Daughter of the Nile*, Eloise Jarvis MeGraw (Puffin Books).
• Older Students: *The Complete Temples of Ancient Egypt*, Richard H. Wilkinson (Thames and Hudson). Colorful photos.
• Videos:
  (1) *Ancient Civilizations for Children: Ancient Egypt*. (Schlessinger Media).
  (2) *Great Cities of the Ancient World: The Pyramids and the Cities of the Pharaohs* (1994). Not Rated.
  (3) *The Great Pharaohs of Egypt* (1997), four-part series. Not Rated. (A&E).
  (4) *The Great Egyptians I and II*, narrated by Bob Brier. (The Learning Channel).
• IMAX Movie: *Mysteries of Egypt* (1999).

LESSON 25 Legend of the Trojan Horse
• All Students:
  (1) *The Children's Homer, The Adventures of Odysseus*, and *The Tale of Troy*, Padraic Colum (Aladdin Paperbacks).
  (2) *The Search for Lost Cities*, Nicola Barber (Raintree-Steck Vaughn, 1998). This is a beautiful and informative library book that gives interesting detail to the excavation work done by Heinrich Schliemann and his wife, Sophia.
• Younger and Middle Students: *Trojan Horse*, Emily Little (Random House).
• Older Students: *Iliad*, Homer.
• Videos:
  (1) *Ancient Civilizations for Children: Ancient Aegean*. (Schlessinger Media).
  (2) *Ancient Mysteries: The Odyssey of Troy* (1995), narrated by Kathleen Turner. Not Rated. (A&E).
  (3) *The Odysssey* (1997). Rated PG-13.

LESSON 26 Ruth and Naomi
• Middle and Older Students: Book of Ruth, the Bible.
• Videos:
  (1) *The Story of Ruth* (1960).
  (2) *People of the Book: Ruth: the Convert* (1996), starring Stuart Whitman Not Rated.

LESSON 27 Gideon
• Middle and Older Students: Judges 6–8, the Bible.
• Video: *Bible Adventures—Gideon/Jonah and the Big Fish*, produced by ShowForth Videos, Bob Jones University Press (for younger students).

Wish List
These are toys, games, and the like, for enrichment. Prices listed may no longer be accurate.
• "The Tiny Perfect Dinosaur Series," Andrew and McMeel ($12.95).
• "The Dinosaur Hunter's Kit," Running Press ($18.95).
• "How to Draw Prehistoric Animals," Watermill Press ($1.85).
• Lego "The Adventurers: Dino Series" (Dinosaur Age).
• "Life in Ancient Egypt Coloring Books," Dover ($2.95).
• "Fun with Hieroglyphics," Catherine Roehrig, Metropolitan Museum of Art, Viking Children's Books ($24.99).

- "Treasure Chest: Ancient Egypt," Running Press ($19.95). This is an educational craft pack.
- "Lift the Lid on Mummies," Running Press ($19.95). A neat, hands-on mummy craft.
- "Take an Egyptian Adventure," Nova Curiosity Kits.
- Lego "The Adventurers: Desert Series," (Egyptian theme).
- "Tabernacle Model to Make." Makes a card-stock scale model of the Tabernacle. Available through Elijah Company ($5.99).
- "A Coloring Book of Ancient China," Bellerophon ($4.95).
- *Then and Now Bible Atlas*, available through the Elijah Company. This would be an excellent resource to own and use throughout this text.

QUARTER 2

LESSON 28 Samson
- Middle and Older Students: Judges 13–16, the Bible.
- Videos:
  (1) *Samson and Delilah* (1949), starring Hedy Lamarr. Won five Academy Awards. Not Rated.
  (2) *Samson and Delilah* (1996), starring Eric Thal. Not Rated.

LESSON 30 Samuel
- Middle and Older Students: I Samuel 1–8, the Bible.

LESSON 31 King Saul
- Middle and Older Students: I Samuel 9–31, the Bible.

LESSON 32 David
- Middle and Older Students: I Samuel 16 – II Samuel, Favorite Psalms, the Bible.
- Video: *King David* (1985), starring Richard Gere. Not Rated, but be careful.

LESSON 33 Solomon
- Middle and Older Students: I Kings 1–11, Proverbs, Ecclesiastes, Song of Solomon, the Bible.

LESSON 35 The Kingdom of Israel Divides
- Middle and Older Students: I Kings 12, the Bible.

LESSON 36 Elijah, the Fiery Prophet
- Middle and Older Students: I Kings 17–19; II Kings 2, the Bible.
- Video: *The Animated Stories from the Bible: Elijah*. (Nest Family Entertainment Series, animated).

LESSON 37 Elisha (Israel's Prophet)
- Middle and Older Students: I Kings 19:19–21; II Kings 2–8:15, 13:14–21, the Bible.
- Videos:
  (1) *The Animated Stories from the Bible: Elisha*. (Nest Family Entertainment Series; animated).
  (2) *Bible Adventures—Naaman the Leper/Samson*, produced by ShowForth Videos, Bob Jones University Press.

LESSON 38 Joel and Obadiah
- Middle and Older Students: Books of Joel and Obadiah, the Bible.

LESSON 39 Homer
- Younger and Middle Students: *The Children's Homer, The Adventures of Odysseus*, and *The Tale of Troy*, Padraic Colum (Aladdin Paperbacks).
- Older Students: *Iliad*, Homer.

LESSON 40 India and Hinduism
- Younger Students: *Count Your Way Through India*, Jim Haskins (Carolrhoda Books, Inc, 1990). A colorful and informative library book on India.
- Older Students: *Handbook of Today's Religions*, Josh McDowell and Don Stewart (Here's Life Publishers, 1983). See the chapter on Hinduism.

LESSON 42 Jonah and Amos
- Middle and Older Students: Books of Jonah and Amos, the Bible.

LESSON 44 Isaiah and Micah (Judah's Prophets)
- Middle and Older Students: Selected portions of Isaiah, II Kings 19–20; Book of Micah, the Bible.

LESSON 45 Israel Falls to Assyria
• Middle and Older Students: II Kings 17, the Bible.

LESSON 46 Hosea (Israel's Prophet)
• Younger and Middle Students: Book of Hosea, the Bible.

LESSON 47 Hezekiah and Sennacherib
• Middle and Older Students: II Kings 18–20 and/or II Chronicles 29–32, the Bible.

LESSON 48 Ancient Native Americans
• Video: *Prehistoric Ohioans.* A library resource that is available in Cincinnati, Ohio.

LESSON 49 The Rise of Athens and Sparta
• Video: *Great Cities of the Ancient World Series: Athens and Ancient Greece* (1994).

LESSON 50 Manasseh
• Middle and Older Students: II Kings 21, II Chronicles 33, the Bible.

LESSON 51 The Powers of Mesopotamia
• All Students: Matthew 27:46, the Bible.
• Younger and Middle Students: *The Search for Lost Cities*, Nicola Barber (Raintree-Steck Vaughn, 1998). Beautiful book with information on many people, including the Assyrians and Babylonians.

LESSON 52 King Josiah
• Middle and Older Students: II Kings 22-23 or II Chronicles 34-35, the Bible.

LESSON 53 Nahum and Zephaniah
• Middle and Older Students: Books of Nahum and Zephaniah, the Bible.

LESSON 54 Jeremiah (Judah's Prophet)
• Middle and Older Students: Any selected portions of the books of Jeremiah and Lamentations, the Bible.

Wish List *(continued)*
There are so few games or toys that depict life from this time period. However, here are a few other ideas that would give children a sense of the cultures they are studying.
• Souvenirs from India.
• Eating at an Indian restaurant.
• Field trip to ancient Native American sites of the Mound Builders.
• Tour of a Buddhist temple.
• Tour of a Jewish synagogue.
• Visit to a worship service of a Messianic Jewish synagogue.

QUARTER 3

LESSON 55 Nineveh Destroyed
• Middle and Older Students: *The Works of Josephus* (Nimrod).

LESSON 56 Habakkuk and Huldah
• Middle and Older Students: Book of Habakkuk, II Kings 22:14, or II Chronicles 34:22, the Bible.

LESSON 57 The Babylonian Captivity
• Younger Students: *Jerusalem, Still Shining*, Karla Kuskin (Harper and Row, 1987). This is a great library book that all ages would appreciate. It describes in children's language the history of Jerusalem well beyond the Babylonian Captivity.
• Middle and Older Students: II Kings 25 or II Chronicles 36:15–21, the Bible.

LESSON 58 Nebuchadnezzar II and the Hanging Gardens
• All Students: *World Book Looks at Wonders of the World* (Chicago: World Book, Inc., 1997). A colorful library resource.
• Middle and Older Students: Daniel 1–4, the Bible.
• Video: *Seven Wonders of the World: Simply the Best*, documentary. (Discovery Channel).

LESSON 59 Daniel
• Middle and Older Students: Any selected portions of the Book of Daniel, the Bible.
• Video: *Daniel and the Lion's Den*. (Hanna-Barbera; animated).

LESSON 60 Aesop's Fables
• Younger and Middle Students: Aesop's fables have been published by many companies, usually available through the library.

LESSON 61 Ezekiel
• Middle and Older Students: Selected portions of the Book of Ezekiel, the Bible.

LESSON 62 Shadrach, Meshach, and Abed-Nego
• All Students: Daniel 3, the Bible.
• Video: *Bible Adventures—Ahab the Pouting King/The Fiery Furnace*, produced by ShowForth Videos, Bob Jones University Press.

LESSON 63 Buddha
• Older Students: *Handbook of Today's Religions*, Josh McDowell and Don Stewart (Here's Life Publishers, 1983). See the chapter on Buddhism.

LESSON 65 Confucius
• Older Students: *Handbook of Today's Religions*, Josh McDowell and Don Stewart (Here's Life Publishers, 1983). See the chapter on Confucianism.

LESSON 66 Belshazzar and Cyrus the Great
• All Students: Daniel 5; Isaiah 44:28–45:1, the Bible.

LESSON 68 Zerubbabel
• Middle and Older Students: Ezra 1–6, the Bible.

LESSON 69 Haggai and Zechariah
• Middle and Older Students: Books of Haggai and Zechariah, Ezra 5:1–2, the Bible.

LESSON 72 Herodotus
• Middle and Older Students: Original works available on the Internet (http://classics.mit.edu).

LESSON 73 Xerxes I
• Middle and Older Students: Book of Esther, the Bible.

LESSON 74 Esther
• Middle and Older Students: Book of Esther, the Bible.
• Videos:
  (1) *The Animated Stories from the Bible: Esther.* (Nest Family Entertainment Series; animated).
  (2) *Esther.* (Veggie Tales).

LESSON 76 Socrates
• Middle and Older Students: *The Book of Virtues*, William J. Bennett.

LESSON 78 Ezra and Artaxerxes
• Middle and Older Students: Ezra 7–10, the Bible.

LESSON 79 Nehemiah
• Middle and Older Students: Book of Nehemiah, the Bible.

Wish List *(continued)*
These are toys, games, and the like, for enrichment. Prices listed may no longer be accurate.
• An Esther doll sold at Christian bookstores.
• A copy of the Hippocratic Oath from anyone you know in the medical field.
• Dinner at a Greek restaurant.
• Treasure Chest "Ancient Greece," Running Press ($19.95). This is an educational craft pack.
• Ancient Arts "Mosaics," Running Press ($18.95). This is a neat craft set for making mosaics of both Greek and Roman design.

QUARTER 4

LESSON 82 Malachi
• Middle and Older Students: Book of Malachi, the Bible.

LESSON 83 Plato and Aristotle
• Middle and Older Students:
  (1) *The Book of Virtues,* William J. Bennett.
  (2) Look for a version of the "Lost City of Atlantis" from the book *Timaeus* by Plato.

LESSON 85 Alexander the Great
• Video: *Conquerors: Alexander the Great,* documentary. (Discovery Channel).

LESSON 86 The Split of Alexander's Empire
• Middle and Older Students: Daniel 8, 11, the Bible.

LESSON 88 Emperor Asoka of India
• Younger Students: *Count Your Way Through India,* Jim Haskins (Carolrhoda Books, Inc.). A beautiful and informative library book on India.

LESSON 89 The Septuagint and the Colossus of Rhodes
• All Students: *World Book Looks at Wonders of the World* (Chicago: World Book, Inc., 1997). A colorful library resource.
• Younger Students: *From Arapesh to Zuni: A Book of Bibleless People,* Karen Lewis. (Wycliffe Bible Translators).
• Video: *Seven Wonders of the World: Magic Metropolis,* documentary featuring Alexandria. (Discovery Channel).

LESSON 90 The Qin Dynasty
• All Students: *The Terra Cotta Army of Emperor Qin,* Caroline Lazo (New Discovery Books, 1993). This is a good library book with pictures and information.
• Videos: *Forbidden City: The Great Within* (1995), documentary with Rod Steiger. (Discovery Channel).
• IMAX Movie: *First Emperor of China* (1995). This is about Qin in the third century B.C.

LESSON 91 Hannibal, Elephants, and the Punic Wars
• IMAX Movie: *Africa's Elephant Kingdom.* This will give students a better appreciation of the amazing elephant.

LESSON 92 The Han Dynasty
• Younger Students: *The Story About Ping,* Marjorie Flack and Kurt Wiese (Viking Press). This is a simple fiction about a duck, but it depicts life on a houseboat.

LESSON 93 The Maccabean Revolt
• Middle and Older Students: See the Apocrypha.
• Video: *Maccabees: The Story of Hanukkah* (Living History Productions, Inc., Animated Hero Classics).

LESSON 94 Spartacus
• Video: *Spartacus* (1960), starring Kirk Douglas. An excellent presentation for mature students.

LESSON 96 Julius Caesar
• Video: *Julius Caesar,* based on the play by William Shakespeare. There are several versions of this film; the 1953 version stars Marlon Brando.

LESSON 98 Cleopatra
• Middle and Older Students: *The Royal Diaries: Cleopatra VII, Daughter of the Nile,* Kristiana Gregory (Scholastic Books, 1999). This is a great presentation of the younger life of Cleopatra. Excellent reading, in my opinion.
• Video: *Cleopatra,* starring Elizabeth Taylor. A must-see for mature children; one of my all-time favorite movies!

LESSON 99 Herod the Great
• All Students: *Herod the Great,* Robert Green (New York: Franklin Watts, 1996). A very well-written library book.
• Videos:
  (1) *That the World May Know.* Set 4 of this tape series contains a segment on Herod in contrast to David in his accomplishments. (Focus on the Family Films).
  (2) *Herod the Great,* in the series *Mysteries of the Bible, Collector's Choice* (A&E). This was a fantastic documentary that I stumbled across while shopping at a large discount store!

LESSON 101 Augustus Caesar and the Roman Empire
• All Students: Luke 2:1–7, the Bible.

LESSON 102 John the Baptist
• Middle and Older Students: Isaiah 40:3; Malachi 3:1, 4:5–6; Mark 1:1–11, 6:14–29; Luke 1, 3; John 2:19–28, 3:22–36.
• Video: *The Animated Stories from the New Testament: John the Baptist.* (Nest Entertainment; animated).

LESSON 103 Jesus Christ, His Birth
- All Students: Matthew 1, 2; Luke 1:26 to Chapter 2.
- Middle Students: *The Bronze Bow*, Speare. A fictional story set in the time period of Christ; usually available at homeschool conventions.
- Video: *The Animated Stories from the New Testament: The King is Born.* (Nest Entertainment; animated).

LESSON 104 Jesus, His Teachings and Miracles
- Middle and Older Students: See the Gospels of Matthew, Mark, Luke, and John.
- Middle and Older Students: *Ben-Hur*, Lew Wallace, as presented in the Illustrated Classic Editions (Moby Books). This scaled-down version was one book my son could hardly put down.
- Older Students: *Ben Hur*, Lew Wallace. This is a classic fiction that takes place during the time of Christ and gives great insight into the time period. Difficult reading.
- Videos:
  (1) *The Animated Stories from the New Testament: The Miracles of Jesus.* (Nest Entertainment; animated).
  (2) *Ben Hur* (1959), starring Charlton Heston. A must-see for the entire family!

LESSON 105 Tiberius Caesar, Pilate, and Herod
- Middle and Older Students: (Luke 20:25); (Matthew 27; Mark 15; Luke 23; John 18:28–40, 19:5–24); (Matthew 14:1–12).

LESSON 106 The Twelve Disciples of Christ
- Middle and Older Students: Matthew 4:18–22, 10:1–4; Mark 1:16–20, 3:13–19; Luke 5:1–16, 27–32, 6:12–16; John 1:35–51.

LESSON 107 Jesus, His Death and Resurrection
- All Students: Matthew 27, 28; Mark 15, 16; Luke 23, 24; John 19, 21; Acts 1:1–11.
- Videos:
  (1) *Jesus*, produced by Campus Crusade for Christ.
  (2) *Jesus of Nazareth*, the 1977 TV miniseries directed by Franco Zeffirelli and featuring an international cast of stars.
  (3) *The Robe* (1953), starring Richard Burton.
  (4) *Greatest Story Ever Told* (1965), starring Max Von Sydow and Charlton Heston.

LESSON 108 Jesus, the Mystery of History (Yesterday, Today, and Tomorrow)
- Middle and Older Students: *Know What You Believe*, Paul Little.
- Older Students: *Evidence That Demands a Verdict*, Josh McDowell.
- Video: *That the World May Know.* This excellent series teaches biblical truths by taking you to historic sites in the Holy Lands. (Focus on the Family Films).

Wish List *(continued)*
These are toys, games, and the like, for enrichment. Prices listed may no longer be accurate.
- Treasure Chest "Ancient Rome," Running Press ($19.95). This is an educational craft pack.
- A trip to the Holy Lands. (We're allowed to dream, aren't we?)
- A visit to Splendid China in Orlando, Florida, to see the scaled-down remake of the terra-cotta soldiers, the Great Wall, and relics of the Han dynasty. It is amazing!
- I heard on the radio once that if you go to Rome, you could enroll in "gladiator school" for a week and re-enact the gruesome lives of the gladiators like Spartacus. (I don't recommend it but thought it was very interesting.)
- The beautiful Barbie doll made to represent Elizabeth Taylor from the movie *Cleopatra*. It is an expensive collector's doll.
- Visit to a "live" Nativity put on during Christmas.
- A new theme park—The Holy Land Experience—is up and running in Orlando, Florida! It is a place where you can walk the streets of Jerusalem, much as Jesus did, and follow His life on earth. The address and phone are: The Holy Land Experience, 4655 Vineland Rd., Orlando, FL 32811, phone (407) 872-2272. Call for more information!

Barber, Nicola. *Treasure Hunters: The Search for Lost Cities*. Austin: Raintree-Steck Vaughn, 1998.

Baxter, J. Sidlow. *Explore the Book*. Grand Rapids, MI: Zondervan, 1966.

Beechick, Ruth. *Adam and His Kin: The Lost History of Their Lives and Times*. Pollock Pines, CA: Arrow Press, 1990.

Beers, Barbara. *The Latin Road to English Grammar*, Vol. II. Redding, CA: Schola Publications, 1994.

Berry, Roger L. *God's World: His Story*. Harrisonburg, VA: Christian Light Publications, Inc., 1976.

Bible Times Crafts for Kids, compiled by Neva Hickerson. Ventura, CA: Gospel Light, 1993.

Demi. *Buddha*. New York: Henry Holt and Company, 1996.

Durant, Will. *Caesar and Christ*. New York: Simon and Schuster, 1944.

Durant, Will. *The Life of Greece*, from the *Story of Civilization* series. New York: Simon and Schuster, 1939.

Durant, Will. *Our Oriental Heritage*, from the *Story of Civilization* series. New York: Simon and Schuster, 1954.

Dyer, Charles H. *The Rise of Babylon*. Wheaton, IL: Tyndale, 1991.

Green, Robert. *Herod the Great*. New York: Franklin Watts, 1996.

Gregory, Kristiana. *The Royal Diaries: Cleopatra VII, Daughter of the Nile*. New York: Scholastic, 1999.

Haneirot Halalu: These Lights Are Holy—A Home Celebration of Chanuka, edited by Elyse D. Frishman. New York: CCAR Press (Central Conference of American Rabbis).

Hart, Avery, and Paul Mantell. *Pyramids! 50 Hands-On Activities to Experience Ancient Egypt*. Charlotte, VT: Williamson Publishing, 1997.

Hart, George. *Eyewitness Books: Ancient Egypt*. New York: Dorling Kindersley, 1993.

Herodotus, transl. by George Rawlinson. From the Web site http://www.classics.mit.edu.

Holmes, Burnham. *Nefertiti: The Mystery Queen*. Austin: Raintree-Steck Vaughn, 1992.

Holy Bible, The. New King James Version. Nashville: Thomas Nelson Publishers, 1982.

Hoobler, Thomas and Dorothy. *Confucianism: World Religions*. New York: Facts On File, 1993.

Kadodwala, Dilip, and Paul Gateshill. *Celebrate Hindu Festivals*. Crystal Lake, IL: Heinemann Library, 1997.

Kid's Discover, "Pyramids." New York: Edpress, 1992.

Kingfisher Illustrated History of the World, The. New York: Kingfisher Books, 1993.

Langley, Myrtle. *Eyewitness Books: Religion*. New York: Alfred A. Knopf, 1996.

Lascelle, Ruth Specter. *A Dwelling Place for God*. Seattle: Rock of Israel, 1990.

Living Bible Encyclopedia in Story and Pictures, The. Art Treasure ed. New York: H.S. Stuttman Co., Inc., 1968.

Marks, Anthony, and Graham Tingay. *The Usborne Illustrated World History: The Romans*. Tulsa: Educational Development Corp., 1990.

Maybury, Richard J. *Ancient Rome How It Affects You Today*. Placerville, CA: Bluestocking Press, 1995.

Mulcahy, John P. *Coins of the Ancient Mediterranean World*. Federal Reserve Bank of Philadelphia.

Murphy, Rich. *Science With Paper: Learning About Bridge Structures Using Paper*. Schenectady: Maranatha Life, 1997.

Nardo, Don. *The Age of Pericles*. San Diego: Lucent Books, 1996.

Nardo, Don. *Life in Ancient Rome*. San Diego: Lucent Books, 1997.

Nardo, Don. *The Persian Empire*. San Diego: Lucent Books, 1998.

Nardo, Don. *The Punic Wars.* San Diego: Lucent Books, 1996.

Nardo, Don. *The Roman Republic.* San Diego: Lucent Books, 1994.

Nardo, Don. *The Trial of Socrates.* San Diego: Lucent Books, 1947.

Old World Civilizations: The Illustrated History of Humankind. San Francisco: Harper Collins, 1994.

Peach, Susan, and Anne Millard. *The Usborne Illustrated World History, The Greeks.* Tulsa: Educational Development Corp., 1990.

Robinson, Charles Alexander, Jr. *Athens in the Age of Pericles.* Norman, OK: University of Oklahoma Press, 1959.

Simpson, Judith. *The Nature Company Discoveries Library: Ancient China.* San Francisco: Weldon Owen, 1996.

Stevens, Carl H., Jr. *Fulfilled Prophecies from the Bible.* Baltimore: Grace Publications, 2000.

Stout, Kathryn. *Guides to History Plus.* Wilmington: Design-A-Study, 1998.

Thompson, George T., and Laurel Elizabeth Hicks. *World History and Cultures in Christian Perspective.* Pensacola, FL: A Beka Book, 1985.

Today's Dictionary of the Bible, compiled by T.A. Bryant. Minneapolis: Bethany House Publishers, 1982.

Unger, Merrill, F. *Unger's Bible Dictionary.* Chicago: Moody Press, 1979.

Vine, W. E. *The Expanded Vine's Expository Dictionary of New Testament Words.* Minneapolis: Bethany House Publishers, 1984.

Wall Chart of World History, The. London: Studio Editions Ltd., 1991.

Walvoord, John F., and Roy B. Zuck. *The Bible Knowledge Commentary: An Exposition of the Scriptures by Dallas Seminary Faculty.* USA: Victor Books, 1985.

Waterlow, Julia. *Look Into the Past: The Ancient Chinese.* New York: Thompson Learning, 1994.

West, Ruth, and Willis Mason West. *The New World's Foundations in the Old.* Norwood, MA: Norwood Press, 1934.

Whitcomb, John C., and Henry M. Morris. *The Genesis Flood: The Biblical Record and its Scientific Implications.* Grand Rapids, MI: Baker Book House, 1961.

Whitelaw, Kevin. "Ancient Riddles: The Sorcery of the Stones or Elvis Meets Merlin in Y2K." *U.S. News and World Report* 129, no. 4 (July 24–31, 2000).

Wilkinson, Philip. *The Unfolding World, Mysterious Places.* Philadelphia: Running Press, 1993.

Wilson, Lisa and Randy. *Celebrations of Faith.* Colorado Springs, CO: Cook Communications, 2001.

Wingate Philippa. *The Usborne Book of Kings & Queens.* Tulsa: Educational Development Corp., 1995.

Wise, Jessie, and Susan Wise Bauer. *The Well-Trained Mind: A Guide to Classical Education at Home.* New York: W.W. Norton and Company, 1999.

World Book Encyclopedia, The. 50th Anniversary ed. Chicago: Field Enterprises Educational Corp., 1966.

World Book Looks at Wonders of the World. Chicago: World Book, Inc., 1997.

World Heritage: Prehistoric Stone Monuments. Chicago: Children's Press, 1993.

QUARTER 1

PRETEST 1

1. What is Genesis?
2. What is Day 4 of Creation?
3. What is Day 7 of Creation?
4. Who are Adam and Eve?
5. Who are Cain and Abel?
6. Who is Jubal?
7. What is the result of Adam's disobedience?
8. Who is Tubal-Cain?

PRETEST 2

1. e
2. c
3. d
4. h
5. g
6. a
7. f
8. b

WEEK 2, ACTIVITY 4

1. 40 days and 40 nights (Gen. 7:12)
2. 600 (Gen. 7:6)
3. a raven (Gen. 8:7)
4. the Lord (Gen. 7:16)
5. 15 cubits (Gen. 7:20)
6. 150 days (Gen. 7:24, 8:3)
7. three (Gen. 8:8, 10, 12)
8. built an altar and made offerings (Gen. 8:20)
9. eight (Gen. 7:13)
10. "I will never again curse the ground for man's sake, . . . nor will I again destroy every living thing, as I have done." (Gen. 8:21)

PRETEST 3

1. Sir C. Leonard Woolley
2. cuneiform
3. ziggurat
4. Mesopotamia
5. Tower of Babel
6. babel
7. idolatry
8. epic

PRETEST 4

1. England
2. rock
3. football
4. heart
5. pets
6. Nile
7. Crete
8. bull

PRETEST 5

1. T
2. F
3. T
4. F
5. T
6. F
7. T
8. T

PRETEST 6

1. Babylonia
2. laws
3. slaves
4. flourished
5. pharaoh
6. China
7. dynasty
8. silkworm

PRETEST 7

1. Egyptian
2. lamb
3. 10
4. worship
5. 3
6. priest
7. Joshua
8. shouted

PRETEST 8

1. Abu Simbel
2. Akhenaten
3. Amenhotep
4. Cairo

5. Carter

6. Nefertiti

7. Ramses

8. Tutankhamen

PRETEST 9

1. Helen

2. Trojan Horse

3. Priam's treasure

4. Naomi

5. Ruth

6. Boaz

7. Gideon

8. Midianites

QUARTER 2

PRETEST 10

1. Where was Samson's strength?

2. Whom did Samson love?

3. How did Samson beat the Philistines?

4. What followed the Shang dynasty in China?

5. How was the Zhou dynasty divided?

6. What was the "Mandate of Heaven"?

7. Who was the last judge over Israel?

8. Who was the mother of Samuel?

WEEK 10, ACTIVITY 29

1. millet – a grain

2. Shang – the second dynasty

3. Zhou – the third dynasty

4. iron – an abundant natural resource in China

5. King Wen – first to overthrow the Shang

6. King Wu – Wen's son who finished taking over the Shang

7. King Bing – left the Western Zhou and started the Eastern Zhou

8. irrigation – a way of watering crops

9. Eastern – division of Zhou dynasty that lasted the longest

10. Western – division of Zhou dynasty that was strong but short-lived

11. Chou – another spelling for Zhou, pronounced JOE

12. cities – these were becoming huge in China

13. poor – lived in huts

14. rich – lived luxuriously

PRETEST 11

Saul:
- I was the first king of Israel.
- I ended my own life.
- I hated David.
- My son was Jonathan.

David:
- I loved Bathsheba.
- I killed Goliath.
- I wrote many of the Psalms.
- I played the harp for Saul.

Solomon:
- I built the Temple.
- I was the wealthiest man in the world.
- I had 700 wives.
- I wrote many of the Proverbs.

PRETEST 12

1. murex snail

2. Phoenicians

3. Israel

4. Rehoboam

5. golden calf

6. Elijah

7. ravens

8. chariot of fire

PRETEST 13

1. Elijah

2. miracles

3. minor

4. locust

5. prophet

6. Esau

7. blind

8. mythology

PRETEST 14

1. T
2. T
3. F
4. F
5. T
6. F
7. F
8. T

PRETEST 15

1. Latins

2. wolf

3. Shakespeare

4. Christ

5. farmer

6. Bethlehem

7. Assyria
8. Samaritans

PRETEST 16

1. Israel
2. Gomer
3. humble
4. proud
5. dead
6. hunters
7. animals
8. dead

PRETEST 17

1. Achaens
2. Acropolis
3. Ashurbanipal
4. Assyrians
5. Athens
6. Catapults
7. Manasseh
8. Sparta

PRETEST 18

1. 3
2. 200
3. 8
4. 16
5. 39
6. 5
7. 2
8. 51

QUARTER 3

PRETEST 19

1. What is a major river in Mesopotamia?
2. Who originally founded Nineveh?
3. What minor prophet wrote *to* God?
4. Which major prophet lived at the time of Habakkuk?
5. What female helped Josiah interpret the Book of the Law?
6. What king first invaded Jerusalem?
7. How many tries did it take Nebuchadnezzar to defeat Judah?
8. What helped the Judeans stay alive during the takeover by Babylon?

PRETEST 20

Nebuchadnezzar II (in pink):

- Had bad dreams
- Built the Hanging Gardens
- Went "mad"

Daniel (in green):
- Ate only veggies
- Sat before lions
- Saw the future

Aesop (in yellow):
- Was once a Greek slave
- Wrote stories
- Was murdered

PRETEST 21

1. Ezekiel
2. dry bones
3. Shadrach
4. Meshach
5. Abed-Nego
6. Buddha
7. nirvana
8. India

PRETEST 22

1. prime
2. round
3. China
4. respect
5. religions
6. party
7. handwriting
8. freedom

PRETEST 23

1. T
2. F
3. T
4. T
5. F
6. T
7. F
8. F

PRETEST 24

1. king
2. two
3. patricians
4. miles
5. Greece
6. Pheidippides
7. father
8. Persians

PRETEST 25

1. floating
2. Daniel

444

3. sea
4. orphan
5. cousin
6. Golden
7. masks
8. Parthenon

PRETEST 26

1. Asclepius
2. Ezra
3. Hippocratic Oath
4. Longimanus
5. Persia
6. philosopher
7. poison hemlock
8. Socrates

PRETEST 27

1. Nehemiah
2. walls of Jerusalem
3. Pericles
4. strategoi
5. Peloponnese
6. Long Walls
7. Peloponnesian War
8. Athenians

QUARTER 4

PRETEST 28

1. Malachi
2. four
3. pupils
4. Academy
5. Aristotle
6. Zeus
7. Alexander
8. tomb

PRETEST 29

1. Alexander the Great
2. Daniel
3. Archimedes
4. Jewish priests
5. Archimedes
6. Alexander the Great
7. General Ptolemy
8. Archimedes

PRETEST 30

1. Emperor Asoka

2. banyan tree
3. Septuagint
4. Alexandria
5. Early Christians
6. Colossus of Rhodes
7. 7,500 clay soldiers
8. Emperor Qin

PRETEST 31

1. What animal did Hannibal use to fight against the Romans?
2. What mountains did Hannibal cross with his war elephants?
3. What substance was scattered across Carthage to ruin it?
4. What was the greatest trade item made by the Chinese?
5. What did the Chinese invent during the Han dynasty?
6. What Seleucid ruler sacrificed a pig on the Jewish altar?
7. What was miraculously provided at Hanukkah?
8. What does the word "Hanukkah" mean?

PRETEST 32

1. slave
2. "sword"
3. Republic
4. three
5. pirates
6. slaves
7. Cleopatra
8. July

PRETEST 33

1. March
2. Brutus
3. Second
4. Ptolemy
5. carpet
6. Mark Antony
7. Great
8. Temple

PRETEST 34

1. T
2. T
3. F
4. F
5. T
6. F

7. T

8. F

PRETEST 35

1. Augustus Caesar issues a decree for a census.

2. Jesus is born in Bethlehem.

3. Angels proclaim the birth of Jesus.

4. Jesus lives as a carpenter in Galilee.

5. Jesus teaches and performs miracles.

6. Pilate sends Jesus to Herod Antipas.

7. Herod Antipas sends Jesus back to Pilate for sentencing.

8. Pontius Pilate washes his hands of the death of Jesus.

PRETEST 36

1. 12 (James, John, Peter, Andrew, Matthew, Philip, Bartholomew, Thomas, James [the son of Alphaeus], Thaddaeus, Simon the Canaanite, Judas)

2. Peter, James, John

3. Peter

4. Judas

5. James and John

6. Passover Feast

7. Place of the skull

8. 40 days

QUARTER 1

WEEK 1: EXERCISE

Days of Creation:
- Day 1 – Day and night
- Day 2 – Heaven
- Day 3 – Earth, seas, seeds, grass, herbs, fruit
- Day 4 – Sun, moon, and stars
- Day 5 – Sea creatures and birds
- Day 6 – Cattle, creeping things, beasts, and mankind
- Day 7 – God rested

WEEK 2: QUIZ

1. T
2. F
3. F
4. T
5. F
6. F
7. T
8. T
9. T
10. F

WEEK 3: EXERCISE

1. c
2. c
3. b
4. a
5. d
6. d
7. b
8. c
9. d
10. c

WEEK 4: QUIZ

1. k
2. a
3. i
4. h
5. g
6. d
7. c
8. e
9. f

10. l
11. j
12. b

WEEK 5: EXERCISE

1. 7
2. 3
3. 6
4. 1
5. 2
6. 4
7. 9
8. 5
9. 8
10. 10

WEEK 6: QUIZ

1. a
2. d
3. c
4. b
5. c
6. b
7. c
8. a
9. b
10. c
11. a
12. b
13. b
14. d
15. c

WEEK 7: EXERCISE

WEEK 8: QUIZ

1. ironmaking
2. 270
3. dinosaurs
4. eternal life
5. heart
6. Joseph
7. Hammurabi
8. 50,000
9. Moses
10. Day of Atonement
11. servant
12. gold
13. Howard Carter
14. Abu Simbel
15. iron

WORKSHEET 1

I.   Copy as directed.

II. 1. c
     2. e
     3. h
     4. i
     5. b
     6. a
     7. d
     8. g
     9. j
     10. f

III. 11. T
     12. F
     13. F
     14. T
     15. F
     16. F
     17. F
     18. T
     19. F
     20. F

IV. 21. b
     22. d
     23. c
     24. c
     25. a

V.   26. after
     27. before
     28. after
     29. after
     30. before

VI. Potiphar's house – Joseph

    City of Ur – Abraham

    England – Mary Mantell

    Giza – Khufu

    Crete – Minoans

    China – Shang dynasty

    Jericho – Joshua

    Sodom and Gomorrah – Lot

    Great Hall – Ramses II

VII. Answers will vary.

1. They demonstrate the ingenuity and abilities of early man (which helps defend Creation).
2. A canopy of water vapor covered the earth. It produced a greenhouse effect.
3. They believed that they might need things from this life to take to the afterlife.
4. Mountains, desert, and an ocean are the three natural barriers around China.
5. They worshiped only one god.

QUARTER 2

WEEK 10: EXERCISE

```
      S C H L I E M A N N   K K     B
    F   H   H   B A B Y L O N I A   U
    E     E A             O   N     L
    R   J   M I N O T A U R S G     L
    T L A W S N     D       S       L
L   I   P     C       Y     O   P   E
A   L   H     E         S   S   H   A
M   E   E M A N D A T E   S     I T P
P   C   T     S           E     L U I
S   R   H   M E R C Y S E A T U I T N
T   E A S T E R N       M       S A G
A   S       P R O P H E T       T N
N   C U N E I F O R M   N       I K
D   E L I L A H H A N N A H     N H
    N H A I R     M       O     E A
    T           S       T       S M
K   I N G W E N   E H E L E N       E
Z   I G G U R A T S       P     N
```

WEEK 11: QUIZ

1. F
2. T
3. F
4. T
5. F
6. T

7. T

8. F

9. F

10. F

11. T

12. T

13. F

14. T

15. F

16. T

17. F

18. T

Bonus: "Circa," which means "about"

WEEK 12: EXERCISE

1. Jubal and Tubal-Cain

2. Noah and the flood

3. Tower of Babel

4. Stonehenge is started

5. Abraham

6. Hammurabi

7. King Tutankhamen

8. Ramses II

9. Gideon

10. Zhou dynasty begins

11. King Saul

12. Solomon

13. Kingdom of Israel divides

14. Elijah

WEEK 13: QUIZ

1. f

2. h

3. l

4. b

5. j

6. n

7. a

8. e

9. d

10. g

11. m

12. i

13. c

14. k

WEEK 14: EXERCISE

The Chocolate Candy Game:
Answers will vary.

WEEK 15: QUIZ

1. d
2. b
3. d
4. b
5. c
6. c
7. b
8. d
9. c
10. a
11. b
12. c
13. d
14. a
15. c
16. b
17. d
18. a
19. b
20. c

Bonus: Latin

WEEK 16: EXERCISE

(2 answer formats)
By number:
1. l – Jubal
2. k – dinosaurs
3. b – Minoans
4. a – Moses
5. g – Amenhotep IV
6. c – Rahab
7. m – Samuel
8. h – Solomon
9. i – The Kingdom divided
10. n – Elijah
11. j – Joel
12. p – Olympics
13. f – Jonah
14. d – Amos
15. o – Israel falls to Assyria
16. e – Hopewells

OR

By letter:

a. Moses   staff
b. Minoans   oval

c.	Rahab	red cord
d.	Amos	plumb line
e.	Hopewells	hill
f.	Jonah	fish fin
g.	Amenhotep IV	sun
h.	Solomon	dollar signs
i.	The Kingdom divided	line underneath
j.	Joel	bug wings
k.	dinosaurs	feet and tail
l.	Jubal	musical note
m.	Samuel	box
n.	Elijah	flame
o.	Israel falls to Assyria	letter "A"
p.	Olympics	five rings

WEEK 17: QUIZ

1. Khufu (Cheops)
2. Rachel
3. tent
4. Joshua
5. Tutankhamen
6. Odysseus
7. Phoenicians
8. David
9. Obadiah
10. Homer
11. reincarnation
12. Bible
13. Samaritans
14. Assyrian
15. mounds
16. Acropolis
17. hooks
18. Babylonians

WORKSHEET 2

I. Copy as directed.

II.
1. 3
2. 1
3. 4
4. 2
5. 5

1. 3
2. 1
3. 5
4. 4

        5. 2

        1. 3

        2. 1

        3. 4

        4. 2

        5. 5

III. 1. d

      2. c

      3. e

      4. a

      5. b

      6. f

IV. 1. e

     2. d

     3. b

     4. c

     5. a

V. 1. c. 925 B.C.

    2. c. 800 B.C.

    3. 776 B.C.

    4. 753 B.C.

    5. 722 B.C.

VI. 1. d

     2. e

     3. a

     4. b

     5. c

     6. f

VII. Answers will vary.

1. • Impatient and sent troops to fight without food

    • Spared king of Amalakites against God's orders

    • Jealous toward David

    • Looked to fortune-tellers instead of to God or the prophets

2. • Sailing

    • Glassmaking

    • Making dye

    • Trading

    • (Phonics)

3. • Elijah and John: Lived away from people; rugged; powerful

    • Elisha and Jesus: Lived around people; performed miracles

4. • Spartans: Warlike, trained children to fight

    • Athenians: Artsy; thinkers; valued education highly

5. • Judah was taken captive to Babylon.

• His countrymen were in sin; he knew God's heart hurt for Judah.

Bonus: Murex

SEMESTER I TEST

I. 1. T
    2. F
    3. F
    4. F
    5. T
    6. F
    7. F

II. 1. b
    2. c
    3. b
    4. d
    5. a
    6. b
    7. d

III. 1. Nile
     2. Tabernacle
     3. Amenhotep IV
     4. iron
     5. Greeks
     6. Gideon
     7. Boaz
     8. Zhou

IV. 1. d
    2. e
    3. a
    4. c
    5. g
    6. h
    7. b
    8. f

V. 1. 4
    2. 1
    3. 2
    4. 5
    5. 3

    1. 4
    2. 3
    3. 1
    4. 2

    1. 4
    2. 1
    3. 3
    4. 2
    5. 5

VI. 1. the *Iliad*
    2. the Vedas
    3. Greeks
    4. Latins
    5. Judah
    6. wife
    7. Samaritans
    8. good
VII. 1. Mound Builders
    2. Jeremiah
    3. Nineveh
    4. Josiah
    5. Athens and Sparta
    6. Manasseh
VIII. Bonus Essay: Possible answers—
    • Stonehenge
    • Jubal – music
    • Tubal-Cain – iron
    • Pyramids
    • Sumerians – plumbing
    • Genealogies kept for generations.

QUARTER 3

WEEK 19: EXERCISE

(2 answer formats)
By number:
1. f – Samuel
2. m – Elijah
3. h – Elisha
4. b – Joel
5. e – Obadiah
6. l – Jonah
7. o – Amos
8. c – Isaiah
9. g – Micah
10. a – Nahum
11. i – Zephaniah
12. d – Jeremiah
13. j – Habakkuk
14. n – Huldah
15. k – Hosea

Israel (star):
    • Samuel, Elijah, Elisha, Amos, and Hosea

Judah (box):
    • Joel, Isaiah, Micah, Zephaniah, Jeremiah, and Huldah

Nineveh and Assyria (squiggles):
- Jonah and Nahum

Others (check mark):
- Obadiah and Habakkuk

OR

By letter:

a.	Nahum	turquoise & squiggles
b.	Joel	black & box
c.	Isaiah	light pink & box
d.	Jeremiah	hot pink & box
e.	Obadiah	light purple & check mark
f.	Samuel	dark green & star
g.	Micah	yellow & box
h.	Elisha	light blue & star
i.	Zephaniah	light green & box
j.	Habakkuk	dark blue & check mark
k.	Hosea	dark purple & star
l.	Jonah	gray & squiggles
m.	Elijah	orange & star
n.	Huldah	brown & box
o.	Amos	red & star

WEEK 20: QUIZ

I.
1. F
2. F
3. T
4. F
5. F
6. T
7. F
8. T
9. F
10. T

II.
11. Manasseh
12. Assyrians
13. Passover feast
14. Zephaniah
15. Jeremiah
16. flood
17. Habakkuk
18. Nebuchadnezzar
19. Daniel
20. Aesop

WEEK 21: EXERCISE

1. b
2. c

3. b
4. b
5. d
6. a
7. c
8. a
9. c
10. d
11. c
12. a
13. d
14. a
15. c
16. d
17. b
18. d
19. c
20. d

WEEK 22: QUIZ

I.   1. c
   2. h
   3. g
   4. i
   5. a
   6. j
   7. b
   8. d
   9. f
   10. e

II. 11. c
   12. a
   13. d
   14. b
   15. d
   16. d
   17. a
   18. b
   19. b
   20. c

Bonus: Supernatural events include seeing men survive the fiery furnace, being restored after seven years of madness, and Daniel interpreting dreams without being told what they were.

WEEK 23: EXERCISE

Answers will vary.

1. Given

2. Tut was probably murdered. The Egyptians were not open to worshiping one god. Tut might have been a religious martyr for his faith.

3. David was only the second king. The Israelites were transitioning from judges to kings. It was a great time for Israel. The capital was moved to Jerusalem.

4. The Kingdom of Israel split because Rehoboam was cruel and listened to peers rather than to his elders. It made a huge difference in the government of the Israelites. They became two separate kingdoms. We would better understand the Bible, particularly the Old Testament, if we understood the two kingdoms. Each had its own prophets.

5. God allowed the Babylonian Captivity because the Judeans were very sinful. It took their home away for 70 years. In the long run, they learned to trust and follow God again.

6. Buddha's life is significant because his peaceful teachings are the basis of the Buddhist religion. Though he never claimed to be a god, he is worshiped. Buddha actually broke away from Hinduism because he saw the unfairness of the caste system.

7. Confucius's teachings were moral, and they developed into a major religion of the world. His intent, however, was not to be worshiped. His beliefs influenced others toward the worship of their ancestors.

WEEK 24: QUIZ

Stump the Teacher:
Answers will vary.

WEEK 25: EXERCISE

Crossword solution (across and down answers):

- ¹EZEKIEL
- ⁵PENTATHLON
- ⁸NINEVEH
- ⁹PYTHAGORAS
- ¹¹GATE
- ¹³ROCK
- ¹⁴PLEBEIAN
- ¹⁷PURIM
- ¹⁸EART(H)
- ²⁰HERODOTUS
- ²²BUDDHA
- ²³MOSES
- ²⁴MINOTAUR

Down answers include: ²ZHUN, ³LATIN, ⁴MESOPOTAMIA, ⁶MASSEH, ⁷CREE, ¹⁰HELLENES, ¹²MEGALITH, ¹⁵ABRAHAM, ¹⁶SAA, ¹⁹HULDAH, ²¹DIONYSIS

WEEK 26: QUIZ

I.
1. Tower of Babel
2. Minoan
3. Abraham
4. Jericho
5. Boaz
6. David
7. Edomites
8. Amos
9. Nineveh
10. Huldah

II.
1. f
2. e
3. i

4. b
5. g
6. c
7. a
8. h
9. j
10. d

WORKSHEET 3

I. Copy as directed.

II. 1. Judah

2. Babylonia

3. Babylonia

4. Greece

5. India

6. Greece

7. China

8. Persia

III. 1. b

2. d

3. a

4. c

5. b

IV. 1. T

2. T

3. T

4. F

5. F

6. T

7. T

8. F

V. Answers will vary.

1. Judaism

a. Believers worship one God.

b. Man is sinful.

c. Man has one life.

2. Buddhism

a. Nirvana is a state of mind.

b. Man is good.

c. Man has more than one life (reincarnation).

3. Confucianism

a. Elders should be respected.

b. Rulers should be honest and well educated.

c. Man is good, and proper living can solve problems.

VI. Answers will vary; look for these points—

1. Aesop: Former slave; wrote fables

2. Pythagoras: Great mathematician; Pythagorean theorem; prime numbers

The Mystery of History

3. Herodotus: Father of history; documented events

4. Socrates: Philosopher during Golden Age; promoted wisdom; sentenced to death

5. Hippocrates: Father of medicine; treated symptoms with diet and exercise

6. Pericles: Great speaker, politician, statesman; inspired Athenians through patriotic speeches; died of plague

VII. Answers will vary. They should include:

- Babylonian Captivity
- Daniel – experienced visions; foretold the future
- Ezekiel - prophesied to Jews still in Jerusalem
- Cyrus – issued decree of freedom
- Zerubbabel – rebuilt Temple
- Inspired by Haggai and Zechariah
- Ezra – restored right living
- Nehemiah – rebuilt wall

Older Students:

- The significance—Judah learned the lesson of sin and disobedience.
- The end result—They were restored through God's grace and love.

QUARTER 4

WEEK 28: EXERCISE

1. F   (example)
2. T
3. T
4. F   Iron was abundant in early China.
5. F   Israel was defeated by the Assyrians in 722 B.C.
6. F   Josiah died before the Babylonian Captivity.
7. T
8. T
9. F   Artaxerxes was nicknamed Longimanus for having a deformed hand.
10. T
11. F   Socrates never wrote his own works.
12. T
13. F   Ezra prayed and fasted for protection.
14. T
15. T
16. T
17. F   Malachi is the last book of the Old Testament.
18. F   Plato's school was the Academy.
19. F   Aristotle tutored Alexander the Great.
20. F   Philip was a prisoner in Thebes.

WEEK 29: QUIZ

I. 1. c
    2. e
    3. c
    4. b
    5. b

II. 1. F

    2. T

    3. T

    4. F

    5. F

III. 1. Buddha

    2. Zerubbabel

    3. Darius I

    4. Xerxes

    5. Pythagoras

IV. 1. c

    2. e

    3. d

    4. b

    5. a

V. Alexander's empire was divided by four generals after his death.

WEEK 30: EXERCISE

1. Noah
2. Abraham
3. Tutankhamen
4. David
5. Israel divides
6. The first Olympics
7. Babylonian Captivity
8. Buddha
9. Confucius
10. Golden Age of Athens
11. Plato
12. Alexander the Great

WEEK 31: QUIZ

I. 1. F

    2. F

    3. T

    4. F

    5. T

    6. T

II. 1. c

    2. c

    3. b

    4. d

    5. c

    6. e

III. 1. c

    2. d

    3. b

4. f

5. e

6. a

IV. 1. Bucephalus

2. Archimedes

3. banyan trees

4. Great Wall

5. Carthage

6. Antiochus Epiphanes

V. Answers will vary.

1. The Egyptians believed that the body needed to be preserved for the next life. They thought it was necessary to bury useful things and people with them for the next life.

2. It was written by 70 men in 70 days. It was the first Old Testament translation. It is what the early Christians used before the New Testament was available.

WEEK 32: EXERCISE

The Chocolate Candy Game:
Answers will vary.

WEEK 33: QUIZ

I. 1. e

2. d

3. c

4. b

5. a

6. g

7. f

II. 1. Mandate

2. Samuel

3. three

4. snail

5. Elijah

6. Esau

7. Isaiah

III. 1. b

2. d

3. c

4. a

5. b

6. c

7. d

IV. 1. T

2. F

3. F

4. F

5. T

6.   F

7.   T

V.   Answers will vary.

1.   The making of silk. It was a profitable export.

2.   They built earth mounds, some of which are still standing.

3.   I could make intricate black and red pottery, perform in the theater, build great temples, be a philosopher, write poetry, make games and toys, and play sports.

WEEK 34: EXERCISE

(2 answer formats)

By number:

1.   d – Nahum
2.   m – Huldah
3.   s – Joel
4.   b – Samuel
5.   o – Jeremiah
6.   g – Daniel
7.   f – Jonah
8.   j – Elijah
9.   i – Malachi
10. k – Isaiah
11. r – Ezekiel
12. a – Obadiah
13. t – Elisha
14. q – Amos
15. l – Hosea
16. e – Micah
17. c – Zechariah
18. p – Habakkuk
19. n – Haggai
20. h – Zephaniah

OR

By letter:

a.	Obadiah	"E" / blue
b.	Samuel	big ears / yellow
c.	Zechariah	"Priest" / pink
d.	Nahum	"N" / blue
e.	Micah	pitchfork / green
f.	Jonah	big fish / blue
g.	Daniel	carrot / pink
h.	Zephaniah	crown / green
i.	Malachi	"Last" / pink
j.	Elijah	flames / yellow
k.	Isaiah	pen / green
l.	Hosea	heart with jagged slash / yellow
m.	Huldah	eye with long eyelashes / green

n.	Haggai	"T" / pink
o.	Jeremiah	tear / green
p.	Habakkuk	mailbox / blue
q.	Amos	straight line / yellow
r.	Ezekiel	scroll / pink
s.	Joel	wings / green
t.	Elisha	bones / yellow

WEEK 35: QUIZ

I. 1. Jubal
   2. rainbow
   3. Stonehenge
   4. pyramids
   5. Abraham
   6. sun
   7. Helen
   8. Moab

II. 1. c
    2. e
    3. h
    4. a
    5. g
    6. b
    7. d
    8. f

III. 1. d
     2. b
     3. d
     4. c
     5. a
     6. c
     7. d
     8 b

IV. 1. T
    2. T
    3. F
    4. F
    5. F
    6. F
    7. T
    8. T

V. Answers will vary.
   1. Great achievements include pyramids, ziggurats, the skills of Jubal and Tubal-Cain, city water systems, written language.
   2. Jesus was born in Bethlehem. Nineveh was destroyed by a flood.
   3. The Jews were spared death; they celebrate this event at the Feast of Purim.
   4. John's life purpose was to teach repentance of sins and to prepare the coming of Jesus Christ.

WORKSHEET 4

I.   Copy as directed.

II.   1. Aristotle

      2. Septuagint

      3. Hannibal

      4. Julius Caesar

      5. Plato

      6. Qin dynasty

      7. John the Baptist

      8. Crucifixion

III.   Greece:

      1. Plato

      2. Archimedes

      3. Aristotle

      4. Hippocrates

      Rome:

      1. Spartacus

      2. Julius Caesar

      3. Mark Antony

      4. Augustus Caesar

      Israel:

      1. Malachi

      2. Judas Maccabee

      3. Herod the Great

      4. John the Baptist

IV.   1. Given

      2. Punic Wars; Carthage (or Hannibal) vs. Rome (or Scipio); circle Rome

      3. Maccabean Revolt; Jews (or Judas Maccabee) vs. Seleucids (or Antiochus Epiphanes); circle the Jews

      4. Servile War; Slaves (or Spartacus) vs. Romans (or Crassus); circle the Romans

      5. Battle of Actium; Octavian (Western Rome) vs. Mark Antony & Cleopatra (or Eastern Rome and Egypt); circle Octavian

V.   1. e

      2. f

      3. a

      4. g

      5. d

      6. c

      7. h

      8. b

VI.   1. Pyramids of Egypt (or Giza)

      2. Hanging Gardens of Babylon

      3. Temple of Diana (or Artemis)

      4. Statue of Zeus

      5. Mausoleum of Halicarnassus

6. Lighthouse of Alexandria (or Pharos)

7. Colossus of Rhodes

VII. 1,500; 25; towers; feet; chariots

VIII 1. F He became mute.

2. T

3. F Jesus allowed Mary and others to worship Him.

4. T

5. F Pilate "washed his hands" of the matter.

6. F Peter, James, and John

7. T

8. T

IX. 1. displacement

2. banyan

3. 422 years

4. Julius Caesar, Pompey, Crassus

5. Octavian, Mark Antony, Cleopatra

6. Gabriel

7. blasphemy (claiming to be God)

8. Matthew

SEMESTER II TEST

I. 1. flood

2. Habakkuk

3. Hanging Gardens

4. lions' den

5. fables

6. Ezekiel

7. Babylonian

8. mathematician

II. 1. T

2. T

3. F

4. F

5. T

6. T

7. F

8. T

III. 1. d

2. h

3. a

4. g

5. b

6. c

7. e

8. f

IV. 1. c
    2. a
    3. b
    4. c
    5. d
    6. d
    7. e
    8. c

V. 1. The Silk Road
    2. Judas Maccabee
    3. Spartacus
    4. The First Triumvirate
    5. Mark Antony
    6. Cleopatra
    7. Herod the Great
    8. Battle of Actium

VI. 1. John the Baptist
    2. miracles
    3. Pilate
    4. Peter
    5. Passover
    6. women

VII. 1. d
    2. e
    3. a
    4. h
    5. c
    6. f
    7. b
    8. g

VIII. Bonus Essay. Answers will vary.

1. The prophets' words always came true.

2. Jesus Christ (the Gospel) because He is the Creator of all things; He has a plan and purpose for the world; He is seeking to reveal Himself to man throughout history; etc.

PHOTO CREDITS

Museum of Biblical Archaeology: pp. 7, 11, 17, 19, 27, 38, 47, 58, 64, 70, 79, 90, 100, 112, 115, 121, 122, 134, 144, 153, 162, 170, 198, 202, 232, 241, 260, 282, 294, 332, 345; North Wind Picture Archives: pp. 36, 135, 207, 230, 269, 280, 302, 322, 336, 343, 356, 378; George Holton/Photo Researchers: p. 77; Jan Halaska/Photo Researchers: p. 111; Lawrence Migdale/Photo Researchers: p. 317. Also, photo by Kathleen D. Mitchell: p. 346; Unice B. and Patricia Hawkins: pp. 41, 263 and cover; David B. Smith: pp. 173, 220; Ron Hobar: pp. xxviii, xxix, xxxi, xxxii; Linda Lacour Hobar: pp. iv, 6, 21, 164, 165, 249, 326, 366, 372.

TRADEMARKS

The following trademarks were referred to in the lessons and activities:

Frisbee® flying discs is a registered trademark of Wham-O, Inc.

Ivory® soap is a registered trademark of The Procter & Gamble Company.

Lego® plastic construction toys is a trademark of The Lego Group.

Play-Doh® modeling compound is a registered trademark of Hasbro, Inc.

Styrofoam® plastic foam is a registered trademark of The Dow Chemical Company.

PRODUCTION CREDITS

Kathryn Dix: project management/editing; Ivy Ulrich-Bonk: page layout; Christy Shaffer: cover design, illustration on p. 382; Tyler H. Hogan: outline maps; Emily Rose: photo research; Penny Baker: proofreading.

Bright Ideas Press
www.BrightIdeasPress.com
877.492.8081
Call or email for a free catalog. Or visit our Web site for articles, reviews, resources, and secure on-line ordering. Check our schedule to see if we're coming to a homeschool conference near you.

The Mystery of History - Volume I

Volume I: *Creation to the Resurrection*
Classical, Chronological, Complete
A User-Friendly Family Curriculum
Written for 4th – 8th graders, Adaptable for Older & Younger Students
The Mystery of History provides a historically accurate, Bible-centered approach to learning ancient history. The completely chronological lessons shed new light on *who* walked the earth *when,* as well as *where* important Bible figures fit into secular history.
Pbk. 512 pages Family BIP-5 $44.95

The Mystery of History - Volume II

Volume II: *The Early Church and the Middle Ages*
Check on availability for this and future volumes.

The Ultimate Geography and Timeline Guide

Are you geographically literate? Far too many Americans are sadly lacking knowledge in this vital subject. This one source book will provide you with everything you need to competently teach geography from kindergarten through graduation. Part lesson plans, part idea book, part unit study, and part inspiration! Whether you are a unit study or textbook fan, a hands-on mom or a classical approach teacher, you'll find much to love about this award-winning curriculum.
Pbk. 352 pages K–12 GC-100 $34.95

Hands-On Geography

Take another look! This long-time favorite introduction to geography went through a massive revision in 2001. New look and layout, loads more ideas and activities make this a book worth getting excited about! Enough material to last families for several years. Written from a Christian perspective, *Hands-On Geography* will motivate you to teach an oft-neglected subject. Includes specific instructions for activities, games, and projects. Appealing to kids and easy for parents.

How can you miss with Around the World Night, Hero Geography, Make Your Own Field Guides as well as reproducible maps and games? Joseph's Journey, a geographic look at a beloved Bible passage, walks parent and student through these familiar verses, illuminating them in a fresh new way. An easy, yet thorough, introduction to a very important subject.
Pbk. 144 pages Grades K–5 BIP-1 $14.95

Student History Notebook of America

The classical, Charlotte Mason, and other educational approaches call for students to keep their own notebooks. The notebook method is flexible, interesting, and memorable! Witness improvements in the quality of students' work as they record information, artwork, daily assignments, and more in their own personal notebook.

Book includes pages for essays, drawings, vocabulary, presidents, states and capitals, and much more. The timeline and 10 outline maps contribute depth as well as hands-on learning. Detailed instructions provide guidance on implementing this type of self-directed learning. great addition to any prepackaged U.S. history curriculum or use as the basis for your own units.
Pbk. 112 pages K–12 BIP-3 $12.95

The Scientist's Apprentice

This exciting, complete one-year curriculum is presented in an easily understandable manner and is just as easy to use. Introductory information for the teacher provides guidance. Experiments, games, crafts, recipes, writing, songs, and more are used to reach different learning styles. Orderly thinking skills, based on the scientific method, are reinforced throughout.

Use the recommended student notebook approach as you spend eight weeks on each of four topics: Astronomy, Anatomy, Earth Science, and Oceanography. The Reading Plan Chart keys every topic in *The Scientist's Apprentice* with the corresponding pages in the nine optional resource books: (4) Magic School Bus titles, (4) DK Eyewitness Explorers titles, and *It Couldn't Just Happen*.

Reproducible pages and a friendly layout make this a practical choice for busy homeschoolers. Teach several grade levels at the same time. More interesting than a text and easier than creating your own study: the work's been done for you. One-year program.
Pbk. 200 pages K–6 BIP-2 $26.95

Over Our Heads in Wonder

A gem of a book! Discover God's "Wonders in the Sky" and His love and power on earth! Parents will appreciate the simplicity of this book while students enjoy the great activities. With 25+ readings/discussions and 50+ projects/experiments encompassing science, the Bible, writing, math, and language arts, there is no shortage of ideas here! Suitable for multi-level teaching, these "any day – anywhere" assignments utilize common household materials and are organized around the different facts of weather and the sky: clouds, rainbows, sun, stars, snow, wind, storms, and air. This book will inspire your whole family. Use this with the laminated cloud chart for a terrific weather unit.
Pbk. 96 pages K–5 BIP-4 $9.95

Laminated Cloud Chart

This sturdy, colorful poster is as beautiful as it is useful! Identify and name clouds with the labeled color photographs. Comes with a black-and-white chart of forecast rules—after you identify the cloud, forecast the weather!
FSS-100 $12.50

Gifted Children at Home: A Practical Guide for Homeschooling Families

Gifted kids are different! Are you meeting their needs? Written by three Christian moms who have chosen to home-educate their intellectually gifted children, this book will not only guide you through perplexing questions but also wholly encourage you with discerning and dependable answers. Provides information and resources that will enable you to make important educational decisions with confidence and success. Topics extensively covered include: assessment, characteristics and learning styles, curriculum considerations, techniques, acceleration/skipping, and much more.
Pbk. 160 pages GG-102 $24.95

See our Order Form on Next Page!

BRIGHT IDEAS PRESS
www.BrightIdeasPress.com

ORDER FORM

Mail your check or money order to:
Bright Ideas Press
P.O. Box 333
Cheswold, DE 19936
Toll Free: 877.492.8081

VISA & MasterCard orders are accepted. See below for information.

SHIPPING TABLE
Prices Good Through
December 31, 2003
Up to $60............ ...$6.00
$61-$150............ ...10%
Over $150............ .FREE

Most orders are shipped within 3 business days. Please allow 3-4 weeks from May-July.

	TITLE	QTY	PRICE	TOTAL
BIP-1	Hands-On Geography		14.95	
BIP-2	The Scientist's Apprentice		26.95	
BIP-3	Student History Notebook of America		12.95	
BIP-4	Over Our Heads in Wonder		9.95	
BIP-5	The Mystery of History – Volume I		44.95	
FSS-100	Laminated Cloud Chart		12.50	
GG-102	Gifted Children at Home		24.95	
GC-100	The Ultimate Geography & Timeline Guide		34.95	

SHIP TO ADDRESS: Please print clearly

NAME:_____

ADDRESS:_____

_____

_____

PHONE:___(____)_____

EMAIL:_____

Special!!
FREE SHIPPING
on orders over $150.00

Subtotal	
←Shipping Cost: See Shipping Table	
Total Amount Due	

Credit Card Information

VISA/MasterCard Number   Expiration Date

Signature

Practical, Fun and Affordable Geography, History and Science Resources!